timeout.com/boston

Published by Time Out Guides Ltd, a wholly owned subsidiary of Time Out Group Ltd.
Time Out and the Time Out logo are trademarks of Time Out Group Ltd.

Previous editions, 1999, 2001

10 9 8 7 6 5 4 3 2 1

This edition first published in Great Britain in 2004 by Ebury
Ebury is a division of The Random House Group Ltd,
20 Vauxhall Bridge Road, London SW1V 2SA

Random House Australia Pty Limited, 20 Alfred Street, Milsons Point, Sydney, New South Wales 2061, Australia
Random House New Zealand Limited, 18 Poland Road, Glenfield, Auckland 10, New Zealand
Random House South Africa (Pty) Limited, Endulini, 5A Jubilee Road, Parktown 2193, South Africa

Random House UK Limited Reg. No. 954009

Distributed in USA by Publishers Group West
1700 Fourth Street, Berkeley, California 94710

Distributed in Canada by Penguin Canada Ltd
10 Alcorn Avenue, Toronto, Ontario, Canada M4V 3B2

For further distribution details, see www.timeout.com

ISBN 1-904978-18-5

A CIP catalogue record for this book is available from the British Library

Colour reprographics by Icon, Crowne House, 56-58 Southwark Street, London SE1 1UN

Printed and bound by Cayfosa-Quebecor, Ctra. De Caldes, KM 3 08 130 Sta, Perpètua de Mogoda, Barcelona, Spain

Edited and designed by
Time Out Guides Limited
Universal House
251 Tottenham Court Road
London W1T 7AB
Tel + 44 (0)20 7813 3000
Fax + 44 (0)20 7813 6001
Email guides@timeout.com
www.timeout.com

Editorial
Editor Lisa Ritchie
Deputy Editor Jenny Piening
Consultant Editor Chris Wright
Listings Checker Paul McMorrow
Proofreader Angela Jameson
Indexer Jonathan Cox

Editorial/Managing Director Peter Fiennes
Series Editor Ruth Jarvis
Deputy Series Editor Lesley McCave
Guides Co-ordinator Anna Norman
Accountant Sarah Bostock

Design
Art Director Mandy Martin
Acting Art Director Scott Moore
Acting Art Editor Tracey Ridgewell
Acting Senior Designer Astrid Kogler
Designer Sam Lands
Junior Designer Oliver Knight
Digital Imaging Dan Conway
Ad Make-up Charlotte Blythe

Picture Desk
Picture Editor Jael Marschner
Deputy Picture Editor Kit Burnet
Picture Researcher Ivy Lahon
Picture Desk Assistant/Librarian Laura Lord

Advertising
Sales Director Mark Phillips
International Sales Manager Ross Canadé
International Sales Executive James Tuson
Advertising Sales (Boston) Sheri Trocchi
Advertising Assistant Lucy Butler

Marketing
Marketing Manager Mandy Martinez
US Publicity & Marketing Associate Rosella Albanese

Production
Guides Production Director Mark Lamond
Production Controller Samantha Furniss

Time Out Group
Chairman Tony Elliott
Managing Director Mike Hardwick
Group Financial Director Richard Waterlow
Group Commercial Director Lesley Gill
Group Marketing Director Christine Cort
Group General Manager Nichola Coulthard
Group Art Director John Oakey
Online Managing Director David Pepper
Group Production Director Steve Proctor
Group IT Director Simon Chappell

Contributors
Introduction Chris Wright. **History** Camille Dodero. **Boston Today** Robert David Sullivan (*Bright young things* Nina MacLaughlin). **Architecture** Joe Keohane. **Literary Boston** Luke Salisbury. **Where to Stay** Caroline McCloskey, Rob McKeown, Lisa Ritchie. **Boston Common & Downtown** Mike Miliard. **Beacon Hill** Rachel O'Malley. **Back Bay & South End** Caroline McCloskey. **North End** Mike Miliard. **The Waterfront & Charlestown** Rachel O'Malley. **Cambridge** Michael Freidson (*Drop out, get rich* Angela Gaimari). **Further Afield** Caroline McCloskey. **Guided Tours** Kristen Paulson. **Museums** Camille Dodero. **Restaurants & Cafés** Rob McKeown. **Pubs & Bars** Chris Wright (*Shakin' things up* Rob McKeown). **Shops & Services** Kristen Paulson (*Sneaker City* Caroline McCloskey). **Festivals & Events** Nina MacLaughlin. **Children** Joe Keohane. **Clubs** Craig Kapilow. **Film** David Valdes Greenwood. **Galleries** David Wildman. **Gay & Lesbian** Lissa Harris. **Music: Rock & Roots** David Wildman. **Performing Arts** David Valdes Greenwood (*The cultural melting pot* David Wildman). **Sport & Fitness** Michael Freidson (*Sox obsessed* Luke Salisbury). **Colonial Villages** Caroline McCloskey. **Massachusetts Coast & Islands** Nina MacLaughlin. **Directory** Angela Gaimari.

Maps JS Graphics (john@jsgraphics.co.uk). Subway map on p284 reproduced with kind permission of the MBTA.

Photography Kent Dayton Photography, except: pages 6, 9, 10, 33, 35, 36, 61, 84 Corbis; page 13 TopFoto; page 14 Bettman/Corbis; page 15 Boston Irish Tourism Association; pages 17, 21, 224, 225 Getty Images; page 32 Ronald Grant/Merchant Ivory Films; page 72 Otis House Museum; page 103 Boston Harbor Cruises; page 121 Dom Miguel Photography; page 181 Associated Press; page 183 Susan Cole Kelly; page 195, 2004 Warner Home Video UK Ltd; pages 200, 201 Boston Gay Pride Committee; page 218 Michael Lutch/Boston Symphony Orchestra; page 230 Minuteman National Historical Park; pages 232, 241 Kindra Clineff/MOTT; page 242 The Preservation Society of Newport County; page 245 Alamy Images.

The Editor would like to thank: Susan Baranyi at Kortenhaus Communications, Namita Raina at the Greater Boston Convention & Visitors Bureau, Barbara Salisbury and all the contributors from the previous editions.

Contents

Introduction

To understand Boston, you must understand its ongoing rivalry with New York, which touts itself as a bigger and brighter version of its civilised sibling. Especially bigger. For reasons we'll address later in this guide, Boston is often called Beantown. Picture a bean sitting beside an apple – a Big Apple at that – and you'll get a sense of Boston's relationship with its swaggering rival.

Size, of course, isn't everything. Boston crams in some of the most beautiful and varied architecture in the US, from neo-classical to postmodern. In Copley Square alone, you can marvel at the splendour of the old Boston Public Library, gaze into the huge looking glass of the John Hancock Tower, or run your eye over the arches and gargoyles of Trinity Church. Stand at the centre point of the Harvard Bridge on a sunny day and you'll see an urban panorama that ranks among the most stunning spectacles in America and beyond.

But there is more to Boston than its good looks. The 'Athens of America' has long served as a centre of literature, art and politics. It is saturated with history, yet this city doesn't only look to its past. Boston and the surrounding area are at the vanguard of America's future: the innovations at the Institute of Contemporary Art, the ground-breaking dramas at the American Repertory Theatre, the robotics and nanotechnology labs at MIT, the literary talent at Boston University, the powerful political thought that still emerges from Harvard.

This mid-sized city is home to the great monoliths of American education, which means that crusty old Boston, known for its Brahmins and the antiquated red bricks that house them, is also a youthful place. Its streets are teeming with the tens of thousands of students who show up every year, demanding to be entertained – so there's a flourishing nightlife. As for dining, the city's culinary arena has undergone an unprecedented revival over the past decade, to the extent that chefs now enjoy the kind of celebrity that used to be reserved for rock stars. If you can't find something that pleases your palate in Boston, you're not looking hard enough.

Bostonians, for all their notorious conservatism, are not given to sitting still. Perhaps because its inhabitants are always measuring themselves against that megalopolis to the south, Boston is a restless place. You can see this in its ever-changing skyline, and in the changing faces of those who fill its streets. You can see it in the Big Dig – the largest and most complex highway project in American history. Today, Bostonians can stand beside the Charles River and gaze at the exquisite new Leonard P Zakim Bunker Hill Bridge and think, 'Eat your heart out, New York.'

Which is not to say Boston aims to emulate its rival. Bostonians treasure the intimacy and ease the city's size affords them. They call their city 'liveable', and it is. But it is also a wonderful place to visit, a place where old and new dovetail perfectly, where, by taking a few steps, you can journey from the 18th century to the 21st and back again. There is actually a better metaphor for the relationship between New York and Boston than the bean and the apple. That city to the south is a sprawling doorstop novel, while this one is a poem, with all its meaning and life compressed onto a single page – to be enjoyed over and over again.

ABOUT THE TIME OUT CITY GUIDES

Time Out Boston is one of an expanding series of Time Out City Guides, now numbering over 45, produced by the people behind London and New York's successful listings magazines. Our guides are all written and updated by resident experts who have striven to provide you with all the most up-to-date information you'll need to explore the city and its sights, understand its history and architecture, and enjoy its best bars and restaurants – whether you're a local or a first-time visitor.

THE LOWDOWN ON THE LISTINGS

Above all, we've tried to make this book as useful as possible. Addresses, telephone numbers, websites, transport information, opening times, admission prices and credit card details are all included in our listings. And, as far as possible, we've given details of facilities, services and events, all checked and correct as we went to press. However, since owners and managers can change their arrangements at any time, we always advise readers to telephone and check opening times and other particulars.

While every effort has been made to ensure the accuracy of the information in this guide, the publishers cannot accept responsibility for any errors it may contain.

PRICES AND PAYMENT

We have noted whether venues accept credit cards, but have only listed the major cards: American Express (**AmEx**), Diners Club (**DC**), Discovery (**Disc**), MasterCard (**MC**) and Visa (**V**). Many businesses will also accept other cards and travellers' cheques.

The prices we've supplied should be treated as guidelines, not gospel. Fluctuating exchange rates and inflation can cause charges, in shops and restaurants particularly, to change rapidly. If prices vary wildly from those we've quoted, please write and let us know. We aim to give the best and most up-to-date advice, so we always want to know if you've been badly treated or overcharged.

THE LIE OF THE LAND

As central Boston is relatively compact, its geography is easy to grasp. To make it even easier, we have divided it into sections. Most of these are in common local usage, but a couple of additional boundaries have been imposed to aid navigation. These areas are defined in our Sightseeing chapters and used throughout the book, both in addresses and chapter subdivisions. We've included cross streets wherever possible to make finding your way around easier. And there are fully indexed maps to the main sightseeing areas of the city, along with the Greater Boston, Trips Out of Town and subway maps at the back of the guide, starting on p272. Venues listed in the book that fall into the area covered have a page and grid reference to take you directly to the right square.

TELEPHONE NUMBERS

The area codes for metropolitan Boston (including Cambridge, Somerville and Brookline) are 617 and 857. Even if you are calling a number within the same area code as the one you are dialling from, you must dial the three-digit code, plus the seven-digit number. The 1 prefix is optional for numbers with the same area code, but must be dialled if you are calling from a different one. We have provided area codes in the listings. For more on Massachusetts area codes and telephone use, *see p258*.

Advertisers

We would like to stress that no establishment has been included in this guide because it has advertised in any of our publications and no payment of any kind has influenced any review. The opinions given in this book are those of Time Out writers and entirely independent.

ESSENTIAL INFORMATION

For all the practical information you might need for visiting the city, including visa and customs information, disabled access, emergency phone numbers, useful websites and the local transport network, turn to the **Directory** chapter at the back of the guide. It starts on page 248.

LET US KNOW WHAT YOU THINK

We hope you enjoy *Time Out Boston*, and we'd like to know what you think of it. We welcome tips for places that you feel we should include in future editions and take notice of your criticism of our choices. You can email us at guides@timeout.com.

There is an online version of this book, along with guides to 45 other international cities, at **www.timeout.com**.

In Context

Features

History

From pilgrims and revolutionaries to modern innovators, Boston has a long tradition of new beginnings.

More than any other city in America, Boston is soaked in history. Sure, Philly's got the fractured Liberty Bell and Washington, DC has the monolithic political monuments. But when people think of Boston, they think of the past, from the Boston Massacre to the Boston Tea Party and the Battle of Bunker Hill. Out-of-town visitors always want to see the sites that begot America, such as Faneuil Hall, the Cradle-of-Liberty-turned-gift-shop, and the Old State House, where the Declaration of Independence was first read to the public in 1776.

Boston has a tradition of influential politics, intellectual curiosity and thoughtful revolution. It's a city with a strong political thrust that has fostered influential leaders since America's inception, from John Adams to John F Kennedy. It's a city of scientific development and technological innovation, from Alexander Graham Bell's telephone to the first ever computer, which was built at MIT. It's a place of academic dominance – Harvard was the first seat of higher education in the country – and the area is known for training and fostering future visionaries, rulers and thinkers. Boston is history: making it, inspiring it and preserving it.

THE PILGRIMS IN 'PARADISE'

Strictly speaking, Boston was not truly 'settled' until the arrival of the Puritans in 1620. Of course, that's the Anglocentric way of looking at it. In fact, the region had human occupants as far back as 7,500 BC. The area was heavily populated with Native Americans by 1497, when John Cabot's explorations in search of the Northwest Passage to the Orient led him to claim Massachusetts for King Henry VII of England. Just over a quarter of a century later, in 1524, Giovanni Verrazano claimed the same land for Francis I of France, thus setting up more than 200 years of squabbling over what had become known as the New World. Word of this 'paradise' reached John Brewster, leader of a strict religious sect known as the Puritans. Facing persecution in England, he began an effort to establish a Puritan colony in America. And so it was that the *Mayflower*, filled with 102 passengers, set sail in September 1620 bound for 'some place about the Hudson River'. It landed nowhere near the Hudson, actually, anchoring instead, after 65 days at sea, at the tip of Cape Cod, near what is now Provincetown. Finding the area too wild for their new town, the Puritans soon moved on, crossing the bay and ultimately establishing their colony on a protected stretch of sandy beach close to several cornfields maintained by local tribes. They called it Plymouth.

Utopia it surely wasn't. Winters were brutal here, and the Pilgrims had little understanding of the land, the kinds of crops that would grow here and what native vegetation was edible.

They also brought diseases with them that wrought devastation on their population and on the Native American tribes. Nearly half of the Pilgrims died of pneumonia and smallpox that first winter. But in the spring local tribes taught them how to plant corn, dig clams and fish for cod. By harvest time, the settlers were sufficiently established to host a three-day feast – celebrated today as Thanksgiving.

Once things were running more smoothly on the new shores, word spread back to England about the Puritans' settlement. By 1630, 1,000 more settlers had arrived. They established Salem, on the north shore of Massachusetts Bay. These new settlers would ultimately form the foundation for what is now Boston. Choosing as their leader John Winthrop, many of them migrated south from Salem to the area now known as Charlestown. This didn't last, however, as the lack of fresh water forced them to relocate to a neighbouring peninsula, known to the natives as Shawmut. Winthrop's settlers bought the narrow 440-acre (177-hectare) peninsula from a hermit bachelor and renamed it Tremontaine after its three surrounding hills. They soon changed their minds and renamed it again. This time they called it Boston, after the Lincolnshire village from which many of them had originally come. As the capital of the Massachusetts Bay Colony, it quickly became the centre of activity.

THIS LAND IS OUR LAND

By 1636 there were some 12,000 colonists, primarily Puritans, spread between the townships of Plymouth, Salem and Boston, with new settlements springing up almost monthly. By 1640 the population of Boston alone was 1,200. In fact, the lack of qualified ministers to keep up with the growing population led Puritan elders to establish America's first training college, which they later named after a young minister, John Harvard, who died and left the college his library. Colonists found Massachusetts curiously easy to settle and rather empty of the anticipated hostile Indians. The fact was, epidemics of smallpox, pneumonia and influenza brought over by early explorers and settlers had decimated the once-robust native population.

Relations with the remaining tribes rapidly deteriorated. The fundamental Puritan notion of a righteous life leading to the accumulation of wealth clashed with native beliefs that it was impossible to own the land. Unlike the French to the north, who converted native populations to Catholicism, the Puritans took a rather more aggressive tack. They attempted to rid Christianity of the heathen devil by burning out the Indians' settlements and appropriating their land. The Algonquin nation, under the leadership of Chief Metacomet (known to colonists as King Philip), retaliated in 1675 by raiding several outlying English settlements. But it was all in vain. Metacomet was betrayed by one of his own warriors the following year and gruesomely executed.

The Indians were not the sole targets of Puritan intolerance. Quakers and Baptists arriving in the colonies were sometimes prevented from leaving their ships; those who practised their faith publicly were hanged for heresy. Such religious paranoia ultimately led to the witch trials of Charleston (1648), Boston (1665) and – most infamously – Salem (1692), where 100 colonists were imprisoned and 19 were hanged in a mass hysteria that became known as the Salem witch trials.

IN COD WE TRUST

By 1700 Boston had grown into the third-largest port of the burgeoning British Empire. Some of the Puritans grew extremely wealthy, thanks primarily to the export of dried cod to the Caribbean and the Mediterranean. (To this day, a carved pine cod – known as 'the Sacred Cod' – hangs above the entrance to the House of Representatives in the State House, pointing towards the party in power.) Some got very rich in a notorious triangular shipping trade where sugar cane was harvested by slaves in the West Indies and then shipped to Boston to be distilled into rum. The Puritans shipped most of the rum to West Africa where it was traded for more slaves who were, in turn, delivered to the Caribbean sugar plantations.

One of the by-products of the city's rum production was molasses (Boston was the largest American producer of the stuff until the early 20th century). Another, more important, consequence was the introduction of slavery to American soil. By 1705 there were more than 400 black slaves – and a small number of free blacks – living in Boston.

At about the same time, England was mired in a serious financial crisis. The crown had incurred enormous expenses during its lengthy (and inconclusive) wars with France. As some of the battles were fought in New England, and as the colonists were virtually voiceless in Parliament, it established the Revenue Act of 1764, which placed heavy duties on silk, sugar and wine from the West Indies. The colonists were irate and began the first of a series of boycotts of the imports involved.

TAXATION WITHOUT REPRESENTATION

Ignoring their protest, Parliament enacted another set of taxes a year later. The Stamp Act required a heavy duty to be paid on all commercial and legal documents printed in the colonies, including newspapers. This was viewed by the colonists as an attempt to remove what little voice they had through the freedom of the press. Again they fumed. Again they felt no sympathy from England. Again they boycotted, but this time, with more force. They branded their protest with the tagline 'No taxation without representation' on the grounds that they had no voice in government in England. They were heard, and the Stamp Act was hastily repealed a year later, but the British still attempted to keep their rebellious cousins in line. They next imposed the Townshend Acts of 1767 – a litany of levies on imported lead, glass, paint, paper and tea.

Britain's attempts to pull political rank enraged the colonists, especially those in Boston. Governmental meeting houses such as Faneuil Hall, the Old South Meeting House and the Old State House became hotbeds for revolutionary plotting. Rebels like Samuel Adams, Daniel Webster, Paul Revere and James Otis gathered secretly to discuss the benefits of splintering off from the British Empire. Prodded by growing public outcry, civil unrest grew so clamorous it carried across the Atlantic and back to the monarch. To quiet the rumblings, George III reluctantly sent troops overseas in 1768, but military occupation in the colonies created more problems than it solved.

Lieutenant General Thomas Gage, commander-in-chief of British forces in the colonies, was faced with a near-impossible situation. Perhaps understandably, he hated Boston and its inhabitants. 'I wish this cursed place was burned,' he wrote in 1770. 'America is a mere bully, from one end to the other, and the Bostonians by far the greatest bullies.'

But it was the British who looked like bullies when, on 5 March 1770, a group of unarmed anti-royalists sparred with English soldiers in front of the Old State House. The Redcoats were antagonised – the gathered assemblage was heckling and throwing things at them. No matter, the Brits came out looking like the bad guys, because during the fray the British troops opened fire. Five colonists were fatally shot, including Crispus Attucks, an African-American slave-turned-martyr who is considered the first casualty of the American Revolution. The colonists were outraged over the attack, and impassioned insurgent Sam Adams dubbed the incident the 'Boston Massacre'. The shooting became a rallying cry for those who supported plans for a revolution.

TEA AND LIBERTY

Word of the incident quickly spread throughout the colonies, causing King George III to fear (and rightly so) that this bloodshed might be the match that would light the powder keg. To avert such an outcome, the king quickly abolished the Townshend Acts – all except for its provisions on tea, which would continue to be taxed under the Tea Act of 1773. This was a little jab from the king to his subjects as George III knew it was the most popular beverage in America. Instead of easing the mood of revolt,

Boston breakthroughs

First North American lighthouse

Boston Light first beckoned ships to shore in 1716. Two years later the beacon's first keeper, George Worthylake, drowned at sea.

First American sighting of a house rat

Occurred in Boston in 1775 – a dubious distinction at best. Not indigenous to the US, the rodents came by ship. As you'll notice if you look around Boston, they took a look and decided to stay.

First African-American schoolhouse

Abiel Smith School became the first public school to educate black children in 1835. It was named after its founding philanthropist, a white businessman.

First painless surgery with a general anaesthetic

In 1846 a dentist named William Morton demonstrated the first surgical use of ether at Massachusetts General Hospital. Dental work is such fun now, thanks to him.

First telephone

On 10 March 1876 Alexander Graham Bell made the very first phone call in history to his assistant, Dr Watson.

First North American subway system

Trains started rolling out of Park Street Station in 1897.

First computer

Developed at MIT in 1931, the infant computer was called a 'differential analyser'.

Fired up: the battles of Lexington and Concord have inspired countless re-enactments.

the move added fuel to the flames and the colonists continued to plot and to boycott.

With the situation growing heated – and with the East India Company (Britain's chief exporter of tea) teetering on the brink of bankruptcy, Parliament attempted to rescue the Asian tea-sellers by exempting them from paying taxes. So while the colonists had to shell out import taxes on tea, the East India Company didn't have to pay tariffs, so it could undercut the prices of local tea merchants and flood the colonial markets. No such luck: every American port slammed shut to English tea ships – except Boston. The state's British governor, Thomas Hutchinson, stuck to the party line, ignoring the incensed citizens, and insisting that all ships could dock in Boston Harbor until the other ports accepted the tea.

The rebels hit back. On the night of 16 December 1773, a group of 60 men, calling themselves the 'Sons of Liberty', disguised themselves as Mohawk Indians (then seen as a symbol of freedom in the New World), stormed the blockaded ships and dumped 342 chests of tea into the harbour. This defiant act, known as the Boston Tea Party, electrified the colonies.

The following September, the first Continental Congress for Independence convened in Philadelphia. Massachusetts sent prominent delegates such as John Adams, John Hancock and Sam Adams to represent it and to help in the writing of the country's manifestos. At the same time, throughout the colonies, local militia began training for a fight.

'BLOWS WILL DECIDE IT'

The first shots of the revolution were fired in Lexington, Massachusetts, on 19 April 1775. British garrisons lodged in Boston heard about an arms store located in the nearby township of Concord. When the Redcoats left Boston to seize the Concord stockpiles on the night of 18 April, rebels Paul Revere, William Dawes and Samuel Prescott set out on horseback to warn the local militia that the British troops were on their way. Paul Revere's ride became one of the most famous acts of the War of Independence – immortalised in Henry Wadsworth Longfellow's 1860 poem (*see p84* **Paul Revere: the ride of his life**). The message was sent, the British marched forth and early the next morning the world's David and Goliath came to blows. The first shot of the battle, called by the rebels the 'shot heard round the world', rang out on Lexington Green where 77 Minutemen – an elite force of local militia members – crouched waiting to ambush 700 Redcoats. The king's men quickly smothered the skirmish, killing eight rebels, and the war was underway. By then, King George was no longer reluctant to go to war. He is said to have told his counsellors: 'I am glad that blows will decide it.'

It was to be a lengthy, bitter fight, marked by heroism on the part of the outgunned, outmanned rebels, and rugged determination on the part of the British. The Americans were led by military leaders who knew only too well that their troops were fighting more with heart than skill. The colonists were plagued by a shortage of ammunition and weaponry. In the first full-scale battle of the revolution, two months after the shots at Lexington, General Israel Putnam is said to have ordered his American troops, 'Don't one of you fire until you see the white of their eyes.' Part of the reason Putnam gave the order was to prevent the troops from wasting scarce ammunition.

That famous command came during the gory battle of Charlestown, which started on 17 June 1775, when the British attacked a group of

The trouble with the Kennedys

Boston's infamous baseball hex isn't the city's only case of really bad juju. There's also the 'Kennedy curse' – aka the chronic misfortunes of America's 'royal family'.

The Kennedys came from humble beginnings. Patrick J Kennedy was a poor immigrant from southern Ireland who pulled himself up by the bootstraps, setting up Boston's only Irish-owned bank. Patrick's son Joseph (born 1888) attended Harvard, married Rose, daughter of popular Boston mayor John 'Honey Fitz' Fitzgerald, and made millions in boat building, the stock market, the motion-picture industry and Prohibition-era bootlegging, later serving as ambassador to Great Britain. But after resigning from the position and losing his first-born in World War II, Joseph devoted himself to the political futures of sons John, Robert and Edward.

John had all the makings of a president. A Harvard graduate, he became a decorated war hero, a Pulitzer Prize winner and a three-term US Senator. In 1960, he beat Richard Nixon to become the 35th US President. During his office, he was a popular leader whose picture-perfect children and beautiful young wife led the media to nickname his government 'Camelot'. But everyone knows what happened next. The Kennedy clan's reversal of fortune began in 1963, when John was shot dead during a Dallas parade. Five years later, younger brother Robert, Attorney General during JFK's presidency, fell to an assassin in his own bid for America's highest office. Youngest son Edward 'Ted' Kennedy also had White House aspirations, but a car accident off the coast of Martha's Vineyard in 1969, which killed his passenger (a young female campaign worker who wasn't his wife), damaged his reputation, and haunted his presidential bid in 1980.

The bad luck didn't stop there. In 1991 Ted's nephew William was indicted for rape, but later acquitted. In 1984 Robert's third son David, who'd battled drug addiction since the age of 13, died from a cocaine overdose at the age of 28; in 1997 his fourth son Michael slammed into a tree while playing football on skis and died. And in 1999 John F Kennedy Jr, a dashing media darling previously linked to the likes of Madonna and Brooke Shields, crashed his plane off the coast and died with the woman he'd wed three years earlier, Carolyn Bessette Kennedy.

Yet, despite the calamities, the family's influence remains strong. Ted is the second most senior member of the US Senate. His son Patrick is a US Representative from Rhode Island. And Joseph's granddaughter Maria is married to the Governor of California, Arnold Schwarzenegger. Joseph must be rolling in his grave: Arnie is a Republican.

colonists who had fortified themselves at the top of Breed's Hill. (This battle was later mistakenly identified as the battle of Bunker Hill, which was, in fact, the next mound over.) Having learned from their mistakes earlier in the war, the unflinching colonists waged a tactically masterful fight: British casualties were more than double that of the Minutemen – more than 1,000 Redcoats were killed compared to 440 rebels. Unfortunately for the Americans, the fight was so heated that they exhausted their ammunition supplies. The Redcoats won that battle, but reports of the bravery of the American troops helped to inspire the spirit of insurrection throughout the colonies.

BIRTH OF A NATION

Meanwhile, in Philadelphia, the Second Continental Congress was establishing a new government. Using as an excuse the fact that King George III had not replied to a petition for redress of grievances sent by the First Continental Congress, the second Congress gradually took on the responsibilities of a national government. In June 1775 the group established a continental army and currency. By the end of July of that year it had also created a post office for the 'United Colonies'.

In August 1775 England issued another proclamation, this one declaring (a bit belatedly) that the colonies were 'engaged in open and avowed rebellion'. Later that year Parliament passed the American Prohibitory Act, which declared that all American vessels and cargoes were the property of the Crown.

It all finally reached a crescendo in Philadelphia on 7 June 1776. On that date the Congress heard Richard Henry Lee of Virginia read a resolution which began: 'Resolved: That these United Colonies are, and of right ought to be, free and independent states, that they are absolved from all allegiance to the British Crown, and that all political connection between them and the state of Great Britain is, and ought to be, totally dissolved.'

The valour (or treachery, depending on your perspective) of the rebels in Boston ultimately resulted in the penning of the Declaration of Independence. The document, still considered one of the world's great governmental manifestos, has been taught in political science classes ever since. Its introductory paragraph is blunt and unapologetic and tells the story of how America viewed its strength in comparison to England's: 'When in the course of human events, it becomes necessary for one people to dissolve the political bands which have connected them with another… a decent respect to the opinions of mankind requires that they should declare the causes which impel them to the separation. We hold these Truths to be self-evident, that all men are created equal; that they are endowed by their Creator with certain unalienable rights, that among these are Life, Liberty and the pursuit of Happiness.'

On 4 July 1776 in Philadelphia, John Hancock of Boston signed his name to the document with a flourish. His is the largest signature by far – he is said to have written large enough that George III could read it without spectacles. Even today in America a 'John Hancock' is an expression for someone's signature.

INNOVATION AND IMMIGRATION

At that point, of course, the war was still far from over. The fight would last for another five years, but while much of it was fought in New England, there were no more battles in Boston. When America finally did achieve its independence in 1781, Massachusetts was one of the original 13 states constituting the fledgling United States of America.

As might be expected, when it was all over, the war relegated the US to England's doghouse and trade was cut off. The loss of the English market caused Boston's status as a major port to suffer. The US economy continued to sputter until Boston embraced whaling and Far East trade; eventually, when the demand for fishing clippers grew, Boston's shipyards – especially Nantucket, New Bedford and Salem – grew into some of the largest in the world. Other Boston inventions that helped the economy were Eli Whitney's cotton gin, Charles Goodyear's vulcanised rubber, Elias Howe's sewing machine and Alexander Graham Bell's telephone.

As the city's wealth and power grew, so did its immigrant population. In the 19th century shiploads of immigrants were turning up on its shores looking for a better life. The Irish arrived in 1845, escaping the potato famine; they were followed by tens of thousands of European immigrants seeking financial opportunity and religious freedom. By 1860 it was estimated that more than 60 per cent of Boston's population had been born elsewhere in the world.

Boston's skinny peninsula could hardly accommodate such an enormous influx of new citizens, so resourceful denizens looked to the fetid swamps of Back Bay for real estate. To make the bogs liveable, two of Boston's three hills were levelled and several feet were shaved off the top of Beacon Hill. But the real work of filling in the marshy Back Bay didn't begin until the mid 1850s, when 3,500 loads of gravel a day were railed in and dumped into the muck. It took 40 years to complete the project – the largest engineering feat of its day. The result was 450 more acres (181 hectares) of land, which doubled the city's size.

THE ATHENS OF AMERICA

'Their hotels are bad. Their pumpkin pies are delicious. Their poetry is not so good,' Edgar Allan Poe once wrote about Bostonians. And Poe was right. For a while, Boston's poetry wasn't so good. But it wasn't just the city's stanzas that lacked finesse; it was the entire notion of crafted aesthetics that escaped the community's inhabitants. Why had the arts been so neglected? In essence, Massachusetts housed many Puritans and Puritans were, well, puritan. They didn't consider the arts a godly practice. As for the other early colonists, many were preoccupied with gaining independence. ('I must study politics and war so that my sons may have liberty to study mathematics and philosophy in order to give their children a right to study painting, poetry, music, architecture,' wrote patriot and future US President John Adams to his wife Abigail in 1780.)

Luckily, economic prosperity in the 19th century was to beget a cultural awakening. When the well-heeled 'First Families of Boston', dubbed 'Brahmins' by writer Oliver Wendell Holmes, began to travel abroad, they realised just how unenlightened their city was. It didn't take the wealthy population long to rectify the situation. In the short span between the 1840s and 1880s, Boston gained a music hall, a magnificent public library, a museum of natural history, a museum of fine arts and a symphony orchestra. These new arts showcases, coupled with the talent they attracted, earned the city the sobriquet 'the Athens of America'.

Athens was also the birthplace of the Olympics, and Boston was one of the first American cities to take sports seriously. In 1897 the first Boston Marathon ran from the nearby town of Hopkinton to Copley Square. Soon afterwards, the newly invented game of baseball swung into the city. Boston's first professional team was called the Somersets, but the name only lasted one season. In 1903 Boston's new team, the Pilgrims, hosted the Pittsburgh Pirates at the World Series; by the time Fenway Park opened in 1912, the Pilgrims were renamed the Red Sox. Six years later the Red Sox won Boston's fifth World Series in 17 years – it would be the last time that century Boston would win a championship. Bostonians have been torturing themselves ever since.

THE WAR AGAINST SLAVERY

Talk about being misunderstood: when Bostonian Wendell Phillips joined the Massachusetts Anti-Slavery Society, his Yankee family wanted to send him to a sanitarium. Fortunately, he withstood their persecution and eventually became one of abolitionism's most revered voices.

Phillips was swayed to anti-slavery when, at the age of 24, he witnessed a lynch mob drag reputed abolitionist William Lloyd Garrison half-naked through the streets. But such savage bigotry was less common in Massachusetts than anywhere else in the country.

In 1800 Boston was home to the oldest and largest population of free black people in America (a full five per cent of its then total population of 25,000) and the black community already had its heroes: Crispus Atticus was a martyr of the Boston Massacre, Peter Salem a hero of Bunker Hill. Although the black population hadn't yet been granted suffrage, they were allowed to earn wages as servants, street cleaners, shipbuilders, blacksmiths and barbers. They could also meet freely, worship as they pleased and educate themselves. The first African Meeting House in America was built on Beacon Hill in 1806, and the first black school, Abiel Smith, in 1835. Taught to young Boston children were the ABCs of Abolition:

A is an abolitionist
A man who wants to free
The wretched slave
And give to all
An equal liberty
B is a Brother with a skin
Of somewhat darker hue,
But in our Heavenly Father's sight
He is as dear as you

Hence, it wasn't surprising that, as tensions over slavery mounted between the North and South, Boston became the centre of the abolition movement. The New England Anti-Slavery Society was founded in 1832, and prominent blacks such as Frederick Douglass, William Nell and Maria Miller Stuart began condemning slavery publicly with the support of wealthy white people. Lewis and Harriet Hayden's house at 66 Phillips Street became a station on the Underground Railroad (a network of abolitionists whose members smuggled slaves from the South to freedom in the North). When the Civil War broke out, the first free black regiment of the Union Army – the 54th Regiment of Massachusetts – was organised on Beacon Hill, trained in Jamaica Plain and sent to battle in the Carolinas. All of those soldiers died in war. Their story was largely forgotten for the better part of a century. It gained attention only in recent years – it is commemorated by a sculpture in the Public Garden and was explored in the 1989 film *Glory*.

SHAMROCK GOVERNMENT

It might be hard to believe in these days of pubs shipped over brick by brick from Dublin, but Boston didn't always ooze unconditional love

Sam Adams: the firebrand brewer

Walk into any Boston pub and you'll see him behind the bar, hoisting a frothy mug: Samuel Adams, the pony-tailed patron saint of Boston beer. Nearly three centuries ago, Adams played a key role in the Revolution and was a signatory of the Declaration of Independence. But since Sam Adams Ale was established in 1984 the Massachusetts-born sparkplug has become better known for his place in the brewing industry than as an architect of the American Revolution. So who was the man behind the brew?

Born in 1722, Adams grew up in Quincy, Massachusetts, a Boston suburb that was also the birthplace of John Hancock. Cousin of future President John Adams, Samuel entered Harvard and studied philosophy, Latin and literature – disciplines that would ultimately serve him well in the colonists' struggle against the Crown. After receiving a Master's degree, Adams inherited his father's brewery in 1748, which was situated on Boston's State Street. Meanwhile, he became ever more active in local politics, sermonising at town hall meetings and running successfully for city offices such as Clerk of the Market and Tax Collector.

But Adams' strengths weren't pecuniary, they were rhetorical. The brewery closed in 1764 due to fiscal mismanagement, and he began to devote himself to politics full time. As a bold and impassioned speaker, he regularly decried Britain in public forums and penned insurgent manifestos denouncing the Crown's control. When the mother country imposed the Revenue Act in 1764 – a tariff on imported sugar, rum, and certain wines – Adams drafted the colonies' angry response, a deed that led him to being elected to the Massachusetts General Court. Then in 1770, after British troops fired into a crowd of rioting civilians, killing five, Adams dubbed the event the 'Boston Massacre', painting the rebelling casualties as martyrs, even though the Redcoats had been provoked.

One of the reasons historians remember Adams as the father of the American Revolution is that he was a major force behind the Boston Tea Party. In 1773, the British repealed the Townshend Acts, a six-year old tax on imported lead, glass, paint, paper and tea. But as a direct insult to the tea-loving colonists, Parliament continued to tax the dried leaves under a new law called the Tea Act and brought in an Asian company that could sell tea for cheap prices, hoping to put colonial tea merchants out of business. On 16 December, the evening before a major tea shipment was due to be unloaded, Adams and about 60 protestors – a group called the Sons of Liberty who were dressed as Native Americans – ran aboard three docked boats and threw 342 crates of tea into the Boston Harbor. This act of insurgence sparked the American Revolutionary War.

When the first Continental Congress was held the following year, Adams was the Massachusetts representative. A pivotal contributor to America's freedom, he helped compose the Articles of Confederation and later was one of the signatories of the Declaration of Independence. From 1789 to 1794 he was governor of Massachusetts, succeeding John Hancock. He died in 1803 aged 81, and today rests in Boston's Old Granary Burying Ground (*see p63*).

But the least-known fact about Samuel Adams? He was a terrible brewer.

for the Irish. When the potato famine of the mid 19th century first sent over 100,000 people from Ireland to Boston, the reported life expectancy of an Irish immigrant living in Boston was 14 years. In this traditionally Brahmin city, blatant discrimination was common. Job postings often bore the clause 'No Irish Need Apply'.

After generations of political struggle, though, prejudices began to subside as the city's Irish political machine fought its way into power. The election of the first Irish-Catholic mayor of Boston, Hugh O'Brien, started to chip away at racial biases – so much so, that eventually Irish leaders couldn't lose a race.

'Boss' James Michael Curley was perhaps the finest example of this relative invincibility. Curley was nicknamed the Purple Shamrock – and as the moniker suggests, he was a colourful character. Curley served as congressman, governor and mayor, and over a checkered 40-year career he bought votes, got re-elected to the position of alderman while in the clink and allegedly acquired the mayoral office after threatening to expose the incumbent, John 'Honey Fitz' Fitzgerald (JFK's maternal grandfather), for having a mistress. And holding true to his crooked ways, Curley spent much of his fourth and last term as mayor in a federal penitentiary, charged with mail fraud.

20TH-CENTURY BLUES

By the late 1940s Boston had lost its major port status to the West Coast and its manufacturing to the South. What's more, Boston became the only major US city in the post-World War II baby boom to see a decline in population (plummeting from 800,000 to 560,000). Both the city's middle and upper classes migrated to the suburbs, and its infrastructure went with them. With downtown crime on the rise and student demonstrations blocking the streets, tourism suffered, and the city entered an economic crisis. By the mid 1960s Boston had officially become one of the worst places to live in America.

Panicked by Boston's decline, city officials attempted to hit the brakes. Under Mayor John Hynes and the newly established Boston Redevelopment Authority (BRA), officials began a 'clean up' of the city's problem areas. The 1960s saw the completion of three massive urban renewal projects with controversial results. The Prudential Tower rose out of Back Bay's abandoned Boston & Maine railyards. The West End, Boston's only ethnically mixed neighbourhood, was razed to make way for a modern apartment complex called Charles River Park. Seedy Scollay Square, home to Boston's then few gay bars and jazz joints, was levelled to make way for the new Government Center. They called it urban renewal. But, basically, much of the city's character was systematically erased in the name of progress.

However inept, though, these first efforts at regeneration did have their positive side, although mainly in reaction to them. Organisations like the Beacon Hill Historical Society were established to protect other neighbourhoods from suffering the fate of the West End. Public outcry caused subsequent developers to be attentive to architectural and historical significance. Today the city maintains many of its most important historical buildings despite the ravages of the planners and developers of the 1960s and 1970s.

Enforced integration in schools sparked the notorious race riots of the 1970s. *See p15.*

DESEGREGATION AND DISCONTENT

In the midst of financial chaos, Boston then entered an emotional and moral morass. The city's 1970s race riots are notorious to this day. Possibly the most striking image from those days was shot on City Hall Plaza, when a white student tried to spear a black passer-by with a flagpole bearing an American flag. Presages of such bigotry began in 1974, when federal Judge Arthur Garrity Jr ordered the city to desegregate its public school system. Before the ruling, proximity had dictated school assignment, leaving poor children (often racial minorities) going to school only with other poor children and receiving a poor education. The court saw this as a violation of civil rights and forced an end to the practice. It ordered a racial integration policy designed to give each school a ratio of black to white children that reflected Boston's overall population. That September, under heavy police security, the Board of Education began busing white students into black neighbourhoods and black students into white neighbourhoods. Huge riots flared up. Crowds of angry white parents and children filled the streets. Rocks were thrown at the black students. Bedlam ensued – most particularly in Irish South Boston and largely black Roxbury. While the violence exposed Boston's ugly underbelly to the nation, critics of busing – future Mayor of Boston Ray Flynn, President Gerald Ford, state politician William Bulger – argued fervently that this fight concerned other issues than racism. Many believed Boston's ethnic ghettos had evolved into close-knit neighbourhoods – both blacks and whites feared losing their hard-earned sense of community. The court disagreed.

Finally, in 1999, precisely 25 years after the racial integration programme began, the Boston School Committee voted to stop using racial quotas for school placement, saying it would never achieve its goal of making the schools truly equal. The ending was anti-climactic, nobody emerged a winner. And in the eyes of many Boston will always be associated with those scenes of racial intolerance and hatred.

BREAKING NEW GROUND

In the 1970s city officials courted the emerging high-tech industry aggressively and, by the mid 1980s, Boston had reinvented itself once again. 'The Massachusetts Miracle' – as the media touted Boston's resuscitated economy – was due largely to the leadership of mayors such as Kevin White and Raymond Flynn. Within the last 15 or 20 years, Boston has become a popular location for the headquarters of national corporations. Around the turn of the century Boston also underwent a major facelift.

Irish Famine Memorial.

The city's Central Artery, a six-lane elevated freeway jutting through downtown, was one of the most congested highways in the country. And so in the early '80s, local planners designed the Big Dig, one of the largest, most technically complicated engineering projects ever undertaken in the United States. Construction began in 1991, giving birth to the Ted Williams Tunnel, a long underground stretch dedicated to one of Boston's most revered athletes, and a new Boston landmark, the Leonard P Zakim Bunker Hill Bridge, the widest cable-stayed suspension bridge in the world.

Boston continues to make national history. The city still produces influential political figures. Governor Michael Dukakis ran for President in 1988, but lost to George Bush Sr. In 2004 US Senator John Kerry received the Democratic nomination for President – another Massachusetts man duelling with a Bush. And in May 2004, after a ruling by the Massachusetts Supreme Judicial Court, the first gay couples were legally married. Once again, Boston is a leader in shaping America.

Key events

1497-1524 Explorations of Massachusetts Bay by John Cabot, Miguel Corte Real and Giovanni Verrazano – among others.
1614 Captain John Smith explores and maps the Massachusetts Bay area.
1620 Puritans set sail aboard the *Mayflower*. They land on Cape Cod on 11 November. They found Plymouth on 10 December.
1630 John Winthrop and his Puritans establish Boston on the Shawmut peninsula.
1636 The first college in the New World is established; it's given the name Harvard College in 1638.
1665 Boston witch trials.
1675 Native American Chief Metacomet (King Philip) raids several Massachusetts Bay Colony settlements. A year later he is captured, drawn, quartered and beheaded.
1692 Salem witch trials.
1706 Benjamin Franklin born on the corner of Milk and Devonshire Streets.
1765 Parliament imposes Stamp Act on all commercial and legal documents, including newspapers. It's repealed one year later.
1767 The Townshend Acts are passed by Parliament, placing duties on any glass, lead, paint, paper and tea imported to the colonies.
1768 Troops are dispatched to Boston by George III to quiet civil unrest.
1770 George III repeals duties levied in the Townshend Act except those on tea. Clash on 5 March between Bostonians and English soldiers results in the Boston Massacre.
1773 Sons of Liberty host the Boston Tea Party on 16 December by dumping 342 chests of East India tea into the harbour.
1774 Boston port is closed and colonists prohibited from meeting publicly. Delegates from Massachusetts are sent to the First Continental Congress in Philadelphia, convened on 5 September.
1775 Battles of Lexington and Concord take place on 19 April, when British march to Concord to take an arms store. Battle of Bunker Hill takes place on 17 June.
1776 British troops evacuate Boston in March. Declaration of Independence signed in Philadelphia on 4 July and first read to the public from the balcony of the Old State House on 18 July.
1783 Slavery is abolished in Massachusetts.
1793 Eli Whitney invents the cotton gin.
1822 Boston becomes a city on 7 January.
1830 Cows stop grazing on Boston Common.
1835 Abiel Smith School is opened, the first black schoolhouse in the USA.
1839 Charles Goodyear invents vulcanised rubber.
1854 Boston Public Library opens, the first free public library in the USA.
1862 The 54th Regiment of Massachusetts, the first black regiment of the Union Army, is commissioned, trained and sent to battle in the Civil War.
1872 The Great Fire of Boston destroys most of what is now downtown Boston.
1876 Alexander Graham Bell introduces the telephone. The Museum of Fine Arts opens.
1897 Park Street and Boylston Street stations open, part of the first subway in the USA.
1897 First Boston Marathon is run.
1912 Fenway Park opens. The Boston Red Sox win the World Series.
1905 James Curley begins his political career as alderman, campaigning from jail.
1931 World's first computer is developed at MIT.
1946 John F Kennedy elected congressman.
1947 Curley serves final term as mayor from a federal penitentiary.
1960 John F Kennedy becomes 35th president of the USA.
1963 John F Kennedy is assassinated.
1974 Federal district court orders the desegregation of Boston schools. Cross-town busing begins.
1980 Boston celebrates 350th anniversary.
1988 Mike Dukakis runs unsuccessfully as Democratic candidate for president.
1990 Boston's population increases in the census for the first time in four decades.
1991 Construction on the Big Dig, the largest highway project in US history, begins.
1993 Thomas Menino is elected mayor, the first non-Irishman to hold the post in 63 years.
1995 The Ted Williams Tunnel, the first completed milestone of the Central Artery/Tunnel Project, opens to traffic.
1999 Race-based admissions end in Boston public schools.
2003 Leonard P Zakim Bunker Hill Bridge opens – the widest cable-stayed bridge in the world. Mitt Romney, a Republican Mormon, takes up his post as governor.
2004 After a ground-breaking court case in November 2003, gay marriage becomes legal in Massachusetts. John Kerry is Democratic presidential candidate.

John Kerry on the campaign trail.

Boston Today

In the midst of a slick makeover, the Hub is hungry for the spotlight.

For a native, watching Boston's behaviour over the past few years has been like witnessing an elderly aunt belting out a Britney Spears number in a karaoke bar. It's too embarrassing for words, but there's also something hopeful about the spectacle.

During the 20th century, Boston's best days already seemed to be behind it. 'I have just returned from Boston. It is the only thing to do if you find yourself up there,' quipped radio comedian Fred Allen in the 1930s.

However, more recently, the Hub (*see p22* **Name calling**) has been working hard to raise its profile. For the better part of a decade, city and state officials struggled to win the right to host the 2004 Democratic National Convention (no major political party had ever met in the city before). The city has also successfully lobbied for such prestigious national sporting events as baseball's All-Star Game and golf's Ryder Cup. At the same time, Boston has undergone a makeover, thanks to the Big Dig highway project, a mammoth new convention centre and an array of recently erected gleaming skyscrapers.

The Bay State has also been thrust into the political spotlight thanks to the presidential campaign of its junior senator, John Kerry, and to a state court ruling that made Massachusetts the first jurisdiction in the United States to recognise gay marriage.

In a few years, Boston may be seen as a trendsetter – or a crazy aunt that the rest of the country does its best to ignore.

THE BIG PIG

The Big Dig is the most expensive public works project in American history, which is why many taxpayers prefer its porcine nickname. Its objective was to replace the city's unsightly elevated expressway with a larger-capacity tunnel, thereby easing traffic jams, reducing air pollution and providing citizens with unimpeded access to Boston Harbor. Begun in 1991, the Dig's original estimated cost was $2.6 billion, but that figure has since risen to nearly $15 billion.

Now completed, the underground highway is one of the most advanced in the nation. Still, it went through a bad batch of publicity just a couple of weeks after the southbound side opened, as water leaks created sheets of ice along parts of the tunnel. The leaks were blamed on sections of the old artery that had not yet been torn down, which raised another question that should have been answered by now: what exactly is going to take the place of the highway system that kept large parts of downtown Boston in darkness for 50 years? We know that the Rose Kennedy Greenway – named after the mother of John F Kennedy – will be a 27-acre ribbon of mostly open land, and that part of the area is tipped for the development of a $70 million botanical garden by the Massachusetts Horticultural Society, but other ideas, such as performance stages and outdoor cafés, were still up in the air as this guide went to press.

'YANKEES SUCK!'

Any discussion of Boston's place in the national consciousness has to involve New York. The

Bright young things

Every September some 250,000 students descend on the Boston area to attend the more than 60 colleges and universities here. This massive young-adult population influences virtually every aspect of city life, and Boston's humming cultural scene owes much to the academic presence: concerts, film screenings, lectures, readings and exhibitions are often tied to the colleges. Boston is home to some of the world's most esteemed writers, poets, and scientists – some studied here and never left, others teach in the renowned universities. These institutions have even helped shape the appearance of the city: it's guaranteed that at one point or other you'll find yourself standing in the shadow of a university building. Be it brick and ivy, or stainless steel and glass, these edifices define the Boston landscape.

On the flip side, the student population is not welcomed with open arms by all Bostonians. Undeniable antipathy exists between the grown-ups and the youngsters who party loud and long and flit around, arrogant and entitled, like they own the place. Yet, love 'em or hate 'em, the young and highly educated give this place its pulse.

The crème de la crème of the area's institutions is Harvard. Founded in 1636, it's the oldest university in the country, and one of the most prestigious. With admission rates hovering around ten per cent of applicants, an air of exclusivity pervades the campus. Tourists stroll amid the ivied, red-brick buildings of Harvard Yard to soak up the heady mix of intellectual endeavour, history and privilege. Harvard undergrads have the reputation of taking their work, and themselves, very seriously. Yet how can you blame them, when the annual tuition, room and board adds up to a cool $39,880? Pulitzer Prize-winning authors and seven US presidents (including George W Bush – maybe he's not so dumb after all?) are among the alumni.

Just down Mass Ave from Harvard in Kendall Square, the Massachusetts Institute of Technology isn't exactly for slackers either. From the development of radar to the Genome Project, MIT pushes the boundaries of technological innovation. The student body stereotype – techno-geeks who get their kicks rebuilding their computers on Friday nights – isn't far off the mark. And although fraternities are a potent campus presence, having a social life at MIT seems like a miracle of science. But who cares when you stand to make millions after graduation?

Boston University, meanwhile, situated on the outskirts of Back Bay near bumping, thumping Lansdowne Street, tends to be more party-intensive than the colleges across the Charles. With a population of more than 16,000 undergrads, BU has a bit of everything – jocks, frat boys, hippies and hipsters, plus a significant faction of designer-clad international students. The actual campus blends blandly into the Kenmore Square and Comm Ave surroundings; the real student centre is the Allston/Brighton neighbourhood with its grocery store-sized liquor stores and countless cheap take-out joints.

Nearby, Berklee College of Music and New England Conservatory groom the country's future rock, jazz and classical stars, ensuring the Boston/Cambridge music scene is always buzzing with innovation.

The list goes on: Boston College, Northeastern, Emerson, Tufts, Wellesley, Brandeis... all are seats of higher education in the Boston area. No wonder the students think they own this town.

one-sided rivalry (New Yorkers certainly don't obsess over Boston) began early in the 20th century, when the Boston Red Sox traded one of the greatest baseball players of all time, Babe Ruth, to the New York Yankees. Boston has never got over it. The Sox haven't won the World Series since 1918, and that's a major source of insecurity for this baseball-mad city. Even non-baseball fans are sensitive about their town's team. When 1.5 million people assembled downtown to celebrate the New England Patriots' victory in the 2004 Super Bowl – the football team's second championship win in three years – the crowd passed the time by lustily chanting 'Yankees suck!'

New York's shadow is just as strong outside the realm of sports. The New York Times Company owns the famously liberal daily newspaper, the *Boston Globe* – though the Hub remains one of the few two-newspaper cities in America, thanks to the *Herald*, a conservative tabloid that still shows the influence of former owner Rupert Murdoch. In the late '90s, Macy's took over the beloved Jordan Marsh department store and, to add insult to injury, replaced it with a small and rather shabby version of its New York emporium. Another indignity came in 2003, when it was announced that the Boston Ballet's 35-year holiday tradition, *The Nutcracker*, would be evicted from the huge Wang Center for the Performing Arts to make room for a road-show production starring New York's Radio City Rockettes. (*The Nutcracker* has found a home in the smaller Colonial Theatre for the 2004 Christmas season, before it relocates to the restored Opera House in 2005.)

But in other respects Boston has some bragging rights over the megalopolis to the south. In 2003 the business magazine *Forbes* ranked Boston third in its 'Best Cities for Singles' report, behind Austin and Denver but well ahead of eighth-place New York, and the Hub took first place in the 'culture' category, thanks to its affordable and plentiful arts offerings. And, of course, Boston snared the 2004 national convention of the Democratic Party, the dominant political force on both American coasts, while New York's booby prize was the gathering of the Republicans.

Boston has also outmatched New York in producing presidential candidates for about 50 years, from John F Kennedy to John F Kerry. The initially harsh coverage of the Kerry campaign by the Boston media may be attributed to fears of backing another 'loser' (the country rejected former Massachusetts Governor Michael Dukakis in 1988).

And while many native Bostonians still grumble about being in New York's shadow, an increasing number of residents are finding some fringe benefits to the symbiotic relationship, including frequently scheduled three-hour train rides to Manhattan (or, for as little as $10, four-hour bus rides), dual memberships in New York and Boston gyms, and the appearance of famous New York DJs in Boston dance clubs.

THE NEW BOSTONIANS

If the chip on Boston's shoulder seems to be shrinking, it may be because most of its current residents were born elsewhere. According to the 2000 Census figures, about one quarter of the city's residents are foreign-born, and another quarter were born outside of Massachusetts. A 2003 study by the respected think tank MassINC showed that the state is attracting young, highly educated workers from other states – many of them from New York, which is probably the only city in America with higher housing costs. On the minus side, Massachusetts is losing middle-class families with children – which can largely be attributed to the scarcity of housing in the minority of suburbs with well-regarded public (state) schools.

The 2000 Census also revealed that Boston's white Anglo population has dipped below 50 per cent for the first time in history. This shift was underscored by the recent elections of Felix Arroyo, the city's first Hispanic city councillor, and Jarrett Barrios, the first Hispanic state senator to be elected in Massachusetts. Most agree that racial tensions have cooled since the 1970s, when attempts to desegregate public schools led to a series of riots in mostly white neighbourhoods, but the image of a city that is unwelcoming towards African-Americans persists to this day.

Boston also has a large gay and lesbian population, which will probably get larger as a result of two related events: the court ruling which permits gay marriage in Massachussetts and the scrambling by almost every other state in the union to rewrite their laws so that the same thing doesn't happen to them.

THE NEW NEIGHBOURHOODS

When the national economy was at its strongest in the 1990s, Boston officials touted big plans for building a completely new neighbourhood on Boston Harbor to take the place of long-extinct factories and shipyards. The Seaport District has a long way to go, thanks to a now erratic economy and the cold feet of developers. But major pieces of the neighbourhood are being filled in. There's the 700,000-square-foot (65,000-square-metre) convention centre, as well as a new federal courthouse. The tipping point for making the area attractive to people other than lawyers and conventioneers may be the Institute of Contemporary Art (currently in the Back Bay, *see p106*), whose ground-breaking modern headquarters is set to be completed by 2006.

A smaller-scale attempt at neighbourhood-building has already been a conspicuous success. The Ladder District (*see p67*) is the fulfilment of Boston's decades-old dream of an upscale area to link the downtown shopping area with the theatre district – and to erase the red-light district known as the Combat Zone. When a cluster of upscale restaurants opened in the area a few years ago, they immediately attracted large crowds of dining connoisseurs. The neighbourhood became increasingly popular and now also has a new 19-screen cinema, an outpost of the posh SportsClub/LA and a gleaming new Ritz-Carlton hotel.

MORIBUND POLITICS

One area where Boston has lost much of its crackle in recent years is in local politics. Mayor Tom Menino's place in office seems to be secure for as long as he wants it, and the City Council has few powers – and little inclination – to act as a countervailing force. Since his 1994 inauguration, Menino has had mostly good fortune. Unemployment is low, crime has plummeted to its lowest levels in 35 years, and school exam scores have been climbing.

Still, it hasn't all been an easy ride for the mayor. Police and firefighters seeking a new contract picketed the mayor's State of the City address in early 2004, and the entire City Council declined to enter the auditorium. On this issue and others, Menino has tried to walk a fine line between old-fashioned city politics (in the form of public employees seeking more

Puritans or rebels?

Thanks to overzealous city censors in the early 20th century, 'Banned in Boston' became a synonym for raciness – and a surefire way to increase book sales. But Boston is certainly not the most buttoned-up city in modern America. Evangelical Protestants, who are leading the charge against the 'decline' in American culture, are virtually non-existent in Boston, and the Roman Catholic Church has largely lost its power to keep its flock away from 'blasphemous' activities. Moral guardians just don't have much clout in a college centre with one of the youngest populations in the United States. (Among major US cities, only Austin, Texas, has a lower average age.) So has Boston finally cast off its Puritan character?

Yes and no. Boston doesn't have many preachers promising hellfire to anyone who enjoys himself on earth, but there are neighbourhood groups warning that there will be hell to pay if anyone disturbs their members' sleep. And the city's large student population only makes local politicians hyper-vigilant against any activity that might lead to rowdiness. (Public urination is an obsession of residents who live near colleges.)

So let's look at the particulars:

Adult entertainment The Combat Zone, Boston's once-thriving red-light district, has been obliterated by rising property values. Two strip clubs and a couple of dirty book stores are all that's left of what used to be a favourite area for bachelor parties. But adult videos and sex toys can be found in more places than ever across the Boston area, with boutiques popping up in such staid neighbourhoods as Coolidge Corner (where the local cinema also hosts an annual amateur-porn festival). Besides risqué theme parties at local dance clubs, there are also events like the biannual Fetish Fair, which brings hundreds of leather-and-leash aficionados to an upscale hotel venue.

Gay life For a city of Boston's size, there are astonishingly few gay bars, and the area's only bath house was shut down by the authorities several years ago. But there are plenty of gay-friendly churches, a queer section in just about every bookstore, and one of the country's largest Gay Pride celebrations in June. Massachusetts is also the first jurisdiction in the United States to recognise the legality of gay marriage.

Alcohol Happy hours and two-for-one drink specials are against the law in Massachusetts, for fear people might get drunk too quickly. And Boston's 2am closing time seems set in stone; even a proposal to let hotel bars stay open an extra hour during the Democratic National Convention drew such howls of outrage that it was immediately abandoned. Teetotallers lost one battle in 2004, as the state finally repealed its law against stores selling liquor on Sundays.

Smoking In 2003, Boston banned cigarette smoking in all bars and restaurants (except for the handful of trendy 'cigar bars'), and the entire state seems ready to follow its lead.

benefits) and catering to newer Bostonians (who would like to see more fiscal restraint). Despite coming from Hyde Park, one of the most conservative neighbourhoods in the city, Menino has sometimes sided with the newer Bostonians in advocating gay rights, and he approved a city programme that distributes clean syringes to drug users in order to limit the spread of HIV and hepatitis.

Politics is somewhat more exciting at the state level. Republican Mitt Romney, a former businessman with a no-nonsense demeanour, won the Governor's office by promising to act as a check against the overwhelmingly Democratic legislature. He has had some successes, most notably in holding off tax increases, yet Romney's strong opposition not only to gay marriages, but also to same-sex civil unions, is something of a risk in mostly liberal Massachusetts – which has fuelled speculation that the Governor may ultimately be more interested in national office.

As for Senator Kerry, his initials and his good looks recall John F Kennedy, and his home on historic Beacon Hill is a symbol of the city's gentrification. He first gained fame as a Vietnam vet turned anti-war protester, coming out of that divisive era with stripes that could satisfy all camps. In contrast to the state's other US senator, blustery liberal Ted Kennedy, Kerry has a cool demeanour and a reputation as a pragmatist rather than an ideologue.

BUSINESS SENSE

Boston is considered the world's third largest city for money management, behind New York and London. Widely viewed as the king of the mutual fund, the city houses the headquarters

While you can still find a few places in smoke-free New York where people puff away in a back room, adherence to the law is almost absolute in Boston – you'll have to stand out on the street if you want a nicotine fix. On the other hand, pot is not exactly a rare substance in the Hub. In October 2003, some 50,000 people attended Hempfest, the 14th annual rally on Boston Common in favour of repealing laws against marijuana – and it's a safe bet that most of those people had a vested interest in the issue.

Noise Boston residents are famous for trying to block or shut down any business that might remind them that they live in a city. But they couldn't stop the city from allowing Bruce Springsteen to play two concerts in Fenway Park in 2003 – with loudspeakers that reportedly carried the music for more than a mile. And after both commuters and underground musicians protested, the MBTA dropped a proposed ban on the use of amplifiers on subway platforms. (Trumpets, however, are still against the rules, apparently because they sound too much like the indecipherable announcements by T personnel.)

Language Are you shitting me? This is a state whose inhabitants are nicknamed 'Massholes', where four-year-olds are taught to yell 'Yankees suck!', and whose junior senator complained to *Rolling Stone* magazine that President Bush 'fucked up' in Iraq. Foul language is one taboo Bostonians threw into the harbour a long time ago.

of world-class financial companies like Fidelity and Putnam. The boom-and-bust high-tech sector continues to be one of the city's biggest growth industries, and Boston is home to 3,000 software and internet companies. Trying to stay ahead of the curve, the city and state are also trying to expand the area's already strong profile in the nascent biotech industry.

The largest employer in the Boston area, however, is the health-care industry, with many well-regarded hospitals here attracting patients from all over the country. According to a 2003 study by the Milken Institute, Massachusetts ranks third in the percentage of its workforce employed in health care, behind Pennsylvania and Rhode Island. Massachusetts General Hospital alone employs nearly 12,000 people – which helps explain the intense competition for apartments on nearby Beacon Hill.

Name calling

Beantown, the Hub... visitors are understandably puzzled by Boston's many monikers, but they all have logical origins. The Native Americans called it **Shawmut**, or 'unclaimed land'. When John Winthrop and his fellow Puritans defied the Indians by claiming it after all, they promptly renamed it **Tremontaine** (three mountains) after the three local hills that dominated the place. In no time, though, the homesick settlers had re-dubbed their village **Boston** (a corruption of St Botolph's Town) after the Lincolnshire village from which most of them had come. A torrent of other names soon followed, all of which have stuck around for centuries.

Take, for instance, **Beantown**. In the 18th century Boston was fairly awash with molasses, a by-product of rum production. Because of its cheap cost and plenitude, the syrup was frequently used by colonial housewives to sweeten ordinary foods. A favourite food of the day was beans that had been stewed in the sugary stuff for hours. Travellers dubbed the town Beantown, for this ubiquitous dish.

In the early 1800s, Boston became America's undisputed capital of culture. It's little wonder, then, that the city became known as the **Athens of America**.

Later in the 19th century, the writer Oliver Wendell Holmes gave the city the moniker that Bostonians love the most. In his popular 1858 essay *The Autocrat of the Breakfast Table*, he described Boston's State House as the 'hub of the Solar System'. In no time, Bostonians had extended the concept, calling their city the hub of the universe – and the **Hub** remains Boston's most popular nickname to this day.

RENTS AND RAVES

Though the office vacancy rate has recently risen, there is still a housing shortage in the Boston area. Thanks to a sluggish economy, Boston's apartment vacancy rate rose to about four per cent in 2003, but job growth is expected to push that figure back down, especially because few affordable units are being added to the market. In 2003 the city's average rent was up to $1,542 per month, with modest one-bedrooms in the Back Bay and Cambridge easily topping $2,000 per month. Condos in safe and well-equipped neighbourhoods now almost all cost above $250,000, and million-dollar units are popping up in the South End and other areas once considered affordable alternatives to downtown living.

In the past, students, lower-wage workers and struggling families looked to nearby areas like Allston, Cambridge or Somerville for cheap housing. But today's high rents are pushing them further away from the centre of city life. They may also be contributing to the number of homeless people in the city. Estimates, which some social agencies feel are conservative, place the homeless population at around 5,000 – almost one per cent of the city's population.

Gentrification has also killed much of Boston's underground party scene, including the all-night raves and ticket-only loft parties popular in the late '80s and early '90s. That was an era of cheap living, when hundreds of local artists took over dusty warehouses and abandoned lofts along the edges of downtown. Gradually the artists' efforts to make their new environs safe and comfortable proved so successful that they caught the attention of those with much deeper pockets. Since the tenants' upheaval, underground parties aren't completely extinct in the Boston area, but they tend to take place in the less expensive sections of the Dorchester neighbourhood, or in nearby cities such as Chelsea and Lynn.

CRIME STORIES

During the 1990s, the Boston Police Department put more police officers on the street, several neighbourhoods organised a series of crime watch schemes, and schools instituted anti-gang programmes. State legislators also provided Massachusetts with the toughest gun control laws in the country. The results have been pretty spectacular: both violent crime and

Give us the money: Boston's heavyweight **Financial District**.

crimes against property have fallen to their lowest levels in 30 years, and homicide is at its lowest level in 40 years.

While garden-variety crimes are down, there are plenty of stories for the tabloids. For example, the saga of South Boston mobster James 'Whitey' Bulger, brother of former State Senate President William Bulger, has been the subject of several books and newspaper stories. Over the course of the 1970s and '80s, Whitey Bulger allegedly became the city's king of drug-trafficking and extortion by becoming an FBI informant and helping put away his rivals in the Italian Mafia. Several FBI agents allegedly helped him and his associates by warning them whenever other law-enforcement figures were trying to gather evidence against them. In 1995, Bulger – personally accused of several brutal murders – was apparently tipped off that an indictment was finally near, and he took off for parts unknown. 'Whitey sightings' have been a staple of crime journalism in Boston ever since.

But the biggest crime story of 2002 was the sexual abuse scandal that wracked the Roman Catholic Church, and particularly the Archdiocese of Boston. Cardinal Bernard F Law resigned amid charges that he covered up crimes by clergy, and in 2003 the archdiocese finally agreed to pay $85 million to more than 500 people who said they were sexually abused by Boston area priests, most of them when they were teenagers, over the previous few decades. The story took another nasty turn in August 2003, when convicted sexual abuser John J Geoghan was strangled to death by another inmate, leading to an investigation into whether prison guards allowed the crime to happen.

THE GOOD LIFE?

'The Pursuit of Happiness', a survey conducted in 2003 by the think tank MassINC, found that 42 per cent of Massachusetts residents rated the quality of life in their state as 'good'; 29 per cent said it was 'very good to excellent' and 28 per cent described it as 'fair to poor'. But about one third of the respondents said they would leave the state if given the opportunity. The top motives for moving were 'to go somewhere with a lower cost of living or lower taxes' and 'to go somewhere with better weather'.

The survey underscored the new challenges facing Boston and Massachusetts. No longer seen as dull or parochial, the Hub is a magnet for artists, entrepreneurs, and free spirits. The trick is getting them to stay here. Some of Boston's problems can't really be changed (it's always going to be the windiest major city in North America), but there's no reason why the city and state can't address the housing shortage, the wobbly state of public schools and the decaying public transit system. Assuming there's any money left after the Big Dig.

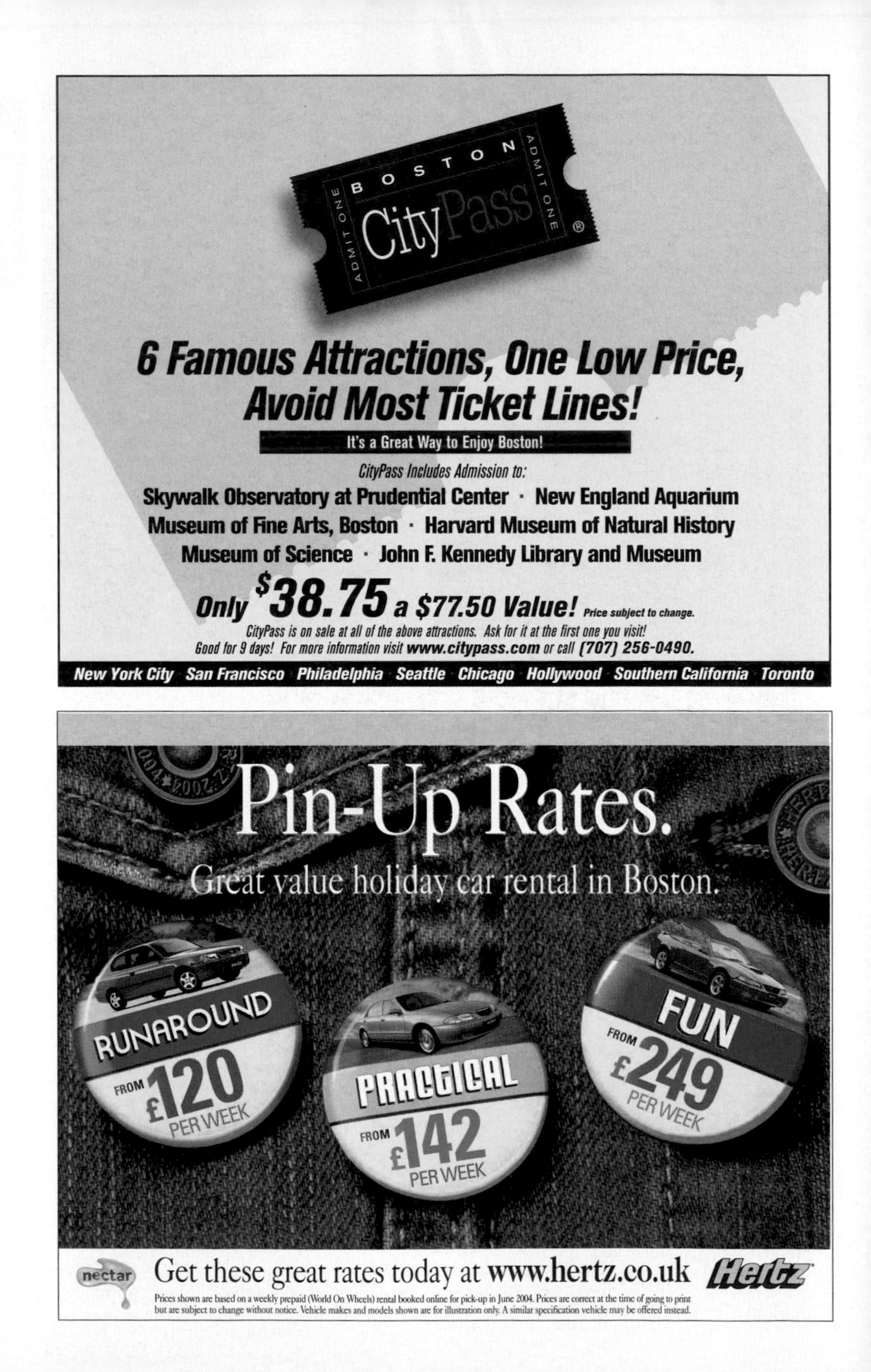
BOSTON
ADMIT ONE
CityPass®
ADMIT ONE
6 Famous Attractions, One Low Price,
Avoid Most Ticket Lines!
It's a Great Way to Enjoy Boston!
CityPass Includes Admission to:
Skywalk Observatory at Prudential Center · New England Aquarium
Museum of Fine Arts, Boston · Harvard Museum of Natural History
Museum of Science · John F. Kennedy Library and Museum
Only $38.75 a $77.50 Value! Price subject to change.
CityPass is on sale at all of the above attractions. Ask for it at the first one you visit!
Good for 9 days! For more information visit www.citypass.com or call (707) 256-0490.
New York City San Francisco Philadelphia Seattle Chicago Hollywood Southern California Toronto
Pin-Up Rates.
Great value holiday car rental in Boston.
RUNAROUND
FROM £120 PER WEEK
PRACTICAL
FROM £142 PER WEEK
FUN
FROM £249 PER WEEK
nectar
Get these great rates today at www.hertz.co.uk
Hertz
Prices shown are based on a weekly prepaid (World On Wheels) rental booked online for pick-up in June 2004. Prices are correct at the time of going to print but are subject to change without notice. Vehicle makes and models shown are for illustration only. A similar specification vehicle may be offered instead.

Architecture

Quaint row houses, ostentatious mansions, a new Gehry – admire one of America's most picturesque cityscapes.

When most people think of Bostonian architecture, chances are they conjure up an image of unbroken swathes of red-brick town houses. What they probably don't know is this elegant unity was born of catastrophe. As with so many other urban centres, it was a string of massive conflagrations that ushered Boston from an era of wooden structures to an era of brick. Fires had plagued Boston since its initial settlement. The city suffered devastating blazes in 1653, 1676, 1679, 1711 and 1761, but it was the Great Fire of November 1872 that was by far the most catastrophic. It started in a hoop skirt warehouse on the corner of Kingston and Summer Streets and rapidly spread, consuming most of Boston's early cityscape. Consequently, very little colonial architecture still exists, and virtually all of Boston is now built of brick – the logical solution for a city that had suffered from so many fires.

In fact, the only 17th-century wooden construction that remains within the city limits is the **Paul Revere House** (*see p83*). Built in 1680 for merchant Robert Howard, it lodged its eponymous inhabitant for 30 years from 1770 to 1800. After periods as a flophouse, souvenir shop, cigar factory and grocery store it was saved from the wrecking ball in 1902 by one of Revere's descendants and restored to its original two-storey frame. Today the house is a National Historic Landmark and museum, furnished with period antiques.

Next to Revere's house is **Pierce/Hichborn House** (*see p83*), a three-storey brick structure built in 1711 for glazier Moses Pierce and later owned by Revere's cousin, shipbuilder Nathaniel Hichborn. Although the Pierce/Hichborn House was constructed only 30 years after its neighbour, there is a stark contrast between the two: organic Tudor gives way to orderly English Renaissance; clapboard to brick; diamond to gridded panes; a cramped winding staircase to one that is perfectly straight. The Pierce/Hichborn House

The **Burrage Mansion** in Back Bay was modelled on the Vanderbilts' Newport pile...

was restored in the 1950s, and four of its rooms are open to the public.

The **Old State House** (*see p66*) is another remnant of Boston's Georgian past. Designed and constructed in 1713, this small building served as the colonial governor's offices – hence the lion and unicorn ornamentation on the façade. It was then used as a public meeting place until the Revolution, when it became the headquarters of the British Army. Topped with a richly ornamented steeple, the three-storey brick building, dwarfed by the surrounding downtown skyscrapers, now houses the Bostonian Society's museum and the State Street T station.

THE BULFINCH BLUEPRINT

Charles Bulfinch (1763-1844) was America's first notable (though never formally trained) architect. Born in Boston to great wealth, Bulfinch travelled extensively in England and Europe, and developed an affinity for the Greek Revival style of architecture fashionable at the time. Inspired, Bulfinch returned to America and began designing his friends' houses for free. This led to public commissions such as designing the new State House (*see p70*) and the remodelling of Faneuil Hall (*see p66*).

Bulfinch is best known for the development of the Federal style – an Americanisation of the Georgian Greek Revival style – and his crowning glory outside of Massachusetts was the US Capitol building in Washington, DC. Typical of this genre is the austere, three-storey brick **Harrison Gray Otis House** (*see p70*), one of the three houses Bulfinch designed for his close friend Otis. Completed in 1796, the flat-faced building, now the Otis House Museum, is a masterpiece of symmetry and proportion. Rooms contain false doors, intricately carved fireplaces and shockingly garish colour schemes – all typical of the period. Though the brick building nearly crumbled in the early 1900s, it was rescued in 1916 by the Society for the Preservation of New England Antiquities and painstakingly restored to its original state. Most of the rooms are now open to the public.

Considered one of Bulfinch's best works, the State House occupies a commanding spot atop Beacon Hill, and its gleaming gold dome can be seen for miles. The building, completed in 1798, has a red-brick façade, supported by white Corinthian pillars and flanked by Palladian windows. The dome – the architect's signatory flourish – originally bore a layer of white wood shingles. In 1802, Paul Revere covered the curvature with copper sheeting and painted it grey. Then, as the nation's wealth grew, a coating of 23-carat gold leaf was applied in 1872. Save for being painted grey again during World War II, for fear of Axis bombers, the dome has retained its elegant finishing touch to this day.

Bulfinch's architectural impact extended beyond his own designs. His influence can be spotted around town in green wooden doors topped with fanlights, wrought-iron grillwork

...which was a copy of a Loire château.

and bay windows – a Boston invention. The preponderance of black shutters you see today are a Victorian afterthought.

VICTORIAN VALUES

Frilly as a doily and intricate as a wedding dress, the Victorian architectural era is manifested nicely in two of Boston's neighbourhoods: the South End and the Back Bay, two areas that didn't exist until the mid-19th century. Gradually, as the city expanded, the surrounding tidal marsh was filled and the soft ground shored up. First to spring up was the bourgeois South End. Stacked with red brick and bay windows, the South End's architecture mostly reflects Beacon Hill's Federal tradition; many of the side streets emulate Bulfinch's beloved English square design. Two wonderfully preserved examples of this can be seen at Union and Rutland Squares. Yet, the South End stands apart from Beacon Hill in several notable ways. The scale of its townhouses is noticeably larger than those on Beacon Hill – simply because 19th-century folk were taller than their 18th-century counterparts. High ceilings, soaring windows and mansard roofs speak of a Victorian preoccupation with slenderness and verticality.

The Back Bay, on the other hand, takes most of its architectural cues from France's Second Empire. This is where much of Boston's upper class moved when Brahmin Beacon Hill became crowded with immigrant families. The area favours Parisian avenues over English squares, and the house façades tend towards marble and sandstone rather than red brick.

Here, both public and private buildings have all the opulence and unnecessary embellishment of a diamond-studded tiara. The **Ames-Webster House** (306 Dartmouth Street), for example, sports an elaborate *porte cochère* that kept the ladies dry as they descended from their carriages. The **Burrage Mansion** (314 Commonwealth Avenue) is a grotesque neo-Gothic confection modelled on the Vanderbilt mansion in Newport, which itself was modelled on Château Chenonceau in the Loire.

Throughout the Victorian era, the city embraced ostentation. The favoured styles of the time were Italian Renaissance, neo-Gothic and neo-Romanesque. An area then known as Art Square was one of the first parcels of land set aside in Back Bay purely to showcase the city's fledgling cultural institutions. Later renamed Copley Square, it housed great examples of institutional architecture, such as the Museum of Fine Arts (later torn down to make way for the Fairmont Copley Plaza), the Museum of Natural History (now the posh Louis Boston department store) and the magnificent **Boston Public Library** (*see p74*).

Charles McKim's (1847-1909) original library is usually attributed to the Italian Renaissance style, though he claimed its ornate stone façade was equally inspired by a library in Paris, a temple in Rimini and the Marshall Fields department store in Chicago. The library was not an easy project. It was finally completed after a ten-year construction period in 1895. The lobby doors were designed by Daniel Chester French (the artist who also created the statue of Abraham Lincoln in the Washington, DC, memorial to the assassinated president, as well as the statue of John Harvard in Cambridge). McKim didn't spare any expense when it came to the library's interior, commissioning murals by John Singer Sargent and Pierre Puvis de Chavannes, and sculptures by Saint-Gaudens.

While the modern wing of the museum (built in 1972 by Philip Johnson; *see p30*) is seen by many as a blight on McKim's work, the historic portion of the structure is worth a visit. Its grand staircase, vaulted reading room and enchanting cloistered garden have all been meticulously restored and lovingly maintained.

RICHARDSON'S GRAND DESIGNS

Henry Hobson Richardson (1838-86) is considered one of the greatest American architects, and was to Victorian Boston what Charles Bulfinch was to Colonial Boston. Although he lived in New York, New Orleans and Paris before moving to Boston – and

Bridging past and present

In 1997 Republican Congressman Tom Petri gave his infamous 'Porker Award' for government waste to Massachusetts Senator Ted Kennedy and then Speaker of the House Tip O'Neil. What did they do to earn this ignominious distinction? The two legendary Massachusetts politicians convinced the US Government to subsidise what came to be known as the Big Dig, a highly controversial civil engineering project whose large-scale ambition was matched only by its skyrocketing cost.

In response to ghastly traffic and a fast-deteriorating elevated highway traversing Boston, planning for the Big Dig started in 1982, and with federal financing in place, construction began in 1991. The project that was expected at the outset to cost around $2.5 billion ultimately consumed more than six times that sum. And you have only to utter the words 'Big Dig' to any Bostonian to get a sense of the headaches and controversy the massive project created.

Still, it is said that there is no beauty without pain, and the Big Dig holds true to that maxim. From an aesthetic standpoint, the project's completion is undoubtedly a success. The hulking, rusting green mass that was the original Central Artery has been torn down and replaced with two wide, sleek subterranean tunnels running the length of the city. The surface area, once a picture of urban blight, will be converted to open green space, with a few areas reserved for commercial and residential development.

In addition to a noticeably smoother flow of traffic, the Big Dig's completion has meant drastically lower noise and pollution levels in the surrounding area. The North End, for example, had lived in the shadow of the highway for so long that some of its inhabitants are vaguely unsettled by the absence of choking smog and the roar of passing trucks. Now, strolling along its historic streets while enjoying a newly unobstructed view of the Boston skyline, you can actually hear strains of music coming from the bars and cafés.

And then there's the Leonard P Zakim Bunker Hill Bridge: a stunner, an architectural marvel and, at ten lanes, the widest cable-stayed bridge in the world. Partly named for Lenny Zakim, a tireless local champion of civil rights, who succumbed to cancer in 1999, and partly for nearby Bunker Hill, a crucial battlefield of the Revolutionary War, the bridge succeeds where many other forward-thinking architectural projects in Boston have failed dismally. The concept of Swiss designer Christian Menn, it bridges the old and the new, seamlessly blending into the greater physical and historical context of Boston. The matching 270-foot (82-metre) towers at each end, for example, are modelled after the Bunker Hill Monument.

Bostonians love this bridge; in fact, at $100 million, it is one of the few components of the Big Dig unanimously considered money well spent. Locals are so besotted with the structure that the state had to erect signs urging drivers to maintain speed, after more than a few motorists came to a halt in the middle of the highway to admire the 'Zakim'.

constructed only two major buildings here – Richardson is inextricably linked to the city because of his masterpieces, the **Trinity Church** (*see p74*) and the lovely **First Baptist Church** (*see p77*). A student of the École des Beaux-Arts in Paris, Richardson was influenced by the heavy lines and solid arcs of medieval French architecture. Richardson introduced himself to Boston by way of his First Baptist Church. Completed in 1871, its mix of stone and wood surfaces is set against a bell tower bas-relief by Frederic Auguste Bartholdi, who is best known as the sculptor of the Statue of Liberty.

Though it was commissioned in 1872, Richardson's finest work, the Trinity Church, didn't open until 1877, and cost almost four times the original budget. However, it seems it was worth the expense, as it is often cited as one of the most successful pieces of architecture in America. As is characteristic of most of Richardson's works, Trinity is crafted with the stone walls and solid arcs prevalent throughout medieval French architecture, and decorated with delicate Byzantine etchings. Richardson modelled the central tower after one in Salamanca, though it had to be built considerably shorter than the original or its weight would have sunk the structure into the marshy Back Bay. The church rests on 4,502 pilings driven into the mud.

Richardson's Romanesque style is evident in a number of flagrant imitations around town, including the **New Old South Church** (645 Boylston Street, at Copley Square) and the **Flour & Grain Exchange Building** (177 Milk Street, near Quincy Market).

THE EMERALD NECKLACE

The impetus to develop Boston's green spaces was spurred on by the development of New York's Central Park in the 1850s. Renowned landscape architect Frederick Law Olmsted (1822-1903), who was responsible for shaping the Manhattan park, designed two major projects for Boston – the **Arnold Arboretum** and the **Back Bay Fens**. In the late 1880s, the Metropolitan Parks Commission (now the Metropolitan District Commission, or MDC) hired Olmsted to fill in the links of the 'Emerald Necklace' – a string of lush green plots stretching from Boston Common to Jamaica Plain. Olmsted added 'jewels' to the Common, the Public Garden, the green swathe in the centre of Commonwealth Avenue, and his existing parks, including **Olmsted Park**, **Jamaica Pond** and **Franklin Park**. The **Charles River Esplanade**, although conceived by Olmsted, wasn't developed until after his death in the 1930s. After the MBTA extended the Orange Line to the South End, the **Southwest Corridor Park** joined the Necklace in the 1980s.

Trinity Church reflected in the **Hancock Tower** (*see p31*).

A bleak irony shrouds the epilogue to Olmsted's career: he also refurbished the grounds of McLean Hospital in Belmont – the sanatorium where he later spent his final days.

CONCRETE PLANS

Boston's first attempt to scrape the sky came in 1915, when a 30-storey, neo-Gothic tower was inexplicably stuck on top of the Customs House. Shortly thereafter, though, the city slumped into a recession. Virtually no important buildings were constructed until the 1960s, when a brutal and controversial effort at urban renewal began. Swathes of buildings in the inner city were torn down and replaced with ugly modern architectural behemoths. The city wiped away several culturally and historically rich communities as the concept of progress eclipsed the concept of beauty – or at least tasteful integration – throughout the 1960s and early 1970s. (Pick up a copy of Jane Holtz Kay's *Lost Boston* for an exasperating tour through all the places that succumbed to the wrecking ball and got replaced with concrete slabs, gas stations and parking lots.)

One of the first great architectural missteps was the **Prudential Center**, a bland cheese grater of a tower that is widely considered to be Boston's ugliest structure. Rising up out of the former site of the Boston & Albany railyards, the dull 52-storey building is, for the city, the bad haircut that never goes away. In an effort to spruce the place up, however, the long-neglected shopping complex at the base of the 'Pru' was renovated and reintroduced in the early 1990s as 'The Shops at the Prudential': a sunny, moderately upscale mall.

Not long after, most of the West End fell prey to anxious metropolitan surgeons. Scollay Square – which in its respectable days was where Alexander Graham Bell invented the telephone, and, later, where debauchees flocked to drink, dance and raid brothels – was razed to make space for another architectural monstrosity: **Government Center** and **City Hall Plaza**.

The respected architect IM Pei designed the master plan for Government Center, which paved red brick over 56 acres (23 hectares) of now prime urban real estate and reduced 22 city streets to six. Architects Kallman, McKinnel and Knowles designed City Hall itself, and Walter Gropius's Architects Collaborative created the adjacent JFK Buildings. Despite the pedigree of the people behind the project, the results are flat and cold. Plonked in the middle of the seemingly barren Government Center is the awkward City Hall, an imposing concrete box that would warm the heart of any homesick ex-Soviet. What to do with it is an inexhaustible reservoir of debate for residents and officials alike.

Gehry has made his mark on MIT: the **Ray and Maria Stata Center**. *See p31.*

Harvard graduate and stolid postmodernist Philip Johnson contributed even more controversy to the city with his stark addition to the Boston Public Library in 1972, which attempted to reinterpret the McKim building's classical lines in a modernist vocabulary. Although it follows the same roof line and uses harmonising granite, it is seen by many as a blemish on the original structure.

NEW HEIGHTS

Today, most of the city's skyscrapers are downtown (the area annihilated by the Great Fire of 1872) and only a handful of historically interesting buildings remain. The **Batterymarch** (60 Batterymarch Street) is a decent example of art deco and the **Winthrop** (276 Washington Street) was Boston's first building to make use of a steel frame.

With the 1980s economic boom came a forest of new skyscrapers, many of which were designed by America's most prominent architects. Three firms in particular have been responsible for shaping modern Boston's appearance: IM Pei Associates, Graham Gund Associates and Philip Johnson.

Besides the stolid fortress of the Government Center complex, IM Pei is also responsible for the new wing of the **Museum of Fine Arts**, **Harbor Towers** on the waterfront (off Atlantic Avenue), the gleaming layout of the **Christian Science Plaza** (*see p78*), the **John F Kennedy Library** (*see p112*) and a number of buildings at MIT in Cambridge.

But Pei's best-loved contribution is the **John Hancock Tower**. According to Pei, the concept behind the severe rhomboid shape was to not overwhelm Copley Square's older buildings. The tower is 62 storeys tall, but only a sliver of it shows from the square. It's made more pleasing to look at by the images of Back Bay and the sky reflected in its glass sides. Though instantly more popular than the Prudential Center with most Bostonians, the Hancock did not escape controversy. While it was still under construction in 1973, a structural flaw caused the windows to pop out and crash down into the street below. Every one of its 10,344 panes had to be replaced – at a cost of $8 million. In addition, the historic Trinity Church was slightly damaged in the process, but, thankfully, no one was hurt.

In addition to his controversial Boston Public Library addition, Johnson also masterminded **500 Boylston Street** and **International Place** (on Atlantic Avenue), which, the joke goes, contains more Palladian windows than the whole of Italy.

The latest addition to Boston's copse of skyscrapers bodes well for the future. At once forward-looking and tasteful, **111 Huntington** (on Huntington Avenue), designed by the firm of Childs Bertman Tseckares and completed in 2002, is a multifaceted tower, stretching some 554 feet (169 metres) skywards to a telescoping cylindrical top. Technically part of the Prudential Center, the mirrored tower might be seen as an attempt to atone for Boston's troubled architectural past.

Other such attempts abound in modern-day Boston. The massive Big Dig project (*see p28* **Bridging past and present**) has sunk the unsightly elevated Central Artery highway underground and will finally rejoin two parts of the city that were divided when the ugly green hulk was constructed in 1959. Boston is also struggling to convert what was a post-industrial wasteland in South Boston into a thriving waterfront district. Rafael Viñoly's slightly airport-like **Boston Convention and Exhibition Center** has been completed, while plans for a new Institute of Contemporary Art are well underway (*see p92* **Future vision**).

CUTTING-EDGE CAMBRIDGE

Bostonians can be forgiven for being a little gun-shy about so-called modern architecture. Some see their apprehension as needless Yankee stubbornness resisting progress, others as the only way to prevent a relapse into ghastly, alienating urban design. Nevertheless, the Boston area does boast an oasis of world-renowned modern architecture – albeit across the river in Cambridge.

The **Massachusetts Institute of Technology** (MIT) dedicates a significant portion of its endowment to commissioning ground-breaking works from the world's great architects. Its campus – which spans from Kendall Square to Massachusetts Avenue by the Charles River – is studded with some of the most innovative designs in the country.

In 1949 **Baker House** (362 Memorial Drive, Cambridge) opened its doors. One of only two works in the country by iconic Finnish architect Alvar Aalto, the six-storey student dorm is distinguished by its curvilinear plan, 'moon garden' (a two-storey dining area with a wood-slatted ceiling, punctuated by cylindrical skylights), and the fact that it is designed in such a way to afford 80 per cent of its rooms a view of the Charles.

1955 saw the unveiling of the **Kresge Auditorium** (48 Massachusetts Avenue, Cambridge). The brainchild of Finnish master Eero Saarinen, the Kresge has an outer shell that is exactly one eighth of a sphere, and 'floats' above its base thanks to a number of intricately placed buttresses.

The MIT campus also features several works by alumnus IM Pei. Chief among them is the 1984 **Wiesner Building** (20 Ames Street, Cambridge) and the 1959 **Green Tower** (on MIT's actual campus), which at 277 feet (85 metres) is the tallest building in Cambridge.

The most recent additions to the MIT landscape are among the most stunning. The Institute enlisted the services of Frank Gehry, best known for his Guggenheim Museum in Bilbao, Spain, to create the **Ray and Maria Stata Center** (32 Vassar Street, Cambridge) – a multicoloured, multifaceted example of his trademark sculptural style. The computer and information sciences complex, nearing completion as this guide went to press, features a 'Toon Town' colour scheme and inverted walls that look ready to topple.

Finally, an architectural pilgrimage to MIT is not complete without a visit to **Simmons Hall** (243 Vassar Street, Cambridge), a ten-storey dorm designed by award-winning New York architect Steven Holl. The exterior is wrapped in recessed square windows connected by strips of anodised aluminium. The combination of the windows, their multicoloured recesses, and the shimmering aluminium makes for a façade that dramatically changes hues when viewed from different angles.

Madeleine Porter and Vanessa Redgrave in the 1984 film of **The Bostonians**.

Literary Boston

From Puritan poets to the contemporary literati, the Boston area has always attracted bookish types.

In 1858, poet and essayist Oliver Wendell Holmes called the Boston State House the 'hub of the solar system'. While the veracity of this assertion is up for debate, there's no doubt that in the 19th century Boston was the centre of America's literary universe – although much of the actual writing took place about 20 miles (30 kilometres) north-west, in Concord. The most important American thinker of that century, Ralph Waldo Emerson, lived and wrote there; his disciple Henry David Thoreau spent two years in an isolated cabin by nearby Walden Pond, which was to inspire his beautiful book *Walden*; Louisa May Alcott penned the American classic, *Little Women*, in the village, and Nathaniel Hawthorne, author of *The Scarlet Letter*, for a time occupied the house where Emerson wrote the seminal essay *Nature*. As well as a literary legacy, Hawthorne left his and his wife's initials in a window pane, etched with a diamond ring. The Concord authors are all buried close to each other on Poet's Ridge in Sleepy Hollow cemetery.

As well as breeding authors, Boston has been the setting for a number of novels, from *The Bostonians*, a send-up of feminism and the occult written in 1885 by part-time resident Henry James, to John P Marquand's Pulitzer Prize-winning *The Late George Apley* (1937), a brilliant depiction of a Brahmin family in the two generations following the Civil War, and David Foster Wallace's mammoth Generation X rehab odyssey, *Infinite Jest* (1996).

The list of poets who were educated or lived in Boston and Cambridge reads like a *Who's Who* of American literature and includes Henry Wadsworth Longfellow, John Greenleaf Whittier, TS Eliot, Robert Frost, ee cummings, Elizabeth Bishop, Robert Lowell and Sylvia Plath. To this list can be added a host of literary figures including black intellectual giant WEB DuBois; psychologist William James (Henry's brother); Henry Adams, whose famous autobiography *The Education of Henry Adams* starts 'under the shadow of the Boston State House'; black nationalist Malcolm X, whose own education began in the Charlestown prison where he copied the dictionary starting with 'aardvark'; and John Updike, unrivalled chronicler of late 20th-century suburban sex. Looking west, Amherst, Pittsfield and Lowell were once home, respectively, to Emily Dickinson, America's finest female poet, Herman Melville, author of *Moby-Dick*, arguably the greatest American novel, and Jack Kerouac, patron saint of wandering literary rebels.

WALDEN.

BY HENRY D. THOREAU,

AUTHOR OF "A WEEK ON THE CONCORD AND MERRIMACK RIVERS."

...pose to write an ode to dejection, but to brag as lustily as chanticleer in the morning, standing on his roost, if only to wake my neighbors up. — Page

Henry David Thoreau.

PROLIFIC PURITANS

The Puritans did not believe in sex, but they did believe in literacy – even for women. Part of God's purpose was reading His Book, and using it as an inspiration to write your own. Consequently, the Puritans left a rich legacy of journals, sermons and historical records. William Bradford (1590-1657), *Mayflower* Puritan and first governor of Plymouth Colony, kept an account of those first harsh years, eventually published in 1856 as *Of Plymouth Plantation 1620-1647*. The first Massachusetts Bay Colony governor, John Winthrop (1588-1649), wrote *The History of New England*, published posthumously in 1790. The most successful Puritan author was Cotton Mather (1663-1728), who chronicled the American Protestant movement in *Magnalia Christi Americana* (1702), but is best remembered for inflaming the Salem witchcraft hysteria. Anne Bradstreet (1612-72) wrote poems in secret but a cousin published them without her knowledge as *The Tenth Muse Lately Sprung Up in America* (1650). An authorised volume with her corrections, *Poems* (1678), was published after her death. The only Puritan poet whose work was published while he was still alive was Michael Wigglesworth (1631-1705), whose *Day of Doom* (1662) is read today only by scholars.

THE NEW ENGLAND RENAISSANCE

In 1807, a group of wealthy Beacon Hill Brahmins established 'a reading room, a library, a museum and a laboratory', which they named the Athenaeum after a temple devoted to the goddess Athena. (The Athenaeum subsequently served as a model for the Boston Public Library.) By 1811 it had published the influential *North American Review*, and over the course of the 19th century, Daniel Webster, Ralph Waldo Emerson, Henry Wadsworth Longfellow and Amy Lowell were all members.

In 1829, Timothy Harrington Carter opened the Old Corner Bookstore at the corner of Washington and School Streets in downtown Boston, and it became a locus of the city's literary scene. Between 1845 and 1865 the Old Corner was owned by William Tichnor and Jamie Fields. Fields focused on printing and encouraging local writers like Emerson, Longfellow, Oliver Wendell Holmes and James Russell Lowell. Tichnor and Fields were the first to bring European authors such as Charles Dickens to America. They were also the founders of the *Atlantic Monthly* magazine, and were the first to pay authors royalties on sales rather than a flat fee.

The first great author of the New England Renaissance was Nathaniel Hawthorne (1804-64). A native of Salem, Hawthorne altered the spelling of his last name to distance himself from his infamous ancestors, William Hathorne, who harassed Quakers, and Judge John Hathorne, who presided over the 1692 Salem witch trials. Themes of guilt and sin recur frequently in Hawthorne's work; his most revered work, *The Scarlet Letter*, examines the fate of a female victim of Puritan society. Hawthorne worked in the Salem Customs House, but wasn't suited for government work. He moved to the village of Lenox in western Massachusetts, where he wrote *The House of the Seven Gables* and met Herman Melville (1819-91), a denizen of nearby Pittsfield. Melville, a New Yorker, had already achieved literary success with two novels of the sea, *Typee* (1846) and *Omoo* (1847). He described his meeting with Hawthorne as the 'shock of recognition' and the subsequent intellectual bond inspired him to finish *Moby-Dick* (1851), and dedicate the novel to his friend. Unfortunately *Moby-Dick* wasn't recognised as the quintessential American novel until the 1920s – well after the deaths of both men.

Also writing in western Massachusetts was Emily Dickinson (1830-86), acknowledged today as one of the greatest American poets of the 19th century. Cloistering herself in Amherst, Dickinson disliked Boston, scoffing at its pomp and pretensions, and rarely visited the city. Only seven of Dickinson's poems were printed in her lifetime, though she wrote more than 1,800 – and only 24 have titles. Drawn to the rhythm of Protestant hymns and transcendentalism, Emily Dickinson used verse to explore her heart and soul; only occasionally, in love poems, did she redirect her gaze outside of herself.

SPIRITUAL SUSTENANCE

The New England Transcendentalists believed spirituality was as essential to the human body as food, intuition was more important than intellectual knowledge, and the purest ideas came from reason, not sensual discovery. Transcendentalism's chief prophet was Ralph Waldo Emerson (1807-82), a Harvard alumni and Boston native born to a line of Unitarian ministers. Emerson deftly wove nature's nuances into a metaphor for the human mind in his first work, *Nature* (1836). He is most noted for his collections of essays (1841, 1844) which include *Self-Reliance*, *The American Scholar* and *The Oversoul.* It took 12 years to sell the initial 500 copies of *Nature*, yet the book resonated immediately with a diverse group of writers who were all members of the Transcendentalist Club. The club met at Emerson's house and produced the *Dial* (1840-42), a quarterly of poetry and essays dedicated to 'literature, philosophy and religion'. Among *Dial*'s most noted contributors were Emerson, Margaret Fuller (journalist, critic and feminist), Amos Bronson Alcott (Louisa May's father and founder of Boston's controversial Temple School and the short-lived utopian community Fruitlands), George Ripley, who founded the Utopian artists' community Brook Farm, and Henry David Thoreau. Thoreau (1817-62) was the most curious member of the group; in an attempt to live according to Emerson's doctrine about nature, he spent two years, two months and two days living in isolation in a cabin by Walden Pond before writing his masterpiece *Walden.* Thoreau's other influential work, *Civil Disobedience* (1849), sprang from another self-imposed isolation – a brief jail sentence for refusing to pay his taxes as part of an abolitionist protest against the expansion of slavery into western territories. *Civil Disobedience* inspired pacifists Leo Tolstoy and Mahatma Gandhi.

Tutored at home by both Emerson and Thoreau, Louisa May Alcott (1832-88) achieved worldwide fame with her novel *Little Women* (1868) and its sequel *Little Men* (1871). Lack of formal education didn't prevent her from making a career of writing – or creating characters Hollywood would still be embracing nearly a century and a half later.

Introspective poetess **Emily Dickinson**.

On the road to Lowell

Jack Kerouac, Villa Muneria garden wall, Tanger – he'd preceded me & Peter O. on Yugoslav freighter by a month to help type Burroughs' Interzone "word-hoard" manuscript assembled for Naked Lunch. Jack left for Paris a week and a half later, On the Road published earlier that year – he'd already written twelve books, Visions, Dreams, Blues, in the "Legend of Duluoz" series, up to Desolation Angels Part I, late 1957.
Allen Ginsberg

Less than an hour north-west of Boston lies the city of Lowell, birthplace of the American industrial revolution, but also of Jack Kerouac, the restless prose-poet Beat bard of the 1950s and '60s.

Kerouac was born in 1922 at **7 Lupine Road**, in a house that still stands. He was an altar boy at **St Jean Baptiste Church** (now the Nuestra Senora del Carmen, at the corner of Merrimack and Austin Streets) where his funeral was held in 1969 – and where he allegedly had his first sexual experience in a confessional. His wake was held at the **Archambault Funeral Home** (309 Pawtucket Boulevard) as was that of his older brother Gerard, who died aged nine and became the subject of Kerouac's novel *Visions of Gerard.* The author is buried at **Edson Cemetery** (on

ENGLISH INFLUENCE

More popular than the Transcendentalists were the Cambridge Poets. Primarily well-heeled academics, the latter were associated with Harvard and influenced by the work of the English Romantic poets. The most important was Henry Wadsworth Longfellow (1807-82). His sing-song verse has now fallen out of fashion, but was so popular in his time that Longfellow became the first literary artist in America to support himself completely from his writing, and the first to earn a place in Poet's Corner in Westminster Abbey. Longfellow snatched Paul Revere from historical obscurity when he canonised the courier in *Paul Revere's Ride*. The poet celebrated the love affair of Priscilla and John Aden in *The Courtship of Miles Standish* (1858) and created a myth around the Native American Hiawatha in *The Song of Hiawatha* (1855) – a poem, incidentally, based not on American Indian lore but the Finnish epic *Kalevala*.

Often enjoying Longfellow's magnificent Craige House at 105 Brattle Street (paid for by the poet's father-in-law) were his Cambridge cronies Oliver Wendell Holmes and James

Gorham Street, two miles south of the Lowell Connector intersection).

Those acquainted with Kerouac's novels will find Lowell somewhat familiar. The clock outside **Lowell High School** (50 Father Morissette Boulevard) is still there, as is the Madonna shrine – the Grotto and Stations of the Cross – near the intersection of Pawtucket and School Streets, which figure so ominously in *Dr Sax*.

As a child Kerouac read prodigiously, and in *Maggie Cassidy* he recounts skipping school to pore over crumbling books 'from the darkest shelf in the Lowell Public Library' (now **Pollard Memorial Library**, 401 Merrimack Street). He also wrote poetry and fiction – by the age of 11 he had completed his first novel. But he did not fit the mould of the delicate, introverted literary youngster. Powerfully built and handsome, Kerouac was a star athlete in high school. His obvious literary talents notwithstanding, he went to Columbia University on a football scholarship.

At Columbia, Kerouac fell in with Allen Ginsberg, William Burroughs, and other form-bending, taboo-breaking writers who would go on to found the Beat movement. Sport was quickly cast aside as Kerouac explored sex, drugs, jazz and literature. Years later, when the one-time football star had begun to make a name for himself as a writer, Columbia coach Lou Little was quoted as saying, 'Whatever happened to Jack Kerouac?'

What happened was Kerouac had adopted the kind of hobo-bohemian lifestyle – travelling, writing, picking up odd jobs – that would one day make him a worldwide literary icon. After serving in the Merchant Marines, Kerouac and his madcap buddy Neal Cassady hit the road in earnest. The resultant meandering literary travelogue *On the Road* found its way into pretty much every book bag and back pocket in America. Overnight, Kerouac had become a star.

The Beats, led in large part by this boy from a working-class Massachusetts mill town, rejected the conformist society they had been born into, ushering in the wild, drug-filled, sex-drenched 1960s. But not without cost. The excesses Kerouac celebrated in his writing killed him at the age of 48.

To this day, thousands upon thousands of fans make the annual pilgrimage to Lowell, the beginning and end of Kerouac's road. In 1988 the city dedicated a commemorative plaza to its most famous son. Eight granite blocks inscribed with his words stand in **Jack Kerouac Park** (part of the Eastern Canal Park, at the corner of French and Bridge Streets). Across the street is **Arthur's Paradise Diner** (112 Bridge Street, 1-978 452 8647, open 6am-1pm Mon-Fri, 6am-noon Sat, Sun). Arthur recalls how a young Jack once ran by naked, earning him the nickname 'Bare-assed Jack'. The Paradise Diner still serves the Boott Mill sandwich, Jack's favourite.

For the **Lowell Celebrates Kerouac!** Festival, *see p184*.

HOW TO GET THERE

Lowell is 26 miles (42km) north-west of Boston. By **car**, take Route 93 North to 495 South. Take exit 35C onto the Lowell Connector. Exit 5B will take you to Thorndike St. The trip takes 40 minutes to an hour.

The MBTA **Commuter Rail** (1-617 222 3200, www.mbta.com) runs from Boston's North Station to Lowell's Gallagher Station. Trains leave approximately once an hour Monday to Friday and once every two hours Saturday and Sunday. The journey time is approximately 45 mins.

Russell Lowell. Holmes (1809-94) was a master of light verse and wrote the popular 'Breakfast table' pieces for the *Atlantic Monthly* (1858). Though Lowell (1819-91) was suspended from Harvard in his senior year (he spent the time with Emerson and Thoreau in Concord), he returned to take Longfellow's professorship when the poet left to write full-time. Lowell became the first editor of the *Atlantic Monthly* and co-edited the *North American Review* with Charles Eliot Norton.

Also influenced by the English were John Greenleaf Whittier (1807-92) and William Cullen Bryant (1794-1878). Whittier's sentimental and homespun poems became the texts for several hymns. His long poem *Snowbound* (1866) is a wonderful description of a New England winter. Bryant was the leading American poet of the 1830s, though his best-known poem, *Thanatopsis* was written in 1815.

BANNED IN BOSTON

The centre of American writing and publishing shifted slightly south in the 1890s. When William Dean Howells – editor, novelist and America's most important critic (his best novel

The Rise of Silas Lapham, 1885, chronicles the career of a Boston businessman) – moved to New York, a literary sphere of influence went with him. The New England generation that followed Emerson, Thoreau and Alcott was less talented and more reactionary. In 1904, Boston appointed a censor to forbid the publication of morally corrupt literature, ushering in a kind of literary Dark Ages that lasted for 40 years – and made Boston the butt of innumerable jokes. Works by such writers as Ernest Hemingway, Sinclair Lewis and Eugene O'Neill were banned. Lillian Hellman's award-winning play, *The Children's Hour* (1935), wasn't allowed to open in Boston because it contained lesbian undertones. Boston did its best to appear to the rest of the country as a prudish old lady.

Yet, despite censorship, Boston and Massachusetts managed to nurture many talented authors, poets and journalists during the first half of the 20th century. Living in the western Massachusetts town of Lenox, New Yorker Edith Wharton (1862-1937), who won a Pulitzer Prize for *The Age of Innocence* (1920), continued Hawthorne's bleak portrait of New England in *Ethan Frome* (1911) and *Summer* (1917). Pulitzer Prize-winner Edwin O'Connor (1918-68) left his native Rhode Island for Boston, finding a job at the *Boston Herald* and fodder for his novel, *The Last Hurrah*, a thinly veiled story about former Boston Mayor James Michael Curley.

TORTURED POETS

Another Pulitzer Prize-winner and well-known literary figure in Boston in the 1950s was poet Robert Lowell (1917-77). Praised for his emotionally rich, confessional verse, Lowell taught at Boston University and Harvard. Notorious for his chronic drinking, manic depression, three marriages and stints at McLean Hospital, a psychiatric facility in Belmont, Lowell had a troubled personal life – something he shared with fellow Boston-born poets Sylvia Plath and Anne Sexton. Lowell was respected for holding open-office hours for aspiring poets during his time at Harvard, and was revered as a source of inspiration for budding talent. At the same time as Lowell's reign as Boston's poet king, poet Elizabeth Bishop also taught at Harvard. Together they helped revitalise Boston's literary scene.

At the other end of the literary spectrum was Lowell native Jack Kerouac (*see p36*). His novel *On the Road* stunned the country with its jazz-influenced writing, lack of literary pretension, and liberating, hell-bent quest for freedom. As Plath wrestled with emotional demons in intellectual fashion, describing that battle in her poems in *Ariel* and in her novel *The Bell Jar*, Kerouac waged a literary revolt assisted by amphetamines, booze, free writing and lots of sex. In their own way, each helped change the way people read: Kerouac, as a spokesman for the Beat movement, heralded the age of hippies, rock 'n' roll, and experimental literature; Plath, who wrote about being misunderstood, even abused, by the men in her life, became a poet laureate for women. Both, it's worth noting, moved away from Massachusetts. Kerouac, however, returned towards the end of his life.

THE CONTEMPORARY SCENE

Today, Boston is a hive of notable thinkers, poets and journalists. Famous writers are always stopping by, some to teach, some to learn and others to gain experience before trying to conquer the world.

Boston University boasts among its faculty Saul Bellow, Derek Walcott, Elie Weisel and Robert Pinsky, former Poet Laureate of the United States. The BU Creative Writing Programme, considered to be one of the best in the country, is run by novelist Leslie Epstein (*King of the Jews*, *Pandemonium*, *San Remo Drive*). Alumni of the course include novelists Sue Miller (*The Good Mother*), Arthur Golden (*Memoirs of a Geisha*), National Book Award-winner Ha Jin (*Waiting*) and Pulitzer Prize-winner Jhumpa Lahiri (*Interpreter of Maladies*). Epstein's father and uncle together wrote the scripts for several classic Hollywood movies including *Casablanca* and *The Man Who Came to Dinner*, while his son Theo has found (non-literary) fame as General Manager of the Boston Red Sox baseball team.

Other literary notables live near Boston: John Updike in Beverly, Norman Mailer in Provincetown and Tracy Kidder in Williamsburg. Novelist and essayist James Carroll kicks around Boston; political gadfly Noam Chomsky teaches at MIT; playwright extraordinaire David Mamet has a home in suburban Boston.

The list of local talent goes on: *Orchid Thief* author Susan Orlean, novelist and Boston native Patricia Powell (*Me Dying Trial*, *A Small Gathering of Bones*) and up-and-coming writer Tom Perrotta (*Election*). Literary critics Helen Vendler and Christopher Ricks have homes and teaching positions in the area. The essayist Sven Birkerts lives here. World-renowned poets resident in Boston at the moment include Frank Bidart, current Poet Laureate of the United States Louise Glück and Seamus Heaney.

Boston may no longer be the hub of the literary universe, but the number of writers who get educated, live and work in and around the city has put it close to the centre of American letters once again.

Where to Stay

Features

Where to Stay

New launches and major revamps have bumped up the choice of stylish accommodation – but it ain't cheap.

Get cosy at **Beacon Hill Hotel & Bistro**. *See p49.*

Hoteliers roll into this town like freshman college students: wide-eyed, eager and dreaming of dollar signs. That's because Boston is a mid-sized American city with an outsized global reputation and there aren't enough rooms to go around – high prices and little bargaining power are the norm. That's the bad news. The good news is that, over the past few years, relief has started to arrive.

Between 2002 and 2004, there were more than 2,000 additions to Boston's reserve of hotel rooms and, if you go back to 1999, the number jumps to over 7,000. Well-received newcomers include the cosy 33-room **Charlesmark** (*see p45*), the stylish 190-room **Nine Zero** (*see p51*) and the large 236-room **Marlowe** (*see p56*).

The recent boom has given this city's many traditionals a swift kick to action. From 2002 to early 2004, some 15 hotels invested nearly $341 million on renovations and restoration of historic architecture. The **Park Plaza** (*see p42*) has gone in for wholesale rebeautification, while the **Ritz-Carlton** (*see p42*) not only nipped and tucked the Back Bay original back to its former glory, but also spawned the spiffy new **Ritz-Carlton Boston Common** (*see p49*). But don't think this is all in the name of vanity: stiff competition is on the horizon as the Regent Battery Wharf and Mandarin Oriental are set to break ground in 2004.

So, when all the rooms are open and the renovations complete, prices are going to drop to reasonable levels, right? Not likely. The average room rate in Greater Boston in 2003 was around $200 per night and rising. Based on the high-occupancy rates of recent years, projections indicate that even after the new hotels are completed, this city will fill up fast. Our advice: book ahead, particularly in the traditionally busy autumn season, and during May and June, when over 60 college graduation ceremonies take place in the Boston area.

CHOOSING A LOCATION

Of course, where you decide to stay depends largely on why you've come here. Back Bay, with its wealth of restaurants, bars and shops, is the most popular with visitors. But there are other exceptional areas of town to set up camp. Picturesque Beacon Hill makes a peaceful and romantic getaway, while the vicinity of Kenmore Square has numerous lively bars and can be a raucous place to let your hair down. Those in town on business could find the Financial District or the Waterfront more convenient. Meanwhile, the funky South End, with its miles of brick rowhouses and cobbled streets, is rapidly emerging as a favourite choice for regular visitors. As in any city, there is also a number of moderately priced, though unexotic, chain options. **Marriott** (1-800 228 9290, www.marriott.com) has convenient locations in Copley Square, Long Wharf, Cambridge and the suburbs; **Sheraton** (1-800 325 3535, www.starwood.com/sheraton) has outposts in Back Bay and Harvard Square, Cambridge, while **Howard Johnson** (1-800 654 2000, www.hojo.com) is a reliable, if unglamorous, budget choice in Fenway.

Bear in mind that many hotels have now adopted a no-smoking policy in all rooms. Smokers are advised to call ahead so they don't end up having to trudge outside every time they want a quick puff.

ABOUT THE LISTINGS

Prices may change according to season and do not include the 12.45 per cent sales tax. Note that, unless otherwise stated, breakfast is not included in the rates.

Back Bay

Deluxe

Four Seasons

200 Boylston Street, at the Public Garden, Boston, MA 02116 (1-617 338 4400/1-800 332 3442/fax 1-617 351 2051/www.fourseasons.com). Arlington T. **Rates** $495-$745 single/double; $1,450-$6,000 suite. **Credit** AmEx, DC, Disc, MC, V. **Map** p277 H5.

Not exactly architecture's gift to Boston, the Four Seasons was built on the former site of the Playboy Club. While it's always commanded unobstructed views of the Public Gardens, the hotel is now flanked by a suddenly hopping Theatre District, a host of exclusive European boutiques and upscale eateries like Excelsior (*see p115*) and Finale (*see p124*). It also has its own renowned eating and drinking options. At press time, the chummy, quaint Bristol Lounge – where evening brandy and afternoon tea are both good propositions – was being redone, and the fêted dining room, Aujourd'hui, was being re-imagined. Service is renowned for its mixture of doting charm and modern ease. Amenities such as a rooftop pool, round-the-clock room service, a printed pet menu and relaxed dress code mean CEOs are as likely to stay here as rockers like Prince and the Stones.

Hotel services *Air-conditioning. Babysitting. Bars (2). Business services. Concierge. Disabled: adapted rooms. Gym. Laundry. Limousine service. No-smoking rooms. Parking (valet $36 per night). Restaurants (2). Swimming pool (indoor).* **Room services** *Bathrobe. Hairdryer. Iron. Kitchenette (in suites). Dataport. Ethernet. Minibar. Newspaper. Room service (24hr). Turndown. TV: cable/pay movies/satellite.*

The best Hotels

For heavenly hosts

Never has the phrase 'urban retreat' been more apt than at the **Monastery Guest House**. *See p47.*

For gastronomes

Boston's adorable mini-grand hotel the **Eliot** houses fêted eatery Clio. *See p42.*

To sample the gay scene

Buzzing bar Fritz is on the ground floor of the hip South End hostelry **Chandler Inn**. *See p53.*

For city slickers

Cool, contemporary and comfortable, **Nine Zero** also has fabulous park views. *See p51.*

To pretend you're a (rich) local

Set up camp at **Beacon Hill Hotel & Bistro** in Boston's most exclusive enclave. *See p49.*

For a bit of culture

Hit the books at **Hotel Marlowe**'s literary soirées. *See p56.*

To pick up design tips

Rich Italian fabrics and four-poster beds re-create a glossy interior-magazine spread in **XV Beacon**, Boston's top boutique property. *See p47.*

For old Brahmin luxury

If the **Ritz-Carlton** was good enough for Churchill, it's good enough for us. *See p42.*

For techies

Science-themed decor and in-room Sony PlayStations keep visiting geniuses amused at the **University Park Hotel @ MIT**. *See p55.*

Ritz-Carlton

15 Arlington Street, at Newbury Street, Boston, MA 02116 (1-617 536 5700/1-800 241 3333/ fax 1-617 536 1335/www.ritzcarlton.com). Arlington T. **Rates** $350-$595 single/double; $395-$3,000 suite. **Credit** AmEx, DC, Disc, MC, V. **Map** p277 H5.

Truly the grande dame of Boston hotels, the Ritz opened in 1927 with the intention of catering to a very select clientele – the Duke and Duchess of Windsor, Winston Churchill and Charles Lindbergh among them – and the hotel has never deviated appreciably from this policy. (That said, it has since stopped screening bookings with the Social Register, the formal directory of old-money families in the US.) The property is the Ritz flagship in America and remains the touchstone for old world charm and knowing service. Some recent nips and tucks have ensured that all 278 French Provincial rooms, the haute-classic dining room (presided over by a former Alain Ducasse protégé) and ladies' lunching legend Ritz Café are all looking as posh and pert as ever.

Hotel services *Air-conditioning. Babysitting. Bars (2). Beauty salon. Business services. Concierge. Disabled: adapted rooms. Gym. Laundry. Limousine service. No-smoking rooms. Parking ($37 per night). Restaurants (2).* **Room services** *Bathrobe. Dataport (high-speed). Hairdryer. Iron. Minibar. Newspaper. Room service (24hr). Turndown. TV: cable/pay movies/videogames.*

Expensive

Boston Park Plaza

64 Arlington Street, at Boston Common, Boston, MA 02116 (1-617 426 2000/1-800 225 2008/fax 1-617 423 1708/www.bostonparkplaza.com). Arlington T. **Rates** $159-$299 single/double; $309-$399 suite. **Credit** AmEx, DC, Disc, MC, V. **Map** p277 J6.

With two ballrooms and a vast, chandeliered lobby, the Park Plaza screams 'fancy old hotel'. Its scale is operatic, and the Plaza's multiple restaurants, bars and shops give it the feel of a self-sustaining principality. On the whole, the guest quarters are surprisingly mediocre, although the renovated rooms, with new bathrooms, are a definite improvement. Draws include a trendy bar, Whiskey Park (*see p146*), and two solid restaurants, the Bonfire Steakhouse and McCormick & Schmick's (*see p119*).

Hotel services *Air-conditioning. Bars (5). Beauty salon. Business services. Concierge. Disabled: adapted rooms. Gym. Laundry. No-smoking rooms. Parking (valet $36 per night). Restaurants (5).* **Room services** *Bathrobe. Dataport. Ethernet. Hairdryer. Iron. Newspaper. Room service (6am-midnight). TV: cable/pay movies.*

Colonnade

120 Huntington Avenue, at the Prudential Center, Boston, MA 02116 (1-617 424 7000/1-800 962 3030/fax 1-617 424 1717/www.colonnadehotel.com). Prudential T. **Rates** $125-$425 single/double; $425-$1,000 suite. **Credit** AmEx, DC, Disc, MC, V. **Map** p277 G7.

The best feature of the Colonnade's vanilla-bland 1970s structure is its rooftop swimming pool – nothing beats it on a sticky summer afternoon. The hotel's 285 rooms are generous in size if somewhat anonymous in decor (though there's always the complimentary rubber ducky for the tub). But what the hotel lacks in charm it makes up for in its location, right next to Symphony Hall and the Prudential Center shopping mall. There's also the useful in-house Brasserie Jo downstairs for morning croissants or evening oysters.

Hotel services *Air-conditioning. Bar. Business services. Concierge. Disabled: adapted rooms. Gym. Laundry. Limousine service. No-smoking rooms. Parking (valet $32 per night). Restaurant. Swimming pool (outdoor). Wireless internet.* **Room services** *Dataport. Ethernet. Hairdryer. Iron. Minibar. Newspaper. TV: cable/pay movies/VCR (on request).*

Hotel Commonwealth

500 Commonwealth Avenue, at Kenmore Square, Boston, MA 02215 (info 1-617 933 5000/ reservations 1-866 784 4000/fax 1-617 266 6888/www.hotelcommonwealth.com). Kenmore T. **Rates** (incl breakfast) $269-$389 single/double, $3,000 suite. **Credit** AmEx, DC, Disc, MC, V. **Map** p276 D6.

A major player in the regeneration of formerly run-down Kenmore Square, this luxury hotel has suffered some teething troubles along the way. When it was unveiled in 2003, the 19th-century-inspired fibreglass façade looked as false and chintzy as the Disneyland castle. However, the developers quickly set about rectifying the mistake; work was still in progress at time of writing. Whatever the outcome, the interior is delightful. A tasteful update of traditional elegance, rooms are decorated in soothing, muted colour schemes and contemporary brocades. A boon for business travellers, the generous period-style writing desks are equipped with all manner of gadgetry: high-speed internet, voicemail and cordless phones you can carry throughout the hotel. Room service is delivered directly from Great Bay, the contemporary seafood restaurant from award-winning restaurateur/chef team, Christopher Myers and Michael Schlow, which shares the building. A bistro with sidewalk tables, which is due to open in autumn 2004, should breathe new life into the square.

Hotel services *Air-conditioning. Bar. Business services. Concierge. Disabled: adapted rooms. Gym. Laundry. No-smoking floors. Parking (valet $32 per night) Restaurant.* **Room services** *Bathrobe. CD player. Dataport (high speed). DVD player. Ethernet. Hairdryer. Iron. Minibar. Newspaper. Room service (6am-11pm Mon-Thur; varies Fri-Sun) Turndown. TV: cable/VCR on request.*

The Eliot Hotel

370 Commonwealth Avenue, at Massachusetts Avenue, Boston, MA 02215 (1-617 267 1607/ 1-800 443 5468/fax 1-617 536 9114/www.eliot hotel.com). Hynes/ICA T. **Rates** $215-$335 single/ double; $235-$415 suite. **Credit** AmEx, DC, MC, V. **Map** p276 E6.

Hotel Commonwealth updates traditional elegance. *See p42.*

Built in 1925, the Eliot was getting a bit rough around the edges until a renovation several years ago. Now it's back to its old self: a 95-room Boston facsimile of a small European city hotel. A tiny yet elegant lobby, an ornate French Revival-style façade, and doormen who transcend their job with shopping tips and guest-name memory combine to make it Back Bay's finest independent hostelry. The large number of suites, with sitting rooms and kitchenettes, is a boon for families. One of Boston's top tables, Clio (*see p115*), is downstairs and Newbury Street's consumer paradise is just steps away.
Hotel services *Air-conditioning. Bar. Business services. Disabled: adapted rooms. Gym. Laundry. Limousine service. No-smoking rooms. Parking (valet $29 per night). Restaurants (2).* **Room services** *Bathrobe. Dataport. Ethernet. Fax. Hairdryer. Iron. Minibar. Newspaper. Room service (24hr). Turndown. TV: cable/pay movies/VCR (on request).*

Fairmont Copley Plaza

138 St James Avenue, at Copley Square, Boston, MA 02116 (1-617 267 5300/1-800 441 1414/fax 1-617 375 9648/www.fairmont.com). Back Bay or Copley T. **Rates** $199-$389 single; $229-$469 double; $479-$669 suite. **Credit** AmEx, DC, Disc, MC, V.
Map p277 H6.

Overlooking Copley Square, this hotel was originally built in 1912 as the sister establishment to New York's Plaza. Although it's never achieved the same social cachet as its forerunner, it has nonetheless retained much of its earnest elegance over the years. The mirrored and gilded lobby is nothing short of spectacular. In contrast, the 379 rooms combine discreet opulence with every modern amenity (a $29 million revamp will soon add high-speed internet and marble bathtubs to the list). The rooms are large and those with views of the square are particularly coveted. Most US presidents since Taft have stayed here (Clinton passed). The Fairmont's restaurant, the Oak Room, is a perennial contender for top steakhouse in Boston, and the Oak Bar (*see p146*) is a must-visit for Martinis as big as bird baths. Service is top-notch, and the concierges seem to know what you're thinking before you do.
Hotel services *Air-conditioning. Babysitting. Bar. Business services. Concierge. Disabled: adapted rooms. Gym. No-smoking rooms. Parking (valet $36 per night). Restaurant.* **Room services** *Bathrobe. Dataport. Ethernet. CD/DVD player (Gold floors only). Hairdryer. Iron. Kitchenette. Minibar. Room service (24hr). TV: cable/pay movies/VCR (on request).*

The Lenox

61 Exeter Street, at Boylston Street, Boston, MA 02116 (1-617 536 5300/1-800 225 7676/fax 1-617 266 7905/www.lenoxhotel.com). Copley T. **Rates** $308-$348 single/double; $695 suite. **Credit** AmEx, DC, Disc, MC, V. **Map** p277 G6.

The privately owned Lenox, which first opened in 1900, boasts a prime location next to the Boston Public Library. The hotel's old-style gold and blue decor has earned it design awards for years. Rooms feature brass chandeliers, dark wood furniture and marble bathrooms; several also boast working fireplaces, as does the charmingly restored lobby. Its rooftop provides one of the best seats in town on Boston Marathon day, when the runners whizz (or

stagger) past to the finish one block away. Besides being a fine business hotel, the Lenox also has two great entertainment spots: upscale New American restaurant Azure and the chic City Bar.
Hotel services *Bars (2). Business services. Concierge. Disabled: adapted rooms. Gym. Laundry. No-smoking rooms. Parking (valet $34 per night). Restaurant.* **Room services** *Dataport. Ethernet. Hairdryer. Iron. Room service (6.30am-midnight). TV: cable/pay movies.*

Moderate

Hotel Buckminster

645 Beacon Street, at Kenmore Square, Boston, MA 02215 (1-617 236 7050/fax 1-617 262 0068). Kenmore T. **Rates** $99-$129 single/double; $139-$169 suite. **Credit** AmEx, DC, Disc, MC, V. **Map** p276 D6.
With its perfectly acceptable rooms and proximity to Kenmore Square's clubs and bars – and, of course, Fenway Park – the Buckminster is one of the best deals in town. Though you probably wouldn't have guessed it, the building was designed by the celebrated American architect Stanford White. None of its 96 rooms will win any design awards, but all come equipped with microwaves, refrigerators, and cheaper versions of the amenities offered by luxury hotels. A weird piece of Buckminster trivia: the first network radio broadcast took place here in 1929.
Hotel services *Air-conditioning. Disabled: adapted rooms. Laundry (self-service). No-smoking rooms.* **Room services** *Dataport. Hairdryer. Iron. Kitchenette (microwave and refrigerator). TV: cable.*

The Charlesmark Hotel

655 Boylston Street, at Copley Square, Boston, MA 02216 (1-617 247 1212/fax 1-617 247 1224/ www.thecharlesmark.com). Copley T. **Rates** (incl breakfast) $119-$299 single/double. **Credit** AmEx, DC, Disc, MC, V. **Map** p277 G6.
Small, hip and inexpensive, the Charlesmark is a welcome alternative to Copley Square's more excessive lodgings. The only obvious concessions to thrift here are the modest size of the rooms and lack of an in-house restaurant; in all other respects, the digs are rather lavish. The 33 rooms are bathed in warm neutral tones, and punctuated with colourful accents: red leather chairs, Italian tiles, a lone poppy. CD players and wireless internet, are standard. What's more, the hotel doubles as an art gallery, and each floor's halls are bedecked with the work of a different artist.
Hotel services *Air-conditioning. Business services. Concierge. Disabled: adapted rooms. Laundry. Parking ($32 per night). No-smoking rooms. Wireless internet.* **Room services** *CD player. Hairdryer. Hi-fi. TV: satellite.*

Copley Square Hotel

47 Huntington Avenue, at Exeter Street, Boston, MA 02116 (1-617 536 9000/1-800 225 7062/ fax 1-617 267 6547/www.copleysquarehotel.com). Back Bay or Copley T. **Rates** $169-$405 single/ double/family; $405 suite. **Credit** AmEx, DC, Disc, MC, V. **Map** p277 G6.
Across the street from the Lenox (*see p43*) is its more modest turn-of-the century sister, the Copley Square. The understated hotel has a distinctly European feel about it, from the snippets of French and German you'll hear in the comfortable lobby lounge to the cosmopolitan crowd sipping cocktails at Saint (*see p116*), the Copley's upscale restaurant/lounge hybrid. True, the corridors are a bit dingy and the decor in the rooms is a bit spare, but it's a solid, comfortable choice.
Hotel services *Air-conditioning. Bar. Disabled: adapted rooms. Laundry. No-smoking rooms. Parking (valet $32 per night). Restaurants(2).* **Room services** *Dataport. DVD player. Iron. Room service (7am-11.30pm). TV: VCR.*

Gryphon House

9 Bay State Road, at Beacon Street, Boston, MA 02215 (1-617 375 9003/fax 1-617 425 0716/ www.innboston.com). Kenmore T. **Rates** (incl breakfast) *Mar-Nov* $185-$245 double. *Dec-Feb* $149-$208 double. **Credit** AmEx, Disc, MC, V. **Map** p276 E6.
The first things you'll notice when you enter this plush Victorian bed and breakfast are its walls. Papered with scenic French wallpaper, they depict the flora and fauna of Africa, Asia and Europe. The eight spacious suites contain many romantic flourishes, including gas fireplaces (in most), silk lampshades and antique furniture. All are equipped with refrigerators and wet bars.
Hotel services *Air-conditioning. No-smoking hotel. Parking (free). Wireless internet.* **Room services** *CD player. Dataport. Hairdryer. Iron. Kitchenette (no cooker). Newspaper. TV: cable/VCR.*

Newbury Guest House

261 Newbury Street, between Gloucester & Fairfield Streets, Boston, MA 02116 (1-617 437 7666/1-800 437 7668/fax 1-617 262 4243/www.hagopian hotels.com). Hynes/ICA T. **Rates** (incl breakfast) $100-$190 single/double. **Credit** AmEx, DC, Disc, MC, V. **Map** p276 F6.
Smack, bang in the middle of Boston's elegant retail strip, this pleasant small hotel is made up of three refurbished townhouses. The 32 rooms are tastefully fitted out with Victorian-style furnishings, wooden floors, high ceilings and bay windows. Continental breakfast is served in a sunny little parlour that opens on to a patio terrace. About half the clientele here are gay men, but everyone is made to feel welcome. Be warned the location can get a bit noisy – light sleepers would do well to request rooms away from the hustle and bustle of lively Newbury Street.
Hotel services *Air-conditioning. Concierge. Disabled: adapted rooms. Limousine service. No-smoking rooms. Parking ($15 per night). Wireless internet* **Room services** *Dataport. Hairdryer. Iron. Newspaper. TV: cable.*

Oasis Guest House

22 Edgerly Road, at Massachusetts Avenue, Boston, MA 02115 (1-617 267 2262/1-800 230 0105/fax 1-617 267 1920/www.oasisgh.com). Hynes/ICA or

The hospitable **Florence Frances**.

Symphony T. **Rates** (incl breakfast) *mid Mar-mid Nov* $69-$89 single/double. *Mid Nov-mid Mar* $90-$140 single/double. **Credit** AmEx, MC, V. **Map** p276 F7.

The name says it all. Though it's just a few blocks from Symphony Hall, the Prudential Center and the city's hottest nightspots, the hotel's location on a leafy, quiet side street in Back Bay makes you forget the busy city outside. The 30 rooms are small but nicely decorated, and most offer private baths. Continental breakfast is served in the cosy lounge, and the two outdoor decks – the only places smoking is allowed – are great places to hang out and relax. The clientele here is a mix of gay and straight and the staff are very welcoming.

Hotel services *Air-conditioning. Guest refrigerator and microwave. Limousine service. No-smoking hotel. Parking ($15 per night).* **Room services** *Dataport. Hairdryer. Iron. TV: satellite.*

Budget

Florence Frances Guest House

458 Park Drive, at Beacon Street, Boston, MA 02215 (1-617 267 2458). Fenway or Kenmore T. **Rates** $80 single; $90 double. **No credit cards**.

Glamorous former actress Florence Frances offers three guest rooms in her 150-year-old townhouse. Each is meticulously decorated according to a different, slightly theatrical theme. The 'Spanish' double room, for example, is bedecked with decorative fans and Spanish paintings, red linens and black lacquered furniture. The rooms are equipped with colour TVs, but no telephone or private bath; instead, guests share a freshly remodelled bathroom that features a toilet-seat inlaid with half-dollar coins. There's a well-stocked bar for guests (Florence herself doesn't drink), a comfortable lounge, a roof terrace, laundry facilities and free parking at the back. The tirelessly gracious hostess is an added feature of your stay here – if you don't mind her participating a little. No smokers, pets or children.

Hotel services *Air-conditioning. Cooking facilities. No smoking hotel. Parking. Payphone.* **Room services** *Hairdryer. Iron. TV.*

Hosteling International Boston

12 Hemenway Street, at Boylston Street, Boston, MA 02115 (1-617 536 1027/1-800 909 4776/ fax 1-617 424 6558). Hynes/ICA T. **Rates** $35 dorm; $99 private single/double. **Credit** MC, V. **Map** p276 E7.

Before you get all excited about the price, be clear about what an American Youth Hostel is. This one, at the edge of Back Bay, can accommodate up to 190 people, but the cheap rooms are dormitory style (some are mixed sex), with up to six beds each. Though bedlinen is included in the price, you may want to consider bringing your own. The saying 'you get what you pay for' was never more apt.

Hotel services *Air-conditioning (private rooms and lounge only). Cooking facilities. Internet access. Laundry (self-service). Payphone. No-smoking. TV room.*

YMCA

316 Huntington Avenue, at Northeastern University, Boston, MA 02115 (1-617 536 7800/fax 1-617 267 4653). Northeastern T. **Rates** (incl breakfast) $46 single; $66 double. **Credit** AmEx, Disc, MC, V. **Map** p276 F8.

The YMCA only takes male guests for most of the year, but goes unisex during the summer months – call to check exact dates. It has a surprisingly friendly atmosphere and, while the rooms look austere, they're comfortable enough and linen is changed daily. There are no phones in rooms, and bathrooms are down the hall, but breakfast in the café (which is sometimes closed on Sundays) is included.

Hotel services *Cafeteria. Gym. Laundry (self-service). No-smoking rooms. Restaurant. Swimming pool (indoor). TV room.*

YWCA/Berkeley Residence

40 Berkeley Street, between Gray & Appleton Streets, Boston, MA 02116 (1-617 375 2524/fax 1-617 375 2525). Arlington or Back Bay T. **Rates** (incl breakfast) $56 single; $86 double; $99 triple. **Credit** MC, V. **Map** p277 H7.

This is the YWCA, which means women only. In fact, Y-chromosome types can barely get in the door. Still, it's a fairly nice example of a no-frills hostel. Thus, the rooms are clean, if a bit threadbare, and each comes with a desk, bureau and closet. Bathrooms are down the hall. Breakfast, included in the price, is served in the surprisingly pleasant restaurant-cum-cafeteria, where dinner is also dished up on the cheap. Weekly, monthly and long-stay rates are available. No phone in rooms.
Hotel services *Laundry (self-service). Payphone. Restaurant. TV room: cable.*

Beacon Hill

Deluxe

XV Beacon

15 Beacon Street, at Park Street, Boston, MA 02108 (1-617 670 1500/fax 1-617 670 2525/ www.xvbeacon.com). Park St T. **Rates** $295-$600 single/double; $995-$2,300 suite; $3,500 private floor. **Credit** AmEx, DC, Disc, MC, V. **Map** p274 K4.
XV Beacon opened to much applause several years ago – and with startlingly high rates. But for the

Let us stay

Most accommodation provides little in the way of spiritual direction beyond the neglected Bible tucked away in the bedside drawer. But the Monastery Guest House in Cambridge brings new meaning to the phrase 'urban retreat'.

It's operated by the Brothers of the Society of Saint John the Evangelist, an order of monks affiliated with both the Anglican and American Episcopal Churches, and profits fund the Society's various ministries. Founded in Oxford, England in 1866, the Society of Saint John emphasises the twin pillars of prayer and service. Although the monks take the traditional vows of celibacy, they also welcome female guests and couples to the Guest House.

Spiritual benefits aside, the Monastery has much to recommend it: a prime location just three blocks from Harvard Square, views of the Charles River, a lovely garden and an affordable price. These perks, coupled with the Monastery's serene environment, attract tourists – though most visitors come for the sanctuary and prayer.

The two wings of guest quarters, which accommodate up to 16 people, combine the personalised hospitality of a bed and breakfast with the no-frills vibe of a hostel. The rooms, primarily singles, are what you might expect of a monastery: small, clean and sparely furnished, but perfectly comfortable. Bathrooms are segregated by gender and shared by each floor. Two common rooms and a well-stocked library are also open to guests. Meals, which are taken in the refectory, are typically eaten in silence.

Should you choose to participate in a retreat, the Monastery offers a vast menu of options, from structured meditation under the guidance of a Brother to a few days of undirected, independent reflection. Weekends are frequently reserved for 'programme retreats', on subjects both universal (forgiveness) and specific (monastic chant). But even if you just want a relaxing break, you can't beat a monastery for peace and quiet.

Monastery of the Society of Saint John the Evangelist

980 Memorial Drive, at John F Kennedy Park, Cambridge, MA 02138 (1-617 876 3037/ www.ssje.org). Harvard T. **Rates** $60 per person; $75 for a directed retreat. **Credit** MC, V. **Map** p278 A3.

influential and discreet crowd it attracts, it justifies every penny and ovation. Deserving of the headlines is Celeste Cooper's design: it melds European small-hotel sophistication, a sense of American (and Boston) history, and contemporary cheek. Striking details include a richly chic use of Italian fabrics, bold mineral tones and four-poster beds. For business travellers, rooms are hard-wired to the nines with fax machines, broadband and multi-line phones – even in-residency business cards with direct dial numbers to hand out to colleagues (or show off to friends). XV's perch just over the crest of Beacon Hill makes it possible to grab the hotel Mercedes and be Downtown in a matter of minutes, stroll to Boston Common, or dart to the T at Park Street with equal ease. Its restaurant, the Federalist (*see p131*), comes off a bit goofier with its drab, mismatched fabrics and white repro busts of former presidents, but the bar is a great place for a brandy, and the power breakfast here is unmatched.
Hotel services *Air-conditioning. Bar. Concierge. Disabled: adapted rooms. Gym. Laundry. Limousine service. No-smoking rooms. Parking (valet $30 per night). Restaurant.* **Room services** *Bathrobe. CD player. Dataport. Ethernet. Fax. Hairdryer. Iron. Minibar. Newspaper. Room service (24hr). Turndown. TV: cable/pay movies/DVD.*

Expensive

Beacon Hill Hotel & Bistro

25 Charles Street, at Chestnut Street, Boston, MA 02114 (1-888 959 2442/www.beaconhillhotel.com). Arlington or Charles/MGH T. **Rates** (incl breakfast) $245-$285 single/double; $365 suite. **Credit** AmEx, DC, Disc, MC, V. **Map** p274 J4.
Singular in chain-clad Boston, BHHB calls itself a hotel but taps the best elements of country inns and bed and breakfasts to make your stay a fine one. The amiable owners, Peter and Cecilia Rait, returned to Boston after years working in hotels and restaurants in Europe, and it shows in the elegant yet relaxed atmosphere. The building is a converted 1830s townhouse on lantern-lit Charles Street. Despite having a mere 12 rooms and one suite, there's room service from early till late, plenty of business assistance and modern perks like flat-screen TVs and broadband internet. A full breakfast, lazy lunch, or wine-soaked dinner at the bistro (*see p131*) is not to be missed.
Hotel services *Air-conditioning. Business services. Disabled: adapted rooms. Laundry. No-smoking hotel. Restaurant.* **Room services** *Dataport. Ethernet. Hairdryer. Iron. Room service (7am-11pm). TV: pay movies/satellite.*

Moderate

John Jeffries House

14 David G Mugar Way, at Charles Street, Boston, MA 02114 (1-617 367 1866/fax 1-617 742 0313/ www.johnjeffrieshouse.com). Charles MGH T. **Rates** (incl breakfast) $95-$125 single/double; $125-$175 suite. **Credit** AmEx, DC, Disc, MC, V. **Map** p274 H3.
This 19th-century B&B is more like a small hotel. The quality of the warm and elegant decor, and amenities like 24-hour coffee and tea service, well exceed the price. The staff here are so welcoming you almost believe they're genuinely glad to see you. The rooms range from small studios to deluxe suites, most of which include kitchenettes. A continental breakfast is served each morning in the common room on the ground floor. Having the shops and restaurants of Charles Street on the doorstep is a further bonus. Dollar for dollar, this is one of the best deals in town.
Hotel services *Air-conditioning. Garden. No-smoking hotel. Parking ($18 per night).* **Room services** *Dataport. Iron. Kitchenette (some rooms). TV.*

Downtown & the Financial District

Deluxe

Ritz-Carlton Boston Common

2 Avery Street, at Tremont Street, Boston, MA 02111 (1-617 574 7100/1-800 241 3333/fax 1-617 574 7200/www.ritzcarlton.com). Boylston T. **Rates** $325-$595 single/double; $395-$4,000 suite. **Credit** AmEx, DC, Disc, MC, V. **Map** p274 K5.
It seems fitting that the oldest Ritz-Carlton in the US abuts the prim Public Gardens, while at the other side of the green swathe, one of the country's newest R-Cs occupies a similar parkside position in an area that's redefining itself. The Downtown district near the Ritz-Carlton Boston Common is undergoing a sea change from shady no-man's-land to the place to be. Contemporary luxury is the angle of the hotel and it comes across in the self-consciously slick feel of Jer-Ne, the bar/restaurant on the ground floor, and in the high-tech features (flat-screen TVs, internet hard-wiring) throughout the hotel. Rooms feel fresh and modern without betraying the timeless class of the Ritz, and the service is highly polished. Quirky touches like a fireplace butler, personally on-call with a selection of hardwoods to get a fire going in-room, add character.
Hotel services *Air-conditioning. Babysitting. Bars (2). Beauty salon. Business services. Concierge. Disabled: adapted rooms. Gym. Laundry. Limousine service. No-smoking floors. Parking ($37 per night). Restaurant. Wireless internet.* **Room services** *Bathrobe. CD player. Dataport (high speed). Hairdryer. Hi-fi. Iron. Minibar. Newspaper. Room service (24hr). Turndown. TV: cable/pay movies/ VCR rental (on request)/videogames.*

Expensive

Jurys Boston

350 Stuart Street, at Berkeley Street, Boston, MA 02116 (1-617 266 7200/fax 1-617 2667203/ www.jurysdoyle.com) Copley T. **Rates** $149-$435 single/double; $435-$750 suite. **Credit** AmEx, DC, Disc, MC, V. **Map** p277 H6.

Puttin' on the glitz: **Nine Zero**. *See p51*.

Jurys was formerly the Boston Police Department building, and it took three years and around $60 million for the Irish company to turn it into a posh four-star hotel. The landmark's severe limestone-and-brick façade conceals a fanciful interior. The design scheme, meant to evoke 'ye olde Ireland', combines dreamy flourishes – a glass staircase, streams and waterfalls, a two-storey fireplace – with memorabilia from the building's crime-fighting past. The 220 rooms feature desks with ergonomic chairs, down quilts and heated towel racks. A gym, Irish pub and coffeeshop are also on the premises, as is the Stanhope Grille, where you can feast on an authentic Irish breakfast.
Hotel Services *Air-conditioning. Bar (2). Business Services. Concierge. Gym. Parking (valet $34 per night). Restaurant.* **Room services** *CD player. Dataport (high-speed). DVD player. Hairdryer. Iron. Newspaper. No-smoking rooms. Room service (24hr). TV: cable.*

Langham Hotel Boston

250 Franklin Street, at Post Office Square, Boston, MA 02110 (1-617 451 1900/1-800 543 4300/fax 1-617 423 2844/www.langhamhotels.com). State T. **Rates** $270-$420 single/double; $500-$1,800 suite. **Credit** AmEx, DC, Disc, MC, V. **Map** p275 L4.
When it was known as Le Méridien, this was hailed as one of Boston's most elegant hotels, and though the name has changed, little else has. The Langham occupies the former Federal Reserve Bank, whose Renaissance Revival architecture sets the mood at decadent; embellishments such as polished bronze, ornate woodwork and coffered ceilings abound. The hotel includes two popular French restaurants, Julien and Café Fleuri, and guests have been known to slaver over its Chocolate Bar – a ridiculously indulgent buffet of cakes, tortes and crêpes.
Hotel services *Air-conditioning. Bar. Business services. Concierge. Disabled: adapted rooms. Gym. Laundry. Limousine service. No-smoking rooms. Parking ($39 per night). Restaurants (2). Swimming pool (indoor).* **Room services** *Dataport. Ethernet. Hairdryer. Iron. Minibar. Room service (24hr). Turndown. TV: cable/pay movies/VCR (on request).*

Millennium Bostonian

26 North Street, at Faneuil Hall Marketplace, Boston, MA 02109 (1-617 523 3600/1-800 222 8888/fax 1-617 523 2454/www.millennium hotels.com). Gov't Center or Haymarket T. **Rates** $229-$309 single/double; $350-$399 junior suite; $499-$599 suite. **Credit** AmEx, DC, Disc, MC, V. **Map** p275 L3.
Formerly the Regal Bostonian, this hotel seems to have fallen off a bit since it became the Millennium – which is unfortunately not reflected in its prices. Still, its great location, close to the throngs at Faneuil Hall Marketplace, continues to attract guests. Housed in two adjoining converted warehouses, and arranged around a central brick courtyard, the hotel has nice enough rooms, with small, covered balconies and well-equipped bathrooms (featuring vast bathtubs) – although the dingy carpets could stand replacing. If noise is a problem for you, ask for a room at the back. The rooftop restaurant, Seasons, has served as a launching pad for some of the city's best-known chefs – it's a good place for a power breakfast or lunch.
Hotel services *Air-conditioning. Bar. Business services. Concierge. Disabled: adapted rooms. Gym. Laundry. Limousine service. No-smoking rooms. Parking (valet $35 per night). Restaurant.* **Room services** *Dataport. Ethernet. Hairdryer. Iron. Minibar. Newspaper. Room service (24hr). Turndown. TV: cable/pay movies.*

Nine Zero

90 Tremont Street, at Park Street, Boston, MA 02108 (1-617 772 5800/1-866 6463 9376/fax 1-617 772 5810/www.ninezero.com). Park St T. **Rates** $279-$489 single/double; $450-$700 suite; $1,800-$3,000 penthouse suite. **Credit** AmEx, DC, Disc, MC, V. **Map** p274 K4.
Since 2002 Nine Zero has filled the previously barren niche of slick urban design hotel. In New York, it wouldn't get much attention – but in Boston it stands out from the crowd. The odd dodgy detail aside (glitzy diaphanous curtains recalling an East London sari shop), it fits the boutique brief with its slick, sexy lines and lots of glass, chrome and dark wood. But most importantly, staying in one of its understated rooms – equipped with all the expected technology, goose-down quilts and your personally requested snacks in the minibar – is an extremely comfortable experience, enhanced in the upper front-facing rooms by spectacular views over Boston Common. It's worth staying in for dinner – Nine Zero's glamorous, grown-up restaurant, Spire, has garnered both local and national praise for its contemporary American menu.
Hotel services *Air-conditioning. Bar. Business services. Concierge. Disabled: adapted rooms. Gym. Laundry. Limousine service. No-smoking rooms. Parking (valet $32 per night). Restaurant.* **Room services** *Bathrobe. CD player. Dataport. Ethernet. Hairdryer. Iron. Minibar. Newspaper. Room service (24hr). TV: cable.*

Omni Parker House

60 School Street, at Tremont Street, Boston, MA 02108 (1-617 227 8600/1-800 843 6664/fax 1-617 523 5716/www.omnihotels.com). Park St T. **Rates** $139-$289 single/double; $189-$339 suite. **Credit** AmEx, DC, Disc, MC, V. **Map** p274 K5.
Established in 1855 as the Parker House, this is the oldest continuously operating hotel in America, but thanks to a recent $70 million facelift, it's ageing quite well, thank you very much. The guest rooms are done in warm neutrals, with cherry-wood furniture and heirloom accents. But the Omni's real claim to fame is its dizzying history: Charles Dickens stayed here, Ho Chi Minh and Malcolm X both worked here, JFK proposed to Jackie in the hotel's restaurant, and the Saturday Club, a group of distinguished authors (including Longfellow, Hawthorne and Emerson), met here once a month for lunch. And that's just for starters.

Hotel services *Air-conditioning. Bars (2). Concierge. Disabled: adapted rooms. Gym (24hr). Laundry. Limousine service. No-smoking rooms. Parking (valet $36 per night). Restaurant. Wireless internet.* **Room services** *Bathrobe. CD player. Dataport. Ethernet. Hairdryer. Iron. Minibar. Newspaper. Room service (24hr). Turndown. TV: cable/pay movies.*

The Tremont Boston

275 Tremont Street, at Stuart Street, Boston, MA 02116 (1-617 426 1400/1-800 331 9998/fax 1-617 482 6730/www.wyndham.com). NE Medical Center T. **Rates** $129-$229 single; $169-$339 double; $219-$389 suite. **Credit** AmEx, DC, Disc, MC, V. **Map** p277 J6.

This art deco-style hotel was built in 1925 as the national headquarters for the business organisation the Elks Club (look out for the authentic elk-head doorknobs), but it's far more happening these days. The prime downtown location makes it ideal for young urban types. The hotel has two popular nightclubs on the premises, plus a decent restaurant and bar, and the surrounding neighbourhood has many other swinging nightlife options.

Hotel services *Air-conditioning. Bar. Concierge. Disabled: adapted rooms. Gym. No-smoking rooms. Parking (valet $30 per night). Restaurants.* **Room services** *Bathrobe. CD Player. Dataport. Ethernet. Hairdryer. Iron. Minibar. Newspaper. Room service (7am-11pm). TV: cable/pay movies/web TV.*

Wyndham Boston

89 Broad Street, at Franklin Street, Boston, MA 02110 (1-617 556 0006/fax 1-617 556 0053/ www.wyndham.com). Aquarium T. **Rates** $265-$375 single/double; $340-$450 suite. **Credit** AmEx, DC, Disc, MC, V. **Map** p275 L4.

Wyndham dropped a lot of cash converting the historic Batterymarch building into an upscale art deco hotel, and it seems to have paid off. As with other Wyndhams, comfort and efficiency are the name of the game, but style plays a significant role here as well. The swanky rooms include 12ft (3.5m) ceilings, Aeron chairs, virtually soundproof walls and cordless telephones. The library downstairs, with its dark oak walls and a fireplace glowing on cold days, is an ideal place to while away a rainy afternoon.

Hotel services *Air-conditioning. Bar. Business services. Concierge. Disabled: adapted rooms. Gym. Laundry. No-smoking rooms. Parking (valet $32 per night). Restaurant.* **Room services** *Dataport. Ethernet. Hairdryer. Iron. Minibar. Newspaper. Room service (24hr). Turndown. TV: cable/pay movies.*

South End

Moderate

Chandler Inn

26 Chandler Street, at Berkeley Street, Boston, MA 02116 (1-617 482 3450/1-800 842 3450/fax 1-617 542 3428/www.chandlerinn.com). Back Bay T. **Rates** $79-$119 single; $139-$169 double. **Credit** AmEx, MC, V. **Map** p277 H7.

Chandler Inn is what you'd call 'straight-friendly': its primary clientele is gay, but all visitors are welcome – as long as they're cool. The Chandler's location in the hip South End is as appealing as its price. This is a great small hotel, with truly lovely staff who go out of their way to help guests. The 56 rooms have been recently refurbished, and are clean and comfortable (if a bit small), although the bathrooms are tiny and nondescript. There's no lobby to speak of, and no restaurant, but Fritz, the gay bar on the ground floor (*see p203*), offers a decent brunch at the weekend. Unless you're there to party, it's a good idea to ask for a room on an upper floor, as Fritz can get outrageously loud at night.

Hotel services *Air-conditioning. Bar. No-smoking rooms.* **Room services** *Dataport. Hairdryer. Iron. Parking ($28 per night). TV: satellite.*

Clarendon Square Inn

198 West Brookline Street, between Tremont Street & Warren Avenue, Boston, MA 02118 (1-617 536 2229/www.clarendonsquare.com). Back Bay T. **Rates** (incl breakfast) $129-$289 double. **Credit** AmEx, DC, Disc, MC, V. **Map** p277 H8.

The centrepiece of this beautifully converted 1860s townhouse is an original Victorian salon with soaring ceilings, period detail and a grand piano. But the place isn't chintzy or doily-strewn; it feels more like a stylish boutique hotel. The rooms feature streamlined furnishings, marble-and-limestone bathrooms and sumptuous linens. Most come with working fireplaces as well. They're also stocked with modern amenities (DVD players, high-speed internet) you wouldn't expect of a place with so much old-world charm. The focus here is definitely on romance, straight or gay; if you're squeamish about sharing the rooftop hot tub with a couple of another sexual orientation, you might be better off hanging out, so to speak, in your private two-person shower.

Hotel services *Air-conditioning. Guest refrigerator. Internet access (high-speed). No-smoking hotel. Parking ($15 per night).* **Room services** *CD player. Dataport. Ethernet. Hairdryer. Iron. TV: cable/DVD.*

Waterfront

Expensive

Boston Harbor Hotel

70 Rowes Wharf, Boston, MA 02110 (1-617 439 7000/1-800 752 7077/fax 1-617 345 6799/ www.bhh.com). South Station T. **Rates** $295-$450 single/double; $570-$2,500 suite. **Credit** AmEx, DC, Disc, MC, V. **Map** p275 M4.

On one side of the Boston Harbor Hotel lies the water – almost half the 230 rooms boast harbour views. On the other, the biggest highway-engineering project in US history, the Big Dig, is finally being wrapped up. Over the next couple of years, hundreds of acres of parkland, meandering boardwalks and a new landmark Institute of Contemporary Art

Cambridge House Bed & Breakfast. *See p56.*

(*see p92* **Future vision**) will be springing up nearby. But in the meantime, once in the hotel there's an airy calm and confident class that draws guests back repeatedly. Elegance comes across in the little things, like Tiffany china in the restaurants. It's a rightful favourite for business travellers and also goes the extra distance for comfort in the form of soundproof glass in the rooms, slippers next to the bed, and concierges who have the town hard-wired.
Hotel services *Air-conditioning. Babysitting. Bar. Business services. Concierge. Disabled: adapted rooms. Gym. Laundry. Limousine service. No-smoking rooms. Parking ($20 per night; valet $25 per night). Restaurants (2). Swimming pool (indoor).* **Room services** *Bathrobe. CD player (on request). Dataport. Ethernet. Hairdryer. Iron. Minibar. Newspaper. Room service (24hr). Turndown. TV: cable/pay movies/VCR (on request).*

Seaport

1 Seaport Lane, at the World Trade Center, Boston, MA 02210 (1-617 385 4000/1-877-732 7678/fax 1-617 385 4001/www.seaport hotel.com). South Station T. **Rates** $159-$300 single/double; $350-$1,700 suite. **Credit** AmEx, DC, Disc, MC, V.

If you're coming to Boston on business, the Seaport is the place for you. Situated directly across the street from the Boston World Trade Center, near the new convention centre and the Financial District, this hotel has every imaginable modern convenience. Even the elevators are equipped with screens that constantly flash stock prices. For the CEOs among us, there's a private yacht available upon request. To cap it all, the Seaport boasts what is arguably the best hotel health and spa club in town. Aura, the hotel restaurant, may look like a sectioned-off part of the lobby, but the excellent continental food and service are a secret not even the locals have caught on to yet. Smokers may want to stay elsewhere though, as they'll be slapped with a stiff fine if they're busted lighting up indoors.
Hotel services *Air-conditioning. Bar. Business services. Concierge. Disabled: adapted rooms. Gym. Laundry. Limousine. No-smoking hotel. Parking ($25 per night; $33 valet). Restaurant. Spa. Swimming pool (indoor). Wireless internet.* **Room services** *Bathrobe. CD/DVD player (on request). Dataport. Ethernet. Hairdryer. Iron. Kitchenette (some suites). Minibar. Newspaper. Room service (24hr). Turndown. TV: cable/VCR.*

Moderate

Harborside Inn

185 State Street (1-617 723 7500/1-888 723 7565/fax 1-617 670 6015/www.harborsideinn boston.com) Aquarium T. **Rates** $149-$169. **Credit** AmEx, Disc, MC, V. **Map** p275 M4.

This renovated mercantile warehouse, with a plum downtown address, is a simple, unpretentious hotel with loads of charm. It's also one of the city's best bargains. The Harborside's rooms have much to

recommend them – high ceilings, exposed brick walls, hand-woven oriental rugs – and the staff are equally gracious. Though the name might suggest otherwise, the hotel has no water views, and unless you're a night owl, you might want to avoid the street-side rooms. The restaurant, Margo Bistro, successfully riffs on classic American cuisine, and hotel guests are invited to dine at a discount after 5pm.
Hotel services *Air-conditioning. Concierge. Laundry. No-smoking rooms. Restaurant. Wireless internet.* **Room services** *Dataport (high speed). Hairdryer. Iron. Newspaper. Room service (11.30am-10pm). TV: cable.*

North

Moderate

Onyx Hotel

155 Portland Street (1-617 557 9955/fax 1-617 557 0005/www.onyxhotel.com) Haymarket or North Station T. **Rates** $149-$249 single/double; $299 suite. **Credit** AmEx, DC, Disc, MC, V. **Map** p274 K3.

The Onyx is the first hotel to land in the North Station area since the Big Dig restructured this neighbourhood, and brings a touch of sophistication to what city planners hope will become the 'new Downtown'. A few doors down from the FleetCenter, the latest 'boutique' offering from the West Coast Kimpton chain is emphatically modern. Black figures prominently in the palette and rooms are tricked out with down quilts, red suede chairs and flat-screen TVs. Off the terrazzo-floored lobby, the Ruby Room slings cocktails in a stylish lounge setting. Oh, and feel free to bring the ferret along: the Onyx is pet-friendly.
Hotel services *Air-conditioning. Bar. Business services. Concierge. Gym. Laundry. Restaurant. Wireless internet.* **Room services** *Dataport. Ethernet. Parking ($30 per night). Room service (24hr). TV: satellite.*

Cambridge

Expensive

Charles Hotel

1 Bennett Street, at Harvard Square, Cambridge, MA 02138 (1-617 864 1200/1-800 882 1818/ fax 1-617 864 5715/www.charleshotel.com). Harvard T. **Rates** $200-$575 single/double; $250-$4,000 suite. **Credit** AmEx, DC, MC, V. **Map** p278 A2.

The Charles doesn't hit you over the head with its luxury – nothing so tacky as that. The glamour here is cool and understated, which may be why it's the hotel of choice for visiting luminaries (everyone from Ben Affleck to the Dalai Lama has slept here). The 296 rooms epitomise New England decorative restraint: all are done in blond woods, with muted carpets and calm fabrics, plus the requisite high-tech amenities. Staff are efficient but unobtrusive and the hotel's two restaurants – the upscale Rialto (*see p137*) and the more relaxed Henrietta's Table – are both excellent. The Regatta Bar, which hosts jazz ensembles, is another draw, as is the sleek cocktail bar Noir (*see p153*).
Hotel services *Air-conditioning. Bars (3). Beauty Salon. Business services. Concierge. Disabled: adapted rooms. Gym. Laundry. Limousine service. No-smoking rooms. Parking (valet $32 per night). Restaurants (2). Swimming pool (indoor).* **Room services** *Dataport. DVD player. Ethernet. Hairdryer. Iron. Minibar. Newspaper. Room service (24hr). TV: cable/pay movies.*

Inn at Harvard

1201 Massachusetts Avenue, at Harvard Square, Cambridge, MA 02138 (1-617 491 2222/1-800 458 5886/fax 1-617 491 6520/www.theinnatharvard.com). Harvard T. **Rates** $199-$475 single/double. **Credit** AmEx, DC, Disc, MC, V. **Map** p278 B2.

This little gem of a place is a stone's throw from Harvard Yard, and it shows. Designed by Harvard alumnus Graham Gund in 1992, the red-brick structure is intended to mimic the architectural style of America's most prestigious university. All 113 rooms are arranged over four floors around a glassed-in courtyard meant to recall an Italian villa. The atrium is the ideal place for morning coffee, afternoon tea or a quiet dinner. The rooms themselves are somewhat predictable, but comfortable enough, with all the usual amenities. One can reach the campus, the T stop and a bevy of pubs and cafés in the shortest of strolls.
Hotel services *Air-conditioning. Business services. Concierge. Disabled: adapted rooms. No-smoking rooms. Parking ($30 per night). Restaurant.* **Room services** *Dataport. Iron. Room service (7am-10pm). TV: cable/pay movies/VCR (on request).*

University Park Hotel @ MIT

20 Sidney Street, Cambridge, MA 02139 (1-617 577 0200/fax 1-617 494 8366/www.hotelatmit.com). Central T. **Rates** $99-$359 single/double; $159-$1200 suite. **Credit** AmEx, DC, Disc, MC, V. **Map** p278 C4.

Resembling a chic high-school science fair, this innovative hotel verges on elegant surrealism. There are robotic sculptures in the lobby, atomic energy signs stitched into the elevator carpet and circuit boards in all the most unexpected places – even engraved into the frosted glass of the light fixtures in the hallways. The rooms are decorated with exactly the kind of geeky flair one would expect from MIT – they're even equipped with Sony PlayStations. The hotel's fabulous restaurant, Sidney's Grille, whips up haute comfort food using fresh local ingredients. Truly unique.
Hotel services *Air-conditioning. Babysitting. Bar. Business services. Concierge. Disabled: adapted rooms. Garden (rooftop). Gym. Laundry. No-smoking rooms. Parking ($25 per night). Restaurant.* **Room services** *Bathrobe. Dataport. DVD player. Ethernet. Hairdryer. Iron. Room service (24hr). Sony PlayStation. TV: cable/pay movies/satellite.*

Moderate

Cambridge House Bed & Breakfast

2218 Massachusetts Avenue, at Rindge Avenue, Cambridge, MA 02138 (1-617 491 6300/1-800 232 9989/fax 1-617 868 2848/www.acambridge house.com). Davis or Porter T. **Rates** $99-$290 single/double. **Credit** AmEx, DC, Disc, MC, V.

A country inn divided from busy Mass Ave by a quaint lawn, the Cambridge B&B occupies an adorable Greek Revival house constructed in 1882. Its 16 rooms are busily furnished with antiques, and two (be sure to request) have working fireplaces for the colder months. The freshly made breakfasts, sweets served with tea or brandy, and changing buffet are a (slightly fattening) delight. Free off-street parking is an added boon.

Hotel services *Air-conditioning. No-smoking rooms. Parking (free).* **Room services** *Dataport. Ethernet. Hairdryer. Iron. TV: cable.*

Hotel Marlowe

25 Edwin H Land Boulevard, at O'Brien Highway (1-617 868 8000/reservations 1-800 825 7040/fax 1-617 868 8001/www.hotelmarlowe.com). Lechmere T then 10mins walk. **Rates** (incl breakfast) $99-$249 single/double; $179-$329 studio suite; $279-$429 executive suite. **Credit** AmEx, DC, Disc, MC, V. **Map** p274 H2.

It would be easy to poke fun at this brash upstart – part of the small California-based Kimpton chain – which opened in 2003. But, like an exuberant, eager-to-please junior employee, while you feel it may be trying a little too hard, it's hard not to warm to its enthusiasm. The exterior may be unremarkable (a boxy, brick courtyard design) and the overdesigned interior verging dangerously on the tacky (leopard print, trompe l'oeil effects, curtains emblazoned with the Declaration of Independence), but the rooms are comfortable and luxuriously equipped, staff are very friendly and the mood is unpretentious – even pets are pampered with special dog and cat packages. It is somewhat off the beaten track, but ideally placed for MIT, and only a short walk and a T stop away from the funky nightlife of Central Square. Tying in with the academic theme, the hotel hosts book readings on the first Wednesday of every month and maintains links with local arts organisations.

Hotel services *Air-conditioning. Bar. Business services. Concierge. Disabled: adapted rooms. Gym. Laundry. Limousine service. No-smoking rooms. Parking ($20 per night; $28 valet). Restaurant. Wireless internet.* **Room services** *Bathrobe. Dataport. DVD player. Ethernet. Hairdryer. Hi-fi. Iron. Minibar. Newspaper. Room service (24hr). Turndown. TV: cable/pay movies.*

Flashy but friendly **Hotel Marlowe**.

Bed & breakfast agencies

Whether you're after a more 'authentic' taste of local life or all the comforts of home in your own apartment, B&B agencies can hook you up with accommodation in Boston and beyond. Rates start from as little as $70 per night off-season for a single room with a shared bath.

Bed & Breakfast Agency of Boston

47 Commercial Wharf, Boston, MA 02110 (1-800 248 9262/UK freephone 0800 895128/fax 1-617 523 5761/www.boston-bnbagency.com). **Credit** AmEx, MC, V.

This agency offers high-quality, child-friendly accommodation in central Boston, from waterfront lofts to rooms in historic Victorian Back Bay homes. It's especially good at finding short-term studios and apartments.

Bed & Breakfast Associates Bay Colony

PO Box 57166, Babson Park Branch, Boston, MA 02157 (1-781 449 5302/1-800 347 5088/fax 1-781 455 6745/www.bnbboston.com). **Credit** AmEx, MC, V.

With a far-reaching list of accommodation in B&Bs, inns, suites and furnished apartments throughout the city and surrounding suburbs, this agency also covers the coast, Nantucket and Martha's Vineyard.

Sightseeing

Features

Introduction

Just look at Boston now.

With its pre-eminent place in US history and impressive cultural reputation, the city has always been a magnet for tourists – you'll see them wandering amid the weathered gravestones of the Granary Burial Ground, or buying knick-knacks at Faneuil Hall Marketplace. It's easy to find the main sights – just follow the Freedom Trail (*see p65* **On the trails...**). But there are more recent entries to the Hub's formidable list of attractions; Boston is being beautified. The last remnants of the ugly Central Artery that cruelly cut through downtown Boston are being swept away and will soon be replaced by parkland and (let's hope) more attractive developments. The long-neglected waterfront is at last being turned into a public asset – you can now walk large stretches of it unimpeded and the Harbor Walk is being extended to a staggering 43 miles (69 kilometres). Formerly seedy areas, such as the Combat Zone (the old red-light district) in the heart of the city have been revitalised with gleaming new entertainment venues, while the South End has truly arrived as a galleries-and-shops hot spot. With world-class developments like the ultra-modern waterfront headquarters of the Institute of Contemporary Art on the horizon (*see p92* **Future vision**), the city is adding to its venerated collection of landmarks.

MAIN AREAS

This book focuses primarily on central Boston, although we have made excursions into further-afield neighbourhoods that have become hip hangouts, or which contain sites of interest. The city is anchored by **Boston Common** and its refined adjunct the Public Garden. On one side of the Common is the area loosely termed **Downtown**, which is both the heart of Revolutionary Boston, containing many notable sites, and the city's commercial centre, housing its mainstream shopping, financial and theatre districts. On the other side, behind the grand, golden-domed State House, genteel **Beacon Hill** seems a world apart, with its quaint brick houses, antiques shops and gas lanterns. To the west of the Public Garden lie **Back Bay** and **South End**, the fashionable and wealthy areas overflowing with cultural, retail and culinary riches. On Boston's northernmost peninsula is one of the oldest parts of the city, the **North End**, whose large Italian population has shaped its distinctive identity, while, across the gleaming new Leonard P Zakim Bunker Hill Bridge (*see p28* **Bridging past and present**) is **Charlestown**, site of the famous battle. Across the Charles River, **Cambridge** offers the cultural buzz and raucous nightlife you'd expect of a major university town. If you have more time to play with, it's worth venturing into the green and pleasant Massachusetts countryside, to relive the Revolution in **Concord** and **Lexington**, or just take a stroll in what feels like wilderness, less than an hour's drive away. In summer, the beautiful beaches of the **Massachusetts coastline** are within easy reach.

ORIENTATION

The official tourist literature calls Boston 'America's walking city', which is apt for two reasons: if you're relatively fit, central Boston is compact enough to traverse comfortably by foot, and driving here is hell. The city's drivers rank among the most aggressive in the country and, while many of the traffic problems have been alleviated by the Big Dig, which put the major roads underground, the meandering streets in some parts of town can be confusing to say the least. Only the areas developed later, such as Back Bay and South Boston, follow logical grids. Mercifully, the subway system (called the MBTA or T) is far-reaching and efficient.

Another aspect that can be confusing for visitors is the geography. Greater Boston is made up of numerous neighbourhoods, suburbs and adjacent cities. Cambridge, although it is only steps away from Boston across the river, is a separately governed city, while Jamaica Plain, which is much further away from the centre of town, is a suburb. While Boston's neighbourhoods are very clearly defined (and many have a history of insularity and racial segregation), these days, locals tend to treat the whole area as their turf; it's common for a Bostonian to go out to a bar in Cambridge, or have dinner in Brookline.

Once you've got a handle on the layout, there are the street names to contend with. These are blithely shortened and contorted, and locals get impatient if you have no idea that Comm Ave is Commonwealth Avenue, Mass Ave is Massachusetts Avenue and Mem Drive is Memorial Drive. Be warned: everything that can be abbreviated probably will be. *See p262* **Learning the lingo**.

Essential Boston

... in 24 hours

• To get a sense of Revolutionary Boston, take in selected downtown highlights of the famous **Freedom Trail** – the Granary and King's Chapel Burying Grounds, whose gravestones bear many famous names, and Faneuil Hall, where the rebellion was born (*see pp61-67*). Swing by the **North End** to see celebrated patriot Paul Revere's house and the Old North Church, which played a key role in his famous ride (*see pp82-87*). Stop for a cappuccino en route at one of the area's Italian cafés, such as Graffiti or Vittoria (*see p128*).
• For lunch, slurp down a dozen cherrystones and a pint of Sam Adams ale at the ancient wooden raw bar of the nearby **Ye Olde Union Oyster House**, reputedly America's oldest restaurant (*see p127*).
• Head to Back Bay in the afternoon for a stroll in the refined English-style **Public Garden**, then on to the shops and galleries of **Newbury Street** (*see p161* **A stroll up Newbury Street**).
• Have cocktails at the Top of the Hub on the 52nd floor of the **Prudential Tower** for a bird's-eye view of Boston and beyond (*see p76*).
• Dine in one of the **South End**'s many fashionable eateries (*see pp119-125*).

... in 48 hours

Day two:
• Wander among the narrow byways of **Beacon Hill**, and tour a historic Bulfinch-designed house (*see pp68-72*).
• Have a picnic on the **Charles River Esplanade** or the grassy stretch on the opposite bank by Harvard Square, Cambridge. Alternatively, grab a burger at student institution Mr Bartley's Burger Cottage (*see p139*).
• Stroll among the hallowed halls of **Harvard University** before browsing in Harvard Square's bookshops, and take in one or more of the Harvard University museums (*see p109*).
• In the evening, diverge from the beaten track to have a meal in restaurant-rich **Inman Square**, Cambridge (*see p98*), or hip **Davis Square** in neighbouring city Somerville (*see p96* **Hip to be (Davis) square**).
• Get into some alternative grooves at legendary live rock venues the **Middle East** (*see p211*) or **TT the Bear's Place** (*see p212*) in Central Square or, if theatre's more your thing, a stimulating production at the **American Repertory Theatre** at Harvard (*see p214*).

... in 72 hours

Day three:
• Do **brunch** – it's a favourite local pastime (*see p115* for recommendations).
• Get a double dose of culture at the Fens' major museums: the wide-ranging **Museum of Fine Arts** and the beautiful, eccentric **Isabella Stewart Gardner Museum** (*see p106*), housed in a magnificent palazzo-style mansion.
• Take afternoon tea (or Martinis) in grand style at the Fairmont Copley Plaza, Copley Square, or the Ritz-Carlton on Arlington Street.
• To complete your tour of the 'Athens of America' stop in at the **Boston Public Library** (*see p74*) and strain your neck to admire Sargent's recently restored ceiling murals, then gaze at the elaborate **Trinity Church** across Copley Square, or if you can't stand any more culture, hunt out a bargain at **Filene's Basement** (*see p164* **Brawls and bargains in the Basement**).
• Have a meal in Chinatown, then catch funky live jazz in atmospheric dive **Wally's** (*see p213*), which has been jumpin' since the 1940s.

... in 96 hours

Day four:
• Explore further afield. Choose quaint colonial villages or glorious beaches – both are accessible in under an hour's drive.
• The archetypal New England town of **Concord** (*see p230*), with its white steepled church and clapboard houses, is brimming with Revolutionary and literary history. Walk through the battleground at the Minuteman National Park, see the homes of literary luminaries Hawthorne, Emerson and Alcott, then their graves at Sleepy Hollow Cemetery. Lunch at the Colonial Inn (the Tap Room serves sandwiches).
• Alternatively, if the weather's hot, head for the magnificent sweep of **Crane Beach** in Ipswich (*see p240*). Lunch on lobster or fried clams at Woodman's seafood shack (*see p241*) and browse through the antiques shops of **Essex** (*see p239*).
• Head back to the city for a slap-up final meal at one of its most glamorous restaurants: choose from No.9 Park, Radius, Excelsior or Clio (*see pp114-143*).

Boston Common & Downtown

You say you want a Revolution – well, it all started here.

Swanning around in the **Public Garden**. *See p62.*

Visitors who come from other parts of the country (say, California) are often struck by the aura of history that permeates Boston. Of course, 17th-century buildings are nothing to Europeans accustomed to medieval cathedrals and Roman aqueducts, but for an American metropolis, Boston is as old as it gets.

The lion's share of historical sites – as well as the modern administrative and financial centres that form the city's backbone – are concentrated within the compact, walkable area between Boston Common and Government Center. In many ways, this is truly the heart of Boston.

Boston Common & The Public Garden

America's oldest public park, the 48-acre (19-hectare) **Boston Common** marks the beginning of the Freedom Trail (*see p65* **On the trails...**). It's also the sprawling anchor of the Emerald Necklace, a string of semi-connected green spaces spread across the city. Established in 1634, the Common was originally a grazing pasture for cattle, and later became a military training ground. British Redcoats also made camp here before heading north-west to Lexington and Concord in 1775. Interestingly, this leafy park had no trees at all to begin with, save one giant specimen that served as a central meeting place for the Puritans who'd settled here (until 1817 the 'Great Elm' was also handy for public hangings, including 'witch' Ann Hibbens). The tree eventually fell victim to a series of ferocious storms that blew through the area in the mid 1800s, but by then the Common's use as a rallying point was an unshakeable tradition.

Today, watched over by the imposing golden-domed Massachusetts State House on Beacon Hill, it remains an arena for public gatherings, sunbathing (in summer) and ice-skating (on the Frog Pond in winter). Massive protests against the Vietnam War were staged here in the 1960s; Pope John Paul II said mass to nearly half a million people on its lawns in 1979, and more recently it's been the site of raucous marijuana legalisation rallies.

Just across Charles Street from the Common is the gorgeous 25-acre (10-hectare) **Public Garden**. Dating from 1837 – it was cultivated on filled-in salt marshes – the Garden is much younger than the Common. It was America's first public botanical garden, a showcase for the then-burgeoning greenhouse technology. In warmer months its tidy English-style flowerbeds explode with colour and there are many rare species of tree.

The Public Garden is also home to a wide array of statuary. The most striking, which stands opposite the footbridge over the Lagoon in the centre of the park, is the regal bronze statue of America's first president, General George Washington, astride his horse. It has been said that the statue features perhaps the

What lies beneath

With six extant 17th-century burial grounds in the city alone – not to mention cemeteries in the suburbs and surrounding areas – Boston is the final resting place for a diverse mix of famous folk, from revolutionary heroes to literary lions and former presidents.

The battered gravestones of the **Granary Burying Ground** (*see p63*) bear the famous names of Declaration of Independence signatories John Hancock and Samuel Adams. Also interred here is Paul Revere, whose 'midnight ride' alerted the militia men in Lexington and Concord that the Redcoats were on their way in 1775. But perhaps the most intriguing plot belongs to Elizabeth Foster, who is widely thought to be the Mother Goose of nursery rhyme renown.

Further afield at the **First Unitarian Church**, on Hancock Street in nearby city Quincy, are crypts of two locally born US presidents – the second, John Adams, and the sixth, John Quincy Adams. And at **Holyhood Cemetery** on Heath Street, in Brookline, lie the parents of 35th president John F Kennedy, Joseph P and Rose Kennedy.

Ichabod Crane is not buried at **Sleepy Hollow Cemetery** in Concord (*see p233*), nor is his creator Washington Irving. But several of the most important 19th-century American writers and thinkers are. Laid to rest near their former homes are novelists Louisa May Alcott and Nathaniel Hawthorne, and essayist chums Ralph Waldo Emerson and Henry David Thoreau.

More modern writers are well represented at **Forest Hills Cemetery** in Jamaica Plain (*see p101*): confessional poet Anne Sexton, playwright Eugene O'Neill and poet ee cummings (uncharacteristically, his name is rendered in capital letters on his headstone).

At **Mount Auburn Cemetery** in Cambridge (*see p98*) you'll find the grave of Henry Wadsworth Longfellow, who's linked to two others mentioned here – not only did he commemorate Paul Revere's ride in verse, he was also Nathaniel Hawthorne's college roommate. Here, too, lies a trio of highly influential women: philanthropist Dorothea Dix, who revolutionised the care and treatment for the mentally ill, Mary Baker Eddy, founder of Christian Science, and Isabella Stewart Gardner, the wealthy socialite and patron of the arts, who founded the magnificent palazzo-style museum to house her collections.

In spooky Salem, the **Burying Point** (on Charter Street) accommodates many of the unfortunate victims of the 1692 Salem Witch Trials, including Giles Corey, the 83-year-old farmer who was crushed to death by heavy stones for refusing to stand trial. There are sinister vibes down in south-western Massachusetts city Fall River too. 'Lizzie Borden took an axe and gave her mother 40 whacks,' goes the old nursery rhyme. 'When she saw what she had done, she gave her father 41.' Lizzie was acquitted of the 1892 crime and, at **Oak Grove Cemetery**, on Prospect Street, reposes with her mother and stepfather, Abigail and Andrew Borden.

In **Edson Cemetery**, on Gorham Street in the mill town of Lowell, is the much-visited grave of Beat writer Jack Kerouac, who drank himself to death at the age of 48 in 1969. Another victim of substance abuse, actor John Belushi, was a native Chicagoan, but the Massachusetts island Martha's Vineyard was his favourite vacation place, and it's here, in historic **Abel's Hill Cemetery**, on South Road in Chilmark, that his body lies. It's said to be in an unmarked plot set somewhat apart from the headstone – a cautionary measure after an overzealous fan tried to disrupt the grave site.

most detailed, true-to-life example of equine anatomy (the only part of the animal missing is its tongue). Unfortunately late-night pranksters regularly remove the good general's sword as a souvenir, keeping statue sword-makers in steady business. Several other monuments pay tribute to war heroes and statesmen, but the most humble statue is also the most charming. A bronze tribute to Robert McCloskey's classic children's book *Make Way for Ducklings*, which is set in the park, depicts a waddling mother duck followed by eight fluffy offspring. Also featured in the book are the famous Swan Boats, which have glided gracefully on the Public Garden Lagoon (powered by pedals and pulleys) since 1877. They operate from mid April to mid September and a 15-minute ride costs $2.50 ($1-$2 concessions).

Beyond the Common

On the north-east corner of Boston Common, across Park Street from the entrance to the T station, is the tall and austere **Park Street Church** (*see p64*). Its primary claim to fame is as the venue of abolitionist William Lloyd Garrison's first anti-slavery speech, thundered from the pulpit on 4 July 1829. Beside the church is the **Granary Burying Ground** (*see below*), where lie the American patriots Paul Revere and John Hancock. Across the street, tucked into a wide alleyway, is the **Orpheum Theatre** (1 Hamilton Place), a refurbished music hall from 1852 with ornate mouldings and proscenium seating. It's played host to everything from the world première of Tchaikovsky's First Piano Concerto (1875) to concerts by the Clash and Willie Nelson.

Just a block or two further up Tremont Street lies the **King's Chapel & Burying Ground**, Boston's oldest cemetery (*see p64*). The chapel itself, the first Anglican church in the city, was mandated by King James II, who wanted to ensure a proper foothold for the Church of England in the new colonies. Nearby, on School Street, is the site of the nation's first public school. Inventor, author, scientist, scholar and patriot Benjamin Franklin, whose statue stands outside, was once a student there (as were Cotton Mather, Samuel Adams, and John Hancock). Later, it became the Boston Latin School.

At the corner of Washington and School Streets is the building known as the **Old Corner Bookstore**, which was the premises of several 19th-century booksellers. Literary lights such as Emerson, Dickinson, Hawthorne, Longfellow, Harriet Beecher Stowe and Dickens all passed through its doors, and works published here include *Walden*, *The Scarlet Letter* and *The Song of Hiawatha*. Across the street is the **Old South Meeting House** (*see p64*), once the largest building in colonial Boston and a sparring ground for anti-British debate before the Revolution.

The regal **King's Chapel**. *See p64*.

Also in the area is the **Boston Irish Famine Memorial**, at the corner of School and Washington Streets, designed by Robert Shure and unveiled in 1998 to commemorate the great famine's sesquicentennial. Although some dismiss it as a bathetic cliché – one statue depicts a family, gaunt and kneeling, imploring the heavens for sustenance, while another shows the same family, this time well fed, striding triumphantly and purposefully into the New World – in a city as indelibly marked by Irish immigration as Boston, it's at least worth a quick look.

Granary Burying Ground

At Tremont & Bromfield Streets (1-617 635 4505). Park St T. **Open** dawn-dusk daily. **Admission** free. **Map** p274 K4.

So named because the adjacent Park Street Church is built on the site of a pre-Revolution storehouse for grain and supplies, the Granary Burying Ground is the third oldest in Boston, established in 1660. In addition to Paul Revere and John Hancock, famous figures buried here are Samuel Adams, Peter Faneuil (the Huguenot merchant who built revolutionary meeting place Faneuil Hall; *see p66*), Benjamin Franklin's parents, Samuel Sewall (famous as the only Salem Witch Trial magistrate to admit later that he was wrong), and the victims of the Boston Massacre (*see p66*). Note that there are two tombstones for Revere – the obvious one is a more recent and elaborate pillar, but beside it is a tiny, ancient headstone that says only 'Revere'.

King's Chapel & Burying Ground

58 Tremont Street, at School Street (1-617 227 2155). Gov't Center T. **Open** *May-Sept* 10am-4pm Mon-Sat. *Oct-Apr* 10am-3pm Sat. Also by appointment. **Admission** free. **Map** p274 K4.

Designed by America's first architect, Peter Harrison, the chapel was built on a plot of land excised from the cemetery next door after a decree from King James II in 1754. Restive Bostonians were reluctant to comply with his fiat that land be sold at a fair price so a church could be founded to foist Anglicanism on the colonies. The adjoining burial ground is Boston's oldest. Eminent Bostonians who've found their final resting place here include Mary Chilton, the first woman to step off the *Mayflower*; John Winthrop, former governor of the Massachusetts Bay Colony; and Elizabeth Pain, said to be the model for the persecuted Hester Prynne in Nathaniel Hawthorne's *The Scarlet Letter*.

Old South Meeting House

310 Washington Street, between Milk & Water Streets (1-617 482 6439). Downtown Crossing or State T. **Open** *Apr-Oct* 9.30am-5pm daily; *Nov-Mar* 10am-4pm daily. **Admission** $5; $1-$4 concessions. **Credit** AmEx, MC, V. **Map** p275 L4.

With its handsome white interior and pew-style seating, this meeting house (built in 1729) was second only to Faneuil Hall as a centre of dissent during Boston's Revolutionary era. Famously, it was the departure point of the Boston Tea Party: after a raucous debate on British taxation on 16 December 1773, the infuriated colonists, disguised as Mohawk Indians, marched to Boston Harbor under cover of darkness and hurled 342 crates of imported tea into the Atlantic in protest.

Park Street Church

1 Park Street, at Tremont Street (1-617 523 3383). Park St T. **Open** *Mid June-Aug* 9.30am-3pm Tue-Sat. **Map** p274 K4.

Built in 1809, the Park Street Church was known as 'Brimstone Corner' during the War of 1812 – not for fiery sermons about hellfire and damnation, but because gunpowder was kept in a crypt in the basement, and thus the smell of sulphur was constant, and sometimes overwhelming. It was here that William Lloyd Garrison gave his first anti-slavery oration and the nation's first Sunday School class was taught (in 1818). Sunday services are still held here.

Quincy Market. *See p67.*

Faneuil Hall & The Cradle of Liberty

Following either Washington Street or Tremont Street further north will bring you to **Government Center**, which is dominated by **City Hall Plaza** (Congress Street, at Court Street). The result of 1960s urban renewal, City Hall Plaza used to be the site of Scollay Square, a boisterous, if somewhat seedy, riot of burlesque shows, jazz joints, penny arcades, movie houses, tattoo parlours and taverns. City planners levelled it and, in its place, built the hulking City Hall stranded in a vast, brick expanse used for public performances and festivals. The concrete monstrosity looked dated soon after it was completed in 1968.

The main attractions for most tourists in this area are the historic colonial edifice **Faneuil Hall** (*see p66*) and the adjacent 19th-century **Quincy Market** (*see p67*). Once the seat of the American Revolution, today Faneuil Hall is little more than part of a glorified shopping mall. Locals refer to it and Quincy Market pretty much interchangeably, but the whole retail/restaurant conglomeration is called Faneuil Hall Marketplace. What would Paul Revere say if he saw Faneuil Hall today? We're guessing he'd think an Abercrombie & Fitch, a pizza stand and a comedy club were poor uses for such illustrious and historical property. He'd probably also frown upon the Marketplace's ugly outdoor bars, which fill up with blustering drunks late on weekend afternoons.

Nonetheless, you must go there. The history of the place renders its current condition secondary. (Interestingly, the conversion is considered a huge success, and representatives from other cities frequently study it for tips on how best to convert their own historic buildings into tourist traps.)

Faneuil Hall (pronounced *fan*-yell) has at least preserved its upstairs meeting room from the early 18th century. In the earliest days of the American struggle for independence the rebels frequently met here – in tense, secret gatherings, under pain of execution for sedition – and fomented their plans for revolution. Because of the role it played, the building itself became known as the Cradle of Liberty. As the war began, Faneuil Hall was the heated centre of the struggle for the minds and hearts of the people of the colonies. It was here that George Washington toasted the giddy new nation on its first birthday. Through the years the walls have heard the nation's most impassioned speakers, from the writer Oliver Wendell Holmes and early US feminist Susan B Anthony, to US Senator Ted Kennedy and President Clinton.

Directly across very busy Congress Street from the Marketplace is the spot where the **Boston Massacre** took place. One of the most significant historical sites in the area, it was under the balcony of the **Old State House** (*see p66*) that British troops fired on protesting rebels, providing the spark needed to inflame the revolution. Today, it is one of the very few buildings connected to the Revolutionary War that is appropriately used – it serves as a museum to the war and those who fought it. Included in its collection is a drawing by Paul Revere of Redcoats firing on rebels, with the Old State House in the background. In typical

On the trails...

For the first-time visitor to Boston, the **Freedom Trail** provides a useful sightseeing starting point. The self-guided two-and-a-half mile (four-kilometre) tour is marked by a red line on the sidewalk, which has wended its way past 16 of the Hub's best-known historical sites for more than 45 years. The Trail begins at the Visitor Information Center on Boston Common (147 Tremont Street, 1-617 426 3115), where you can pick up a map or rent a device for an audio tour, and ends at the Bunker Hill Monument in Charlestown (*see p93*).

More recently, historical organisations have jumped on the bandwagon with specialised rambles. The **Black Heritage Trail** traces the history of African Americans in Boston from the 19th century onwards. Guided tours (1-617 725 0022) are offered daily from Memorial Day (May) to Labor Day (September), but a map (available online at www.afroammuseum.org/trailmap.htm) lets you do it yourself. Starting at the Robert Gould Shaw and 54th Regiment Memorial, a plaque in front of the State House that commemorates the valour of a young Boston Brahmin and the black regiment he commanded in the Civil War, the tour takes you past, among other sites, the country's first public school for African-American children – the Abiel Smith School – and winds up at the African Meeting House (1805), the oldest black church in the US (for both, *see p68 and p112*).

The **Women's Heritage Trail** is comprised of nine separate, self-guided walking tours flung across Boston's neighbourhoods (for maps, visit www.bwht.org). In the North End, for example, stop by the birthplace of Rose Fitzgerald Kennedy, matriarch of the American political dynasty. Downtown, see the statue of Mary Dyer, who was hanged on Boston Common in 1660 for her Quaker beliefs. On Beacon Hill, visit the homes of *Little Women* author, suffragette and abolitionist Louisa May Alcott and Rebecca Lee Crumpler, who's generally considered to have been the first African-American woman doctor.

The **Irish Heritage Trail** is a self-guided tour (get a map at www.irishheritagetrail.com) that hits museums, statues and memorials celebrating everyone from Boston's first Irish-born mayor, Hugh O'Brien to John Boyle O'Reilly, the 'poet, patriot, prisoner, sportsman and orator' who was one of the most influential Irish Americans of the 19th century. It winds up at the John F Kennedy Library & Museum in Dorchester (*see p112*) – a fitting conclusion for this tribute to 'the capital of Irish America'.

New England Holocaust Memorial.

Boston fashion, however, even this building is not sacrosanct. Almost unthinkably, its basement serves as an entrance to the T.

From the marketplace, walk north up Congress Street and you come to Blackstone Block (the block of streets off Blackstone Street, between Hanover Street and North Street). Cosy pubs, and one of the city's most famous restaurants, **Ye Olde Union Oyster House** (*see p127*), line this cobblestoned area, making it an agreeable place to recover from a long afternoon's sightseeing with a pint of Harpoon IPA (a popular local brew) and a plate of raw shellfish (or some fish and chips).

Across the street in **Carmen Park** (at Congress and Union Streets) is the **New England Holocaust Memorial**. Six glass towers covered with six million etched numbers pay tribute to those who were killed. At night, steam rises out of the transparent towers and the dancing vapours make the monument particularly haunting.

Faneuil Hall

15 State Street, at Congress Street (1-617 242 5642). Gov't Center, Haymarket or State Street T. **Open** 9am-5pm daily. **Admission** free. **Credit** (shops) AmEx, MC, V. **Map** p275 L4.

Built for the city by the wealthy merchant Peter Faneuil in 1742, the hall was later remodelled by ubiquitous Boston architect Charles Bulfinch. It had a dual function as marketplace (on the ground floor) and meeting hall (upstairs). During Revolutionary times it became known as the 'Cradle of Liberty' – colonial heroes like Samuel Adams regularly roused the Boston populace against the British here. These days, as a nod to its history, Faneuil Hall hosts the occasional political debate and symposium, but the rest of the time it serves as a mishmash marketplace – the ground floor is full of tacky souvenir shops and there's a comedy club on the second level.

Old State House

206 Washington Street, at State Street (1-617 720 3290/www.bostonhistory.org). State T. **Open** 9am-5pm daily. **Admission** $5; $1-$4 concessions. **Credit** AmEx, MC, V. **Map** p275 L4.

Incongruously but elegantly set in the midst of modern skyscrapers and congested traffic, this former legislative house is the oldest surviving public building in Boston. It was built in 1713 for the British governor (notice the lion and unicorn still standing regally atop the building's façade) and the colonial legislature. Proclamations, including the Declaration of Independence, were read in this building, often from the balcony on the east side. The area below the balcony was the scene of the Boston Massacre on 5 March 1770 (commemorated by a ring of cobblestones), when British soldiers fired on an unruly crowd, killing five men. Among them was Crispus Attucks, a black man recorded as the first casualty of the American Revolution. After Independence the

State House continued as the seat of Massachusetts government until Bulfinch finished his new legislative building on Beacon Hill.

Quincy Market

At Chatham & Quincy Streets (1-617 338 2323). Gov't Center, Haymarket or State Street T. **Open** *Food hall* 10am-9pm Mon-Sat; noon-6pm Sun. **Credit** varies. **Map** p275 L3.

Built in the 1820s when Boston's population was rapidly outgrowing the smaller marketplace in Faneuil Hall, Quincy Market was originally right on the harbour (the shoreline has changed over time). Today, the neoclassical Colonnade building is lined with fast food stands. On either side of the central hall, rows of carts loaded with souvenirs and crafts lure tourists to part with still more dollars, as do the street performers who flock to the place. Flanking the Colonnade are the North and South Markets, which are likewise filled with shops.

The Financial District

If there is one section of the Hub that feels ever-so-slightly like its dreaded competitor, New York, it's the Financial District. Down here, in an area bordered roughly by Congress, Purchase and State Streets, is a concrete labyrinth of one-way streets. During the day Boston's business types fill the byways of this money-making district – the heart of America's trust fund industry. Shiny, square, featureless buildings sprinkle the area around **Post Office Square Park** (between Pearl and Congress Streets). At 185 Franklin Street is the giant edifice of the **New England Telephone Building**, which is where the world's first telephone exchange was developed.

Although the Financial District used to empty pretty quickly after hours, a few hip restaurants and eclectic bars have popped up amid the skyscrapers, giving outsiders an incentive to enter the area after nightfall.

Chinatown & The Theatre District

Originally known as South Cove, Chinatown is a small neighbourhood lined with Asian bakeries, tailors, antique shops and, of course, restaurants. Towards the end of the 19th century, Chinese immigrants began arriving in the city to work on the railroads and to provide cheap labour in factories. By the early 20th century there were over 1,000 mostly Asian residents in Chinatown, and the number expanded hugely after World War II. Today the area is contained within a few blocks next door to the Theatre District, and roughly based around Kneeland, Essex, Beach and Tyler Streets. It's still the best place in the city to gawp at roasted ducks hanging in storefront windows or to get a taste of authentic Asian cuisine *(see p128-131)*.

Remnants of the **Combat Zone** (the once notorious red-light district that was located around Washington Street between Essex and Kneeland Streets) linger in the form of a handful of X-rated video stores, a couple of peepshows and the only strip joint left within city limits. Be alert if you're in this area after dark.

Next door to Chinatown, on Tremont Street, is what's known as the **Theatre District**. You can find almost any sort of entertainment within this block, from cabaret to serious drama. The imposing Wang Center is where the big shows play, but there are several more intimate and elegant theatres situated close by as well.

The Ladder District & Downtown Crossing

As neighbourhood appellations go, we've heard worse (the Meatpacking District?) but the recently resurrected term 'Ladder District' has a funny ring to it (and no, it's not the exclusive province of window cleaners and kitten-saving firemen). Bordered by Boylston and School Streets, the small side streets running between main thoroughfares Tremont and Washington appear, from an aerial view, to be rungs on a ladder. The name had been in wide use for almost a century, but at one point or another the more prosaic 'Downtown Crossing' came to embrace the entire swathe between Boston Common and Chinatown. Over the past few years, however, as trendy restaurants such as **Mantra** (52 Temple Place, 1-617 542 8111) and nightspots like hip pool hall **Felt** (533 Washington Street, 1-617 350 5555) cropped up where once there were only dodgy alleyways, the area began to assert its independence and PR for some of its fashionable ventures nudged 'Ladder District' back into general use. Flashy developments have spruced up the district considerably, including slick cineplex **Loews Boston Common** (*see p194*) and the new **Ritz-Carlton Boston Common** (*see p49*). The extensive renovation of the gorgeous rococo **Opera House** on Washington Street (*see p217*) has crowned the neighbourhood's rejuvenation.

Downtown Crossing, where Winter Street meets Washington Street, before continuing south as Summer Street, is the city's gritty centre of modern consumerism. It's here, not touristy Quincy Market, where real Bostonians shop for basics like CDs, clothes and electrical goods in the mid-priced department stores, discount outlets and chains.

Beacon Hill

It's traditionally known as the home of Boston's elite – but there's another story behind the quaint, well-kept façades of 'Brahmin land'.

The **State House**. *See p70.*

Since its development in the late 18th century, Beacon Hill has been a lofty address – literally and figuratively. Originally three grassy hills (the other two were subsequently levelled), the area was known as Tremontaine, giving nearby Tremont Street its name. In Revolutionary times, it was little more than pasture land for cattle owned by politico John Hancock, who had his 'country estate' there, and the painter John Singleton Copley, who owned a substantial share. But when construction on Charles Bulfinch's new State House began in 1795, well-to-do Bostonians with a nose for real estate began buying and building on the South Slope of Beacon Hill. The name derives from the beacon lit when enemy ships were sighted out at sea by a lookout posted at the summit.

Today the area bounded by Beacon, Bowdoin and Cambridge Streets and Storrow Drive maintains much of its original character, with tightly packed townhouses, narrow brick pavements and old-fashioned gas lanterns. While it's historically home to Boston's old, aristocratic families, there's another side to the Hill. Together with the neighbouring West End, the North Slope was a centre of immigrant struggle and social change.

Beacon Hill

When young, well-to-do Charles Bulfinch left his family in Boston in 1786 for a European tour, he was expected to return home and begin life as a businessman. Bulfinch did return home, but instead of starting in business, inspired by his travels, he thought he'd give his friends a few pointers on designing their homes first. The result of this 'help' changed the architectural landscape of Boston forever. While Bulfinch's distinctive stamp can be seen throughout the city, it is most apparent in Beacon Hill, from the new State House, modelled after Somerset House in London, to the Federalist brick houses with classic Boston bow fronts (so called because they bulge in the middle).

Beacon Hill is closely associated with the 'First Families of Boston' – or FFBs as they came to call themselves – the descendants of the original Puritan settlers who had become the American aristocracy. Repugnantly exclusive, they were dubbed the 'Brahmin caste of New England' in 1861 by the writer Oliver Wendell Holmes – the sobriquet 'Boston Brahmin' stuck and is still used today. Later, local wit JC Bossidy delivered a mocking toast at a Harvard dinner which perfectly sums up their snobbish Yankee airs:

And this is good old Boston
The home of the bean and the cod
Where the Lowells talk to the Cabots
And the Cabots talk only to God

While many of the FFBs had moved to Beacon Hill to escape encroaching immigrants in the North End, the neighbourhood wasn't their sole preserve for long, as further waves of immigrants arrived in Boston, spreading out into the nearby West End. To distance themselves further, a number of wealthy families took flight to mansions in the freshly filled in marshland of Back Bay.

In the 19th century, Boston's free black community was concentrated in the West End, between Pinckney and Cambridge Streets, and on the North Slope of Beacon Hill, between Joy and Charles Streets. The **Black Heritage Trail** (*see p65* **On the trails...**) takes in the area's historical sites, although as most of the buildings featured are private residences, visitors can only enter two of them. Together, the **African Meeting House** (8 Smith Court) and the adjacent **Abiel Smith School** (46 Joy Street) form the **Museum of Afro American History** (*see p112*). The Meeting House is the oldest surviving black church in the nation. Built by African-American artisans in 1806, it played an important role in the anti-slavery movement in the 19th century. Abolitionist William Lloyd Garrison founded the New England Anti-Slavery Society here in 1832 – earning it the moniker 'the black Faneuil Hall'. At the end of the century, when Boston's black population shifted further south, the building became a Jewish synagogue. The interior has been restored to its mid-19th-century appearance since its acquisition by the Museum of African American History. The Abiel Smith School was named after a 19th-century white businessman who bequeathed $2,000 to the city for the education of black children. A few years after it was built in 1834, the school was at the centre of controversy over segregated schooling and, following much protest and legal wrangling, in 1855 children were allowed to attend the school closest to their homes – regardless of race. The Abiel Smith School subsequently closed. After extensive restoration in 2000, it opened to the public, and houses a historical exhibition.

Today, the Hill's residents are a mix of Boston's elite – the descendants of the Brahmins of Holmes's day as well as newer money. While the neighbourhood is still tremendously wealthy, the neat proportions of its understated houses make it more quaint than outwardly opulent. This has been the case ever since the Beacon Hill Historic District came into existence in 1955, and enforced strict architectural restraints that required the neighbourhood to maintain its rustic charm. This is especially evident in the byways of the Hill, such as **Acorn Street** (between Mount Vernon and Chestnut Streets), probably one of the tiniest and quaintest lanes in town – and reportedly the most photographed – which retains some of its original cobblestones.

Abiel Smith School.

Other points of interest on Beacon Hill include the **Otis House Museum** and the **Charles Nichols House Museum** (both designed by Bulfinch and open for touring), as well as the beautiful private library **Boston Athenæum** (10½ Beacon Street), which contains some of George Washington's books. Art and architecture tours of the building are held twice a week, but must be booked in advance. There is also a gallery open to the public on the ground floor (*see p104 and p112*).

At the foot of the hill lies the area's main thoroughfare, Charles Street, lined with antiques shops, restaurants and a handful of chic boutiques. Nearby is one of the city's most popular tourist attractions, Cheers (*see p151*). Formerly the Bull and Finch Pub, it is credited with inspiring the long-running TV sitcom. While the exterior is satisfyingly familiar – as it was featured in the opening shot for *Cheers* – be warned, the interior looks nothing like the television set and is best avoided by all but die-hard fans. A more authentic bet for sampling the Boston neighbourhood bar experience is the unpretentious **Sevens Pub** (77 Charles Street, *see p151*).

Antique hunting on **Charles Street**.

Nichols House Museum

55 Mount Vernon Street, at Joy Street (1-617 227 6993/www.nicholshousemuseum.org). Park St T. **Open** *Feb-Apr, Nov, Dec* noon-4pm Thur-Sat. *May-Oct* noon-4pm Tue-Sat. **Admission** $5; free under 12s. **No credit cards. Map** p274 J4.

The Nichols House Museum, also a Bulfinch design, was occupied from 1885 to 1960 by slightly wacky spinster, writer and landscape architect Rose Standish Nichols – the last of her family to live there. In 1961 the house was turned into a museum. One of the few Beacon Hill homes still open to the public, and furnished with sumptuous oriental rugs, Flemish tapestries and American, European and Asian art, it provides a glimpse of how the other half lived in the late 19th century.

Otis House Museum

141 Cambridge Street, at Staniford Street (1-617 227 3956). Charles/MGH T. **Open** *Tours only* 11am-5pm Wed-Sun. **Admission** $8; $24 family. **Credit** AmEx, MC, V. **Map** p274 J3.

A Harvard graduate who was known as 'the irrepressible social lion', Harrison Gray Otis had his house built by Bulfinch, his childhood friend and neighbour, in 1796. Both a mayor of Boston and also a representative in the US Congress, Otis only lived at this residence with his young wife for four years (believe it or not, it was considered only a 'starter home' for the new couple). Bulfinch designed two more houses for his friend (both on Beacon Hill, but further up the slope toward the more fashionable side). A tour of Harry's house takes about 45 minutes and offers an interesting picture of the life of a Boston socialite. Even the fire bucket (all neighbourhood residents were obliged to rush to the scene of a fire with one in hand to create a water chain) is still in place, hanging behind the grand staircase.

State House

Beacon & Park Streets, Beacon Hill (1-617 727 3676/www.mass.gov/statehouse). Park St T. **Open** 9am-5pm Mon-Fri. **Tours** 10am-3.30pm Mon-Fri. Call ahead for reservations. **Admission** free. **Map** p274 K4.

Designed by Bulfinch and begun in 1795, the magnificent structure was completed three years later. It replaced the old legislative building across the common, which had been the headquarters of the British government (*see p66*). The dome was originally covered in copper by Paul Revere & Sons, later sheathed in 23-carat gold and, during World War II, blacked out due to a fear of air raids. To this day, the shining bulb is one of Boston's best-known landmarks. The building is the seat of government for the state, and the stomping ground of the Senate and House of Representatives of the Massachusetts State Legislature.

Of the statues that adorn the front vista of the State House, that of Major General 'Fighting Joe' Hooker arguably has the most interesting background. A native of Hadley, Massachusetts, he not only distinguished himself as a Civil War general,,

Where the other half live

Lodged between Pinckney and Mount Vernon Streets, Louisburg (Bostonians pronounce the 's') Square is the most coveted Beacon Hill address. The city's only remaining private garden square (although it's actually more oval), Louisburg follows the classic London model of terraced houses arranged around a central gated park. Built in the mid 19th century, its red-brick, bow-fronted houses are in the Greek Revival style – the line-up creates a striking, gently undulating effect. Privately owned and run by an association of home owners, the Louisburg Square Proprietors, the square contains some of the city's highest-priced property and has an impressive literary pedigree. Former residents include Louisa May Alcott, who moved to No.10 after the financial success of *Little Women*. Novelist and influential *Atlantic Monthly* editor William Dean Howells resided at No.4 and No.16 at different points, while poets Sylvia Plath and Robert Frost lived just outside the exclusive enclave (at 9 Willow Street and 88 Mount Vernon Street, respectively). While Louisburg has been home to members of the Kennedy clan, the most illustrious current resident is US Senator and Democratic presidential candidate John Kerry, at No.19 – the oldest and most spectacular house on the square. Since they moved into the former convent in 1996, Kerry and his wife, philanthropist and ketchup heiress Teresa Heinz, have stirred up controversy among their blue-blood neighbours. After receiving a parking ticket, the couple paid an undisclosed sum to have a fire hydrant in front of their property removed so they could park their Jeep in the spot. And in the run-up to the 2004 election, sniffy fellow residents complained the Secret Service agents in black government vehicles guarding the couple's $13 million mansion were hogging precious parking spaces, scaring their domestic staff and disturbing the rarefied atmosphere with noise and exhaust fumes from idling motors. Bet they voted in the hope of getting him into the White House and out of the square.

Get a taste of old Boston high society at the **Otis House Museum**. *See p70.*

but also became notorious for his bodily appetites (ironically, the statue next to him is of the Quaker Mary Dyer, who no doubt would have condemned his exploits). An accomplished boozer, Major Hooker would allow loose women to prowl his troops' tents at night. These nocturnal guests became known as 'Hooker's Ladies', and later, simply as 'hookers' – a little known piece of etymological trivia.

The West End

This area north of Cambridge Street is hardly ever referred to by its old name and is unrecognisable as the neighbourhood of 50 years ago. The West End was once a large residential area that formed a bridge between the North End and Beacon Hill. For many years an immigrant district, its winding streets and cramped tenements housed a considerable low-income black, Jewish, Irish, Italian and Polish population. Despite the problems that such neighbourhoods tend to endure – overcrowding and a run-down infrastructure being the most basic – the West End was a gritty but solid niche for many families, who dearly loved their neighbourhood. And ironically, in a city that has had such difficulties with integration, it was one of Boston's true melting pots, with families from a wide range of backgrounds living and working side by side. The area was also known as a destination for visiting sailors, who patronised its shady bars and shadier brothels. However, in the 1960s, under the flag of 'urban renewal', city planners levelled the neighbourhood in favour of building luxury high-rises and expanding Massachusetts General Hospital. In the process, some 7,000 residents were displaced and the historic architecture was demolished.

On a positive note, the heart-wrenching loss of the West End has become a cardinal example of what not to do when seeking to improve a neighbourhood, and other communities whose homes were targeted for 'urban renewal' banded together to stop the planners.

Bordering what remains of the West End is the **FleetCenter** (*see p223*), a stadium on the former site of the late, lamented Boston Garden sports arena. Though the garden was mildewed, rickety and weathered, it was fondly regarded as the place where the Boston Celtics won numerous NBA Championships in the 1980s, and where Boston Bruins legend Bobby Orr regularly sprayed ice with his skates. The FleetCenter remains the only arena in town where both major sporting events and big rock concerts – from the likes of Justin Timberlake all the way to Aerosmith – are staged.

Along the Charles River Dam between Boston and Cambridge is the **Museum of Science** (*see p112*). Featuring the Hayden Planetarium, the huge, dome-shaped Omni Theater for viewing its spectacular nature films, and with countless interactive exhibits to encourage properly hands-on learning, it's educational and popular with kids.

Back Bay & South End

These elegant districts have it all – chic shopping, hip dining and arts aplenty, from cutting-edge galleries to venerable cultural institutions.

Whether you want to see it, eat it, hear it or buy it, it's a safe bet you'll find 'it' here, in Boston's Back Bay and the South End. Together, these neighbourhoods contain an embarrassment of cultural, culinary and retail riches, and form the cosmopolitan core of Boston. Reviewing the attractions here is like ticking off a laundry list: elegant mansions (check), swanky boutiques (check), hip restaurants (check), provocative galleries (check). These neighbourhoods have all the accessories of the wealthy, urbane, elitist districts they're frequently accused of being. But there is one deliciously atonal note here – the fact that Boston's commercial and cultural centre was built on landfill is a gorgeous piece of irony of which many tourists are unaware.

Though one might imagine a more genteel pedigree for the Back Bay and South End of today, only 150 years ago there was nothing here but a vast expanse of uninhabitable swamp. The entire area, from the Public Garden to the Fens, was submerged, making it, quite literally, the Back Bay; today's neighbourhood of the same name – just under a square mile (2.5 square kilometres) – constitutes only a small chunk of that space. The huge task to fill it in with gravel began in the mid 1850s and took 40 years to complete – but the neighbourhood was an instant hit with Boston's high society.

Because Back Bay's sights are so densely concentrated, they're best covered on foot. Stroll past Commonwealth Avenue's formidable homes, Newbury Street's chi-chi shops, and Copley Square's historic landmarks. And that's just for starters; the truly ambitious will wend their way to the gardens and museums of the Fens, and check out the wildlife at one of Kenmore Square's clubs before calling it a night.

Though it remains less commercially developed than its famous neighbour, the South End has (with all the subtlety of a crashing anvil) outgrown its cult status and become a bona fide player in city life. The area has the fresh, invigorated feel of a place hitting its stride. There's plenty of action here. The booming art and restaurant scenes, coupled with some magnificent Victorian architecture, provide plenty of incentive to explore this lively village.

Roughly defined, the Back Bay's centre is the area stretching from the Charles River to the north, Huntington Avenue to the south, the Public Garden to the east, and Kenmore Square to the west. If you are coming by T, take the Green Line and exit at Copley.

Copley Square

One of Boston's most picturesque spots, Copley Square is anchored by two major landmarks: the **Trinity Church** and the **Boston Public Library**. Positioned on either end of the plaza, the buildings are engaged in a permanent stand off. Music festivals often take place in the square on spring and summer weekends, and it's also the finishing point for the annual Boston Marathon. No guidebook on Boston would be complete without a shot of the neo-Romanesque Trinity Church, completed in 1877. The church, with its exquisite Moorish details, took five years to build. Despite ongoing renovations it remains open to tourists. Directly opposite the church, kids skateboard down the entrance ramps of the Boston Public Library – a neo-classical masterpiece. The original 19th-century McKim structure radiates a kind of graceful authority. However, critics still turn their noses up at the modern wing of the building, which is often derided as clunky and visually oppressive (*see also pp25-31*).

Just across St James Avenue from Copley Square, but light years away in terms of architectural styles, is New England's tallest building, the 62-storey **John Hancock Tower** designed by IM Pei. Sleek, shiny and cold, the structure stands in stark contrast to its historic neighbours. Though regarded as one of the most dazzling examples of modern architecture in the city, the Hancock had an ignominious start. During construction in 1973 a design flaw caused dozens of the Tower's 500-pound (225kg) windows to spontaneously pop out of their frames and shatter on the sidewalk below; miraculously, no one was hurt, but every single pane had to be replaced, and the frames that held them redesigned, at terrific expense. What's more, it was discovered that the foundations of the Trinity Church had been damaged during the Tower's construction. After a 12-year legal battle, the church was awarded $11.6 million in restitution. The Tower's only tourist attraction, its observation deck, closed its doors in September 2001.

Boston Public Library

700 Boylston Street, at Copley Square (1-617 536 5400/www.bpl.org). Copley T. **Open** 9am-9pm Mon-Thur; 9am-5pm Fri, Sat; 1-5pm Sun. **Admission** free. **Map** p277 G6.

Founded in 1848 and completed in 1895, this is the oldest public library in the country, and one of the grandest. The massive shrine to literature is divided into two parts: The original Research Library, designed by Charles McKim, and Philip Johnson's General Library extension, which was added in 1972. The McKim building's elegant granite exterior is generally classified as Italian Renaissance Revival, although McKim claimed it was equally inspired by a library in Paris, a temple in Rimini and the Marshall Fields department store in Chicago. At the heart of it is an Italianate courtyard. Graced by a fountain and garden, it's a wonderful sanctuary, particularly on sunny spring days. Inside, each floor houses a warren of reading rooms and galleries. Make your way to the third floor, where you'll find John Singer Sargent's epic mural cycle, *Triumph of Religion*, as well as several galleries devoted to the fine arts, and a well-curated collection of rare books and manuscripts. The library's star attraction, though, is down a flight. Monumental reading room Bates Hall runs the entire length of the building, and features a majestic barrel-arched ceiling punctuated by half-domes at each end. Downstairs, the library's restaurant, Novel, and the Map Room Café, are popular lunch spots. The Johnson building, adjacent to the old library, is as blunt and lacking in detail as McKim's is packed with flourishes.

Trinity Church

206 Clarendon Street, at Copley Square (1-617 536 0944/www.trinityboston.org). Copley or Back Bay T. **Open** 9am-6pm daily. **Admission** $4. **Map** p277 H6.

Commanding, flamboyant and vaguely macabre, Trinity Church is the visual centrepiece of Copley Square. When the original Episcopal church on Summer Street was destroyed by a fire in 1872, Henry Hobson Richardson won the contract to design the new building in Copley Square. Deviating from the Gothic Revival style prevalent at the time, Richardson's Romanesque creation was inspired by the 11th-century churches of southern France. It proved to be his masterpiece. The central tower, which was added later (partly designed by Stanford White, who worked under Richardson), was modelled after Salamanca Cathedral in Spain. Fashioned out of red sandstone and pink granite, the heavily ornamented exterior features a series of low reliefs depicting biblical scenes, including the baptism of Jesus. Inside, the church's most striking feature is its art. Several British and American artists contributed stained-glass windows and frescoes to the interior, and their styles are dramatically distinct. If

Boston Public Library. *See p74*.

you catch them at the right time of day, John LeFarge's layered opalescent windows produce a shimmery effect that is particularly effective. The church's $42 million restoration project is being financed in part by money from the Hancock Tower, which settled generously when it became apparent that the Tower's crushing weight was accelerating the historic landmark's descent into Back Bay.

Boylston Street

Traditionally treated as little more than an access route separating Newbury Street and Copley Square, the Back Bay stretch of Boylston Street is finally crawling out from the shadow of its flashy neighbours and becoming a destination in its own right. Until quite recently, the stretch was dominated by a sad collection of office buildings and parades of underwhelming shops. But as Newbury and Copley have reached their commercial saturation points, several high-profile retailers and restaurants have bled over to Boylston, joining the street's few veteran attractions.

Architecturally, Boylston Street is a bit of a mishmash: traditional Back Bay style meets brutal modernism. This is particularly true at its south-western end, around the monolithic Hynes Convention Center and its neighbour, the **Prudential Center** (*see p76*). This shopping mall and apartment complex is clustered around the huge tower universally known as 'The Pru'. While the building itself is unremarkable, and most of the shops in the mall are mainstream chains, it's worth zipping up to the Skywalk Observatory on the 50th floor, for the fantastic view. Next door is **Shreve, Crump & Low** (*see p171*), the oldest jeweller in America. Renowned for its work in silver, Shreve's has bedecked wealthy Bostonians in diamonds and pearls since 1796 (the original store was across the street from Paul Revere's workshop in the North End). Also at this end of Boylston Street is the **Boylston Fire Station** (955 Boylston Street, at Massachusetts Avenue). Dating from 1887 and built in the same Romanesque style as Trinity Church, it is still operational today, and houses two fire engines. Part of the building was once a police station, but in 1976 that section became the **Institute of Contemporary Art** (*see p106*), a sleek modern gallery that exhibits both big-name and up-and-coming artists; the ICA will relocate to the waterfront in 2006.

Fans of ostentatious architecture should pause to gaze up at the **Berkeley** (420 Boylston Street, at Berkeley Street). Built in

Uncommon wealth: Boston's grand boulevard, **Commonwealth Avenue**. *See p77.*

1906, the office building looks like a giant wedding cake, with gleaming white spires and fussy adornments. Considerably less chintzy, at the other end of Boylston and abutting the Public Garden, is the **Arlington Street Church** (351 Boylston Street, at Arlington Street, www.ascboston.org). One of Back Bay's earliest buildings, the church was built in the mid 19th century by Arthur Gilman, and boasts 16 Tiffany stained-glass windows. Boylston Street carries on to the downtown area, and beyond the Public Garden it becomes a rather trendy dining and nightlife destination.

Prudential Center & Tower

800 Boylston Street, between Dalton & Exeter Streets (1-800 746 7778/Skywalk Observatory 1-617 859 0648/www.prudentialcenter.com). Prudential, Hynes/ICA/Copley T. **Open** *Skywalk Observatory* 10am-10pm daily. *Shops* 10am-9pm Mon-Sat; 11am-6pm Sun. *Food court* 7am-9pm Mon-Sat; 9am-7pm Sun. **Admission** *Skywalk Observatory* $7; $4 concessions. **Credit** *Skywalk Observatory* AmEx, Disc, MC, V. *Shops & restaurants* varies. **Map** p277 G6.

This is a standard-issue American shopping mall/ office complex hybrid. It's also very crowded, and not recommended for agoraphobes. The mall (*see p160*) forms the base for the 52-storey tower above. Since the closing of the John Hancock observatory deck, the Pru's Skywalk Observatory on the 50th floor has been Boston's lone skyscraper viewing platform. From a height of 700ft (215m), you can appreciate how history and industry commingle in Boston: meticulously arranged Victorian rowhouses collide with ungainly condominium high-rises, and the Hancock Tower gleams like a knife. It's a revealing, 360-degree perspective of the city – and beyond. On a clear day, you can see as far as 80 miles (129km) in any direction. If you prefer to take in the view sitting down, book a table at the classic Top of the Hub Restaurant & Lounge, two floors up.

Newbury Street

The city's hype merchants like to call Newbury Street 'Boston's Rodeo Drive', after the exclusive Beverly Hills shopping street. There's no doubt that Newbury is the city's premier shopping strip, but it's also a major player in the city's cultural milieu, housing a large percentage of the city's commercial art galleries. The street's personality changes palpably from one end to the other. Generally speaking, the Arlington Street end, closer to the Common, is more conservative and upscale. The shops here – European labels, high-end jewellers, the occasional furrier – are geared toward an older clientele, or at least a wealthier one. This end is anchored by **Louis Boston** (*see p159*), an imperial palace of a department store that occupies the former Museum of Natural History between Boylston and Newbury Streets. Things relax somewhat as you approach Massachusetts Avenue, where a more laid-back, collegiate vibe prevails. Reflecting the considerable student population (Berklee, BU and several other colleges are nearby), the shops, and the prices, become less exclusive while the number of tattoos increases. So does the traffic, especially in summer, when convertibles and SUVs crawl along the street, in-line skaters and skateboarders zipping between them. Here, the bohemian epicentre is **Trident Booksellers and Café** (*see p119*), a popular alternative bookstore and hangout where patrons can acquire essays on Taoism and breakfast burritos in one fell swoop.

Commonwealth Avenue & Beacon Street

For a look at how well-heeled Bostonians have lived for the past hundred years, head away from Newbury Street toward the river, and the architectural eye candy of Back Bay's handsome residential neighbourhood. The area from Commonwealth Avenue to Beacon Street is bursting with fantastic examples of 19th-century Victorian architecture, and is best investigated on foot.

The area's grandest residential street, **Commonwealth Avenue** (or Comm Ave as it's universally known), runs parallel to Newbury Street. Elegant mansions and townhouses line the thoroughfare, designed in 1865 to resemble a Parisian boulevard. The wide, tree-lined central promenade is dotted with statues, memorials and gardens; in the spring, when the magnolias are in bloom, it's almost absurdly picturesque. It's also a popular stroll for locals, who try not to get too close to the many homeless who also enjoy the space in the warmer months. On the corner of Clarendon Street is another Back Bay landmark – the striking tower of Henry Richardson's 1871 **First Baptist Church**. Like much of Richardson's other work, it was designed in the Romanesque style, and some joke that it was his warm-up to creating the more lavish Trinity Church in Copley Square.

Criss-crossing Comm Ave are a series of streets that run in alphabetical order (Arlington, Berkeley, Clarendon, Dartmouth, and so on). Cut down one of these streets, going north towards the river, and you'll come to Marlborough Street. Because of its rather odd configuration of one-ways, Marlborough is the quietest of the Back Bay's streets. It's also one of the prettiest, and well worth a stroll, just for the meditative aspects. The French Academic-style residence at 273 Clarendon Street, between Marlborough and Beacon Streets, is the birthplace and former home of the Massachusetts Audubon Society, one of the country's first environmental organisations. Over on Beacon Street, the **Gibson House Museum**'s meticulously preserved interiors are frozen in the Victorian era. It looks like something out of a Merchant-Ivory film, and it is: they filmed *The Bostonians* here in 1983.

First Baptist Church

110 Commonwealth Avenue, at Clarendon Street (1-617 267 3148/www.firstbaptistchurchof boston.org). Copley T. **Open** 11am-2pm Tue-Fri. **Admission** free. **Map** p277 H5.

Completed in 1871, a year before Richardson began work on Copley Square's Trinity Church, this building is a similar mix of stone and wood surfaces. Richardson commissioned the bas-relief encircling the top of the belltower from Frédéric Auguste Bartholdi, the sculptor of the Statue of Liberty.

Gibson House

137 Beacon Street, between Arlington & Berkeley Streets. (1-617 267 6338/www.thegibsonhouse.org). Arlington T. **Tours** 1pm, 2pm, 3pm Wed-Sun. **Admission** $5; concessions $2-$4. **No credit cards. Map** p277 H5.

Though the 1859 façade of Gibson House is unspectacular, the interior offers a rare glimpse of how wealthy Bostonians lived 100 years ago. Tours take in four floors of the six-storey house, with its original Victorian furnishings, down to details such as the household dinner service (members of the Gibson family lived here until the 1950s). The kitchen and servants' quarters will give you an upstairs/downstairs perspective.

Massachusetts Avenue

The main sights on the Back Bay stretch of this major thoroughfare – commonly referred to as Mass Ave – are located between Boylston Street and Huntington Avenue, where three local institutions are clustered, like Boston's pearls, in a row. **Berklee College of Music**, at the corner of Mass Ave and Boylston Street, is one of the country's top music schools, and its

Around the world in 80 seconds

It was not the brainchild of Rem Koolhaas. It is not outfitted with lasers, strobe lights or any other type of space-age gadgetry. Paul Revere did not stop here on his way to alert the townspeople of British invasion. Nonetheless, Boston's Mapparium, the world's largest walk-in globe, has earned its own place among the city's landmarks.

Located in the Mary Baker Eddy Library in the Christian Science Plaza, the Mapparium is, essentially, a three-storey model of the globe, built to scale. The room, a perfect sphere, runs 30 feet (ten metres) in diameter. Visitors are able to traverse the earth by way of the glass bridge that bisects it. This in itself is a bit eccentric, but several unusual features up the oddball quotient considerably. For one thing, there are the weird acoustics. Sound bounces off the room's non-porous glass walls, amplifying it tenfold. The effect is pleasantly hallucinatory – whispers across the room register directly in your ear.

Another baffling feature is the map itself. Instead of depicting the world's current geography, the 608 stained-glass panels re-create the planet as it was back in the mid 1930s, when the project was completed. Most of the borders are outdated; several of the countries shown have long since been swallowed up by larger, hungrier, hardier entities. It is, as the piped-in voice overhead reminds us, 'a world that no longer exists'. Then what, one wonders, is the point?

The point is, it looks cool. Built in 1935 for the then-astronomical sum of $8,900, the Mapparium was originally conceived as a symbol of the *Christian Science Monitor*'s global audience. Its creator, Boston-based architect Chester Lindsay Churchill, designed the rest of the library as well. Ironically, it is the map's obsolescence that gives it a new and unexpected relevance today. Over the years, as its geography has grown increasingly antiquated, the map has become a gentle reminder that boundaries, and the powers that dictate them, are in a state of constant flux. There's a lesson here for every Ozymandias: the weak shall inherit the earth.

Despite its geographical nostalgia, the Mapparium has made a few concessions to the 21st century. Decades spent on display had taken their toll, so in 1998 the library embarked on a four-year plan to restore and enhance its original lustre. Today, a number of technological improvements breathe new life into the old globe. A proper lighting system, capable of generating 16 million colour combinations (but which, thankfully, doesn't) invigorates the map panels without overwhelming them, and a multimedia presentation, *The World of Ideas*, has also been installed. Don't be put off by its New Agey title – at seven minutes, the show is brief, and totally doctrine-free.

The map itself, however, remains unchanged. Though it could easily have become just another kitschy relic, the enigmatic 70-year-old globe still has a surprising dignity about it. As the Mapparium's admirers know, standing in the centre of world is an uplifting, if slightly surreal, experience.

The Mapparium at the Mary Baker Eddy Library

200 Massachusetts Avenue, at Clearway Street (1-617 450 7000/www.marybakereddylibrary.org). **Open** 10am-5pm Tue, Wed, Sat, Sun; 10am-9pm Thur, Fri. **Admission** $5; $3 concessions; free under-6s. **Credit** AmEx, Disc, MC, V. **Map** p276 F7.

Performance Center puts on shows by both students of the college, who may go on to become the virtuosos of tomorrow, and more current big-name acts.

Further down, the triangle of land formed by Mass Ave and Huntington is dominated by the imposing **Christian Science Plaza** (175 Huntington Avenue), the world headquarters of the Church of Christ, Scientist, an organisation established by Mary Baker Eddy, based on a system of spiritual, prayer-based healing. The compound's administration, broadcasting and Sunday school buildings, designed by IM Pei's firm, surround the plaza with its dramatic 670-foot (200m) reflecting pool. The main attraction here, the behemoth Mother Church, is actually two churches, each distinct in size, style and atmosphere. The Romanesque original, built in 1894, is warm, sun-drenched and relatively intimate, with lovely opalescent stained-glass windows. The main attraction, however, is the 1906 Extension Church, a spun-sugar confection of Byzantine and Renaissance details, with soaring 108-foot (33m) ceilings, and one of the largest organs in the country, containing 13,290 pipes ranging in height from half an inch (1cm)

to 32 feet (10m). The interior of the church is astonishingly vast – it can accommodate a whopping 3,000 worshippers. Behind the church is the 1930s Christian Science Publishing Society building, home of the **Mapparium** (*see p78* **Around the world in 80 seconds**), one of Boston's more unusual sights. The two galleries upstairs, devoted to the life of Mary Baker Eddy and the *Christian Science Monitor*, respectively, are enlivened by high-tech gadgetry and interactive exhibits.

Almost directly across Mass Ave is **Symphony Hall**, home of the Boston Symphony Orchestra (*see p219*). The attractive, unfussy building, which was completed in 1900, was partly inspired by the Leipzig Gewandhaus in Germany. It was also the first music and concert hall designed with acoustical considerations kept particularly in mind: during planning, the architects McKim, Mead and White consulted with a Harvard physicist in order to achieve the best possible sound. The free, hour-long tours cover the ground breaking acoustics in detail, and also provide a bit of history on the building and the 125-year-old Boston Symphony Orchestra.

South End

A five-minute stroll south of Copley Square casts you into the Landmark District near the junction of Clarendon and Tremont Streets. This is the core of the South End, and the name derives from its status as a protected neighbourhood since 1983. It's an attractive, smartly arranged part of the city – the original street plan was laid out by celebrated Boston architect Charles Bulfinch, and the South End contains the largest collection of Victorian cast iron-girded row-house properties in the country.

While elaborately designed Back Bay was occupied by the upper crust, its near neighbour, with its neat, English-style squares, such as Worcester Square and Union Park, was built for the mercantile class.

In the 20th century, however, the area became depressed and fell into disrepair. By the mid-70s, many original buildings had been demolished; others fell victim to arson. But through the efforts of concerned citizens, who founded the South End Historical Society, the South End was restored and subsequently gained its protected status.

Sandwiched between the swank commercial gloss of Back Bay and the working-class neighbourhood of Roxbury, the South End was a shabby-chic 'gay ghetto' in the '80s, where enterprising young urbanites found affordable period apartments in the heart of the city. Now as sought-after as its Back Bay neighbour but a lot more trendy, it still has a large gay population. The high concentration of style-conscious residents in part explains the growth of hip eateries and chic, independently owned home and gift shops in the area. Rainbow flags flying outside many businesses proclaim the area's gay pride and diversity.

The South End's two parallel main road arteries, Tremont Street and Washington Street, are at the centre of the area's thriving restaurant and bar scenes.

The neighbourhood is also experiencing an art boom. While there has been an artist presence here since the 1960s, in recent years the area south of Washington Street (SoWa) has exploded with showrooms and studio spaces. The burgeoning scene is beginning to rival Newbury Street; the converted warehouse at 450 Harrison Avenue alone houses a dozen exhibition spaces (*see p197*). The **Jorge Hernandez Cultural Center** (85 West Newton Street, 1-617 927 0061; *see also p215*) in a converted 19th-century church, is a dynamic local institution. Its bi-weekly salsa and flamenco bashes are wildly popular, and the adjacent three-storey **Center for Latino Arts** exhibits the work of contemporary Latino artists. Two other churches in the vicinity merit a mention for their frequent classical or gospel concerts: the baroque **Church of the Immaculate Conception** (775 Harrison Avenue, 1-617 536 8440), and the **Ebenezer Baptist Church** (157 West Springfield Street, 1-617 262 7739), founded by former slaves.

Another South End site of cultural significance is the recently erected statue honouring **Harriet Tubman**, a runaway slave and one of the key organisers of the Civil War-era Underground Railroad, an escape route to the north for southern slaves seeking freedom. Tubman ended up living in the South End and her house still stands today at 566 Columbus Avenue.

The landmark around these parts is the **Boston Center for the Arts**, a sprawling cultural village that occupies the block of Tremont Street in between Berkeley and Clarendon Streets. The complex was originally a 19th-century organ factory. Today, the arts centre has three theatres and a large, light-filled gallery that displays an eclectic range of contemporary and experimental art. It's also home to the Boston Ballet. The building's centrepiece is the Cyclorama, a circular, domed structure built in 1884 to exhibit the huge painting by Dominique Philippoteaux of the Civil War battle of Gettysburg. The painting went on tour five years later, but never returned – it's now on display in Gettysburg. The Cyclorama itself has served as a rollerskating arena, flower market and factory, and now it hosts weddings, trade shows, and the occasional performance. With the new addition of the Theatre Pavilion and Atelier 505 – a development of upscale condos, retail shops and a parking garage – the already massive BCA is about to get even bigger, and the South End's gentrification will be complete.

Just behind the BCA and a short walk up Clarendon Street is the cheap and deservedly popular local watering hole called the **Delux Café** (*see p147*). From Clarendon Street take a walk up Appleton or Chandler Streets, two of the most desirable roads in the neighbourhood. The South End is a great neighbourhood in which to simply wander, stumbling across tiny parks or the occasional public garden sandwiched in between buildings.

When you reach Columbus Avenue, it's hard to believe that this drab main road was once touted as the finest residential avenue in the city. But that was 1869, and times have changed. **Charlie's Sandwich Shoppe** (*see p123*) hasn't been around quite that long – but the 1930s-time-capsule lunchroom, complete with counter stools and no-nonsense staff, is well worth a pitstop.

The Fens & Kenmore Square

Many maps of the city provided for tourists crop off – or worse, omit altogether – the section of Boston known as the Fens, a loosely connected group of public parks and byways. It's a glaring omission: some of Boston's most celebrated cultural institutions reside here.

It's impossible to talk about this area of Boston without mentioning **Frederick Law Olmsted** (1822-1903). Generally acknowledged as the father of landscape architecture, Olmsted is perhaps best known as the designer (along with Calvert Vaux) of New York's signature green space, Central Park. But one of his greatest endeavours was designing the Boston park system (his offices were based in the suburb of Brookline from 1883). Collectively known as the Emerald Necklace, it's a string of nine green spaces that stretch through, and offer a respite from, some of the city's busiest districts. It is feasible to walk the Necklace from end to end (it's about a seven-mile/11-kilometre trek from Boston Common to Franklin Park), although sensible walking shoes and a motivated frame of mind are essential.

Walking through the rose-vined archways of the Fens' **James P Kelleher Rose Garden** – established in 1930 – can be a heady and head turning experience, especially in late April or May, when the flowers blush in crimson and pink. Two exceptional museums are located nearby. The **Museum of Fine Arts** (*see p106*) has a wide range of works, including paintings by Degas, Renoir, Rembrandt, Sargent and Picasso, as well as art ranging from African sculpture to 16th-century Chinese furniture and Egyptian artefacts. Located just across the street from the MFA, the **Isabella Stewart Gardner Museum** (*see p106*) is another, equally impressive, showcase. The elegant palazzo-style mansion has a stunning central courtyard garden, and its three floors of galleries house a collection of antique furnishings and masterpieces by Rembrandt (again), Botticelli and Whistler, among others. Continuing further along the Riverway portion of the Emerald Necklace is the Olmsted Park, which features a well-travelled path for cyclists and pedestrians, and straddles the Boston-Brookline Border.

Near the Fens, **Kenmore Square** sits at the confluence of three major roadways: Commonwealth Avenue, Brookline Avenue and Beacon Street. The square can be easily identified by the giant Citgo sign on Beacon Street. Since its arrival in 1940 (the neon was added in the 1965), the sign has become a beloved point of reference for locals; attempts to remove it in 1983 were met with such fierce resistance that they were ultimately dropped.

Over the years, Kenmore Square's function as a transportation corridor, combined with the seasonal nature of the visitors and inhabitants of its two main tenants, Boston University and Fenway Park, have engendered the area with a sense of impermanence and confusion. The abundance of students created a natural market for cheap eateries and bars, which all contributed to the square's slightly seedy air. But that's about to change, however. Several ambitious development projects, which began with the unveiling of the four-star Commonwealth Hotel in 2003, hope to transform Kenmore. Soon, a slew of upscale condos, shops and restaurants will modernise the dingy strip, and tree-lined brick promenades will make the area more appealing to pedestrians and visitors. It will, however, retain its status as a hub of Boston nightlife.

At night, Kenmore's large student population heads for **Lansdowne Street**, the city's nightclub row. Whatever you're looking for – be it a cheesy techno warehouse or an upscale martini bar – the chances are that you'll find it here. **Avalon** (*see p190*) and **Axis** (*see p191*) are the flashy dance clubs of the masses, packed to the gills with gyrating college girls and the boys who pursue them. Next door at the **Modern** (36 Lansdowne Street, 1-617 536 2100), young professionals sip pricey cocktails and try to approximate boredom in a minimalist lounge setting. If dodging frat boys is your top priority, head upstairs to the **Embassy** (*see p192*), a nightclub that caters to the international set. Nearby, a more laid-back atmosphere prevails at **Bill's Bar** (*see p144*), where the retro vibe and underground music draws a hip, eclectic crowd. Not up for a trendy scene? Confused what's cool? Shoot pool at **Jillian's** (*see p146*) or sing along with the duelling pianos at **Jake Ivory's** (1 Lansdowne Street, 1-617 247 1222).

Just steps from Lansdowne sits historic **Fenway Park**, home of the Boston Red Sox (*see p222*). The celebrated baseball stadium opened on 20 April 1912, just days after the *Titanic* sank. It may have been an omen, as the Sox haven't won a World Series since 1918. Nonetheless, some of the all time greats have played here, including Babe Ruth, Ted Williams, Cy Young and Roger Clemens, and Bostonians are notoriously, masochistically, loyal to the home team. The most famous part of the stadium is its 37-foot-high (11 metre) left-field wall, affectionately known as the Green Monster. Persistent rumours of plans to tear it down have finally been put to rest by the addition of new seats in this section.

The North End

Colonial history and immigrant traditions coexist in the Italian quarter.

Locals shoot the breeze in Boston's answer to Little Italy.

What do Paul Revere and great pasta have in common? It may seem an unlikely combination, but this vibrant area is famous for both. Settled in the early 1600s, the North End is Boston's oldest neighbourhood and for decades it has been the city's Italian quarter.

The area played a starring role in Revolutionary history. It was from his North Square home that silversmith Paul Revere made his famous midnight ride to warn rebel troops in Lexington and Concord of the arrival of British Redcoats in nearby Boston Harbor. As the childhood home of John F Kennedy's grandfather, John Fitzgerald, the North End also has links with that most famous of Boston political dynasties.

The early township at the tip of Shawmut Peninsula was a maze of two- and three-storey clapboard houses called saltboxes, but a number of fires – notably the devastating blaze of 1676 – ushered in the age of brick. The area's other memorable disaster was the great molasses flood. On 15 January 1919 an enormous tank of molasses that was being stored on Commercial Street for the purpose of rum-making exploded and sent 2.5 million gallons (9.4 million litres) of the stuff cascading through the streets. Rising to waves of up to 40 feet (12 metres), the deluge crushed houses and vehicles and dragged 21 people (and 12 horses) to a sugary grave. Some claim that on a hot day you can still smell molasses on Commercial Street.

The neighourhood was originally a blue-blood bastion, but in the mid to late 19th century there was an influx of European immigrants. First came the Irish, then German, Russian and Polish Jews, followed by a smattering of Portuguese fishermen and, finally, the Italians. By 1920, 90 per cent of the population of the area was from central and southern Italy.

Today, almost half of its residents are of Italian descent. Despite a wave of high-income professionals moving into recently converted loft apartments, and crowds of diners and tourists, the North End retained its old-world character. With its tightly clustered red-brick row houses hung with wrought-iron fire escapes, traditional cafés and retro neon signage, all it needs is a Tony Bennett soundtrack to feel like a scene out of *Goodfellas*.

Spurning the supermarket age, locals still buy their provisions from *salumerias*, bakeries and greengrocers (*see p87* **Topor's taste of Italy**). Stooped old women lean on canes as they test the freshness of market-stand tomatoes; elderly men cluster in modest social clubs or, when the weather is warm, drag their folding chairs to the sidewalk to play backgammon and argue with gesticulating hands. Passers-by greet each other and chat in the streets and storefronts, often in Italian. In summer, thronging street festivals in honour of various saints take over the neighbourhood nearly every weekend.

Perhaps the North End has retained its distinctive identity in part because, until recently, it was literally cut off from the rest of the city. Since the late 1950s, the massive iron girding holding up the elevated six-lane Central Artery created a 40-foot (12-metre) wall, separating the North End and waterfront from the rest of downtown Boston. But the massive engineering project, the Big Dig, has remedied that. In late 2003, as the work inched toward completion, the traffic that once congested the Central Artery was rerouted underground to the southbound I-93 tunnel – allowing the unsightly and noisy hulk of steel to be dismantled. While it's not yet clear what exactly will replace the towering, car-choked wall, the 27 acres (11 hectares) of open space is earmarked for greenery and limited commercial development.

As its long-overdue reconnection with the rest of the city begins, people are noticing a change in the North End. The noise from the overhead traffic has been silenced, and some even sense a different quality to the light. Let's hope this new atmosphere – and newly revealed views of the rest of the city – won't usher in skyrocketing rents and insensitive developers.

North Square

Three of the Freedom Trail's sites (*see p65* **On the trails...**) are in the North End. The best known of these is the house of the area's most famous former resident, **Paul Revere**, at 19 North Square. Revere owned the house for 30 years and worked as a silversmith in a workshop on nearby Clark's Wharf; some of his handiwork can be seen in the house today. While the building is a rare example of wooden 17th-century colonial architecture, in the end it is Revere's own history that makes it worth a visit.

More impressive architecturally is the three-storey brick mansion on the other side of the courtyard, the **Pierce/Hichborn House**. It was built in 1810, and Revere's cousin Nathaniel Hichborn bought it to be closer to his relative. The contrast between the two houses is fascinating – Revere's being far more primitive than Hichborn's, showing how the nation's wealth had advanced over the course of a century (*see below*).

Once Walt Whitman's place of worship, the **Sacred Heart Church** (*see p84*) is across the cobblestoned North Square plaza from the Pierce/Hichborn House. It's also worth taking a glance at the **Mariners' House** (11 North Square, between Moon and Prince Streets). This was a hotel that rented rooms to sailors from the 1870s up until 1997.

While Revere's story is the area's main claim to fame, another American legend has its roots here. Congressman and former Boston mayor John 'Honey Fitz' Fitzgerald was born on Ferry Street and later lived at 4 Garden Court. There, he reared a daughter named Rose, who later married a fellow named Kennedy. Her sons included President John F Kennedy, Attorney General Robert F Kennedy and Senator Ted Kennedy, who still serves in the US Congress. Despite the family's many personal tragedies and misdemeanours, the liberal Kennedy clan remains undefeated in Massachusetts elections. *See also p10* **The trouble with the Kennedys**.

Paul Revere House & Pierce/Hichborn House

19 & 29 North Square, between Richmond & Prince Streets (1-617 523 2338/www.paulreverehouse.org). Haymarket T. **Open** *Apr-Oct* 9.30am-5.15pm daily. *Nov-Mar* 9.30am-4.15pm daily. **Admission** $3; $2 concessions. **Credit** (shop only) AmEx, MC, V. **Map** p275 L3.

Haymarket. *See p85.*

Sightseeing

Paul Revere: the ride of his life

Of all America's founding fathers, only George Washington is more famous among US schoolchildren than Paul Revere. Part of the reason for his mass popularity is the incredibly catchy poem written in 1860 by another Bostonian, Henry Wadsworth Longfellow. *Paul Revere's Ride* is one of the first poems many American children learn, for the simple reason that it is both historical and, well, kind of fun:

Built in 1680 – making it the oldest surviving structure in downtown Boston – the Paul Revere House was constructed on the site of the Second Church of Boston parsonage, the home of Puritan preacher Increase Mather and his family, including son Cotton (*see p33*). The two-storey clapboard building may seem modest, but its leaded diamond panes and extravagant Elizabethan overhang indicate it was home to families of means. Revere bought the house from its first owner, wealthy merchant Robert Howard, and lived here with his wife, children (he had 16 over 30 years, but only eight lived in the house at any one time) and mother from 1770 until 1800. The third storey was removed in the 19th century, when the house fell into disrepair (at various times, it served as a flophouse, candy store, cigar factory and bank). In 1902 it was nearly demolished, but the fortuitous intercession of Revere's great-grandson saved the place from the wrecking ball; six years later, the Paul Revere House opened to the public, one of the very first 'house museums' in America. While 90 per cent of the structure and several doors and windows are still intact more than three centuries on, none of the furnishing is original. However, some of Revere's exquisite silverwork is on display.

Across the courtyard – where sits a 900lb (408kg) iron bell cast by Paul Revere and his sons – is the Pierce/Hichborn House, one of the oldest brick buildings in Boston and a prime example of early Georgian architecture. It was built in 1711 for local glass cutter Moses Pierce, and purchased later by Revere's cousin, Nathaniel Hichborn, a shipbuilder.

Sacred Heart Church

12 North Square, at Prince Street (1-617 523 5638). Haymarket T. **Open** 6am-8pm daily. **Admission** free. **Map** p275 L3.

Founded in 1833, this was originally known as the Seamen's Bethel, a place of worship for sailors and fishermen (in the 19th century, the wharves and waterfront reached a little further inland, so the church was nearby). These days it's Catholic – the only formally designated Italian church in the North End – and the 10am Mass each Sunday is celebrated in the mother tongue.

Hanover & Salem Streets

With more than 100 restaurants packed into just a few blocks, the North End has been a popular dining destination with Bostonians and

Listen my children, and you shall hear
Of the midnight ride of Paul Revere,
On the eighteenth of April, in Seventy-five;
Hardly a man is now alive
Who remembers that famous day and year...

Let's start at the beginning. Revere was a silversmith in Boston at the time of the Revolution. He was also one of the key rebels in the city, heavily involved in overthrowing the British government in the American colonies. Revere's drawings (he was an artist, too) of the Boston Massacre were widely published throughout the colonies, and helped to inflame the anger against the British.

Despite his artistic efforts, Revere's primary role was as a messenger. He frequently travelled between Boston and Philadelphia – where the Continental Congress was meeting to form the country's early government – carrying messages from Boston's rebels to the leaders. By 1775 the Boston colonists had created an extensive underground network to monitor British troops occupying the area, and to alert the rebel leaders of any activity by the Redcoats. In particular, the well-positioned Old North Church at the top of a hill was a prime spying spot. The sexton, Robert Newman, had offered to signal by placing lanterns in the church's steeple – one lantern meant the troops were moving on the ground; two would mean they were coming in from the ocean: 'One if by land, two if by sea.'

On the night of 18 April 1775, Newman placed two lanterns in the steeple to signal that the British were crossing the Charles River on their way to Charlestown. From there they would set out to Lexington and Concord, where rebels were assembling. Revere and two other horsemen (William Dawes and Samuel Prescott) hit the road. Their mission was to beat the British to Lexington and then to Concord, to warn the militia and give them enough time to mount a defence.

The three succeeded in arriving in Lexington in time to gather the Minutemen and to rouse Patriot leaders John Hancock and Samuel Adams, both of whom were spending the night at a Lexington inn. But as the three rebels headed for Concord they encountered a British patrol. The two other riders escaped and rode on, though only Prescott ultimately reached Concord. Interestingly, Revere, who was well-known to the British for his work with the rebels, was held for several hours and then deprived of his horse. He finally walked into Concord. Now, there's something nobody ever tells US schoolkids.

tourists alike for decades. In the vicinity of these two main drags, you can find everything from traditional cafés and humble trattorias to chic *nuovo Italiano* eateries. (*See also pp114-143.*)

Once you've had your fill, waddle down to one of the more notorious sites in the area – the **Joseph A Langone Funeral Home** (383 Hanover Street). This is where the funeral was held for Nicola Sacco and Bartolomeo Vanzetti, two Italian anarchists who were executed in 1927 following a controversial robbery and murder trial that preyed on the xenophobia of the era. Many believed the two were innocent. What's indisputable is that their case was railroaded through the court system to appease the angry, anti-immigrant zeitgeist, and the story of their fate remains a cause célèbre among anti-death-penalty groups worldwide.

Nearby on Prince Street is **St Leonard's Church** (1-617 523 2110), the first Italian Catholic church in New England. It houses the beautiful Peace Garden and still functions as a place of worship. Not far from St Leonard's is **St Stephen's Church**, the only remaining place of worship in Boston designed by Charles Bulfinch. Unlike the Italians, other immigrants didn't leave a lasting legacy. Salem Street is so named because it was once called Shalom Street – in the mid-19th century it was the primary home of the neighbourhood's Jews. There used to be five synagogues in the North End. None remain, and virtually all traces of Jewish influence have vanished.

Separated from the North End for decades by the Central Artery, but linked in spirit, is **Haymarket**, an open-air produce and fish market, situated behind Blackstone Block to the north of Faneuil Hall. On Fridays and Saturdays it's a bustling, colourful scene, punctuated by the cries of charismatic stallholders.

St Stephen's Church

24 Clark Street, at Hanover Street (1-617 523 1230). Haymarket T. **Open** 7.30am-5pm daily. **Admission** free. **Map** p275 L2.

This Bulfinch-designed church wasn't built from scratch, but remodelled from an existing structure in 1804. Shortly thereafter the church's congregation purchased a set of bells cast by Paul Revere's

Sightseeing

St Francis of Assisi presides over the courtyard of the **Old North Church**.

foundry for $800. Those who are most familiar with elaborate cathedral architecture will find this church's colonial plainness unusual. The building was renovated in 1965, when it was painstakingly returned to its original appearance. The church also has a part in the history of the Kennedy clan – JFK's mother, Rose, was baptised here. It was also the site of her funeral.

The Prado

In 1933 the North End's favourite son got his own memorial. The **Paul Revere Mall**, located in the quaint, brick-paved park known as the Prado, features as its centrepiece a statue of Revere first designed by Cyrus E Dallin in 1865 but only cast in 1940. The mall (between Hanover and Unity Streets) serves as a social hub in warm weather, where locals play cards, gossip and argue over sport scores. In the square, engraved tablets on the walls list famous residents and places in the neighbourhood.

The remaining two Freedom Trail stops are in this area – the **Old North Church**, and **Copp's Hill Burying Ground**. The latter is the highest point in the North End, and a good spot for taking pictures of the USS Constitution across the harbour in Charlestown. Nearby is a symbol of the sometimes eccentric rudeness of some Bostonians. You'll note that **44 Hull Street** barely looks like a house. In fact it's the narrowest in Boston – only ten feet (three metres) wide. According to local lore, the sole purpose its original owners had in building it was to block their neighbours' view. Welcome to Boston, pal.

Copp's Hill Burying Ground

Charter Street, at Snowhill Street. North Station T. **Open** dawn-dusk daily. **Admission** free. **Map** p275 L2.

The final resting place of roughly 10,000 early Bostonians, this cemetery was developed on the most northern hill of the Shawmut Peninsula in 1659. Once the site of the community's mill, it was originally called Windmill Hill. The British used the site's geographical advantage to launch cannon balls at the rebel army during the Battle of Bunker Hill; it is said that they warmed up by using some of the cemetery's gravestones for target practice.

Perhaps the most famous Bostonians to be interred here are the Puritan preachers and arch-conservative theologians Cotton Mather and his father Increase. Cotton Mather was famed for his literary prolificacy. He is believed to have written more than 400 books and pamphlets. Both Cotton and Increase fell out of favour in subsequent years over their handling of the Salem Witch Trials. Both were influential enough to have halted the Salem inquisition, but neither condemned the mass hysteria that occurred among the religious residents of Salem until it was far too late.

Also buried on Copp's Hill is the slave and soldier Prince Hall, an early African-American leader in Boston. Hall lived in the free black community that originally settled the hill, and earned fame for his bravery in the Battle of Bunker Hill.

Old North Church

193 Salem Street, at Hull Street (1-617 523 6676). Haymarket T. **Open** 9am-5pm daily. **Admission** $2. **Map** p275 L2.

Originally called Christ Church in Boston, the city's oldest church was built in 1723 in the style of Christopher Wren. It played a critical role in the earliest days of the American Revolution: it was from Old North's steeple that lanterns were hung to warn the Minutemen of the movements of British troops. One lantern was to be displayed if the troops were seen moving by land, two if they were coming in by sea. They came by sea, and two it was – spurring Paul Revere to take his midnight ride (*see p84* **Paul Revere: The ride of his life**). In fact, the steeple wasn't part of the original church, but was added in 1740. Replacement steeples were built in 1806 and 1954 after hurricanes knocked the previous versions down. In the original window where the two lanterns were hung sits a third lantern, lit by President Ford on 18 April 1975, symbolising hope for the nation's next century of freedom. More trivia about the church: its 175ft (53m) spire has been used as a reference point by sailors for hundreds of years. It still appears on modern nautical maps. Famous visitors to the church have included US presidents James Monroe and Theodore and Franklin Roosevelt, as well as Queen Elizabeth II. Finally, the bust of George Washington inside the church is said to have been the first memorial ever dedicated to the country's founding father.

Topor's taste of Italy

'Spinosi pasta has changed my life!' Michele Topor may be of Polish descent, but she has embraced *la dolce vita* with the zeal of a religious convert. A North End resident for more than 30 years, she knows almost everyone in the neighbourhood – which quickly becomes evident on her Market Tour as she exchanges the tenth *buongiorno* in the first half-hour.

Topor has studied in Bologna and Florence, and is considered one of Boston's authorities on Italian food and wine. A three-and-a-half-hour tour of around ten of the area's food shops and producers may sound daunting, but time literally flies as you keep up with her energetic pace, accompanied by her effervescent synopsis of the culinary history of Italy and the North End.

In the late 19th and early 20th centuries, the quarter drew thousands of immigrants from Italy's central and southern regions, and food-shopping remains much the same as it was in those days. (Indeed, some of these shops have been around since the early part of the 20th century.) Topor buys ingredients almost daily, and considers her rounds to be 'as much socialising as anything'. She leads you to establishments tucked away on winding side streets (many of which keep erratic hours, according to the owner's whim) with the savvy of a long-time local.

Bypassing the always-mobbed **Mike's Pastry** (a tourist hot spot that attracts more visitors than the Old North Church and Paul Revere House combined, she says), Topor ushers you to the lesser-known **Maria's** (46 Cross Street, *see p172*), which, she says, is the best *pasticceria* in Boston. Entering some shops feels like being initiated into a secret society: **Alba** greengrocers (18 Parmenter Street) has no sign above the door and no prices on the produce. But heaven help you if you touch anything: the rules are to point and let the proprietor pick. Visiting other businesses reveals wonderful stories. The two owners of competing meat markets

Sulmona and **Abruzzese** (32 Parmenter Street and 94 Salem Street) grew up in the same region of Italy and share the same last name, but didn't meet until they emigrated to the North End. They're now best friends.

From sweet shop to delicatessen, Topor scans the shelves and display cases, pointing, grabbing and enthusing about the merits of each product while dispensing pinches of wisdom: that the coffee-laced tiramisu gets its name from Italian slang for 'pick-me-up' or that one should *never* buy a prefilled cannoli.

Perhaps the best part of the tour are the samples at each stop – from freshly made pastries like *sfogliatelle* and sweet, fruit-shaped marzipan, to the warming *liquori* limoncello that rounds things off nicely.

Michele Topor's North End Market Tours

For listings, *see p104*.

The Waterfront & Charlestown

Dramatic developments are afoot along Boston's historic harbour.

Christopher Columbus Park.

At heart, Boston is just a big seaside town. The Hub has always been known for fresh seafood, ocean-whipped winds and water views. After years of neglect – due in part to a declining fishing industry – Boston's waterfront is on the rise again. This time the focus is on its huge stretches of prime, underdeveloped property. The fish might not be jumpin', but the buyers are.

The Waterfront

Referred to as the 'final frontier' in Boston's urban development, the Waterfront's 43 miles (69 kilometres) of coastline continue to evolve at a quickened pace. Boston Harbor, once known for its 'dirty water', has improved immensely after a clean-up costing almost $4 billion.

The Seaport District is taking shape. Not far from the new Seaport Hotel, the massive new Convention and Exhibition Center has been completed. Boston's **Institute of Contemporary Art** recently snatched up a lease along Fan Pier (*see p92* **Future vision**). Meanwhile, in the wake of the Big Dig, there are plans not only to add to the Emerald Necklace – the city's chain of green spaces – but also to unify the Sapphire Necklace – open spaces along the water meant for the public to enjoy. Scheduled for completion in 2008, the Harbor Walk will be a 43-mile (69 kilometre) continuous footpath with features including public art, beaches and observation decks.

Long Wharf & the Aquarium

Almost directly behind Faneuil Hall Marketplace lies **Long Wharf**. It was originally known as Boston Pier when, in 1710, a group of merchants first built brick warehouses here. The shoreline has changed quite a bit since then: when the **Customs House**, Boston's first skyscraper, was built (in 1847, in the style of an Italian Renaissance campanile) it stood on the edge of the water. The landmark now lies on State and India Streets, several blocks inland. The green space at the border of Long Wharf is **Christopher Columbus Park**. A huge wooden arbour, with vine-covered trellises and benches from which to admire the waterfront views, gives the spot an unexpectedly romantic air. Long Wharf is the place to go to find tickets for whale-watching cruises or tours of the Boston Harbor Islands (*see p89*). The striking glass **New England Aquarium** sits on neighbouring Central Wharf; while every city seems to have an aquarium these days, this is one of the country's best.

New England Aquarium

Central Wharf, at Atlantic Avenue & Milk Street (1-617 973 5200/www.neaq.org). Aquarium T. **Open** *July, Aug* 9am-6pm Mon, Tue, Fri; 9am-8pm Wed, Thur; 9am-7pm Sat, Sun. *Sept-June* 9am-5pm Mon-Fri; 9am-6pm Sat, Sun. **Admission** $15.95; $8.95-$13.95 concessions. **Credit** AmEx, Disc, MC, V. **Map** p275 M4.

One of the finest aquariums in the world, the New England Aquarium's huge indoor penguin exhibit (constructed so almost all of the balconies overlook it) is a hoot. But its colossal 187,000-gallon salt-water replica of a Caribbean coral reef – 40ft/12m in diameter and three storeys tall – is its breathtaking centrepiece. The cylindrical tank is alive with moray eels, stingrays, gigantic sea turtles and menacing sharks. There's also an outdoor sea otter enclosure, and a display where you can stick your hands into the cold water of a tidal basin and get up close and personal with starfish, sea urchins and hermit crabs. The IMAX theatre offers state-of-the-art 3D glasses to put viewers in the middle of the action.

Boston Harbor Islands

Some of the waterfront's least-exploited assets are these 34 small islands left by a retreating glacier about 12,000 years ago. In the 1990s Congress designated them national parkland, and they provide a thriving wildlife habitat. Rare and endangered species of birds such as the plover and osprey have been spotted here, and grey and harp seals live in the harbour. Although only five of the islands are currently accessed by public ferry, special arrangements can be made to visit most of the others (1-617 223 8666, www.bostonislands.com). The islands' fate has recently become a hot topic as waterfront renovation booms. There have been murmurs of developments, such as B&Bs, amphitheatres, shops, and even a water slide – which will no doubt lead to extensive debate among environmentalists, state agencies and businesses. Not that the islands have been untainted idylls – in the past they've played host to prostitution, gambling and garbage dumping (indeed, Gallops Island is currently closed due to the presence of asbestos building debris). Largely unvisited aside from the fairly well-trafficked Fort Warren on Georges Island, the islands make a pleasant escape from the city on a warm afternoon.

Short of bringing your own boat, you can catch a Harbor Express commuter boat (1-617 222 6999, www.harborexpress.com) from T Wharf (alongside Long Wharf Marriott). The 28-acre (11-hectare) **Georges Island** is dominated by Fort Warren, a massive structure used during the Civil War as a Union training base and a prison for captured Confederate soldiers (including, most famously, the vice-president of the Confederacy, Alexander Hamilton Stephens). You can either take a guided tour or explore it on your own.

Bumpkin Island, covering about 35 acres (14 hectares), is tucked away in Hingham Bay and doesn't see much traffic. From the early part of the 20th century to the 1940s it was used to quarantine children with polio. Today it's one of four islands, along with Peddocks, Grape and Lovells, where camping is permitted. In all cases, reservations must be made in advance with park officials by calling the number above. Also note that, inexplicably – chalk it up to prim New England culture – alcohol is not permitted on the islands.

Grape Island has never been developed; the remains of a 19th-century farmhouse are the only clue that the 50-acre (20-hectare) island was once inhabited. It has pristine shell and gravel beaches, campsites, and berries to pick.

Lovells Island covers 62 acres (25 hectares) and has a public swimming beach, hiking trails, wooded hills and dunes. **Peddocks Island**, at 188 acres (76 hectares), is the largest of the archipelago. During the 1960s a 4,100-year-old skeleton was excavated on its shores. It's the only island with residents all year round; when

The best Views

For the energetic

At 221 feet/67 metres, **Bunker Hill Monument**, offers sweeping views of the Boston skyline. *See p93.*

For tipplers

The **Top of the Hub Lounge** on the 52nd floor of the Prudential Tower gives a bird's-eye view spanning up to 80 miles (129 kilometres). If cocktails aren't on your itinerary, stop at the Skywalk Observation Deck two floors below. *See p76.*

Off the beaten track

If you find yourself in Southie on a summer's day, ascend the **Dorchester Heights** Georgian Revival tower to see the ocean, Harbor Islands, and downtown Boston stretching below. *See p101.*

In a peaceful setting

Perched atop Mount Auburn in the lovely Cambridge cemetery, the 62-foot (18-metre) **Mount Auburn Tower** (open from April to October, depending on weather conditions), commands a view of the Charles River and Boston skyline. *See p98.*

From your car

True, you have to pay a $1 toll to enjoy this vista, but it's worth it. Directly after the toll booth as you enter Boston from the **eastbound Mass Pike**, see the entire city laid out before you. It's especially pretty at night – but keep an eye on the traffic!

the Harbor Islands were first turned into a state park, the state granted the residents – most of them fishermen – life-long leases; upon their death the land reverts back to state ownership. Peddocks, with its salt marshes and woods, is great for picnicking, camping and hiking.

Fort Point Channel

Fort Point, 16 December 1773: a group of 60 colonists disguised as Mohawk Indians dumps 342 chests of tea into Boston Harbor in protest at the tea tax imposed by King George III. Due to shifts in the coastline, the actual site is inland on Pearl Street, by what is now **Carl's Deli** (147 Pearl Street, 1-617 542 1965), and the original ships involved are long gone, but re-enactments have been taking place to the delight of visiting schoolchildren at the **Boston Tea Party Ship and Museum** (a ship docked on the Congress Street Bridge, 1-617 338 1773, www.bostonteapartyship.com). Due to a recent fire it's currently closed, but the site will reopen in summer 2005, complete with two additional tall ships and a renovated museum space almost twice its original size.

The eastern side of Fort Point Channel, between Northern Avenue and Summer Street, is called **Museum Wharf** – home to the much-loved **Children's Museum** (*see p187*). Focusing on early childhood education and teaching resources, the museum specialises in hands-on displays to entertain children of all ages. If you're hungry, stop by the **Milk Bottle** (312 Congress Street) – a Fort Point landmark. This restaurant, shaped like a giant milk bottle, has a take-away window that has been dishing out ice-cream, french fries and the like since 1934.

In the late 1970s, the warehouses of this former industrial area attracted artists and, although many have been forced out by developers over the last decade, there is still a large live/work building at 300 Summer Street, which contains the **Fort Point Arts Community Gallery** (1-617 423 4299, www.fortpointarts.org). Snippets of public art dot the neighbourhood, especially the Summer Street bridge. The area isn't known for its nightlife, but retro bar and restaurant **Lucky's** (*see p149*) is a recent addition.

Continuing along Northern Avenue you come to South Boston's pier area. This is the place to discover the city's traditional seafood restaurants, including **Jimmy's Harborside** (242 Northern Avenue, 1-617 423 1000) and the **No Name restaurant** (15 Fish Pier, Northern Ave, 1-617 338 7539) for fried seafood galore, and **Anthony's Pier 4** (140 Northern Avenue, 1-617 423 6262), where you can eat baked cod, finnian haddie and salty oyster crackers among the driftwood and fishing nets. It's also the site of Legal Seafoods' headquarters – a two-ton, 45-foot-high (14-metre) steel fish adorns its roof at 1 Seafood Way. Beer lovers may want to consider a free tasting at the **Harpoon Brewery** (306 Northern Avenue, 1-866 427 7666, www.harpoonbrewery.com).

The Charles River Basin

Some of Boston's most exhilarating panoramas are viewed from the banks of the Charles. The Charles River Basin runs from the river's end at the Museum of Science to the Boston University Bridge. Bicycle paths and grassy banks line both sides of the river. One of the best views of the city skyline is from the Cambridge side of the basin along Memorial Drive between the Boston University and Longfellow Bridges.

On the Boston side the **Charles River Esplanade** is the grassy park, criss-crossed by walking paths, between the Longfellow and Harvard bridges. It's anchored by the **Hatch Memorial Shell**, a pavilion best known for the annual Fourth of July concert by the Boston Pops, an extravaganza which attracts hundreds of thousands of concert-goers each year (*see p182*). On summer weekends, it can get quite crowded here – sun-worshippers lie on towels, impeding the frolicking of frisbee players, dog walkers, cyclists and skaters, and the river is dotted with sailboats. Further up the path behind the Hatch Shell is **Charlesbank Park**, a lovely space with room to roam alongside tennis courts and a children's playground.

Charlestown

For many years Charlestown has been known as the tough, working-class neighbourhood on the edge of the Boston skyline – insular, with Mob ties and a predominantly Irish Catholic population. But that reputation, like that of many old-time Boston neighbourhoods, is changing fast. Over the last two decades it's been infiltrated by young professionals, lured by its elegant properties and close proximity to downtown Boston. Even so, the neighbourhood maintains a small-town feel with its tight, winding streets, clapboard 'triple-decker' three-family houses and corner pubs. Locals are still referred to as 'townies', a nickname that dates back to colonial times.

Charlestown's prosperity once reflected the ebb and flow of business in the Navy Yard, which employed 47,000 workers at the start of World War II. It opened for business in the late 1800s when the new republic, desperate to respond to attacks on merchant ships by Barbary pirates off the coast of North Africa,

The exhilarating view from the top of **Bunker Hill Monument**. *See p93*.

decided to beef up its Navy. From that point on the Navy Yard became one of the most critical and, during wartime, busiest shipbuilding and repair yards in the country. Due to lack of demand it closed shop in 1974 and some tough years followed. Today the **Charlestown Navy Yard** serves as a museum of American naval history. The most famous ship in the yard (if not in the country) is the USS *Constitution* – 'Old Ironsides' – built in 1797; its neighbour is the USS *Cassin Young*, a destroyer which saw action in the Pacific during World War II (*see p93*). The adjacent **USS Constitution Museum** (*see p93*) includes an interactive

Future vision

You'd think Boston would need a break from monstrous construction projects after the Big Dig. But giraffe-necked cranes will remain a part of the cityscape indefinitely, since the next major building effort is scheduled to break ground as early as 2005. The Fan Pier project will transform a 21-acre (8.4-hectare) site by Boston Harbor into a premier commercial and residential development. But arguably the most exciting feature will be the spectacular new Institute of Contemporary Art (ICA).

At the vanguard of modern art since its 1936 inception, the ICA introduced seminal 20th-century artists like Andy Warhol, Cindy Sherman, and Robert Rauschenberg to the Bay State. In more recent years the edgy visual-arts venue has upheld this pioneering tradition by showing emerging artists like conceptual thinker Cornelia Parker, videographer Bill Viola and photographer Nikki S Lee. As the champion of modern sensibilities, it's fitting that the ICA's new structure will be Boston's first art museum built in nearly 100 years – since the Museum of Fine Arts leapt from Copley Square to its present Huntington Avenue home.

To design its new physical identity, the ICA hired Diller + Scofidio, the husband-and-wife architectural firm from New York that created the Viewing Platforms at New York's Ground Zero. The blueprint is unlike anything else in Boston: a four-storey glass-and-metal edifice topped with a rectangular glass cantilever hovers over the harbour like a spaceship.

One of the wonders of the new ICA's design is that it will look different depending upon the viewer's perspective. From the street side the sleek construction will appear smooth and luminous, like a translucent box wrapped up in a metal ribbon; but from the waterfront the cantilever's supports won't be entirely visible – so from a distance, the orthogonal glass will appear to float over the water's edge like a levitating slab of ice. Then at night, when the artificial lights go on inside, the galleries will glow like a spacecraft above the water, adding an ethereal presence to the seaport skyline.

The interior design is equally impressive, tripling the current space. Fitted with adjustable walls, the galleries will be equipped with 16-foot (five-metre) ceilings and overhead skylight systems that allow the art to be viewed in natural light. The waterfront wall of the Long Gallery, the ICA's main showcase, will be made of lenticular glass – a series of microscopic vertical lenses that are transparent at 90-degree angles, but opaque from any other angle – intended to create the optical illusion of the outside world following you.

Also in the ICA's plans are a 300-seat theatre and a digital media centre that protrudes from the base of the galleries like a chute aimed at the ocean. In a city that prides itself on its past, the project suggests Boston might finally be embracing the future.

galley where visitors can load and fire a cannon or simulate steering a square-rigger at sea.

From the yard you can see the obelisk of the **Bunker Hill Monument** (*see below*) shining in the near distance. It commemorates one of the bloodiest and most famous battles of the Revolutionary War and its summit commands spectacular views. The Visitor Center in the Bunker Hill Pavilion (*see below*) offers an educational multimedia presentation on the battle, which shows every 30 minutes.

Not far from Bunker Hill, reflecting '80s gentrification, are the first two restaurants of Boston chef Todd English: **Olives** and **Figs** (for both *see p133*). For more down-to-earth refreshment, stop at the **Warren Tavern** (2 Pleasant Street, at Main Street, 1-617 241 8142). Named after Dr Joseph Warren, a popular revolutionary who died in the final clash in the Battle of Bunker Hill, the tavern was built just after most of Charlestown burned down in the late 1700s, making it one of the oldest structures in the area. Paul Revere presided over Masonic meetings as a grand master here, and George Washington visited as president. After closing in the 1960s, the tavern reopened in 1972, and has thrived ever since.

Charlestown Navy Yard

Entrance at Gate 1, Constitution Road, Charlestown (1 617 242 5601/www.nps.gov/bost/Navy_Yard.htm). North Station T then 15mins walk/92, 93 bus. **Open** *Visitor Center* 9am-5pm daily. **Admission** free. **Map** p275 M1.

Established at the point where the Mystic and Charles Rivers converge as the 18th century turned into the 19th, this was once the country's premier navy dockyard. Just before you enter through the yard's main gate, stop by the helpful Visitor Center to your right, which provides free leaflets with maps and information about the site. The yard's most famous occupant is the USS *Constitution* (free tours are given of the ship and its 44 guns daily). The ship earned her nickname – 'Old Ironsides' – during the War of 1812, when a sailor watched as shots fired by a British cannon bounced off her hull (which is actually made of oak). The sailor is said to have shouted, 'Her sides are made of iron!' The name stuck to the ship, and on the same day 'Old Ironsides' is credited with scuppering two British frigates, the Guerriere and the Java. The USS *Constitution* has largely remained in dry dock since the late 19th century, although she did set sail for the first time in 116 years in 1997 – the year of her bicentennial – and she is towed out into Boston harbour and turned around once a year, to ensure that her hull weathers evenly. The *Constitution*'s neighbour is the restored naval destroyer USS *Cassin Young*, which during World War II served in the Pacific theatre to provide early warning of air attacks to the rest of the fleet, and thereby suffered kamikaze suicide attacks by Japanese fighter pilots.

USS Constitution Museum

Building 22, Charlestown Navy Yard, off Constitution Road, Charlestown (1-617 426 1812/ www.ussconstitutionmuseum.org). North Station T then 15min walk/92, 93 bus. **Open** *May-Oct* 9am-6pm daily; *Nov-Apr* 10am-5pm daily. **Admission** free. **Map** p275 M1.

Located inside the Charlestown Navy Yard, this museum is worth a detour as it offers exhibits related to the ship itself and to naval history in general. The interactive portion includes computer games that allow players to devise an escape from an enemy ship, and to see an attack through the eyes of various crew members. Children will enjoy swinging in the sailors' hammocks.

Bunker Hill Monument

Monument Square, Breed's Hill, Charlestown (1-617 242 5641). Community College T. **Open** 9am-5pm daily. **Admission** free.

A towering 221ft-high (67m) granite obelisk designed by Solomon Willard dominates the picturesque residential Monument Square. It commemorates the Battle of Bunker Hill, one of the earliest, and goriest, of the Revolutionary War. In fact, the battle was misnamed – it actually took place on Breed's Hill. On 17 June 1775, when the British 'Committee of Safety', which had planned to fortify Bunker Hill, awoke to find rebel forces entrenched on the neighbouring mound, they stormed Breed's Hill in waves. The American army, led by General William Prescott, was a motley crew of locals with a hodgepodge of ammunition. The rebels were ultimately forced to retreat, but of the 2,200 British ground forces, almost half were counted as casualties, compared to 440 American soldiers. Considered a major turning point in the war effort, the battle emboldened the fledgling nation, and sent a warning to the British that the colonies would not fold easily. The cornerstone of the monument was laid in 1825 by the Marquis de Lafayette, the French officer viewed by the American revolutionaries as the only foreign leader brave enough to offer his help in their fight. Dedicated in 1842 by Daniel Webster, it is part of the Boston National Historical Park. Park rangers give free informative talks hourly (between 10am and 4pm; call ahead in winter months to check the frequency of their presentations). Climb the monument's 294 steps (it takes about 15 minutes) for a breathtaking view of Boston.

Bunker Hill Pavilion

55 Constitution Road, next to Charlestown Navy Yard, Charlestown (1-617 241 7575). North Station T then 15min walk/92, 93 bus. **Open** 9am-5pm daily. **Admission** $2-$4. **Credit** AmEx, Disc, MC, V. **Map** p274 K1.

Come face to face with Revolutionary soldiers in a multimedia presentation called 'Whites of Their Eyes', which explores and explains the Battle of Bunker Hill. Using a variety of screens and modern technology to simulate battle sounds, the story is poignantly narrated by actors.

Cambridge

Soak up the laid-back, intellectual vibe in Student Central.

The city just across the river from Boston used to be referred to regularly as 'the People's Republic of Cambridge' because it boasted a diverse and decidedly liberal – if not outright lefty – population of academics, artists, immigrants and students. That balance still exists, but new additions such as Starbucks, McDonald's and Gap are encroaching on once-cool areas. Rising housing costs, triggered by the end of rent-control, has threatened the bohemian atmosphere. Multiculturalism used to be a mantra here, but lately many groups, like the Portuguese, have settled on the outskirts of town, far from the T.

Still, a vital, intellectual vibe exists, if only because Cambridge is an academic centre, boasting two of the world's best universities – Harvard and MIT – just a few miles apart. The area was only briefly anything other than a college town. It was founded in 1630 by one of the first waves of Puritans. Originally called Newtowne, it was a farming community for six years before the city elders established the country's first college in 1636. A short time later, the institution was renamed after the clergyman John Harvard who, upon his death in 1638, left the university half his estate and all the books from his personal library. Newtowne was then renamed after that other famous university town in England, where many of the settlers had received their education.

The hunger for knowledge will always be a Cambridge staple. But these days students can choose to buy their texts at an independent bookseller, sipping a Fair Trade roast, or at a major chain, downing pricey mochaccinos.

Harvard University

Harvard has more than 400 buildings scattered around Cambridge and Boston, but for the university you've seen in the movies, head to **Harvard Yard** (tours available by calling 1-617 495 1573), a grassy, tree-lined quadrangle surrounded by colonial red-brick buildings that date back to 1720. First-year students still live in dormitories in the Yard, and you'll find them studying and reading (or flirting or sleeping) on the grassy sections of the quad.

As you enter the Yard (opposite the Harvard T) by the gate on Massachusetts Avenue, look for **Massachusetts Hall**'s two buildings down on the left. Built between 1718 and 1720, during the Revolutionary War, the Hall sheltered the soldiers of the fledgling Continental Army. Today the president of the university, vice-presidents and other university officials live on the lower floors, while the upper floors are occupied by first-year students. The hall just edges out the **Wadsworth House** (built in 1726) as the oldest building in the Yard, though the latter yellow clapboard structure is more picturesque. This building served as temporary headquarters for George Washington when he was leading the nation's army in 1775.

John Harvard keeps an eye on the campus.

University Hall, designed by Charles Bulfinch in 1813, sits directly in front of the Yard's most popular sight: the statue of John Harvard. Cast in 1884 by Daniel Chester French (who also sculpted the Lincoln Memorial in Washington, DC), it's known as the 'statue of three lies'. Its inscription reads 'John Harvard,

Founder, 1638', three times untrue since John Harvard was a donor, not a founder; the college was set up in 1636; and nobody knows what he really looked like – French used a Harvard student as a model. Touching John Harvard's shoe is rumoured to bring good luck, so students (and tourists) line up accordingly.

On the quiet square directly behind University Hall you'll find the imposing, classically styled **Widener Library**, the oldest university library in the country and the largest academic library in the world. It holds more than 13 million volumes. Getting through the doors of the library without a student ID is almost as difficult as getting into the college itself, but anyone can appreciate the *Titanic* tie-in of the place. Harry Elkins Widener, after whom the library is named, graduated from Harvard in 1907, then went down with the famous ship when he failed to swim 50 yards (46 metres) to reach a lifeboat. The following year his mother donated $2 million to Harvard for this library. Legend has it that she stipulated all undergraduates must pass a 50-yard swimming test.

Though most visitors to the campus don't venture beyond the main quad, it's worth exploring further in order to see the neo-Gothic **Sanders Theatre** (45 Quincy Street) and the **Carpenter Center for the Visual Arts** (24 Quincy Street), designed in 1963 by the French modernist architect Le Corbusier. Other notable buildings on campus include the **Science Center**, just north of the central quad – which is one of several at Harvard designed by Josep Lluis Sert; the others are the **Peabody Terrace** (1964; 900 Memorial Drive), **Holyoke Center** (1967; 1350 Massachusetts Avenue), and the **Center for the Study of World Religions** (1959; 42 Francis Avenue).

Outside Harvard Yard

The extraordinary collections on display in the **Harvard art museums** (*see p109*), to the east of the Yard on Quincy Street, are definitely worth a visit. In addition, the **Museum of Natural History** (26 Oxford Street, 1-617 495 3045), the **Peabody Museum of Archaeology and Ethnology** (*see p110*), and the **Semitic Museum** (6 Divinity Avenue, 1-617 495 4631) are all located a couple of blocks north of the Yard.

Lying between Harvard Yard and Memorial Drive is the **Harvard Lampoon Castle** (44 Bow Street), offices of the satirical publication the *Harvard Lampoon*, which has spawned countless writers and comedians, including John Updike and Conan O'Brien. Not open to the public, the Castle is still worth seeing from the outside. It is wedged on to a tiny sliver of land between Mount Auburn and Bow Streets, but architects Wheelwright & Haven made the most of the awkward site in 1909, creating a cartoonish, miniaturised castle that reflects its mischievous inhabitants.

Harvard Square

As cool as it is, Cambridge (and neighbouring Somerville) is all about being square. The town is divided into small neighbourhoods, which are themselves divided into a matrix of squares –

Drop out, get rich

With all the distractions in town, it's not unusual for some Harvard students to stray from their studies. But ditching the books isn't always the end of the world; in fact it's been the making of some Harvard alumni. The university's most famous dropout is also one of the richest men in the world: **Bill Gates** gave up his studies in 1977 to build Microsoft. In a recent speech to current students, Gates confessed his 'terrible habit of not ever attending classes'. He and fellow Harvard classmate **Steve Ballmer** donated a $25 million computer science building to the university. Another dropout who gave generously to his alma mater is **Edwin H Land**, the founder of the Polaroid Company. It's said that Harvard does not name buildings after corporations, but some think the Science Center resembles the shape of a Polaroid camera.

Hollywood hunk **Matt Damon** never finished his Harvard degree, but went on to co-author the screenplay for *Good Will Hunting*, about a genius janitor at MIT. Not exactly an academic overachiever, **George W Bush** followed in pop's footsteps and followed up his Yale undergrad studies with a Harvard Business school degree. His famous undergrad C-average was matched by that of another US President, **Franklin Delano Roosevelt**, during his Harvard tenure.

Let it be a lesson to students everywhere: if you're ambitious enough, there's no shame in leaving the hallowed halls behind to pursue entrepreneurial endeavours. Just don't tell the folks it was our idea.

Hip to be (Davis) square

Utne magazine called it one of the 15 hippest places in the country. The *Hipster Handbook* said its inhabitants were super-cool. And locals have known for years that this is the 'new Central Square'. But **Davis Square**, in the city of Somerville, just north of Cambridge, hasn't let the attention go to its head. The result is a refreshingly down-to-earth hangout minus the big ego – at least for now; get here while the vibe lasts.

Largely residential, Somerville doesn't have much in the way of tourist attractions (the only major landmark is **Tufts University** on the Medford border). During the day Davis Square resembles the tiny, 1950s burg in *Back to the Future*, with serene coffeeshops, indie record stores and the lovingly restored chrome-and-neon **Rosebud Diner** (*see p143*) – although the Starbucks spoils the illusion somewhat. At night the unusually polite students from Tufts University bring the town into the noughties as they hit the local pubs, bars and nightclubs.

The T lets you off right in the square, where you'll find an old-time ice-cream parlour (**JP Licks**, *see p142*), an Italian diner (**Mike's Restaurant**, *see below*) and picnic benches that host artists and their sketchpads. The **Somerville Theatre** (55 Davis Square, 1-617 625 4088) shows festival and second-run films you might have missed, while the neighbouring **Someday Café** (51 Davis Square) is the square's original coffee spot.

From there, most of the highlights are on two streets. Walk south on Elm to find the **Diesel Café** (No.257, 1-617 629 8717), whose Accelerator coffee (a vanilla latte with almond flavour) will give you the energy to rummage through **McIntyre and Moore Booksellers** (No.255, 1-617 629 4840), an antiquarian treasure trove open until 11pm. Further down the street is popular Irish bar the **Burren** (No.247, 1-617 776 6896) and **Jimmy Tingle's Off Broadway** (No.255, 1-617 591 1616), a small theatre run by the local social commentator/comedian. Nearby, **Gargoyles on the Square** (No.219, 1-617 776 5300) is a great contemporary neighbourhood bistro. One of Boston's best barbecue joints, **Redbones**, is tucked away on Cheshire Street (*see p143*), and on Elm's parallel street, Highland Avenue, is the vintage-fashion addict's secret weapon, **Poor Little Rich Girl** (*see p171*).

In the opposite direction from the square, due north on Holland Street, lie the area's nightclubs, including **Johnny D's** (*see p210*), which features live music – from Cajun to rock to Britpop – seven nights a week, and **Orleans** (65 Holland Street, 1-617 591 2100), a jazz, lounge and house joint. Afterwards, head back to the Square itself, where local institution **Mike's Restaurant** (No.9, 1-617 628 2379) serves late-night meatballs and cheesy garlic bread. What more could you ask for?

though many are little more than glorified intersections. The best-known, and certainly one of the most popular of these, is Harvard Square. It's a people-watcher's paradise, as the bustle of aristocratic Harvard students (some actually wearing their sweaters tied over their shoulders), mohawked punks, camera-toting tourists, homeless panhandlers and harried, suit-wearing businesspeople creates a diverse and colourful street scene.

Coming out of the Harvard Square T station, the biggest local landmark is right in front of you: **Out of Town News**, which stocks a wide selection of periodicals from all over the world, is the area's popular meeting place. Right next to it is a pedestrianised space known as 'the Pit' – not much to look at when nobody's around, but it has been a haven for street kids since punk rock broke in the 1970s.

There are usually street performers on every corner of the square when the weather is fine, but a favourite spot is outside the local branch of the chain **Au Bon Pain** (111 Massachusetts Avenue, at Harvard Square, 1-617 354 4144). This is an ideal place to relax outdoors and observe local street life. An added bonus are the numerous chess experts who set up at the outdoor tables; for a buck or two they'll let you challenge them, or for a few more, you can get a one-on-one lesson.

The streets of Harvard Square are lined with restaurants, cafés and shops, though the influx of mega-chains over the past 15 years has largely diminished the neighbourhood feel. Though it may not be the bohemian enclave it once was, Harvard Square still has a lot to offer, including the independent cinema **Brattle Theatre** (*see p193*). The other top-line arts venue in the area is the legendary **Club Passim** (*see p209*), a folk club that helped to launch the careers of Joan Baez and Suzanne Vega, among others. Other highlights in the area are **Cardullo's** (*see p173*), a wonderful gourmet food shop, and **Leavitt & Peirce** (1316 Massachusetts Avenue, 1-617 547 0576), an old-fashioned tobacconists that's been in the same location for more than 100 years.

Bibliophiles will be in heaven in Cambridge, which is said to have the most booksellers per square mile of any city in America. Among the best-loved are **Grolier Poetry Book Shop** (*see p163*); and the **Harvard Book Store** (*see p164*), a scholarly shop where you can happily get lost for hours among the shelves. You'll find graphic novels at **Newbury Comics** (36 John F Kennedy Street, 1-617 491 0337, www.newburycomics.com), located in the Garage mall, which also houses **Tokyo Kid** (1-617 661 9277, www.tokyokid.com), a mine of all things anime.

From Harvard Square it's a short stroll to the **Charles River**. Just walk down John F Kennedy Street and you'll soon run directly into the river embankment. There are walking paths in both directions. It's especially pleasant on summer Sundays when Memorial Drive is closed to traffic, and scores of runners, bladers and bikers take over the street.

In the opposite direction, at Garden Street and Mass Ave, is the lovely grassy **Cambridge Common**, established in 1631. William Dawes rode across it before the battles of Lexington and Concord; it's also where George Washington took control of the Continental Army in 1775 and a plaque marks the elm tree under which the troops were mustered. Nearby, **Christ Church** (*see p97*) is the site where George and Martha Washington once worshipped. Right next to the church is the **Old Burying Ground**, also known as 'God's Acre'. It first began life as a cemetery in 1635, and thus contains the remains of early settlers.

Brattle Street was once called Tory Row, and several of the mansions of its former wealthy merchant residents remain. The further you venture from Harvard Square on Brattle, the older and grander the houses become. The **Longfellow National Historic Site** is a 28-room mansion where the poet lived from 1837 until his death in 1882. It is also one of the many spots in Cambridge where George Washington spent time during the Revolutionary War. A few doors down is the headquarters of the Cambridge Historical Society, which, appropriately, has set up shop in the oldest house in Cambridge, the 1688 **Hooper-Lee-Nichols House** (159 Brattle Street, 1-617 547 4252).

Another pleasant walk, with a more modern slant, is along Mass Ave north of Harvard Square towards Porter Square. Starting at the Cambridge Common, the broad avenue passes Harvard Law School and an array of small independent restaurants and shops, before running into Porter Square.

Christ Church

Zero Garden Street, at Massachusetts Avenue, Cambridge (1-617 876 0200). Harvard T. **Open** 7am-6pm Mon-Fri, Sun; 7am-3pm Sat. **Map** p278 A2.

Designed in 1761 by the country's first trained architect, Peter Harrison, Christ Church was a hotbed of rebel activity during the Revolutionary War. The walls are still peppered with bullet holes. While much here is original to the building, the organ's pipes are not. The originals were melted down to make bullets during the war.

Old Burying Ground

Massachusetts Avenue, at Garden Street, Cambridge (Cambridge Historical Commission 1-617 349 4683). Harvard T. **Open** dawn-dusk daily. **Map** p278 A2.

Beautiful **Mount Auburn Cemetery**.

This was one of the country's first cemeteries. It contains the remains of several early Puritan settlers as well as Revolutionary War victims and veterans.

Kendall Square

Harvard notwithstanding, some very bright folks attend that other top Cambridge college, the **Massachusetts Institute of Technology** in Kendall Square. MIT was founded in 1861 and rose to prominence during World War II when radar was invented in its labs. The architecture of its various buildings is wildly diverse, ranging from the neo-classical walls of Building 10 to some striking modern structures, including the new Frank Gehry-designed Ray and Maria Stata Center (*see p31*). MIT also boasts its fair share of impressive museums, from the cutting-edge **List Visual Arts Center** to the multimedia **MIT Museum** (for both *see p111*). One of the most amusing exhibitions in the latter is the 'MIT Hall of Hacks' installation, chronicling the various pranks pulled by MIT students over the years.

MIT doesn't have the same connection with Kendall Square that Harvard has with its square, so the area doesn't really have a striking identity. But you'll find some good restaurants and bars and a popular art house cinema, the **Kendall Square Cinema** (*see p194*).

Central Square

The polar opposite of bland Kendall, Central Square is characterised by never-ending hustle and bustle, from the early morning rush hour to late-night club crawls. Once a lower-income section of Cambridge, Central Square still has an African-American and immigrant community. Over the past few years, though, it's become a desirable neighbourhood for recent college grads and young professionals – high-rise condos and the ubiquitous chains have followed. On the plus side, so have some great restaurants.

The many inexpensive ethnic eateries in the area, and a profusion of nightclubs and bars, make Central Square a popular place for an evening out. Fabled rock clubs the **Middle East** (*see p211*) and **TT the Bear's Place** (*see p212*) share the same block. Other hangouts, like the working-class **Cantab Lounge** (*see p209*), the Rat Packy **Good Life** (*see p147*), and the ultra-chilled lounge bar **ZuZu** (*see p212*) put spins on familiar themes. Irish pub **Phoenix Landing** (*see p154*), for example, holds electronica and reggae nights.

During the day, an assortment of Indian markets, record shops, cheap clothing stores, cafés and one sexual fetish shop make it an interesting browse for the alternative shopper.

About a mile (one-and-a-half kilometres) from Central is **Inman Square**, an area distinguished primarily by a high concentration of reasonably priced restaurants, including Portuguese places run by the local immigrant community (*see pp114-143*). Unfortunately the square isn't accessible by T, but it's worth making the trip nonetheless.

A short drive to the edge of Cambridge brings you to **Fresh Pond**, at the end of Fresh Pond Parkway (take the 72 bus from Harvard T). The Pond was used in the 1800s as an ice source and today is a peaceful reservoir with a two-mile (four-kilometre) perimeter and constantly changing scenery. To its south lies the vast **Mount Auburn Cemetery**, the country's first garden cemetery. This is a lovely and peaceful place, where many of the city's most famed residents, including Charles Bulfinch, are buried.

Mount Auburn Cemetery

580 Mount Auburn Street, at Aberdeen Avenue, Cambridge (1-617 547 7105/www.mountauburn.org). Harvard T then 71 or 73 bus. **Open** *Cemetery* 8am-5pm daily. *Greenhouse* 8am-4pm Mon-Fri; 8am-noon Sat. **Admission** free.

This is the final resting place for Oliver Wendell Holmes, Winslow Homer, Charles Bulfinch, Henry Wadsworth Longfellow and some 86,000 others. In fact, the cemetery is now so full that locals who want to spend eternity at Mount Auburn have to settle for cremation. But there's plenty of life here too. There are 4,000 types of trees and 130 species of shrub alone on its 174 acres (70 hectares), and excellent free guided tours to help you distinguish them.

Further Afield

Hang out in Malcolm X's old haunt or visit JFK's boyhood home.

Vibrant **Jamaica Plain**.

Roxbury

Ten years ago, Roxbury was an unlikely stop for tourists. The inner-city neighbourhood had fallen on hard times: crime was up, employment was down, and the warehouses and factories that had once generated a booming trade in manufacturing were boarded up and long abandoned. But thanks to grass-roots activism by residents and a boost in state funding, the area is experiencing something of a renaissance.

Founded in 1630 by British colonists, Roxbury flourished first as a farming community, and later as a bustling industrial centre. During the 1950s, the neighbourhood became famous for its swinging jazz scene. It was during this period that Roxbury's most notorious resident moved to town. For several years, Malcolm Little, aka Malcolm X, lived here with his half-sister, Ella. One of his favourite haunts, **Bob the Chef's Café** (*see p120*), still serves soul food and live music on the Roxbury-South End border.

One of the sights worth visiting is the beautiful **First Church of Roxbury** (10 Putnam Street, at Dudley Street, 1-617 445 8393, Roxbury Crossing T), near John Eliot Square. Built in 1803, this is the oldest wooden church in Boston and the bell in its tower was cast by patriot and silversmith Paul Revere. Also in the area, the **Shirley-Eustis House**, is one of the few remaining examples of pre-revolutionary architecture. The **Eliot Burying Ground** (Eustis Street, at Washington Street), established in 1630, is another surviving site. Several colonial governors, as well as Reverend John Eliot (whose interest in Native Americans inspired him to translate the Bible into Algonquin), are buried here. Reflecting Roxbury's more recent history as an almost exclusively black neighbourhood is the **Museum of the National Center for Afro-American Artists** (*see p109*).

Shirley-Eustis House

33 Shirley Street, at Massachusetts Avenue (1-617 442 2275/www.shirleyeustishouse.org). 1 bus. **Open** *June-Sept* noon-4pm Thur-Sun. *Oct-May* by appointment only. **Admission** $5; $3 concessions. **No credit cards.**

This house was built between 1747 and 1751 for the Royal Colonial Governor William Shirley; ironically, it later served as barracks for Revolutionary forces during the war. Another governor, Dr William Eustis, subsequently lived here, and several major figures – both George Washington and Benjamin Franklin among them – have dropped in for a visit. With its refurbished marble floors and lovely period furniture, the well-preserved residence, spread over an acre (half a hectare) of land, gives a glimpse of life in pre-Revolutionary Roxbury.

Jamaica Plain

Defying every stuffy Bostonian stereotype, the lively village of Jamaica Plain, or JP, as it's more commonly called, radiates an earthy, bohemian charm. It contains the city's largest Latino population and its highest concentration of artists, as well as having a thriving queer community. Recently there's been an influx of hip young professionals, causing rents to rise and boutiques and yoga studios to set up shop alongside Latino bakeries and barber shops – yet there's surprisingly little friction here. The area around the main drag, Centre Street, is literally vibrant: streets are lined with rambling Victorian houses painted in splashy tropical colours, and murals decorate the sides of commercial buildings. Check out the lush jungle scene outside Petal & Leaf (467 Centre Street, between Roseway and South Huntington Streets), and the tropical sunset adorning a building at Centre and Hall Streets.

The best spot for people watching is **JP Lick's** (*see p142*), an ice-cream place with a rabid local following – pretty much everybody passes through at some point – and the **Centre Street Café** (669 Centre Street, 1-617 524 9217) is a great place for a relaxed lunch. Situated on the tree-lined Jamaica Pond, and blessed with acres of parkland, JP is easily one of the most verdant parts of the city. In the spring, the **Arnold Arboretum**, a sprawling botanical park, explodes with blossom, attracting walkers, joggers and cyclists. **Franklin Park**, a somewhat careworn 527-acre (213-hectare) spread, features a woodland preserve, golf course and zoo. Frederick Law Olmsted, who designed the park, considered it to be his masterwork, which makes its current disrepair all the more unfortunate. Across from Franklin Park is the **Forest Hills Cemetery**, which contains the graves of several literary icons and colonial heroes.

Arnold Arboretum

125 Arborway, at Routes 203 & 1 (1-617 524 1718/ www.arboretum.harvard.edu). Forest Hills T. **Open** *Grounds* dawn-dusk daily. *Visitors' centre* May-Oct 9am-4pm Mon-Fri, 10am-4pm Sat, noon-4pm Sun. Nov-Apr 10am-2pm Sat, Sun. **Admission** free. Free public tours one Sat each month.

The arboretum is named after James Arnold, who financed its development and left it, along with his fortune, to Harvard University. He asked that it

Strange sights indeed

They're not on the Freedom Trail, but urban adventurers may want to venture into the 'burbs to check out these monuments to local colour, kitsch – or just plain weirdness.

Laugh if you must, but plumbing is a crucial element of modern civilisation – and grossly overlooked by those of us privileged enough to enjoy it. In light of this oversight, the **American Sanitary Plumbing Museum** (39 Piedmont Street, at Davis Street, Worcester, 1-508 754 9453) pays loving tribute to all manner of bathroom fixtures, including toilets, bathtubs, foot baths, wash basins and elaborate shower heads.

From the I-93, it's hard to miss the enormous, rainbow-striped gas tank resting majestically on the Dorchester waterfront. But a quick glimpse at this landmark, the world's largest copyrighted art work, doesn't do justice to its bizarre legacy. In 1971, Boston Gas commissioned Corita Kent, a nun, activist and artist, to transform its plain white tank into a masterpiece. The real mystery is whether Kent – a vocal anti-war activist – deliberately incorporated the profile of revolutionary leader Ho Chi Minh into the left edge of the tank's blue stripe. According to local legend, Kent surreptitiously included the image as a statement against the Vietnam War. But we'll never know for sure, because Kent – who died in 1986 – never confirmed or denied the rumours.

In East Boston, a 35-foot (ten-metre) bronze-and-copper rendering of the Blessed Virgin Mary looms at the top of a hill overlooking, oddly enough, the airport (**Madonna Queen National Shrine**, 111 Orient Avenue, at Selma Street, 1-617-569-2100). It's a strange, stark image, trimmed with golden spurs and surrounded by a bleak stone plaza. Erected in 1954, the statue is a replica of one near Rome by the Jewish sculptor Arrigo Minerbi, who created the original as thanks to a group of Catholic priests who had offered him refuge in Italy during World War II. All in all, it's one of the more unsettling sights in town, and not to be missed by those with a taste for religious iconography and/or extreme kitsch.

With such winning visuals as a 12-foot (3.5metre) orange dinosaur, a three-storey 'Leaning Tower of Pizza' and a herd of lifesize fibreglass cows to its credit, the stretch of Route 1 running between Boston and Saugus is not known for its subtlety. Instead, the overdeveloped strip has become a shrine to clichéd Americana: pretty much everything here is outsized and in bad taste, from theme restaurants to miniature golf courses and discount shopping emporiums.

should grow 'all the trees [and] shrubs... either indigenous or exotic, which can be raised in the open air.' Today, the arboretum's living, breathing tree museum is a bountiful resource for botanists and other scholars, but it's also a spectacular public park.

Forest Hills Cemetery

95 Forest Hills Avenue, at Route 203 (1-617 524 0128). Forest Hills T. **Open** dawn-dusk daily. **Admission** free.

Literary giants ee cummings, Eugene O'Neill and Anne Sexton are all buried here, as is the abolitionist William Lloyd Garrison. The Sculpture Path, which includes work by artists across the country, gives the cemetery the feel of an open-air museum.

Loring-Greenough House

12 South Street, at Centre Street (1-617 524 3158/ www.lghouse.org). Green St T then 15min walk/ 39 bus. **Open** *June-Aug* 10am-noon Tue; noon-3pm Sat-Sun. *Sept-May* 10am-noon Tue, Sat; or by appointment. **Admission** $5. **No credit cards**.

This house, originally built as a country home for Joshua Loring, a wealthy officer of the British navy, was confiscated after the Revolutionary War; it subsequently housed five generations of the Greenough family. In 1924 it was turned into a museum.

Sam Adams Brewery

30 Germania Street, at Brookside Ave (1-617 368 5080/www.samadams.com). Stony Brook T. **Tours** 2pm Thur; 2pm, 5.30pm Fri; noon, 1pm, 2pm Sat; 2pm Wed (May-Aug only). **Admission** $2. **No credit cards**.

This small-batch brewery, named after the brewer turned-revolutionary, offers tours that walk you through the brewing process, beginning with the selection of ingredients and ending with the finished product – which you're invited to sample.

Brookline

Located four miles (six kilometres) west of downtown Boston, Brookline is one of Boston's prettiest and most affluent suburbs. In addition to great restaurants and shopping, several sights make a trip worthwhile. One is for garden lovers – the **Frederick Law Olmsted National Historic Site** (99 Warren Street, at Dudley Street, 1-617 566 1689) is the former home of the creator of the Emerald Necklace (*see p29*). Not surprisingly, it's flanked by lush gardens, and contains some of Olmsted's design plans. The grounds are open from 10am to 4.30pm Friday to Sunday; call for tour info. Another major attraction is the birthplace and boyhood home of former President **John F Kennedy**. The small house was carefully restored after JFK's death under the supervision of his mother, Rose. On a more whimsical note, the **Larz Anderson Auto Museum**, in the vast Larz Anderson Park, exhibits America's oldest car collection (*see p112*).

John F Kennedy Birthplace

83 Beals Street, at Harvard Avenue (1-617 566 7937/www.nps.gov/jofi). Coolidge Corner T. **Open** *May-Nov* 10am-4.30pm Wed-Sun. **Tours** every half hour from 10am-3pm. **Admission** $3; free under-17s.

The former home of the country's 35th president has been restored to its appearance at the time of his birth, in 1917. It was donated by the Kennedy family.

South Boston

This blue-collar, Irish-Catholic, conservative-Democrat community, known as 'Southie', remained virtually unchanged for almost a century, but like every corner of the city, it's being colonised by young, university-educated folk looking for affordable rents. And the development of the South Boston Waterfront District will no doubt push property values up further. Southie's signature triple-decker homes and New York-style grid system of streets reflect its past as a purpose-built immigrant district, dating from the early 1800s. Dominated by organised crime in the 20th century, it gained a reputation as one of Boston's toughest neighbourhoods. But the mood on Southie's two main thoroughfares is changing. Smart new eateries have been popping up on East and West Broadway. **Woody's L Street Tavern** (658 East 8th Street, at L Street, 1-617 268 1335), has been given a facelift, but is still recognisable as the dive where Matt Damon and Ben Affleck hung out in *Good Will Hunting*.

While there is not much in the way of tourist sights, the **Dorchester Heights Monument** (Thomas Park, south of Broadway and G Street) built in 1898, is worth a visit. The spot marks the site of a former military encampment used by the troops of General George Washington when he was pushing the British out of Boston. It is said that when Washington brought his forces up to Dorchester Heights on 17 March 1776, he had the cultural prescience to order the troops to use the password 'Saint Patrick'. This explains why St Patrick's Day here is also called Evacuation Day.

Castle Island Park and Fort Independence

East end of William J Day Boulevard at Shore Road (1-617 268 5744). Broadway T then 9 or 11 bus. **Open** 6am-11pm daily. **Admission** free.

South Boston lays claim to one of the city's most appealing shoreline parks: Castle Island, although it has been attached to the mainland since the 1930s. First fortified by the British in 1634 and originally called Castle William, the island's main attraction is Fort Independence, a bastioned granite fort, which provided harbour defence from the Revolutionary War to World War II. The island's green spaces and ocean air make for a pleasant outing.

Guided Tours

Whether by land or by sea – or a combination of both – there are myriad ways to explore the city.

Boston's tours can get pretty hokey. You might be urged to rub a lion's tail for luck, asked to quack like a duck, or be subject to corny asides meant for the 'ladies' on the tour. Happily, you'll receive some useful knowledge mixed with the guides' bad puns and constant use of superlatives.

Bicycle tours

Boston Bike Tours

Information 1-617 308 5902/www.bostonbiketours.com. Tours meet at the beginning of the Freedom Trail on Boston Common, Downtown. Park Street T. **Tours** *Apr-Oct* 10.30am, 2.30pm Mon, Wed-Sat; 11am Sun. **Rates** $20 including bike rental; *Sun* $25. **Credit** AmEx, MC, V. **Map** p274 K4.

This company offers interesting two-and-a-half-hour bike tours (four hours on Sundays) through historic neighbourhoods and parks. Bicycles, plus helmets and water are supplied.

Boat tours

Bay State Cruise Company

Information 1-617 748 1428/www.baystatecruises.com. Tours leave from 200 Seaport Boulevard, at World Trade Center, South Boston. South Station T then 7 bus. **Tours** *Entertainment cruise* June-Sept 8.30pm Fri, Sat. *Ferry* May-Sept 8am, 9.30am, 1pm, 5.30pm daily. **Rates** *Entertainment cruise* $16-$25; *ferry* $18-$58; $14-$39 concessions. **Credit** AmEx, MC, V. **Map** p275 N5.

Entertainment cruises feature local talent playing jazz, blues and rock. Bay State also offers fast ferry services to points along Cape Cod and Rhode Island.

Boston Harbor Cruises

Information 1-617 227 4321/1-877 733 9425/www.bostonharborcruises.com. Tours leave from 1 Long Wharf, next to the New England Aquarium, Waterfront. Aquarium T. **Tours** *USS Constitution Cruise* Apr-Nov every hour on the half hour 10.30am-4.30pm. *Historic Sightseeing Cruise* May-Sept 11am, 1pm, 3pm daily. *Sunset Cruise* May-Sept 7pm daily. **Rates** $12-$18; $9-$16 concessions. **Credit** AmEx, MC, V. **Map** p275 M4.

BHC provides a variety of themed sightseeing, entertainment and meal cruises, as well as whale-watching excursions (call for schedules, which vary with the season).

Charles Riverboat Company

Information 1-617 621 3001/www.charlesriverboat.com. Tours leave from Lechmere Canal, at CambridgeSide Galleria, 100 CambridgeSide Place, at Charles Street, Cambridge. Lechmere T then 5mins walk. **Tours** *June-Aug* 10am, 11.30am, 1pm, 2.30pm, 4pm daily. *Apr, May, Sept* 10am, 11.30am, 1pm, 2.30pm, 4pm Sat, Sun. **Rates** $10; $6-$9 concessions. **Credit** MC, V.

The Charles River tour departs from the Lechmere Canal at the CambridgeSide Galleria mall (handy if you want to do a spot of shopping first), then cruises the Charles River basin, taking in the sights along the way. Other tours, including Boston Harbor by paddleboat, are available.

Odyssey Cruises

Information 1-617 654 9700/1-888 741 0281/www.odysseycruises.com. Tours leave from Rowes Wharf, at Boston Harbor Hotel, Waterfront. State or Aquarium T. **Tours** *Lunch cruise* 11am daily. *Dinner cruise* 6pm Mon-Thur; 7pm Fri, Sat; 5pm Sun. *Midday cruise* 2.45pm Mon-Thur; 3pm Fri, Sat. *Moonlight cruise* midnight (subject to

Whale-watching with **Boston Harbor Cruises**.

availability; call in advance). **Rates** $32-$89. **Credit** AmEx, DC, Disc, MC, V. **Map** p275 M4.
Take brunch, lunch or dinner on the water. Odyssey offers meal cruises with musical entertainment.

Speciality tours

Art and Architecture Tour of the Boston Public Library

Information 1-617 536 5400/www.bpl.org/guides. Tours meet at Boston Public Library's Dartmouth Street entrance, Copley Square. Copley T. **Tours** 2.30pm Mon; 6pm Tue, Thur; 11am Fri, Sat; 2pm Sun. **Rates** free. **Map** p277 G6.
It's easy to join in one of these informal 50-minute surveys of the McKim Building, dubbed a 'cigar box' by its contemporaries. What did they know? Its Mitford granite, Iowa sandstone and Siena marble are exquisite. You'll see seals sculpted by Augustus St Gaudens, Pierre Puvis de Chavannes' murals and spectacular ceiling panels painted by John Singer Sargent.

Boston Athenæum Tour

Information 1-617 227 0270/www.boston athenaeum.org. Tours meet at 10½ Beacon Street, Beacon Hill. Park Street T. **Tours** 3pm Tue, Thur. **Rates** free. **Map** p275 K4.
This independent library and historic landmark has an art collection that includes works by John Singer Sargent. Athenæum docents conduct hour-long art and architecture tours for bookworms on Tuesdays and Thursdays. Advance reservations are required.

Fenway Park Tour

Information 1-617 236 6666/www.redsox.com. Tours meet at Fenway Park, Gate D, Yawkey Way and Van Ness Street, Fenway. Kenmore T. **Tours** hourly 9am-4pm daily; game days 9am-3 hrs before game. **Rates** $10; $8-$9 concessions. **Credit** AmEx, Disc, MC, V. **Map** p276 D7.
'Thumpin' Theodore' and 'Teddy Ballgame' – the colourful nicknames of legendary Boston Red Sox Player Ted Williams are a fraction of the lore you'll reap during this intensive hour. A highlight is the view from atop the 'Green Monster', the Park's trademark green-hued 37-foot-tall (11m) left-field wall.

Michele Topor's North End Market Tours

Information 1-617 523 6032/www.northend markettours.com. Tours leave from 6 Charter Street, at Hanover Street, North End. Haymarket T. **Tours** 10am, 2pm Wed, Sat; 10am, 3pm Fri. **Rates** $47.25. **Credit** AmEx, Disc, MC, V. **Map** p275 L2.
Vivacious guide Topor likes to make eye contact, so you can't nap on this three-and-a-half-hour culinary tour. But you won't want to, since the former nurse and longtime neighbourhood resident will bombard you with tips on the Italian language, cooking, and proper nutrition. The tour takes in around 10 shops and producers – and you'll enjoy samples at most stops. Wear comfortable footwear and bring a notebook. *See p87* **Topor's taste of Italy**.

Themed vehicles

Boston Duck Tours

Information 1-617 723 3825/www.bostonduck tours.com. Tours leave from the Prudential Center, Huntington Avenue, Hynes/ICA or Prudential T; or from the Museum of Science, Science Park, Charles River Dam, Science Park T. **Tours** *Apr-Nov* every 30-60mins, 9am-sunset. **Rates** $24; $15-$21 concessions. **Credit** AmEx, Disc, MC, V. **Map** p277 G7/p274 H2.
Travel by land *and* sea – in a restyled World War II amphibious landing craft remodelled as a tour vehicle. Manned by so-called conDUCKtors the tours are informative and especially fun for kids.

Boston Old Town Trolley Tours

Information 1-617 269 7150/www.trolleytours.com. Tours leave from Old Atlantic Avenue, at New England Aquarium, Waterfront. Aquarium T. **Tours** *Apr-Oct* every 15-20mins 9am-5pm daily; *Nov-Mar* every 25-30mins 9am-4pm daily. **Rates** $35; $23 concessions; free under-12s. Specialised tours up to $50. **Credit** AmEx, Disc, MC, V. **Map** p275 M4.
One of these faux trolley cars (they ride on wheels, not rails) always seems to be passing you no matter where you are. This company offers a host of seasonal specialised tours – from a chocolate tour to a John F Kennedy tour. You can leave and rejoin the tour at will, which is useful if you want to get a better look at a particular building or neighbourhood.

Walking tours

For the Black Heritage Trail and self-guided walking trails, *see p65* **On the trails...**

Boston by Foot

Information 1-617 367 2345/www.bostonbyfoot.com. Tours leave from a variety of locations; call in advance. **Tours** *May-Oct* departure time varies according to tour. **Rates** $10 adults; $8 children. **Credit** (advance purchases only) MC, V.
Boston by Foot offers a broad array of 90-minute historical and architectural tours, and its several hundred volunteer tour guides encourage questions. Tours focus on neighbourhoods or themes, like Victorian Back Bay or Literary Landmarks. Themed or group tours are available upon request.

WalkBoston

Information 1-617 367 9255/www.walkboston.org. Tours leave from a variety of locations; call in advance. **Tours** departure times vary according to tour. **Rates** $5. **No credit cards**.
This group offers a shifting menu of offbeat tours based on demand, including the only one that circumnavigates the new addition to Boston's skyline – the majestic cable-stayed Zakim Bridge (*see p28*). One of the bridge's architects sometimes leads the tour, which runs between the North End and Charlestown. Other tours include Dorchester Lower Mills, Jamaica Plain, the upper Charles River, South Boston, and Alewife.

Museums

If the famously unpredictable weather turns nasty, gawp at fine-art masterpieces, dusty archaeological collections or wacky curiosities.

John F Kennedy Library & Museum: IM Pei's modernist temple to JFK. *See p112.*

John Singer Sargent, the late 19th-century realist painter and renowned portraitist, didn't spend much time in the United States or even Boston, the city where he had his first solo show at the age of 21. Yet Sargent is a consummate New England artist. For one, he befriended Isabella Stewart Gardner, matriarch of Boston's fine-arts scene (*see p107* **Gardner's world**), and painted a portrait of her that still hangs in the **Gardner Museum**'s Gothic Room. But, more importantly, Sargent's serene realism and wistful scenes capture New England's quaint, sweetly conservative character, which is probably why his work is a standard in the region. There are major Sargent murals at the **Boston Public Library** and the **Museum of Fine Arts**, plus pieces in Harvard's **Fogg Museum** and Andover's **Addison Gallery of American Art**.

Considering Boston's Sargent fixation, along with its undying devotion to the Impressionists and preserved artefacts, it's no surprise that the city's cluster of museums gets criticised for being stuck in the past. But Boston is not only a richly historical place, it's also the home of an academic community built on progress. So contemporary works appear at many of the university galleries and museums like MIT's **List Visual Arts Center**, Brandeis's **Rose Art Museum** and Harvard's **Sert Gallery**. And developments like the construction of a new Institute of Contemporary Art along Boston's waterfront (*see p92* **Future vision**) and a major addition to the Museum of Fine Arts herald much promise for the city's visual-arts future. For museums further afield in Concord, Salem, Plymouth and elsewhere on the Massachusetts coast, *see pp230-246.*

Visual arts museums

Addison Gallery of American Art

Phillips Academy, Main Street, Andover (1-978 749 4027/www.andover.edu/addison). **Open** 10am-5pm Tue-Sat; 1-5pm Sun. **Admission** free.

Though it's situated at a boarding school in suburban Andover, don't let the setting put you off. This mid-sized museum is worth the 40-minute drive if you can get your hands on a car. Some aesthetic snobs sneer at photography, but the Addison regards picture-taking as a fine art, featuring prints by Ansel Adams, Man Ray, Walker Evans and others. The permanent painting collection is categorically New England, with major works by Winslow Homer, James Abbott McNeill Whistler and John Singer Sargent. If you get a giggle out of miniature *objets d'art*, there's also a basement of model ships enumerating the history of American sailboats.

DeCordova Museum & Sculpture Park

51 Sandy Pond Road, off Route 2 or 128, Lincoln (1-781 259 8355/www.decordova.org). **Open** 11am-5pm Tue-Sun. **Admission** $6; $4 concessions; free under-12s. **Credit** MC, V.

West of Boston on a sprawling site, the DeCordova Museum and Sculpture Park presents a gallimaufry of modern works and styles, including photography, painting, installation art and digital montage. The recently expanded castle-like premises (the former estate of Boston entrepreneur Julian de Cordova, 1850-1945) is the largest contemporary art museum in the region. Devoted to New England talent, the DeCordova holds renowned annual shows of the most accomplished artists in the area. On the grounds outside, an ever-changing array of enormous sculptures bespeckle the 35 acre (14 hectare) outdoor park, a grass-and-stone terrain on which visitors can picnic or listen to concerts.

Institute of Contemporary Art

955 Boylston Street, at Massachusetts Avenue, Back Bay (1-617 266 5152/www.icaboston.org). Hynes/ ICA T. **Open** noon-5pm Tue, Wed, Fri; noon-9pm Thur; 11am-5pm Sat, Sun. **Admission** $7; $5 concessions; free under-12s; free to all 5-9pm Thur. **Credit** AmEx, MC, V. **Map** p276 F7.

Currently in a converted 19th-century brick fire station, the ICA plans to move into a state-of-the-art new glass building along Boston's waterfront by 2006 (*see p92* **Future vision**). With no permanent collection until that relocation, the ICA now stages a changing programme of exhibitions. One of the few institutions in this smart yet culturally conservative city willing to take big intellectual and political risks with the content of its shows, the ICA aims to be an 'experimental laboratory'. It upholds this mission by consistently introducing rising stars to Boston, sometimes even the US. This is evidenced by a new project series entitled 'Moment', featuring emerging artists, which is slotted into the museum's main programme.

Isabella Stewart Gardner Museum

280 The Fenway, at Palace Road, Fenway (1-617 566 1401/www.gardnermuseum.org). Museum of Fine Arts T. **Open** 11am-5pm Tue-Sun. **Admission** $11 Sat, Sun; $10 Mon-Fri; $5-$7 concessions; free under-18s. **Credit** AmEx, Disc, MC, V. **Map** p276 D8.

Built in the style of a 15th-century Venetian palace, everything in this lavish museum, from the luxuriant greenhouse-style courtyard to the scalloped archway framing John Singer Sargent's *El Jaleo*, is part of the exhibition. Isabella Stewart Gardner, an eccentric arts patron who lived and entertained here early in the 20th century (*see p107* **Gardner's world**), wanted the arrangement of the paintings, tapestries, objects, ceilings, and terraces to engage the imagination. So every piece in the 2,500-piece collection – a medley of sculptures, rare books, and artworks created by the likes of Rembrandt, Botticelli and Raphael – is meticulously placed according to Gardner's personal instructions. And since the museum was the site of the largest American art heist back in 1990 – when two thieves dressed as police officers took five Degas pieces, three Rembrandts and a Vermeer – the security staff is so vigilant it'll pounce if you so much as look at an artwork in a funny way. And don't even think about touching.

Mills Gallery & Cyclorama

Boston Center for the Arts, 539 Tremont Street, at Clarendon Street, Back Bay (1-617 426 8835/ www.bcaonline.org). Back Bay T. **Open** *exhibitions* noon-5pm Wed, Thur; noon-10pm Fri, Sat; noon-5pm Sun. **Admission** free. **Map** p277 H7.

Expect the unexpected at the Mills Gallery, which focuses on presenting new works by artists with ties to Boston and New England, and which has been the site of conceptual shows like 'Restroom: Privacy and Consciousness', an exhibition that included hanging used soap bars and a week's worth of urine samples. Next door, the 23,000-square-foot (2,137-square-metre) Cyclorama is a circular, domed structure built in 1884 to exhibit the huge painting by Dominique Philippoteaux of the Civil War battle of Gettysburg. The painting went on tour five years later never to return – it's now on display in Gettysburg – and today large, experimental works show up in the space.

Museum of Fine Arts

Avenue of the Arts, 465 Huntington Avenue, at Museum Road, Fenway (1-617 267 9300/ www.mfa.org). Museum of Fine Arts T. **Open** 10am-4.45pm Mon, Tue; 10am-9.45pm Wed-Fri (only West Wing Galleries open after 4.45pm Thur, Fri); 10am-5.45pm Sat, Sun. **Admission** $15; $6.50-$13 concessions; free under-6s; free under-17s weekends & school holidays; free to all 4.45-9.45pm Wed. **Credit** AmEx, Disc, MC, V. **Map** p276 D8.

The distinguished grandpa of the New England art world, the MFA is the largest, oldest and most expansive of Boston's mainstream museums. With

Gardner's world

There are many famous tales about **Isabella Stewart Gardner**, founder and namesake of the eponymous museum. She bedecked her slippers with rubies. She was the inspiration for Isabel Archer, the heiress protagonist in Henry James's *Portrait of a Lady*. When artist James McNeill Whistler promised her a painting and then reneged on the deal, the feisty woman took matters into her own hands and pilfered the piece.

But it's difficult to distinguish fact from fiction in Gardner's life. A favourite subject of local gossip columns, she never bothered to quash untrue rumours and even liked to joke, 'Don't spoil a good story by telling the truth.'

What's known about Gardner, the grande dame of the Boston arts world, is that she was born in 1840 to a moneyed New York family. At 20, after attending private schools in New York and Paris, she wed John 'Jack' Gardner, a financier from Boston. In 1863 'Mrs Jack', as she came to be nicknamed, gave birth to a son. The boy died of pneumonia two years later. After the loss, Isabella suffered from depression, so Jack brought his grieving wife to Europe, where her adoration for the arts turned into a lifelong commitment. 'We were a very young country and had very few opportunities of seeing beautiful things,' she wrote in 1917 about the inspiration of the Gardner Museum. 'So I determined to make it my life work if I could.'

Back in the States, Gardner's eccentric ways made her an anomaly among aristocrats. A legendary socialite, she settled in among enlightened artists, hosting fabulous dinner parties for the likes of painter John Singer Sargent, writer Henry James, and philosopher George Santanaya. When Gardner's father passed away in 1891, he left her a sizeable inheritance, which she used to procure masterpieces like Vermeer's *The Concert* and Titian's *Europa*. With their growing art collection, the Gardners decided they would open a museum. But when Jack died suddenly in 1898, Gardner took on the job alone, buying land in the Fens and hiring architect Willard T Sears to turn their vision into a reality. Not surprisingly, Gardner didn't want to build a typical, staid museum with simple white walls and high ceilings. Rather, she wanted to design a setting that was as intricate and stunning as the works it housed. So after designing a 15th-century Venetian-style palazzo, she personally installed her 2,500-piece panoply of artworks – sculptures, paintings, *objets d'art*, rare books, furniture – and organised them not by chronology or origin, but in ways that would enhance their aesthetic presentation. In some cases, her arrangements created awe-inspiring optical illusions.

The Isabella Stewart Gardner Museum first opened on New Year's Day 1903, with its widowed owner residing on the fourth floor, where she lived until her death in 1924. But even in the last decade of her life Gardner continued to scandalise. When the Red Sox won the World Series in 1912, the unabashed baseball fan appeared at Symphony Hall sporting a white headband with the words 'Oh you Red Sox' in red letters. A newspaper scribe later snickered that it looked 'as if the woman had gone crazy'. Somewhere, Gardner was probably smiling.

For the **Isabella Stewart Gardner Museum**, *see p106*.

Sightseeing

extensive holdings ranging from Asian art to American Colonial and Federal portraits, and with smaller collections studded by gems (European Impressionists and ancient Egyptian artefacts significant among them), the institution has been historically obsessed with Monet – not only do more than 30 of his dreamy masterpieces permanently align the walls, but the French Impressionist shows up in blockbuster exhibitions more often than the Red Sox lose in the playoffs. The MFA is currently undergoing renovations planned for completion in 2009: British architect Norman Foster was hand-picked to expand the MFA's historic building. But with progress comes sacrifice: the museum has had to close various wings during the construction, which could be a disappointment if the branch housing your favourite period isn't accessible. Also, check out the MFA's film programme, which hosts some of Boston's favourite film festivals (*see p194*).

Museum of the National Center of Afro-American Artists

300 Walnut Avenue, at Cobden Street, Roxbury (1-617 442 8614/www.ncaaa.org/museum.html). Ruggles T then 22 bus. **Open** 1-5pm Tue-Sun. **Admission** $4; $3 concessions. **No credit cards.**

The Museum of the NCAAA has been affiliated with the Museum of Fine Arts since the late 1960s, and is the only place in New England committed exclusively to African, Caribbean and Afro-American visual arts. The neo Gothic Victorian mansion in Roxbury houses diverse exhibitions including its permanent display 'Aspelta: a Nubian King's Burial Chamber' and shows like 'Final Exposure: Portraits from Death Row', a stark black-and-white photography series of prisoners awaiting execution.

Worcester Art Museum

55 Salisbury Street, Worcester (1-508 799 4406/ www.worcesterart.org). **Open** 11am-5pm Wed-Fri, Sun; 10am-5pm Sat. **Admission** $8; $6 concessions; free under-17s; free to all 10am-noon Sat.
No credit cards.

The WAM prides itself on having been the first American museum to purchase works by Claude Monet and Paul Gauguin. It has a good eye for the new and presents small but often rewarding contemporary exhibitions alongside selections from its large permanent collection, which is organised geographically and ranges from Egyptian antiquities and Antioch floor mosaics to European Impressionist painting and Early American art.

University collections

Boston College

McMullen Museum of Art

140 Commonwealth Avenue, at College Road, Chestnut Hill (1-617 552 8100/www.bc.edu/art museum). Chestnut Hill T. **Open** 11am-4pm Mon-Fri; noon-5pm Sat, Sun. **Admission** free.

This is a somewhat conservative but genuinely erudite place. With a permanent collection of Flemish tapestries and Italian sacrosanct scenes, the McMullen's idea of curatorial adventure is surrealist painting and street photography. The museum tends to show work that's consistent with the Irish-Catholic college's academic character: Celtic works, microscopic photos of geological formations, and more Madonna pictures than a celebrity-gossip mag.

Brandeis University

Rose Art Museum

415 South Street, Waltham (1-781 736 3434/ www.brandeis.edu/rose). Brandeis/Roberts Commuter Rail. **Open** noon-5pm Tue-Sun. **Admission** free.

This facility offers a fine collection of 20th-century art, with a focus on post-World War II American work. Pieces by de Kooning, Johns, Rauschenberg and Warhol are on display, and there are also contemporary paintings, installations and a terrific programme of changing exhibitions.

Harvard University

Though Harvard's museums all have separate specialties – from the Museum of Natural History's stuffed triceratops to the Fogg's Kiki Smith sculpture *Pee Body* – they're all authorities in their respective fields. The museums are easy to navigate and accessible by public transportation, and if you're planning on visiting the lot, pick up a Harvard Hot Ticket (available at any of the museums listed below). The pass costs $10 for adults or $8 for concessions and is valid for one year from the date of purchase so you can visit the museums at your leisure. If you're only interested in visual arts, a $6.50 ticket ($5 concessions) admits you to the Sackler, the Fogg and the Busch-Reisinger. Entry to the **Semitic Museum** (6 Divinity Avenue, 1-617 495 4631), containing ancient artefacts, is free.

Arthur M Sackler Museum

485 Broadway, at Quincy Street, Cambridge (1-617 495 9400/www.artmuseums.harvard.edu). Harvard T. **Open** 10am-5pm Mon-Sat; 1-5pm Sun. **Admission** *with Fogg Art & Busch-Reisinger Museums* $6.50; $5 concessions; free under-18s; free to all Wed & 10am-noon Sat. **Credit** AmEx, Disc, MC, V. **Map** p278 B2.

The Sackler is the place to peruse ancient objects, from Romanic gambling artefacts to Alexander the Great coins. With two floors of display cases and one floor for special exhibitions, the museum is dedicated to Asian, Islamic, and later Indian art. It houses the widest collection of Chinese jades outside China, an unrivalled showcase of Korean ceramics, and an outstanding collection of Thai illuminated manuscripts. The large permanent collections are displayed on a rotating basis.

DeCordova Museum and Sculpture Park. *See p106.*

Fogg Art Museum & Busch-Reisinger Museum

32 Quincy Street, at Broadway, Cambridge (1-617 495 2397/www.artmuseums.harvard.edu). Harvard T. **Open** 10am-5pm Mon-Sat; 1-5pm Sun. **Admission** *with Arthur M Sackler Museum* $6.50; $5 concessions; free under-18s; free to all Wed & 10am-noon Sat. **Credit** AmEx, Disc, MC, V. **Map** p278 B2.

As Harvard's oldest museum, the Fogg is the unofficial anchor of the university's fine-arts system. Arranged around a Renaissance-style courtyard, the cathedral-like interior is a meditative backdrop for its permanent collection, an assemblage that spans from the Impressionists to British Pre-Raphaelites and the Boston area's most important Picasso collection. Contiguous to the Fogg is Harvard's Busch-Reisinger Museum, the only place in the western hemisphere devoted to the art of German-speaking Europe. With a special emphasis on German Expressionism and Bauhaus artists, the gallery space hangs works by Klee, Kandinsky, Beckmann and Klimt.

Peabody Museum of Archaeology & Ethnology and the Museum of Natural History

11 Divinity Avenue, at Kirkland Street, Cambridge (1-617 496 1027/www.peabody.harvard.edu). Harvard T. **Open** 9am-5pm daily. **Admission** $7.50; $5-$6 concessions; free to all 9am-noon Sun; *May-Sept* free to all 3-5pm Wed. **Credit** AmEx, MC, V. **Map** p278 B2.

The Peabody features fossils and anthropological artefacts from as far back as the Paleolithic period, with exhibitions on North American Indians and Central America. In fact, the museum has so many artefacts that it recently discovered a rare Native American bear-claw necklace acquired by early-19th-century explorers Lewis and Clark in one of its storage rooms. Despite its scientific bent, the building retains the Victorian character of early museum exhibits by displaying relics with descriptive rather than interpretive label texts. Connected to the Peabody is Harvard's Museum of Natural History, which exhibits dinosaur fossils, mineral and rock collections and a menagerie of life-sized stuffed animals – lions, tigers and pheasants – that used to belong to George Washington. A highlight of the museum is the world's only mounted kronosaurus, a 42ft-long (12m) prehistoric marine reptile.

Sert Gallery

24 Quincy Street, in the Carpenter Center for the Visual Arts, Cambridge (1-617 495 9400/ www.artmuseums.harvard.edu). Harvard T. **Open** 10am-5pm Mon-Sat; 1-5pm Sun. **Admission** free. **Map** p278 B2.

A window-encased lobby above the Harvard Film Archive in the Carpenter Center for the Visual Arts – the only building in North America designed by Le Corbusier – the Sert Gallery is an exhibition space of modern and contemporary art with a strong emphasis on photography.

MIT

Compton Gallery

77 Massachusetts Avenue, at MIT Campus, Cambridge (1-617 253 4444). Kendall/MIT T. **Open** 9am-5pm Mon-Fri; noon-5pm Sat. **Admission** free. **Map** p278 C4.

Nestled under MIT's famous dome, the Compton features alternating shows that draw on the institute's historical collection of art and scientific objects. Note that MIT's campus itself also merits attention: sculpture by Louise Nevelson, Alexander Calder and Henry Moore dot its grounds, and buildings by Eero Saarinen, Alvar Aalto and IM Pei are joined by a Frank Gehry computer centre (*see p31*).

List Visual Arts Center

20 Ames Street, at Main Street, Cambridge (1-617 253 4680/web.mit.edu/lvac). Kendall/MIT T. **Open** noon-6pm Tue-Thur, Sat, Sun; noon-8pm Fri. **Admission** free. **Map** p278 C4.

Located on the Wiesner Building's first floor, the List holds rotating shows of challenging, conceptual art. From new-media installations and flashing digital displays to 'haunted hallways', the exhibitions always push the boundaries of contemporary art.

MIT Museum

265 Massachusetts Avenue, at MIT Campus, Cambridge (1-617 253 4444/web.mit.edu/museum). Central T. **Open** 10am-5pm Mon-Fri; noon-5pm Sat, Sun. **Admission** free. **Map** p278 C4.

A ten-minute stroll from MIT's Killian Court, this technological outpost boasts exploding chairs, robotic hands and historical lasers from NASA research. Alexander Graham Bell did research on the MIT campus, so there's a retrospective of early telephonic devices. Also on display are the kinetic sculptures of Arthur Ganson – ingenious, frequently hilarious machines that seem to have minds of their own – and the world's largest collection of holographic art, featuring a morphing Michael Jackson album cover and a woman transmogrifying into a tiger. And since you might expect a little dry-humoured peculiarity from MIT's museum, there's an exhibition that traces the, um, exciting evolution of the slide rule.

Strobe Alley

4th Floor, Building Four, 77 Massachusetts Avenue, at MIT Campus, Cambridge. Kendall/MIT T. **Open** 24hrs daily. **Admission** free. **Map** p278 C4.

Hidden on the fourth floor (go upstairs and walk straight ahead), this narrow passage presents an indefinite show of the photographs of Harold ('Doc') Edgerton, the pioneer of high-speed photography. (Edgerton shot the famous images of a bullet explosively tunnelling through an apple and a crown-shaped splat of milk.) Since the Strobe is quick to exhaust, it's a good excuse to venture beyond Building Four's imposing columns and experience MIT's 'Infinite Corridor', an amazingly long passage that's also a kind of living art installation.

Art schools

Massachusetts College of Art

Bakalar, Huntington & President's Galleries

621 Huntington Avenue, at Longwood Avenue, Fenway (1-617 879 7333/www.massart.edu). Longwood T. **Open** 10am-6pm Mon-Fri; 11am-5pm Sat. **Admission** free.

The only publicly funded school in the US solely dedicated to the fine and decorative arts. Not only do its galleries showcase artists with international reputations, but its student and faculty shows push limits and generate excitement without the name-recognition factor.

School of the Museum of Fine Arts

Grossman Gallery

230 The Fenway, at Museum Road, Fenway (1-617 369 3718). Museum of Fine Arts T. **Open** 10am-5pm Mon-Wed, Fri, Sat; 10am-8pm Thur. **Admission** free. **Map** p276 E9

Just across Museum Road from the MFA, this gallery also boasts a worthy exhibition programme, featuring established artists as well as works by Museum School students.

Other museums

For the **USS Constitution Museum** and the **New England Aquarium**, *see pp88-93*.

Boston Athenæum

10½ Beacon Street, between Bowdoin & Somerset Streets, Beacon Hill (1-617 227 0270). Park Street T. **Open** *Gallery* 9am-5pm Mon-Fri; 9am-4pm Sat. **Admission** free. **Map** p275 K4.

Founded in 1807 as a literary society, the Boston Athenæum published America's first literary magazine and acquired an extensive library of books and works of art. By the dawn of the 20th century, it had helped establish Boston's Museum of Fine Arts and moved into its current home, a giant five-storey building on Beacon Street. Although much of the library is accessible only to members or scholars, the ground-floor gallery is open to the public, and a guided tour of the building's art and architecture can be booked in advance (*see p104*).

Boston Public Library

For listings see p104.

This is America's oldest public library. The original structure, an Italian Renaissance-style building designed by Charles McKim, was extended when an annex designed by Philip Johnson was built in the early 1970s. Along with books and periodicals, the BPL features several galleries exhibiting everything from rare books and manuscripts to photographs of Boston's changing cityscape. Of more interest, perhaps, are permanent fixtures such as the bronze doors designed by Lincoln Memorial architect Daniel Chester French and several newly restored murals by John Singer Sargent.

John F Kennedy Library & Museum

Columbia Point, at Morrissey Boulevard, Dorchester (1-866-535-1960/www.jfklibrary.org). JFK/UMass T then free shuttle bus. **Open** 9am-5pm daily. **Admission** $10; $7-$8 concessions; free under-12s. **Credit** AmEx, Disc, MC, V.

A looming concrete-and-glass monolith designed by IM Pei, the Kennedy Library overlooks the outer harbour from the top of the Columbia Point peninsula. Inside is an extensive display of memorabilia dedicated to the assassinated 35th US president. Included in the permanent exhibition is a timeline of the Kennedy family, films of JFK press conferences and the president's desk. Along with Kennedy memorabilia, the museum also contains books and manuscripts that once belonged to Ernest Hemingway.

Larz Anderson Auto Museum

Larz Anderson Park, 15 Newton Street, Brookline (1-617 522 6547/www.mot.org). Cleveland Circle or Reservoir T then 51 bus. **Open** 10am-5pm Tue-Sun. **Admission** $5; $3 concessions; free under-5s. **No credit cards**.

When Isabel Anderson, the socialite wife of former ambassador Larz, died in 1948, she bequeathed her entire estate to the town of Brookline. It's now the 64-acre (26-hectare) Larz Anderson Park, and in the couple's former carriage house, this non-profit museum displays their impressive collection of vintage motorcars and carriages – acquired over nearly 40 years – as well as other automotive exhibits.

Museum of Afro American History

African Meeting House, 8 Smith Court, off 46 Joy Street, Beacon Hill (1-617 742 5415/www.afroammuseum.org). Charles/MGH T or Park St T. **Open** *June-Aug* 10am-4pm daily. *Sept-May* 10am-4pm Mon-Sat. **Admission** free. **Map** p308 G4.

This museum is essentially two structures of historical significance: the African Meeting House, the oldest black church in the country and the place where the New England Anti-Slavery Society was founded in the 1830s; and the recently restored Abiel Smith School, the nation's first public school for African American children. Though there are exhibitions, interactive touch-screen computers and historic artefacts about African Americans in New England on display, the museum is primarily a historic landmark. Both buildings are stops on the Black Heritage Trail walking tour (*see p65* **On the trails...**).

Museum of Bad Art

Dedham Community Theater, 580 High Street, Dedham (1-781 444 6757/www.museumofbadart.org). **Open** 6-10pm Mon-Fri; 1-10pm Sat, Sun. **Admission** free.

Buried in the basement of a suburban movie theatre is the world's only museum dedicated to abysmally bad art, from laughable renderings of kissing trees, a disproportionate nude with hairy armpits, and a ghastly woman with aquamarine skin. The MOBA acquired much of its permanent collection from trash piles, including *Lucy in the Field With Flowers* – a hilarious portrait of a saggy-breasted grandma angrily gathering daisies in tall grass that became the original inspiration for the museum. So bad it's good.

Museum of Science & Charles Hayden Planetarium

Science Park, between Storrow & Memorial Drives, West End (1-617 723 2500/www.mos.org). Science Park T. **Open** 9am-5pm Mon-Thur, Sat, Sun; 9am-9pm Fri. **Admission** *Museum of Science* $13; $10-$11 concessions. *Charles Hayden Planetarium & Mugar Omni Theater* $8.50; $6.50-$7.50 concessions. **Credit** AmEx, Disc, MC, V. **Map** p277 H2.

From the Gemini Space Ship capsule (which orbited Earth more than 200 times in 1965) to the Thomson Theatre of Electricity (which houses a giant Van de Graaf generator), Boston's Museum of Science is committed to providing an interactive and educational experience, making science accessible to the average person through exhibitions that explain all things scientific in straightforward terms, and via hundreds of different hands-on installations. At the Charles Hayden Planetarium, audiences relaxing in ergonomic seats watch the dome-shaped ceiling as the Zeiss Star Projector creates a realistic night sky before their eyes.

Eat, Drink, Shop

Features

Restaurants & Cafés

After decades in the doldrums, Boston's back on the gastronomic map.

Charlie's Sandwich Shoppe. *See p123.*

How far has Boston come as a food town? Chefs now rank with the Kennedy clan (Senator Ted, the late John-John), the Red Sox (shortstop Nomar and pitcher Pedro) and locally bred actors (Matt and Ben) as the select few who enjoy first-name status. Long-time Cambridge resident Julia Child was awarded the Legion of Honour by the French government for her services to cuisine. Many Bostonians will debate the merits of the latest tasting menu at Ken's (Oringer) **Clio** (*see p115*) or where to procure the best Cubano sandwiches with the kind of bluster once reserved for rebelling against the British.

And that's exactly what has occurred in the last decade: an edible revolution. Though New England was the site of the country's first regional cuisine, Boston spent much of the last century earning a not-so-savoury reputation for bland meat-and-potato cooking. That changed as a gifted crop of chefs began to take the message Julia Child first delivered to heart, mixing humour, respect for tradition, good products and a sense of adventure into their own brand of creative American cooking.

There's certainly a democratic quality to eating here. A new generation of home-grown chefs like Chris Schlesinger of **East Coast Grill** (*see p137*) has given even the highest level of dining a casual ethos. Talents groomed elsewhere, like Rene Michelena of **Saint** (*see p116*), have added vitality by setting up shop here. Global flavours also abound in Boston thanks to a bewildering number of ethnic communities and the large foreign academic contingent. Afghan, Ethiopian, Korean, Moroccan, Tibetan and Brazilian cuisines are readily available alongside authentic Thai, Chinese and Vietnamese stalwarts. Add to that the Portuguese influence (thanks to immigrant fishing communities on the North Shore), soul food and slow-and-low, real-deal barbecue found at places like **Redbones** (*see p143*).

'Eating local' is a catch phrase. Seafood from Georges Bank, traditional breads made from potato or corn, heritage breeds of turkey, and wild game are still as beloved as they were by the settlers. Many places serve cod, scallops, or lobsters caught that morning. Seasonal produce is grown by small collectives, and some restaurants, like **L'Espalier** (*see p117*), have their own farms and herb gardens. Dramatic changes in weather mean everyone from the gifted burrito spinners at **El Pelon Taqueria** (*see p119*) to Todd (English, of **Olives**, *see p133*) must constantly tweak their menus to reflect what is available. In the autumn, chefs make use of hard squash, corn, figs, quail and pheasant. In the winter, apples, potatoes and turnips take the spotlight. Spring brings fiddlehead ferns, fava beans and English peas. Summer's the time for heirloom tomatoes, verbena, wild oysters and all kinds of berries.

In 2003, Alan Richman, the feared former *GQ* restaurant critic and *Globe* sportswriter, who in the 1990s derided chefs and restaurants here in an article entitled 'the Boston Glob', went on record saying that Boston was perhaps the upcoming food city in the US. Mr Richman clearly didn't eat around enough. Any well-fed local knows Boston is already there.

For the restaurants listed, we've given an approximate price range for main courses.

Back Bay

Contemporary

Audubon Circle

838 Beacon Street, at Park Drive (1-617 421 1910). Kenmore T. **Open** 11.30am-11pm daily. **Main courses** $10-$17. **Credit** AmEx, DC, Disc, MC, V.

Don't look for a sign outside this laid-back hangout – the only identifying symbol is a cryptic circle and a dot. The modern interior is equally understated, and the kitchen turns out an accomplished menu of grills, a great burger and salads.

Clio

Eliot Hotel, 370 Commonwealth Avenue, at Massachusetts Avenue (1-617 536 7200). Hynes/ICA T. **Open** 5.30-10.30pm Tue-Sun. **Main courses** $28-$39. **Credit** AmEx, Disc, MC, V. **Map** p276 F6.

In the refined Eliot Hotel, quietly buzzing Clio, with its leopard-print rug and enormous vases full of blooms, provides a glamorous backdrop for chef Ken Oringer's excellent cooking. An antidote to the profuse and ingredient-intensive cuisine that earned Boston its spot on the gastronomic map, his focused flavours and small, sculptural presentations wouldn't be out of place in New York: a dramatically spare plate of foie gras; steak seared with spices and served over a little vegetable ragout; two perfect scallops on pedestals of salt.

Excelsior

272 Boylston Street, at Charles Street (1-617 426 7878). Boylston T. **Open** 5.30pm-10pm Mon-Thur, Sun; 5.30pm-11pm Fri, Sat. **Main Courses** $30-$40. **Credit** AmEx, MC, V. **Map** p277 J5.

Lydia Shire wowed Bostonians for years with her creative American cuisine and flash interiors at Biba. She also knew when to call it quits – and then reinvent herself. Excelsior is the result. Adam Tihany's design combines Brahmin-era glamour with a touch of jet-set swagger: tones of burgundy and chocolate offset with modishly colourful rugs and a bar with fetching waitresses in pink cheongsam. Menu favourites include a swordfish chop with fiery grits, lobster pizza at the bar, and the his-and-hers steak preparations.

Restaurant L at Louis Boston

234 Berkeley Street, at Newbury Street (1-617 266 4680). Arlington T. **Open** noon-3pm Mon-Sat; 6pm-10pm Tue-Sat. **Main courses** $15-$28. **Credit** AmEx, MC, V. **Map** p277 H5.

Louis is a destination clothier occupying a historic Back Bay building (*see p159*). Pint-sized L is its attempt to transmute its cutting-edge style into edible form. Boston-bred chef Pino Maffeo is a protégé of New York City's Patricia Yeo and has begun to come into his own here. His muscular cooking melds European technique with Asian ingredients and occasional derring-do. L has one of Boston's unsung wine lists and a hidden bar for sampling it.

The best Brunch spots

Among Boston's many food fetishes is a big-time love of brunch. People plan where to have their Sunday morning Bloody Mary or fix of eggs Benedict days, sometimes weeks, in advance. Here's where to have yours with the locals:

The Blue Room
Every fluffy omelette, leafy salad and sinful cookie is wrought with stand-out New American panache. *See p136.*

Charlie's Sandwich Shoppe
The archetypal greasy spoon, Charlie's has a 30-minute limit on table time, but the breakfast sandwiches and rich flapjacks are worth the rush. *See p123.*

East Coast Grill
Hearty helpings of egg dishes, home-made sausages, and hashes turned out with Latin-American flair. The DIY Bloody Mary bar is great for Sunday morning hangovers. *See p137.*

S&S Restaurant
This decades-old deli-cum-diner has a classic roster that includes high-rise piles of French toast, three-egg plates and fruit salad. *See p139.*

Tremont 647 & Sister Sorel
The adjoining eateries are a weekend magnet for breakfast pizza, skillet-fried eggs and home-made sausage. *See p120.*

Excelsior. *See p115.*

Saint

90 Exeter Street, at Blagden Street (1-617-236 1134). Copley T. **Open** 5pm-2am daily. **Main Courses** $8-$22. **Credit** AmEx, DC, Disc, MC, V. **Map** p277 G6.

This space underneath the Copley Square Hotel likes to call itself a 'nitery'. It is one of those rare venues that winningly fuses the debauched nature of a nightclub with the chef-led devotion to food of an eatery. Models, celebs and Euro-chic twentysomethings inhabit the black leather couches and velvet-clad nooks on busy nights. But the presence of chef Rene Michelena, one of Boston's great talents, means foodies come early, clamouring for his roster of tapas-sized dishes like Balinese-style short ribs with black sesame and tamarind. His food is an ethereal combination of Asian dynamism and Italian lustiness – ask for an improvised tasting.

Sonsie

327 Newbury Street, between Hereford Street & Massachusetts Avenue (1-617 351 2500). Hynes/ICA T. **Open** 7am-11.30pm Sun-Thur; 7am-12.30am Fri-Sat. **Main courses** $17-$35. **Credit** AmEx, MC, V. **Map** p276 F6.

Sonsie is possibly the premier hangout for the Newbury Street elite and those who want to meet them. The restaurant is crowded elbow-to-elbow with Back Bay denizens, from the beautiful to the beery. The eclectic menu features Northern Italian pasta dishes and American staples like burgers and grilled chicken. The front of the restaurant has tables facing the windows, so everybody can keep an eye on who's promenading along chic Newbury.

American

Capital Grille

359 Newbury Street, at Massachusetts Avenue (1-617 262 8900). Hynes/ICA T. **Open** 5-10pm Mon-Wed; 5-11pm Thur-Sat; 4-10pm Sun. **Main courses** $18-$35. **Credit** AmEx, DC, Disc, MC, V. **Map** p276 F6.

It's easy to picture: wood panelling, giant Martinis at the bar; porterhouse steaks dry-ageing in a meat locker; a list of major-league and expensive red wines. In classic steakhouse fashion, you order vegetables separately, if at all. The handy location at the tip of Newbury Street means you can roll next door and keep the cocktail train going at Sonsie (*see above*) after dinner.

Grill 23 & Bar

161 Berkeley Street, at Stuart Street (1-617 542 2255). Arlington T. **Open** 5.30-10.30pm Mon-Thur; 5.30-11pm Fri; 5-11pm Sat; 5.30-10pm Sun. **Main courses** $30-$40. **Credit** AmEx, DC, Disc, MC, V. **Map** p277 H6.

Dry-aged meats, a blockbuster wine list, and chummy service? Check. What separates the clubby and cavernous Grill from the pack is having chef Jay Murray at the helm of it all. Besides keeping the béarnaise at its buttery finest, he turns out a menu of adventurous seafood dishes and creative departures (from straight-up beef) like roast rack of lamb or pork tenderloin. One of the great non-chain steakhouses in the US.

Asian

Brown Sugar

129 Jersey Street, at Queensbury Street (1-617 266 2928). Kenmore T. **Open** 11am-10pm Mon-Thur; 11am-11pm Fri, Sat. **Main courses** $10-$20. **Credit** DC, Disc, MC, V. **Map** p276 D8.

Good Thai food is served in this pretty-but-casual room in the quiet West Fens, just across the park from the Museum of Fine Arts. Appetisers are particularly vivid and sharp and the Thai iced coffee and tea are standard-setting.

Kashmir

279 Newbury Street, at Gloucester Street (1-617 536 1695). Hynes/ICA T. **Open** noon-11pm daily. **Main courses** $13-$19. **Credit** AmEx, Disc, MC, V. **Map** p276 F6.

This below-street-level restaurant is probably a standard-bearer among Indian eateries in the Hub – while it's not quantum distances beyond the competition, it is still the most handsome and serves some of the finest food. Curries are well balanced, delicate yet energetic; specials such as tandoori rack of lamb are presented with flair.

Shino's Express Sushi

144 Newbury Street, at Dartmouth Street (1-617 262 4530). Copley T. **Open** noon-9pm Mon-Wed, Sun; noon-9.45pm Thur-Sat. **Set meals** $6-$11. **Credit** AmEx, MC, V. **Map** p277 G6.

This is the equivalent of a sushi diner, with great-value lunch specials. The decor is basic, but service is fast and friendly. Most importantly, it's always busy, as turnover is key when raw fish is involved.

Uni

Eliot Hotel, 370A Commonwealth Avenue, at Massachusetts Avenue (1-617-536 7200). **Open** 5.30-10.30pm Tue-Sun. **Sushi** $12-$27. **Credit** AmEx, Disc, MC, V. **Map** p276 F6.

Chef Ken Oringer has been doing all-sashimi tasting menus at his vaunted Clio for years. Now his obsession has spawned a new venture, Uni. Once the leopard-clad lounge of Clio (*see p115*), this tiny restaurant-within-a-restaurant is a paean to things raw, swimming-fresh and Japanese – seafood from Tokyo's Tsukiji market is flown in daily. A single chef toils behind the four-seat sushi bar.

European

L'Espalier

30 Gloucester Street, at Newbury Street (1-617 262 3023). Hynes/ICA T. **Open** 5.30-10pm Mon-Sat. **Set meals** $68, $85. **Credit** AmEx, DC, Disc, MC, V. **Map** p276 F6.

Chef/owner Frank McClelland serves exquisite food at breathtaking prices in a Back Bay brownstone. Known for its intimacy, hyper-attentive service and an unequalled seven-course set-price meal, L'Espalier is the location of up to three marriage proposals a night (be very careful who you bring with you) and is not quite matched by anything else in the city. For those without the investment-banker budget, there's a less expensive sister restaurant, Sel de la Terre, on the harbour (*see p125*).

Tapeo

266 Newbury Street, between Fairfield & Gloucester Streets (1-617 267 4799). Copley or Hynes/ICA T. **Open** 5.30-10.30pm Mon-Wed, Sun; noon-11pm Thur-Sat. **Main courses** $18-$24. **Tapas** $5.40-$7.50. **Credit** AmEx, DC, MC, V. **Map** p276 F6.

Fun, sexy and tasty in a way perhaps only a Spanish restaurant can be, Tapeo is the place to go for tapas in the Back Bay. Downstairs is a kitschy sherry bar; upstairs is a spacious dining room with witty decor. The menu is consistently excellent, especially if you like garlic – tapas run from simple marinated olives to sizzling baby eels. You don't really need to order entrées, though there's a spectacularly presented baked fish in salt. The list of Spanish wines is extensive. The place is often crowded, so arrive early or book a table.

Latin

Bomboa

35 Stanhope Street, at Clarendon Street (1-617-236 6363). Back Bay T. **Open** 5.30pm-midnight Tue-Sat; 5.30-10pm Mon, Sun. **Main courses** $22-$29. **Credit** AmEx, MC, V. **Map** p277 H6.

This French-Brazilian restaurant on the edge of the Back Bay has been buzzing since day one. The food is vibrant but inconsistent in its wide palette of Latin, Asian and European flavours. Zebra-striped banquettes, the long zinc bar and a glowing fish tank match the eclectic crowd, which runs the gamut from pro athletes to guests from the nearby Ritz. Sexy and chic, Bomboa also has a Latin cocktail list and a late-night weekend scene with no equal (*see p148* **Shakin' things up**).

Casa Romero

30 Gloucester Street, at Newbury Street (1-617 536 4341). Arlington T. **Open** 5-11pm daily. **Main courses** $14-$27. **Credit** Disc, MC, V. **Map** p276 F6.

This restaurant is such a hidden jewel that most locals can't even find it. Everyone's heard of it, of course, but its behind-the-beaten-path entrance (located in an alley between Newbury Street and Commonwealth Avenue) helps to keep this upmarket Mexican restaurant obscure enough that you can still manage to snag a table without a reservation on most nights. The house speciality, *puerco adobado*, is a cut of pork marinated in oranges and smoked chipotle peppers, which is spicy and sweet at the same time. Wash down this fine fare with the excellent sangria or a Margarita.

Chef Rene Michelena of **Saint**. *See p116.*

SAFFRON
Restaurant & Bar
Contemporary Indian Cuisine
Saffron, we simply have nothing to compare it with,
and so we grasp for words to describe it,
but end up feeling we haven't quite captured the true sensation.
Saffron showcases two romantic & intimate dining areas
both with sweeping glass facades overlooking Newbury Street.
"...a rack of lamb marinated in spices and roasted tandoori-style is a marvel... The edges crackle; the interior of the lamb chops is moist."
"...Kiwi rice pudding is served beautifully with white raspberries. A delicious scoop of Kulfi is drizzled with mango and raspberry puree"
"...a swirl of exotic aromas and tastes"
Alison Arnett
The Boston Globe
Introducing our late night menu & 'a little night music' until 1am!
Saffron, 279 A Newbury Street, Boston
Mon.-Thurs. -11am-10:30pm;
Fri-Sat.-11am-11pm; Sun-11am-10:30pm.
Reservations accepted at (617) 536.9766
Available for private parties & catering
www.saffronboston.com

El Pelon Taqueria

92 Peterborough Street, at Kilmarnock Street (1-617 262 9090). Fenway or Kenmore T. **Open** 11.30am-9.30pm daily. **Main courses** $5-$6. **Credit** AmEx, MC, V. **Map** p276 D7.

El Pelon may be small, but this tiny Fenway taqueria packs a punch. Every item on the menu makes extraordinary use of ordinary ingredients and blows the doors off bland superchain Mexicana. The salsa here, for example, is good enough to eat with a spoon. When the cilantro (coriander) jumps up and dances on your tongue, you know the stuff is fresh.

Seafood

McCormick & Schmick's

Boston Park Plaza Hotel, 34 Columbus Avenue, at Arlington Street (1-617 482 3999). Arlington T. **Open** 11am-11pm daily. **Main courses** $10-$24. **Credit** AmEx, Disc, MC, V. **Map** p277 J6.

McCormick & Schmick's has perfected the odd role of a West Coast seafood chain on the East Coast. Offerings here are so fresh, they print an additional daily menu. Combined, the two menus list around 40 species of seafood as well as their origins. Continuing the fresh concept, the restaurant uses no frozen goods or additives: all fruit juices are freshly squeezed, and even the potatoes are mashed with a frequency bordering on fanaticism. The clubby atmosphere is more steakhouse than anything.

Cafés & coffeehouses

Armani Cafe

214 Newbury Street, at Exeter Street (1-617 437 0909). Copley T. **Open** 11.30am-10pm Mon-Wed, Sun; 11.30am-11pm Thur-Sat. **Main courses** $10-$27. **Credit** AmEx, Disc, MC, V. **Map** p277 G6.

Black-clad waiters serve a young Euro crowd at the fashionista's fave pitstop. Restaurateur Seth Woods recently took over the kitchen, adding some spiffy leather seating, and upping the ante on the food end.

Espresso Royale Caffe

44 Gainsborough Street, between Huntington Avenue and St Stephens Street (1-617 859 7080). Symphony or Northeastern T. **Open** 7am-11pm Mon-Fri; 8am-11pm Sat, Sun. **Credit** AmEx, Disc, MC, V. **Map** p276 F8.

With several universities and cultural institutions within a stone's throw, Espresso Royale has taken on the role of 'great place to meet'. The sandwiches aren't recommended, but all the liquids – especially the flavour shots – are.

Other locations: 286 Newbury Street, at Gloucester Street (1-617 859 9515); 736 Commonwealth Avenue, at St Mary's Street (1-617 277 8737).

Parish Café

361 Boylston Street, at Arlington Street (1-617 247 4777). Boylston T. **Open** 11.30am-1am Mon-Sat; noon-1am Sun. **Main courses** $9-$14. **Credit** AmEx, DC, MC, V. **Map** p277 H5.

This sandwich specialist's menu is made up mostly of other people's recipes, but in the best of ways. Top chefs like Chris Schlesinger of East Coast Grill, Nadsa de Monteiro of Elephant Walk, and Michael Schlow of Radius all have their own between-the-bread takes sold here. And, with a patio peering back down Boylston Street towards the Public Garden, the people-watching is grade A.

Tealuxe

108 Newbury Street, at Clarendon Street (1-617 927 0400/www.tealuxe.com). Copley T. **Open** 9am-10pm Sun-Thur; 9am-11pm Fri, Sat. **Credit** AmEx, DC, Disc, MC, V. **Map** p277 H6.

At Tealuxe everyone from little old ladies to pierced-and-painted punks can choose from hundreds of bins full of leafy goodness and share in the pleasures of a nice pot of tea. The Newbury Street location also offers tasty grilled sandwiches and scones.

Other locations: Zero Brattle Street, at Harvard Square (1-617 441 0077); 256 Harvard Street, Brookline (1-617 739 4832); 1223 Center Street, Newton (1-617 244 3155).

Torrefazione Italia Café

85 Newbury Street, at Clarendon Street (1-617 424 0951). Copley T. **Open** 7am-8pm Mon-Thur; 7am-9pm Fri; 8am-9pm Sat; 9am-8pm Sun. **Credit** AmEx, DC, Disc, MC, V. **Map** p277 H6.

The clientele is sophisticated and well kempt, and all the plates and glasses are gorgeous Raffaellesco ceramics, but it's not just about appearances here. Style meets substance, as Torrefazione pulls the most consistent espresso-based drinks outside of the North End – with fine *crema*, body and never too much foam – so many make the pilgrimage here.

Trident Booksellers & Cafe

338 Newbury Street, at Hereford Street (1-617 267 8688). Hynes/ICA T. **Open** 9am-midnight daily. **Main courses** $10. **Credit** AmEx, DC, Disc, MC, V. **Map** p276 F6.

If your idea of a good time is getting a bite to eat, sipping a cup o' joe or a carrot juice with ginger and flipping through a vast selection of magazines, say hello to your new home.

South End

Contemporary

Claremont Café

535 Columbus Avenue, at Massachusetts Avenue (1-617 247 9001). Mass Ave T. **Open** 9am-3pm, 5.30-10pm Tue-Thur, Sun; 9am-3pm, 5.30-10.30pm Fri, Sat. **Main courses** $16-$25. **Credit** AmEx, MC, V. **Map** p276 G8.

The Claremont has been eclipsed in fame by the slew of high-ambition bistros in the neighbourhood. But this is unfair, as this very consistent restaurant turns out good, sharp-flavoured food – particularly on the appetiser menu – at moderate prices. There's seating outside during warm weather.

The Dish

253 Shawmut Avenue, at Milford Street (1-617 426 7866/www.southenddish.com). Back Bay T. **Open** 5-10pm Mon-Thur, Sun; 5-11pm Fri, Sat. **Main courses** $11.95-$15.95. **Credit** AmEx, MC, V. **Map** p277 J7.

The epitome of a neighbourhood restaurant, the Dish is small, intimate, loud, full of personality and staffed by spunky locals who would just as soon hand in their notice as serve a plate that didn't look right. The miscellaneous menu and eclectic hand-picked wine list are to match.

Franklin Café

278 Shawmut Avenue, at Hanson Street (1-617 350 0010). Back Bay T. **Open** 5.30pm-1.30am daily. **Main courses** $12-$19. **Credit** AmEx, DC, MC, V. **Map** p277 J7.

Small, full and friendly, the Franklin keeps its growing gay and straight clientele happy. It's the perfect neighbourhood restaurant in one of the hippest confines in the city, so it stands to reason the seared tuna, chicken livers with soy sauce, turkey meatloaf and Sidecars are equally dandy. Food is served well past midnight to a funky soundtrack.

Hamersley's Bistro

553 Tremont Street, at Clarendon Street (1-617 423 2700). Back Bay or Copley T. **Open** 6-10pm Mon-Fri; 5.30-10.30pm Sat; 5.30-9.30pm Sun. **Main courses** $24-$39. **Credit** AmEx, DC, Disc, MC, V. **Map** p277 H7.

Join the crowd at **Tremont 647**.

Chef and owner Gordon Hamersley's eponymous bistro is unmatched for his hearty New England execution of regional French fare. The roast chicken with garlic, lemon, and parsley is the stuff of poultry legend. The eatery even won Julia Child's seal of approval for its uttery unpretentious and delicious food. As a cheeky salute, Hamersley's serves sausages during Red Sox season (just take a look at the owner's cap if you wonder who thought of that idea) and Moroccan and Indian influences show up ever so subtly.

Tremont 647 & Sister Sorel

647 Tremont Street, at West Brookline Street (1-617 266 4600/www.tremont647.com). Back Bay T. **Open** 5.30-10pm Mon-Thur; 5.30-10.30pm Fri; 10.30am-2pm, 5.30-10.30pm Sat; 10.30-3pm, 5.30-10pm Sun. **Main courses** $18-$26. **Credit** AmEx, DC, MC, V. **Map** p277 H8.

Chef Andy Husband's buzzing South End tandem – adventurous American restaurant Tremont 647 and adjoining bar/café Sister Sorel – is a neighbourhood staple. The food folds Southern, Latin, Thai and even Tibetan influences into the mix to create big, bold yet approachable flavours. The heavy-handed cocktails and great weekend brunch are further draws – the urbane crowd often digs into a meal, has a breakfast Martini or three and is still there come dinnertime.

Union

1357 Washington Street, at Union Park Street (1-617-423 0555). Back Bay T/Union Park Silver Line bus. **Open** 5.30-11pm Mon-Wed, Sun; 5.30pm-midnight Thur-Sat. **Main Courses** $14-$37. **Credit** AmEx, MC, V. **Map** 277 J8.

Named after its fashionable location – near Union Park's English-style gardens – Union is the finest-hour achievement of restaurateur Seth Woods. It's an American update of the brasserie with just enough swagger to keep the hipsters happy. The American part comes in the Gallic staples wrought from New England ingredients; the swagger comes across in the black leather banquettes, clean lines and striking flower arrangements.

American

Bob the Chef's Café

604 Columbus Avenue, at Massachusetts Avenue (1-617 536 6204). Mass Ave T. **Open** 5-10pm Mon-Thur; 11am-11pm Fri-Sun. **Main courses** $12-$15. **Credit** AmEx, DC, MC, V. **Map** p276 G8.

On the South End/Roxbury border, Bob's used to be a funky caféteria-style soul food restaurant and cult favourite. It counts one-time local Malcolm X among its clientele. It's since gone a bit upscale – you could say it's now more Southern supper club – with spot lighting, framed art and some very bistro-looking tables. You'll probably find better versions of grits, fried chicken and greens up the road in Dorchester or Mattapan – but you will have to search and you won't get live jazz to boot.

Queens of cuisine

Though smaller than some of its restaurant-scene rivals, such as Chicago and LA, Boston may well have the most talented group of female chefs in the US – if not the world. That's no easy feat in a business where masculinity, egos and brutish behaviour in the kitchen are the stereotype. Not only do women have to possess superior talent, they must also toe the line between quiet strength and firm reserve to get a shot at being top toque. They also tend to cook food that is less showy (with some exceptions: see Lydia Shire), more sensuous, but every bit as well crafted as that of their male counterparts, and often more timeless in its taste. To dine well in Boston, you'll certainly want to meet the ladies:

Barbara Lynch and Cat Silirie (No.9 Park, The Butcher Shop, B&G Oysters): Restraint, a hint of bygone-age glamour and lusty flavours are the hallmarks of this chef/sommelier duo. Few food/wine pairs can match their synergy and their ability to marry the rustic and elegant. Modern Boston classics-in-the-making.

Ana Sortun (Oleana): The humble and talented Sortun's food is perhaps the most unusual of the bunch. She canvasses the heady cuisines of North Africa, the spicy roasts of Armenia, historical Persian cooking and sunny Mediterranean flavours for inspiration. Give her a gargantuan persona and she'd be famous. As it is, she is simply a great cook with a warm, inviting restaurant. What else really matters?

Lydia Shire (Excelsior and Locke-Ober): And then there was Lydia (*pictured*). She's worked as a butcher and truck driver, spun dough in Chinatown and helped Adam Tihany design her latest babe of an eatery, Excelsior. Her food is even gutsier than that of many male counterparts – a gale-force combination of tastes that can summon Provençal countryside, pungent Bangkok streets and salty New England coastlines in succession. She helped spank Boston out of the culinary doldrums in the 1980s, pretty much before anyone but Jasper White.

Jody Adams and Michela Larsen (Rialto): Restaurateur Michela Larsen has seen talents like Todd English and Barbara Lynch pass through her kitchens, but smartly settled on chef/owner Jody Adams as a partner. Their brand of hospitality has a spark of passion, an intellectual streak to match the Cambridge clientele at Rialto, and of course, Jody's sexy, earthen cooking.

Marisa Iocco and Rita D'Angelo (Bricco): The term 'cult following' could have been invented for 'the Girls', as they've been known for nearly a decade. They first came to fame at the late Galleria Italiana, where they helped discover and groom chefs like Rene Michelena, Barbara Lynch and Felino Samson. They're stand-alone talents as well: Iocco is one of the most instinctively gifted and creative Italian cooks around, and D'Angelo is a bewitching host and GM.

Joanne Chang (Flour): A Harvard grad and consultant by training, this sweet-smiling, beautiful, marathon-running Taiwanese-American woman became the top pastry chef in town while at Mistral. But her SoWa bakery, Flour, has put American goodness, European technique and her engaging wit to the best use: keeping a wide-ranging crowd happy and stuffed with sweet things.

Charlie's Sandwich Shoppe

429 Columbus Avenue, at Pembroke Street (1-617 536 7669). Back Bay T. **Open** 6am-2.30pm Mon-Fri; 7.30am-1pm Sat. **Main Courses** $4-$8. **No credit cards. Map** p277 G7.

This greasy spoon on a windy stretch of Columbus Avenue is pure Americana. There are chrome stools at the counter, a paper coffee cup for take-out tips and fast-talking waitstaff who have worked here for decades. Regulars are known by name but they still have to wait in line for a table with you – and Bill Clinton. It's worth it for turkey hash, cranberry French toast, pistachio muffins and big fluffy omelettes slung with a side of tough love.

Rouge

480 Columbus Avenue, at West Newton Street (1-617 867 0600). Back Bay or Mass Ave T then 10mins walk. **Open** 5.30-10pm Mon-Thur, Sun; 5.30-10.30pm Fri-Sat. **Main Courses** $16-$25. **Credit** AmEx, MC, V. **Map** p277 G7.

Chef/owner Andy Husbands has a knack for affordable but sophisticated cooking served with just the right amount of cool. Rouge is his second restaurant and has a seasonal American focus and some fine low-and-slow-smoked barbecue staples that reveal his early training at East Coast Grill. The VW Bug-sized bar/lounge is a moody haunt for sipping Margaritas and Mint Juleps.

Tim's Tavern

329 Columbus Avenue, at Dartmouth Street (1-617 437 6898). Back Bay T. **Open** 11am-11pm Mon-Sat. **Main courses** $7-$15. **Credit** AmEx, Disc, MC, V. **Map** p277 H7.

Like Charlie's (*see above*), Tim's is a leftover from the time before the South End was a latte-loving, hipster-strewn kinda place, and not a single soul complains. The tables are formica, the groove and R&B on the jukebox are mostly unchanged since the 1970s, and the Bud is served in plastic cups. It's all as it should be and comes with the opportunity to sample a behemoth of a hamburger or some fine buffalo wings and ribs. Possibly the only place in town where you can spot hip hoppers, policeman, yuppies, and gay artists mingling over french fries and beer.

African

Addis Red Sea

544 Tremont Street, at Clarendon Street (1-617 426 8727). Back Bay or Copley T. **Open** 5-11pm Mon-Fri; noon-11pm Sat, Sun. **Main courses** $8-$13. **Credit** AmEx, MC, V. **Map** p277 H7.

After more than a decade, this Ethiopian eatery is still Boston's most exotic place to eat. Low wooden stools surround woven-grass tables, and food is delivered without cutlery – the spongy sourdough bread injera serves as both utensil and mild-tasting foil for the spicy chicken, lamb and lentil stews. Don't miss the red-pepper cottage cheese as an appetiser, and use the diced tomato salad to cool your palate. The house beer is an African take on mead.

Asian

Pho Republique

1415 Washington Street, at West Dedham Street (1-617 262 0005). Back Bay T/Union Park Silver Line bus. **Open** 5.30pm-12.30am daily. **Main courses** $14.50-$19. **Credit** AmEx, MC, V. **Map** p277 H8.

Imagine what it would feel like to step into a restaurant off a crowded street in Hanoi and find a modish crowd dining on *pho* and drinking lemongrass Martinis like tomorrow would never come. That's pretty much the vibe at Pho Republique, plus a DJ in the corner on some nights and random flame jugglers passing through on others. The food here is healthy and hearty; the drinks are inspirational (*see p148* **Shakin' things up**); the decor is as funky as you're going to see in Boston; and there's usually a pretty hip scene going on.

European

Aquitaine

569 Tremont Street, at Union Park (1-617 424 8577). Back Bay or Copley T. **Open** 5.30-10pm Mon-Wed; 5.30-11pm Thur, Fri; 10am-3pm, 5.30-11pm Sat; 10am-3pm, 5.30-10pm Sun. **Main courses** $19-$29. **Credit** AmEx, DC, MC, V. **Map** p277 H7.

The wine racks stretch to the ceiling and the crowd stretches the imagination at this South End hot spot. The food is part classic continental and part Left Bank, and there's a hearty hominess to it that appeals to the locals. Bistro all-stars like steak frites (possibly the best in town), vegetable tartlets, and plats du jour such as *choucroute* are hard to fault; but do scan the menu for roasts and monkfish, as chef/owner Seth Woods does great things with them.

Mistral

223 Columbus Ave, between Berkeley & Clarendon Streets (1-617 867 9300/www.mistralbistro.com). Back Bay T. **Open** 5.30-11pm Mon-Sat; 5.30-10pm Sun. **Main Courses** $22-$44. **Credit** AmEx, DC, Disc, MC, V. **Map** p277 H6.

A little bit of swish Saint Tropez on the edge of the South End, Mistral has been an A-list staple since opening in 1997. Jamie Mammano's Mediterranean-by-way-of-Boston cuisine is well crafted and full of sunny flavours, but can be pricey. Better to grab a cushiony perch in the café, where industry and entertainment power-brokers congregate, and enjoy the scene over thin-crust pizza and Cosmos.

Latin

Botucatu Restaurant

57 West Dedham Street, at Tremont Street (1-617 247 8394). Back Bay T. **Open** 11.30am-10pm daily. **Main courses** $9-$14. **Credit** Disc, MC, V. **Map** p277 H8.

Tell a Brazilian you're going out for an authentic, no-frills South American/Brazilian supper and he or she will probably ask why. Well, Botucatu is why.

Slick Italian **Teatro**. *See p127.*

The food is cheap and true to its roots: empanadas stuffed with spicy chicken and ground beef, *tostones* (fried plantain) with carrot sauce, fresh heart of palm salads and a Brazilian version of chicken-fried steak called *bife a Milaneza*. What makes the experience even more special is an 'anything can happen' atmosphere that rarely fails to deliver. People start singing, free beers or snacks are brought to the table for no apparent reason. It's all too wonderful.

Seafood

B&G Oysters

550 Tremont Street, at West Dedham Street (1-617 423 0550). Back Bay T. **Open** 11.30am-11pm Mon-Fri; 2-11pm Sat, Sun. **Main Courses** $11-$22. **Credit** AmEx, DC, Disc, MC, V. **Map** p277 H8.
Local gal Barbara Lynch's second act is an upscale version of the down-home oyster bar. It's a labour of love with a killer location (the heart of the South End) and diminutive size (two dozen seats) whose initials (B for Barbara, G for Garrett) are a reference to the owners. From before noon until 11pm weekdays, a shucker slings bivalves harvested daily from nearby Wellfleet, Cotuit, or Blue Point, as well as 'foreign' ones like kumamotos from the West Coast. The kitchen serves lobster stew, lobster rolls and seafood chowders. On the opposite corner is Lynch's chic charcuterie/wine bar the **Butcher Shop** (522 Tremont Street, 1-617 423 4800).

Legal Seafoods

26 Park Plaza, at Park Square (1-617 426 4444/ www.legalseafoods.com). Boylston or Arlington T. **Open** 11.30am-11pm Mon-Thur; 11.30am-midnight Fri, Sat; 11.30am-10pm Sun. **Main courses** $14-$40. **Credit** AmEx, DC, Disc, MC, V. **Map** p277 J6.
Legal is that rare thing – a tourist magnet that hasn't lost credibility with locals. This huge, thronged restaurant has enjoyed years of success by following one simple rule: start with something fresh out of the ocean and don't screw it up.
Other locations: 255 State Street, at Long Wharf (1-617 227 3115); Copley Place (1-617 266 7775); Prudential Center, 800 Boylston Street (1-617 266 6800); 5 Cambridge Center at Kendall Square, Cambridge (1-617 864 3400); 20 University Road at Harvard Square, Cambridge (1-617 491 9400).

Cafés & coffeehouses

For **Flour**, *see p138* **Bakery-cafés**.

Finale

Park Square Building, 1 Columbus Avenue, at Arlington Street (1-617 423 3184). Boylston or Arlington T. **Open** 11.30am-11pm Mon-Wed; 11.30am-midnight Thur, Fri; 6pm-midnight Sat; 4-11pm Sun. **Credit** AmEx, MC, V. **Map** p277 J6.
If you have a sweet tooth, this is your ultimate fantasy: an eatery that specialises in dessert, with a velvety, moody atmosphere to match the calorific indulgence. There's also a fine menu of small plates

to quell savoury cravings, plus dessert wines and cordials to stand up to the artfully plated chocolate bombes, tropical fruit concoctions and mousses.

Garden of Eden Café

571 Tremont Street, at Union Park Street (1-617 247 8377). Back Bay T. **Open** 7am-10.30pm Mon-Thur; 7am-11pm Fri, Sat; 7am-10pm Sun. **Main courses** $8-$18. **Credit** AmEx, MC, V. **Map** p277 H7.

Expanded from its original storefront sliver, Garden of Eden is the kind of sunny, family-run café that's so much a part of the South End neighbourhood that one wonders what people did before it was around. Guests spread out their *Sunday Globe* or hold weekday meetings on an old kitchen table. It combines deli, grocer, café and bistro, and the Mediterranean-American kitchen keeps 'em coming back.

Downtown & the Financial District

Contemporary

Radius

8 High Street, at Summer Street (1-617 426 1234). South Station T. **Open** 11.30am-2.30pm, 5.30-10pm Mon-Thur; 11.30am-2.30pm, 5.30-11pm Fri; 5.30-11pm Sat. **Main courses** $32-$43. **Credit** AmEx, DC, MC, V. **Map** p275 L5.

A table at Radius – chef Michael Schlow and restaurateur Christopher Myers' glamorous collaboration – is still one of the most sought-after reservations in town. The restaurant, housed in a former bank, manages to feel both lived in and of the moment. Fashionable twentysomethings, CEOs and foodies mingle in a room that mixes tones of slate with splashes of lipstick red. The kitchen deals in classy plays on regional New England game, seafood and produce. It's a shame the bar isn't busier, as the view of the dining room is as fetching as the tipples.

American

Durgin Park

340 Faneuil Hall Marketplace, at Congress Street (1-617 227 2038/www.durgin-park.com. Gov't Center, Haymarket or State T. **Open** 11.30am-10pm Mon-Sat; 11.30am-9pm Sun. **Main courses** $6-$37. **Credit** AmEx, DC, Disc, MC, V. **Map** p275 L3.

This huge, multi-level, no-frills eatery has never had any trouble filling its tables. In fact, Durgin Park has been packing them in for over 130 years. The formula is simple: large portions of well-prepared Yankee comfort food, friendly service and a prime spot in Quincy Market. An oasis of authenticity in the midst of a thronging tourist industry, this is the perfect place to bring your aching feet and increasingly cranky kids after a hard day's T-shirt shopping. Try the chicken livers sautéed in white wine for lunch, the prime rib for dinner, and don't leave without sampling the baked beans.

Locke-Ober

3 Winterplace, off Winter Street (1-617 542 1340/ www.locke-ober.com). Downtown Crossing or Park St T. **Open** 11.30am-2.30pm, 5.30-10pm Mon-Thur; 11.30am-2.30pm, 5.30-11pm Fri; 5.30-11pm Sat. **Main Courses** $32. **Credit** AmEx, Disc, MC, V. **Map** p274 K4.

Some things never change. Along with the weight of 129 years of history, this storied dining room still bears carved mahogany, stained glass and silver plate covers. Other things change for the better. Chef/owner Lydia Shire and designer Adam Tihany and have done for this one-time Brahmin classic what Viagra has done for Hugh Hefner: extended its glory days indefinitely. The restaurant is so delightful, even the strained attempts at cool can be forgiven. The menu mixes updates on crab Louis, lobster stew and fried calf's liver with the odd trendy Asian-inflected entry. We prefer the classics.

Silvertone Bar & Grill

69 Bromfield Street, at Tremont Street (1-617 338 7887). Downtown Crossing or Park St T. **Open** 11.30am-11pm Mon-Thur; 11.30am-midnight Fri; 6-11pm Sat. **Main courses** $7-$18. **Credit** AmEx, DC, Disc, MC, V. **Map** p274 K4.

The dining-room side of this funky subterranean spot plays host to a hip audience appreciative of the eclectic wine list and the kitchen's finesse with everyday dishes such as grilled chicken and macaroni and cheese. Nothing too fancy or out of control here; just consistently tasty, updated comfort foods. The space is dimly lit and tightly packed, but somehow rarely gets stuffy. The vibe is effortlessly cool.

European

Les Zygomates

129 South Street, at Kneeland Street (1-617 542 5108). South Station T. **Open** 11.30am-2pm Mon-Wed; 11.30am-2.30pm, 6-10.30pm Thur; 11.30am-2pm, 6-11pm Fri; 6-11pm Sat; 6-10.30pm Sun. **Main courses** $19-$24; **Set meal** $29. **Credit** AmEx, DC, Disc, MC, V.

This Francophile bistro, complete with tiled floor, zinc bar and live jazz, has two owners: one, a Paris-trained American cook who turns out straightforward versions of French classics such as rabbit, venison and sweetbread vol-au-vents; the other, a European oenophile who keeps the wine list stocked with new names and unusual varieties and hosts weekly wine tastings. As wine is available by the 'taste' (two ounces), you can sit at the bar, order appetisers and sample your way down the list.

Sel de la Terre

255 State Street, at Long Wharf (1-617 720 1300). Aquarium T. **Open** 11.30am-2.30pm, 5.30-10pm daily. **Main courses** $24. **Credit** AmEx, DC, Disc, MC, V. **Map** p275 M4.

Even packed with the throngs of tourists, Sel shines. The less expensive sister restaurant to the acclaimed L'Espalier in the Back Bay (*see p117*), it sets the tone

Eat, Drink, Shop

with an accomplished artisan bread basket, and salads that will make you fall in love with vegetables all over again. Later it kicks into gear with authentic Provençal cuisine described by fans as 'transcendent'. The menu here is structured so that all main dishes cost the same.

Teatro

177 Tremont Street, at Essex Street (1-617 778 6841). Boylston T. **Open** 5pm-midnight Mon-Sat; 4pm-11pm Sun. **Main courses** $12-$21. **Credit** AmEx, DC, Disc, MC, V. **Map** p274 J5.

It took only a matter of weeks for this Theatre District spot to be adopted as a Teflon dinner haunt. Looks help, for sure, with a vaulted ceiling detailed in gold leaf, chic key-lime banquettes, and black marble tables offset with ergonomic white chairs. Euros sipping Bellinis mix with the odd State House politician and businessmen drinking beer at the bar. They all seem to agree that the mid-priced menu (roast monkfish, braised pork, thin-crust pizza, freshly rolled pastas) is on target whether one has a hot date or a Sunday night pang for bolognese.

Seafood

Todd English's Kingfish Hall

Faneuil Hall Marketplace, at Congress Street (1-617-523 8862). Aquarium T. **Open** 11.30am-10pm daily. **Main courses** $23-$40. **Credit** AmEx, DC, Disc, MC, V. **Map** p275 L3.

More is more at this Faneuil Hall seafooder from celebrity chef Todd English. Gold leafing and tiles by designer Todd Oldham decorate the bar, blown-glass shaped like squid hang from above, and the booths on the second-floor rotate. The fun-house feel is a perfect foil for English's larger-than-life flavours. Latin and Asian influences are applied to local seafood of the highest calibre – line-caught fish from the Atlantic, Maine scallops harvested by deep-sea divers – and the raw bar is first-rate. Thunderously loud, but nobody's complaining.

Ye Olde Union Oyster House

41 Union Street, at Hanover Street (1-617 227 2750/www.unionoysterhouse.com). Gov't Center or Haymarket T. **Open** 11am-10pm Mon-Sat; 11am-9.30pm Sun. **Main courses** $17-$33. **Credit** AmEx, DC, Disc, MC, V. **Map** p275 L3.

Tourist trap or throwback? It's hard to tell in 'America's oldest restaurant' (established 1826). Sure, it's next to Faneuil Hall and draws hordes of out-of-towners, but, as long as you turn a blind eye to the gift shop, the wooden booths, white-washed walls, lobster tank and servers with 'Bah-ston' accents have an air of authenticity – even Kennedys still show up here on occasion. The affable shuckers keep up the patter while they put on a show behind the ancient semicircular wooden oyster bar – which remains tops for cherrystones and clams casino. The Lazy Man's Lobster (the meat baked with seasoned breadcrumbs, sherry and butter in a casserole) is another winner.

North End

European

Bricco

241 Hanover Street, between Cross & Parmenter Streets (1-617-248 6800). Haymarket T. **Open** 5-11pm daily. **Main courses** $23-$36. **Credit** AmEx, MC, V. **Map** p275 L3.

Bostonians have gone ga-ga over Marisa Iocco and Rita D'Angelo – known to fans as 'the Girls' – for nearly a decade now. After a year-long sojourn in their native Abruzzi, they're back at the helm of this soigné North Ender. Iocco cooks a passionate and distinctive brand of regional Italian; her pillowy gnocchi, silken pastas and absurdly rich bread pudding are without equal. D'Angelo roams the room, air-kissing with her European clientele as if it were Milan and chit-chatting comfortably with the Bostonian locals as she has since her days as a BU student. Come midnight, a DJ spins lounge and the bar buzzes with the lithe and stylish.

Monica's

143 Richmond Street, at Hanover Street (1-617 227 0311). Haymarket T. **Open** 5.30-9.30pm Mon-Thur, Sun; 5.30-11pm Fri, Sat; 5-9.30pm Sun. **Main courses** $15-$30. **Credit** AmEx, MC, V. **Map** p275 L3.

Inspired by the cooking and traditions of their Argentinian/Italian family, the Mendoza clan has expanded its North End empire over the past few years to encompass three warm and inviting businesses. Monica's Restaurant is the flagship property; the home-made pastas and soups make for comfortable Italian eats without hitting too deep in the wallet. Monica's Salumeria sells imported and domestic food, including freshly prepared daily selections. And Monica's Pizzeria boasts the 'Best Sauce in the North End'.

Pizzeria Regina

11½ Thatcher Street, at North Margin Street (1-617 227 0765). Haymarket T. **Open** 11am-11.30pm Mon-Thur; 11am-midnight Fri, Sat; noon-11pm Sun. **Main courses** $12-$25. **No credit cards. Map** p275 L2.

One thing that strikes most visitors to the North End is that there's no pizza. But that's a misconception. There's pizza, it's just hiding in this winding back-street – and you can smell it from around the corner, where the queue begins. Pizzeria Regina has become a chain, but this is the original, which opened in 1926. The pizza may not be the best in town, but the place has an authentic North End atmosphere, and it's fun to roll through several pies – and many more pitchers of Bud – in a rough-and-tumble series of booths that hasn't changed in decades.

Pomodoro

319 Hanover Street, at Prince Street (1-617 367 4348). Haymarket T. **Open** 2-11pm Tue-Fri; 11am-11pm Sat; 3-11pm Sun. **Main courses** $15-$18. **No credit cards. Map** p275 L2.

The smell of sizzling garlic permeates this tiny storefront restaurant, owned by the Italian food expert (an Irish lass, no less) Siobhan Carew. The simple, excellent specials and pasta dishes stand out from those found at the run-of-the-mill Italian joints that clutter Hanover Street.

Prezza

24 Fleet Street, at Hanover Street (1-617 227 1577). Haymarket T. **Open** 5.30-10pm Mon-Thur; 5-10.30pm Fri, Sat. **Main courses** $26-$38. **Credit** AmEx, DC, Disc, MC, V. **Map** p275 L2.

The achievement of a local boy made good, Prezza is Anthony Caturano's urbane stab at next-generation cooking for the North End set. His food is bold in the contemporary American sense, earthy and personal, but he's not above asking Mom or Grandma for some help with an old Abruzzi recipe or fresh fruit tart. Dad takes care of the wine list, which is full of American boutique finds, and the crowds have happily beaten a path to a slightly hard-to-find address to experience it all.

Sage Restaurant

69 Prince Street, at Salem Street (1-617 248 8814). Haymarket T. **Open** 5.30-10pm Mon-Sat. **Main courses** $20-$28. **Credit** AmEx, Disc, MC, V. **Map** p275 L2.

Sage is the love-child of Tony Susi, a native North Ender whose family has been in the restaurant business for decades. He's earned a rabid following for this kiss-on-both-cheeks kind of a place. White beans, pork roasts, fresh egg pastas and panna cotta all get fine treatment at his eight-table eatery. Make a reservation if possible.

Taranta

210 Hanover Street, at Cross Street (1-617 720 0052). Haymarket T. **Open** 5.30-10pm daily. **Main courses** $16-$30. **Credit** AmEx, MC, V. **Map** p275 L3.

Regional Italian gets a double shot of character at this unsung labour of love in the North End. Owner Jose Duarte is a self-taught cook who can summon the Moorish-influenced tastes of Sicily in one dish and then infuse another with the rustic flavours of his own country – Peru. The results are always likeable and sometimes inspired – and, besides, it's hard not to love someone who makes his own *limoncello*, hand-shaves *bottarga* (dried fish roe) and can wax poetic about Sardinian wine.

Trattoria a Scalinatella

253 Hanover Street, at Parmenter Street (1-617 742 8240). Haymarket T. **Open** 5.30-9.30pm Mon-Thur, Sun; 5.30-10pm Fri, Sat. **Main courses** $20-$35. **Credit** AmEx, MC, V. **Map** p275 L3.

To reach this North End hideout involves locating an unmarked door and climbing a rail-thin staircase to a discreet entrance. The first thing you'll see as you walk in is a few chefs hard at work – and those brows will furrow if you make too many demands on the highly personal cooking. Specials change nightly according to what has come in from the farms and local waters. Order from the menu or, even better, simply choose a wine with the help of the gregarious host-owner and let the kitchen make all the decisions for you. Scalinatella is as eclectic and exclusive as they come.

Cafés & coffeehouses

Café Graffiti

307 Hanover Street, between Parmenter and Prince Streets (1-617 367 3016). Haymarket T. **Open** 6am-midnight daily. **No credit cards**. **Map** p275 L3.

Even without the cigarette smoke that used to shroud the room, Graffiti is a seamlessly Italian café. There is textbook espresso made with pride by a barista, loud guys with well-coiffed black hair – and out-the-door crowds when Champions League soccer matches or the Series A is on TV. Always busy and a fun place to hang out.

Caffe Vittoria

296 Hanover Street, at Prince Street (1-617 227 7606). Haymarket T. **Open** 8am-midnight Sun-Thur; 8am-2.30am Fri, Sat. **No credit cards**. **Map** p275 L2.

Vittoria claims to be the oldest Italian café in the North End, and it's got the 'practice makes perfect' goods to back up the assertion. It's a bit of a tourist trap, but the pastries and desserts are incredible and the cappuccinos are the best and most perfectly proportioned in Boston.

Chinatown

Asian

Apollo Grill & Sushi

84 Harrison Avenue, at Kneeland Street (1-617 423 3888). Chinatown T. **Open** 11.30am-2pm, 5pm-4am Mon-Fri; 5pm-4am Sat, Sun. **Main courses** $15-$20. **Credit** AmEx, DC, Disc, MC, V.

A pit in your table is set ablaze and an elegant Asian waitress appears bearing platters of meat, lettuce, rice, bean paste and kim chee. The rest is up to you. Now this is living. Korean barbecue is to American barbecue what Sumo wrestling is to the World Wrestling Federation: just as exciting, but drenched in tradition and a hell of lot classier. Here, it makes for an extremely tasty repast and can be offset with decent sushi or tempura for good measure. The performance is best attended in large groups.

Chau Chow City

83 Essex Street, at Ping On Street (1-617 338 8158). Chinatown T. **Open** 8am-3am daily. **Main courses** $8-$15. **Credit** AmEx, DC, Disc, MC, V. **Map** p274 K5.

Dim sum enthusiasts swear by Chau Chow City. Check it out if you're in the mood for a real Chinatown experience. Carts of luscious *shui-mai* (dumplings), soups and other tasty nibbles get wheeled around from table to table, while an ever-more-excitable crowd shouts constantly. Unless

Elegant **No.9 Park** is one of Boston's top tables. *See p131.*

you're a seasoned dim sum expert, you won't know what anything is or what it costs. Luckily, it always ends up being pretty cheap, and what you don't know can't hurt you.

King Fung Garden

74 Kneeland Street, at Harrison Avenue (1-617 357 5262). Chinatown T. **Open** 11am-11pm daily. **Main courses** $4.75-$28. **No credit cards**.

It's a run-down-looking shack that's too bright inside, and if you want a beer you'll have to bring your own, but this off-the-beaten-path dive also happens to be the first place where those in the know will look for a table. The breathtaking scallion pancakes and Peking-style pork dumplings are rumoured to be purchased by far fancier places around town and sold at ten times what King Fung charges. For the ultimate treat, call 24 hours in advance and ask them to get a Peking duck ready – it easily serves four and costs less than a slice of duck breast across the street.

Peach Farm

4 Tyler Street, at Beach Street (1-617 482 1116). Chinatown T. **Open** 11am-3am daily. **Main courses** $10-$30. **Credit** Disc, MC, V. **Map** p274 K5.

This long-running seafood specialist serves Hong Kong-style cooking in a series of small rooms with too-bright neon lighting. Pick your fish from the tank in the kitchen and be sure to order anything involving scallops, the salt-and-pepper squid and seasonal greens like pea shoots.

Penang

685 Washington Street, at Kneeland Street (1-617 451 6373). Chinatown T. **Open** 11.30am-11.30pm Mon-Thur, Sun; 11.30am-midnight Fri, Sat. **Main courses** $15-$25. **Credit** MC, V. **Map Map** p274 K5.

It's getting a bit old now, but the simple wooden tables and dark atmosphere of Penang retains an edge to it in decor-averse Chinatown. The food here is Malaysian, and that means you'll find specialities from different ethnic groups: Malay, Chinese, Indian, and the famed Nonya cooks. Typical dishes include a coconut milk-rich noodle dish called *laksa*, the Indian flatbread *roti*, meant for dunking in curry, and peanut pancakes for a great Asian finale. Adventurous palates should ask for the Chinese menu, full of unlikely flavours. Come late at night and you'll be temporarily transported to the New Asia of Kuala Lumpur or Bangkok as many expat students flow in to *makan* (eat).

Pho Pasteur

682 Washington Street, at Kneeland Street (1-617-482 7467). Chinatown T. **Open** 10am-10.30pm daily. **Main courses** $5.25-$10. **Credit** AmEx, Disc, MC, V. **Map** p274 K5.

The original Pho Pasteur is a wee bolthole with hardly any design to speak of – and that's probably why it remains the best of the bunch. Atmosphere comes in the form of wafting scents of star anise and cinnamon: a tell-tale sign of good noodle soup, as any Vietnamese native will tell you. Here they serve the beef and chicken versions, plus regional dishes worth trying like Saigon staple *banh xeo*, a turmeric-stained and crêpe-like concoction folded around pork, bean sprouts and mung beans, wrapped with herbs in lettuce, and dunked into dipping sauce. It's best to come for lunch.

Other locations: 119 Newbury Street, at Dartmouth Street (1-617 262 8200); the Garage, 36 John F Kennedy Street, at Harvard Square, Cambridge (1-617 864 4100).

Taiwan Café

34 Oxford Street, at Beach Street (1-617 426 8181). Chinatown T. **Open** 11am-1am daily. **Main courses** $9-$12. **No credit cards**. **Map** p274 K5.

Down a Chinatown side street and up a flight of stairs, Taiwan Café is obscure in location and culinary leanings. It serves Taipei-style cooking, a more nuanced take on Chinese, with healthy doses of saltiness, pungency, and chilli snap. Chances are, you'll be the only non-native occupying a round table and chasing your dish on the Lazy Susan – which is a very good thing.

Beacon Hill

Contemporary

Beacon Hill Bistro

Beacon Hill Hotel, 25 Charles Street, at Chestnut Street (1-888 959 2442/www.beaconhillhotel.com). Charles/MGH or Arlington T. **Open** 7-10am, 11.30am-3pm, 5.30-11pm Mon-Fri; 10am-3pm, 5.30-11pm Sat; 10am-3pm, 5.30-10pm Sun. **Main courses** $15-$24. **Credit** AmEx, DC, Disc, MC, V. **Map** p306 F4. **Map** p274 J4.

Peter and Cecilia Rait serve three meals a day at this amiable bistro on the ground floor of their Charles Street hotel. There's an in-the-neighbourhood vibe that feels by turns Beacon Hill and small-city Europe. Tastes are a local take on bistro and, while not as inspired as it was on opening, the menu lures a certain type of tweedy customer for repeated visits.

The Federalist

XV Beacon, 15 Beacon Street, at Park Street (1-617 670 1500/www.xvbeacon.com). Park St T. **Open** 7-10.30am, 11.30am-2pm, 5.30-10.30pm daily. **Main courses** $28-$50. **Credit** AmEx, DC, Disc, MC, V. **Map** p274 K4.

Though the Boston press sometimes likes to use the Fed as a whipping boy, this restaurant is a genuinely fun yet elegant fine dining experience. Yes, it's expensive. And the room would seem stuffy were it not for the almost palpable spirit of pleasure that presides. The food can be extravagant and sometimes outrageous, but every bite rings true. The service is so good it's almost comical. Just don't try charging the meal to a room you're not really staying in – it may add up to grand larceny.

Upper Crust

20 Charles Street, at Beacon Street (1-617 723 9600). Arlington or Charles/MGH T. **Open** 11.30am-10pm Mon-Thur, Sun; 11.30am-10.30pm Fri, Sat. **Main courses** $10-$18. **Credit** AmEx, DC, MC, V. **Map** p274 J4.

Upper Crust managed the nifty trick of opening up next to Todd English's already-entrenched gourmet pizzeria, Figs (*see p133*) and coming out just as busy. The space is compact, simple, and hip: nothing but a wooden floor, an abstract tin sculpture hanging from the ceiling and a common table, at the head of which you can watch cooks hand-toss the dough. It's a formula that captures the everyday appeal of pizza and injects it with enough youthful Bostonian cockiness to make having a slice fun again.

Other locations: 286 Harvard Street, at Coolidge Corner, Brookline (1-617 734 4900).

European

No.9 Park

9 Park Street, at Beacon Street (1-617 742 9991). Park St T. **Open** 11.30am-2.30pm, 5.30-10pm Mon-Fri; 5.30-10pm Sat. **Main courses** $27-$45. **Credit** AmEx, DC, Disc, MC, V. **Map** p274 K4.

Understated elegance is given 21st-century Bostonian form at Barbara Lynch's No.9 Park. From the Bulfinch building it inhabits to the lusty, haute yet approachable transformation of European peasant fare, it is fast becoming a modern classic. Lynch was born and bred in the South Boston projects, but rolls handmade pasta like an Italian *nonna* and creates such distinctive dishes as prune gnocchi with foie gras and *vin santo* glaze. There's a touch of the Gallic afoot in the timeless grace of the place and a well-edited use of classic sauces like Choron, which often shows up as a velvety cloak for Maine lobster. Thoughtful details also keep the place full: a daily cheese cart, affable servers, the trademark Palmyra cocktail and Pear Martini, and a bar that serves the full menu to whispering couples and single diners. Sommelier Cat Silirie's wine list alone is worth several visits.

International

Lala Rokh

97 Mount Vernon Street, at Charles Street (1-617 720 5511). Charles/MGH or Arlington T. **Open** noon-3pm, 5.30-10pm Mon-Fri; 5.30-10pm Sat, Sun. **Main courses** $14-$20. **Credit** AmEx, DC, MC, V. **Map** p274 J4.

Raw power

The Atlantic coastal waters flowing past Rhode Island, Cape Cod, Massachusetts and Maine are a frightful proposition for swimmers most of the year: brackish, rough and chilly. But they are ideal for producing clean-tasting shellfish – tiny cherrystones, oysters of every size and shape, the streamlined razor clam – making Boston one of the best places in the world to eat them in their unadulterated (read: raw) form. Menus list them according to the towns from which they come, and the taste changes by the day, season, year, even from shell to shell. East Coast oyster varieties to look out for include Wellfleet, Cotuit, Blue Point and Malpeque, but always consult your shucker. Some people like them plain; others with any combination of mignonette, tabasco and lemon. Any eatery worth its sea salt will have one or two of these accompaniments on hand, but the half-dozen below also serve 'em with real know-how and, in some cases, chutzpah.

B&G Oysters

Why didn't other chefs think of this first? No.9 Park's Barbara Lynch beat her star chef brethren to it when she opened B&G, an old-school oyster bar with new-school verve. There are two dozen seats, maximum – the prime ones are at the inlaid-tile bar where a female shucker tears through up to more than 700 oysters, including many rare varieties, per night. A trendy crowd and non-stop serving hours from 11.30am to 11pm weekdays. *See p124.*

Central Kitchen

An unlikely entry, with no more than a few varieties (often Wellfleets) on hand depending on the night, but the blue-tiled bar at this groovy, no-nonsense Central Square hangout is a perfect stage for downing the slippery-salty things by the dozen. Cheap cava makes a fine foil, and the bartenders (who sometimes turn their hand to the shucking) pour a fine Martini too. *See p138.*

Jasper White's Summer Shack

White is the Godfather of seafood cookery in New England. His Summer Shack (*pictured*) serves up to a dozen varieties of oysters every which way – buttermilk-fried, shucked with multiple mignonettes, stewed as the early settlers would have had them – and with some blue-collar sass to boot. *See p140.*

McCormick & Schmick's

This clubby Seattle-based rival to local chain Legal Seafoods uses its size and buying power in the best of ways: to get oysters sweet and fresh in taste from every corner of the country. This is where to come to do the East vs West taste test, as it brings in unlikely specimens from Rhode Island to Vancouver. *See p119.*

Todd English's Kingfish Hall

Loud-mouthed barflies, fast-talking bartenders, and shuckers who work underneath a tiled fresco done by a fashion designer. It's all in a day's work at the raw bar of Todd English's fish house in Faneuil Hall. Interesting mignonettes and swimming-fresh products make the place hard to fault. *See p127.*

Ye Olde Union Oyster House

Even the biggest Boston food snob can't decry oysters and clams on the half (though they may slag off other things) at Ye Olde. And if they do, there's a centuries-long customer history to prove them wrong. Hands-down the tastiest stop on the Freedom Trail. *See p127.*

A remarkable warren of rooms on a Beacon Hill side street, this place serves pretty, piquant food from the Persian recipes of the owner's mother, who also mails packets of hard-to-find spices over from the Middle East. Dishes feature unusual ingredients such as pomegranate juice and sturgeon; service is helpful, and the experience is one of the most unique and romantic in the city.

Charlestown

Contemporary

Figs

67 Main Street, at Monument Avenue (1-617 242 2229). Community College T. **Open** 5.30-10pm Mon-Thur; 5.30-10.30pm Fri; 5-10.30pm Sat; 5-9.30pm Sun. **Main courses** $11-$19. **Credit** AmEx, DC, MC, V. **Map** p274 K1.

After Todd English moved his influential bistro Olives (*see below*) into its current digs in nearby City Square, he promptly opened an upmarket pizzeria in its tiny original space, making the city's connoisseurs of clam and oregano pizza very happy indeed. And subsequent expansion means he's making them happy in Beacon Hill and Newton too. This place is popular and nearly always full, so be prepared to wait for a table.

Other locations: 42 Charles Street, Beacon Hill (1-617 742 3447); 1208 Boylston Street, Newton (1-617 738 9992).

Olives

10 City Square, at Main Street (1-617 242 1999). Community College or North Station T then 10mins walk. **Open** 5.30-9.30pm Mon-Fri; 5-10pm Sat; 4-8.30pm Sun. **Main courses** $19-$32. **Credit** AmEx, MC, V. **Map** p274 K1.

Todd English has influenced Boston cooking like nobody since culinary grande dame Julia Child. His totally unrestrained and powerfully flavoured approach to Italian ingredients and sauces, and his layers of taste upon taste create a kind of magic that has kept the house full every night for years while inspiring all kinds of imitators. English's 'empire', as it's called, is big now – a chain of Figs pizzerias; Olives in Aspen, New York and Washington, DC – and his divided attention takes its toll here and there. Still, there's nothing quite like it.

European

Mezé Estiatorio

100 City Square, at Park Street, Charlestown (1-617 242 6393). Community College or North Station T then 10mins walk. **Open** 11.30am-2.30pm, 5-10pm Mon-Wed; 11.30am-2.30pm, 5-11pm Thur-Sat; 11am-3pm Sun. **Main courses** $18-$30. **Credit** AmEx, DC, Disc, MC, V. **Map** p274 K1.

Owner Paul Delios became a foodie cult favourite with his still-great **Paolo's Trattoria** down the road (251 Main Street, 1-617 242 7229). Mezé is his second act, a vital paean to his Greek-American heritage and the first Greater Boston eatery in years to give Greece the culinary attention it deserves. Rabbit stews, lamb roasts, yogurt dips, and a slew of meze are all for the taking. Break bread in the raucous taverna-style bar or in the more adult dining room. Be sure to plunder the ouzo selection and Greek wines on offer.

Waterfront

Seafood

The Barking Crab

88 Sleeper Street, at Northern Avenue (1-617 426 2722). South Station T then 10mins walk. **Open** 11.30am-9pm Sun-Wed; 11.30am-10pm Thur-Sat. **Main courses** $9-$24. **Credit** AmEx, MC, V. **Map** p275 M5.

Without being outright wacky, the Barking Crab is its own kind of fun – especially in the summertime, when its outdoor lobster tent provides bench seating, live music, beer in plastic cups, lobster in a paper basket and steamer clams in a bucket. In winter the food moves indoors to a marine-themed room with a fireplace. This is not the city's best or most reliable seafood restaurant, but it remains a perennial favourite with both tourists and a large contingent of locals.

Allston/Brighton

Asian

Rangoli

129 Brighton Avenue, at Harvard Avenue, Allston (1-617 562 0200). Harvard Avenue T/57 bus. **Open** 11.30am-3pm, 5-10.30pm Mon-Fri; 5-10.30pm Sat, Sun. **Main courses** $10-$11. **Credit** AmEx, Disc, MC, V. **Map** p278 5A.

While most of Boston's Indian restaurants serve North Indian staples such as chicken tikka masala and tandoori dishes, Rangoli – a pleasant but unassuming place on busy Brighton Avenue – was the first to make a speciality of South Indian food. Others have followed in its footsteps, but Rangoli is still a bargain and a treat, with foot-long *dosai* (fried chickpea-flour pancakes) wrapped around potatoes and chicken.

European

Tasca

1610 Commonwealth Avenue, at Washington Street, Brighton (1-617 730 8002). Washington Street T. **Open** 5-11pm Mon-Thur; 5pm-midnight Fri; 4pm-midnight Sat; 4-11pm Sun. **Tapas** $3-$7. **Credit** AmEx, Disc, MC, V.

What happens when an Irishman opens a tapas bar? You get a friendly, convivial Spanish-looking restaurant serving a slightly blander version of the

salty and piquant tapas available downtown. Dishes are a dollar or two cheaper than other tapas bars, and the free valet parking is a convenience.

Brookline

Contemporary

The Fireplace

1634 Beacon Street, at Washington Street, Brookline (1-617 975 1900). Washington Square T. **Open** 11am-10pm Mon-Thur, Sun; 11am-11pm Fri, Sat. **Main courses** $16-$26. **Credit** AmEx, DC, Disc, MC, V.

The feel-good atmosphere of the Fireplace has been an instant hit in Brookline since the day it opened. Owner Jim Solomon is the goofy-cool uncle you never had. He plays a dual role as host and co-chef (his kitchen counterpart is always changing but capable), and can easily be spotted in this multi-tiered room with picture windows looking on to Beacon Street. The menu is highly seasonal and champions New England staples like squash, cod, pumpkin and wild berries whenever possible.

Washington Square Tavern

714 Washington Street, at Beacon Street, Brookline (1-617 232 8989). Washington Square T. **Open** 5.30-10pm Mon-Thur, Sun; 5.30-11pm Fri, Sat; 11.30am-2.30pm Sun. **Main courses** $13-$21. **Credit** MC, V.

Twinkling Christmas lights, bookshelves, groovy tunes and an avant-garde menu that fuses New American cuisine with French and Asian influences attract a flood of food adventurers to this hip and sparkling little jewel in the middle of nowhere.

American

Zaftigs

335 Harvard Street, at Babcock Street, Brookline (1-617 975 0075). Coolidge Corner T. **Open** 8am-10pm daily. **Main courses** $9.95-$12.95. **Credit** AmEx, Disc, MC, V.

Probably the most popular breakfast spot in Brookline, if not the whole Boston area, Zaftigs updates the Jewish deli for a slightly more calorie-conscious 21st-century crowd. There's a huge menu and a 45-minute wait for a table on Saturday or Sunday mornings. Book if you can.

Asian

Dok Bua

411 Harvard Street, at Fuller Street, Brookline (1-617 277 7087). Coolidge Corner T then 10mins walk/66 Bus. **Open** 11am-11pm daily. **Main courses** $6-$10. **Credit** AmEx, DC, Disc, MC, V.

In an unassuming Brookline village storefront, Dok Bua does a fine job at obscuring what lies within: a family-run market and café serving impressive Thai food with the kind of hot-sour-salty-sweet verve that normally gets lost in translation when it's recreated in restaurant kitchens in the West.

Oishii Sushi

612 Hammond Street, at Boylston Street, Chestnut Hill (1-617 277 7888). Chestnut Hill T. **Open** 11.30am-3pm, 5-9.30pm Tue-Fri; 11am-9.30pm Sat, Sun. **Main courses** $7-$15. **Credit** AmEx, MC, V.

Arrive a little before or after the meal-time rush at Oishii if you don't want to wait for a seat. There are just over a dozen of them, mostly at the counter, and the ex-Nobu chefs who preside ever so humbly over the raw fish turn out creative maki rolls, sashimi fresh enough to compete in LA or NY, and impromptu omakase menus that draw celebrity chefs on their lunch breaks.

European

Taberna de Haro

999 Beacon Street, at St Mary's Street, Brookline (1-617 277 8272). St. Mary's T. **Open** 5.30-10pm Mon-Thur; 5.30-11pm Fri, Sat. **Main Courses** $10-$15. **Credit** AmEx, MC, V.

Veal sausage with a lemony mayo, garlicky frogs' legs, tender lamb racks – the menu at this Spanish restaurant is rambling and completely appealing. An L-shaped tapas bar and wooden tables are the setting for a raucous scene, lovingly watched over by the chef/owners, Julia and Deborah de Haro. Gentle and elegant, they last ran a restaurant in Madrid. It certainly shows, from the authentic Spanish cooking to the top list of regional wines and sherries.

Jamaica Plain

European

Bella Luna

405 Centre Street, at Perkins Street (1-617 524 6060). Stony Brook T then 15mins walk/39 bus then 5mins walk. **Open** 11am-10pm Mon-Wed, Sun; 11am-11pm Thur-Sat. **Main courses** $12-$21. **Credit** AmEx, DC, Disc, MC, V.

Definitely funky. This colourful restaurant is strong in the pizza, pasta, sandwich department, and even stronger in the daily specials. Downstairs is a cool candlepin bowling alley – yes, there is such a thing – called the Milky Way that serves Bella Luna pizzas and has an entertainment line-up from live acts to karaoke (*see also p211 and 226*).

Latin

El Oriental de Cuba

416 Centre Street, at Paul Gore Street (1-617 524 6464). Stony Brook T then 15mins walk/39 bus then 5mins walk. **Open** 8am-9pm Mon-Thur, Sun; 8am-10pm Fri, Sat. **Main courses** $7-$8. **Credit** AmEx, MC, V.

When a restaurant has been in a neighbourhood for years and there's still a queue out the door, chances

Taiwan Café. *See p131.*

are it's a winner. El Oriental de Cuba is just such a champion. For non-Spanish speakers, the spicy sauces and overall *Cubano* experience can be an adventure, culinary and cultural. For the Hispanic clientele, it's just a well-executed meal. Its Cuban sandwich – a hot pressed roll packed with roast pork, ham, Swiss cheese, lettuce, tomatoes and other condiments – is the real deal.

Cafés & coffeehouses

Coffee Cantata

605 Centre Street, at Pond Street, (1-617 522 2223). Green St T then 10mins walk. **Open** 7am-7pm Mon-Fri; 8am-6pm Sat; 8am-5pm Sun. **No credit cards.**
Just to step inside this zero-pretension bistro-and-beans is to be blown away. The aroma of fresh brewing coffee mixed with the rest of this café's tasty offerings is so delicious you'll be ready to eat the air. The reality that follows is pretty good too.

South Boston

American

Amrheins

80 West Broadway, at A Street (1-617 268 6189). Broadway T. **Open** 11am-10pm Mon-Thur; 11am-11pm Fri, Sat; 9am-8pm Sun. **Main courses** $11-$18. **Credit** AmEx, Disc, MC, V.
You don't stay in business more than 100 years without doing a few things right. Amrheins, one of Boston's oldest restaurants, had the first draught-beer pump system in Boston, and Southie's finest continue to rest their glasses on the oldest hand-carved bar in America. Waitresses who call everyone 'buddy' serve hometown favourites including the enormously popular giant home-made chicken pie and lobster and scallop pie. Dessert? Boston cream pie or Guinness, naturally.

Cafés & coffeehouses

Café Arpeggio

398 West Broadway, at F Street (1-617 269 8822). Broadway T then 9 bus or 10mins walk. **Open** 6am-10pm daily. **No credit cards.**
This peaceful oasis, pleasantly out of place amid the pizza joints and pharmacies, provides respite for residents of South Boston looking for a freshly brewed cup of latte, home-baked pastries, home-churned ice-cream and tasty sandwiches. Plenty of light to read by and comfortably upholstered chairs to boot.

Cambridge

Contemporary

Blue Room

1 Kendall Square, between Cardinal Madeiros Avenue & Hampshire Street (1-617 494 9034). Kendall/MIT T. **Open** 5.30-10pm Mon-Thur; 5.30-10.30pm Fri, Sat; 11am-3pm, 5.30-10pm Sun. **Main courses** $17-$24. **Credit** AmEx, DC, Disc, MC, V.
Kendall Square's Blue Room – which is actually purple, green and peach-themed – brings New American ideas to the table with a globally influenced menu of grills, salads, and heady stews.

Cambridge, 1

27 Church Street, at Harvard Square (1-617 576 1111). Harvard T. **Open** 11.30am-1am daily. **Main Courses** $13-$25. **Credit** AmEx, Disc, MC, V. **Map** p278 B2.

Pizza parlour cool is the currency of Cambridge, 1, and there are queues nightly as a result. Exposed brick walls, sleek timber tables and bartenders who DJ from their iPods set the scene. Good cooking and better ingredients drive a menu of fab salads (iceberg wedge with blue cheese drizzle); thin-crust pizzas with toppings like mashed potato and prosciutto, bolognese sauce, or your basic pepperoni or cheese; and satisfying pints of Toscanini's ice-cream to round off the meal.

East Coast Grill

1271 Cambridge Street, at Prospect Street (1-617 491 6568/www.eastcoastgrill.net). Central T then 10mins walk/83 bus. **Open** 5.30-10pm Mon-Thur; 5.30-10.30pm Fri, Sat; 11am-2.30pm, 5.30-10pm Sun. **Main courses** $15-$26. **Credit** AmEx, Disc, MC, V. **Map** p278 C2.

The East Coast Grill did for dining what rock 'n' roll did for music – shook it up and made it fun again. Almost two decades on, Chris Schlesinger's Inman Square classic is still jamming with a daily menu written on a blackboard that mixes spice rubs, grilled local catches, Asian sambals and Latin-American flavours, and usually comes out a winner. Don't pass on side dishes like mashed sweet potatoes and pulled pork, served vinegar-spicy in the style of the Carolinas. You can even buy the kitchen a six-pack of beer off the menu – how's that for a light-hearted approach to eating out?

Rialto

Charles Hotel, 1 Bennett Street, at Harvard Square (1-617 661 5050/www.rialto-restaurant.com). Harvard T. **Open** 5.30-10pm Mon-Fri; 5.30-11pm Sat; 5.30-9pm Sun. **Main courses** $20-$36. **Credit** AmEx, DC, MC, V. **Map** p278 A2.

Chef/owner Jody Adams has become the grande dame of Harvard Square thanks to her highly personal cuisine: voluptuously flavoured renditions of Southern Mediterranean cooking with an East Coast twist, made from local seafood and produce. The same tempered worldliness is afoot in the dining room, whose overstuffed banquettes and dimly lit surrounds could use a revamp, and in the groups of profs, suited brokers and Boston's growing youth contingent out to plunder the menu and wine list. Those in the know bring their date to drink – or full-on dine – in the moody lounge by the entrance.

UpStairs on the Square

91 Winthrop Street, at John F Kennedy Street (1-617 864 1933). **Open** 11.30am-2.30pm, 5-10pm Mon-Thur; 11.30am-2.30pm, 5-11pm Fri-Sat; 11am-2pm, 5-10pm Sun. **Main courses** $16-$39. **Credit** AmEx, DC, MC, V. **Map** p278 A2.

For many years a classic known as UpStairs at the Pudding (named after the theatre it resided above), this second-level eatery has moved across Harvard into a delightful brick house on a small green. Although it's been reborn with a slightly altered name, all its zany elegance is intact. There's something a bit madcap about the multi-floor and multi-room set up – one look at the collection of pink and green tones, leopard prints and chandeliers and you'll understand what we mean. But the continental-goes-modern-Bostonian food is hard to fault and the wine list is full of finds from Napa and the lesser-known regions of Europe.

American

B-Side Lounge

92 Hampshire Street, at Windsor Street (1-617 354 0766/www.bsidelounge.com). Kendall/MIT T. **Open** 5.30pm-midnight Mon-Wed; 5.30pm-1am Thur-Sat; 11am-midnight Sun. **Main courses** $14-$20. **Credit** AmEx, MC, V. **Map** p278 C3.

Funky, brash and stashed on a no-man's-land corner of Cambridge, the B-Side has managed to retain its cult status among hipsters despite garnering widespread acclaim when it first opened. There's a lack of pretension that's very 'neighbourhood bar', and a user-friendly yet creative American menu – think London gastropub gone Stateside. Where to seat yourself in the eclectic crowd? Groups prefer the retro-style booths, while regulars sidle up to the three-sided bar and plunder a lengthy list of classic

What's the catch? The **East Coast Grill.**

cocktails whose recipes date back to the 19th century (*see p148* **Shakin' things up**). As you might expect from the name, the music here is tops.

Cambridge Common

1667 Massachusetts Avenue, at Sacramento Street (1-617 547 1228). Harvard or Porter T. **Open** 11.30am-midnight Mon-Wed, Sun; 11.30am-1am Thur-Sat. **Main courses** $10-$14. **Credit** AmEx, DC, Disc, MC, V. **Map** p278 B1.

Handy for comfort food such as chicken pie and meatloaf, all at family prices. The only frills come in the amount of blue cheese melted on the chips or the generous size of the Cosmopolitans – which obviously nobody complains about as they slide into the big wooden booths at this welcoming retreat.

Central Kitchen

567 Massachusetts Avenue, at Essex Street (1-617 491 5599). Central T. **Open** 11.30am-2.30pm, 5.30-11pm Mon-Fri; 5.30-11pm Sat, Sun. **Main courses** $18-$26. **Credit** AmEx, MC, V. **Map** p278 C3.

On a good night, this is your all-round, all-time-great vibrant bistro, complete with waiters with good attitudes who love food and wine. And a chef who laughs. And chalkboard specials that are very hard

Bakery-cafés

In Boston, the hybrid eatery known as the bakery-café has done for neighbourhoods what the diner, coffeehouse and corner pub could only accomplish in part – serving as an all-day, one-stop repository for caffeine, indulgence and comfort. They can be found across the city, from affluent suburbs like Arlington to the most raw, urban corners. Some attract one kind of customer – say, a tweedy academic or a vintage-sneakered hipster. Others are a mixed milieu. Whether bike messenger, businessman or graphic artist, they all come for calorific sweets, good cappuccino and a where-everyone-knows-your-name atmosphere.

Carberry's Bakery & Coffeehouse

187 Elm Street, at Tenney Street, Somerville (1-617 666 2233). Davis T. **Open** 7am-8pm Mon-Sat; 7am-7pm Sun. **Credit** AmEx, MC, V.

Carberry's began life as an Icelandic bakery and has become a fine modern American bakery-café over the years. It has soaring windows and plenty of outdoor seating. But the real draw for its eclectic clientele (coffeehouse hipsters and stroller-pushing parents) is pastry chef/baker Greg Case, formerly of Hamersley's Bistro, and now an independent maestro in charge of the many home-baked pies, cookies, brownies and cakes that fly off the shelves.

Other locations: 74 Prospect Street, at Central Square, Cambridge (1-617 576 3530).

Flour

1595 Washington Street, at East Concord Street, South End (1-617 267 4300). Mass Ave T/East Concord Silver Line bus. **Open** 7am-7pm Mon-Fri; 8am-6pm Sat; 9am-3pm Sun. **Credit** AmEx, Disc, MC, V. **Map** p277 H9.

The SoWa (South of Washington Street) district is regaining some of its old lustre, and Joanne Chang's cheery bakery-café is part of that transformation. Hospital workers from the nearby Boston Medical Center, local artists and long-time fans of this Harvard grad-turned-pastry-chef linger over wooden common tables. Sandwiches and soups of the day are written on a chalkboard and at the counter you can choose from upscale versions of Pop Tarts, cheddar scones, banana bread, double-chocolate cookies and to-die-for tarts.

Hi-Rise Bakery

208 Concord Avenue, at Huron Avenue, Cambridge (1-617 876 8766). Harvard T then 10mins walk/72 bus. **Open** 8am-8pm Mon-Fri; 8am-5pm Sat; 8am-3pm Sun. **Credit** MC, V. **Map** p278 A1.

It's worth the leafy walk from Harvard to visit baker Rene Becker's shop in affluent residential 'Huron Village'. Inlaid pebble floors, wood-block tables and an adjacent baker's kitchen make for lots of fun. It serves as a second living room for Harvard profs, local families and downtown types who make the pilgrimage for the homey sweet stuff. This is the rare American bakery that plunders historic recipes for ideas, and it has become one of the country's best. Yeasted corn bread, oatmeal-dried cherry cookies, and an upscale version of the Oreo are just a few sweet staples. For breakfast? Don't miss toasted slices of New England brown bread. For lunch? Generous sandwiches on thick-crusted wheat or sourdough loaves. To drink? Small-batch birch and ginger beers if cappuccino isn't your thing.

Other locations: 56 Brattle Street, at Harvard Square, Cambridge (1-617 492 3003).

to choose between. On a bad night, it's none of those things, though. There is one dish here, however, that does everything right and will never change and never fail to please if not redeem: the fabulous Mussels from Brussels. This is a huge bowl of mussels and frites drizzled with such a tasty sauce that you'll be slurping it up when the food is gone regardless of how crude you look.

Charlie's Kitchen

10 Eliot Street, at Harvard Square (1-617 492 9646). Harvard T. **Open** 10.30am-1am Mon-Wed, Sun; 10.30am-2am Thur-Sat. **Main courses** $4-$10. **Credit** MC, V. **Map** p278 A3.

Double cheeseburgers, pencil-thin fries, omelettes and lobster rolls. It's hard to go wrong at this leftover from the '60s in over-gentrified Harvard Square. By day it's a funky diner of sorts. But by night it transforms into a hidden party venue where people linger over drinks and there's a loud-mouthed, small-town bonhomie in the air.

Mr Bartley's Burger Cottage

1246 Massachusetts Avenue, at Harvard Square (1-617 354 6559/www.mrbartleys.com). Harvard T. **Open** 11am-9pm Mon-Sat. **Main courses** $6-$13. **No credit cards**. **Map** p278 B2.

A hallowed ground-beef depot and student hangout since the '60s, the always-busy Bartley's has an encyclopedic roster of thick burgers with larky names (such as the Bill Clinton), soda-pop classics like a raspberry lime rickey, and milk shakes to make everyone feel like a child again. The decor is as basic and busy as a dorm room (peeling radical posters, local memorabilia) and the menu verbose enough to be an undergrad term paper. It's all part of the substantial, greasy, stomach-bursting fun.

S&S Restaurant

1334 Cambridge Street, at Inman Square (1-617 354 0777). Harvard or Kendall/MIT T then 15mins walk, or Lechmere T then 69 bus. **Open** 7am-11pm Mon-Wed; 7am-midnight Thur, Fri; 8am-midnight Sat; 8am-10pm Sun. **Main courses** $8-$15. **Credit** AmEx , MC, V. **Map** p278 C2.

A great basic deli where breakfast is served until closing time. Join the queue at this 80-year-old Inman Square institution for bagels and overflowing omelettes on Sunday mornings, or slide into a booth for late-night comfort food and ridiculously rich desserts. Fancier daily specials are sometimes over-ambitious and seafood is often overcooked, but basics such as onion-packed chopped liver and piled-on pastrami never fail.

Asian

Common Market

Porter Exchange, 1815 Massachusetts Avenue, at Porter Square. Porter T. **No credit cards**. **Map** p278 B1.

This is actually a conglomeration of six small restaurants in the old art deco Sears & Roebuck building which, in its reincarnation as the Porter Exchange shopping complex, has become the heart of 'little Asia' for North Cambridge. It's the place to find excellent Japanese fare at rock-bottom prices. Take a seat at the sushi bar at grocer **Kotobukiya** (1-617 492 4655, open noon-8.30pm Mon-Sat, noon-6pm Sun) for fast, fresh nori rolls. Or belly up to a big bowl of noodle soup at **Tampopo** (1-617 868 5457, open noon-9pm daily), or a curried cutlet at **Café Mami** (1-617 547 9130, open noon-9pm daily).

Elephant Walk

2067 Massachusetts Avenue, at Walden Street (1-617 492 6900/www.elephantwalk.com). Porter T. **Open** 5-10pm Sun-Thur; 5-11pm Fri, Sat. **Main courses** $13-$27. **Credit** AmEx, DC, Disc, MC, V.

Elephant Walk's two restaurants are singular – not just for Boston, but on a global level. The Cambodian cooking here wraps Hindi, Thai, French and Chinese influences into a nuanced whole; recipes are from the decades-old family repertoire of Longteine de Monteiro, who learned to cook in Phnom Penh and later fled the country in the time of the Khmer Rouge. The Cambridge location is comfortable, sexy and exotic, the Brookline branch is simply cosy – at both, the golden age of a near-lost cuisine lives on.

Other locations: 900 Beacon Street, at Park Drive, Brookline (1-617 247 1500).

European

Atasca

279 Broadway, at Columbia Street (1-617 354 4355). Central T. **Open** 5-10pm Tue-Thur, Sun; 5-11pm Fri, Sat. **Main courses** $15-$27. **Credit** AmEx, DC, Disc, MC, V. **Map** p278 C3.

The coastal towns of New England have long been enriched by Portuguese fishermen and their families, and East Cambridge is another traditional hub. Strewn with knick-knacks and warmly lit, this boîte is the heart of the Portuguese restaurant scene. Grilled seafood, clam dishes and hearty stews are all signatures, and the owner has a savvy cellar of Portuguese wines that go way beyond Vinho Verde – but who could resist a bottle of that to start?

Other locations: 50 Hampshire Street, Cambridge (1-617 621 6991).

Centro

720 Massachusetts Avenue (enter through the Good Life in winter), at Pleasant Street (1-617 868 2405). Central T. **Open** 5.30-10pm Tue, Wed; 5.30-11pm Thur-Sat; 4.30-9pm Sun. **Main courses** $14-$19. **Credit** AmEx, DC, Disc, MC, V. **Map** p278 C3.

Meet the little restaurant that could. The triumph and pride of Central Square, this tiny ten-table Italian doesn't even have its own door in winter due to heating issues. It shares a kitchen and bar with the ever-happening jazzy nightclub the Good Life (*see p147*). And it rocks so hard that even the most notoriously venomous local restaurant reviewer couldn't help but bestow three stars upon it (out of four). So, what's to love? Everything, really. But especially pork chops that open your eyes; soft polenta that will make you close them and sigh; and service that treats you the same whether you're wearing a slutty she-devil outfit or an Armani suit.

International

Baraka Café

80 Pearl Street, at Williams Street (1-617 868 3951). Central T. **Open** 11.30am-2.30pm, 5.30-10pm Tue-Sat; 5.30-10pm Sun. **Main courses** $9-$17. **No credit cards. Map** p278 C4.

How this lusty, colourful, exotic Tunisian restaurant remains such a secret even to Central Square locals is as much a mystery to us as how the owner sometimes manages to cook for and wait on eight tables while simultaneously yapping away into a cordless phone crunched between her head and shoulder. Everything is lovingly and perfectly prepared, from the fresh mint green tea to the ever-evolving savoury menu and the astonishing flourless chocolate torte with star anise, black pepper, saffron and ginger.

Chez Henri

1 Shepard Street, at Massachusetts Avenue (1-617 354 8980). Harvard or Porter T. **Open** 6-10pm Mon-Thur; 5.30-10pm Fri, Sat; 5.30-9pm, Sun. **Main courses** $16-$29. **Credit** AmEx, DC, MC, V. **Map** p278 A1.

Sometimes the French and Cuban fusion comes together wonderfully, for instance when a moist, tangy duck tamale garnishes a meal-sized warm spinach salad. At other times, this popular little bistro splits its dishes with flair – as in the bouillabaisse with a side dish of *tostones* (fried plantain). The menu changes constantly, though duck tamale is a staple. Boisterous in the winter and quieter in the summer, Chez Henri and its adjoining bar (*see p148* **Shakin' things up**) qualify as a first-class neighbourhood find. The lovingly prepared crème brûlée is to die for.

Oleana

134 Hampshire Street, at Elm Street (1-617 661 0505/www.oleanarestaurant.com). Central T then 10mins walk. **Open** 5.30-10pm Mon-Thur, Sun; 5.30-11pm Fri, Sat. **Main courses** $23-$28. **Credit** AmEx, MC, V. **Map** p278 C3.

Few cooks can boast of doing something original in this day and age, but Ana Sortun is one of them. Her Cambridge restaurant Oleana is one of the only places where you can experience the grills of Turkey, spice cookery of North Africa and haunting flavours of Armenia, turned out with the personalised stamp of a learned modern chef. Go heavy on the meze menu (dishes tend to lose focus when they get sized up to main courses) and definitely don't miss the desserts. The exotic leanings of the place extend to cocktails, Lebanese wines, an arrack selection and Turkish musicians who turn the garden into a slice of Istanbul during the warmer months. Service can be slow.

Latin

Forest Café

1682 Massachusetts Avenue, at Sacramento Street (1-617 661 7810). Harvard or Porter T. **Open** 5-10pm Mon-Wed, Sun; 11.30am-10pm Thur-Sat. **Main courses** $12-$19. **Credit** AmEx, DC, Disc, MC, V. **Map** p278 B1.

The closest many Cantabridgians will come to Mexico's two coastlines is this long, narrow barroom. Here the daily catch comes served with sauces of pumpkin seed and cilantro (coriander) while shrimp soak up garlic and herbs. Non-fish-eaters can enjoy a smoky mole chicken or enchilada, and it all comes at bar-room prices.

Midwest Grill

1124 Cambridge Street, at Norfolk Street (1-617 354 7536). Central or Lechmere T then 15mins walk. **Open** 11.30am-11.30pm daily. **Main courses** $16-$22. **Credit** AmEx, Disc, MC, V. **Map** p278 C2.

This Brazilian restaurant is a carnivore's dream. In the churrascaria tradition of primal dinner theatre, everything is grilled and the spits are taken from table to table, where waiters lop off peppery sausages and crispy chicken parts or carve from melting tenderloins and joints. The accompanying salad bar – with rice, beans and hearts of palm – is the only concession to nutritional balance.

Seafood

Jasper White's Summer Shack

149 Alewife Brook Parkway (1-617 520 9500). Alewife T. **Open** 11.30am-3pm, 5-10pm Mon-Fri; noon-11pm Sat; 3-9pm Sun. **Main courses** $8-$20. **Credit** AmEx, DC, Disc, MC, V.

Iconic chef Jasper White has got back in the business in a super-sized way with Summer Shack. His 220-seater draws inspiration from the raw oyster-slinging, clam-frying, lobster-steaming shacks found along the Eastern seaboard. The picnic tables in the dining room and fruit pies for dessert are much the same. But this 'shack' is all about excess, so there's a well-lit bar with Margaritas, TVs blaring Sox games, and sea-salty tastes ranging from low (Rhode Island-style calamari, served greasy with vinegar peppers) to high (pan-roasted lobster with chervil and cognac). If you can't get up to Maine for a meal, this is just as good. There's also a newer Back Bay outlet above Kings bowling alley (*see p226*) that's not quite as much raucous fun.

Other locations: 50 Dalton Street, at Boylston Street, Back Bay (1-617 867 9955).

Cafés & coffeehouses

For **Hi-Rise Bakery**, *see p138* **Bakery-cafés**.

LA Burdick

52D Brattle Street, at Farwell Place (1-617 491 4340/www.burdickchocolate.com). Harvard T.

Moody **Baraka Café**.
See p140.

The big scoop

Cold-weather Boston and hot-weather ice-cream? Yup. Back in the '70s novelist and *New Yorker* scribe Calvin Trillin cemented them as synonymous when he gushed about Steve Herrell's burgeoning local business – particularly the master ice-cream maker's innovative blending methods with Heath Bars and candy. The city has since become the highest per-capita consumer of the cooling treat in the US, and has continued to produce local cafés that hand-churn sorbets, ice-cream, and now yoghurt to year-round crowds – with no bona fide rival outside Italy. Don't imagine Ben & Jerry's doesn't take a few pages from the Hub's book on the occasional weekend trip from Vermont. The perennial cream of the crop are:

Christina's Homemade Ice Cream

1255 Cambridge Street, at Inman Square, Cambridge (1-617 492 7021). Central T then 10mins walk/83 bus. **Open** 11.30am-10.30pm Mon-Fri, Sun; 11.30am-11pm Sat. **Medium ice-cream** $3. **No credit cards. Map** p278 C2.

This Inman Square storefront has a cheery, small-town atmosphere and flavours that please adults, children – and adults who want to feel like children – with a range spanning Gingersnap Cookie, Sweet Corn, Khulfi and Hot Chocolate. Our personal favourite.

Emack & Bolio's

290 Newbury Street, at Gloucester Street, Back Bay (1-617 536 7127/ www.emackandbolios.com). Hynes/ICA T. **Open** 11am-11.30pm Mon-Thur; 11am-midnight Fri, Sat; noon-11.30pm Sun. **Medium ice-cream** $4. **No credit cards. Map** p276 F6.

Since expanding to other cities, the Newbury Street stalwart hasn't lost its mojo and serves one of the creamier examples around. Oreo Cookie ice-cream was, in fact, invented here in 1975 and it also has a series of flavours co-created by rock stars, like Purple Cow by Deep Purple's Glenn Hughes (black raspberry ice-cream with chocolate chips and blueberries) and the Sugar Ray Chip by Sugar Ray's Mark McGrath (vanilla with an array of chips). The café has a patio wrapped in a wrought-iron fence so one can lick, spoon and people-watch in peace.

Other locations: 1663 Beacon Street, at Winthrop Road, Brookline (1-617 731 6256).

Herrell's

15 Dunster Street, at Massachusetts Avenue, Cambridge (1-617 497 2179/ www.herrells.com). **Open** noon-midnight daily. **Medium ice-cream** $3.65. **No credit cards. Map** p278 B2.

Though the former hands-on master is no longer present, his namesake ice-creamery still uses his recipes, and the product has substantial style and emphatic taste. Flavours include Hearts & Flowers (vanilla with rose water and lavender), Negative Chocolate Chip (chocolate ice-cream with white chips) and Earl Grey.

Other locations: 155 Brighton Avenue, at Harvard Avenue, Allston (1-617 782 9599).

JP Lick's

659 Centre Street, at Green Street, Jamaica Plain (1-617 524 6740). Green Street T then 10mins walk/39 bus. **Open** *Oct-Apr* 6am-11pm Mon-Thur, Sun; 6am-midnight Fri, Sat. *May-Sept* 6am-midnight daily. **Medium ice-cream** $4. **No credit cards.**

Cow-patterned booths, zany tiled floors, and playful seasonal flavours like Cherry Garciaparra (for the Red Sox shortstop), Cape Cod (cranberry and vodka) and Tiramisu keep this Jamaica Plain-based mini-chain at the top of things. JP Lick's also serves as the neighbourhood's unofficial morning-coffee meeting place, and offers further temptation in the form of sinful brownies and home-made soft serve ice-cream in adult-oriented flavours such as Cinnamon Latte.

Other locations: 352 Newbury Street, at Hereford Street, Back Bay (1-617 236 1666); 311 Harvard Street, at Coolidge Corner, Brookline (1-617 738 8252).

Toscanini's

1310 Mass Avenue, at Linden Street, Cambridge (1-617 354 9350). Harvard T. **Open** 8am-11pm Mon-Fri; 9am-11pm Sat; 10am-11pm Sun. **Medium ice-cream** $3.95. **No credit cards. Map** p278 B2.

If you can't get to one of the sleek parlours in Cambridge, Toscanini's now sells by the pint in many speciality markets. The sophisticated flavours (Burnt Caramel, Cake Batter, White Coffee) and smooth quality of the product recall the best *gelati* in Italy.

Other locations: 899 Main Street, at Massachusetts Avenue, Cambridge (1-617 491 5877).

Open 8am-11pm Tue-Sat; 8am-10pm Sun, Mon. **Credit** AmEx, Disc, MC, V. **Map** p278 A2.
This world-class chocolate shop and café is the flagship of Swiss-trained chocolatier Larry Burdick, who works from his home base in New Hampshire. As well as the finely crafted truffles, it offers hot chocolate like one would find in Paris, Viennese pastries and the de rigueur croissant. Brown paper covers the tables and one can watch the Harvard intelligentsia in the slightly musty mirrors on the walls. The truffles and cute signature chocolate mice are sold in wooden gift boxes, which make wonderful, if expensive, presents.

1369 Coffee House

1369 Cambridge Street, at Hampshire Street (1-617 576 1369). Central T. **Open** 7am-10pm Mon-Thur; 7am-11pm Fri; 8am-11pm Sat; 8am-10pm Sun. **No credit cards. Map** p278 C2.
This is a hangout for everyone from bicycle couriers on a break to Cantabridgian musicians. At 1369 they know how to crank out high-power java, and the scene here is always buzzing.
Other locations: 757 Massachusetts Avenue, at Inman Street, Cambridge (1-617 576 4600).

Somerville

American

Redbones

55 Chester Street, at Davis Square (1-617 628 2200). Davis T. **Open** 11.30am-10.30pm Mon-Thur; 11.30am-11.30pm Fri, Sat; noon-10.30pm Sun. **Main courses** $8-$19. **No credit cards.**
Ranked among the best of the Boston area's barbecue spots, this Davis Square favourite is stocked with slow-cooked succulent ribs and brisket in the classic Southern style. Flaky fried catfish, spongy cornbread and spicy corn pudding are among the 'lighter' offerings. Huge platters, such as the nearly foot-high pile of ribs and brisket called the 'Barbecue Belt', will put you in a meat coma. As good as Southern cooking gets this far north.

RF O'Sullivan's

282 Beacon Street, at Sacramento Street (1-617 492 7773) Porter T. **Open** 11am-11pm Mon-Sat; noon-11pm Sun. **Main courses** $7-$8. **Credit** MC, V. **Map** p278 B1.
Want a great cheeseburger and an ice-cold beer with a side of blue-collar sincerity? O'Sullivan's meets all your criteria. The fist-sized patties are sweet, meaty and primal and come on a towering bun. Sam Adams is the favoured local brew accompaniment.

Rosebud Diner

381 Summer Street, at Davis Square (1-617 666 6015). Davis T. **Open** 8am-11pm Mon-Thur, Sun; 8am-midnight Fri, Sat. **Main courses** $7-$13. **Credit** AmEx, MC, V.
A restored dining car from 1941, the Rosebud Diner is a beacon of old-fashioned Americana – albeit with somewhat updated prices – amid the bars and eateries of gentrified Davis Square. Meals are still good value and traditional diner fare (hamburgers, clam chowder, steak tips) is dished up in an atmosphere of shiny chrome and pink neon that's straight out of *American Graffiti*.

Meat's on the menu at **Redbones.**

European

Dali

415 Washington Street, at Beacon Street (1-617 661 3254). Harvard T. **Open** 5.30-11pm daily. **Main courses** $19-$25. **Tapas** $4-$9. **Credit** AmEx, DC, MC, V. **Map** p278 C2.
Dali, one of the best Spanish eateries in the Boston area, also features some of the most accomplished flamenco-dancing waiters you'll find this side of the Atlantic. The atmosphere is animated, from the chatter at the bar to the lively Spanish music. There's usually a queue (reservations are only accepted for parties of six or more) for those waiting to try the dizzying array of savoury and creative tapas. The sangria's great, but don't miss the exceptional list of wines and sherries. Ask for one of the booth tables if it's intimacy you're after.

Cafés & coffeehouses

For **Carberry's Bakery & Coffeehouse**, *see p138* **Bakery-cafés**.

Pubs & Bars

Quirky dives, slick cocktail lounges and enough Irish pubs to rival Dublin... there's no shortage of watering holes in the Hub.

Boston's economy may have flagged somewhat in the past year or two, but the arrival of spanking-new pubs and bars continues apace. Now that Boston, Cambridge and Somerville have joined Brookline in a total ban on cigarettes in bars, watering holes are no longer shrouded in tobacco smoke – but the drinks are still flowing freely.

Many of the newer establishments in the city are aggressively upmarket, as if, in a collective act of boozy defiance, Bostonians have decided to embrace elegance and indulgence as never before. After all, who has the time to worry about economic indicators when you're trying to decide whether to have the Champagne Prague or the Lynchburg Lemonade? And of course there are plenty of extremely popular low-key bars in the area, places where you're as likely to get Guinness slopped on your shoe as be jabbed with a cocktail stick.

The legal drinking age in Boston is 21, but carry photo ID if you look under 30. And remember, the subway service ends at 12.30am – a good half an hour before most bars' last call – so you may have to fork out for a taxi.

Back Bay

An Tua Nua

835 Beacon Street, at Park Drive (1-617 262 2121). Kenmore T. **Open** 11am-1am Mon-Wed; 11am-2am Thur-Sun. **Credit** AmEx, MC, V.

An Tua Nua (Gaelic for 'the new beginning') is a rather odd hybrid of Irish pub and dance club, meaning that it's a fine place to either stop in for a quiet afternoon pint or shoehorn yourself into a seething mass of sweaty BU co-eds bumping and grinding to the latest dance hits.

Audubon Circle

838 Beacon Street, at Park Drive (1-617 421 1910). Kenmore T. **Open** 11am-1am daily. **Credit** AmEx, DC, Disc, MC, V.

With its slate counters, wooden bar-back and subdued lighting, Audubon is one of the more stylish drinking establishments in Boston, with an agreeable laid-back vibe. It does terrific food too (*see p115*).

Bill's Bar

5 Lansdowne Street, at Brookline Avenue (1-617 421 9678/www.billsbar.com). Kenmore T. **Open** 9pm-2am Mon, Wed-Fri; 10pm-2am Tue, Sat, Sun. **Credit** AmEx, MC, V. **Map** p276 D7.

Among the many nightclubs dotting Lansdowne Street, Bill's offers welcome respite from the clang and clatter of their large, twitching-room-only dancefloors. It's more intimate, and there's live music several nights a week – from reggae to rock. The off-evenings are still lively though, with DJs spinning the likes of Korn and Metallica (*see p209*).

Blue Cat Café

94 Massachusetts Avenue, at Newbury Street (1-617 247 9922). Hynes/ICA T. **Open** 5pm-1am daily. **Credit** AmEx, MC, V. **Map** p276 F6.

This spacious room has the look and feel of a French brasserie, but without the bright lighting. Although the tall brick walls are lined with photographs of jazz greats, the DJs here supplement their daily servings of classic jazz with acid jazz, house and techno. The crowd is a mix of college students and local residents.

Bomboa

35 Stanhope Street, at Clarendon Street (1-617 236 6363) Copley T. **Open** 5.30pm-2am Mon-Sat; 5.30pm-midnight Sun. **Credit** AmEx, DC, MC, V. **Map** p277 H6.

Because of this trendy yet friendly restaurant bar's location, at the point where several neighbourhoods converge, the crowd is an interesting mix of gay, straight, artistic and professional. The food is tasty (*see p117*), but the focus after midnight is on music and cocktails. Bomboa's extensive mixed-drinks menu features 16 different Martinis and various tropical concoctions. For aficionados of the spirit, Thursday is Vodka Night.

Boston Beer Works

61 Brookline Avenue, at Lansdowne Street (1-617 536 2337). Fenway or Kenmore T. **Open** 11.30am-1am daily. **Credit** AmEx, DC, Disc, MC, V. **Map** p276 D7.

With its cleverly positioned location right across the street from Fenway Park, Boston Beer Works can be overrun with baseball fans between April and September. But it's worth popping in here any time of year, if only for the beer which is made on the premises: brews like the crisp Fenway Pale Ale and the hearty Boston Red. There's a menu of above-par burgers and other munchables.

Bristol Lounge

Four Seasons Hotel, 200 Boylston Street, at Arlington Street (1-617 351 2071). Arlington T. **Open** 11am-1am daily. **Credit** AmEx, DC, Disc, MC, V. **Map** p277 F5.

A 'proper attire required' kind of place in the swanky Four Seasons Hotel. The bar is full of the sort of plush furniture low-tier royalty might have in their drawing rooms. And there's no telling just who one might see here: George Clooney reclining in one of the comfortable armchairs, Ted Kennedy sipping a glass of Jameson's by the fire, Gwyneth Paltrow enjoying subtle jazz piano.

Bukowski's Tavern

50 Dalton Street, at Boylston Street (1-617 437 9999). Hynes/ICA T. **Open** 11.30am-2am Mon-Sat; noon-2am Sun. **No credit cards**. **Map** p276 F6.

This tiny bar caters to a hip, young crowd, the kind that likes to enjoy a drink while listening to music that would drown out a tactical nuclear explosion. Still, if the bartender can hear you above the racket, the choice of beers here (more than 100 different kinds) makes it all worthwhile. If your taste runs to spirits, though, forget it. As one employee so aptly put it, 'It's all about beer.'

Other locations: 1281 Cambridge Street, at Inman Square, Cambridge (1-617 497 7077).

Kitsch 'n' cosy **Delux Café**. *See p147.*

Daisy Buchanan's

240A Newbury Street, at Fairfield Street (1-617 247 8516). Copley T. **Open** 11am-2am daily. **No credit cards. Map** p276 G6.

A favourite haunt of the romantically challenged, Daisy Buchanan's often resembles the set of the television game show *The Dating Game*. Although it can be interesting watching guys with enormous pecs pursuing girls with enormous, um, eyelashes, if you are not large of pec or lash you should probably keep walking.

Dillon's

955 Boylston Street, at Hereford Street (1-617 421 1818). Hynes/ICA T. **Open** 11am-2am daily. **Credit** AmEx, MC, V. **Map** p276 F6.

This used to be called Barcode and, apart from the name, not much has changed. You'll still find the same chattery PR people and expensively dressed international students sipping unpronouncable cocktails beneath its huge, languorous fans. It could be Dillon's elegant decor that attracts so many elegant people – or, more likely, the enormous mirror behind the bar.

Jillian's

145 Ipswich Street, at Lansdowne Street (1-617 437 0300). Kenmore T. **Open** 11am-2am daily. **Credit** AmEx, Disc, MC, V. **Map** p276 D7.

A whizz-banging, whirring, ding-donging megaplex, Jillian's is the kind of place where beer is barely necessary for those seeking intoxication. With a full arcade, a mock casino, pool tables galore, and other assorted amusements, the sensory overload at this three-storey fantasy land is hangover-inducing before you've even started drinking.

The Oak Bar

Fairmont Copley Plaza, 138 St James Avenue, at Copley Square (1-617 267 5300). Back Bay or Copley T. **Open** 4.30pm-1am daily. **Credit** AmEx, Disc, MC, V. **Map** p277 H6.

So this is how the other half live. From the high ceilings and the panelled walls to the plush furniture, the Oak Bar in the Fairmont Copley Plaza Hotel simply oozes class. Sink back into an easy chair and slurp down one of the delicious cognacs out of a magnificent snifter. Then get the hell out of there before you spend your entire holiday allowance. (Although the adjacent Oak Room does serve great steaks.)

Other Side Cosmic Café

407 Newbury Street, at Massachusetts Avenue (1-617 536 9477). Hynes/ICA T. **Open** 11.30am-midnight Sun-Thur; 11.30am-1am Fri-Sat. **Credit** MC, V. **Map** p276 E6.

At the tail end of Newbury Street, across Mass Ave from the trendy parts of Back Bay, the Other Side has become a sort of Galapagos Island of Newbury Street bars, attracting a different kettle of clientele. Scruffy and bohemian, this crowd is equally at home sipping carrot-based concoctions or beer. A good place to head if you can't face another Martini.

Sonsie

327 Newbury Street, between Hereford Street & Massachusetts Avenue (1-617 351 2500). Hynes/ICA T. **Open** 11.30am-1am daily. **Credit** AmEx, MC, V. **Map** p276 F6.

Known mainly as a restaurant (*see p116*), the tasteful Sonsie is a premier hangout for the Newbury Street elite and those who want to meet them.

TC's Lounge

1 Haviland Street, at Massachusetts Avenue (1-617 247 8109) Hynes/ICA T. **Open** 9am-2am Mon-Sat; noon-2am Sun. **No credit cards. Map** p276 F7.

This is the quintessential dive – cheap beer, great jukebox, 50-year-old furniture, a vending machine with snacks and an electric log fireplace. What more could you ask for in a bar? The clientele here is a mix of students from nearby Berklee College of Music, punk rockers and old-time regulars.

The Tikki Room

1 Lansdowne Street, at Ipswich Street (1-617 351 2580). Kenmore T. **Open** 5pm-2am Tue-Sat. **Credit** AmEx, Disc, MC, V. **Map** p276 D7

With its tropical theme and extensive list of flavoured-rum cocktails, this is where Bostonians go in mid-winter, as if the illusion of beaches and summer breezes might make them forget that they haven't been able to feel their toes for the last three months. Tends to attract a young crowd.

29 Newbury Street

29 Newbury Street, at Arlington Street (1-617 536 0290). Arlington T. **Open** 11.30am-1am daily. **Credit** AmEx, DC, MC, V. **Map** p277 H5.

Though primarily a restaurant, 29 has a thriving little bar where Boston's PR and media power players convene to chug Martinis and call each other 'darling'.

Whiskey Park

Park Plaza Hotel, 64 Arlington Street, at St James Avenue (1-617 542 1482). Arlington T. **Open** 4pm-2am Mon-Sat; 8am-2am Sun. **Credit** AmEx, DC, Disc, MC, V. **Map** p277 J6.

The Boston branch of a group of sleek drinkeries in New York, LA and Chicago founded by Cindy Crawford's hubby Randy Gerber, Whiskey Park is a playground for the rich and nearly famous. It features plush, overstuffed leather furniture, subdued lighting and high-quality but expensive drinks.

South End

For **Wally's**, *see p213*.

Anchovies

433 Columbus Avenue, at Braddock Park (1-617 266 5088). Back Bay T. **Open** 4pm-1am daily. **Credit** AmEx, MC, V. **Map** p277 G7.

Though it can get lively as the night wears on, this narrow, cosy, dimly lit neighbourhood bar is the perfect spot to enjoy a quiet drink and a no-frills appetiser at the end of a busy day. The low-key locals are regularly joined by the city's media types.

Clery's

113 Dartmouth Street, at Columbus Avenue (1-617 262 9874). Back Bay or Copley T. **Open** 11.30am-2am daily. **Credit** AmEx, Disc, MC, V. **Map** p277 H7.

Large, labyrinthine and lively, Clery's is one of the few remaining joints in the South End where you can still order a Bud without feeling like a pariah. The clientele is generally a mix of sporty youngsters and an unbuttoned after-work crowd, with a few locals thrown in for good measure. Clery's serves solid but unspectacular American food.

Delux Café

100 Chandler Street, at Clarendon Street (1-617 338 5258). Back Bay T. **Open** 5pm-1am Mon-Sat. **No credit cards. Map** p277 H7.

A shrine to all things kitsch, Delux is a good choice if you're in the mood to cosy up with the young and hip. And cosy up is right, too: the bar is as small as it is popular, the latter thanks largely to some fine microbrews and even finer food.

Franklin Café

278 Shawmut Avenue, at Hanson Street (1-617 350 0010). Back Bay T/East Berkeley Silver Line bus. **Open** 5.30pm-2am daily. **Credit** AmEx, Disc, MC, V. **Map** p277 J7.

This smallish, low-key restaurant bar is almost always packed to the gills with local foodies and trendies. The conversation is loud, the food is great, and the cocktails flow like there's no tomorrow. Be prepared to wait for a table if you show up after 6pm. *See also p120.*

The Red Fez

1222 Washington Street, at Perry Street (1-617 338 6060). Back Bay T/East Berkeley Silver Line bus. **Open** 4pm-2am daily. **Credit** AmEx, DC, Disc, MC, V. **Map** p277 J8.

Though people generally come to Fez for the upscale Middle Eastern food, there's also a long bar here, which is often crowded. While the drinks list – good wines, great cocktails – is impressive enough, it's worth checking this place out just for the colourful, quasi-Middle Eastern decor.

Downtown & Government Center

Bell in Hand Tavern

45-55 Union Street, at Congress Street (1-617 227 2098). Gov't Center or Haymarket T. **Open** 11.30am-2am Mon-Sat; noon-2am Sun. **Credit** AmEx, DC, Disc, MC, V. **Map** p275 L3.

Built in 1795, this is 'the oldest tavern in the US', as a plaque outside attests. Yet there's little 'ye olde' nonsense going on here; the unpretentious decor has been described as 'Woolworthian'. The clientele is largely young regulars and you'll find them nose to elbow Tuesday to Saturday, when the bar has live music. Outside is the haunting Holocaust Memorial.

Top five Irish pubs

Brendan Behan Pub

The bar that launched a thousand imitators: popular Behan's kicked off the Irish pub craze. *See p156.*

Doyle's

Politicians and locals rub shoulders at this big, beautiful boozer which has pulled pints for over 100 years. *See p157.*

The Phoenix Landing

This Irish pub/dance club hybrid plays everything from jazz to hip hop – without a Michael Flatley imitator in sight. *See p154.*

Tir Na Nog

The mahogany bar, bookcases and live folk nights make it worth squeezing into this tiny watering hole. *See p156.*

Matt Murphy's

A good pint of Guinness, some fine fiddling – but it's the top-notch comfort food that makes this pub stand out. *See p157.*

Bishop's Pub

1 Boylston Place, between Charles & Tremont Streets (1-617 351 2583). Boylston T. **Open** 4pm-2am Tue-Fri; 6pm-2am Sat. **Credit** AmEx, MC, V. **Map** p274 J5.

Situated in 'the Alley' – an area with lots of night-spots – Bishop's is a pit-stop for the giggling clouds of hairspray that float from club to club. Things don't really get started here until after 11pm, when you'll be lucky if you can breathe, let alone move.

The Black Rose

160 State Street, at Commercial Street (1-617 742 2286). Gov't Center or State T. **Open** 11.30am-2am Mon-Fri, Sun; noon-2am Sat. **Credit** AmEx, DC, MC, V. **Map** p 275 L4.

There are Irish Republican proclamations and photos of Republican patriots adorning the walls of the Black Rose. But don't let that put you off. If you fancy a singsong, this is the place to head: there's live Irish music every night, and a very friendly crowd.

The Good Life

28 Kingston Street, at Summer Street (1-617 451 2622). Downtown Crossing T. **Open** 11.30am-2am Mon-Sat. **Credit** AmEx, DC, MC, V. **Map** p274 K5.

One of several upmarket spots that have helped to drag downtown Boston out of late-night wasteland. This is one of the most popular – and for good reason. With its orange vinyl walls, wood panelling, Rat Pack soundtrack and *Goodfellas* ambience, the Good Life is a smirky tribute to lounge bars of the '50s. **Other locations**: 720 Massachusetts Avenue, at Pleasant Street, Cambridge (1-617 868 8800).

Shakin' things up

Boston may be a tradition-bound city, but it's anything but staid when it comes to drinking. Thanks to a quirky combination of jet-set students, old world academics and innovative mixologists, Boston is at the vanguard of the modern American cocktail craze – arguably the biggest of its kind since the Jazz Age.

Forget Cosmos: Latin tipples like the Caipirinha have been de rigueur here for a decade now – years before they became A-list party drinks in New York or London – especially at Chez Henri and, before that, the late Division Sixteen. Current info-age favourite, the Espresso Martini, was a Hub staple by the mid 1990s. Restaurants like No.9 Park devote entire evenings to vintage tipples. And in this town it's not only die-hard cocktail connoisseurs who know bartender schedules off by heart, in order to plan nights around where to find a good Sidecar or Pomegranitini. But here's where to grab a stool night in and night out:

Bar at Chez Henri

Equal parts homey Cambridge bar and Latin adventurer, the darkly moody Bar at Chez Henri concocts textbook Mojitos (mixed one drink at a time) and a rare Hemingway favourite from Cuba called the Periodista – think edgy Sidecar with a sultry Latin-American twist. *See p140.*

Pho Republique

This moody South-east Asian lounge serves exotic tipples like Mango and Lemongrass Martinis. Try the coconut-milk variation – it's a White Russian with a chic New Asian pedigree. *See p123.*

Bomboa

Zebra-striped banquettes, a zinc-topped bar, Espresso Martinis and Latin drinks – Pisco Sours from Peru, Passionfruit Caipiroshkas, and dozens more. *See p117.*

Excelsior

Lydia Shire was playing chef-behind-the-bar back in the 1980s. Now her swish restaurant serves up such exotic drinks as the Bajito (a Mojito mixed with basil that strikes a haunting herbaceous note). *See p115.*

B-Side Lounge

This hipster hideaway near Inman Square has free hard-boiled eggs at the bar, leather booths and a cocktail list that reads like an encyclopedia of American drinking history. Very *Great Gatsby*-esque. *See p152.*

No.9 Park

The house specialities, Pear Martini and Palmyra, have kick, subtle sweetness, just the right hit of sour lemon acidity, and a timeless class that would've made them contenders decades ago. *See p131.*

The Green Dragon

11 Marshall Street, at Union Street (1-617 367 0055). Gov't Center T. **Open** 11am-2am daily. **Credit** AmEx, DC, Disc, MC, V. **Map** p275 L3.

A stone's throw from the Bell in Hand (*see p147*), this bar dates back (though not in its present form) to 1773. The spot on which it stands is 'the birthplace of American freedom', where the sons of liberty gathered over a few pints to plot the downfall of the British. There's a glass case on the wall containing some of the implements – muskets and so on – which were used to achieve that end. Still, this is a congenial gaff with live music, attentive staff, carpeted nooks and faded wallpaper.

Hennessy's

25 Union Street, at Quincy Market (1-617 742 2121). Gov't Center or Haymarket T. **Open** 11am-2am daily. **Credit** AmEx, MC, V. **Map** p275 L3.

A warm, brightly lit place, with peat fires and *seisiún* music, and a welcoming refuge from the bustle of nearby Quincy Market. If you're aching to hear voices that ring with the musical cadences of Ireland, you can pop in here to have a nice drop of Guinness.

Jacob Wirth

31-37 Stuart Street, at Washington Street (1-617 338 8586). Boylston or NE Medical Center T. **Open** 11.30am-11pm Sun-Thur; 11.30am-midnight Fri-Sat. **Credit** AmEx, DC, Disc, MC, V. **Map** p 277 J6.

Besides serving some of the best Bratwurst in town, this eccentric, German-themed bar has a weekly singalong (Fridays 8pm to midnight), hosted by ivory-tinkling wag Mel Stiller, which has been a favourite of locals for the past 15 years.

JJ Foley's

21 Kingston Street, at Summer Street (1-617 338 7713). Downtown Crossing T. **Open** 8am-2am daily. **Credit** AmEx, MC, V. **Map** p274 K5.

This low-key Irish bar is an institution in Boston – a hangout for bike messengers, tattooed masses, business suits and borderline bums. Anyone who has lived in Boston for long has met someone at Foley's, or broken up with someone at Foley's, or met and broken up with them there on the same evening – or knows someone who has.

Other locations: 117 East Berkeley Street, at Cortes Street, South End (1-617 338 8935).

The Kinsale

2 Center Plaza, Government Center (1-617 742 5577). Gov't Center T. **Open** 11am-2am Tue-Sat; 11am-1am Sun. **Credit** AmEx, MC, V. **Map** p274 K3.

Built in Ireland and shipped to the Hub piece by piece, the Kinsale is Irish pub as theme park, but one could do a lot worse. The Guinness is top notch and the Irish staff are unfailingly pleasant. The Kinsale's central location means it can get crowded fast, but great pub grub and occasional live music more than make up for any stepped-on toes or spilled suds.

The Littlest Bar

47 Province Street, at Bromfield Street (1-617 523 9766). Downtown Crossing or Park St T. **Open** 8.30am-2am daily. **No credit cards**. **Map** p274 K4.

There may be smaller bars than this one (it measures 16ft/5m from end to end), but we don't know of any. Maximum occupancy is 34. It draws a crowd of doggedly loyal regulars, including members of Boston's political and cultural elite (note the 'Seamus Heaney peed here' sign outside the men's room). That said, the patrons seem willing to make room at the bar for newcomers – or they would if they could.

Locke-Ober

3 Winterplace, off Winter Street (1-617 542 1340/www.locke-ober.com). Downtown Crossing or Park St T. **Open** 11.30-10pm Mon-Fri; 5.30-11pm Sat. **Credit** AmEx, Disc, MC, V. **Map** p274 K4.

This Boston institution, established in the 19th century, has long been known as a place where the mythical Boston Brahmin came to smoke cigars and make power deals. Today, thanks to the smoking ban, the cigar smoke has dissipated. Locke-Ober has been taken over by Lydia Shire, one of Boston's most celebrated celebrity chefs, but the bar still hasn't lost its leathery, lineny elegance. Be prepared to shell out.

Lucky's

355 Congress Street, at A Street (1-617 357 5825) South Station T. **Open** 11.30am-2am Mon-Fri; 6pm-2am Sat, Sun. **Credit** AmEx, Disc, MC, V.

Nestled in the belly of a beautiful old warehouse, Lucky's is easily missed. The only sign to look for is the orange glow radiating from the basement windows. Once inside you may feel as though you've been transported back to the '50s, when men were men and bars were dens of iniquity. Staying true to

its retro theme, the big night at Lucky's is Sinatra Sunday – when young hipsters flock to hear the Al Vega Trio pay tribute to Ol' Blue Eyes. Lucky's also features live funk, soul and R&B from Wednesday to Saturday, beginning around 9.30pm.

Mr Dooley's

77 Broad Street, at State Street (1-617 338 5656). South Station or Downtown Crossing T. **Open** 11.30am-2am Mon-Fri; 11am-2am Sat, Sun. **Credit** AmEx, DC, Disc, MC, V. **Map** p275 L4.

Named after the fictional, opinion-rich barkeep of writer FP Dunne's syndicated newspaper columns, this financial district mainstay has a loyal clientele of journalists and politicians and lives up to its own billing as 'a great place for a pint and a chat'.

Peking Tom's Longtang Lounge

25 Kingston Street, at Summer Street (1-617 482 6282). Downtown Crossing T. **Open** 11am-2am Mon-Fri; 5.30pm-2am Sat, Sun. **Credit** MC, V. **Map** p274 K5.

A funky twist on a Chinese restaurant. Surrounded by simple, earthy decor, one can sip a Scorpion Bowl on a cosy chair in the front lounge area. The cocktail menu offers interesting hybrids such as the Bonsai Rita , and you can snack on Shrimp Shu Mai, tuna rolls and more. If you're looking for action, Peking Tom's comes alive from Thursday to Saturday after 10pm, when the DJs start spinning.

Pravda 116

116 Boylston Street, at Tremont Street (1-617 482 7799). Boylston T. **Open** 5pm-2am Wed-Sat. **Credit** AmEx, MC, V. **Map** p274 J5.

This is how the other half live in Russia: slick, upscale decor, pricey vodka and hordes of well-dressed lovelies saying 'Nyet' to a stream of romantic propositions. But fear not, brown booze aficionados, there's beer as well as vodka on sale. The bar has a dress code – so save the jeans, boots and flannels for tomorrow's hangover.

Rock Bottom

115 Stuart Street, at Tremont Street (1-617 523 6467). Boylston T. **Open** 11.30am-midnight Mon-Thur, Sun; 11.30am-1am Fri, Sat. **Credit** AmEx, MC, V. **Map** p277 J6.

It's not often you get to down a pint of real ale in a place that models itself on the watering holes of the American Southwest. But then Rock Bottom is nothing if not eclectic. As well as offering a wide selection of microbrew beers, this place allows you to wash down your steak and salad with a Tom Collins, if you so wish.

Silvertone

69 Bromfield Street, at Tremont Street (1-617 338 7887). Downtown Crossing or Park St T. **Open** 11.30am-2am Mon-Fri; 5pm-2am Sat. **Credit** AmEx, Disc, MC, V. **Map** p274 K4.

With its nifty 1940s-ish decor, pleasing jazz soundtrack and affable bar staff, Silvertone has attracted a loyal cadre of followers. Tucked away on a gloomy side street near Downtown Crossing, it's not really the kind of place you stumble across. But those who find it come back – the bar very often has standing room only. It also serves excellent comfort food (try the meat loaf). *See p125.*

Les Zygomates

129 South Street, at Kneeland Street (1-617 542 5108). South Station T. **Open** 11.30am-1am Mon-Sat. **Credit** AmEx, DC, Disc, MC, V.

Pronounced 'Zee-go-maht', this is one of Boston's most elegant wine bars. Some visitors may be intimidated by the upmarket atmosphere and the telephone directory sized wine list. *See also p125.*

Beacon Hill

Beacon Hill Tavern

228 Cambridge Street, at Charles Street (1-617 742 6192). Gov't Center T. **Open** 11am-2am daily. **Credit** AmEx, DC, MC, V. **Map** p274 H3.

During the week the Tavern is a place where young urban professionals and State House denizens gather to compare power suits. At the weekend regulars let their hair down a little – but just a little. Stay away if you have an aversion to khaki.

Cheers

84 Beacon Street, at Arlington Street (1-617 227 9605/www.cheersboston.com). Arlington T. **Open** 11am-1am daily. **Credit** AmEx, DC, Disc, MC, V. **Map** p274 H5.

Formerly the Bull and Finch Pub, Cheers is credited with inspiring the popular sitcom of the same name – but expect no Sams, Norms or Carlas. They don't know your name here, nor do they really want to. And they're only glad you came if you brought your wallet with you. Only obsessive fans will want to line up with the dozens of other tourists waiting for a spot inside to eat expensive hamburgers and drink pricey beer in a place that looks absolutely nothing like the bar in the TV show. The only part of this pub you'll recognise is the stairwell, as it provided the exterior shot. The replica Cheers in Faneuil Hall Marketplace (1-617 227 0150) feels even less authentic. Remember the episode of *Cheers* where Norm sat at one of the bar's outside tables eating a hamburger while throngs of tourists marched by clutching novelty baseball caps? No, of course not. The food may repeat on you later, but comparisons with the TV bar end there.

Sevens Pub

77 Charles Street, at Mount Vernon Street (1-617 523 9074). Charles/MGH T. **Open** 11.30am-1am Mon-Sat; noon-1am Sun. **No credit cards.** **Map** p274 J4.

Though often prohibitively crowded, this unpretentious little Beacon Hill pub is also a good spot to seek respite from a hard day of relentless sightseeing. Find a booth in the corner, settle down with a Guinness or a Bass and you might just find the Freedom Trail ends right here.

The 21st Amendment

148 Bowdoin Street, at Beacon Street (1-617 227 7100). Park St T. **Open** 11.30am-2am daily. **Credit** AmEx, MC, V. **Map** p274 K4.

On the surface, there's nothing particularly interesting about this small, low-ceilinged bar. Right across the street, however, is the State House, which leads to the happy spectacle of power brokers, tourists and local ne'er-do-wells sharing a drink together.

North

Anthem

138 Portland Street, at Merrimac Street (1-617 523 8383). Haymarket or North Station T. **Open** 11.30am-1am daily. **Credit** AmEx, Disc, MC, V. **Map** p274 K3.

This bar aspires to a kind of warehouse-chic ambience. The long copper-top bar is often the resting place for such classic concoctions as the Sidecar or Mint Julep. If you are looking to just lounge around, head downstairs to Anthem's cavernous, stylish basement bar with its velvet couches, plasma televisions and several secret VIP rooms.

Grand Canal

57 Canal Street, at Causeway Street (1-617 523 1112). Haymarket or North Station T. **Open** 11am-1.30am daily. **Credit** AmEx, DC, Disc, MC, V. **Map** p274 K2.

The Grand Canal boasts one of the finest façades in the city. There's something very English about the place, although the no-frills menu is decidedly American. Live music (on Friday and Saturday nights) and a cheery pub atmosphere have made this bar enormously popular with a young crowd.

Cambridge

B-Side Lounge

92 Hampshire Street, at Windsor Street (1-617 354 0766). Central or Kendall/MIT T. **Open** 5.30pm-1am Mon-Wed, Sun; 5.30pm-2am Thur-Sat; 11am-2am Sun. **Credit** AmEx, MC, V. **Map** p278 C3.

Formerly the Windsor Tap, a real dive, the B-Side is now a faux dive, complete with red-neon decor and free hard-boiled eggs at the bar. The menu is out of this world – wash it down with a bottle of Pabst Blue Ribbon and you'll feel right at home with the trendy Cantabrigians who flock here. *See also p137.*

Cambridge Brewing Company

Building 100, 1 Kendall Square, at Hampshire Street (1-617 494 1994). Kendall/MIT T. **Open** 11.30am-1am Mon-Fri; noon-1am Sat; 3pm-1am Sun. **Credit** AmEx, MC, V.

Located in the industrial-turned-entertainment complex One Kendall Square, this bar boasts some of the finest own-brews in the region – the Tall Tale Pale Ale is a winner. In the summer you can sit at the tables outside, where trees adorned with twinkling fairy lights create a romantic setting. Or maybe that's just the beer talking.

Cambridge Common & Lizard Lounge

1667 Massachusetts Avenue, at Sacramento Street (1-617 547 1228). Harvard or Porter T. **Open** 11.30am-1am Mon-Wed; 11.30am-2am Thur-Sat; 11am-1am Sun. **Credit** AmEx, DC, Disc, MC, V. **Map** p278 B1.

This is a low-key, get-a-couple-down-you kind of place. Off the beaten track (between Harvard and Porter Squares), it attracts mostly regulars, as well as the poets, jazz players and Marlene Dietrich-lookalikes who frequent the Lizard Lounge club downstairs (*see p210*).

The Enormous Room

567 Massachusetts Avenue, at Norfolk Street (1-617 491 5550). Central T. **Open** 5.30pm-1am Mon-Wed, Sun; 5.30pm-2am Thur-Sat. **Credit** AmEx, Disc, MC, V. **Map** p128 C3.

Even with a capacity of 85, the room never really feels enormous enough – a queue starts to form outside as early as 9pm. If you do get in, you'll find a long, dark space filled mostly with twentysomething students pursuing an exotic, near-Eastern evening of intrigue. Different DJs do variations on the same theme – acid, techno, house or jazz, depending on the night. Save for some sofas at the front, seating is on bi-level platforms strewn with oriental rugs and pillows. If you are good at eating with your hands while lying down, you can sup upon a platter of Moroccan appetisers.

The Field

20 Prospect Street, at Massachusetts Avenue (1-617 354 7345). Central T. **Open** noon-1am Mon-Thur, Sun; noon-2am Fri, Sat. **No credit cards**. **Map** p311 C3.

This place manages to give the feel of a real Dublin pub, probably because it doesn't try too hard. Irish and American kids jostle and bob along happily to the music and chat each other up in the front room, sit in the considerably more sedate back room, or have a game of pool or darts.

Grafton Street

1230 Massachusetts Avenue, at Plympton Street (1-617 497 0400). Harvard T. **Open** 11am-1am daily. **Credit** AmEx, MC, V. **Map** p278 B3.

This relative newcomer to the Irish pub set overflows in summer, when its big French windows allow interaction with Harvard Square's fascinating parade. Expect no leprechaun logos or fiddledy-dee music at this place – Grafton Street stresses upscale modernism over traditional Irish stereotypes. Serves haute pub grub and cocktails.

Grendel's Den

89 Winthrop Street, at John F Kennedy Street (1-617 491 1160). Harvard T. **Open** 11.30am-1am Mon-Sat; 4pm-1am Sun. **Credit** AmEx, Disc, MC, V. **Map** p278 A2.

This unpretentious little basement bar – which recently underwent a major overhaul – continues to attract throngs of intelligent, well-behaved Harvard

Big night out: the **Enormous Room** fills up fast. *See p152.*

students. From 5pm to 7.30pm (9pm to 11.30pm Sundays), everything on the menu is half price after the purchase of a $3 drink. Even tomorrow's leaders need a bargain now and then.

Hong Kong

1236 Massachusetts Avenue, at Plympton Street (1-617 864 5311). Harvard T. **Open** 11.30am-2am daily. **Credit** AmEx, DC, Disc, MC, V. **Map** p311 B2

Despite the kitsch 1950s-style sign out front, this Chinese restaurant-cum-bar – a Harvard institution – is lacking in eye-candy decor. The downstairs restaurant is Chinesey enough, but the first-floor bar is a modest affair where darts, Budweiser and wonton soup are not strange bedfellows.

John Harvard's Brew House

33 Dunster Street, at Massachusetts Avenue (1-617 868 3585). Harvard T. **Open** 11.30am-12.30am Mon-Wed; 11.30am-1am Thur; 11.30am-1.30am Fri, Sat; 11.30am-midnight Sun. **Credit** AmEx, DC, Disc, MC, V. **Map** p278 B2.

A longtime favourite with the local student body, this large basement brew pub in Harvard Square offers basic American cooking and a selection of its own ales – try the delicious Old Willy's IPA.

Miracle of Science Bar & Grill

321 Massachusetts Avenue, at State Street (1-617 868 2866). Central T. **Open** 7am-1am Mon-Fri; 9am-1am Sat, Sun. **Credit** AmEx, Disc, MC, V. **Map** p278 C4.

Sister bar to Audubon Circle in Boston (*see p144*), the Miracle of Science boasts ultra-modern design, good beer and a comfortable atmosphere, with huge windows looking out over Mass Ave. In honour of the many MIT students who frequent the place, the bar serves drinks in laboratory beakers.

Noir

Charles Hotel, 1 Bennett Street, at Harvard Square, Cambridge (1-617 661 8010). Harvard T. **Open** 4pm-2am daily. **Credit** AmEx, MC, V. **Map** p278 A2.

This lovely little lounge in the Charles Hotel stays true to its name: the decor is 1940s film noir and the colour scheme is black. To say the lighting is minimal is an understatement. The candlelit atmosphere makes this a perfect place for a romantic drink. This is the only bar in Cambridge open until 2am seven nights a week, and if you want a smoke, you can even take your libation outside while you puff.

Join the regulars at well-loved Cambridge pub the **Plough & Stars**.

People's Republik

880 Massachusetts Avenue, at Lee Street (1-617 492 8632). Central or Harvard T. **Open** noon-1am Mon-Wed, Sun; noon-2am Thur-Sat. **No credit cards. Map** p278 C3.

In the spot that used to house the divey little bar Drumlins, the People's Republik has jazzed things up considerably. In the daytime you'll find postal workers from down the street cosying up to the bar. At night, though, it becomes a seething cauldron of youth. With old Russian and Chinese communist propaganda posters on the walls, and a giant mock bomb above the window, the Republik plays around with a revolutionary theme, which has led local wags to rename it 'Kremlin's'.

The Phoenix Landing

512 Massachusetts Avenue, at Brookline Street, Cambridge (1-617 576 6260). Central T. **Open** 11am-1am Sun-Thur; 11am-2am Fri, Sat. **Credit** AmEx, DC, Disc, MC, V. **Map** p278 C3.

Invariably packed, loud and steamy, this was one of the first Irish bars in the area to realise the potential of combining a dance club with a pub. The Landing offers live music (on Tuesday nights) as well as showcasing up-and-coming local DJs. Besides pulling a very decent pint of Guinness, the bar shows English football at weekends, coupled with delicious, artery-clogging full Irish breakfasts. *See also p192.*

Plough & Stars

912 Massachusetts Avenue, at Hancock Street (1-617 441 3455). Central T. **Open** 11.30am-1am Mon-Sat; noon-1am Sun. **Credit** AmEx, Disc, MC, V. **Map** p278 B3.

The spiritual forefather of Greater Boston's thriving Irish pub business, the Plough has been going for 30 years and many of the regulars who line the bar have been around since the beginning. In the daytime the Plough offers the best pub grub in town. At night the tiny bar is transformed into a hotbed of clashing elbows and live music. *See also p211.*

Redline

59 John F Kennedy Street, at Eliot Street (1-617 491-9851). Harvard T. **Open** 11am-1am Sun-Wed; 11am-2am Thur-Sat. **Credit** AmEx, DC, Disc, MC, V. **Map** p278 A3.

Situated in the spot where the fabled Crimson Sports Bar & Grille used to be – a place where the Bud flowed freely and the sports coverage never stopped

– Redline has tried to up the ante a little, with a granite bar top, a red-and-black colour scheme and cosy booths, not to mention a full lunch and dinner menu. After 10pm a DJ shows up and the place transforms into a mini disco. But there are still a couple of large-screen TVs, so the Harvard students who continue to flock here can catch a game from time to time.

Rialto

Charles Hotel, 1 Bennett Street, at Harvard Square. (1-617 661 5050). Harvard T. **Open** 5pm-12.30am daily. **Credit** AmEx, DC, MC, V. **Map** p278 B2.

Not your 'let's-pop-in-for-a-quickie' kind of place, Rialto serves hefty cocktails (not to mention excellent food in the restaurant, *see p137*) with prices to match. As it's nestled in the elegant Charles Hotel and a stone's throw from Harvard's John F Kennedy School of Government, you're just as likely to find yourself sipping a G&T beside foreign dignitaries as expense account-wielding out-of-towners and well-heeled locals.

River Gods

125 River Street, at Kinnaird Street (1-617 576 1881). Central T then 10mins walk. **Open** 3pm-1am daily. **Credit** AmEx, MC, V. **Map** p278 B3.

The Irish owners serve a great pint of Guinness, but you won't find any shamrocks hanging on the walls here. River Gods is a contemporary, swanky yet cosy bar. The small space fills up quickly at around 9pm, as the DJs, who rotate nightly, do their thing. The beer selection is good, cocktails are reasonably priced and tasty food is served nightly until 10pm.

Shay's Lounge

58 John F Kennedy Street, at Mount Auburn Street (1-617 864 9161). Harvard T. **Open** 11am-1am Mon-Sat; noon-1am Sun. **Credit** AmEx, MC, V. **Map** p278 B2.

Owned and operated by English expats, Shay's is one of the nicer bars in the area. Sunk a few feet below the sidewalk and with a nifty outdoor patio, the bar itself is rather poky. It attracts a lively mix of academics, artists and die-hard regulars. Though many quaff from Shay's extensive beer menu, this is primarily a wine bar and there are no spirits.

Temple Bar

1688 Massachusetts Avenue, at Sacramento Street (1-617 547 5055). Harvard or Porter T. **Open** 5pm-1am Mon-Fri; 11am-1am Sat, Sun. **Credit** AmEx, DC, Disc, MC, V. **Map** p278 B1.

Despite its name, an Irish pub this ain't. Emblematic of the current vogue for neo-lounge bars, it attracts the nouveau-riche, mobile-phone-wielding, Martini-clinking crowd. The atmosphere is serene and the food a little classier than your usual pub grub (lobster bisque, artichoke pizza).

Toad

1912 Massachusetts Avenue, at Porter Square (1-617 497 4950). Porter T. **Open** 5pm-1am Mon-Wed, Sun; 5pm-2am Thur-Sat. **No credit cards. Map** p278 B1

You'd miss Toad if you blinked. But if you want to get intimate with Cambridge residents, this friendly, low-key bar is the place to hang out. Toad defies physical laws by successfully combining nightly live music, huge popularity and a minuscule size.

Zu Zu

474 Massachusetts Avenue, at Brookline Street (1-617 864 3278). Central T. **Open** 5.30pm-1am Mon-Wed, Sun; 5.30pm-2am Thur-Sat. **Credit** AmEx, Disc, MC, V. **Map** p278 C3.

Sandwiched between the two entrances of its big brother, the Middle East *(see p211)*, Zu Zu is one of the gems of Central Square. With its muted red and orange tones, this is a great place to have a drink, nosh on some Middle Eastern mezes and make some selections from the best jukebox in town. Zu Zu is known as a haven for local musicians, and when they're not sipping the bar's creative cocktails, they're playing. Every night, starting at 10.30pm, Zu Zu features eclectic live music (no cover charge), from Latin to pure rock 'n' roll.

Somerville

The Burren

247 Elm Street, at Davis Square (1-617 776 6896). Davis T. **Open** 11.30am-1am Mon-Fri; 9am-1am Sat, Sun. **Credit** AmEx, MC, V.

Since its launch in the mid-1990s, the Burren has enjoyed enormous success – so much so that it has expanded, opening up a huge back room to accommodate the pub's many devotees. In the daytime a scattering of people can be found eating beef-and-Guinness stew at the bar's wooden tables. At night the place is packed largely with students from nearby Tufts University, who show up to hear classy Irish musicians jam in the pub's *seisiúns*.

The Independent

75 Union Square, at Stone Avenue (1-617 440 6022). Harvard T then 86 bus. **Open** 4.30pm-1am Mon-Sat; 11am-1am Sun. **Credit** AmEx, DC, Disc, MC, V.

Yet another Irish pub that has chosen to forego flouting its 'Oirishness' in favour of comfort and low-key elegance. While the restaurant here is known for its tasty food, the adjoining bar can get pretty brash in the evenings. Favoured among locals, the Independent boasts a fine wine list, Guinness (of course) and a friendly atmosphere.

Orleans

65 Holland Street, at Davis Square (1-617 591 2100). Davis T. **Open** 11am-1am Mon-Sat; 10.30am-1am Sun. **Credit** AmEx, Disc, MC, V.

Half restaurant, half lounge, with no walls between the two, this large open space aspires to a casual ambience. The large floor-to-ceiling windows are especially nice during the warmer months when they are opened up for street viewing. The student party crowd begins to trickle in at around 10pm when the DJ starts spinning.

PJ Ryan's

239 Holland Street, at Teele Square (1-617 625 8200). Davis T. **Open** 4pm-1am Mon-Thur; noon-1am Fri; 10am-1am Sat, Sun. **Credit** AmEx, Disc, MC, V.

A relative newcomer to Somerville, PJs does the Irish pub thing right. No shamrocks on the wall here; instead a couple of Jack Yeats paintings, a perfectly pulled pint and live music at the weekend create the right vibe. With its intimate size, dark-wood panelling and homey feel, it's the perfect place to grab a beer and watch the world go by through its large front windows. Take note: on Tuesdays PJs has a very popular trivia night that can make getting through the door a challenge.

Sligo Pub

237A Elm Street, at Davis Square (1-617 623 9651). Davis T. **Open** 8am-1am daily. **No credit cards**.

Its spruced-up new sign and façade notwithstanding, the Sligo is one of the last bastions of Davis Square's blue-collar traditions. It's a throwback to another era – from the oldies on the jukebox to the small glass that accompanies your bottle of Miller High Life. Though the number of Buddy Holly-bespectacled Tufts students has increased here lately, it still serves generous shots of the hard stuff to guys who look like they've been regulars since Eisenhower was president.

Thirsty Scholar Pub

70 Beacon Street, at Washington Street (1-617 497 2294). Harvard T. **Open** 11am-1am daily. **Credit** AmEx, MC, V.

With its exposed brick walls and little nooks and crannies, the Thirsty Scholar is the perfect place for an intimate drink. Not that you'd particularly want to shut yourself off from this pub's patrons, who rank among the friendliest – and probably the most literate – in the area. Many distinguished local writers have flocked here to get sozzled and discuss the finer points of literaure.

Tir Na Nog

366A Somerville Avenue, at Union Square (1-617 628 4300). Porter T. **Open** 2pm-1am Mon-Thur; 11.30am-1am Fri-Sun. **Credit** Disc, MC, V.

This is a terrific little pub, with bookcases lining the walls, a marvellous mahogany bar and a friendly crowd. But it's tiny, and on nights when it hosts live Irish or folk music it can begin to feel like the inside of a bean burrito. Having said that, you couldn't hope to have the life squeezed out of you by a nicer bunch of people.

Toast

70 Union Square, at Washington Street (1-617 623 9211/www.toastlounge.com). Davis Square T then 87 bus. **Open** 5.30pm-1am Wed-Sun. **Admission** $5. **Credit** AmEx, DC, Disc, MC, V.

This New York-style lounge comes in three parts. The small front room, with its minimalist decor, has the feeling of a waiting-room – waiting, that is, to pluck up the courage to venture into the next room. The second room is the largest and loungiest, with large, high-back red sofas fluffed with big pillows. And, if you don't fall asleep on one of the sofas, the third room is where the music and people are. The DJ spins dance and techno nightly (*see p192*).

Allston

Model Café

7 North Beacon Street, at Cambridge Street (1-617 254 9365). Harvard Ave T/57 or 66 bus. **Open** 3pm-2am Mon-Sat; 5pm-2am Sun. **No credit cards**.

The Model started off as an unpretentious little neighbourhood dive and then one day, through no fault of its own, became suddenly enormously pretentious, playing host to the cream of the counter-cultural community (who inexplicably started calling it the 'Mow-*dell*'). Nowadays the trendy crowd and the divey neighbourhood crowd share the place. The jukebox is among the best around.

Sunset Grill

130 Brighton Avenue, at Harvard Avenue (1-617 254 1331). Harvard Ave T/57 or 66 bus. **Open** 11.30am-1am daily. **Credit** AmEx, DC, Disc, MC, V.

For the no-nonsense ale lover, this may be the only bar in town worth a visit. The beer menu is huge: 380 bottled beers, 112 on tap. The decor is nothing spectacular, and unless you have a thing about college students, the clientele won't knock your socks off. But with all that ale inside you, who cares?

Wonder Bar

186 Harvard Avenue, at Commonwealth Avenue (1-617 351 2665). Harvard Ave T/57 or 66 bus. **Open** 5pm-2am daily. **Credit** AmEx, Disc, MC, V.

On the premises of what used to be a famously grungy music club, Wonder Bar makes no bones about wanting to move in higher circles. At the door a dress code proclaims, among other things, that 'shirts must be tucked and buttoned'. Inside, the bar's black-and-white tiled floor, slo-mo ceiling fans and jazz trio all attest to the encroachment of Martini sensibilities on a Bud Lite neighbourhood.

Jamaica Plain

Brendan Behan Pub

378 Centre Street, at Sherridan Street, Jamaica Plain (1-617 522 5386). Stony Brook T. **Open** noon-1am Mon-Sun. **No credit cards**.

This is one of the jewels of Boston's popular Irish pub scene. Named after the Irish playwright, the Behan has kept up the tradition by regularly hosting readings and storytellings. Patrick McCabe has read here, as has JP Donleavy. Behan's is not a fancy place – it's small and dimly lit, with no food on offer – but this too is part of its charm. It's effortlessly Irish, which can't always be said of the many imitators it has spawned. This is the real deal. Sadly, the pub no longer holds its standing-room-only *seisiúns*, but devoted regulars still come here for a quiet drink and a game of cribbage.

Boston's old Irish charmer, **Doyle's**.

Doyle's

3484 Washington Street, at Williams Street (1-617 524 2345). Green Street T. **Open** 9am-1am daily. **No credit cards.**

One of the oldest Irish pubs in Boston, Doyle's has been in the business for more than a century and oozes an effortless charm without any 'Dublin 23 Miles' signs. It's a rambling place, with high ceilings, huge murals and, invariably, a chatty crowd. It also serves hearty food at low prices.

Flann O'Brien's

1619 Tremont Street, at Wigglesworth Street (1-617 566 7744). Brigham Circle T. **Open** 11am-1am daily. **No credit cards.**

Though somewhat out of the way in the Brigham Circle area, O'Brien's is worth the trip. Irish immigrants and locals alike have found this an ideal spot to let their hair down and have a bit of mad fun.

Brookline

Matt Murphy's

14 Harvard Street, at Webster Place, Brookline (1-617 232 0188). Brookline Village T. **Open** 11.30am-2am Sun-Fri; 11.30am-1am Sat. **No credit cards.**

Like many Irish bars, Matt Murphy's prides itself on pouring a good pint of Guinness, and features a fair amount of fiddly-dee-type music (along with jazz, blues, and reggae). What makes it such a hit among locals, though, is its grub. The fish and chips (served in newspaper, no less) is better than fast-food fare has a right to be, the shepherd's pie is the best in town and the place even makes its own ketchup. However, while it's not as youth-oriented as some of the city's Irish bars, Murphy's still gets its customers moving once the music starts – if they're capable of moving after dinner, that is.

Shops & Services

Conveniently compact retail districts and a new crop of style-conscious stores make it easy to spend, spend, spend.

While Boston is not known as a major shopping destination (why come here for a spree when the overflowing cornucopia of New York is just a few hours' drive away?), it does offer a less frenetic browsing experience than the Big Apple: on a fine day, a relaxed stroll past the immaculate townhouses of Newbury Street or the South End is extremely pleasant. And recently the city's retail landscape has much improved, as scattered pockets of independent interiors/gift shops and boutiques have sprouted up with an air of sophisticated style to rival New York. While chains and mainstream designer shops dominate the main retail areas, such as Newbury Street and Downtown Crossing, the large student population ensures the survival of quirky boutiques and numerous second-hand clothing shops. Some of the most interesting hunting grounds aren't in Boston proper, but in surrounding neighbourhoods – still, far flung in this small city isn't so far.

There is no sales tax on clothing in Massachusetts (there is a five per cent sales tax on other goods), making it a better place to shop, in terms of price, than many of its surrounding states, most of which have high sales taxes.

SHOPPING AREAS

For an easy one-day outing, stick to the major shopping areas. The **Back Bay** has the highest concentration of shops, with two major malls and the city's most famous shopping drag, **Newbury Street** (*see p161* **A stroll up Newbury Street**), all within walking distance. Unfortunately, the prices tend to reflect the area's high rents. The most upmarket retailers are at the Arlington Street end. Around the corner, the relatively new **Heritage on the Garden**, at the corner of Arlington and Boylston Streets, is a couture clutch including the ultra-luxe Hermès and La Perla.

A short stroll up Boylston Street brings you to the mainstream retail cluster at **Copley Square**, comprising the Prudential Center mall and its more upmarket neighbour, the Copley Place mall, which are connected by an enclosed bridge. In direct contrast, the shops in the **South End** are tiny independents, sometimes inconveniently spaced apart. Thanks to the stylish gay population, the area has become a centre for chic home and gift shops.

The crowded **Downtown Crossing** is the first stop for many shoppers, most of whom are succumbing to the siren's call of **Filene's Basement** (*see p160)*. A few ancient independent retailers are tucked away on the side streets (the 'rungs' off main streets Washington and Tremont, which gave rise to the recently resurrected moniker the Ladder District. **Washington Street**, the main downtown drag, has a slightly rough edge and is dominated by department stores, discount outlets and uninspiring vending carts.

Although it's just across Boston Common, genteel **Beacon Hill** feels like another world, with steep cobblestoned streets and correspondingly steep prices at its antique shops and handful of chic boutiques.

In the opposite direction, near the waterfront, **Faneuil Hall Marketplace** is one of the region's most popular shopping attractions. It's often overcrowded on fine days and the shops are mainly chains or catering to tourists, but the cobblestoned setting is charming. From here, head north to investigate the traditional Italian food shops and cafés of the nearby **North End**.

Across the Charles River in Cambridge, **Harvard Square** has a concentrated collection of discount bookshops to cater to the famous university's student body. But some of the more interesting shops, including offbeat record and book stores, are located on the walk up Massachusetts Avenue between Central and Porter Squares. The Porter Exchange, in the old art deco Sears & Roebuck building in Porter Square (1815 Massachusetts Avenue), now houses Japanese shops and eateries (*see p139*).

It's also worth exploring further afield in neighbouring cities and suburbs such as **Davis Square**, Somerville, and **Jamaica Plain** – for offbeat independent shops.

One-stop

Department stores

Filene's

426 Washington Street, at Summer Street, Downtown (1-617 357 2100/www.filenes.com). Park St or Downtown Crossing T. **Open** 9.30am-8pm Mon-Tue; 9am-9pm Wed-Fri; 8am-9pm Sat; 11am-7pm Sun. **Credit** AmEx, Disc, MC, V. **Map** p274 K5.

Browse thousands of tomes at **Brattle Book Shop**. *See p163.*

Filene's itself is an unremarkable mid-range department store selling brand-name clothing, cosmetics, china, furniture, homewares and luggage. The real attraction is below ground level – the separately owned discount store Filene's Basement (*see p160*).

Lord & Taylor

760 Boylston Street, at Exeter Street, Back Bay (1-617 262 6000/www.lordandtaylor.com). Copley T. **Open** 10am-9pm Mon, Tue, Thur, Fri; 9am-9pm Wed; 9am-8pm Sat; 11am-7pm Sun. **Credit** AmEx, Disc, MC, V. **Map** p277 G6.

A classic department store with a conservative air, selling designer and brand-name men's, women's and children's clothing, sportswear and shoes, as well as cosmetics, jewellery and accessories. The end-of-season sales offer huge savings, with up to 75% discounts.

Louis Boston

234 Berkeley Street, at Newbury Street, Back Bay (1-617 262 6100/www.louisboston.com). Arlington T. **Open** 11am-6pm Mon; 10am-6pm Tue, Wed; 10am-7pm Thur-Sat. **Credit** AmEx, MC, V. **Map** p277 H5.

You could easily spend a whole day, and an entire inheritance, at this five-floor couture playhouse in the former Museum of Natural History building. As well as men's and women's collections from top international designers and hot young talent, it has its own upmarket house label and a wide selection of boutique make-up lines and fragrances. Despite the rarefied atmosphere – no humble sales assistants here, they're 'consultants' – the market-style ground floor displays a surprisingly affordable collection of chic gift items, from CDs to toiletries and home accessories. Its chi-chi Restaurant L is frequented by local socialites, but don't try to go for tea – it only serves lunch and dinner (*see p115*).

Macy's

450 Washington Street, at Summer Street, Downtown (1-617 357 3000/www.macys.com). Park St or Downtown Crossing T. **Open** 9.30am-8pm Mon-Sat; 11am-7pm Sun. **Credit** AmEx, MC, V. **Map** p274 K5.

Macy's replaced Boston institution Jordan Marsh in 1996 (there's even a plaque outside commemorating the dearly departed store), but in fact it was more of a conversion than a hostile takeover, since Federated Department Stores, Macy's umbrella company, already owned Jordan's. Macy's sells brand-name clothing, cosmetics, housewares, furniture, and lingerie, but those expecting the scale or choice of the famous New York store will be disappointed by this Boston outpost.

Neiman Marcus

5 Copley Place, at Dartmouth Street, Back Bay (1-617 536 3660/www.neimanmarcus.com). Back Bay or Copley T. **Open** 10am-8pm Mon-Sat; noon-6pm Sun. **Credit** AmEx, DC, Disc, MC, V. **Map** p277 G6.

Situated in the posh Copley Place mall, Neiman Marcus bills itself as a 'high-end speciality store'. As well as the big international names in clothes (Gucci, Marc Jacobs, DKNY), shoes (Manolo Blahnik, Tod's), cosmetics and accessories, you'll find furs and precious jewellery. A good place to indulge in some luxury retail therapy.

Saks Fifth Avenue

Prudential Center, 800 Boylston Street, Back Bay (1-617 262 8500/www.saks.com). Copley T. **Open** 10am-8pm Mon-Sat; noon-6pm Sun. **Credit** AmEx, DC, Disc, MC, V. **Map** p276 G6.

The Bostonian branch of the Manhattan-born store is known for its old-world service and contemporary designer labels (Donna Karan, Calvin Klein and Michael Kors, to name a few). It also sells shoes, accessories, lingerie and cosmetics, and has a full-service beauty salon.

Shopping malls

CambridgeSide Galleria

100 Cambridgeside Place, off Edwin Land Boulevard, Cambridge (1-617 621 8666/www.cambridgeside galleria.com). Lechmere T then 5mins walk or Kendall/MIT T then free shuttle bus. **Open** 10am-9.30pm Mon-Sat; 11am-7pm Sun. **Credit** varies. **Map** p274 H2.

The only major retail oasis within striking distance of the curiously shop-free Kendall Square, the Galleria is good for stocking up on inexpensive basics from the likes of J Crew, Old Navy and Abercrombie & Fitch. It also has one of the Boston area's only two Apple Stores (*see p166*) – a bonus for students from nearby MIT. There's a free shuttle-bus service to and from the Kendall T stop every 20 minutes.

Copley Place

100 Huntington Avenue, at Copley Square, Back Bay (1-617 369 5000/www.simon.com). Back Bay or Copley T. **Open** 10am-9pm Mon-Sat; 11am-7pm Sun. **Credit** varies. **Map** p277 G6.

A boon in inclement weather, this upmarket mall connects to its more pedestrian counterpart at the Prudential Center (*see below*) via a human Habitrail. It boasts an 11-screen cinema, two hotels and 100 stores including Armani Exchange, Gucci, Louis Vuitton and a branch of the Cape Cod contemporary crafts showroom, the Artful Hand Gallery.

The Mall at Chestnut Hill

199 Boylston Street, off Route 9, Chestnut Hill (1-617 965 3037/www.mallatchestnuthill.com). Chestnut Hill T then 15mins walk or Kenmore T then 60 bus. **Open** 10am-9.30pm Mon-Fri; 10am-8.30pm Sat; noon-6pm Sun. **Credit** varies.

This is the place for ladies who lunch. Instead of mall muzak, jazz pianists tickle the ivories. The retail menu is a mix of big chains like Banana Republic and higher-end stores such as Coach, and a scaled-down outpost of New York designer department store Barneys. Continuing the Big Apple theme, it also has New England's only two Bloomingdale's stores – one for clothing and accessories, and one across Route 9 for housewares. For a full-scale mall fix, while you're in the area you may want to check out the nearby **Atrium Mall** (300 Boylston Street, Chestnut Hill, 1-617 527 1400, www.atrium-mall.com), which houses Tiffany & Co and MAC.

The Shops at Prudential Center

800 Boylston Street, between Fairfield & Gloucester Streets, Back Bay (1-617 236 3100/www.prudential center.com). Copley, Hynes/ICA or Prudential T. **Open** 10am-9pm Mon-Sat; 11am-6pm Sun. **Credit** varies. **Map** p276 F6.

Packed with workers from the landmark 52-floor office tower, this shopping centre gets a bit manic at lunchtime. It's a mix of high-end, bland chains and vending carts selling tourist tat. Highlights include Saks (*see above*) and the city's only branch of make-up market Sephora. There are some convenient facilities, such as six cash machines, a barber shop and a post office. There are also plenty of places to eat, from pizza stands to sushi restaurants.

Discount

Downtown Crossing has a concentrated cache of discount stores: as well as the fabled **Filene's Basement** (*see below*), **TJ Maxx** (350 Washington Street, 1-617 695 2424), is fertile bargain-hunting ground for mid-range brand-name and designer clothing (Liz Claiborne, Polo, Tommy Hilfiger) for men, women and children, plus gifts, homewares and accessories. In the same building, **Marshalls** (1-617 338 6205) offers similar fare. Reductions for both range from around 20 to 50 per cent. Across the street, DSW (*see p172*) has a huge range of branded shoes at discounts of up to 50 per cent.

Filene's Basement

426 Washington Street, at Summer Street, Downtown (1-617 542 2011/www.filenes basement.com). Downtown Crossing or Park St T. **Open** 9.30am-8pm Mon-Fri; 9am-8pm Sat; 11am-7pm Sun. **Credit** AmEx, Disc, MC, V. **Map** p274 K5.

Bargain-junkies go into overdrive at Filene's Basement, where wooden bins and rails are stuffed to capacity with mid-range to designer-label clothing, accessories, homewares and bridal attire from stores across the country – all at knock-down prices. And because of its Automatic Mark Down System, the longer an item languishes on the rails, the cheaper it gets: every 14 days stock is reduced an additional 25% – up to 75% – so check the stamped date on the price tag. Be warned: scuffles over bargains can get quite aggressive. (*See also p164* **Brawls and bargains in the Basement**).

Antiques & collectibles

Autrefois Antiques

125 Newbury Street, between Clarendon & Dartmouth Streets, Back Bay (1-617 424 8823/www.autrefoisantiques.com). Copley T. **Open** 10am-5.30pm Mon-Sat. **Credit** AmEx, MC, V. **Map** p277 G6.

This prominent retailer of French and Italian furnishings from the 18th to the 20th centuries

A stroll up Newbury Street

What Bond Street is to London and Madison Avenue is to New York, Newbury Street is to Boston – except, unlike the British capital and the US fashion capital, Boston's 'posh' shopping street doubles as its main shopping drag. On this eight-block stretch between the Public Garden and Charlesgate Street (although the only business past Mass Ave is the appropriately named **Other Side Cosmic Café**), you'll find everything from mainstream chains to exclusive designerwear and expensive antiques. Newbury's cross streets are as easy as ABC, ascending the alphabet with the street's numbers, from Arlington to Hereford. Originally residential, the street's earliest buildings were constructed between 1857 and 1892.

In 1905 the first retail shop opened at No.73, although history doesn't record its wares. But Newbury Street's evolution into the city's elegant shopping strip didn't really begin until after the construction of the Ritz-Carlton hotel in the 1920s. Businesses catering to hotel guests and their visitors sprung up in the lower end of the street, especially clothing stores and dress shops – what used to be quaintly termed the 'carriage trade'. And to this day, in general the higher the price tags, the lower the address. Here are our highlights from end to end:

Begin your stroll at the Arlington Street end with a peek in the window of prohibitively pricey **Chanel** (No.5, 1-617 859 0055) and **Burberry** (No.2, 1-617 236 1000). Funkier designer fashions can be found at **Alan Bilzerian** (No.34, *see p167*). Boston hairdresser **Mario Russo** (No.9, *see p176*) is where local celebrities get their locks lopped. Rise above earthly consumerism (if only for a moment) to gaze at the Gothic Revival **Emmanuel Church** (No.15), one of the first buildings in Back Bay. On a Sunday-morning stroll, you may hear the strains of a Bach cantata floating on the air, part of the 10am service.

While its address is actually credited to Berkeley Street, **Louis Boston** (*pictured, see p159*), on the corner of Newbury, is arguably the strip's showpiece. Built in 1862, the designer department store's French Academic-style edifice once housed the Museum of Natural History. Louis' **Restaurant L** (*see p115*) is a lovely place for lunch.

Crossing Clarendon, homesick Brits should stop at **TeaLuxe** (No.108, *see p119*) for a cup of tea and sympathy (it also has a large outdoor patio). Simple skincare emporium **Kiehl's** (No.112, *see p175*) is generous with samples. For those seeking accessories, **Kate Spade** (No.117, *see p171*) delivers darling bags at dear prices, and at No.123, **Arche**'s (*see p171*) sleek shoes combine comfort with French chic.

Travel back in time at Newbury's numerous antique stores. **Autrefois** (No.125, *see p160*) sells restyled chandeliers; while **Brodney** (No.145, *see p163*) proffers estate jewellery and porcelain. Joshua Winter's 1991 mural depicting 50 famous Bostonians is just across Dartmouth Street.

Traversing Exeter Street, amid Chainville Central, is **Emporio Armani** and the **Armani Café** (No.214, *see p119*) – where the Euro set come to see and be seen.

Crossing Gloucester Street, end your stroll on a high note near Hereford Street: **Newbury Comics** (No.332, *see p178*) is a local favourite for well-priced CDs. For streetwise gear, stop into **Ozone** (No.336, *see p168*). And if your feet are aching after all this exercise, maybe they can squeeze you in for a quick pedicure at **Giuliano** (No.338, *see p175*).

specialises in lamps and chandeliers, which are converted from old candelabras.
Other locations: 130 Harvard Street, at Cyprus Street, Brookline (1-617 566 0113).

Brodney Antiques and Jewelry
145 Newbury Street, at Dartmouth Street, Back Bay (1-617 536 0500). Copley T. **Open** 10am-6pm Mon-Sat. **Credit** AmEx, DC, MC, V. **Map** p277 G6.
Visiting this shop – for serious collectors and curious shoppers – is like entering a heavily gilded past era. Brodney sells antique and estate jewellery, sculpture, paintings, porcelain and silver. Expect unusual finds – we spotted a whimsical statue of the Greek god Pan and fabulous vintage gold charm bracelets on our last visit.

Cambridge Antique Market
201 Monsignor O'Brien Highway, at Third Street, Cambridge (1-617 868 9655). Lechmere T. **Open** 11am-6pm Tue-Sun. **Credit** Disc, MC, V.
Antique furniture, homewares, china, toys, clothing and decorative pieces fill the plethora of stalls in this dusty, five-level warehouse.

Machine Age
354 Congress Street, at A Street, South Boston (1-617 482 0048/www.machine-age.com). South Station T. **Open** noon-5pm Tue-Sat. **Credit** AmEx, MC, V. **Map** p275 M5.
A giant showroom with an exceptional selection of modern-classic designs – Herman Miller, Charles Eames and George Nelson – and a miscellany of 20th-century artefacts, located in a neighbourhood dominated by photography and graphic-design studios. Locals with friends visiting take them to the store as if it's a museum, which it almost is.

Marcoz Antiques
177 Newbury Street, between Dartmouth & Exeter Streets, Back Bay (1-617 262 0780). Copley T. **Open** 10am-6pm Mon-Sat. **Credit** AmEx, Disc, MC, V. **Map** p277 G6.
Not cheap, but tasteful, elegant and well worth a look. European furniture from the 18th and 19th centuries and stylish *objets d'art* are specialities.

Art supplies & stationery

Paper Source
338 Boylston Street, at Arlington Street, Back Bay (1-617 536 3444/www.paper-source.com). Arlington T. **Open** 10am-7pm Mon-Fri; 10am-6pm Sat; 11am-6pm Sun. **Credit** AmEx, Disc, MC, V. **Map** p277 H5.
The emphasis is on craft in this store specialising in fine handmade papers, beautiful but pricey stationery, embellishments such as ribbons, rubber stamps and stickers, and bookbinding supplies. Although staff are far from fawning, you'll get knowledgeable advice if you ask.
Other locations: 1361 Beacon Street, at Coolidge Corner, Brookline (1-617 264 2800); 1810 Massachusetts Avenue, at Porter Square, Cambridge (1-617 497 1077).

Pearl Arts & Crafts
579 Massachusetts Avenue, between Essex & Pearl Streets, Cambridge (1-617 547 6600/www.pearl paint.com). Central T. **Open** 9am-7pm Mon-Thur, Sat; 9am-8pm Fri; noon-6pm Sun. **Credit** AmEx, Disc, MC, V. **Map** p278 C3.
This art supplier is the real deal, and many of its multi-pierced staff are themselves working artists. The store has three floors of art and crafts supplies in all media, from doll's house staples to professional drafting boards and art books.

Bookshops

Border's Books and Music
10-24 School Street, at Washington Street, Downtown (1-617 557 7188). Gov't Center, Park St or State T. **Open** 7am-9pm Mon-Fri; 8am-9pm Sat; 10am-8pm Sun. **Credit** AmEx, Disc, MC, V. **Map** p274 K4.
This large downtown branch of the massive chain is a pleasant place to browse. The relaxed atmosphere is aided by comfy reading areas and a café.

Brattle Book Shop
9 West Street, at Washington Street, Downtown (1-617 542 0210/www.brattlebookshop.com). Downtown Crossing or Park St T. **Open** 9am-5.30pm Mon-Sat. **Credit** AmEx, MC, V. **Map** p274 K5.
Established in 1825, this cosy and well-regarded general bookshop situated in the heart of downtown Boston stocks around 250,000 books and boasts a particularly impressive antiquarian selection.

Comicazi
380 Highland Avenue, at Cutter Avenue, Somerville (1-617 666 2664/www.comicazi.com). Davis T. **Open** 11am-9pm Mon-Sat; noon-6pm Sun. **Credit** AmEx, MC, V.
Vintage and modern comics, plus pop, superhero and sci-fi memorabilia and toys fill this British-owned shop, two blocks from Davis Square. There are comics for kids aged five to 50, from classic Batman to crime noir and horror, such as *Stray Bullets* and *Dark Days*.

Grolier Poetry Book Shop
6 Plympton Street, at Massachusetts Avenue, Cambridge (1-617 547 4648/www.grolier poetrybookshop.com). Harvard T. **Open** noon-6.30pm Mon-Sat. **Credit** AmEx, Disc, MC, V. **Map** p278 B2.
Dedicated exclusively to verse, this delightful shop has around 17,000 titles, many international, and is frequented by local poets including Stephen Dobyns, Frank Bidart, Bill Knott and Jorie Graham. In an effort to promote public interest in poetry Grolier's hosts poetry readings and organises an annual poetry festival and the Grolier Poetry Prize Annual. A Harvard Square institution since 1927, the Grolier was once a cliquey hangout that relied on the trust fund of one of the owners' wives for financial support, but by the 1950s it had become a profit-making operation. Recently, though, there have been

Brawls and bargains in the Basement

'I Just Got a Bargain.' Trumpeted on jumbo-sized shopping bags, the slogan encapsulates the barely contained excitement Filene's Basement inspires in its devotees. A Boston legend, commonly referred to as merely 'the Basement', it was founded by Edward A Filene in 1908 to sell excess merchandise from his father's department store upstairs (the stores have been completely separate since 1987). Soon other retailers were offloading their unsold goods on Filene – and so the 'off-price' store was born. There are now 24 branches across the country, but this is the original.

Filene developed the Automatic Mark Down System that incubates thrilling bargains. Price tags are marked with the date an item is put out. The longer it remains unsold, the further its price is 'automatically' reduced – up to an additional 75% off the already discounted price. As in Filene's day, unsold goods are donated to charity. The store is three levels deep including a stockroom disconcertingly called 'the Morgue'.

rumours it might be forced to closed due to competition from the big bookseller chains, but as we went to press, the doors were still open.

Harvard Book Store

1256 Massachusetts Avenue, at Harvard Square, Cambridge (1-617 661 1515/www.harvard.com). Harvard T. **Open** 9am-11pm Mon-Thur; 9am-midnight Fri, Sat; 10am-10pm Sun. **Credit** AmEx, Disc, MC, V. **Map** p278 B2.

Founded in 1932, the Harvard Book Store has two floors of new books, publishers' overstock and used paperbacks. It specialises mainly in academic texts. Great customer service and good prices distinguish the shop – each month, a 'Select 70' titles are discounted by 20%.

The Harvard Coop

1400 Massachusetts Avenue, at Harvard Square, Cambridge (1-617 499 2000/www.thecoop.com). Harvard T. **Open** 9am-10pm Mon-Sat; noon-7pm Sun. **Credit** AmEx, Disc, MC, V. Map p278 B2.

The Coop was founded in 1882 by a group of Harvard students selling books, scholarly supplies and coal for those cold Cambridge winters. Only those affiliated with participating universities are eligible for membership entitling them to rebates (the fee, $1, hasn't gone up since 1882), but everyone can take advantage of the bargain tables selling cut-price books. The store is divided into two buildings: the main Massachusetts Avenue building is exclusively devoted to books and has an attractive gallery café overlooking the ground floor. The Palmer/Brattle Street building, connected by an enclosed walkway, sells Harvard and MIT T-shirts, caps, cufflinks, ties and the like – even handmade university-themed needlepoint cushions (no stylish dorm room is complete without one!).

Other locations: 3 Cambridge Center, at Kendall Square, Cambridge (1-617 499 3200).

WordsWorth Books

30 Brattle Street, at Harvard Square, Cambridge (1-617 354 5201/www.wordsworth.com). Harvard T. **Open** 9am-11.15pm Mon-Sat; 10am-10.15pm Sun. **Credit** AmEx, Disc, MC, V. **Map** p278 A2.

You can stay up late reading at this bi-level independent discount bookshop with more than 100,000 titles, reduced by 10% to 30%. The store will ship books worldwide.

Children's books

Curious George Goes To WordsWorth

1 John F Kennedy Street, at Harvard Square, Cambridge (1-617 498 0062/1-800 899 2202). Harvard T. **Open** 9am-9pm Mon-Sat; 10am-8pm Sun. **Credit** AmEx, Disc, MC, V. **Map** p278 B2.

The children's arm of WordsWorth is named after the little monkey whose creator, Margret Rey, used to frequent the old bookstore. It's a colourful shop

Basement shoppers enjoy the thrill of the chase. Collectors scour the store daily for a particular designer; nearby office workers hunt frequently during their lunch hour. Mayor Menino walks down from City Hall regularly to snap up designer ties.

Customers often become deeply emotionally attached, particularly those who attend its bridal gown sales. Instituted in 1947, these are held twice annually, generally on the Friday after Valentine's Day and in mid-August. Gowns retail from $249 to $699 – but some are worth $10,000. Brides and their relatives often send ecstatic stories about their bargains to the store, along with the wedding snaps. Many save their tags as proof of their extraordinary finds.

One woman wrote about how she found a bridal gown with 'Maria' mysteriously written on the lining. It happened to fit her daughter Maria perfectly. Another bought a wedding dress for $12 in 1946. Subsequently, five of her friends also wore 'the buy of her life' when it was their turn to walk down the aisle.

The Basement also attracts its share of peeping Toms. Before the addition of dressing rooms, the store's central staircase was a prime spot for men watching women change in their lunch hour. In 1972, an escalator was installed, spoiling their furtive fun. Although the store introduced dressing rooms in 1991, some people still enjoy changing in the open.

Wily bargain-seekers are known for trying to beat the system, squirrelling away items such as brassieres in men's shoes, so they can retrieve them later when they're further marked down. One man wrote 'hole in leg' on the tags of suits to discourage competing shoppers. It is rumoured that former Massachusetts Governor Dukakis used to hide clothing. (Beware, transgressors: a crew works all night to put things back.)

There are skirmishes, but the Basement also has its share of love stories. In 1958, one man let a woman have a shirt if she would have coffee with him. She said yes, and yes again – six months later they were married.

full of classic books such as *Madeline*, *Thomas the Tank Engine* and *Winnie the Pooh*, as well as stuffed animals, toys, art and art supplies.

Second-hand & rare books

Ars Libri

500 Harrison Avenue, at Randolph Street, South End (1-617 357 5212/www.arslibri.com). Back Bay T or East Berkeley Silver Line bus. **Open** 9am-6pm Mon-Fri; 11am-5pm Sat (Aug closed Sat). **Credit** AmEx, MC, V. **Map** p277 J8.

A wonderful resource for scholars and collectors, Ars Libri claims to have the largest stock of rare and out-of-print art books in America. As well as reference tomes on all media and periods of art history, there are beautifully illustrated works, from Renaissance architectural treatises to contemporary artists' books, plus exhibition catalogues and periodicals. The Mario Diacono gallery hosts regular exhibitions on the premises.

Peter L Stern & Co

55 Temple Place, between Tremont & Washington Streets, Downtown (1-617 542 2376). Downtown Crossing or Park St T. **Open** 9.30am-5.30pm Mon-Fri; 9am-4pm Sat. **Credit** AmEx, Disc, MC, V. **Map** p274 K5.

This antiquarian bookseller is the place to track down well-loved mystery and detective authors, such as Sir Arthur Conan Doyle. It also specialises in firsts of 19th- and 20th-century American and British literature, from Hemingway to Herman Melville, plus a smattering of manuscripts and signed authors' photographs. Staff are friendly and eager to help.

Cameras & film-processing

Most pharmacy chains offer fast, inexpensive film developing and there's a **Walgreen's** or **CVS** located in just about every part of town (check the phone book for your nearest branch).

Calumet Photographic

65 Bent Street, at First Street, Cambridge (1-617 576 2600). Lechmere T. **Open** 8am-6pm Mon-Fri. **Credit** AmEx, Disc, MC, V.

This is where local photojournalists buy their gear – the *Boston Globe* has an account here. It has an extensive range of professional photographic equipment for sale or to rent, and an impressive digital department.

Colortek

727 Atlantic Avenue, at Beach Street, Downtown (1-617 451 0894/www.colortek.org). South Station T. **Open** 8.30am-7pm Mon-Fri. **Credit** AmEx, Disc, MC, V.

A highly regarded professional chain with convenient locations. Services include film and digital processing, E6 slide processing, slide duplication and exhibition-quality copy work.

Sneaker city

Massachusetts' domination of the footwear industry dates back to the 17th century, when cobblers in the North Shore hamlet of Salem were considered the best in the business. By 1768, Massachusetts was exporting more than 12,000 pairs of shoes to other US colonies – roughly double the production of any other region. Today the state continues to be a player in the lucrative worldwide industry, with several prominent athletic-shoe makers based in the Boston area. What's more, some of these companies, including Reebok, New Balance and Saucony, have local outlets stocked to the gills with discounted gear.

Originally a British company, **Reebok** (named for an African gazelle) now keeps its world headquarters in Canton, Massachusetts, about ten miles (16 kilometres) south of Boston. The company's sprawling 42-acre (17-hectare) compound contains all the necessary ingredients for developing sneaker wizardry: an indoor track, tennis and basketball courts and seven outdoor athletic fields. Known for its use of innovative materials and highly technological designs, as well as for splashy ads featuring athletes such as Allen Iverson and Venus Williams, Reebok is an industry heavyweight, second only to Nike in revenue.

Less conspicuous by far is **New Balance**, the world's third-bestselling sports-shoe manufacturer. Thanks to its virtually non-existent advertising campaign and emphasis on function rather than fashion, the company has long projected an independent, nerdy-cool image that has distinguished it from its mass-marketed competitors. New Balance was started in 1906 by William Riley, a cobbler in Belmont who specialised in arch supports and orthopaedic footwear. Today, the emphasis on fit over flash continues, and the Boston-based brand is particularly known for stocking hard-to-find sizes, which run up to 22 (US) and range in width from 2A to 6E.

While Reebok and New Balance are full-blown athletic-shoe titans, **Saucony** is more of a niche brand, controlling only about one per cent of the market. When a successful Cambridge cobbler acquired the Saucony Shoe Manufacturing Company in 1968 (the name wasn't formally truncated until 1998), no one blinked an eye. It wasn't until the 1980s that, on the basis of some enthusiastic press, sales picked up and Saucony earned its reputation as a serious runner's shoe company. Now based in Peabody, Massachusetts, Saucony has enjoyed a steady increase in sales over the past few years, and its fantastically comfortable, retro-styled kicks are slavered over by bespectacled Buddy Holly wannabes and hardcore marathoners alike.

New Balance Factory Store

40 Life Street, at North Beacon Street, Brighton (1-877 623 7867). Harvard Ave T then 10mins walk/64, 86 bus. **Open** 9.30am-7pm Mon-Sat; noon-6pm Sun. **Credit** AmEx, Disc, MC, V.

Reebok Factory Outlet

1 Technology Center Drive, Stoughton (1-781 341 4603. **Open** 10am-9pm Mon-Fri; 9am-9pm Sat; 11am-6pm Sun. **Credit** AmEx, Disc, MC, V.

Saucony Factory Outlet

1036 Cambridge Street, at Columbia Street, Cambridge (1-617 547 4397). Central T then 15mins walk/CT2, 69, 85 bus. **Open** 10am-6pm Mon-Fri; 10am-5pm Sat; noon-5pm Sun. **Credit** AmEx, MC, V.

Other locations: 636 Beacon Street, at Kenmore Square, Fenway (1-617 236 4400); 251 Newbury Street, between Fairfield & Gloucester Streets, Back Bay (1-617 267 6503).

EP Levine

23 Drydock Avenue, at Summer Street, South Boston (1-617 951 1499/www.cameras.com). South Station T. **Open** 8.30am-5.30pm Mon-Fri. **Credit** AmEx, Disc, MC, V.

This reputable professional photo shop sells and rents new and used equipment, as well as products for digital imaging. Adjacent to the shop is Exposure Place, two full photography studios available to rent, with darkroom access.

Electronics

Apple Store

CambridgeSide Galleria, 100 Cambridgeside Place, off Edwin Land Boulevard, Cambridge (1-617 225 0442/www.apple.com). Lechmere T then 5mins walk or Kendall T then free shuttle bus. **Open** 10am-9.30pm Mon-Sat; 11am-7pm Sun. **Credit** AmEx, Disc, MC, V. **Map** p274 H2.

The latest desktops, portables, accessories, Apple software and covetable gadgets.

Other locations: The Mall at Chestnut Hill, 199 Boylston Street, off Route 9, Chestnut Hill (1-617 965 5806).

Bang & Olufsen

30 Newbury Street, at Arlington Street, Back Bay (1-617 262 4949). Arlington T. **Open** 10am-6pm Mon-Sat; noon-5pm Sun. **Credit** AmEx, Disc, MC, V. **Map** p277 H5.

Sleek, contemporary Danish-designed audio, video and telephone equipment and accessories.

Tweeter

350 Boylston Street, at Berkeley Street, Back Bay (1-617 262 2299/www.tweeter.com). Arlington T. **Open** 10am-7pm Mon-Sat; noon-6pm Sun. **Credit** AmEx, Disc, MC, V. **Map** p277 H6.

A 1970s Boston success story that grew into a nationwide chain, Tweeter offers a moderate to high-end inventory of audio and video equipment, regular 'WiseBuys' cheap deals and a 30-day satisfaction guarantee.

Other locations: 874 Commonwealth Avenue, at St Paul Street, Brookline (1-617 738 4411); 104 Mount Auburn Street, at John F Kennedy Street, Cambridge (1-617 492 4411).

Fashion

Boutiques

Alan Bilzerian

34 Newbury Street, between Arlington & Berkeley Streets, Back Bay (1-617 536 1001). Arlington T. **Open** 10am-6pm Mon-Wed, Fri, Sat; 10am-7pm Thur. **Credit** AmEx, MC, V. **Map** p277 H5.

In a league of its own in Boston, this long-standing designer boutique for men and women serves up cutting-edge international labels with a side order of individuality. Expect to find an eclectic mix of Lanvin, Italian line Carpe Diem, Martin Margiela, Yohji Yamamoto and Ann Demeulemeester.

Allston Beat

348 Newbury Street, between Hereford Street & Massachusetts Avenue, Back Bay (1-617 421 9555). Hynes/ICA T. **Open** 11am-9pm Mon-Thur; 11am-10pm Fri, Sat; noon-8pm Sun. **Credit** AmEx, MC, V. **Map** p276 F6.

Goths everywhere love to shop at this local alternative institution, owned by a Brit. It's Clubwear Central, selling such labels as Pimpgear, Doc Martens, Lip Service and other trendy lines in artificial fabrics and 'pleather'. A good spot for funky accessories and body jewellery.

Cibeline

85 Holland Street, at Davis Square, Somerville (1-617 625 2229/www.cibelinesariano.com). Davis T. **Open** 11am-7pm Tue-Fri; 10am-6pm Sat; noon-6pm Sun. **Credit** AmEx, MC, V.

Local designer Cibeline Sariano creates sexy, classic clothing for women, not stick insects. Audrey Hepburn-inspired cocktail dresses, bustiers and suits can be custom-tailored for a small fee. The shop is also a great source of accessories and gifts, men's ties and handbags by other designers in the area.

Dapper **Bobby from Boston**. *See p169.*

Gipore

176 Newbury Street, between Dartmouth & Exeter Streets, Back Bay (1-617 424 1500/ www.gipore.com). Copley T. **Open** 11am-7pm Mon-Fri; 10am-7pm Sat; noon-5pm Sun. Also by appointment. **Credit** AmEx, Disc, MC, V. **Map** p277 G6.

Thanks to the owner's Italian connections, you can find some designers making their first US appearance at this women's boutique. Browse through clothes and accessories by the likes of Coccapani, Twin Set, Alessandro Dell'Acqua and Paola Frani, and shoes by Luciano Padovan and Vivian Lee. Gipore does good lines in slinky lace underwear and sexy eveningwear. It also offers a taste of *la dolce vita* with extra services such as free in-store styling, cappuccino, and custom-fitting of your purchases by a tailor.

Jasmine Sola

37 Brattle Street, at Harvard Square, Cambridge (1-617 354 6043/www.jasminesola.com). Harvard T. **Open** 10am-7pm Mon-Wed; 10am-8pm Thur-Sat; noon-7pm Sun. **Credit** AmEx, DC, Disc, MC, V. **Map** p278 A2.

This women's boutique is the young fashionistas' favourite. The lively, youthful collections culled from New York and Europe include labels such as Juicy Couture, Custo Barcelona and Sharagano. The jeans selection alone includes Diesel, Miss Sixty and Earl Jean. The clothes are expensive, but there's always at least one sale rack at the back of the store. Shoes (Steve Madden, Kenneth Cole), accessories and bath and beauty products are also sold.

Other locations: 344 Newbury Street, at Massachusetts Avenue, Back Bay (1-617 867 4636); Chestnut Hill Mall, 199 Boylston Street, off Route 9, Chestnut Hill (1-617 332 8415).

Market

558 Tremont Street, at Clarendon Street, South End (1-617 338 4500). Back Bay T. **Open** 11am-7pm Mon-Thur, 11am-8pm Fri, Sat; noon-6pm Sun. **Credit** AmEx, Disc, MC, V. **Map** p277 H7.

Market is a good place to find a pair of smart trousers or Euro swimwear. This friendly men's European designer sportswear and accessories store is a favourite with 'metrosexuals' (in other words, men who own more moisturiser than their girlfriends) in their 20s to 40s. Expect clothing by Hugo Boss, Gaultier, Cavalli and Dolce & Gabbana, and accessories by Gucci and Dior.

Ozone

336 Newbury Street, at Hereford Street, Back Bay (1-617 421 4464). Hynes/ICA T. **Open** noon-8pm Sun-Thur; 11am-9pm Fri, Sat. **Credit** AmEx, MC, V. **Map** p276 F6.

The stock is weighted in the boys' favour at this urban streetwear store on Newbury Street. Ozone offers labels such as Triple Five Soul, Kitchen Orange, Paul Frank, and local designers such as Tank Theory, as well as shoes and accessories by Kangol and Diesel.

Turtle

619 Tremont Street, at Dartmouth Street, South End (1-617 266 2610). Back Bay T. **Open** 11am-7pm Tue-Fri; 10am-7pm Sat; noon-5pm Sun. **Credit** AmEx, Disc, MC, V. **Map** p277 G8.

Women's clothing, jewellery, and accessories by emerging local artisans and designers. When we last visited, we found handbags made from recycled car-seat upholstery and handmade felted-wool scarves.

Wish

49 Charles Street, at Mount Vernon Street, Beacon Hill (1-617 227 4441/www.wishstyle.com). Charles/MGH T. **Open** 10am-7pm Mon-Wed, Fri; 10am-8pm Thur; 10am-6pm Sat; noon-6pm Sun. **Credit** AmEx, Disc, MC, V. **Map** p274 J4.

You'll wish you had more money in this women's fashion store. Many of the clothes, predominantly by American designers such as Trina Turk, Nanette Lepore and Milly, have a vintage-preppy air – think *Sex and the City*'s Charlotte. Great for dresses, it's also the place to find cult jeans such as Seven.

Formaggio Kitchen. *See p173.*

Mainstream chains

Newbury Street, Faneuil Hall Marketplace or one of the city's malls (*see p160*) are the places to head for the affordable, good-quality national chains such as **Gap**, its more upmarket sibling **Banana Republic**, **Ann Taylor** womenswear and **Victoria's Secret** lingerie. Recently, Swedish superstore **H&M** arrived on Washington Street near Downtown Crossing – a welcome source of cheap, trendy clothes for the city's cash-strapped students. Below are some notable big names.

Brooks Brothers

46 Newbury Street, at Berkeley Street, Back Bay (1-617 267 2600/www.brooksbrothers.com). Arlington T. **Open** 9am-7pm Mon-Fri; 10am-6pm Sat; noon-6pm Sun. **Credit** AmEx, DC, Disc, MC, V. **Map** p277 H5.

The yachting map in the window and the 'Country Club' collection proclaim Brooks Brothers' status as the province of preppies for generations. The men's, women's and boys' clothes may be too conservative for some tastes, but the classic Oxford cloth button-down shirts and cotton boxer shorts are hard to beat for quality and price.

Other locations: 75 State Street, at Court Street, Downtown (1-617 261 9990); The Mall at Chestnut Hill, 199 Boylston Street, off Route 9, Chestnut Hill (1-617 964 3600).

The Original Levi's Store

Prudential Center, 800 Boylston Street, between Fairfield & Gloucester Streets, Back Bay (1-617 375 9010). Copley, Hynes/ICA or Prudential T. **Open** 10am-9pm Mon-Sat; 11am-6pm Sun. **Credit** AmEx, DC, Disc, MC, V. **Map** p276 F6.

A full range of jeans and casual separates by the San Francisco original. The shop also offers a custom-made jeans service.

Lucky Brand

229 Newbury Street, at Fairfield Street, Back Bay (1-617 236 0102/www.luckybrandjeans.com). Copley T. **Open** 10am-7pm Mon-Sat; noon-6pm Sun. **Credit** AmEx, Disc, MC, V. **Map** p276 G6.

Streetwise cuts and distressed finishes elevate these jeans above the mainstream – though not quite to cult status. The California brand also includes trend-conscious casual clothes for men, women and kids.

Urban Outfitters

11 John F Kennedy Street, at Massachusetts Avenue, Cambridge (1-617 864 0070/www.urbanoutfitters.com). Harvard T. **Open** 10am-10pm Mon-Thur; 10am-11pm Fri, Sat; noon-8pm Sun. **Credit** AmEx, Disc, MC, V. **Map** p278 B2.

Inexpensive, fun and funky clothes, furnishings, gifts and toys for young hipsters. The late-night hours are a bonus, and this branch has the chain's only bargain basement, with rock-bottom prices.

Other locations: 361 Newbury Street, at Massachusetts Avenue, Back Bay (1-617 236 0088).

Vintage & second-hand

Bobby from Boston

19 Thayer Street, at Harrison Avenue, South End (1-617 423 9299). Back Bay T or East Berkeley Silver Line bus. **Open** noon-6pm Mon-Sat. **No credit cards. Map** p277 J8.

This fabulous vintage emporium in the warehouse gallery complex is well known to Japanese jeans collectors, movie wardrobe professionals and local rockers. Bobby Garnett is Boston's guru of hip vintage men's fashion and collectable Levi's. Here you'll find both $20 501s and $500 'big E' red-tags, vintage American sportswear and lots of cool men's suits, including English labels from the 1960s. If you want head-to-toe '80s Polo, Bobby's sells whole ensembles.

The Closet

175 Newbury Street, between Dartmouth & Exeter Streets, Back Bay (1-617 536 1919). Copley T. **Open** 10am-6pm Mon-Sat; noon-5pm Sun. **Credit** AmEx, MC, V. **Map** p277 G6.

Styles are no more than two years old at this contemporary designer re-sale shop for both sexes. How do they keep the turnaround high? After 30 days, wares are discounted by 25% and after 60 days, by 50%. Couture comes in regularly at pretty serious discounts – we found flawless Chanel courts for a song.

Garment District & Dollar-a-Pound Plus

200 Broadway, at Davis Street, Cambridge (1-617 876 5230/www.garment-district.com). Kendall/MIT T. **Open** *Garment District* 11am-7pm Mon, Tue, Sun; 11am-8pm Wed-Fri; 9am-7pm Sat. *Dollar-a-Pound Plus* 9am-7pm Mon, Tue, Fri-Sun; 9am-8pm Wed, Thur. **Credit** AmEx, Disc, MC, V.

This second-hand department store is a regular haunt for the city's students and hipsters. The draw is a huge selection of vintage and designer-restyled gear, along with racks and racks of old blue jeans. It also sells cheap new clothing and accessories, and if you've got a costume party to go to you can pick up a fetching mullet wig or a feather boa. The Dollar-a-Pound adjunct is for those who don't mind stains, missing zippers, and rooting through clothing strewn on the floor.

Great Eastern Trading Co

49 River Street, at Central Square, Cambridge (1-617 354 5279). Central T. **Open** noon-7pm Mon-Fri; 11am-6pm Sat; 1-5pm Sun. **Credit** AmEx, Disc, MC, V. **Map** p278 C3.

Great Eastern Trading was one of the first vintage stores in the city, and it still maintains a high standard of second-hand clothing and accessories, mostly from the 1970s.

Keezer's

140 River Street, between Jay & Kinnaird Streets, Cambridge (1-617 547 2455/www.keezers.com). Central T. **Open** 10am-6pm Mon-Sat. **Credit** MC, V. **Map** p278 B3.

Established in 1895, Keezer's is the oldest second-hand clothing store in the country and a cherished local resource. Max Keezer started the company by going into Harvard dorms in order to buy barely worn fine clothing from allowance-starved heirs. The shop now sells second-hand and end-of-the-line men's suits (members of the Boston Pops and the Boston Symphony Orchestra buy their tuxedos here), sports coats, overcoats and casualwear, all in good or mint condition, and with at least 50% off. Since they get designer stuff from Neiman's, Louis Boston and Saks, you may find Armani, Zegna and Brooks Brothers among the labels.

Poor Little Rich Girl

416 Highland Avenue, at Davis Square, Somerville (1-617 684 0157). Davis T. **Open** noon-7pm Mon-Sat; noon-6pm Sun. **Credit** AmEx, Disc, MC, V.

Now hip Davis Square has another draw to add to its numerous bars and eateries – this small shop has become the secret weapon of many a cash-poor fashion addict. While the bulk is consignment stock from mainstream labels such as Anthropologie and J Crew, around 25% is from the 1940s to '80s. Vintage shop-hounds can sniff out vertigo-inducing graphic-patterned finds from the '60s, and there have even been tales of bagging perfectly preserved Courrèges pieces. Housewares, handbags, shoes and jewellery are also sold, and vintage music is played to go with the clothes.

Fashion accessories

Moxie (*see p172*) and **Turtle** (*see p168*) both sell interesting bags and accessories.

Kate Spade

117 Newbury Street, between Clarendon & Dartmouth Streets, Back Bay (1-617 262 2632/ www.katespade.com). Copley T. **Open** 10am-6pm Mon-Sat; noon-5pm Sun. **Credit** AmEx, Disc, MC, V. **Map** p277 G6.

The queen of American modern-classic accessories delivers two floors of ladylike, retro-cool designs. Upstairs are the famous handbags and the luggage Spade designed for Song airlines. Downstairs, check out Jack Spade – a line of men's bags designed by her husband Andy – and women's shoes.

Jewellery & watches

Cartier

40 Newbury Street, at Arlington Street, Back Bay (1-617 262 3300). Arlington T. **Open** 10am-6pm Mon-Sat. **Credit** AmEx, MC, V. **Map** p277 H5.

This venerable jewellery house has a sleek Boston store (the only Cartier in New England).

Dorfman Jewelers

24 Newbury Street, between Arlington & Berkeley Streets, Back Bay (1-617 536 2022). Arlington T. **Open** 10am-5.30pm Mon-Sat. **Credit** AmEx, MC, V. **Map** p277 H5.

With its tiny emerald-cut windows and shiny gold coat of arms above the door, the store itself looks like a well-set jewel. It sells unique jewellery in contemporary and classic styles.

Shreve, Crump & Low

330 Boylston Street, at Arlington Street, Back Bay (1-617 267 9100/www.shrevecrumpandlow.com). Arlington T. **Open** 10am-5.30pm Mon-Wed, Fri, Sat; 10am-7pm Thur. **Credit** AmEx, MC, V. **Map** p277 H5.

This traditional jewellery and luxury gift shop is the oldest in North America, though the current Back Bay premises date from the 1920s; when Shreve's was founded in 1796, it was located across the street from silversmith patriot Paul Revere's workshop. Whether you're buying a diamond bracelet or a bottle of fountain-pen ink, your patronage is always welcomed here. Loyal customers have included the Kennedy family and Winston Churchill. While you're here, take a moment to look up at the beautiful art deco silver gilt ceiling.

Other locations: The Mall at Chestnut Hill, 199 Boylston Street, off Route 9, Chestnut Hill (1-617 965 2700).

Tiffany & Co

Copley Place, Huntington Avenue, at Copley Square, Back Bay (1-617 353 0222). Back Bay or Copley T. **Open** 10am-6pm Mon, Tue; 10am-7pm Wed-Sat; 11am-5pm Sun. **Credit** AmEx, DC, Disc, MC, V. **Map** p277 G6.

Its location in the busy and very touristy (albeit swanky) Copley Place mall saps the glamour from the experience of shopping at Tiffany's – but you'll still walk out with that little blue box.

Time and Time Again

273 Newbury Street, between Fairfield & Gloucester Streets, Back Bay (1-617 266 6869/www.timepiece.com). Copley T. **Open** 11am-6pm Mon-Sat. **Credit** AmEx, MC, V. **Map** p276 F6.

An impressive stock of second-hand watches, including the largest selection of used Rolexes in Boston. The shop also repairs vintage timepieces.

Shoes

Posh department stores **Louis**, **Neiman Marcus**, and **Saks Fifth Avenue** *(see p160)* are good sources of designer shoes. **Jasmine Sola** *(see p168)* sells a wide range of trendy women's footwear, **Alan Bilzerian** *(see p167)* has a small selection of cutting-edge designs, and bag lady **Kate Spade** *(see above)* also does a neat line in footwear. The shoe department at **Filene's Basement** *(see p160)* sometimes yields fantastic bargain finds.

Arche

123 Newbury Street, at Clarendon Street, Back Bay (1-617 422 0727). Copley T. **Open** 10am-7pm Mon-Fri; 10am-6pm Sat; noon-5pm Sun. **Credit** AmEx, DC, Disc, MC, V. **Map** p277 H6.

How do the French do it? These *chaussures* are stylish, comfortable, durable and worth the hefty investment, *non*? Don't expect towering heels – the streamlined slip-ons and Mary Janes are lower to the ground, but very chic nonetheless.

Camper

139B Newbury Street, at Dartmouth Street, Back Bay (1-617 267 4554/www.camper.es). Copley T. **Open** 10am-7pm Mon-Sat; noon-6pm Sun. **Credit** AmEx, Disc, MC, V. **Map** p277 G6.
This is the local headquarters of the sought-after Spanish brand of funky, comfy walking shoes.

DSW Shoe Warehouse

385 Washington Street, at Winter Street, Downtown (1-617 556 0052/www.dswshoe.com). Downtown Crossing or Park Street T. **Open** 10am-8pm Mon-Sat; 11am-6pm Sun. **Credit** AmEx, Disc, MC, V. **Map** p274 K5.
You could land a DC 10 in this vast self-service store, which carries a plethora of shoes for men, women and children at up to 50% off department store prices. To make shopping easier, similar styles (dressy, casual) are displayed together, women's shoes are arranged from highest to lowest heel, and bright stickers indicate special widths. Accessories and handbags are also sold.

John Fluevog

302 Newbury Street, between Gloucester & Hereford Streets, Back Bay (1-617 266 1079/www.fluevog.com). Hynes/ICA T. **Open** 11am-7pm Mon-Sat; 1-6pm Sun. **Credit** AmEx, Disc, MC, V. **Map** p276 F6.
Funky young professionals, creative types and celebrities hoard this fun Canadian-based label – Madonna wore Fluevogs in her *Truth or Dare* video. Most styles are unisex.

Moxie

73 Charles Street, between Mount Vernon & Pinckney Streets, Beacon Hill (1-617 557 9991). Charles/MGH T. **Open** 11am-6pm Mon-Wed; 11am-7pm Thur, Fri; 10am-6pm Sat; noon-5pm Sun. **Credit** AmEx, MC, V. **Map** p274 J4.
This hip little boutique stocks a tempting mix of fashionable shoes, bags and accessories from big names such as Isaac Mizrahi, Anne Klein, Cynthia Rowley, L'Autre, Kate Spade and Marc Jacobs. The overall style leans towards colourful and girly, and prices are mostly high.

Fetish & sex

Grand Opening!

Suite 32 Arcade Building, 318 Harvard Street, at Coolidge Corner, Brookline (1-617 731 2626/ www.grandopening.com). Coolidge Corner T. **Open** 10am-7pm Mon-Wed; 10am-9pm Thur-Sat; noon-6pm Sun. **Credit** AmEx, Disc, MC, V.
A small 'sexuality boutique' selling sex toys and tools especially, though not exclusively, for women. As for the cheeky double entendre name, well, we'd prefer not to dwell on it…

Hubba Hubba

534 Massachusetts Avenue, between Brookline & Pearl Streets, Cambridge (1-617 492 9082). Central T. **Open** noon-8pm Mon-Sat. **Credit** AmEx, Disc, MC, V. **Map** p278 C3.
A locally renowned fetish store that caters to almost every conceivable kink. Come here for all your leather, latex and PVC needs.

Florists

Artemisia Floral Studio

327 Summer Street, at Fort Point Channel, South Boston (1-617 426 4265/www.artemisiaboston.com). South Station T. **Open** 9am-6pm Mon-Fri. **Credit** AmEx, MC, V.
Unique designs for special events and every day, from Dutch imports to African flowers. The store also sells antiques, collectibles, candles and lighting fixtures, and offers an interior-design service.
Other locations: Hotel Commonwealth, 506 Commonwealth Avenue, at Kenmore Square, Fenway (1-617 266 3030).

Winston Flowers

131 Newbury Street, between Dartmouth & Clarendon Streets, Back Bay (1-617 541 1100/ 1-800 457 4901/www.winstonflowers.com). Copley T. **Open** 8am-6pm Mon-Sat; 10am-5pm Sun. **Credit** AmEx, Disc, MC, V. **Map** p277 H6.
With five branches in and around Boston, Winston Flowers specialises in contemporary floral design. The basement in the Boylston Street store offers discontinued, end-of-season and sample items, such as vases, pots and baskets, reduced by 50% to 70%.
Other locations: 141 Congress Street, Downtown; 569 Boylston Street, Back Bay; 49A River Street, Beacon Hill; Route 9 at Florence Street, Newton. For all call 1-800 457 4901.

Food & drink

Bakeries & confectioners

See also p138 **Bakery-cafés**.

LA Burdick Handmade Chocolates

52D Brattle Street, at Farwell Place, Cambridge. (1-617 491 4340/www.burdickchocolate.com). Harvard T. **Open** 8am-10pm Mon, Sun; 8am-11pm Tue-Sat. **Credit** AmEx, Disc, MC, V. **Map** p278 A2.
Larry Burdick's truffles and signature chocolate mice are made by hand in Walpole, New Hampshire, using the highest-quality chocolate from France (the fabled Valrhona), Switzerland and Venezuela. They're not cheap, but the wooden gift boxes make great gifts. The dual shop/café serves superb hot chocolate and pastries (*see p140*).

Maria's Pastry Shop

46 Cross Street, at Hanover Street, North End (1-617 523 1196). Haymarket T. **Open** 7am-6pm Mon-Sat; 7am-1pm Sun. **Credit** AmEx, Disc, MC, V. **Map** p275 L3.

Wall-to-wall gifts and gewgaws at **Black Ink**. *See p174.*

While most people looking for cannolis and other Italian confections follow the masses to **Mike's Pastry** (300 Hanover Street, 1-617 742 3050, www.mikespastry.com), peel off from the pack and ferret out this bolthole of a bakery. North End locals consider it the best because of its commitment to traditional Italian cooking methods. Besides hand-filling cannolis, bakers craft a host of amaretti, rare pastries and sweet breads according to family recipes that have been handed down through generations.

Gourmet grocers

Cardullo's Gourmet Shop

6 Brattle Street, at Harvard Square, Cambridge (1-617 491 8888/www.cardullos.com). Harvard T. **Open** 8am-8pm Mon-Fri; 9am-9pm Sat; 11am-6pm Sun. **Credit** AmEx, Disc, MC, V. **Map** p278 A2.

Family owned since the 1950s, this wonderful little shop is so stuffed to the gills with gourmet foodstuffs from around the globe it can be tricky to navigate. As well as fancy oils, vinegars, preserves, chocolates, wines and the like, homesick Brits can find such national delicacies as Hobnob biscuits and Marmite – at vastly inflated prices.

DeLuca's Back Bay Market

239 Newbury Street, at Fairfield Street, Back Bay (1-617 262 5990). Copley or Hynes/ICA T. **Open** 8am-9pm Mon-Fri; 8.30am-9pm Sat, Sun. **Credit** AmEx, MC, V. **Map** p276 G6.

Established in 1905, Boston's oldest gourmet grocer sells superior-quality fruit and veg, meat, fish, caviar, champagne, freshly baked bread, home-made pasta sauces and more. The shop's motto is, 'What we don't have, we get.' Its Newbury Street location attracts an upmarket clientele.

Other locations: 11 Charles Street, at Beacon Street, Beacon Hill (1-617 523 4343).

Formaggio Kitchen

244 Huron Avenue, at Appleton Street, Cambridge (1-617 354 4750/www.formaggiokitchen.com). Harvard T then 72 bus. **Open** 9am-7pm Mon-Fri; 9am-6pm Sat; 9am-3.30pm Sun. **Credit** AmEx, Disc, MC, V.

Ever been to a speciality store that's been the subject of a poem in the *New Yorker*? Here's your chance. This off-the-beaten-track shop has become one of the top gourmet grocers in the US. Owner Ihsan Gurdal scours the world for rare farmhouse cheeses, then ages them in his own cheese caves. Besides hundreds of cheese varieties, there are artisanal oils from Liguria and Provence, rare Italian *mostarda*, honeys from Turkey and sea salt from Brittany. TV chef Julia Child was a regular customer, and restaurants like California's French Laundry often stock up here. Grilled sandwiches and salads are great for take-outs, and there are all sorts of sweet temptations including Belgian chocolates and French pastries.

Other locations: 268 Shawmut Avenue, at Milford Street, South End (1-617 350 6996).

Buckaroo's Mercantile: a rich source of vintage gems and cheesy novelties.

Liquor stores

Bauer Wine and Spirits

330 Newbury Street, between Hereford Street & Massachusetts Avenue, Back Bay (1-617 262 0363). Hynes/ICA T. **Open** 10am-11pm Mon-Sat; noon-8pm Sun. **Credit** AmEx, Disc, MC, V. **Map** p276 F6.

Established in 1960, this is one of Boston's most highly respected vintners. Manager Howie Rubin, a famous local wine connoisseur, selects fine wines from every major region in the world, and has a well-stocked liquor department to boot.

Blanchard's

103 Harvard Avenue, at Brighton Avenue, Allston (1-617 782 9500/www.blanchards.net). Harvard Avenue T/57 or 66 bus. **Open** 9am-11pm Mon-Sat; noon-6pm Sun. **Credit** MC, V.

Blanchard's not only takes pride in its comprehensive wine selection, but also claims to stock the largest selection of beer in the whole of New England. There's a wine-tasting room and wine consultants on the staff. Every imaginable liquor, as well as cigars, are also sold. Delivery is available within the Greater Boston area.

Brix

1284 Washington Street, at Savoy Street, South End (1-617 542 2749/www.brixwineshop.com). Back Bay T/Savoy Silver Line bus. **Open** 11am-9pm Mon-Thur; 11am-10pm Fri-Sat. **Credit** AmEx, MC, V. **Map** p277 J8.

Brix looks more like a hip bar than a liquor store, and encourages customers to linger and chat. This friendly wine 'boutique' has cork floors, lighted display shelves, regular wine tastings and reasonably priced bottles.

Gift shops

Aunt Sadie's General Store

18 Union Park Street, at Washington Street, South End (1-617 357 7117/www.auntsadiesinc.com). Back Bay T/Union Park Silver Line bus. **Open** 10am-6pm Mon-Sat; 11am-5pm Sun. **Credit** AmEx, Disc, MC, V. **Map** p277 J8.

This spacious store sells what the owner describes as 'urban folk' – a charming mix of new and vintage home accessories. Goods include designer dog beds, hand-dipped candles produced in the adjacent workshop and exclusive, Baskit men's underwear.

Black Ink

5 Brattle Street, at Harvard Square (1-617 497 1221). Harvard T. **Open** 10am-8pm Mon-Sat; 11am-7pm Sun. **Credit** AmEx, MC, V. **Map** p278 B2.

A great place to grab a stylish gift, this shop is packed with an eclectic mix of unusual and amusing toys and gewgaws, household items, bath goods, stationery and a wide range of rubber stamps.

Other locations: 101 Charles Street, at Revere Street, Beacon Hill (1-617 723 3883).

Buckaroo's Mercantile

1297 Cambridge Street, at Inman Square, Cambridge (1-617 492 4792/www.buckmerc.com). Central T then 83 or 91 bus. **Open** noon-8pm Mon-Wed; noon-9pm Thur-Fri; 11am-10pm Sat; noon-7pm Sun. **Credit** AmEx, Disc, MC, V. **Map** p278 C2.

This quirky variety store sells a mix of vintage items and retro reproductions, including furniture, clothing, jewellery and bags. Great for fun, kitschy oddities like Last Supper-themed pens, Elvis charm bracelets, lucky dice shot glasses and winking 1960s sex-kitten hologram postcards. The owner makes nearly half of the merchandise, including fabulously decorated lampshades. Due to the out-of-the-way location, prices are very reasonable, and late opening hours make it an essential pitstop if you're dining in one of Inman Square's many eateries.

Health & beauty

Beauty shops

The only branch of make-up and skincare supermarket **Sephora** within Boston's city limits is located in the Prudential Center mall. *See p160.*

Beauty and Main

30 Brattle Street, at Harvard Square (1-617 868 7171/www.beautyandmain.com). Harvard T. **Open** 11am-7pm Mon-Sat; noon-6pm Sun. **Credit** AmEx, Disc, MC, V. **Map** p278 A2.

Men are comfortable enough to request women's cosmetics for themselves at this store, where staff gently instruct without pushing. Stock includes make-up and skincare by such luminaries as Trish McEvoy, NARS, Laura Mercier and Mario Badescu, Fragrances include Creed (created for Princess Grace to wear on her wedding day) and Darphin, and there's a selection of relaxing scented candles. **Other locations**: 95 Union Street, at Herrick Road, Newton (1-617 243 0036).

Colonial Drug

49 Brattle Street, at Harvard Square, Cambridge (1-617 864 2222). Harvard T. **Open** 8am-7pm Mon-Fri; 8am-6pm Sat. **Credit** AmEx, MC, V (minimum $40). **Map** p278 A2.

A unique, family-run business, this apothecary still looks just as it did in the 1950s, but these days the emphasis is more on luxurious scents and unguents than bromide and hot-water bottles. In particular, it specialises in hard-to-find perfumes (stocking over 1,000 fragrances, including Hermès, Guerlain and Patou), and beauty lines such as Beauté Pacifique, Decléor and Orlane.

Fresh

121 Newbury Street, between Clarendon & Dartmouth Streets, Back Bay (1-617 421 1212). Copley T. **Open** 10am-7pm Mon-Sat; noon-6pm Sun. **Credit** AmEx, Disc, MC, V. **Map** p277 H6.

As well as its own line of unisex cosmetics and skincare based on natural recipes, using ingredients like rice, soy and milk, this Boston-born beauty company sells an excellent selection of imported products and fragrances. Fresh has been so succesful it now has branches in New York and London, and cosmetics counters in various upmarket department stores.

Kiehl's

112 Newbury Street, between Clarendon & Dartmouth Streets, Back Bay (1-617 247 1777/www.kiehls.com). Copley T. **Open** 10am-7pm Mon-Sat; noon-6pm Sun. **Credit** AmEx, MC, V. **Map** p277 H6.

A gleaming Harley-Davidson in the window funks up this branch of the simply packaged, pharmacy-style brand, which has a devoted following. The excellent skin- and haircare products for men and women are a lot cheaper in the US than abroad.

Beauty salons & spas

Giuliano

338 Newbury Street, between Hereford Street & Massachusetts Avenue, Back Bay (1-617 262 2220/www.giulianodayspa.com). Hynes/ICA T. **Open** 8am-8pm Mon-Wed; 8am-9pm Thur, Fri; 8am-6pm Sat; 10am-6pm Sun. **Credit** AmEx, Disc, MC, V. **Map** p276 F6.

Giuliano styles itself as a 'full-service salon and wellness centre', and it's not just hype. The place leaves

Boston-born beauty: Fast expanding **Fresh**.

no treatment stone unturned – you can get a facial or manicure, learn partners' massage or undergo more dramatic procedures like microdermabrasion or tooth bleaching.

G Spa

2nd Floor, 35 Newbury Street, at Arlington Street, Back Bay (1-617 267 4772). Arlington T. **Open** 10am-8pm Mon-Fri; 10am-6pm Sat; 11am-6pm Sun. **Credit** AmEx, MC, V. **Map** p277 H5.

The entrance may be a bit tricky to figure out, but once inside you don't have to go anywhere else to be totally transformed. You can have your hair, nails and make-up attended to, and even outfit yourself in the latest fashions by the likes of Marc Jacobs, D Squared and Blue Cult. The handy 'quickie' services take 25 minutes or less and don't require an appointment, while upstairs is the 'splurge' floor for more involved services, like waxing.

Le Pli Salon and Day Spa

Charles Hotel, 5 Bennett Street, at Harvard Square, Cambridge (1-617 547 4081/www.lepli.com). Harvard T. **Open** 9am-5pm Mon, Tue; 9am-8pm Wed-Fri; 9am-5pm Sat; 10am-5pm Sun. **Credit** AmEx, MC, V. **Map** p278 A2.

Le Pli offers a wide range of hair and skin treatments in an elegant spa setting in Cambridge.

Hairdressers

We've listed a selection of snippers below, but Newbury Street has about 70 hair salons, so snagging a walk-in appointment shouldn't be a problem. Some of Boston's prestigious salons charge through-the-roof prices, but the average for a cut by skilled stylists is $40-$85.

Blade

603 Tremont Street, at Dartmouth Street, Back Bay (1-617 267 2200). Back Bay T. **Open** 11am-8pm Tue-Fri; 9am-5pm Sat. **Credit** MC, V. **Map** p277 H8.

A stylish barber shop, Blade offers traditional clipper cuts, hot lather shaves and facials, in a relaxed neighbourhood environment and at very reasonable prices.

Carriage House Salon

33 Church Street, at Massachusetts Avenue, Cambridge (1-617 868 7800/www.carriagehousesalon.com). Harvard T. **Open** 10am-5pm Mon; 10am-7pm Tue-Fri; 9am-5pm Sat. **Credit** AmEx, MC, V. **Map** p278 A2.

Curly girls and guys flock to the only shop in town that offers the Ouidad-system 'Carve & Slice' cut (not as painful as it sounds). Though it isn't cheap ($85), the technique promises to make the most of curly locks rather than clipping them as though they were straight. Cuts for non-kinky types are also offered, plus nail services and skin treatments.

Ecocentrix

30 Newbury Street, between Arlington & Berkeley Streets, Back Bay (1-617 262 2222). Arlington T. **Open** 10am-5pm Tue; 10am-7.30pm Wed, Thur; 10am-7pm Fri; 9am-5pm Sat. **Credit** Disc, MC, V. **Map** p277 H5.

Local award-winners with a reputation for hip, style-savvy cuts and colour.

Mario Russo

3rd Floor, 9 Newbury Street, at Arlington Street, Back Bay (1-617 424 6676/www.mariorusso.com). Arlington T. **Open** 9am-4pm Mon; 10am-6pm Tue-Sat; 11am-5pm Sun. **Credit** AmEx, MC, V. **Map** p277 H5.

Voted best salon in the city for two years running, this is where celebrities get shorn when they're in town. The fashion-conscious salon caters to well-heeled locals, and also sells its own line of luscious olive-based products.

Other locations: Louis Boston, 234 Berkeley Street, at Newbury Street (1-617 266 4485).

Safar Coiffures

235 Newbury Street, at Fairfield Street, Back Bay (1-617 247 3933). Copley T. **Open** 9am-5.30pm Mon, Tue, Sat; 9am-7pm Wed-Fri. **Credit** AmEx, MC, V. **Map** p276 G6.

One of the most established salons on Newbury Street, the luxurious three-floor Safar has a young, Euro-expat clientele, who are likely to pop into Armani afterwards for a browse. Colour is a speciality, and facials, manicures, pedicures and waxing are also offered.

Home & design

Cocoon

170 Tremont Street, at Avery Street, Downtown (1-617 728 9898/www.cocoonhome.com). Boylston T. **Open** 11am-7pm Mon-Sat; by appointment Sun. **Credit** AmEx, MC, V. **Map** p274 K5.

This family-run store exudes global chic, with its eclectic antique and modern home furnishings and gorgeous arrangements of exotic plants and flowers. We can't name-drop any brands, since the owner relishes discovering new lines and designers off the beaten path. As this guide went to press, the shop was preparing to relocate, so check the website for up-to-date information.

Fresh Eggs

58 Clarendon Street, at Columbus Avenue, South End (1-617 247 8150). Back Bay T. **Open** noon-6pm Tue, Wed; noon-7pm Thur, Fri; 11am-6pm Sat; noon-5pm Sun. **Credit** AmEx, Disc, MC, V. **Map** p277 H6.

This airy, modern shop promises to supply everything for your nest – kitchenware, linens, carpets, furniture, custom lighting, dressing-gowns and soaps. The style is low-key and casual.

Lekker

1317 Washington Street, at Union Park Street, South End (1-617 542 6464/www.lekkerhome.com). Back Bay T/Union Park Silver Line bus. **Open** 10am-7pm Tue-Sat; noon-6pm Sun. **Credit** AmEx, Disc, MC, V. **Map** p277 J8.

Want a new image? Pop into one-stop shop **G Spa**. *See p176.*

Lekker is the Dutch word for tasty and enticing, and it sums up this store's stock of well-designed, affordable merchandise not usually found in the US. Expect an East-meets-West mélange of Chinese antiques, Dutch furniture and accessories like linens, scented candles and kitchen utensils, with the emphasis on simplicity.

The Urban Slipper

48 South Street, Jamaica Plain (1-617 971 0870/ www.theurbanslipper.com). Green Street T then 39 bus or 15mins walk. **Open** 11am-6pm Tue, Wed; 11am-7pm Thur-Sat; 11am-5pm Sun. **Credit** AmEx, MC, V.

An outpost of big-city chic in suburban Jamaica Plain, the Urban Slipper has a hip mix of contemporary items for the home, from funky furniture and decorative ceramics to groovy patterned lamps and loungewear from California.

Laundry & dry-cleaning

King Lee's

227 Newbury Street, at Fairfield Street, Back Bay (1-617 267 9732). Copley T. **Open** 7am-7pm Mon-Thur; 7am-6pm Fri, Sat; 8.30am-5pm Sun. **Credit** MC, V. **Map** p276 G6.

This 30-year-old establishment offers laundry, dry-cleaning (including specialist suede and leather), a wash-and-fold service, a seamstress, and shoe repair on site.

Luggage

Large department stores such as Filene's (*see p158*) and Macy's (*see p159*) have luggage departments – Filene's Basement (*see p160*) often has great deals on big-name brands. **Travel 2000** in the Prudential Center mall (1-617 536 3101, *see p160*) sells a wide selection.

Music

Musical instruments

Daddy's Junky Music

159-165 Massachusetts Avenue, between Boylston Street & Huntington Avenue, Back Bay (1-617 247 0909). Hynes/ICA T. **Open** 11am-9pm Mon-Fri; 10am-7pm Sat; noon-6pm Sun. **Credit** AmEx, Disc, MC, V. **Map** p276 F7.

This regional chain grew from a single music shop in New Hampshire. There's a large selection of new and second-hand gear, with best price guaranteed on keys, drums, guitars, amps, PA systems and more. Also offers rentals and repair.

Records, tapes & CDs

Cheapo Records

645 Massachusetts Ave, at Prospect Street, Cambridge (1-617 354 4455). Central T. **Open** 10am-6pm Mon-Wed; 10am-9pm Thur-Fri; 10am-6pm Sat; 11am-5pm Sun. **Credit** AmEx, MC, V. **Map** 278 C3.

Central Square old-timer Cheapo is stuffed with a huge selection of old vinyl, in every category from African to zydeco by way of rare soul. As with neighbour Skippy White's across the street (*see below*), the owner works on the premises and is an expert on soul and R&B with many tales about personal encounters with the artists sold.

Newbury Comics

332 Newbury Street, between Hereford Street & Massachusetts Avenue, Back Bay (1-617 236 4930). Hynes/ICA T. **Open** 10am-10pm Mon-Thur; 10am-11pm Fri-Sat; 11am-8pm Sun. **Credit** AmEx, Disc, MC, V. **Map** p276 F6.

Don't let its name fool you. While it still sells comics and all manner of pop-culture paraphernalia, the emphasis is on CDs (both new and used) at this hip regional chain. New releases are a lot cheaper here than at the big-name retailers.

Other locations: 1 Washington Mall, Government Center, State Street (1-617 248 9992); The Garage, 36 John F Kennedy Street, at Harvard Square, Cambridge (1-617 491 0337).

Nuggets

486 Commonwealth Avenue, at Kenmore Square, Fenway (1-617 536 0679). Kenmore Square T. **Open** 11.30am-8pm Mon-Sat; noon-7pm Sun. **Credit** AmEx, Disc, MC, V. **Map** p276 D6.

Nuggets has a decent selection of new and used rock, new wave, soul, and jazz records and CDs at reasonable prices. It's near Boston University, so there's a good turnover of music. The shop also has a large selection of used music magazines and soundtracks.

Skippy White's

538 Massachusetts Avenue, between Norfolk & Prospect Streets, Cambridge (1-617 491 3345). Central T. **Open** 10am-6pm Mon-Wed, Sat; 10am-9pm Thur, Fri; 11am-5pm Sun. **Credit** MC, V. **Map** p278 C3.

Skippy White's has been an institution for collectors of R&B, blues, jazz, gospel, soul and oldies since 1961. As well as rare vinyl, it also carries a small selection of contemporary hip hop to keep up with the times. Like Central Square stalwart Cheapo (*see above*), it's owner-operated by an aficionado with many an anecdote about soul and R&B legends.

Twisted Village Records

12B Eliot Street, at Harvard Square, Cambridge (1-617 354 6898). Harvard T. **Open** noon-8pm Mon-Sat; noon-6pm Sun. **Credit** MC, V. **Map** p278 A3.

Go downstairs to find the best new re-releases of 1960s garage, psychedelic, mod and soul around. There's also an excellent listening station, so you can try before you buy.

Virgin Megastore

360 Newbury Street, at Massachusetts Avenue, Back Bay. (1-617 896 0950/www.virginmega.com). **Open** 10am-midnight daily. **Credit** AmEx, Disc, MC, V. **Map** p276 F6.

A multi-storey emporium of music, books, DVDs and the like at the funkier end of Newbury Street. With late hours, in-store DJ, loads of listening stations and top-floor café, it's perfect for loitering.

Sport

City Sports

11 Bromfield Street, at Washington Street, Downtown (1-617 423 2015/www.citysports.com). Park Street T. **Open** 10am-8pm Mon-Fri; 10am-5pm Sat; noon-6pm Sun. **Credit** AmEx, DC, Disc, MC, V. **Map** p274 K5.

This branch of the area's ubiquitous sporting goods chain boasts the company's only bargain basement, with goods at half price or less. Although only open on weekdays, the basement is an ideal hunting ground for cheap running shoes.

Other locations: throughout the city

Toys & games

Henry Bear's Park

361 Huron Avenue, between Standish & Chilton Streets, Cambridge (1-617 547 8424). Harvard T then 72 bus. **Open** 9.30am-7pm Mon-Wed, Fri; 9.30am-8pm Thur; 9.30am-6pm Sat; noon-6pm Sun. **Credit** AmEx, Disc, MC, V.

A charming neighbourhood store that sells a variety of educational and interactive toys for toddlers through to teens. Every Thursday at 11am is story hour, with children and parents gathering to hear a new or classic yarn.

Other locations: 685 Massachusetts Avenue, at Pleasant Street, Arlington (1-781 646 9400).

Jack's Joke Shop

226 Tremont Street, at Stuart Street, Downtown (1-617 426 9640/www.jacksjokes.com). Boylston or Chinatown T. **Open** 9am-5.30pm Mon-Sat. **Credit** MC, V. **Map** p277 J6.

Established in 1922, Jack's is the oldest joke shop in America. The rascally old owner-operators flog their huge supply of jokes, pranks, novelties and magic to a wonderfully diverse clientele.

Stella Bella Toys

1360 Cambridge Street, at Inman Square, Cambridge (1-617 491 6290). Central T then 83 bus. **Open** 9.30am-7pm Mon-Sat; 10am-5pm Sun. **Credit** AmEx, Disc, MC, V. **Map** p278 C2.

A quaint store that specialises in a wide array of educational developmental toys. It also offers fun activities such as sing-alongs and storytelling.

Arts & Entertainment

Features

Festivals & Events

Everyone knows Boston's tea parties are pretty wild, but the rest of its cultural calendar is lively too.

Given its revolutionary pedigree, it's hardly surprising that Boston's calendar features more than its fair share of historical re-enactments. And in the city where American independence began, you can be sure the Fourth of July is going to be a big deal. But Boston's rebels aren't confined to the 18th century. Alongside traditional celebrations such as the Boston Tea Party Re-enactment (*see p185*) and the Boston Harborfest (*see p182*) are events such as the Fetish Fair Fleamarket (*see p182*) and the Massachusetts Cannabis Reform's Freedom Rally on Boston Common (*see p184*). This cultured metropolis is also known for its arts events – notably the alcohol-free New Year's Eve programme, First Night, which has become a model for more than 200 cities worldwide.

Unless otherwise specified, the festivals and events listed below take place annually. Precise dates are difficult to pin down in advance as they're often weather-dependent. The best way to confirm the specifics is by phoning the **City of Boston Special Events Line** (1-800 822 0038), or visiting www.cityofboston.gov/mayor/spevents or the individual contacts provided.

Spring

Boston Massacre Re-enactment

Old State House, State Street, at Washington Street, Downtown (1-617 720 1713/1-617 720 3290/www.bostonhistory.org). State T. **Admission** free. **Map** p275 L4. **Date** 5 Mar.

A gathering to watch the 'cowardly' Redcoats take potshots from the balcony of the Old State House at five Patriot heroes below – marking the first bloodshed of the Revolution. Costumes, muskets and – let's hope – blanks are supplied courtesy of the Massachusetts Council of Minutemen and Militia.

New England Spring Flower & Garden Show

Bayside Exposition Center, 200 Mount Vernon Street, at Morrissey Boulevard, Columbia Point (1-617 536 9280/www.masshort.org). JFK/UMass T. **Admission** $7-$20. **Date** 2nd wk in Mar.

Hyping itself as the third-largest flower show in the world, this century-old tradition celebrates flora, shrubs, bushes and blossoms. The Massachusetts Horticultural Society sponsors five acres of landscaped gardens, flower arrangements and horticultural displays. Beauty in bloom.

St Patrick's Day Parade & Evacuation Day

Dorchester Street & Broadway, South Boston (1-617 536 4100). Broadway T. **Admission** free. **Date** 17 Mar.

Boston is considered the capital of Irish America, and Southie is the Irish capital of Boston. Everyone and their dog wears a shamrock on the 17th, making this both the best and worst place to be. A legal holiday for the city, the day begins with South Boston's Irish community hosting one of the largest St Patrick's Day parades in America, complete with floats, marching bands, war veterans and, of course, waving politicians. Evacuation Day also gets a formal nod when a smaller ceremony commemorates the day the British left town in 1776. But the real festivities begin in the late afternoon, when local pubs froth with green beer, bibulous merrymaking and high cover charges. By midnight, the downtown streets are so full of soused pedestrians that hailing a taxi is tantamount to catching a fly ball at Fenway.

Lantern Hanging

Salem Street at Hull Street, North End (1-617 523 6676/www.oldnorth.com). Haymarket T. **Admission** free. **Map** p275 L2. **Date** Sun before 19 Apr.

'One if by land, two if by sea,' goes the famous line in Longfellow's poem *Paul Revere's Ride*, and two lanterns are ceremoniously hung in the steeple of the Old North Church to commemorate sexton Robert Newman's warning that the British troops were heading towards Concord.

Boston Marathon

Finishes at Copley Square, Back Bay (1-617 236 1652/www.bostonmarathon.org). Copley T. **Admission** free. **Map** p277 G6. **Date** 3rd Mon in Apr.

These days, Patriot's Day in Boston has less to do with nationalism and more to do with thousands of feet pounding 26 miles of pavement. The race begins in Hopkinton (south-west of Boston), wraps around the campus of Boston College and finishes in Copley Square – and you can be sure at least one running Elvis will make the arduous trek. Thousands of spectators come out to sniff the adrenaline.

Patriot's Day Re-enactments

Various sites in Concord & Lexington (1-978 459 6150/1-800 443 3332/www.merrimackvalley.org). **Admission** free. **Date** 3rd Mon in Apr.

In Boston, Paul Revere gallops around, yelling about British invasion. In Lexington, on Lexington Green, there's a full-scale re-enactment of the skirmish that produced the 'shot heard round the world'.

The **Boston Pops Fourth of July Concert** always ends with a bang. *See p182.*

James Joyce Ramble

Start/finish at Endicott Estate on East Street, Dedham (1-781 329 9744/www.ramble.org). **Admission** race registration $20. **Date** last Sun in Apr.

The brainchild of a local runner and Joyce fan who realised that struggling through *Finnegans Wake* was comparable to training for a race, this annual six-mile (10-km) run/walk takes place in Dedham (a south-western suburb of Boston) every spring. While the event is fundamentally a road race, the James Joyce Ramble pays tribute to its namesake by punctuating the contest with an ensemble of Joyce-reading players. Mile one features *Finnegans Wake*, mile three *A Portrait of the Artist as a Young Man* and mile six, appropriately enough, *The Dead*. Proceeds go to charity and past post-race festivities have featured an awards ceremony, a small concert, free food and perhaps, purely in homage to Joyce of course, free beer.

Lilac Sunday

Arnold Arboretum, Arborway at Centre Street, Jamaica Plain (1-617 524 1718/www.arboretum.harvard.edu). Forest Hills T. **Admission** free. **Date** 2nd Sun in May.

The name says it all – float through the Arboretum when 400 varieties of fragrant lilacs are in bloom. Refreshments are available to buy, or bring a picnic.

Summer

Boston Pride

Various locations throughout the city (1-617 262 9405/www.bostonpride.org). **Admission** free. **Date** 1st wk in June.

Beginning with an AIDS awareness walk, New England's largest Gay Pride includes lectures, concerts and parties. It culminates in a parade through the South End on Saturday and a festival on Sunday.

Bunker Hill Celebrations

Various locations in Charlestown (1-617 242 5642/www.nps.gov/bost). Community College or North Station T. **Admission** free. **Date** wknd in mid June.

A weekend of historical talks and re-enactments of the famous battle of Bunker Hill – complete with military costumes and muskets – finishing with a grand parade through Charlestown.

Nantucket Film Festival

Various locations in Nantucket (1-508 325 6274/www.nantucketfilmfestival.org). **Admission** $50 1day; $250 1wk. **Date** 3rd wk in June.

Agents, actors and fans converge on Massachusetts' most exclusive vacation spot, Nantucket Island, for an insider's look at the silver screen. Screenwriting workshops and social events punctuate screenings.

Boston Harborfest

Various locations in Boston (1-617 227 1528/ www.bostonharborfest.com). **Admission** varies. **Date** 4th wk in June.

A maritime and colonial festival of fireworks, open-air concerts and (yet more) historical re-enactments in the Fourth of July week, taking place in over 30 harbourside venues. The Chowderfest (a celebration of New England's traditional bivalve soup, in which top restaurants vie for the title of 'Boston's Best Clam Chowder') is the best part.

Boston Pops Fourth of July Concert

Charles River Esplanade, Back Bay (1-617 266 1492/ www.bso.org/pops). Arlington or Copley T. **Admission** free. **Map** p274 H4. **Date** 4 July.

Not surprisingly, the Fourth of July attracts as many as a million visitors to the birthplace of American independence – most of whom plant themselves along the banks of the Charles River. The Boston Pops are an American institution, and this concert is the centre of the universe for fans. Frantically territorial families show up at dawn to claim their grassy patch for the day. Technically, the event is non-alcoholic, but regulars are savvy enough to conceal their drinks in plastic cups. In the early evening – after everyone is tuckered out from a day of guarding blankets (and hiding beer) – the Pops play. Their finale always includes the *1812 Overture* and an incredible fireworks display.

Turning of the USS Constitution

Viewing along Boston Harbor (1-617 426 1812/ www.ussconstitutionmuseum.org). **Admission** free. **Date** 4 July.

'Old Ironsides', so called because the Royal Navy's cannonballs bounced off her oaken flanks and still a commissioned naval vessel, makes her annual sail around Boston Harbor not for the tourists but in order to turn and re-dock in the opposite direction at the Charlestown Naval Yard. This is all done to ensure that the ship weathers evenly.

Bastille Day

French Library & Cultural Center, 53 Marlborough Street, at Berkeley Street (1-617 912 0400/www. frenchlib.org). Arlington T. **Admission** Call for details. **Date** mid July.

This 60-year-old non-profit organisation throws a street party on an evening before or after Bastille Day, with French cuisine, a live band, children's activities – and plenty of *joie de vivre.*

ArtBeat

Davis Square, Somerville (1-617 625 6600 ext 2985/www.somervilleartscouncil.org/programs/ artbeat). Davis Square T. **Admission** $3. **Date** wknd in mid July.

Reputedly one of the hippest 'hoods in the Boston area, Davis Square is full of artists, writers, musicians, performers and sundry other bohemian types. And every year, Somerville exalts its artists with a weekend-long celebration of all that's artsy. With concerts, dance, food, film and performances.

Edgartown Regatta

Edgartown, Martha's Vineyard (1-508 627 4361/ www.edgartownyc.org). **Admission** free. **Date** wknd in mid July.

The Edgartown Yacht Club sponsors races for four categories of vessels. Even for those who don't have a boat, it offers an excuse to take the short ferry ride out to the white-sand beaches of Martha's Vineyard and wander around the holiday island.

Boston Globe Jazz & Blues Festival

Various venues & locations around Boston (1-617 929 3460/https://bostonglobe.com/promotions/ jazzfest). **Admission** varies. **Date** 3rd wk of July.

Boston's broadsheet newspaper puts on a week-long string of jazz and blues concerts featuring big-name artists. Copley Square in Back Bay is the best place to catch free evening shows.

Feast of the Blessed Sacrament

New Bedford (1-508 992 6911/www.portuguese feast.com). **Admission** free. **Date** last wknd in July.

The largest Portuguese cultural event in America. The harbour town of New Bedford hosts this celebration featuring a parade, entertainment and music, most with a Madeiran flavour.

Fetish Fair Fleamarket

Sheraton Boston Hotel, 39 Dalton Street, at Boylston Street, Back Bay (1-617 876 6352/ www.nla-newengland.org/fff.html). Hynes/ICA T. **Admission** $5 1day; $10 2days. **Map** p276 F7. **Date** early Aug & late Dec.

For review, *see p185.*

Gloucester Waterfront Festival

Various locations in Gloucester (1-978 283 1601/ www.cape-ann.com/events.html). **Admission** free. **Date** mid Aug.

One of the towns that put Boston's fishing industry on the map, Gloucester hosts this annual festival in celebration of the sea, with a Yankee Lobster Bake, whale watching and musical entertainment. Those with a slightly bent sense of humour will enjoy the greasy pole competition, in which contestants (most quite intoxicated) traverse a telephone pole slathered in axle grease in search of fame, glory and the flag that dangles at the pole's end; most, though, get only splinters, unspeakable bruises and a bath in the ocean for their troubles.

Provincetown Carnival Week

Various locations in Provincetown (1-508 487 2313/ 1-800 637 8696/www.ptown.org). **Admission** varies. **Date** 3rd wk in Aug.

This very gay-friendly town celebrates itself each year with a small, Mardi Gras-like event marked by extravagant costumes, wild antics and a parade down Commercial Street. Though the carnival is not strictly gay, expect drag queens and high camp.

Caribbean Carnival

Franklin Park, Dorchester (1-617 298 1370/www. bostoncarnival.com). Forest Hills T. **Admission** free. **Date** wknd in late August.

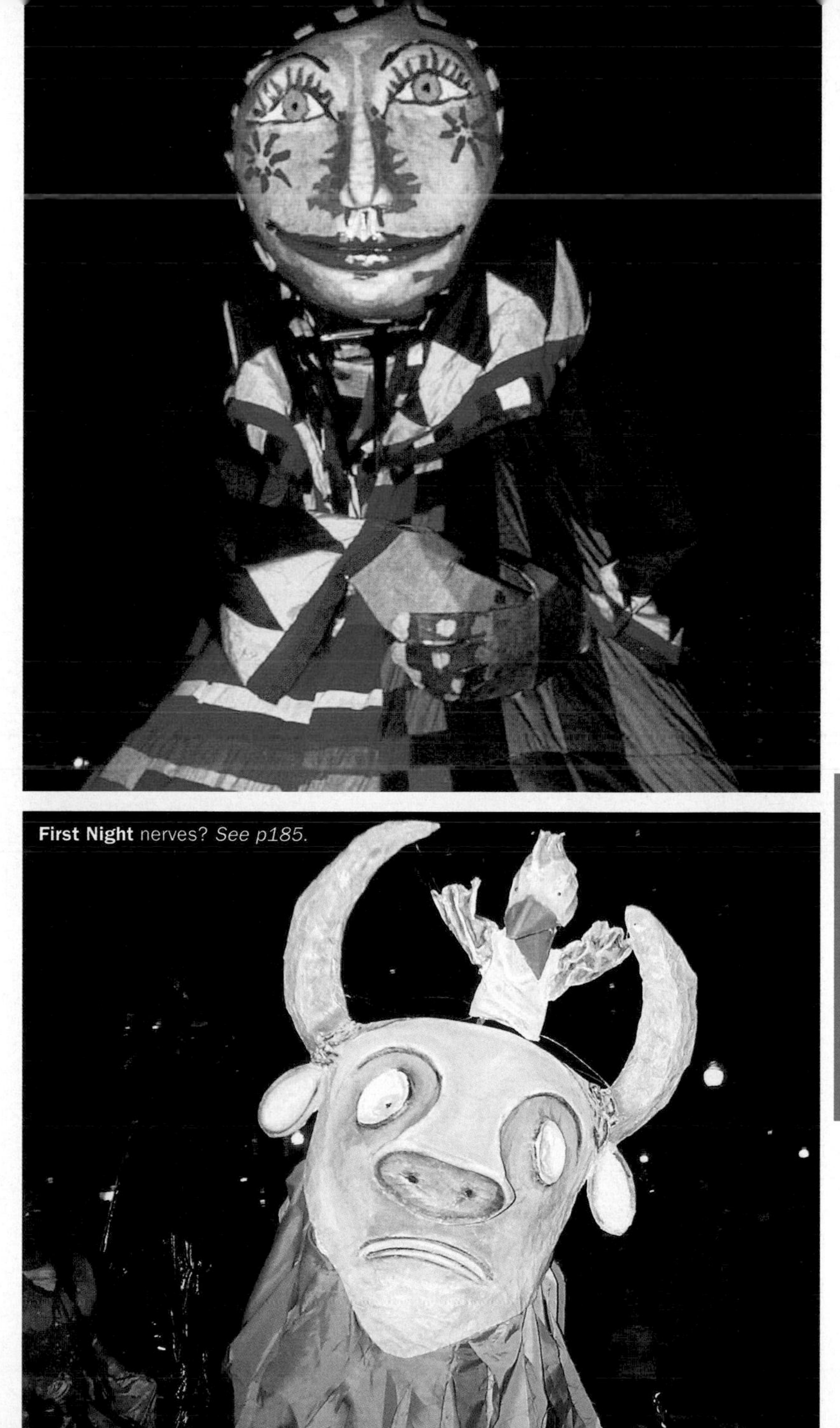

First Night nerves? *See p185.*

Franklin Park in the Dorchester end of Roxbury hosts this lively celebration of Caribbean culture that runs to ethnic foods, arts, music, dance and, of course, a colourful parade.

Autumn

Boston Tattoo Convention

Boston Center for the Arts, 539 Tremont Street, South End (1-617 445 9090/www.bostontattoo convention.com). **Admission** $15 1day; $35 3days. **Map** p277 H7. **Date** wknd in Sept.

Up until 2001, you had to cross the Massachusetts state line in order to get a tattoo. But once it was legalised, it didn't take long for Boston to establish itself as a hub for body art – as the Tattoo Convention proves. Hundreds of tattoo artists descend on the city for the three-day event, which includes contests, vendors, galleries, performances and numerous ink-slingers setting up shop.

King Richard's Faire

Carver, near Plymouth (1-508 866 5391/1-952 238 9915/www.kingrichardsfaire.net). **Admission** $24; $12 concessions. **Date** wknds in Sept & Oct.

Drink deep from the chalice of the 16th century with wenches, beggars, jugglers, knights and of course King Richard himself, late home from the Crusades. Packed with period revelry, Carver's re-creation of an English marketplace teems with fire-eaters, street brawls, singing executioners and Siberian tigers.

Boston Film Festival

Loews Copley Place, 100 Huntington Avenue, at Dartmouth Street, Back Bay (1-617 331 9460/ www.bostonfilmfestival.org). Copley or Back Bay T. **Admission** $10 per film. **Map** p277 G7. **Date** 2nd wk in Sept.

An annual festival of lectures, panels and screenings, this two-weekend showcase integrates feature-length films, shorts and independent works. There's a strong local contingent of participants, many from nearby colleges. Past entries include Oscar-winning *American Beauty* and Billy Ray's *Shattered Glass*.

Massachusetts Cannabis Reform's Freedom Rally

Boston Common, Downtown (1-781 944 2266/ www.masscann.org). Park St T. **Admission** free. **Map** p274 J5. **Date** 2nd or 3rd Sat in Sept.

Every year, the city of Boston broods over issuing permits to this annual drug-fest. Nonetheless, the rally always takes place, and thousands of stoners sneak spliffs on to the Common, a handful of edgy bands play and booths manned by left-leaning activist groups preach to the converted. It goes without saying, but people inevitably end up getting arrested. Bring your lawyer's phone number.

Lowell Celebrates Kerouac! Festival

Various locations in Lowell (1-877 537 6822/ http://ecommunity.uml.edu/lck/index.htm). **Admission** varies. **Date** 1st wk in Oct.

Most famous for *On the Road*, an American traveller's ode to wanderlust, whisky and boisterous escapades, Jack Kerouac was born and buried in this former mill town north-west of Boston. While he never claimed to have taken much from Lowell, once a year, the town commemorates its sole tie to the Beat Generation with a five-day festival of open mics, jazz and poetry readings.

Topsfield Fair

207 Boston Street, Route 1, Topsfield (1-978 887 5000/www.topsfieldfair.org). **Date** 1st 2wks of Oct.

Established in 1818, Topsfield is the oldest agricultural fair in the country. Head north of Boston for a slice of the Massachusetts heartland, complete with giant pumpkins and pig races.

Harvard Square Oktoberfest

Harvard Square, Cambridge (1-617 491 3434/ www.harvardsquare.com/events/oktoberfest). Harvard T. **Admission** free. **Map** p278 B2. **Date** mid Oct.

Harvard Square is transformed for a weekend into a Bavarian township, with bands, dancers, ethnic food and, of course, beer gardens. Some 200 regional artisans and merchants display their wares.

Head of the Charles Regatta

Charles River, between the Eliot Bridge and the Boston University Bridge (1-617 868 6200/ www.hocr.org). Central or Harvard T. **Admission** free. **Date** wknd in mid Oct.

This is one of the most spectacular boat races anywhere. The hundreds of thousands of fans lining the bridges and river banks along the Charles are a sight to be seen, as are the thousands of rowers who converge on Cambridge for this world-class regatta. Fans bring blankets and picnic baskets to the banks of the Charles to cheer their favourite teams.

Salem's Haunted Happenings

Locations throughout Salem (1-978 744 3663/1-877 725 3662/www.salemhauntedhappenings.com). **Admission** varies. **Date** 2nd half of Oct.

As you'd expect from a place that's famous for witches, spooky Salem hosts a wicked Halloween. The town is also a haven for modern pagans. A huge costumed parade kicks off two weeks of jack-o'-lantern carving, haunted-house tours, candlelit vigils, modern witchcraft ceremonies, magic shows and a psychics' fair. Leave your scepticism at home – but bring your wallet.

Winter

Christmas on Cape Cod

Various locations on Cape Cod (1-508 862 0700/ www.capecodchamber.org). **Admission** free. **Date** 4th wk in Nov.

Experience a New England Christmas in proper old-fashioned style by attending a series of open houses, parades and the lighting of the Pilgrim Monument in Provincetown. Wrap up warm as those coastal breezes can get mighty chilly in winter.

Christmas Stroll

Various locations on Nantucket (1-508 228 1700/ www.nantucketchamber.org/visitor/events.html). **Admission** free. **Date** 1st wknd in Dec.

On Nantucket Island, most of the shops start their off-season hibernation in mid October, but for one gloriously festive weekend in December, everything reopens, traffic resumes to midsummer status, and people wander up and down the Christmas-tree-lined streets, getting their holiday shopping done island-style. Watch the women in mink stream off the ferries, and enjoy the old-time cheeriness of carollers and Christmas trees on the cobblestone streets. It's a final hurrah before the place shuts down for the long, bleak winter.

Christmas Tree Lighting

Prudential Center, 800 Boylston Street, between Dalton & Exeter Streets, Back Bay (1-800 746 7778). Copley, Prudential or Hynes/ICA T. **Admission** free. **Map** p276 F6. **Date** 1st Sat of Dec.

The Prudential Center has the most magnificent tree in the city, swaddled in colourful lights. The lighting is the semi-official kick-off for the holiday season and there's usually a singalong.

Boston Common Tree Lighting

Boston Common, Downtown (1-617 635 4505/ www.cityofboston.gov). Park St T. **Admission** free. **Map** p274 J5. **Date** 1st wknd in Dec.

Fifty of the Common's trees are strung with fairy lights. A nativity scene and menorah are usually set up near Park St 'T' station. A local dignitary (often the mayor) flicks the switch.

Boston Tea Party Re-enactment

Old South Meeting House, 310 Washington Street, Boston (1-617 482 6439/www.oldsouthmeeting house.org). State House T. **Admission** $5; free for those in colonial attire. **Map** p275 L4. **Date** mid Dec.

'Patriots' gather for a town meeting at the Old South Meeting House to scream about nasty old King George III. Fife and drum in hand, the excitable group marches to a replica tea ship on the waterfront and does the dirty deed. Because of fire damage, the Boston Tea Party Ship & Museum (Congress Street Bridge, 1-617 338 1773) – where another tea party re-enactment used to take place – is in the process of major renovations. Due to open in spring/summer 2005, the new museum (twice as large as the old one, including two traditional tall ships) will resume its own annual tea-tossing ceremony.

Fetish Fair Fleamarket

Sheraton Boston Hotel, 39 Dalton Street, at Boylston Street, Back Bay (1-617 867 6362/www.nla-new england.org/fff.html). Hynes/ICA T. **Admission** $5 1day; $10 2days. **Map** p276 F7. **Date** early Aug & late Dec.

New England's biggest fetish/leather/BDSM event, the Fleamarket attracts people with all sorts of sexual preferences. For 22 years, the event was held at the Park Plaza, one of Boston's oldest grand hotels, but following a critical article in the *Boston Globe*, the Plaza withdrew its hospitality and the FFF has found a new home at the Sheraton. As well as browsing a hardware store's worth of 'tools', participants can attend discussion groups and classes – great for, um, bonding. Past lectures have covered such stimulating topics as 'Flogging 101' and 'Female Genotorture'. The highlight of the winter event is the Saturday night Fetish Masquerade Ball.

First Night

Events at locations throughout the city (1-617 542 1399/www.firstnight.org). **Admission** $15. **Date** 31 Dec.

Boston was the first city in the country to offer this alcohol-free alternative to ringing in the New Year in its usual drink sodden fug, as long ago as 1976. First Night is celebrated citywide, with performances and exhibitions at nearly 50 venues, from poetry readings to rock concerts. The event kicks off with the carnival-style Grand Procession in Back Bay in the early evening (on a different Boston-related theme each year) and culminates in a midnight fireworks display on the harbour. The massive ice sculptures in Copley Square are another signature feature. Leave the bubbly at home.

Boston Wine Expo

Seaport World Trade Center Boston, 200 Seaport Boulevard, at Northern Avenue, South Boston (1-877 946 3976/www.wine-expos.com/boston). South Station T. **Admission** $70 1day; $92 2days. **Date** 3rd wknd in Jan.

Oenophiles might like to make their way to the harbourside World Trade Center for the country's largest consumer wine event. The grape fest features tastings from over 400 domestic and international wineries, celebrity-chef demonstrations and educational seminars.

Chinese New Year

Beach & Tyler Streets, Chinatown (1-888 733 2678/ www.bostonusa.com). Chinatown T. **Admission** free. **Map** p274 K5. **Date** late Jan or early Feb, depending on lunar calendar.

Dragons dance and fireworks explode in a swirl of colours and sounds at the nation's third-largest celebration of the first day of the Chinese calendar. Festivities last for three weeks and much of the action takes place in and around Beach and Tyler Streets in Boston's Chinatown.

Beanpot Hockey Tournament

FleetCenter, Causeway Street (1-617 624 1000/ www.fleetcenter.com). North Station T. **Admission** $20-$40. **Map** p274 K2. **Date** 1st & 2nd Mon in Feb.

Skaters from Harvard, Northeastern and Boston Universities, along with Boston College (also a university despite its name) go helmet-to-helmet in this annual ice hockey clash. It's the only sports match in Boston where you'll hear anything chanted other than 'bullshit', as an audience of rival college students assault one another with fusillades of jeers and cheers and the occasional witticism. The winning team gets a trophy shaped like a, um, bean pot.

Children

'I'm bored!' should be an easily avoidable refrain in Boston.

Kids have a tendency to break out in hives at the mere mention of the word 'historical'. And although Boston is, among many things, a profoundly historical city, a number of its Revolutionary relics – such as the **USS Constitution** – are nonetheless great fun for children. Putting the past aside, there are countless ways to keep them entertained: in summer they can pet animals at the zoo, or even catch a ball game at the sublime **Fenway Park** (*see p222*); in winter you can take them skating alongside locals at the **Frog Pond** in Boston Common, where the trees are spectacularly lit from December.

If the city's often unpredictable weather puts a damper on outdoor activities, kids can learn about dinosaurs at the **Museum of Science** (*see p112*) or dig through Grandma's Attic at the **Children's Museum**.

For additional ideas, try the Calendar section in Thursday's edition of the *Boston Globe*, which lists a broad selection of activities for children in the coming week. Or check out the *Parents' Paper*, available at select newsstands, street boxes and, more reliably, online at www.boston.parenthood.com.

Another good resource is the Greater Boston Convention & Visitors Bureau's *Kids Love Boston* publication ($3.25), a fount of useful tips (1-888 733 2678/www.bostonusa.com).

Attractions & activities

Animals & nature

The **New England Aquarium** (*see p88*) on Boston's waterfront is one of the best in the country, and kids will love seeing the penguins, sea otters and sharks, as well as getting close to smaller fry – such as starfish and hermit crabs – in a tidal basin they can put their hands in.

Charles River Canoe & Kayak

Soldier's Field Road, Boston side of the Charles River, upstream of Eliot Bridge (1-617 462 2513/ www.ski-paddle.com). Harvard T, then 86 bus to Smith Playground. **Open** *May-Oct* 4pm-sunset Thur; 1pm-sunset Fri; 10am-sunset Sat, Sun. **Rentals** $6-$24 per hr; $24-$72 per day. **Credit** Disc, MC, V. **Map** p278 A3.

Paddle around Boston's waterways and see the city anew. If you're feeling adventurous, try taking one of the guided day trips ($115-$125).

Franklin Park Zoo

1 Franklin Park Road, Jamaica Plain (1-617 541 5466/www.zoonewengland.com). Forest Hills T, then 16 bus. **Open** *Apr-Sept* 10am-5pm Mon-Fri; 10am-6pm Sat, Sun. *Oct-March* 10am-4pm daily. **Admission** $9.50; $8 concessions; $5 2-15s. **Credit** AmEx, Disc, MC, V.

Franklin Park is Boston's best place to observe animals – except perhaps the bleachers at Fenway Park. The mid-sized zoo's Tropical Forest, complete with gorillas, pygmy hippos, leopards and tropical birds, is the main draw here. There are also lions in the Kalahari Kingdom, and wallabies and emus on the Outback Trail. Little ones can meet llamas, goats and chickens out in the Contact Corral, and, for the full tactile experience, actually pet various friendly and fluffy creatures at the new Franklin Farm.

Swan Boats

Public Garden, opposite the Ritz-Carlton, 15 Arlington Street at Newbury Street, Back Bay (1-617 522 1966/www.swanboats.com). Arlington T. **Open** *Mid Apr-mid June* 10am-4pm daily; *mid June-Aug* 10am-5pm daily; *first half of Sept* noon-4pm Mon-Fri; 10am-4pm Sat, Sun. **Admission** $2.50; $1 children. **No credit cards. Map** p274 H5.

Kids usually find these Victorian swan-shaped, pedal-powered boats irresistible. A staple of the Public Garden since 1877, they were inspired by their designer Robert Paget's, love of *Lohengrin*, and the Grail knight who crosses a river in a swan drawn boat to defend the innocence of his beloved. The boats even feature in Robert McCloskey's classic children's book *Make Way for Ducklings*, which makes a fun souvenir (available from most bookshops). The Lagoon the boats navigate isn't very big, but the 15-minute cruise is an essential Boston tourist experience. For more water-based fun in summer, swing through the Common afterwards and let the kids play in the Frog Pond. In winter when it's iced over, five bucks gets a pair of skates and an afternoon of gliding, slipping and sliding.

Museums

Boston is filled with museums – and there are some wonderful ones for kids. In addition to those listed below, the **Museum of Science** (*see p112*) has many memorable options for children, including a planetarium, an Omni Theater and a Friday night observatory, while the **Museum of Fine Arts** (*see p106*) hosts a 'Family Place' programme on weekends between October and May, featuring a variety of entertaining children's activities.

Forever blowing bubbles at the **Children's Museum**.

Children's Museum

300 Congress Street, at Museum Wharf, Downtown (1-617 426 8855/www.bostonkids.org). South Station T. **Open** 10am-5pm Mon-Thur, Sat, Sun; 10am-9pm Fri. **Admission** $9; $7 2-15s; *5-9pm Fri* $1 for all. **Credit** AmEx, Disc, MC, V. **Map** p275 M5.

Four floors of fun. Kids can shop in the Latin-American *supermercado*, play with bubbles, wander through the big maze, board the Minnow and learn about boats, explore dolls' houses or the costumes in Grandma's 1959 attic. The changing exhibits are always educational, but kids will be having too much fun to notice. As well as a gift store, there's a shop selling inexpensive crafts.

Harvard Museum of Natural History

26 Oxford Street, at Harvard Square, Cambridge (1-617 495 3045). Harvard Square T. **Open** 9am-5pm daily. **Admission** $7.50; $6 concessions; $5 3-18s; free for all Sun 9am-12pm; *May-Sept* also free Wed 3pm-5pm. **Credit** AmEx, MC, V. **Map** p278 B2.

Kids can explore this vintage museum, see an actual Dodo skeleton, behold various botanic and geological wonders, meet a 42ft (13m) crocodile, peer up at a pair of massive whale skeletons, and quite possibly pick up some knowledge into the bargain.

USS Constitution & Museum

Charlestown Navy Yard, off Constitution Road, Charlestown (1-617 426 1812/www.ussconstitution museum.org). North Station T then 15min walk/ 92, 93 bus. **Open** *Museum* May-Oct 9am-6pm daily; Nov-Apr 10am-5pm daily. *Ship* Apr-Oct 10am-4pm Tue-Sun; Nov-Mar 10am-4pm Thur-Sun. **Admission** free.

The legendary old frigate was built in 1797 and went on to become one of the most celebrated warships of its era, taking part in over 30 engagements ranging from an Ottoman polacre to a French brig and British privateer. Today, 'Old Ironsides' is the oldest commissioned warship in the world. Kids can explore the ship, ask questions of guides decked out in period garb, then go on to the adjacent museum to learn about the vessel's stormy history.

Theatre

These theatres, which specialise in performances geared towards children of all ages, let kids act out rather than act up.

Artbarn Community Theater

50 Sewall Avenue, at Beacon Street, Brookline (1-617 975 0050/www.artbarn.org). Coolidge Corner T. **Open** Call for performance times and classes. **Tickets** $5-$7. **No credit cards**.

A theatre specialising in providing affordable opportunities for kids to get involved in theatre. From toddlers to high-schoolers, these diverse young actors work to entertain, as well as build confidence and self-esteem. If there's not enough time to commit to a term's classes, drop in for one of the performances.

Free your tadpoles at the **Frog Pond**. *See p186.*

Boston Children's Theatre

647 Boylston Street, at Dartmouth Street, Back Bay (1-617 424 6634/www.bostonchildrenstheatre.org). Copley T. **Open** *Box office* noon-6pm Mon-Fri. Call for performance times. **Tickets** $10-$22 by phone only, except on day of performance. **Credit** MC, V. **Map** p277 G6.

One of the country's oldest theatre organisations, the BCT puts on three main stage shows a year in a number of venues around the city. Productions – by kids, for kids – coincide with the school holidays. Acting classes are offered year round. There are performances for under-fives in Copley Square on Wednesday nights in the summer.

Puppet Showplace Theatre

32 Station Street, at Washington Street, Brookline (1-617 731 6400/www.puppetshowplace.org). Brookline Village T. **Open** *Box office* June-Aug 10am-4pm Mon-Fri; Sept-May 10am-4pm Tue-Sun. Call for show times. **Tickets** $8. **Credit** AmEx, MC, V.

Some of the world's most popular fairy tales, from *Cinderella* to *Jack and the Beanstalk*, are shown here, along with more contemporary stories – all performed by the theatre's professional puppeteers. There are increasingly popular adult shows too.

Tours

For the child-friendly **Boston Duck Tours** and **Boston Old Town Trolley Tours**, *see p103.*

Boston by Little Feet

Information 1-617 367 2345/www.bostonbyfoot.com. Meet at the Samuel Adams statue on Congress Street. State House T. **Tours** 10am Mon, Sat; 2pm Sun. **Tickets** $8. **No credit cards**. **Map** p275 L4.

This hour-long tour for kids aged between 6 and 12 is organised by the acclaimed Boston by Foot tour group. It provides a child's-eye view of sites along the Freedom Trail.

Boston Spirits Walking Tour

Information 781 235 7149/www.newengland ghosttours.com. Meet at the Visitors Center on Boston Common, 147 Tremont Street, Downtown. Park Street T. **Tours** depart 7.30pm on select non-winter evenings; reservations required. **Tickets** $15; $12 children. **Map** p274 K5.

A 90-minute tour of Boston's haunted hotspots, such as Boston Common, the Athenaeum and the Central Burying Ground, with Jim McCabe, a local folklore and occult expert.

Make Way For Ducklings Tour

Information 1-617 426 1885/www.historic-neighborhoods.org. Tours leave from the Historic Neighborhoods Foundation, 286 Congress Street. Downtown Crossing T. **Tours** *July, Aug* Fri & Sat; times vary; call in advance. **Tickets** $8; $6 children. **No credit cards**. **Map** p275 M5.

Trace the route of Jack, Kack, Mack, Nack, Quack, Pack and Mr and Mrs Mallard from *Make Way for Ducklings,* Robert McCloskey's celebrated children's book. The tour quacks and waddles through Beacon Hill, the Boston Common and the Public Garden – where you'll have the chance to take pictures with bronze statues of the book's main characters. There is also an annual Ducklings Day parade through Boston with fully fowled participants, see www.ducklingsday.org for further details.

Babysitting

Parents in a Pinch

45 Bartlett Crescent, Brookline (1-800 688 4697/1-617 739 5437/www.parentsinapinch.com). Washington Street T. **Open** *Office* 8am-5pm Mon-Fri. **Rates** placement fee $65 weekdays, $45 evenings & weekends; plus sitter salary $10-$13 per hr. **Credit** AmEx, MC, V.

This 15-year-old agency can refer up to 150 nannies offering short-term childcare.

Nanny Poppins

100 Cummings Center, Beverly (1-617 227 5437/1-978 927 1811/www.nannypoppins.com). **Open** *Office* 9am-5pm Mon-Fri. **Rates** placement fee $30 day/evening; plus sitter salary $10-$18 per hr. **Credit** AmEx, Disc, MC, V.

Nanny Poppins provides families with full and part-time nannies and babysitters on call, and offers the most comprehensive background check in the industry. If your children's first language is not English, there are babysitters and nannies available for hire who can speak a range of different tongues, even including sign language.

Eating out

An army, however small, marches on its stomach. These restaurants will entertain kids' taste buds, and fortify them for a busy day in and around Beantown. For the best ice-cream places, *see p142*.

Fire + Ice

50 Church Street, at Harvard Square, Cambridge (1-617 547 9007). Harvard T. **Open** 11.30am-midnight Sun-Thur; 11.30am-1am Fri, Sat. **Main courses** $7.95-$16.95. **Credit** AmEx, Disc, MC, V. **Map** p278 A2.

Don't let the sleek, trendy interior fool you. Picky children can choose the ingredients for themselves and watch the meal being cooked right before their eyes. Although it's an all-you-can-eat type of place, smaller childrens' less ravenous appetites may not justify the $15.95 fixed dinner price.

Other location: 205 Berkeley Street, at St James Street, Back Bay (1-617 338 4019).

Full Moon

344 Huron Avenue, between Lake View Avenue and Fayerweather Street, Cambridge (1-617 354 6699). Harvard T, then 72 bus. **Open** 11.30am-2.30pm, 5-9pm Mon-Sat; 9am-2.30pm, 5-9pm Sun. **Main courses** $12-$18. **Credit** MC, V.

Twice winner of the *Parents' Paper* Clean Plate Club Award, Full Moon is stocked with lots of baskets of educational toys, a chalkboard, dolls' houses and so on. While the kids play and munch, you can sample the butternut squash soup, washed down with a glass of Chianti. Booking is recommended, as this is a popular venue with families.

Hard Rock Cafe

131 Clarendon Street, at Stuart Street, Back Bay (1-617 424 7625). Back Bay T. **Open** 11am-1am daily. **Main courses** $11-$21. **Credit** AmEx, DC, Disc, MC, V. **Map** p277 H6.

Noisy, boisterous and filled with memorabilia from the golden age of rock. Kids can be as raucous as they want in one of the most popular burger joints in town and nobody will get angry.

Maggiano's Little Italy

4 Columbus Avenue, at Arlington Street, Back Bay (1-617 542 3456). Arlington T. **Open** 11.30am-10pm Mon-Thur; 11.30am-11pm Fri; noon-11pm Sat; noon-9pm Sun. **Family style meals** $13.95-$23.95 per person; **Main courses** $12-$32.95. **Credit** AmEx, Disc, MC, V. **Map** p277 J6.

A big, bustling Italian restaurant that offers 'family style' meals for parties of four or more. Kids can choose from a vast array of appetisers, pastas, entrées and desserts, and help themselves to the generous quantities brought out by friendly, unflappable servers. A little pricey at first glance, but you can subsist for a week on the leftovers.

Marché Mövenpick Boston

Prudential Center, 800 Boylston Street, between Dalton & Exeter Streets, Back Bay (1-617 578 9700). Prudential or Hynes Convention Center T. **Open** 11.30am-midnight daily. **Main courses** $4-$25. **Credit** AmEx, DC, Disc, MC, V. **Map** p276 F6.

Arranged like an indoor marketplace, Mövenpick's is filled with different food stations, from the Pasta Island to the Seafood Bar and the Grill & Rotisserie.

Clubs

Where to go to get down.

Let's face it, though it has picked up somewhat in recent years, attracting some of the hottest DJs in the business, Boston's club scene still can't compete with New York. For the most part, this can be blamed on the city's 2am closing time. The only after-hours club in town is Rise (306 Stuart Street, 1-617 423 7473, www.riseclub.us), which stays open until the sun comes up, but only admits members and their guests – although if you strike up a conversation with the right person in a club, you might be able to wangle your way in.

That said, with reasonable expectations it is possible to have a good night out in Boston. As in the rest of the nation, hip hop rules the roost, and the once-popular Euro sound is less of a force. In smaller venues, house and techno are slowly returning to prominence, and drum 'n' bass is still popular. In addition, many of the city's best nightspots are also known for their live music (*see pp207-213*).

THE CODE

The law allows entry for 18-year-olds, but the clubs usually like to know their clientele has finished high school, so to get into most of them you have to be aged 21 – or at least 19. Dress codes are looser than they used to be, and tend to be enforced at the discretion of the doormen. As a good general rule, avoid caps, sneakers, athletic wear of all kinds – basically, anything that might identify you as a potential meathead.

Toast of the town. *See p192.*

THE SCENE

There are two main club districts in Boston. Lansdowne Street, a one-block stretch bordering Fenway Park is the city's clubbing heartland. Packed with nightspots, it has a suitably neon-lit, hedonistic atmosphere on weekend evenings. Hordes of college students and suburbanites descend on the area on Friday and Saturday nights. Downtown, the Theatre District near Chinatown is club headquarters for the Prada-wearing international set. Here you'll normally find a high concentration of seemingly perfect-looking people with money to burn. If that's your scene, this is your place. Nearby, Boylston Place (known to its fans as 'the Alley') offers a sort of nightlife mall, with bars, restaurants and clubs lining the street – on most weekend nights, drunken twentysomethings wobble from one to another. Cambridge and Somerville also offer a number of bars with DJs playing non-commercial music. Central Square in particular is noted for underground sounds.

Clubs and specifically designated nights change at a rapid pace in this town, so call ahead to check that low-key spot still plays jazzy downtempo instead of the latest tracks from Nellie. At all the places listed below, credit cards are only accepted at the bar – admission at the door is cash only.

Aria

246 Tremont Street, at Stuart Street, Downtown (1-617 338 7080/www.ariaboston.com). Boylston T. **Open** 11pm-2am Tue-Sat, Sun. **Admission** $8-$15. **Credit** AmEx, MC, V. **Map** p277 J6.

Small enough to be simultaneously both exclusive and jam-packed, this velvet-upholstered dance club under the Wilbur Theatre is popular with designer-clad international students, who put bottles of bubbly on Daddy's credit card and groove to a hip hop dominated soundtrack.

Avalon

15 Lansdowne Street, at Ipswich Street, Fenway (1-617 262 2424/www.avalonboston.com). Kenmore T. **Open** 10pm-2am Thur-Sun. **Admission** $10-$15. **Credit** AmEx, Disc, MC, V. **Map** p276 D7.

Lights, camera, action: **Hollywood KTV/Ekco Lounge**.

With a capacity of 2,000 and an impeccable sound and light system, Avalon remains the crown jewel of Boston's nightlife. Prior to 10pm it features big-ticket rock, hip hop and electronic acts, after which it transforms into a world-class nightclub. International Thursday caters to a mainstream/Top 40 hip hop crowd. Friday's Avaland night has been voted best club night in America by several dance music magazines. Virtually every big-name DJ in the world – from Sasha and Digweed to Paul Oakenfold and Derrick Carter – regularly perform here. The crowd encompasses all races and sexual orientations. Saturday is called TRA (Total Request Avalon) with a mix of city-dwellers and bridge-and-tunnel (read: suburban) types pre-selecting the music via Avalon's website. The Sunday gay night, now in its 23rd year, is an institution.

Axis

13 Lansdowne Street, at Ipswich Street, Fenway (1-617 262 2437). Kenmore T. **Open** 10pm-2am Mon, Thur-Sat. **Admission** $10. **Credit** AmEx, Disc, MC, V. **Map** pp276 D7.

Rising from the ashes of Boston's once-dilapidated dance scene, Axis has reinvented itself once again as a centre for electro-pop, new wave and punk. Static, the long-running gay house night (with an eye-popping drag show) keeps on trucking, but these days the top DJs play almost exclusively in Avalon (*see p190*). Local radio station WFNX runs Next on Fridays, spinning bands like the Rapture, Peaches, Oasis and the Chemical Brothers. Also on Saturdays, head upstairs to I/D (the top half of Axis), where DJs Damian and Gibby run Start, one of the most popular indie/dance/electro/punk nights in town. Thursdays tend to be more progressive house dominated. Friday nights are presided over by legendary DJ David James, known for his retro '80s new wave/synth pop sound. Tip: patrons can move back and forth between Axis and Avalon with no additional cover charge on Fridays.

The Big Easy

1 Boylston Place, between Charles & Tremont Streets, Back Bay (1-617 351 7000/www.bigeasyboston.com). Boylston T. **Open** 9pm-2am Thur-Sat. **Admission** $5-$8. **Credit** AmEx, MC, V. **Map** p277 J5.

A large, New Orleans-style dance club with DJs and cover bands playing alternative and Top 40 dance, new R&B and hip hop. Two lounges upstairs offer nuzzling room and pool tables.

The Club at Il Panino

295 Franklin Street, at Broad Street, Downtown (1-617 338 1000). Downtown Crossing or State T. **Open** 11pm-2am Fri-Sun. **Admission** $15. **Credit** AmEx, Disc, MC, V. **Map** p275 L4.

With five floors, Il Panino offers a multitude of music options on any given night. Sundays feature a mix of hip hop, house and international music. On Fridays, Brazilian, Latin, international and house dominate, while on Saturdays, Russian dance music, house and hip hop tend to be the focus of the night. The crowd has become significantly younger in the last few years (21-25) but the Euro/international crowd remains as loyal as ever. Don't wear sneakers and leave hats and caps at home if you want to get in.

Hollywood KTV/Ekco Lounge

41 Essex Street, Chinatown (1-617 338 8283/www.hollywoodboston.com). Chinatown or Boylston T. **Open** 10pm-2am Tue-Sat. **Admission** varies. **Credit** (bar only) AmEx, Disc, MC, V. **Map** p274 K5.

Hollywood KTV at the Ekco Lounge continues to tweak its entertainment schedule. Several days of the week seem to have a topsy-turvy schedule, but two weekend stalwarts show no sign of shifting. The Pill, a Brit-pop indie-rock night takes place on Fridays and has a devoted fan base throughout the city. On the following day, the weekend reaches its climax when Club Hollywood – voted Boston's best women's night by *Boston* magazine – packs the place with DJs playing hip hop and popular house.

While on the third Saturday of each month the club hosts Glitter Switch, a raucous drag/karaoke night (*see p205* **The girly show**). Live bands perform once a month. Call ahead to check the entertainment and dress code (none on Friday or Saturday).

Embassy

36 Lansdowne Street, at Ipswich Street, Fenway (1-617 262 2424). Kenmore T. **Open** 10pm-2am Thur-Sat. **Admission** $10-$15. **No credit cards.** **Map** p276 D7.

Dark and almost always crowded, with reserved tables and a VIP elevator, the Embassy club, located upstairs from Avalon, is Euro, Euro, Euro and young, young, young. Thursday is the Latin lounge night, complete with free entry to the bigger club below, Friday is Urban Grooves, while Saturday is the best of the classic Euro nights.

Man Ray

21 Brookline Street, at Green Street, Cambridge (1-617 864 0400/www.manrayclub.com). Central T. **Open** 9pm-2am Wed-Fri; 10pm-2am Sat. **Admission** $5-$15. **Credit** AmEx, MC, V. **Map** p278 C4.

This underground club has the most interesting queues outside on Wednesday and Friday nights, if somewhat sombre in range of colour – lots of shrouds, corsets, hip boots and full vinyl ensembles laced up tight. And acres and acres of black. As well as the dedicated Goth/industrial nights, there's a Thursday gay night and a campy disco/new wave night on Saturday, but the Goths and fetishists don't always stick to the schedule. The theme on Friday varies from week to week. If possible, try to make it down to the long-running Hell night (2nd Friday of the month), quite possibly Man Ray's most debauched event. The dress code is strictly enforced to keep out potential troublemakers and overexcitable voyeurs (there's an in-house whipping post, and a lot of flesh on view). Wear black and only black – call or visit the website for guidelines.

The Phoenix Landing

512 Massachusetts Avenue, at Brookline Street, Cambridge (1-617 576 6260). Central T. **Open** 11am-1am Mon-Thur, Sun; 11am-2am Fri, Sat. **Admission** free-$5. **Credit** AmEx, DC, Disc, MC, V. **Map** p278 C3.

Hip hop and Guinness may not seem like the most obvious of night life combinations, but the Phoenix Landing is a successful, if somewhat strange, marriage of dance club and Irish pub. The decor may be on the basic side, but this little joint remains a major cornerstone of Boston's underground dance scene, presided over by top-notch local, national and international DJs. Expect everything from live jazz, hip hop, reggae, house, techno, drum 'n' bass right through to classic '80s new wave. Visit during the week to hear underground music, or at weekends if mainstream tunes are more your preference. The clientele is varied, but the majority is young, casually dressed and ready to hit the (tiny) floor.

Tequila Rain

145 Ipswich Street, at Lansdowne Street, Fenway (1-617 437 0300/ www.tequilarainboston.com). Kenmore T. **Open** 5pm-2am Mon-Thur; 11.30am-2am Fri-Sun. **Admission** free-$5. **Credit** AmEx, MC, V. **Map** p276 D7.

If wet T-shirt contests, girls'/boys' nights out and strawberry daiquiris are your ideal night out thing, you've just found your new favourite club. Located on the first floor of Jillian's, a massive entertainment complex with pool tables, darts, and a brand new bowling alley, Tequila Rain is a Tex-Mex bar, grill and dance club that's very popular with an early to mid-20s crowd. In the back room, fun-lovin' clubbers get down to Top 40 and dance hits from the 1970s to the present in front of a bank of giant video screens. While the atmosphere is casual, men in sleeveless shirts, athletic gear, sneakers or, bizarrely, hats, will be turned away – but women can wear anything, or practically nothing.

Toast

70 Union Square, at Washington Street, Somerville (1-617 623 9211/www.toastlounge.com). Davis Square T then 87 bus. **Open** 5.30pm-1am Wed-Sun. **Admission** $5. **Credit** AmEx, DC, Disc, MC, V. **Map** p278 C2.

One of the newer lounges doubling as a dance club, tiny, intimate Toast screams 'swanky New York hot spot'. Wednesday is gay and Thursday lesbian. Given the area's diverse ethnic mix, the owners cleverly designated Friday as an international night. Prescription Saturdays are in the running as one of the best house nights in town – think funky, bouncy, vocally tribal soul – with guest DJs every week. There's no set dress code, but going too casual might make you feel out of place.

Tonic

1316 Commonwealth Avenue, Brighton (1-617 566 6699). Long Ave T. **Open** 5pm-1am Mon-Fri; 10.30pm-1am Sat, Sun. *DJs* 9pm-1am Thur-Sat. **Admission** free. **Credit** AmEx, DC, Disc, MC, V.

Given the substantial student population in the Allston/Brighton area (Boston University and Boston College are both close by), it was only a matter of time before a bar mixing the local pick-up scene with a Euro accent would open. The ground-floor Met Lounge features a DJ playing mainly Top 40, R&B and hip hop, with the occasional commercial house tune. The spacious loft-style top level is for chilling out, with a 70ft (21m) oval bar, TVs and decent food.

Vapor/Chaps

100 Warrenton Street, at Stuart Street, Downtown (1-617 695 9500). Boylston T. **Open** 3pm-2am Mon-Sat; noon-2am Sun. **Admission** $4-$8. **Credit** Amex, MC, V. **Map** p277 J6.

Boston's long-running gay club has mellowed to a more mixed scene. As this guide went to press it was undergoing refurbishment, but Wednesdays and Sundays are set to continue as gay nights, with the rest of the week catering to a varied crowd. Phone in advance, as specific details may change.

Film

There's plenty of action if you like to watch.

Loews Boston Common. See p194.

Just after *Good Will Hunting* made local boys Matt Damon and Ben Affleck Oscar-winning heroes, the Massachusetts Film Council was forced to shut its doors when it lost state funding. It seemed like a major blow to Boston's shot at becoming a film hub. But heavy hitters like Clint Eastwood kept coming, film programmes have taken off, and festivals are thriving. For the foreseeable future, Boston will remain on the map – and on the screen.

FILM-MAKING

College students don't just dabble in film here, they major in it: at Emerson College, with its hyped LA connections, as well as at other institutions such as Boston University, the Art Institute of New England and Massachusetts College of Art. But there are alternatives to the traditional degree route. The **Boston Educational Film and Video Association** at the Film Shack Studio complex (227 Roxbury Street, Roxbury, 1-617 989 0588, www.befva.org) runs classes taught by professional filmmakers. Most local Adult Education Centers in Boston (1-617 267 4430) and Cambridge (1-617 547 6789) also offer a number of affordable film education choices.

WHERE TO VIEW

Boston has a wide variety of screening venues to cater to all tastes, from glitzy stadium theatres to funky repertory houses, which are among the nation's best for art-house fare.

The oldest of Boston's art-house cinemas is the **Coolidge Corner Movie Theatre** (*see p194*), a double-screen art deco venue in Brookline. Across the river in Cambridge, the single-screen **Brattle Theatre** (*see p193*) screens restored classics and imaginative double bills, and has steadily built up a loyal following for its scheduling.

For newer independent releases, Boston cinephiles usually go to the Landmark chain's outpost in Cambridge, the **Kendall Square Cinema** (*see p194*). But the Kendall, as locals call it, has been joined on the indie scene by a surprising venue. The **Loews Copley Place** (*see p194*), situated in a shopping mall, traded in its programming of Hollywood blockbusters for a mix of Independent Film Channel offerings, foreign films, recent hits and some family fare.

If you don't mind waiting a week or two before seeing new releases, the **Somerville Theatre** (55 Davis Square, 1-617 625 4088) and the **Capitol Theater** in Arlington (204 Massachusetts Avenue, 1-781 648 6022) screen second-run films for about half the price of regular theatres ($4-$6).

For the location of your nearest cinema or information on films currently showing, check local listings or call the free AOL MovieFone Line at 1-617 333 3456.

Cinemas

Art-house screens

Brattle Theatre

40 Brattle Street, Harvard Square, Cambridge (1-617 876 6838/www.brattlefilm.org). Harvard T. **Tickets** $9; $6 concessions. **No credit cards. Map** p278 A2.

Built as a theatre in 1890 by the Cambridge Social Union, the slightly ragged Brattle became a movie house in the '50s, when it offered Humphrey Bogart marathons as a stress reliever for students during exam weeks. In the half century since then, it has kept Bogart in the annual line-up, while toasting new directors, bringing back short-lived cult hits, and offering film seasons with themes like Hong Kong Action and Female Directors.

Coolidge Corner Movie Theatre

290 Harvard Street, at Beacon Street, Brookline (1-617 734 2500/www.coolidge.org). Coolidge Corner T. **Tickets** $9; $5.50 concessions. **No credit cards.**
Originally a church, the Coolidge was transformed into an art deco movie palace in 1933, but fell into disrepair. After putting up with the cinema's shabby seats and dim lighting for years, Coolidge fans have been rewarded with new seats and beautifully restored fixtures. Local filmmakers get exposure in the new screening room upstairs, while the best indie films grace the balcony and ground-floor theatres.

Harvard Film Archive

Carpenter Center for the Visual Arts, 24 Quincy Street, at Harvard University, Cambridge (1-617 495 4700/www.harvardfilmarchive.org). Harvard T. **Tickets** $7; $5 concessions. **No credit cards. Map** p278 B2.
Want a fix of Fassbinder or a taste of Truffaut? This is where the most serious-minded filmgoers and the coolest art kids head, in search of experimental film.

Kendall Square Cinema

1 Kendall Square, at Broadway, Cambridge (information 1-617 499 1996/621 1202/tickets 1-617 333 3456/www.landmarktheaters.com). Kendall/MIT T. **Tickets** $9.25; $5.50 concessions. **Credit** AmEx, MC, V.
The best line-up of art-house films on eight screens, gourmet goodies and knowledgeable staff.

Loews Copley Place

100 Huntington Avenue, at Dartmouth Street (1-617 266 1300/266 2533). Copley T. **Tickets** $9; $6 concessions. **Credit** AmEx, MC, V. **Map** p277 G7.
Having reinvented itself with an emphasis on art-house and indie fare, Copley Place now attracts fewer mall rats and more serious film fans. Some of the theatres have seats graduated in reverse in front of a raised screen, making for a surreal experience.

Museum of Fine Arts

465 Huntington Avenue, at Museum Road, Fenway (1-617 369 3770/369 3306/www.mfa.org). Museum T. **Tickets** $9; $8 concessions. **Credit** AmEx, MC, V. **Map** p276 E9.
The MFA promotes an intellectually stimulating programme of films in its Remis Auditorium. The focus is on local and foreign features and documentaries, and it hosts well-attended French, Jewish, and International Film festivals each year.

Other screens

AMC Fenway

Landmark Center, 201 Brookline Avenue, at Beacon Street, Fenway (1-617 424 6266/www.amctheatres.com). Fenway T. **Tickets** $9.50; $6 concessions. **Credit** AmEx, MC, V. **Map** p276 D7.
This is where moviegoers head for mindless fun: things that go boom, lighter-than-air romance and predictable schmaltz. With fast food, comfy chairs, and 13 huge screens, it's all about entertainment.

Circle Cinemas

399 Chestnut Hill Avenue, at Beacon Street, Brookline (1-617 566 4040/www.showcasecinemas.com). Cleveland Circle T. **Tickets** $9.25; $6.25 concessions. **Credit** Disc, MC, V.
This first-run cinema has the advantage of comfortable high-backed, deep-cushioned tilting chairs.

Loews Boston Common

175 Tremont Street, at Boylston Street, Downtown (1-617 423 5801/www.enjoytheshow.com). Boylston or Chinatown T. **Tickets** $10; $6.50 concessions. **Credit** AmEx, MC, V. **Map** p274 K5.
This state-of-the-art complex boasts 18 screens, all with stadium-style seating. Loews shows the real blockbusters simultaneously on multiple screens.

Loews Harvard Square

10 Church Street, at Massachusetts Avenue, Cambridge (1-617 864 4580/www.enjoytheshow.com). Harvard T. **Tickets** $9; $6 concessions. **Credit** AmEx, MC, V. **Map** p278 B2.
For a while, this Loews transformed itself into an almost-art-house venue, with an emphasis on foreign and indie films, but it now blends arty fare with the hottest hits. While the main screen is huge, the other four are small and oddly configured.

Film festivals

Though it's still a long way from becoming the home of the next Sundance, Boston has its share of film festivals. The MFA hosts several annual genre festivals. In the autumn, Loews theatres and the Independent Film Channel sponsor the **Boston Film Festival** (1-617 421 4499, www.bostonfilmfestival.org). The ten-day event takes place in mid September at the Loews Copley Square and shows a substantial roster of short films as well as feature films. Also in autumn is the **New England Film and Video Festival**, run by the Boston Educational Film and Video Association (*see p193*), offering a programme of independent shorts, features and documentaries at the Coolidge Corner Movie Theatre.

The **Boston Underground Film Festival** (1-617 975 3361, www.bostonundergroundfilmfestival.com) screens bizarre and provocative cinematic fare in various venues (season varies; call or see website for dates), while the **Independent Film Festival of Boston** (www.ifsboston.org) in spring premières indie films headed for general release.

Down on the Cape, the **Provincetown Film Festival** (1-508 487-3456) blends indie and queer sensibilities in a packed June weekend, while the **Nantucket Film Festival** (1-508 325 6274, www.nantucketfilmfestival.org) also held in June, is a favourite excursion for Boston film-lovers, who take in shorts, documentaries and staged readings of unproduced scripts.

On the scene

Although the majority of films set on the East Coast are shot in New York, the photogenic Boston area, with its historical and cultural connections, has seen its share of action.

While Cambridge was the setting for 1918 silent picture *Brown of Harvard*, Boston got its close-up 50 years later in the original *Thomas Crown Affair* starring Steve McQueen and Faye Dunaway, which was shot in 90 different locations in and around the city, including Beacon Hill (the address of McQueen's swanky apartment), Pier 4 in South Boston and, further afield, Crane Beach in Ipswich. But it was slushy romance *Love Story* in 1970, with its Harvard campus shots and beautiful student couple Ryan O'Neal and Ali MacGraw, that brought the city truly filmic fame. Follow in the doomed lovers' footsteps by strolling on the Weeks Footbridge or visiting Emerson Hall – renamed Barrett Hall for the flick. (Incidentally, Tommy Lee Jones, who appeared in the film, attended the university in real life, rooming with former US Vice-President Al Gore.)

In the '80s, it was the small screen that brought Boston into the spotlight with long-running sitcom *Cheers*. A visit to the namesake pub (*see p151*), formerly the Bull and Finch, which provided the opening shot for the programme, is still on many tourists' to-do list – although the interior looks nothing like the set. While you won't find the bar where TV's Ally McBeal and colleagues let their hair down, you can gawp at the 19th-century Congregational House at 14 Beacon Street, used as the exterior of the law firm.

Good Will Hunting (1997) launched the careers of Matt Damon and Ben Affleck, and brought a legion of fans to their on-screen hangout, Woody's L Street Tavern in rough-edged Southie.

The close proximity of Boston's gritty and grand neighbourhoods is a boon for filmmakers. The elegant architecture and historic institutions of Back Bay and Beacon Hill have starred in many movies. Copley Square is the backdrop for explosive action in 1994's *Blown Away*, in which Jeff Bridges works for the Boston bomb squad. In *Amistad* (1997), Anthony Hopkins' John Quincy Adams addresses the Supreme Court in the Senate and House Chambers of the State House. Appropriately, Fenway Park – home of

perennial heartbreak kids the Red Sox – appears in *Field of Dreams* (1989).

New England's coastline also captures filmmakers' imaginations, from Martha's Vineyard, which became 'Amity Island' in *Jaws* (1975), to Gloucester, which was the real-life setting for fishermen's tragedy *The Perfect Storm* (2000) – Dorchester-born star Mark Wahlberg's Massachusetts accent had the ring of authenticity. More recently, Rockport was the coastal home of conjoined twins Matt Damon and Greg Kinnear in *Stuck on You* (2003).

The latest film drawing attention to Boston is Clint Eastwood's much-lauded (if melodramatic) *Mystic River* (2003, *pictured*), based on local writer Dennis Lehane's novel. The film's seemingly small fictional neighbourhood is actually a composite whose locations make for a tour of the entire city: South Boston's Miller's Market, Jamaica Plain's Franklin Park, East Boston's Monmouth Street and the Tobin Bridge over the titular river itself.

Galleries

The visual arts scene is buzzing, if you know where to look.

Art aficionados will find no shortage of visual stimuli in a city where culture reigns supreme. In addition to the major museums and renowned university collections (*see p109*), the commercial gallery scene is undergoing vibrant expansion. While the bulk still nestles amid the antiques shops, designer boutiques and hair salons of Newbury Street, there are substantial contemporary clutches in nearby South End, as well as scattered experimental outposts in Cambridge and further-flung, up-and-coming areas such as Somerville, which has become the site of a nascent art scene.

Back Bay

Long the centre of Boston's commercial art scene, as well as its main upscale retail drag, Newbury Street offers both the cream of the crop and the bottom of the barrel: traditional galleries, blue-chip art emporiums and heady experimental spaces share stylish brownstones with tourist traps selling hotel-lobby art.

Barbara Krakow Gallery

10 Newbury Street, at Arlington Street (1-617 262 4490/www.barbarakrakowgallery.com). Arlington T. **Open** 10am-5.30pm Tue-Sat. **Admission** free. **Map** p277 H5.

This is one of the most prestigious and long-standing galleries in the city, and Barbara Krakow is the reason why. Her continued enthusiasm for the new – both local and international – along with her good taste in well-established contemporary artists guarantee there's always a lot worth seeing here, from Sol LeWitt to Annette Lemieux and Julian Opie.

Chase Gallery

129 Newbury Street, between Clarendon & Dartmouth Streets (1-617 859 7222/www.chasegallery.com). Copley T. **Open** 10am-6pm Mon-Sat. **Admission** free. **Map** p277 G6.

The huge second-storey picture window gives artists a stunning showcase for bustling foot traffic to gawp at. Best known for showing work in a variety of media by renowned national artists, the gallery also prides itself on helping up-and-coming local painters such as Melora Kuhn get a foothold on the Newbury Street scene.

Copley Society of Boston

158 Newbury Street, at Dartmouth Street (1-617 536 5049/www.copleysociety.org). Copley T. **Open** 10.30am-5.30pm Tue-Sat. **Admission** free. **Map** p277 G6.

Founded in 1879, the Copley Society is the country's oldest non-profit art association, but it's a much hipper organisation than the trad-sounding name might imply. With a mandate of promoting the advancement and understanding of the visual arts, the society draws on a pool of more than 600 members for participation in its frequently changing exhibitions. The Society also provides access to the works and personal papers of artists from the last two centuries, including Henry Ossawa Tanner and Jackson Pollock.

Gallery NAGA

67 Newbury Street, at Berkeley Street (1-617 267 9060/www.gallerynaga.com). Arlington T. **Open** 10am-5.30pm Tue-Sat. **Admission** free. **Map** p277 H5.

Besides its fine line-up of Boston and New England-based contemporary painters, including Ken Beck, Paul Rahilly, Louis Risoli and pioneer holographer Harriet Casdin-Silver, NAGA is best known for exhibiting the work of furniture makers – unusual pieces that, while not always functional, are always a pleasure to look at.

Howard Yezerski Gallery

14 Newbury Street, at Arlington Street (1-617 262 0550/www.howardyezerskigallery.com). Arlington T. **Open** 10am-5.30pm Tue-Sat. **Admission** free. **Map** p277 H5.

A well-known fixture on the Newbury Street scene for the past 20 years, Yezerski manages to embody the upscale milieu of the area while still presenting some of the most provocative and decidedly non-commercial work to be found anywhere in the city. You might find an entire exhibition given over to monochrome paintings or bizarre, creeping floor-to-ceiling abstract sculpture.

International Poster Gallery

205 Newbury Street, at Exeter Street (1-617 375 0076/www.internationalposter.com). Copley T. **Open** 10am-6pm Mon-Sat; noon-6pm Sun. **Admission** free. **Map** p277 G6.

A walk through this gallery specialising in one-of-a-kind poster art from around the globe takes you on a vivid trip through the past – from the flowery romanticism of the Belle Epoque to sleek German Futurism, art deco and 1960s psychedelic pop.

Judy Ann Goldman Fine Art

14 Newbury Street, at Arlington Street (1-617 424 8468). Arlington T. **Open** 10.30am-5pm Tue-Sat. **Admission** free. **Map** p277 H5.

The work here is often challenging, however Goldman is always willing to talk you through it. This adventurous gallery owner has brought avant-garde artists from LA, Japan and Miami and introduced them to the Boston art scene. The gallery is known for encouraging young local talent.

Mercury Gallery

8 Newbury Street, at Arlington Street (1-617 859 0054/www.mercurygallery.com). Arlington T. **Open** 10am-5.30pm Mon-Sat. **Admission** free. **Map** p277 H5.

Visiting this gallery is like stepping back in time to Newbury Street in the late 1920s. In those days, the building was a car dealership, and it retains original architectural details. The Mercury specialises in American figurative expressionism and includes works from as far back as the 1930s, but also features artists who are hard at work right now, notably respected photographer Phillip Jones.

The Photographic Resource Center

832 Commonwealth Avenue, at Amory Street (1-617 975 0600/www.bu.edu/prc). BU Central T. **Open** 10am-6pm Tue, Wed, Fri; 10am-8pm Thur; noon-5pm Sat, Sun. **Admission** $3. **No credit cards**.

Although exclusively devoted to the medium of photography, this space manages to present some of the most varied and scintillating shows in the city. Past exhibitions have included the photographic efforts of rock stars (including Lou Reed) and an eerie show featuring pictures taken during seances. A non-profit organisation on the campus of Boston University, the PRC offers regular workshops and lectures.

Robert Klein Gallery

38 Newbury Street, at Berkeley Street (1-617 267 7997/www.robertkleingallery.com). Arlington T. **Open** 10am-5.30pm Tue-Fri; 11am-5pm Sat. **Admission** free. **Map** p277 H5.

Devoted exclusively to fine-art photography, this gallery deals in established 19th- and 20th-century photographers such as Edward Weston, Charles Sheeler and Sally Mann. With over 3,000 images in its inventory, there are bound to be pleasant surprises for even the most knowledgeable of collectors.

South End

An upwardly mobile, multicultural area where once you found only a disparate collection of galleries, the South End has become one of the top destinations for art in the city. A former fabric factory on Albany Street is now a bustling warren of galleries and artists' studios, while a varied collection of commercial and experimental spaces from around the city have found homes in an old warehouse on the corner of Thayer Street and Harrison Avenue, locally referred to as the SoWa galleries building (SoWa stands for South of Washington Street). The galleries there coordinate their schedules so all openings are held on the first Friday evening of every month – making for a can't-miss monthly open-house bash.

The Allston Skirt Gallery

No.303, 450 Harrison Ave, at Thayer Street (1-617 482 3652/www.allstonskirt.com). East Berkeley Silver Line bus/Back Bay T. **Open** 11am-5pm Wed-Sat. **Admission** free. **Map** p277 J8.

Founders and respected Boston art scenesters Randi Hopkins and Beth Kantrowitz are known for their canny, cutting-edge curating. The duo has presented such artists as controversial Brooklyn conceptual art queen Danica Phelps and local photographer Pia Schacter.

Bernard Toale Gallery

450 Harrison Avenue, at Thayer Street (1-617 482 2477/www.bernardtoalegallery.com). East Berkeley Silver Line bus/Back Bay T. **Open** 10.30am-5.30pm Tue-Sat. **Admission** free. **Map** p277 J8.

Toale's place on the Boston art scene is solid, chiefly because of his unimpeachable taste. A visit here promises riches, including the likes of Jocelyn Lee, whose photographs celebrate the way real women, not fashion models, look in bikinis and lingerie; and the highly textured paintings of Ambreen Butt.

Clifford-Smith Gallery

Third Floor, 450 Harrison Avenue, at Thayer Street (1-617 695 0255/www.cliffordsmithgallery.com). East Berkeley Silver Line bus/Back Bay T. **Open** 11am-5.30pm Wed-Fri. **Admission** free. **Map** p277 J8.

A welcome feature of the South End's art scene for several years now, Clifford-Smith has always been

Qingping Gallery Teahouse.

willing to take informed, exciting risks. This sometimes includes offbeat concepts such as a show of photographs of and for dogs – during which the entire space was filled with yapping canines.

Genovese/Sullivan Gallery

450 Harrison Avenue, at Thayer Street (1-617 426 9738). East Berkeley Silver Line bus/Back Bay T. **Open** 10.30am-5.30pm Tue-Sat. **Admission** free. **Map** p277 J8.

This gallery merits a visit not only because it is one of the most art-friendly spaces in the city (the rooms are expansive, the ceilings tall), but also because of the curatorial acumen of its owners, David Sullivan and Camellia Genovese. Among the artists affiliated with the gallery is the sculptor Pat Keck, who creates seemingly simple works of diabolical complexity, and Catherine Carter, who is well known for her eye-popping black and white Op Art stencil paintings.

MPG

Suite 315, 450 Harrison Avenue, at Thayer Street (1-617 357 8881/www.mpgallery.net). East Berkeley Silver Line bus/Back Bay T. **Open** 11am-5pm Tue-Sat, or by appointment. **Admission** free. **Map** p277 J8.

MPG stands for Michael Price Gallery – mover and shaker Price has had several premises, including a high-profile stint on Newbury Street, before moving to his latest location in the South End. He maintains a long-standing policy of actively encouraging and fostering first-time and student artists, and runs an annual national competition for emerging artists. Price has eclectic taste in contemporary art – in the past he's shown luminaries such as Louise Bourgeois, Helen Frankenthaler and Henry Moore, while recent works include the textural canvases of Jennifer Hodges and the moody rustic Americana paintings of Dmitri Cavender.

The NAO Project

3rd Floor, 535 Albany Street, at Plympton Street, South End (1-617 451 2977/www.naoproject gallery.info). Copley T. **Open** *July, Aug* by appointment only. *Sept-June* noon-5pm Thur-Sat. **Admission** free. **Map** p277 J9.

NAO has only around five exhibitions a year, and has shown engaging work such as the stunning glass sculpture of Mags Harries and the paintings and drawings of Heidi Whitman, whose stop-action sketches of items such as sweaters in gradually entropic breakdown are fascinating to behold.

Qingping Gallery Teahouse

231 Shawmut Avenue, at Dwight Street (1-617 482 9988/www.qingping.org). Back Bay T. **Open** noon-midnight daily. **Admission** free. **Map** p277 J7.

Modern art from the Chinese mainland is displayed alongside oriental antiquities in this creaky, quirky, two-level space decked out with couches, chessboards and fish tanks. Owner Wu Jianxin enjoys pouring you a cup of traditional jasmine tea and telling stories about artists like lithographist Su Xinping and silk-screen painter Zhou Jirong.

Somerville

Brickbottom Gallery

1 Fitchburg Street, off O'Brion Highway (1-617 776 3410/www.brickbottomartists.com). Lechmere T then 10mins walk. **Open** noon-5pm Thur-Sat, or by appointment. **Admission** free.

The denizens of this bustling artists' colony live and work in their own studio spaces. The gallery exclusively shows the work of Brickbottom artists, which ranges from painting to sculpture and conceptual art.

Gallery 108

108 Beacon Street, at Washington Street (1-617 441 3833/www.gallery108.com). Harvard T then 10mins walk. **Open** noon-6pm Tue, Thur, Fri; 2-6pm Wed; noon-5pm Sat. **Admission** free. **Map** p277 H5.

Curator/painter/writer Kate Ledogar enjoys courting controversy: an exhibition with a performance artist changing clothes in the street-level window was temporarily shut down by the police in 2003; and in a column she wrote for the *Weekly Dig*, she reviewed a show of her own paintings – unfavourably.

Alternative views

Until recently, Boston's galleries were largely mired in a patrician fine arts tradition, but an explosion of radical art spaces is shaking up the somewhat staid scene. Fusing video, music, unusual installations and outrageous performance art, these low-budget venues provide an outlet for a new generation of edgy and experimental young artists, many of whom are influenced by pop-culture trends such as underground comics and rock-band poster art. Often housed in unusual spaces, they're likely to pop up in out-of-the-way parts of the city, where overheads are cheaper and more risks can be taken.

Hallspace, located in lower Roxbury (31 Norfolk Avenue, 1-617 989 9985, www.hallspace.org) is a long, narrow room that really does resemble a hallway. The space tends to feature installation art, bizarre sculpture, and playfully pervy fare such as its 'Adults Only' show.

Housed in the Distillery (*pictured*), an old South Boston factory that has been colonised as an artists' live/work complex, the **Artists Foundation Galleries & Video Room** (516 East Second Street, 1-617 464 3559, www.artistsfoundation.org) showcases a mix of media from installations to photography. There's also a room devoted to video art.

Studio Soto in Fort Point Channel (63 Melcher Street, 1-617 426 7676, www.studiosoto.com) survived the building boom of the late 1990s, which priced many artists out of what was once a thriving creative community. Experimental shows have seen cars decorated by hip hop artists, and prints made by ink-covered dancers who rolled on paper like human printing presses.

The tiny storefront **Out of the Blue Gallery** in Central Square (106 Prospect Street, Cambridge, 1-617 354 5287, www.outofthe blueartgallery.com) has also commandeered

the walls of every available venue in the area, such as the nearby 1369 Coffee House (*see p143*) and the Middle East rock club (*see p211*). Out of the Blue also sponsors open mics and wild events like punk-rock lingerie fashion shows.

Also in Cambridge is the **Zeitgeist Gallery** (1353 Cambridge Street, at Inman Square, 1-617 876 6060, www.zeitgeist-gallery.org), where on any given day you might find the political art of Bread and Puppet, paintings by local rock musician Peter Wolf or unknown comics from Robert Crumb, all accompanied by atonal jamming, slam poetry or the occasional nude dancer.

Out in Jamaica Plain, the **Gallery @ Green Street** (141 Green Street, 1-617 522 0000, www.jameshull.com) provides visual relief for bored commuters – it's literally built into the Green Street T stop on the Orange Line. Known for its affordable art sales, the non-profit, artist-funded and -run gallery reaches people outside of contemporary art's traditional audience.

Gay & Lesbian

For a city at the vanguard of gay civil rights, the scene is surprisingly small – but it's anything but staid.

Boston's gay and lesbian population is one of the largest in the United States, and also one of the most integrated. Though certain neighbourhoods are more welcoming than others, Boston is generally the kind of place where you can walk downtown hand in hand with your same-sex paramour and no one will bat an eyelid, let alone turn their head.

But while the strict social and religious mores of its founders have long since given way to a kind of laissez-faire liberalism, Boston has inherited from its Puritan ancestry a tendency toward aloofness. The city is infamous among gay travellers for its 'attitude' problem. Still, many gay and lesbian residents, most of whom are from somewhere else, adopt a frosty demeanour only because it's the local custom – given half a chance, they'll lower their guard.

In November 2003 the eyes of the nation turned to the gay community in Massachusetts, as a local lesbian couple, Julie and Hillary Goodridge, became the lead plaintiffs in a historic legal victory for gay civil rights. The Massachusetts Supreme Judicial Court ruled that preventing gay couples from marrying violated the state constitution. The pair were among the first same-sex couples to wed in May 2004 when gay marriage became legal in Massachusetts.

Leading the nation on gay rights has been a Massachusetts tradition that goes back decades before the 2003 decision. In 1972 Bostonian Elaine Noble became the first openly gay or lesbian person to win a seat in any state legislature. Some 15 years later the first two openly gay members of the US Congress (Gerry Studds and Barney Frank) represented suburban Boston. In 1990 Massachusetts became one of the first states to pass a comprehensive gay rights law. More recently it has been at the vanguard in developing programmes to protect gay youth from harassment in schools.

Take **Pride**. *See p201.*

While Boston's gay community often feels transient and youth-oriented, it's rooted in 400 years of history. The first governor of the state of Massachusetts, John Winthrop, wrote love letters to a man he had left behind in England. Later, at least one lesbian from Boston, Deborah Sampson, fought for Independence alongside the Minutemen. Using the name Robert Shurtleff, Sampson wooed many a maiden, and no one knew she was a woman until she was wounded in battle.

In the 19th century the 'Athens of America' is said to have been rife with men-loving literary men. Much has been read into Herman Melville's dedication of *Moby-Dick* to Nathaniel Hawthorne, and Ralph Waldo Emerson's diary chronicles an obsession with a Harvard classmate. Better documented are the so-called 'Boston Marriages' – socially sanctioned relationships between women. Writer Sarah Orne Jewett and poet Amy Lowell, among others, took female partners. By the end of the century Boston's art scene also included a strong queer presence. Isabella Stewart Gardner, the widow who founded the museum that continues to bear her name (*see p106*), surrounded herself with a posse of gay admirers including architect Ralph Adams Cram and the painter John Singer Sargent.

Still, gay culture remained underground until after World War II, when Boston's first gay bars started springing up among the strip joints and burlesque houses of Scollay Square (this teeming, saucy neighbourhood is no more; it's now the sterile cementscape of Government Center). In a reference to the sleazy area of New York City, lower Washington Street became known as 'Gay Times Square', while Bay Village – sandwiched between Chinatown and the South End – became a haven for gay Bostonians. Most of these areas were razed in a neo-Puritan attempt at 'urban renewal' back in the 1960s, but by then Boston's homosexual network was well established.

The gay community took to the streets after the 1969 Stonewall riots in New York kicked off gay emancipation across the country, and organised what became one of the country's first annual Gay Pride parades in 1971. For the first few years, the parade involved only a few hundred people and had a militant tone. These days, **Boston Pride** is basically a massive party that lasts for the entire month of June, and includes art exhibits and Boston Harbor party cruises. The event regularly draws crowds in excess of 100,000 from all over New England, and corporate sponsors vie for space at the post-march fair (*see p181*).

NEIGHBOURHOODS

The South End is no longer the magnet it once was for young men wanting to get their first taste of living in a 'gay ghetto'. But even if straight people seem to be buying into the area more than they once did, the South End has by far the largest concentration of gay-owned businesses in Boston. Most shops are adorned with the rainbow-striped flags signalling they are gay-friendly. The streets are lined with little shops that mix kitsch with quality in equal measure. Gay men set the tone on Tremont Street. Flirting with a waiter or salesperson of the same sex will not always get you better service, but it's still a no-risk strategy.

A few of the adjacent neighbourhoods also have a large gay presence. To the north, Bay Village is a tiny enclave of small brick houses; to the west, the Fens is a notorious cruising area (be warned, it can be risky after dark).

The up-and-coming neighbourhood of Jamaica Plain – Boston's answer to New York's Brooklyn – is home to a growing lesbian population, and across the river, Cambridge and Somerville are especially queer-friendly.

INFORMATION

There are two weekly newspapers, both free. *Bay Windows* is the primary paper for the gay community, covering local and national news in a fairly straightforward manner. *In Newsweekly* is a bit saucier, with an emphasis on gay nightlife throughout the New England area. Both are distributed on Thursdays in book stores, cafés and gay bars throughout Boston, Cambridge and Somerville, and are also available online. Boston's *Weekly Dig* and the *Boston Phoenix*, two free alternative weeklies, also feature plenty of articles related to gay and lesbian issues in their pages.

Bars & clubs

For a city of its size, Boston has surprisingly few gay bars. The problem doesn't seem to be homophobia; rather, the city's powerful neighbourhood groups make it difficult to open any establishment that might lead to nocturnal sidewalk loitering. Boston isn't a late-night town: the city's legally mandated 2am closing time shuts the party down early, and the T stops running at 12.30am, forcing club-goers to cab it or compete for scarce parking spots. Lesbian nightlife options are particularly sparse, and the lack of a seven-day-a-week bar for the ladies is a perennial complaint.

Though Boston's bar scene can't compete with the likes of New York or Montreal, there are plenty of places to see and be seen, or just kick back and enjoy a casual pint.

Avalon

15 Landsdowne Street, between Brookline Avenue & Ipswich Street, Fenway (1-617 262 2424/www.avalonboston.com). Kenmore T. **Open** 10pm-2am Sun. **Admission** $10-$15. **Credit** (bar only) AmEx, MC, V. **Map** p276 D7.

Sunday at Avalon has been Boston's biggest gay night out for as long as anyone can remember. The club has a huge dancefloor with platforms for go-go boys. The music is mostly techno and hip hop, but the cover charge also grants entry to Axis next door, which offers alternative music. College kids usually dominate the scene here.

Buzz

67 Stuart Street, at Tremont Street, Downtown (1-617 267 8969/www.buzzboston.com). Boylston T. **Open** 10pm-2am Sat. **Admission** $10. **Map** p277 J6.

The rest of the week it's Europa, a haven for straight modish Euro types. But on Saturdays it's Buzz – two floors' worth of circuit boys and gym rats showing off their abs to the pulsing beat of loud, loud house music. Non-dancers can check out the club's three bars, pool table, and various lounge areas.

Club Café

209 Columbus Avenue, at Berkeley Street, South End (1-617 536 0966/www.clubcafe.com). Back Bay T. **Open** 11am-2am daily. **Admission** free. **Credit** AmEx, DC, Disc, MC, V. **Map** p277 H6.

A massive bar/lounge/restaurant complex, and one of gay Boston's mainstays. At the front, the lights of the piano bar and restaurant draw an older, professional crowd of very cruisy gay men and a few buttoned-down lesbians. Moonshine, the men's video bar in the back, is a preppy, collegiate version of the posh scene at the front. The crowd peaks at about midnight, after which people drift towards dance clubs and bedrooms.

Club Hollywood

41 Essex Street, at Harrison Avenue, Downtown (1-617 338 8283). Chinatown T. **Open** 10pm-2pm Sat. **Admission** $10. **Credit** (bar only) AmEx, Disc, MC, V. **Map** p274 K5.

This Saturday dance party at the Ekco Lounge is Boston's biggest, sexiest lesbian night, with two packed, energetic dancefloors – it was voted best women's night by *Boston* magazine. Hollywood also hosts occasional live acts, and a drag-king karaoke show, Glitter Switch, on the third Saturday of the month (*see p205* **The girly show**). A plus: the friendly go-go dancers actually look as if they might be lesbians on their nights off.

Dedo Lounge & Bistro

69 Church Street, at Park Plaza, Back Bay (1-617 338 9999). Arlington T. **Open** 5.30pm-1am Tue-Sun. **Admission** free. **Credit** AmEx, MC, V. **Map** p277 J6.

Formerly Luxor. The upstairs lounge has been given an impressive facelift, and is a nice spot for an after-work Martini. Downstairs, a romantic little New American bistro with a late-night bar menu.

The Eagle

520 Tremont Street, at Berkeley Street, South End (1-617 542 4494). Back Bay T. **Open** 3pm-2am Mon-Fri; 1pm-2am Sat; noon-2am Sun. **Admission** free. **No credit cards**. **Map** p277 J7.

Boston's premier 'last call' destination, the Eagle has a decor befitting a leather-and-Levi's bar, but as the evening wears on it attracts South End professionals looking for a quick one before heading home. At 2am some patrons pair up in the nightly 'sidewalk sale' along Tremont Street.

Encore Lounge

At the Tremont Hotel, 275 Tremont Street, at Stuart Street, South End (1-617 338 7699). Boylston or NE Medical Center T. **Open** 4pm-2am Mon-Fri, Sun; noon-2am Sat. **Admission** free. **Credit** AmEx, MC, V. **Map** p277 J6.

Not gay as such, but a piano bar in the Theatre District isn't going to be totally hetero, is it?

Fritz

At the Chandler Inn, 26 Chandler Street, at Berkeley Street, South End (1-617 482 4428). Back Bay T. **Open** 11am-2am Mon-Sat; noon-2am Sun. **Admission** free. **No credit cards**. **Map** p277 H7.

A neighbourhood bar that attracts all types, including out-of-towners staying at the Chandler Inn upstairs. Brunch is served till 3pm at weekends.

Jacque's

79 Broadway, between Piedmont & Winchester Streets, Back Bay (1-617 426 8902/www.jacques cabaret.com). Arlington T. **Open** 11am-midnight Mon-Sat; noon-midnight Sun. **Admission** $6-$8. **No credit cards**. **Map** p277 J6.

The oldest gay bar in town, featuring drag-queen shows from Tuesday to Saturday and live rock 'n' roll from Friday to Monday. It's hardly glamorous, but the filthy banter and discount-store outfits can add up to an entertaining evening, and once in a while there's a performer who's shockingly good. Lots of straight people show up here at weekends.

Machine

Below the Ramrod, 1254 Boylston Street, at Ipswich Street, Back Bay (1-617 266 2986). Kenmore T. **Open** noon-2am daily. **Admission** free-$8. **No credit cards**. **Map** p276 D7.

This glitzy club features a dancefloor with state-of-the-art lighting, a video lounge and a separate room with pool tables. The cover charge also includes the Ramrod bar upstairs (*see below*), which has an older and sometimes over-attentive clientele.

Man Ray

21 Brookline Street, at Green Street, Cambridge (1-617 864 0400/www.manrayclub.com). Central T. **Open** 9pm-2am Wed-Fri; 10pm-2am Sat. **Admission** $5-$15. **Credit** AmEx, MC, V. **Map** p278 C3.

Campus Thursday – 19-plus despite the studenty name – is the official gay night here, but general sexual anarchy reigns at Man Ray most nights of the week. The dancefloor at the front tends to draw large mobs of shirtless college boys, while a goth/punk/lesbian crowd congregates in the back. Fetish Fridays are also worth checking out – just don't show up wearing khakis.

Paradise

180 Massachusetts Avenue, just off MIT campus, Cambridge (1-617 494 0700/www.paradise cambridge.com). Central T then 10mins walk/1 bus. **Open** 7pm-1am Mon-Wed, Sun; 7pm-2am Thur-Sat. **Admission** free. **No credit cards**. **Map** p278 C4.

It's just on the other side of the Charles River from Boston, but Paradise has the feel of the only gay bar in a small town. The crowd is racially mixed and includes all age groups. Upstairs, there are porn videos and often-shirtless bartenders. Go-go dancers circulate among the customers – discreet fondling is available for a suitable tip. Downstairs, there's also a small dancefloor.

The Ramrod

1254 Boylston Street, at Ipswich Street, Back Bay (1-617 266 2986). Kenmore T. **Open** noon-2am daily. **Admission** free. **No credit cards**. **Map** p276 D7.

This is the headquarters of Boston's leather scene, and such master-and-slave groups as the Leather Knights. At weekends the back room is restricted to men who are bare-chested or wearing leather gear. Because the Ramrod also serves as a neighbourhood bar, the front area isn't so intimidating.

Toast

70 Union Square, at Washington Street, Somerville (1-617 623 9211/www.toastlounge.com). Davis Square T then 87 bus. **Open** 7pm-1am Thur. **Admission** $5 **Credit** AmEx, MC, V. **Map** p278 C2.

It's easy to miss the entrance to Toast, tucked away below sidewalk level on Union Square. On Thursday nights this swanky lounge goes lesbian, with good-sized crowds and plenty of eye candy. Plush, high-backed booths are a romantic spot for private tête-à-têtes, if you can hear your date over the thumping bass from the dancefloor.

Vapor/Chaps

100 Warrenton Street, at Stuart Street, Back Bay (1-617 695 9500). Boylston T. **Open** 3pm-2am Wed; noon-2am Sun. **Admission** $4-$8 **Credit** AmEx, MC, V. **Map** p277 J6.

One of the area's landmark gay clubs, Vapor/Chaps was undergoing extensive refurbishment as this guide went to press. While Friday and Saturday nights will be straight-oriented, Boston's longest-running Sunday tea dance and a hot dance-and-drag Wednesday-night line-up look set to continue – but ring to check before you show up in case of changes.

Bookshops

Calamus Bookstore

92B South Street, at East Street, Downtown (1-617 338 1931/www.calamusbooks.com). South Station T. **Open** 9am-7pm Mon-Sat; noon-6pm Sun. **Credit** AmEx, Disc, MC, V. **Map** p275 L5.

A replacement for proprietor John Mitzel's former venture, Glad Day Bookshop (a victim of rising rents in the Back Bay), this place is spacious, and has all the books, magazines and videos you'll need. But the out-of-the-way location has kept it from re-creating Glad Day's entertaining and cruisey atmosphere.

We Think the World of You

540 Tremont Street, between Berkeley & Clarendon Streets, Back Bay (1-617 574 5000/www.wethinktheworldofyou.com). Back Bay T. **Open** 10am-6pm Mon-Fri; 11.30am-5.30pm Sun. **Credit** AmEx, DC, Disc, MC, V. **Map** p277 H7.

This shop sells queer novels, biographies, magazines and erotica, plus CDs, greeting cards and lots of gift items emblazoned with rainbows. The staff are friendly and attentive.

Gyms & spas

There are no euphemisms in this category, since the city's only '24-hour gym' (read: bathhouse) was shut down by the city in 2000.

Étant

524 Tremont Street, at Clarendon Street (1-617 423 5040/www.etant.com). Back Bay T. **Open** 11am-7pm Mon-Fri; 9am-6pm Sat; by appointment only Sun. **Treatments** $12-$180. **Credit** AmEx, Disc, MC, V. **Map** p277 H7.

Though Étant bills itself as a 'spa for well-being', it's basically a nice little place where you can book a massage, get a facial or 'align your energy systems' through polarity therapy. The menu also includes acupuncture, hair removal and body wraps. Call ahead to make an appointment.

Metropolitan Fitness

209 Columbus Avenue, at Berkeley Street, Back Bay (1-617 536 3006/www.bostonfitness.com). Back Bay T. **Open** 5.30am-11pm Mon-Wed; 5.30am-10pm Thur, Fri; 8am-8pm Sat; 9am-8pm Sun. **Rates** *Membership* $75 mth; $45 2wks; $30 1wk; $15 day pass. **Credit** AmEx, Disc, MC, V. **Map** p277 H6.

Where the South End boys with attitude work out. The Metropolitan has the latest weight-training and cardio equipment and a very good aerobics staff. It's best at off-peak hours if you're the type who just wants to get the workout over with. Otherwise, it can be a little like a gay bar with weights.

Restaurants & cafés

Any restaurants or cafés in the South End are, by virtue of their location, gay-friendly. The eateries listed below are popular with queer patrons. For Dedo Lounge and Bistro, *see p202*. For restaurants, we've given approximate prices.

City Girl Caffé

204 Hampshire Street, at Inman Square, Cambridge (1-617 864 2809). Central T then 10min walk. **Open** 11am-9pm Tue-Fri; 10am-9pm Sat; 11am-4pm Sun. **Main courses** $10. **Credit** MC, V. **Map** p278 C2.

A tiny, friendly, funky lesbian-owned and -operated café in the heart of Inman Square. Serves fresh homemade pizza, pasta, sandwiches and salads, and a decent cup of coffee. There's also a small selection of wines and beers.

Club Café

209 Columbus Avenue, at Berkeley Street, South End (1-617 536 0966/www.clubcafe.com). Back Bay T. **Open** 12.30-2.30pm, 5.30-10pm Mon-Wed; 12.30-2.30pm, 5.30-11pm Thur, Fri; 5.30-11pm Sat; 11am-2.30pm, 5-10pm Sun. **Main courses** $10-$22. **Credit** AmEx, DC, Disc, MC, V. **Map** p277 H6.

The restaurant is almost incidental to the bar, which is one of the few places in town where gay men and lesbians really mix – or at least occupy adjacent bistro tables. The dining area, with a New American menu, is usually filled with couples. But Sunday brunch feels more like a town meeting with South Enders trading stories about the night before.

Dartmouth Café

160 Commonwealth Avenue, between Exeter & Dartmouth Streets, Back Bay (1-617 266 1122). Copley T. **Open** 5pm-1am Mon-Fri; 10am-1am Sat, Sun. **Main courses** $12-$16. **Credit** AmEx, Disc, MC, V. **Map** p277 G5.

Formerly a South End favourite (Geoffrey's, on Tremont Street), this eatery relocated to its present location in the Back Bay in 2001. The new, renamed restaurant is bigger, with outdoor patio seating and a cosy fireplace. From Sunday to Thursday it hosts movie nights in front of a large-screen TV.

Diesel Café

257 Elm Street, at Davis Square, Somerville (1-617 629 8717/www.diesel-café.com). Davis Square T. **Open** 7am-midnight Mon-Thur; 7am-1am Fri; 8am-1am Sat; 8am-midnight Sun. **No credit cards**.

There's always a sizeable lesbian contingent at the Diesel – drawn, no doubt, by the posse of cute androgynous baristas (or is it the vegan cake?). But this popular coffee-and-lunch spot, across the street from Starbucks, is often jam-packed with a grab bag of Davis Square locals fuelling up on high-octane espresso, plunking away on their laptops, or lining up shots at one of the two pool tables. To blend in with the students, stop by the book shop next door and grab a volume from the Queer Theory section.

Francesca's Café & Espresso Bar

564 Tremont Street, at Clarendon Street, South End (1-617 482 9026). Back Bay T. **Open** 8am-11pm Mon-Thur, Sun; 8am-midnight Fri, Sat. **Main courses** $4-$10. **No credit cards**. **Map** p277 H7.

A chic hangout for posh South Enders and coffee purists, with a view of Tremont Street. Breakfast, pastries and light-lunch fare are served with attitude.

Garden of Eden

571 Tremont Street, at Clarendon Street, South End (1-617 247 8377/www.goeboston.com). Back Bay T. **Open** 7am-10.30pm Mon-Thur; 7am-11pm Fri, Sat; 7.30am-10.30pm Sun. **Main courses** $6-$14. **Credit** AmEx, MC, V. **Map** p277 H7.

The girly show

Boston is home to a lively burlesque, drag and cabaret scene that is sometimes overtly queer, but more often a postmodern pastiche of raw sexuality, humour and gender identities that were made to be broken. In addition to the established acts and regular venues listed here, there are plenty of solo performers enjoying their 15 minutes of fame, and one-time-only shows that draw crowds of scenesters in the know. To catch up on the local cabaret scene grab a copy of *In Newsweekly* or *Bay Windows* and peruse the weekly listings.

Boston's famous burlesque house at Scollay Square is long gone, along with the old neighbourhood itself. But its naughty *joie de vivre* lives on in the saucy ladies of **Thru The Keyhole Burlesque** (www.thruthekeyhole.com), who claim to offer 'classical striptease and vaudevillian-style antics with a nod (a wink, and a shimmy) to postmodern feminism and social satire'. The Keyhole Cuties (*pictured*) frequently charm pan-sexual audiences at the **Milky Way** (*see p211*) and the **Paradise** (*see p203*) with their signature brand of retro bump-and-grind, an innocently bawdy show that is equal parts Lucille Ball and Madeleine Kahn – only in pasties.

Novices and pros alike rock the mic at the drag-king karaokefest **Glitter Switch** (www.truthserum.org/glitterswitch.htm), where moody host-with-the-most Heywood Wakefield (aka Truth Serum Productions promoter Aliza Shapiro) holds court in a formidable pair of mutton-chop sideburns. Glitter Switch, held on the third Saturday of the month just before the dancing gets under way at **Club Hollywood** (*see p202*), draws a regular crowd of unevenly talented would-be drag kings looking to strut their stuff on stage, as well as the occasional guest star or professional troupe passing through town.

Sunday nights at the **Milky Way** are a grab bag of queer open-mic events, poetry slams, film showings, and appearances by local and visiting performance and spoken-word artists. Boston's own drag-king and high-femme revue, **All the Kings' Men** (www.djdee.com/kings) takes the stage now and then, with choreographed gender-bending ensemble numbers that leave your average lip-sync routine in the dust.

Boston's drag-queen scene has less vibrancy and cachet than the fledgling king scene, but the grande dames of glitz have one thing the city's studs and femmes don't: a home. **Jacque's** (*see p203*), the venerable drag cabaret showcase, has been the centre of the Boston drag universe since 1938. What Jacque's lacks in class, it makes up for in sheer persistence. The notorious bar exudes a seamy, desperate glitter that can at times be almost beautiful, and is not to be found elsewhere in Boston. And with drag shows and/or live rock 'n' roll every night of the week, it's a reliable standby.

Yet another café with excellent views of the foot traffic on Tremont Street, and a gourmet market next door. It's got all the essentials for breakfast, plus sandwiches, pastries and fresh fruit. Strangers often find themselves sharing the large wood-block tables and making new friends.

Laurel

142 Berkeley Street, at Columbus Avenue, Back Bay (1-617 424 6711/www.laurelgrillandbar.com). Back Bay or Arlington T. **Open** 11.30am-2.30pm, 5.30-10pm Mon-Fri; 5.30-10pm Sat; 11am-2.30pm, 5-9pm Sun. **Main courses** $8-$17. **Credit** AmEx, MC, V. **Map** p277 H6.

One of the more reasonably priced eateries in the Back Bay, with an eclectic menu of variable quality. A friendly, chatty crowd tends to gather at the stone-topped bar in the front of the restaurant, and local gay social groups sometimes meet there for dinner or cocktails.

To Go Bakery

314 Shawmut Avenue, at Union Park, South End (1-617 482 1015). Back Bay T. **Open** 6.30am-12.30pm Mon-Fri; 7am-1pm Sat; 8am-1pm Sun. **No credit cards**. **Map** p277 H8.

Locals swear by the coffee at this tiny corner shop/café, which also offers tasty scones and elaborate cakes. When the weather is nice, customers linger on the benches outside.

Shops & services

Boomerangs

716 Centre Street, at Harris Avenue, Jamaica Plain (1-617 524 5120). Green Street T then 10mins walk/39 bus. **Open** 10.30am-7pm Mon-Sat; noon-6pm Sun. **Credit** AmEx, Disc, MC, V.

A resale store that is operated by the AIDS Action Committee (www.aac.org). It offers one-stop shopping for glamorous drag outfits and disco CDs. **Other locations**: 298 Washington Street, Brighton (1-617 787 0500).

Grand Opening!

Suite 32, Arcade Building, 318 Harvard Street, at Coolidge Corner, Brookline (1-617 731 2626/ www.grandopening.com). Coolidge Corner T. **Open** 10am-7pm Mon-Wed; 10am-9pm Thur-Sat, noon-6pm Sun. **Credit** AmEx, Disc, MC, V.

Boston's best sex boutique offers books, movie rentals, workshops and classes on sexuality, and plenty of high-quality toys for girls and boys. What the super-friendly salespeople don't know about sex isn't worth knowing, and proprietrix Kim Airs dispenses good advice (and ten-inch sparkly glitter dildos) like a pervy favourite auntie.

Liquid Hair Studios

640 Tremont Street, at West Newton Street, South End (1-617 425 4848/www.liquidhairstudios.com). Back Bay T. **Open** 11am-8.30pm Tue-Fri; 10am-6.30pm Sat. **Haircuts** $25-$75. **Credit** AmEx, Disc, MC, V. **Map** p277 G8.

This salon caters to South End queens who like a little atmosphere and chat but don't want to pay Newbury Street prices for it.

Marquis Leather

92 South Street, between Beach Street & Tufts Street, Downtown (1-617 426 2120). South Station T. **Open** 10am-11pm daily. **Credit** AmEx, MC, V. **Map** p275 L5.

Marquis Leather recently relocated from the South End to this new store in (appropriately enough) the loft-apartment-laden Leather District. In addition to renting and selling every video known to male homodom, Marquis supplies the neighbourhood with magazines, toys, leather accessories and lube.

Mike's Movies

630 Tremont Street, at Clarendon Street, South End (1-617 266 9222/www.mikesmoviesboston.com). Back Bay T. **Open** noon-11pm Mon-Thur, Sun; noon-11pm Fri; 10am-11pm Sat. **Credit** AmEx, Disc, MC, V. **Map** p277 H7.

The whole local neighbourhood seems to come here to rent out the latest Hollywood blockbusters, foreign films, and camp and cult classics. Meanwhile, the gay boys make use of a generous, discreetly placed porn section. Mostly rental.

The Movie Place

526 Tremont Street, at Berkeley Street, South End (1-617 482 9008). Back Bay T. **Open** 10am-11pm daily. **Credit** (for rentals over $20) AmEx, Disc, MC, V. **Map** p277 J7.

More exclusively gay, this is the best place in town for hard-to-find camp and what appears to be every single episode of *I Love Lucy*. Throw in a visit to the porn section, and there's no limit to what you can put together for an evening in front of the box.

Santa Fe Styling Company

528 & 546 Tremont Street, at Berkeley Street, South End (hair 1-617 338 8228/tanning 1-617 338 5095). Back Bay T. **Open** *Salon* 9.30am-7pm Wed-Sat. *Tanning* noon-8pm Mon-Sat; noon-5pm Sun. **Credit** AmEx, Disc, MC, V. **Map** p277 J7.

Santa Fe specialises in buff-boy homocuts. The nice thing about this place is that everybody's welcome and it doesn't cost an arm and a leg to get a few highlights. Just up the street, its tanning centre has both stand-up booths and beds. Products for sale include creams and colour enhancers plus a line of skimpy men's bathing trunks.

Teddy Shoes

548 Massachusetts Avenue, at Brookline Street, Cambridge (1-617 547 0443/www.teddyshoes.com). Central T. **Open** 10am-6pm Mon-Thur, Sat; 10am-7pm Fri. **Credit** AmEx, Disc, MC, V. **Map** p278 C3.

At Teddy's, drag-worthy PVC thigh-highs go toe-to-toe with ballet slippers and ballroom-dancing gear. Behind the unprepossessing storefront lies a massive collection of fetish shoes, platforms, and stilettos, in sizes up to a truly manly 15 – and you know what they say about men with big feet.

Music: Rock & Roots

Boston's underground music scene rocks on – across the river in Cambridge.

Back in the late 1970s and early '80s there was something known as Boston rock, when a cache of kinetic punk and garage bands exploded out of such clubs as the legendary Rat in Kenmore Square, and other small dives in the downtown and Back Bay areas. You won't find them today – a luxury hotel stands on the site of the Rat. Skyrocketing property values, rising liquor-licence costs and a city government bent on ridding the streets of safety-pinned, leather-jacketed delinquents caused club after club to close. But Boston's underground rock scene didn't die; it stumbled across the Charles River to Cambridge and Somerville, where clubs like the **Middle East** and **TT the Bear's Place** have gained a national reputation.

Passed on to a younger generation, the punk sound mutated into emo, grunge, metal rap and a hundred other variations. Meanwhile older rockers turned to traditional blues and country. Groups influenced more by Hank Williams than Wendy O Williams took root in some of the smaller Cambridge venues like the **Lizard Lounge** and **Plough & Stars**. The result is a renaissance of sounds in the small clubs of Cambridge and Somerville. It hasn't been confined to American roots – the **Middle East** has belly-dancing nights, and organisations such as Worldmusic bring in anything from flamenco artists to Tuvan throat singers to play larger venues like the Somerville Theatre.

Meanwhile, on the other side of the Charles, Boston itself, with the exception of a few surviving rock clubs in Allston and the Lansdowne Street area, has become the province of large-capacity venues like the FleetCenter, Avalon and the Orpheum, where you are likely to see huge MTV acts such as Justin Timberlake or Coldplay. In general, when it comes to major touring groups, contacting the US ticket leviathan Ticketmaster (1-617 931 2000) is your best bet. For smaller clubs, deal directly with the venues.

Major venues

Beer and wine are sold at most big-venue shows, but cigarette smoking is not permitted anywhere in closed arenas and theatres; open-air venues allow smoking outside the seating areas. As for stronger stuff: don't. Security teams frown on illegal substances and their users.

FleetBoston Pavilion

290 Northern Avenue, at Fan Pier, South Boston (1-617 728 1600/www.fleetbostonpavilion.com). South Station T, then 7 bus or free shuttle during shows. **Open** *Box office* noon-5pm Mon-Fri; noon-3pm during weekend shows. **Tickets** prices vary. **Credit** AmEx, Disc, MC, V.

Formerly Harborlights, and since corporatised into name hell, this is a pleasant, tented venue situated on the edge of Boston Harbor. The summer schedules tend to be strong on older artists – the B52s, Go-Go's and Psychedelic Furs' '80s nostalgia tour stopped off here, and Bob Dylan played a remarkable show. But it's also the place to see current pop and jazz stars such as Norah Jones and Björk. Being essentially an outdoor venue, the Pavilion does tend to avoid loud rock, with the occasional exception of crossover acts like Radiohead.

FleetCenter

1 FleetCenter, Causeway Street, at Friend Street, Boston (information 1-617 624 1000/tickets 1-617 931 2000/www.fleetcenter.com). North Station T. **Open** *Box office* 11am-7pm daily. **Tickets** prices vary. **Credit** AmEx, DC, Disc, MC, V. **Map** p274 K2.

Built next door to the now-demolished Boston Garden, which was the legendary scene of historic concerts by the Who and the Stones, as well as an Alan Freed package bill that turned into one of the first high-profile rock 'n' roll riots in 1958. The home of the Bruins hockey team and Celtics basketball team leans towards booking mainstream stars such as Tina Turner, Mariah Carey and Ricky Martin, with occasional concessions to rock acts such as AC/DC, Aerosmith and KISS.

Orpheum Theatre

1 Hamilton Place, at Tremont Street, Downtown (1-679 0810/NEXT Ticketing 1-617 423 6398). Park Street T. **Open** *Box office* 10am-5pm Mon-Sat; *NEXT Ticketing* 24hrs daily. **Tickets** $20-$50. **Credit** AmEx, MC, V. **Map** p274 K4.

A Boston landmark, built in 1852 as the Boston Music Hall, the 3,000-seat Orpheum was the first home of the Boston Symphony Orchestra (*see p219*); in its early incarnation, the venue's acoustics were said to be the best in the world. Since then it has showcased everything from movies to boxing matches. These days it mainly hosts big-name rock, pop and comedy tours.

Somerville Theatre

55 Davis Square, Somerville (1-617 625 4088/ Ticketmaster 1-617 931 2000/www.somerville theatreonline.com). Davis T. **Open** *Box office* 3-9pm daily. **Tickets** prices vary. **No credit cards**.

A converted movie house (and in fact it still serves mainly as a second-run cinema), the Somerville Theatre is situated in the middle of the newly chic Davis Square neighbourhood. It enjoys the patronage of New England's hippie jam-rock underground and is also the gig of choice for top of the bill folkies like Arlo Guthrie and Billy Bragg.

Worcester Centrum Centre

50 Foster Street, at Worcester Center Boulevard, Worcester (1-508 755 6800/Ticketmaster 1-617 931 2000/www.centrumcentre.com). **Open** *Box office* 9.30am-5.30pm Mon-Sat. **Tickets** prices vary. **Credit** AmEx, Disc, MC, V.

A slightly less sprawling arena than the FleetCenter – the only regular occupants are the minor-league IceCats hockey team – the Centrum has hosted shows by greats such as David Bowie. Although acts that play here often greet their fans with a cheery 'Hello, Boston!', the venue is actually a good hour's drive away, and if you don't plan the route well, the directions can be challenging. In other words, allow some time for getting lost.

Music clubs

Abbey Lounge

3 Beacon Street, between Cambridge & Fayette Streets, Somerville (1-617 441 9631/www.schnockered.com). Central T then 83 bus. **Open** *Shows* 9pm-1am Wed-Sat. **Admission** $5-$7. **No credit cards.**

Once the grungiest of the grungy bars-cum-rock clubs, the Abbey was known for its split room, with a clientele of grizzled neighbourhood regulars on one side and a crowd of young rockers in vintage rags enjoying rock bands on the other. Recently, however, new management has taken steps to remove the Berlin Wall separating them and augment the usually dirt-cheap beer selection with a wine bar. It is unlikely that this addition will affect the garage and roots-rock vibe of the club, though, as one of the new owners is also a member of a rock band that has played the room for years.

Avalon

For listings, see p190.

Most nights, the massive sound system and slick lighting attract a disco crowd to one of the biggest dance clubs in the city. But its alter ego as a live music venue is just as strong. From its earliest days, when it was known as the Boston Tea Party, this industrial space (with an industrial sized capacity of 2,000-people) has hosted just about everybody in the rock pantheon. Contemporary bookings have included Snoop Dogg, Macy Gray, Sonic Youth, PJ Harvey and the Chemical Brothers.

Asgard

350 Massachusetts Avenue, at Central Square, Cambridge (1-617 577 9100). Central T. **Open** 11am-1am Mon-Wed; 11am-2am Thur-Fri; 10am-2am Sat; 10am-1am Sun. **Admission** free. **Credit** AmEx, MC, V. **Map** p278 C3.

One of the newest additions to the Cambridge roots-rock scene, this ambitious Irish club boasts a large capacity, great local bands like Woodpile and Ray Mason, and to top it all, no cover charge.

Big in Boston

Boston has produced its fair share of chart-topping rock bands. The first goes back as far as 1966: garage rockers **Barry and the Remains** had the distinction of opening for the Beatles on their final US tour. The 1970s brought fame to local live workhorses **Aerosmith**, ragged rockers who hit it big in 1973 with the power ballad *Dream On.* They went on to have huge-selling hard-rock albums, including *Toys in the Attic*, and eventually nearly imploded from rock star excess, before finding sobriety and rediscovering the power ballad in the early '80s. In 1976 **Boston** (the band, not the city) tamed heavy metal to the tune of mainstream success, and went directly from the recording studio to huge stadium tours, ironically playing barely a note in the small clubs of the town they named themselves after. After paying their dues at clubs like the now defunct Rat, the **Cars** won pop stardom in 1978, and went on to become the standard bearers of the new wave sound. Their music had a ubiquitous presence on MTV throughout the 1980s, and though not critical faves, they were ultimately more commercially successful than their peers Blondie and Talking Heads. The 1990s brought the development of underground credibility to pop music, and British magazines like *NME* and *Melody Maker* had no small part in building the popularity of Boston bands such as **Dinosaur Jr**, the **Pixies**, the **Throwing Muses**, the **Lemonheads** and **Morphine**, all of whom attained stardom in the UK and throughout Europe before gaining a measure of commercial success back home. The most recent success stories from Boston have been in the realms of heavy metal: the hard-rocking suburban outfit **Godsmack**, whose January 2002 album *Awake* received a Grammy nomination, and alternative metal gurus **Staind** have become a huge presence on MTV and in the rock charts.

Lounging at the **Lizard**. *See p210.*

Bill's Bar

For listings, see p144.

A dance club for part of the week, Bill's is one of the few Boston clubs still standing that features live, local hard-rock acts regularly. It's also the only club left on the Lansdowne strip that still has dedicated live music nights – its 'Monsta Monday' is a long-running format featuring local and some national hardcore and metal rock.

Cantab Lounge

738 Massachusetts Avenue, at Inman Street, Cambridge (1-617 354 2685). Central T then 5mins walk. **Open** 8am-1am Mon-Wed; 8am-2am Thur-Sat; noon-1am Sun. **Admission** free-$8. **No credit cards. Map** p278 C3.

The Cantab has been around for at least half a century, without ever having had a facelift. It looks like a roadhouse, loaded with character – and characters. On Tuesday Bluegrass nights the incredibly proficient string department at Berklee College of Music shows off its chops. Prepare to retrieve your jaw from the floor. Pickers from all over the country are drawn to this finger-flying showcase of near superhuman prowess. Every Thursday, Friday and Saturday night, Little Joe Cook – a one-time doo-wop chart-topper who's been the resident blues guru here for decades – plays with his long-time band, the Thrillers. On Mondays, local folkie Geoff Bartley hosts his open-mic folk and acoustic programme.

Club Passim

47 Palmer Street, at Church Street, Cambridge (1-617 492 7679/www.clubpassim.org). Harvard T. **Open** 11am-11pm daily. *Box Office* 6.30-10pm daily. **Admission** $5-$20. **Credit** AmEx, Disc, MC, V. **Map** p278 A2.

As CBGBs was to New York punk, so Club Passim was to the counter-culture folk scene of the 1960s. This legendary spot was the epicentre of the folk revival even before Joan Baez got her start here (renting the room herself and introducing Bob Dylan in between sets). First known as Club 47, it served as an irregularly open but regularly busted jazz joint. Over the past 40 years, Passim has been the launching ground for folkies from Baez and Taj Mahal to Suzanne Vega and Shawn Colvin. Change happens, even here, and the vibe is more hippie/vegan than beatnik these days (it's proudly alcohol-free), but the club still plays host to legions of singer-songwriters in the 1960s tradition. Its newest addition is an on-site restaurant, Veggie Planet.

Harpers Ferry

158 Brighton Avenue, at Harvard Avenue, Brighton (1-617 254 9743/www.harpersferryboston.com). Harvard Avenue T/57 bus. **Open** 1pm-2am daily. **Admission** $5-$20. **No credit cards.**

Situated right in the middle of Boston University and Boston College territory, this one-time (and still occasional) biker bar isn't exactly where you'd expect to find Bo Diddley – though it has actually been known to happen. Other than that, don't expect to hear much in the way of blues. Although it's one of the few clubs left over from the blues boom of the 1960s, you are now far more likely to hear college jam bands playing their own careful variations on the Grateful Dead/Phish musical repertoire. On the plus side, the sound system is superior, there's plenty of room surrounding the bar, and there are pool tables in the room behind the stage.

Jacque's Cabaret

79 Broadway, at Piedmont Street, Back Bay (1-617 426 8902). Arlington T. **Open** 11am-midnight Mon-Sat; noon-midnight Sun. **Admission** $6-$8. **No credit cards. Map** p277 J6.

Even though it's just steps away from the Theatre District, Jacque's has remained a well-kept secret and a bastion of New England surrealism. Local punk and glam acts discovered this seedy transvestite hangout a few years ago and began gigging alongside the drag queens' lip-synch acts. The renovated basement hosts art exhibitions and art-rock bands, ranging from local kids to out-of-town avant-rockers. The mix of patrons has not diluted the place's warped ambience.

Johnny D's Uptown Restaurant & Music Club

17 Holland Street, at Davis Square, Somerville (1-617 776 2004/www.johnnyds.com). Davis T. **Open** 11.30am-1am Mon-Fri; 9am-1am Sat, Sun. **Admission** $8-$15. **Credit** (bar only) AmEx, Disc, MC, V.

The city's best roots-music club, Johnny D's is family owned (must have been fun growing up) and a favourite hangout for enthusiasts of all stripes. The acts are presented in a lounge/restaurant setting, so get there early to secure a table. There's a dancefloor right in front of the stage for spectators, which is also used for the club's Monday salsa nights from 9pm to midnight (lessons provided). There's a traditional jazz brunch on Saturday and Sunday, and a Sunday blues jam from 4.30pm to 8.30pm.

Kirkland Café

421-427 Washington Street, at Beacon Street, Somerville (1-617 491 9640). Harvard T then 86 bus. **Open** 11.30am-1am daily. **Admission** $5-$10. **Credit** (bar only) MC, V.

This place is heavy on grunge and plain old rock 'n' roll, with occasional rockabilly and surf nights. Booking agent Micky Bliss often holds court between bands with his impressive command of the Hammond organ. Blue collar to the bone, and utterly immune to trends, this is where local rock dinosaurs go to revisit their musical youth. It has the hootenanny atmosphere that only seems to evolve in places where payday still means something.

Linwood Grille

81 Kilmarnock Street, at Queensberry Street, Fenway (1-617 247 8099). Fenway/Kenmore T. **Open** 6pm-2am daily. **Admission** $5-$6. **Credit** (bar only) DC, Disc, MC, V. **Map** p276 D8.

When the Rat closed in 1997, the soundman and a bunch of the regulars moved a few blocks away to this dive/baseball bar, and gradually the Linwood took over the defunct club's specialities – heavy metal, garage-punk and surf. It has played host to hip national underground bands such as the Kitty Kill and Nashville Pussy, and is well known for bringing local bands together for benefits (including a stirring tribute to Joey Ramone) and for its political consciousness-raising and other causes.

Lizard Lounge

1667 Massachusetts Avenue, at Harvard Street, Cambridge (1-617 547 0759/547 1228). Harvard T. **Open** 9pm-2am daily. **Admission** $5-$9. **Credit** (bar only) AmEx, Disc, MC, V. **Map** p278 B1.

Situated just below a busy burger-and-brew gaffe, this renovated basement was opened by folks who wanted to emulate the in-the-round set-up of a Nashville club. Decorated to look like a retro-groovy bohemian salon (velvet drapes, gilt mirror frames, red Persian rugs), it's the kind of room where you can choose from several variations on the Martini, and catch deft, independent singer-songwriters, as well as jazz, experimental and rootsy rock acts. The late Mark Sandman, one of Boston's most

The mighty **Middle East** is the heart of the city's rock scene. *See p211.*

well-respected underground music icons, played here regularly; members of his band, Morphine, in their many incarnations, along with the harder-edged side of the local acoustic music community, continue to call this place their home.

The Middle East

472 & 480 Massachusetts Avenue, at Brookline Street, Cambridge (1-617 864 3278/www.mideast club.com). Central T. **Open** 11am-1am Mon-Wed, Sun; 11am-2am Thur-Sat. **Admission** $7-$10. **Credit** AmEx, Disc, MC, V. **Map** p278 C3.

Although it's in Cambridge, this is now Boston's musical heart. Low-key and friendly, the three-room club is a unique mix of all-round cultural endeavour, where you're just as likely to run into the former mayor as, say, former J Geils Band frontman Peter Wolf. It's a favourite of local heroes and regularly hosts national rock, punk, ska and alternative touring bands. The main live room, carved out of what was once a downstairs bowling alley, is frequently the site of shows you won't see anywhere else. The Corner has free music seven nights a week (not to mention belly dancing) in a restaurant setting. The upstairs rock room, decorated with glow-in-the-dark cartoon art, features mostly local rock.

Milky Way Lounge & Lanes

403-405 Centre Street, at Perkins Street, Jamaica Plain (1-617 524 3740/www.milkywayjp.com). Stony Brook T then 15mins walk/39 bus then 5mins walk. **Open** 6pm-1am daily. **Admission** $5-$10. **Credit** AmEx, DC, MC, V.

Converted a few years ago from a World War I-era bowling alley – which is still in use – this is a funky, bohemian basement club with a clientele of local art-schoolers and off-centre rock types partial to Bettie Paige haircuts and 1970s vintage threads. The live music nights, with alternative and underground rock and funk bands, are on Thursday and Friday. Saturday is a popular Latin night, and draws a mixed crowd of all ages. Monday is usually given over to film screenings or offbeat comedy performances. Tuesday is Rock Star Karaoke Night – besides belting out the usual loungy staples, you can humiliate yourself with renditions of the Cure, Echo and the Bunnymen or the Strokes.

O'Brien's

3 Harvard Avenue, at Cambridge Street, Allston (1-617 782 6245). Harvard Ave T/57, 66 bus. **Open** 11am-1am daily. **Admission** $5. **No credit cards.**

One of the last tattered remnants of an area that used to be called Allston Rock City. The student ghettos of Allston had long hidden in their midst a tremendous punk/hardcore/metal scene, and O'Brien's – a pine-panelled relic from decades past – is their only remaining stage in the neighbourhood. Always in danger of being closed down for overcrowding (the capacity is only 50), O'Brien's suffers from patchy booking, but you can still find big-draw local bands here. Bring earplugs, because it doesn't get any rawer or louder than this.

Paradise Rock Club

969 Commonwealth Avenue, at Babcock Street, Brookline (Main Room 1-617 562 8800/lounge 1-617 562 8814/tickets 1-617 423 6398/www.the dise.com). Babcock Street T. **Open** *Main Room* from 7pm, days vary. *Lounge* 6pm-2am daily. **Admission** *Main Room* $8-$20. *Lounge* free-$10. **Credit** AmEx, MC, V.

If you've just heard their single on the radio, they'll probably play here soon; and if they're playing the FleetCenter, chances are they were here a couple of years ago. U2, Echo and the Bunnymen and Alanis Morissette all played formative gigs at this club, and the tradition continues. A new smaller stage in the front room caters to up-and-coming local rock acts, and the recent addition of a kitchen serving pizza, nachos, burgers, and other bar fare makes Paradise even more of a heavenly destination.

Plough & Stars

912 Massachusetts Avenue, at Hancock Street, Cambridge (1-617 441 3455). Central T. **Open** 11.30am-1am daily. **Admission** free-$3. **Credit** (bar only) AmEx, Disc, MC, V. **Map** p278 B3.

The Plough is so cosy it's practically suffocating when the room is full of punters, but the local scenesters and regulars seem to accept the conditions with good humoured equanimity. There's music here every night, generally of the rootsy, surf-rockabilly variety. Morphine played here regularly for years before breaking out on the national level. The atmosphere is magical and the staff lovely, but the squeeze can be too much, especially when you have to shove past the bassist to get to the loo.

Roxy

279 Tremont Street, at Stuart Street, Downtown (1-617 338 7699). Boylston T. **Open** 9pm-2am Thur-Sat. **Admission** $10-$15. **Credit** (bar only) AmEx, MC, V. **Map** p277 J6.

The Roxy is a 1930s ballroom with dual identities as a concert hall and dance club. The venue's music events are irregular but often noteworthy, from punk, reggae and funk deities such as Joe Strummer, Jimmy Cliff and George Clinton to current chart climbers of every genre. A three-sided balcony offers good views, but even from the back of the ballroom you can usually see the stage.

Skybar

518 Somerville Avenue, at Park Street, Somerville (1-617 623 5223/www.esporecords.com/skybar.html). Porter T then 83 bus. **Open** 11am-1am Tue-Sun. **Admission** $5-$7. **Credit** (bar only) MC, V.

Masterminded by WBCN DJ Shred, this club has found its own distinctive hard rock/experimental niche while remaining somewhat off the beaten path. By day a blue-collar local hangout, it comes alive in the evening with a parade of up-and-coming yet unique bands you've probably never heard of. The underground sound waves often seem to clash with the club's mirror ball/dancefloor light show, but true rock 'n' roll believers don't seem to mind. The club also sponsors comedy shows on Tuesday nights.

Foxy **Roxy**. *See p211.*

TT the Bear's Place

10 Brookline Street, at Massachusetts Avenue, Cambridge (1-617 492 2327/Ticketmaster 1-617 931 2000/www.ttthebears.com). Central T. **Open** 6pm-1am daily. **Admission** $3-$15. **Credit** AmEx, MC, V. **Map** p278 C3.

One of Boston's oldest rock venues, TTs has been a regular stop for headliners for more than 25 years. British art rocker Robyn Hitchcock and former Dream Syndicate frontman Steve Wynn insist on playing this club whenever they're in town. Faithfulness is generally rewarded and musicians remain as loyal to TT the Bear's Place as it has been to them. Though the club has been somewhat overshadowed more recently by the mighty Middle East next door (*see p211*), it still manages to score many a booking coup. But if the band is giving you a headache there is refuge to be found in the shape of two pool tables. Despite what are possibly the worst sightlines of almost any major club in the Boston area, TT's stubbornly remains a local favourite.

Western Front

343 Western Avenue, at Putnam Avenue, Cambridge (1-617 492 7772). Central T. **Open** 5pm-1am Tue-Sun. **Admission** $3-$10. **No credit cards**. **Map** p278 B3.

A hotspot for reggae and Caribbean music, with a little avant garde jazz thrown in for good measure, the Western Front attracts an eclectic, racially mixed crowd of rastas, poets, jazz types and, salting the exotics, ordinary neighbourhood folks. With a couple of bars and comfortable seating throughout, this is an atmospheric, friendly place to be.

ZuZu

474 Massachusetts Avenue, at Central Square, Cambridge (1-617 864 3278 ext 237/www.mideastclub.com/zuzu). Central Square T. **Open** 5.30pm-12.45am Sun-Wed; 5.30pm-1.45am Thur-Sat. *Music begins* 10.30pm Sun-Wed; 11.30pm Thur-Sat. **Admission** free. **Credit** AmEx, D, MC, V. **Map** p278 C3.

Born as an upscale eating addition to the Middle East club, with which it shares real estate, this small room has grown into a premium live venue for low-key acts like local Tom Waits-esque bluesman Frank Morey, solo performers and 1970s funk and Latin. Manager Lilli Dennison, a rock scene impresario and former co-owner of the club Lilli's, began with a Monday night feature she called the Unhappy Hour, and now has live music throughout the week, presenting such notable solo performers as Bill Janovitz of Buffalo Tom, Kay Hanley of Letters to Cleo, and Tanya Donnelly of Belly.

Jazz

Hotel lounges

The Regattabar

Charles Hotel, 1 Bennett Street, at Harvard Square, Cambridge (1-617 661 5000/www.charleshotel.com). Harvard T. **Open** 7pm-1am Tue-Sat. **Tickets** $12-$36. **Credit** AmEx, Disc, MC, V. **Map** p278 A2.

Situated in the distinctly swish Charles Hotel, just off Harvard Square, the Regattabar offers table seating, a decent light snacks menu and an essential line-up of events. In a typical season performers include

Kenny Barron, Tommy Flanagan, Dave Holland, John Schofield and estimable local artists. Non-jazz fare tends towards blues and Latin music. The 'stage' is in a corner at floor level, under a low ceiling that restricts both sightlines and consistent sound. It's best to book ahead and get a table close to the action if you can.

Scullers Jazz Club

Doubletree Guest Suites Hotel, 400 Soldiers Field Road, at River Street, Boston (1-617 562 4111/ www.scullersjazz.com). Central T then taxi. **Open** from 11am-2am Mon-Sat; call for show times. **Tickets** $10-$30. **Map** p278 B4.

High above the Charles River, Scullers has a great view of the water. Unfortunately, its location (at the intersection of two major thoroughfares) cuts it off from public transport and foot traffic. Still, the music can be very impressive, and there are light snacks and cocktails to go with the hefty line-up.

Other venues

Bob the Chef's Café

604 Columbus Avenue, at Northampton Street, South End (1-617 536 6204/www.bobthechef.com). Massachusetts Avenue T. **Open** 5.30pm-midnight Mon-Thur; 11.30am-midnight Fri-Sat; 10am-midnight Sun. *Live Jazz* 7.30pm-midnight Thur-Sat; 10am-3pm Sun. **Tickets** $3-$7. **Credit** AmEx, Disc, MC, V. **Map** p277 G8.

For decades, this South End restaurant has been a favourite late-night stop for authentic soul food. It was expanded and renovated a few years ago and started to introduce jazz nights on the weekends. The combo is worth the trip, although some of the worn-down charm of the old place has been lost.

Good Life

28 Kingston Street, at Summer Street, Downtown (1-617 451 2622). Downtown Crossing T. **Open** 11.30am-2am Mon-Sat. *Live music* 9.30pm-1.30am Tue-Sat. **Admission** free. **Credit** AmEx, DC, MC, V. **Map** p274 K5.

Opened during the Martini-lounge revival of the 1990s, this place has grown from a self-consciously trendy facsimile of a Rat Pack-era lounge for yuppies to a culturally cross-pollinated favourite, serving up well-priced American comfort food and live jazz in all genres, along with the classic cocktails.

Other location: 720 Massachusetts Avenue, at Prospect Street, Cambridge (1-617 868 8800).

Ryles Jazz Club

212 Hampshire Street, at Inman Square, Cambridge (1-617 876 9330/www.rylesjazz.com). Central T then 83 bus. **Open** 8pm-1am Tue, Wed; 8pm-2am Thur-Sat. **Tickets** $6-$15. **Credit** AmEx, Disc, MC, V. **Map** p278 C2.

There's jazz in the comfortable downstairs room here, with sandwiches and snacks (as well as a Sunday jazz brunch) and windows looking out on to Inman Square. Jazz trumpeter/promoter Frank Vardaros fills the room by booking his personal heroes, such as Maynard Ferguson and Arturo Sandoval. The action upstairs varies depending on the night – salsa and merengue on Thursday, Brazilian jazz on Friday and Latin dancing on Saturday.

Wally's

427 Massachusetts Avenue, at Columbus Avenue, South End (1-617 424 1408). Massachusetts Avenue T. **Open** *Dining* 11am-2am daily. *Music* 9pm-2am Mon-Sat; 3.30-7.30pm Sun. **Admission** free. **No credit cards. Map** p277 G8.

This legendary hole-in-the-wall opened as long ago as 1947. The sole survivor of the once-thriving jazz and blues district at the edge of Roxbury, Wally's is still owned and operated by the grandsons of the original owner, James 'Wally' Walcott, and retains its down-to-earth character. It's a customary haunt for students from Berklee and the New England Conservatory, and when former Berklee-ites like Roy Hargrove or Branford Marsalis drop in, it's easy to see how the club has provided a rite of passage for generations of young players.

Sax appeal: **Ryles Jazz Club.**

Performing Arts

Take in some high culture, edgy fringe or a showstopper hot from Broadway.

In the last two years, Boston – a city known for being grudging in its acceptance of change – has experienced a burst of reinvention in the arts. The **Boston Symphony Orchestra**, already an international powerhouse, raised its profile with the appointment of conductor James Levine, and two major regional theatres, the **Huntington** and the **American Repertory**, changed guard at the top, infusing their seasons with fresh energy.

One catalyst for these changes has been the need to keep up with the newly established Broadway in Boston, a booking company that brings New York hits like *Hairspray* and the *Lion King* to the Theatre District. But some imports have caused grumbles: the Wang Center's new Christmas-season tenants are the Radio City Music Hall Rockettes, displacing the Boston Ballet's long-running *Nutcracker* – a seismic change on the local calendar.

For fans of edgier fare, the fringe theatre community is in full bloom (*see p220* **Fringe benefits**), and ensembles like ImprovBoston keep the comedy stages rolling.

TICKETS

Generally speaking, getting tickets means either travelling to a venue and buying them from the box office, or shelling out some extra dough to buy them over the phone or on the web. That means swallowing hard and dealing with monster-sized ticket agencies like **Ticketmaster** (1-617 931 2000) and **TeleCharge** (1-800 447 7400). Between the two, most tickets for Theatre District events (plays, musicals and dance performances) are available, but with inescapable – and annoying – service fees.

When your search for tickets seems impossible but you don't want to resort to scalpers, try **Back Bay Tickets** (40 Dalton Street, at Boylston Street, 1-617 536 9666). Sometimes – for a higher fee – they can make the impossible happen. For last-minute and discounted tickets, the place to go is **BosTix** (1-617 723 5181). It has two outlets, at Copley Square and Faneuil Hall. Last-minute tickets go on sale at 11am daily at Copley and every day but Sunday at Faneuil Hall. Tickets are half the full price and available only on the day of the performance. You can also buy full-priced tickets for advance shows here, but bear in mind it's cash only, whatever you're buying.

Theatre

Boston's Theatre District, where touring shows and blockbusters can be found, runs south along Tremont Street from the Boylston T stop to the Mass Pike. The big equity repertory companies anchor their own neighbourhoods well away from the theatre district.

American Repertory Theatre

Loeb Drama Center, Harvard University, 64 Brattle Street, at Hilliard Street, Cambridge (1-617 547 8300). Harvard T. **Open** *Box office* 10am-5pm Mon; 10am-7.30pm Tue-Sun. **Tickets** $35-$69. **Credit** AmEx, MC, V. **Map** p278 A2.

As recipient of a Tony for best regional theatre, the American Repertory Theatre is one of the nation's most respected companies. But it isn't resting on its laurels: under new artistic director Robert Woodruff, the ART is attracting heavyweight artists such as Philip Glass and Anne Bogart to its stage, who join past luminaries like David Mamet.

Charles Playhouse

74 Warrenton Street, at Stuart Street, Downtown (1-617 426 6912/www.blueman.com). Boylston or NE Medical Center T. **Open** *Box office* 10am-6pm Mon, Tue; 10am-8pm Wed, Thur; 10am-9pm Fri, Sat; noon-6pm Sun. **Tickets** $43-$53. **Credit** AmEx, MC, V. **Map** p277 J6.

If it ain't broke, don't fix it. That's the rule at the Charles Playhouse, which has kept its popular acts running for years: among them are the Blue Man Group – a comical performance art troupe whose messy, noisy, colourful antics make them a hot ticket – and the comic murder-mystery *Shear Madness*, the longest-running non-musical in the US.

Colonial Theatre

106 Boylston Street, at Tremont Street, Downtown (1-617 426 9366/www.broadwayinboston.com). Boylston T. **Open** *Box office* 10am-6pm Mon-Sat; noon-6pm Sun (only when evening performance). **Tickets** $25-$100. **Credit** AmEx, MC, V. **Map** p277 J5.

A good place for big musicals, the Colonial was built in 1900 and is the oldest continuously operating theatre in Boston. The fan-shaped auditorium means there's scarcely a bad seat in the house.

Huntington Theatre Company/ Boston University Theatre

264 Huntington Avenue, at Massachusetts Avenue, Back Bay (1-617 266 0800). Symphony T. **Open** *Box office* 11am-5pm Mon-Fri; noon-4pm Sat, Sun. **Tickets** $38-$64. **Credit** AmEx, Disc, MC, V. **Map** p276 F8.

Just a few years ago, the Huntington had a reputation for playing it safe – elegant productions of tame material. Over the last few years it has shaken off that stigma. Now a black comedy by Christopher Durang is as likely to grace the stage here as a revival of a Eugene O'Neill play. Broadway actors appear alongside the cream of the local acting crop.

Lyric Stage

YWCA Building, 140 Clarendon Street, at Copley Square, Back Bay (1-617 437 7172). Arlington or Back Bay T. **Open** *Box office* 11am-5pm Tue, Sun; noon-7pm Wed-Sat. **Tickets** $24-$40. **Credit** AmEx, Disc, MC, V. **Map** p277 H6.

An intimate house where every seat has a good view, the Lyric is a moderately priced way to see excellent stagings of classics and recent off-Broadway hits.

Publick Theater

Christian Herter Park, 1175 Soldiers Field Road, Brighton (1-617 782 5425). Harvard T then 86 bus. **Open** *Box office* noon-7pm Tue-Sun. **Tickets** $15-$30. **Credit** MC, V.

Bring a pillow for your bench seat (and, depending on the season, some bug spray or a blanket) and settle in by the Charles River at this open-air theatre in Christian Herter Park. Typical summer line-ups include a little Shakespeare and a frothy musical.

The cultural melting pot

Boston is often portrayed as a city of culturally elite WASPs, but in fact, less than half the population is from white Anglo stock. The city's rich stew of ethnic diversity is reflected in, and celebrated by, its non-profit multicultural centres. These emerged in the 1970s out of a trend for grass roots, community-oriented arts, and today showcase some of the Boston's most interesting events, from underground theatre and performance art to ethnic festivals and offbeat visual art exhibitions.

The **Boston Center for the Arts** (*see p217*) is a high-profile arts complex serving the whole city, but the centre is also dedicated to uniting the South End's Cape Verdian, Asian and Haitian communities, among others, and events include cultural festivals, exhibitions by local artists, workshops and seminars.

Housed in an imposing Bulfinch-designed 19th-century courthouse, the **Cambridge Multicultural Arts Center** (41 Second Street, Cambridge, 1-617 577 1400, www.cmacusa.org) was founded by the city council in 1978 to help the diverse population get beyond racial and ethnic stereotypes and encourage understanding. Jazz and world music events, spoken word performances and dance take place in its magnificent theatre – which is a spectacle in itself with internal galleries, marble façades and a high, ornate ceiling.

Another architectural gem, the **Jorge Hernandez Cultural Center** (85 West Newton Street, South End, 1-617 927 0061), has recently come under the umbrella of the Center for Latino Arts (*see below*). The funky 19th-century church (*pictured*) has a huge stage and spacious dancefloor, perfect for the Friday salsa dance nights that are a

staple of the venue. The programme of events ranges from family-oriented hip hop shows, Middle Eastern performance art, burlesque, jazz and even film. Next door, the recently renovated three-storey **Center for Latino Arts** has a gallery and a busy programme of performing-arts events.

Spontaneous Celebrations (45 Danforth Street, Jamaica Plain, 1-617 524 6373, www.spontaneouscelebrations.org) grew out of a grass roots festival known as Wake Up the Earth, which began in 1979 to celebrate the defeat of a proposed interstate highway extension through the middle of town. While the festival continues annually, the venue offers free arts training for young people and features everything from dance, music, performance art, multimedia and experimental events to weekly classes in capoeira, yoga and kick-boxing.

The Opera House

539 Washington Street, at Avenue de Lafayette, Downtown (1-617 426 9366). Chinatown T. **Open** *Box office* at the Colonial Theatre 10am-6pm Mon-Sat; noon-6pm Sun. **Tickets** prices vary. **Credit** AmEx, MC, V. **Map** p274 K5.

Once upon a time the jewel of Boston, the 1928-built Opera House languished for more than a decade after the demise of the Boston Opera Company in 1991. In 2004, after a multi-million dollar renovation, its doors reopened – with fixtures gleaming again – to welcome Disney's *Lion King*.

Shubert Theatre

265 Tremont Street, at Stuart Street, Downtown (1-617 482 9393). Boylston or NE Medical Center T. **Open** *Box office* 10am-6pm Mon-Sat. **Tickets** prices vary. **Credit** AmEx, MC, V. **Map** p277 J6.

This is the last remnant of a national chain of Shubert theatres. Now partnered with the Wang Center, the Shubert is home to Boston Lyric Opera and world music. The programme is diverse here, from touring theatre shows, to dance troupes like Mark Morris, and a high-profile reading series of American plays.

Wang Center for the Performing Arts

270 Tremont Street, at Stuart Street, Downtown (Box office 1-617 482 9393/Boston Ballet 1-617 695 6955/www.wangcenter.org). Boylston or NE Medical Center T. **Open** *Box office* 10am-6pm Mon-Sat. **Tickets** $15-$100. **Credit** AmEx, MC, V. **Map** p277 J6.

What do Elvis Costello, *Casablanca* and *Beauty and the Beast* have in common? They all fit into the eclectic programming of the Wang Center, a 3,700-seat performance space that has dominated the local scene since 1925, when it was the Metropolitan Theatre. The Boston Ballet still calls it home – when the stage is not occupied by Broadway shows on tour, pop concerts, and big-screen movie nights.

Wilbur Theatre

246 Tremont Street, at Stuart Street, Downtown (1-617 423 4008/www.broadwayinboston.com). Boylston or NE Medical Center T. **Open** *Box office* 10am-6pm Mon-Sat; noon-6pm Sun (only when evening performance). **Tickets** prices vary. **Credit** AmEx, MC, V. **Map** p277 J6.

With the advent of booking company Broadway in Boston, the Wilbur's stage is kept busy with travelling productions headed to or from Manhattan's theatreland. The fare is a little more varied than at the Colonial (*see p214*), with short-run offerings both familiar (*Nunsense*) and unique (Cirque Eloize).

Alternative theatre

The Boston Center for the Arts' complex in the South End is the hub of fringe theatre in Boston, as available spaces are at a premium. But the thriving small theatre scene always finds a space to make sure the show goes on.

Boston Center for the Arts

539 Tremont Street, at Berkeley Street (1-617 426 5000/tickets 1-617 426 2787/www.bcaonline.org). Back Bay or Copley T. **Open** 9am-5pm Mon-Fri. **Tickets** $10-$35. **Credit** AmEx, MC, V. **Map** p277 J7.

Resident companies SpeakEasy Stage Company, Sugan Theatre, Pilgrim Theater, and Theater Offensive all call the BCA home, but almost every small company in town has performed in its three original spaces. In September 2004, a multi-million dollar expansion will add two more spaces.

Boston Theatre Works

Suite 11, 325 Columbus Ave, at Dartmouth Street, South End (1-617 728 4321/tickets 1-617 939 9939/www.bostontheatreworks.com). Back Bay T. **Open** *Box office* noon-6pm Tue-Fri (noon-5pm Sat; noon-2pm Sun during production weeks). **Tickets** $14-$19. **Credit** AmEx, Disc, MC, V. **Map** p277 H7.

Boston Theatre Works put its roots down in this recently opened venue and soon became the company to watch, with classics by Shakespeare and Tennessee Williams, as well as world premières of edgy contemporary fare.

Peabody House Theater Co-operative

Elizabeth Peabody House, 277 Broadway, at Route 28, Somerville (1-617 625 1300). Sullivan Square T. **Open** *Box office* 10am-5pm Mon-Fri. **Tickets** $10-$20. **No credit cards**.

Off the beaten path in location and fare, the Peabody is one of the most consistently daring small theatres, choosing unusual or seldom-performed plays, and commissioning new works by local writers.

Outside Boston

When it comes to theatre, you don't have to stay in Boston to catch an interesting performance. Since 1978, one of the largest theatre companies in the Boston area has been the respected **Merrimack Repertory Theater** troupe in Lowell, which performs in Liberty Hall at **Lowell Memorial Auditorium** (50 East Merrimack Street, 1-508 484 3926). In Newburyport, there's the **Firehouse Center for the Performing & Visual Arts** (1 Market Square, 1-978 462 7336), which features small-scale local productions. And in Beverly, the **North Shore Music Theatre** (62 Dunham Road, 1-978 922 8500) puts on acclaimed productions and popular concerts.

Dance

Ballet Theatre of Boston

1151 Massachusetts Ave, at Harvard Street, Cambridge (1-617 354 7467), Harvard T. **Open** *Box office* 10am-6pm Mon-Fri **Tickets** prices vary. **Credit** MC, V. **Map** p278 B3.

Playing at **Symphony Hall**.
See p219.

José Mateo's innovative modern dance company finally has a home of its own, after years of renting local venues. The historic Old Cambridge Baptist Church serves both as studio space for instruction, and as a performance space. At Christmas, the 250-seat Sanctuary Hall is always packed for Mateo's popular spin on the *Nutcracker*.

Boston Ballet

For listings, *see* **Wang Center for the Performing Arts,** *p217. Information 1-617 695 6950/Box office 1-617 695 6955.*

While its *Nutcracker*, one of the most attended ballet productions in the world, adjusts to life after the Wang Center, the Boston Ballet continues to reign as one of the top companies in the United States, with Kirov-influenced productions of *Swan Lake* and *Le Corsaire*, and contemporary gems from Mark Morris and Christopher Wheeldon. The *Nutcracker* will continue its festive run at the Colonial Theatre in 2004, moving to the Opera House in 2005.

Dance Complex

536 Massachusetts Avenue, at Brookline Street, Cambridge (1-617 547 9363/www.dancecomplex.org). Central T. **Open** 9am-9.30pm Mon-Thur; 9am-8pm Fri; 9am-6pm Sat; 10am-5pm Sun **Tickets** $10-$15. **No credit cards**. **Map** p278 C3.

This community-run group hosts artists-in-residence who teach classes and perform for the masses. Local choreographers premiere new and unusual work far from the classical repertory. Feel like taking a class while you're in town? Anyone's welcome to drop into any of their classes; just bring $10 and your sweats.

Cutler Majestic Theatre at Emerson College

219 Tremont Street, at Boylston Street, Downtown (TeleCharge 1-617 233 3123). Boylston T. **Open** *Box office* TeleCharge 10am-6pm daily. **Tickets** $15-$85. **Credit** AmEx, MC, V. **Map** p277 J5.

Recently re-dedicated and restored to its deco-era beauty, the renamed Cutler Majestic is still home to dance, including touring flamenco companies and student productions, but it now also stages higher profile plays with New York aspirations.

Green Street Studios

185 Green Street, at Central Square, Cambridge (1-617 864 3191). Central T. **Open** *Box office* 8.30am-6.30pm daily. **Tickets** $10-$15. **No credit cards**. **Map** p278 C3.

This choreographer-run centre is a hub for new dance work, as well as for training in ballet, yoga and international dance forms as diverse as Hawaiian and Bulgarian.

Impulse Dance Company

Information 1-617 469 8787/www.impulsedance.com. **Open** *Box office* 10am-4pm Mon-Fri. **Tickets** $10-$25. **No credit cards**.

Urban, innovative, local – this edgy dance troupe based at the Brookline Community Center for the Arts is making waves at venues all over the city.

Classical music & opera

Classical music tends towards the highbrow in Boston, where the respected and wealthy **Boston Symphony Orchestra** (BSO) reigns supreme. Opera, having struggled in recent years, is experiencing growth as the **Boston Lyric Opera** sells out its runs, and dozens of chamber ensembles and choirs take advantage of the many local conservatories.

Boston Lyric Opera

Information 1-617 542 6772/bookings 1-800 447 7400. **Tickets** $33-$152. **Credit** AmEx, MC, V.

Once considered the new kid in town, Boston Lyric Opera now dominates the local scene with a diverse repertoire that spans the well-trodden path of Puccini and Verdi as well as new work by composers like Philip Glass.

Boston Philharmonic

Information 1-617 236 0999. **Tickets** $15-$63. **Credit** AmEx, Disc, MC, V.

Though the BSO is Boston's classical institution, a hardy band of loyalists champion the Philharmonic, with its mix of freelance professionals, students and amateurs who play side by side. Since its inception in 1979 the orchestra has been led by conductor Benjamin Zander, whose conducting style is electric and whose programming is decidedly a matter of personal taste – an entire season of Mahler, for example. The Philharmonic's concerts are often broadcast live on radio.

Boston Pops

Information 1-617 266 1492/bookings 1-617 226 1200. **Tickets** $19-$75. **Credit** AmEx, DC, Disc, MC, V.

With a heart-throb conductor willing to pose in a Santa suit, and artists like Bette Midler popping up in the mix, no one could accuse the Pops of being highbrow. During the summer season, while the BSO performs out of town, the seats at Symphony Hall are removed and replaced with large circular tables where champagne is served to the accompaniment of pop classics. Without question middle America's favourite 'classical' music.

Boston Symphony Orchestra & Symphony Hall

301 Massachusetts Avenue, at Huntington Avenue, Back Bay (information 1-617 266 1492/bookings 1-617 226 1200). Symphony or Mass Ave T. **Open** *Box office* 10am-6pm Mon-Sat. **Tickets** $26-$95. **Credit** AmEx, Disc, MC, V. **Map** p276 F8.

The BSO has a long and venerable history, but it really came into its own under the stewardship of Serge Koussevitzky, music director from 1924 to 1949. (Koussevitzky's most famous personal protégé was the young Leonard Bernstein.) Today, the BSO is one of the nation's premier orchestras. Its performers are top notch (the orchestra's annual trips to Carnegie Hall in New York are invariably sell-outs). Its Symphony Hall home is acoustically and architecturally impressive, and its profile has grown even more prominent with the appointment of James Levine as the 14th musical director.

Emmanuel Music

Emmanuel Church, 15 Newbury Street, Back Bay (1-617 536 3356). Arlington T. **Tickets** prices vary; cheapest $18. **Credit** MC, V. **Map** p277 H5.

Craig Smith has cemented a place for Emmanuel as a presenter of serious and inventive classical music for three decades. Known for twice completing cycles of all 200 Bach cantatas, this innovative ensemble has linked its musical performances to choreographers Mark Morris and acclaimed stage directors including Peter Sellars.

FleetBoston Celebrity Series

Information 1-617 482 6661. **Tickets** prices vary. **Credit** AmEx, MC, V.

The Celebrity Series began in 1938 with the likes of the Ballets Russes de Monte Carlo and Rudolf Serkin. These days the organisation books more than 70 events between October and May each year in venues such as Symphony Hall. Performers include classical musicians (the St Petersburg Philharmonic, Renée Fleming), dancers (Mark Morris, American Ballet Theatre) and jazz exponents (Wynton Marsalis, Lincoln Center Jazz Orchestra).

Jordan Hall

290 Huntington Avenue, at Gainsborough Street, Back Bay (1-617 536 2412/585 1260). Mass Ave or Symphony T. **Open** *Box office* 10am-6pm Mon-Fri; noon-6pm Sat. **Tickets** free-$100. **Credit** Disc, MC, V. **Map** p276 F8.

Whether you fork out for a Celebrity Series event or stroll into one of 100 free annual New England Conservatory concerts, you'll enjoy the echoes of history in a building that since 1903 has presented artists as diverse as the Von Trapp Family Singers, Bela Bartok and Yo Yo Ma .

Early music

As well as the ensembles listed below, the **Isabella Stewart Gardner Museum** (*see p106*) has one of the oldest museum music programmes in the US – and its own chamber orchestra – while the **Museum of Fine Arts'** (*see p106*) concert series is particularly renowned for its baroque performances.

Boston Cecilia

1773 Beacon Street, at Dean Road, Brookline (1-617 232 4540). Dean Road T. **Open** *Box office* (phone only) 9am-5pm Mon-Fri. **Tickets** $15-$60. **Credit** MC, V.

Fringe benefits

Out-of-towners heading to Boston for a show tend to cluster in the Theatre District, taking in touring productions of Broadway fare. But Bostonians – and savvy visitors – know that much of the most vital theatre in town is performed by the fringe companies. Whether ensuring acclaimed Off Broadway plays find a Boston audience or reinventing classics in unexpected ways, fringe companies often feature the city's best home-grown acting and directing talent.

The **Theater Offensive** (1-617 621 6090) has been around for 15 years and continues to be the reigning diva of fringe. TTO commissions new work and presents the latest shows by queer artists like Noel Alumit and Peggy Shaw. Often shaggy and loose, the performances have a vibrancy that compensates for lack of polish. Slightly younger, **SpeakEasy** (1-617 482 3279) has gone from a cult favourite to the head of the fringe class, routinely selling out its Boston premières of New York hits like *Bat Boy*.

These two veterans are joined by up-and-coming troupes **Boston Theatre Works** (1-617 728 4321) and **Rough & Tumble** (www.rough-and-tumble.org). BTW packs 'em in for its innovative renditions of Shakespeare plays as well as contemporary fare and premières in its annual Unbound Festival. Rough & Tumble creates movement-based original pieces that are whimsical, moving, and utterly singular.

Many of the fringe companies have a focused mission. The **Sugan Theatre Company** (1-617 497 5134) features exclusively the work of Irish playwrights, like award-winning Ronan Noone, while **Centastage** (1-617 536 5981) performs only the work of local playwrights and, in its increasingly popular and exuberant cabaret series, local songwriters.

Coyote Theatre (1-617 695 0659) mixes new work with Off Broadway hits, while finding time to work with children in a mentoring programme, and **TheatreZone** (1-617 887 2336) pushes the envelope on a shoestring budget, with plays like *Bash*. But arguably, no one makes as big a splash on the fringe scene as gender-blasting playwright-actor Ryan Landry, whose **Gold Dust Orphans** troupe (1-617 265 6222) performs outrageously campy yet incisive comedies in the nightclub space Machine (*see p203*).

For more than 125 years, this ensemble has sung the great works of the baroque era, often performed with period instruments. In recent years its repertoire has been spiced up with contemporary works by Boston composers and 20th-century greats.

Handel and Haydn Society

Horticultural Hall, 300 Massachusetts Avenue, at Huntington Avenue, Back Bay (1-617 266 3605). Symphony T. **Open** 10am-6pm Mon-Fri. **Tickets** $25-$74. **Credit** AmEx, Disc, MC, V. **Map** p276 F8.

Established nearly 200 years ago, this is a storied chorus, having presented the American premieres of Handel's *Messiah* (which it has now sung 150 times), Haydn's *The Creation*, and Verdi's *Requiem*. Under the direction of Grant Llewellyn that tradition continues, with variety that includes Italian masterworks and contemporary jazz.

New music

With the wealth of universities in the Boston area and the number of established composers teaching at them, it follows that all those composers are going to need groups to play their music. Here's a sampling to watch out for:

Composer and BU faculty member Theodore Antoniou guides BU's resident contemporary music ensemble **Alea III** (1-617 353 3349) through its annual series of engrossing concerts featuring old and new music.

Boston Musica Viva (1-617 354 6910) director Richard Pittman schedules a balanced mix of 20th-century works from Prokofiev to Harbison, but the group's lifeblood is premières of new music, mainly by American composers.

David Hoose, music director of **Collage New Music** (1-617 325 5200), is one of the most respected contemporary conductors in Boston. In a typical four-concert season series, Collage performs a well-programmed mix of both established composers and world premières.

A collective of respected local composers and players were behind the founding of the group called **Dinosaur Annex** (1-617 482 3852), whose emphasis is on new works by artists like Charles Ives, Gyorgi Lyetti, and Judith Weir.

Schools

Boston University College of Fine Arts

855 Commonwealth Avenue, near Boston University Bridge, Brookline (1-617 353 3350). BU West T. **Open** *Box office* 9am-5pm Mon-Fri. **Tickets** free-$15. **Credit** AmEx, MC, V.

Free faculty recitals include performances by resident ensembles such as the Atlantic Brass Quintet, Muir String Quartet and Alea III. Student performances by the Boston University Opera Institute are also highly regarded.

New England Conservatory

290 Huntington Avenue, at Gainsborough Street, Fenway (1-617 585 1100/www.newengland conservatory.edu). Mass Ave T. **Open** *Box office* 9am-5pm Mon-Fri. **Tickets** free-$100. **Credit** Disc, MC, V. **Map** p276 F8.

The big daddy of Boston music schools, founded in 1867, boasts a $33-million endowment and credits itself with supplying 44% of the players of the BSO from its faculty. For the average concert-goer, that means a year-round calendar of excellent (and free) faculty and student recitals.

Comedy

Boston has a well-deserved reputation as a comedy hot spot. Janeane Garofalo, Jay Leno, and Conan O'Brien all tried out their acts here before they were famous. The laughs keep coming with popular comedy venues on both sides of the river.

Back Alley Theater

1253 Cambridge Street, at Inman Square, Cambridge (1-617 576 1253). Central T. **Open** 8pm-late Wed-Sat; 7pm-late Sun. **Admission** free-$12. **Credit** MC, V. **Map** p278 C2.

The ever-popular comedy group ImprovBoston always attracts a crowd as it whips up something off-the-cuff here every weekend.

Comedy Connection

Upstairs at Faneuil Hall, 15 State Street, at Congress Street, Downtown (1-617 248 9700). Government Center or State T. **Open** *Box office* 9am-10pm daily. **Admission** $12-$35. **Credit** AmEx, MC, V. **Map** p275 L4.

Whether your taste runs to Margaret Cho and Jay Mohr, or old standbys like Rita Rudner and Bobcat Goldthwait, you'll find your favourite comics stopping by this Faneuil Hall institution.

Comedy Studio

Hong Kong Restaurant, 1236 Massachusetts Avenue, at Bow Street, Cambridge (1-617 661 6507). Harvard T. **Open** from 8pm Thur-Sun. **Admission** $7-$10; $5 students (except Sat). **No credit cards**. **Map** p278 B3.

This dark bird's nest on the top floor of a Chinese restaurant is a haven for alternative comedy. It offers a wide variety of stand-up and sketch routines, and unpredictable humour including the popular 'Thursday Night Fights' – a comedy-debate series characterised by foul language and personal attacks.

Nick's Comedy Stop

100 Warrenton Street, at Stuart Street, Downtown (1-617 482 0930). Boylston T. **Open** 7pm-2am Thur-Sat. **Admission** $10-$14. **Credit** AmEx, MC, V. **Map** p277 J6.

A great place to catch tomorrow's big names. Or tomorrow's bartenders and waiters. At the longest running comedy venue in Boston, the headliners are often well-known faces from television, but up-and-comers get their shot (and hecklers) here too.

Sport & Fitness

It's all a game in this sports-mad city.

'Thank God we have the Patriots,' said one Boston sports fan recently, 'otherwise, we'd have to kill ourselves.' That about sums it up. This city is passionate about sports but, besides the New England Patriots football team, which has won two Super Bowls in three years, it seems doomed to mediocrity. The beloved Red Sox haven't won a baseball World Series since 1918, the year before they sold Babe Ruth to the New York Yankees and incurred 'the Curse of the Bambino' (*see p223* **Sox obsessed**). As for basketball, the Celtics – currently looking for a new coach after the last one had 'philosophical differences' with owner Danny Ainge – haven't won a championship since 1986 . And the Bruins haven't brought home ice hockey's Stanley Cup since Bobby Orr scored the cup-winning goal against the New York Rangers, in 1972. Still, Boston remains undaunted as one of the most face-painted, logo-wearing, sports-crazed cities in America.

Spectator sports

In addition to the beleaguered teams already mentioned, Boston also has a professional soccer team, the New England Revolution, but locals have yet to take to the game the rest of the world calls football. College sports are very popular too, especially Boston College football and basketball, and Boston University hockey. Harvard-Yale football games always draw a crowd, but mostly alumni. The **Head of the Charles Regatta** (*see p184*) in October is a big draw, attracting international crowds.

For local sporting information, look no further than the two daily newspapers, the *Boston Globe* and the *Boston Herald*. Both have nationally recognised sports sections that report on professional goings-on in great detail. The *Globe* also publishes daily listings of local and national television and radio coverage, and it has a free pro sports score information line (1-617 265 6600). Sports radio is also popular, particularly WEEI on 850 AM.

Baseball

'Cowboy Up!' This was the battle cry chanted in 2003, coined by Red Sox first baseman Kevin Millar, who defined it as acting bravely in the face of adversity. That year his team was supposed to go to the World Series, hoping to end an 85-year losing streak. What happened? They were beaten in the play-offs. By whom? The New York Yankees, of course, in a battle that included swearing, spitting and 72-year-old Yankees bench coach Don Zimmer charging Sox pitcher Pedro Martinez, who promptly threw the old man to the ground. Despite (or perhaps because of) the cursed, 'Yankees suck' mythology, even visitors continue to bow before the 'Green Monster' of historic Fenway Park. Once inside the stadium they'll drink warm, expensive beer and stuff their faces with the eponymous tasty tubular treat, the Fenway Frank. But what locals really crave is a taste of victory. The baseball season runs from April to October. Book early for a Red Sox-Yankees face-off – and choose your ball-cap wisely.

Fenway Park

Yawkey Way, Fenway (1-617 267 9440/booking line 1-877 733 7699/tours 1-617 236 6666/ www.redsox.com). Kenmore T. **Open** *Box office* 9am-5pm Mon-Fri & game days; 10am-2pm Sat. *Tours* 9am-4pm daily; game days 9am-3 hrs before game. **Tickets** *Game* $12-$75; *Tours* $8-10. **Credit** AmEx, Disc, MC, V. **Map** p267 D7.

Basketball

There was a time in the not-too-distant past when the **Celtics** were gods. Then Larry Bird retired in 1992 and the heavens closed. Bird's heir apparent, Len Bias, died of a cocaine overdose before he even had a chance to put on a uniform. After that tragedy, a promising all-star named Reggie Lewis died unexpectedly of a heart ailment. Then the beloved Boston Garden, which nurtured 16 championship-winning Celtics teams, was torn down and replaced with the sterile FleetCenter. Rick Pitino, once a respected coach at the University of Kentucky, was given the keys to the city in the hope that he might be able to turn things around. He didn't. In 2001 Jim O'Brien replaced him, but then he quit too. As this guide went to press, the Celtics had an interim coach and a roster full of almost-stars (Paul Pierce, Raef LaFrentz) slapped together in the hope that they would stick. A rebuilding year? More like a rebuilding era. But, hey, the entrance fee is well worth it just for a peek at Bird's No.33 jersey hanging from the rafters.

FleetCenter

1 Causeway Street, at Friend Street, Boston (1-617 624 1000/www.fleetcenter.com). North Station T. **Open** *Box office* 11am-7pm daily. **Tickets** $10-$150. **Credit** AmEx, DC, Disc, MC, V. **Map** p274 K2.

Football

Led by quarterback Tom Brady, the **New England Patriots** won the Super Bowl in 2002 and 2004, a double-whammy that has jubilant locals calling out 'Dynasty!' to pay homage to their position of power. And although a third victory is uncertain (the team is currently restructuring), the devotion of football-lovers remains unabated. The team's success has also spawned four cool superstars: besides the pin-up Brady, sweet girls and tough guys love cornerback Ty Law, linebacker Tedy Bruschi, and unlikely hero Adam Vinatieri. He's got the least glamorous position – field goal kicker – but he socked the game-winning score at the last minute in both Super Bowls. The man will never have to buy a drink in this town again. If you don't feel like travelling to the stadium in Foxborough (well outside of Boston in the suburbs), you can catch the excitement in one of Boston's many sports bars (one of the best is the **Rack**, 24 Clinton Street, Downtown, 1-617 725 1051).

Gillette Stadium

1 Patriot Place at Route 1, Foxborough (1-800 543 1776/Ticketmaster 1-617 931 2222). **Open** *Box office* 9am-5pm Mon-Fri. **Tickets** $49-$99. **Credit** AmEx, MC, V.

Ice hockey

Once known as the 'Big Bad **Bruins**', this team had a rough, fearless style of play that struck fear into the hearts of all who entered the rink. That was then; this is now. Coaches seem to get fired every year or two. Local players tell the newspapers it's 'impossible' to win a game. And there aren't as many fights in the stands since ticket prices have skyrocketed and the drunken yahoos of old can't afford to get in. Still, thanks to some nifty teamwork by captain Joe Thornton, things may turn around soon. Either way, Bruins games are enjoyable and the fans are great. Phone the FleetCenter (*see above*) for tickets, or look on www.bostonbruins.com. Tickets range from $19 to $99.

Sox obsessed

'Baseball is not a matter of life and death, but the Red Sox are,' said former *Globe* columnist Mike Barnacle. For Bostonians, it's true. You'll be hard pressed to find a male native of Boston who will not talk your ear off about the local baseball club – its history, its curse, its futility – and many female natives do the same.

How did a sports team come to dominate the dreams and nightmares of an entire region? If you've never seen a baseball game, you might wonder how this event that provides seven or eight minutes of action stretched over three hours can keep people awake, let alone ruin their lives. But the fascination goes beyond what's actually happening on the field. The game lives on myriad levels. There is today's outcome, the team's standing in the division, how much the other club is detested, each player's statistics, and how each statistic compares with the statistics of everyone who ever played. The lifeblood of baseball is numbers.

Yet to be a Red Sox fan is a special curse. Every Sox fan can tell you how long it has been since the club won the World Series – not since 1918, when Germany had a Kaiser and the Russian Tsar was alive. And, more importantly, when the Red Sox had the greatest player of all time, Babe Ruth. Owner Harry Frazee sold him to New York in 1919, and since then the Yankees have won 26 world titles and Boston none (before selling Ruth, the Red Sox were in five Word Series and won them all; since selling him, they have been in four and lost them all). Any fan can tell you where he or she was when Mookie Wilson's ground ball went through Bill Buckner's legs in the '86 World Series, when Bucky Dent's pop fly cleared the left field wall in the '78 play-off with the Yankees, how Jim Lonborg couldn't pitch on just two days' rest in '67... They are consumed by frustration and they don't keep it to themselves.

Then there is Fenway Park. Bostonians regard their attractive but outdated stadium as a shrine. The little brick venue in Kenmore Square embodies the magic of childhood, memories of hot summer days, the joy of hope and sorrows of love.

If you can wrangle a ticket, you'll partake of a quintessential Boston experience. As to understanding the action, any fan will be able to tell you more than you want to know.

Losing lineup: Can the **Red Sox** break the famous curse? *See p223.*

Soccer

The New England Revolution play in Gillette Stadium, also home to the New England Patriots, but the team doesn't enjoy anything close to the popularity of the US football team. In 2003 the Revolution were one goal away from the championships, yet despite their obvious talent you can almost always get a ticket ($16-$32). Phone the stadium for details (*see p223*) or check out the Revolution's website at www.revolutionsoccer.net.

Horse racing

Rockingham Park

Rockingham Park Boulevard, Salem, New Hampshire (1-603 898 2311/www.rockinghampark.com). **Open** *late May-early Sept* post time 1.05pm Wed, Fri, Sat, Sun; simulcast noon-midnight daily. **Admission** $2.50. **No credit cards.**

Although it's just over the border in New Hampshire, Rockingham Park is only a half-hour drive from Boston. Once host to Seabiscuit, the park offers simulcast horse racing from around the country as well as live races.

Suffolk Downs

111 Waldermar Avenue, at junction of routes 1A & 145, East Boston (1-617 567 3900). Suffolk Downs T. **Open** *May-Nov* post time 12.45pm Mon-Wed, Fri, Sat; simulcast noon-midnight daily. **Admission** $2-$4. **No credit cards.**

Live racing takes place on a seasonal basis, between May and November, but the track is open daily for simulcast racing.

Greyhound racing

Wonderland Greyhound Park

190 VFW Parkway, Revere (1-781 284 1300/www.wonderlandgreyhound.com). Wonderland T. **Open** post time 7.15pm Tue, Fri; 6pm Thur, Sat; 6.30pm Sun; simulcast noon-1.30am daily. **Admission** $2-$4. **No credit cards.**

Despite suffering from flagging interest in recent years, this 70-year-old institution still offers plenty in the way of interesting spectacles – in its stands as much as out on the track. Open seven days a week for live and/or simulcast racing.

Marathon running

The 107-year-old **Boston Marathon** takes place every April on Patriot's Day (a relatively obscure holiday marking Paul Revere's famous ride through the colonies warning that the British were coming). The city more or less shuts down on the day of the race to prepare for the arrival of more than 20,000 runners (a figure that doesn't include the number of unregistered runners who jump into the race) and tens of thousands of spectators. Great views of the runners can be had in the last four miles of the race. It finishes at Copley Square, but the area is

always mobbed. If you walk a mile or so from Copley you can cheer in the winners in slightly less crowded conditions (*see also p180*).

Active sports & fitness

The best cities to visit for active sports all have one thing in common: locals who get out there and make it look fun – whatever the time of year. Boston offers sports for all seasons, from ice-skating on the Common's Frog Pond in winter to rowing on the Charles River in summer. Even inclement weather is no obstacle to these rugged New Englanders as they head out running along the Charles or cycling along the Minuteman Bikeway.

GENERAL INFORMATION

Metro Sports magazine, a free regional publication available in most sports shops, publishes information about outdoor activities. *New England Runner*, $3.95, also available in sports stores, is an excellent resource for local road races and multi-sport events. The *Boston Globe* publishes activities listings on Saturdays, but it's not a comprehensive directory of weekend events. For sporting equipment or clothing, check out **Niketown** (200 Newbury Street, at Exeter Street, 1-617 267 3400) or **City Sports** (480 Boylston Street, between Berkeley & Clarendon Streets, 1-617 267 3900), a chain with several locations throughout the city.

Boating & sailing

Boston Harbor Sailing Club

58 Batterymarch Street, at Rowes Wharf, Downtown (1-617 720 0049/www.bostonharborsailing.com). Aquarium T. **Open** *May-Oct* 9am-8pm daily. **Rates** *Rental* $75-$417 per day. *Lessons* $769 per wk. *Skippered charter* $65-$184 per hr. **Credit** MC, V. **Map** p275 M4.

The BHSC is popular with locals, particularly college students, as it offers boat rentals for qualified sailors and one-on-one lessons for beginners.

Boston Sailing Center

54 Lewis Wharf, at Atlantic Avenue, Downtown (1-617 227 4198/www.bostonsailingcenter.com). Aquarium or Haymarket T. **Open** *Apr-Oct* 9am-sunset daily. **Rates** *Lessons* $720-$1,125 per wk. *Skippered charters* $110-$180 per hr. **Credit** MC, V. **Map** p275 M3.

Offers boat rentals, lessons or charters in which you can lean back and let someone else do the work

Charles River Canoe & Kayak

2401 Commonwealth Avenue, Newton (1-617 965 5110/www.ski-paddle.com). Riverside T. **Open** *Apr-Oct* 10am-sunset Mon-Fri; 9am-sunset Sat, Sun. **Rates** *Rental* $13-$18 per hr. **Credit** Disc, MC, V.

To join the hordes on the river in summer, rent a slim boat from the company's boathouse in Newton, or between May and October from its kiosk in Boston (Soldier's Field Road, upstream from the Eliot Bridge). Call the number above or visit the website for opening times.

Community Boating

21 David G Mugar Way, on the banks of the Charles River, between the Hatch Shell & the Longfellow Bridge, Back Bay (1-617 523 1038/www.community-boating.org). Charles/MGH T. **Open** *Apr-Oct* 1pm-sunset Mon-Fri, 9am-sunset Sat, Sun. **Rates** 2-day pass $100. **Credit** MC, V. **Map** p274 H4.

Offers boat rentals, but requires that customers have some level of boating experience.

Bowling

Massachusetts is famous for candlepin bowling, a variation of the game characterised by smaller balls and more pins. It may not sound exciting, but, as many venues serve up food, drink and other entertainment, it makes for a good, clean, fun night out.

Kings

10 Scotia Street, at Dalton Street, Back Bay (1-617 266 2695). Hynes/ICA T. **Open** 5pm-2am Mon-Thur; 11.30am-2am Fri-Sun. **Rates** $6.50 per person per game ($5.50 before 6pm); shoes $4. **Credit** AmEx, MC, V. **Map** p276 F7.

Want to bowl? Looking for billiards? Or maybe all you need from life is a damn good Mai Tai. Kings has it all in a slick nightclub setting – just come early and expect to wait in line.

Lucky Strike Lanes at Jillian's

145 Ipswich Street, at Lansdowne Street, Fenway. (1-617 437 0300/www.bowlluckystrike.com). Kenmore T. **Open** 11am-2am daily. **Rates** $5.95 per person per game ($4.50 before 5pm); shoes $3.50. **Credit** AmEx, MC, V. **Map** p276 E7.

This ten-pin bowling alley – or self-styled 'upscale bowling lounge' is located within the Jillian's entertainment complex. As if bowling weren't entertainment enough, there's also a wall-to-wall video screen showing the day's must-see sporting event, and others at the end of each of the 16 lanes showcasing artwork and cartoons by up-and-coming talent. Food is also available.

Milky Way Lounge & Lanes

403-405 Centre Street, at Perkins Street, Jamaica Plain (1-617 524 3740/www.milkywayjp.com). Stony Brook T then 15mins walk/39 bus then 5mins walk. **Open** 6pm-midnight Mon-Thur; 5pm-12.45am Fri, Sat; 5-11pm Sun. **Rates** $25 per hr per lane; after 8pm there may be an additional cover charge. **Credit** AmEx, MC, V.

With its packed programme of live bands and DJs, cocktail bar and restaurant as well as its original 1950s candlepin lanes, you might forget that you came to the retro-style Milky Way to bowl.

Sacco's Bowl Haven

45 Day Street, at Davis Square, Somerville (1-617 776 0552). Davis T. **Open** 9am-11.30pm Mon-Fri; 10am-11.30pm Sat; noon-11.30pm Sun. **Rates** $2.50 per person per game ($2.25 before 5pm); shoes $1. **No credit cards**.

Sacco's Bowl Haven attracts a mix of blue-collar types and urban hipsters to its 15 candlepin lanes – especially after 9pm for the black-light extravaganza (set to chart music) that's de rigueur in American alleys on weekend nights.

Cycling & mountain biking

Let's face it, cyclists aren't the most popular people in most cities. But in Boston, they fight for their rights. **Critical Mass** (www.boston criticalmass.org) aims to provide safety in numbers for urban cyclists. On the last Friday of the month at 5.30pm, a huge group departs from Copley Square, taking over the streets and forcibly holding up motorised traffic.

Designated trails in and around Boston keep cyclists off the road and also provide an escape route from the city's congestion. **Pierre Lallement Bike Path** runs parallel to the Orange Line. The four-mile (six-kilometre) stretch runs through the Southwest Corridor Park from Copley Place to Franklin Park. The **Paul Dudley White Charles River Bike Path** is an 18-mile (29-kilometre) stretch between the Science Museum and Watertown. The **Minuteman Bikeway** (www.minute manbikeway.org) offers cyclists an 11-mile (18-kilometre) ride from Alewife or Davis T to Lexington and Bedford. Mountain-bikers should make for the lush and lovely **Blue Hills Reservation** – 7,000 acres (2, 800 hectares) spread through Quincy, Dedham, Milton and Randolph, south of the city. There are 125 miles of trails, some designated for mountain biking, some for pedestrians only. Stop at the park office at 695 Hillside Street, Milton (1-617 698 1802), for mountain-bike maps. For more information on all of the paths listed above, visit www.state.ma.us/mdc/activ.htm.

The MBTA allows bikes on the Commuter Rail, Blue, Orange and Red lines at no extra charge in off-peak hours. See www.mbta.com/traveling_t/usingthet_bikes.asp for the rules.

For bike rentals in Boston, try **Community Bicycle Supply** in the South End (496 Tremont Street, 1-617 542 8623), or **Back Bay Bicycles** (366 Commonwealth Avenue, 1-617 247 2336). In Cambridge, there's **Cambridge Bicycle** (259 Massachusetts Avenue, Cambridge, 1-617 876 6555), which also stocks *Ride*, a locally produced 'zine chronicling the New England bike-racing scene.

Fitness centres & gyms

There are over 150 fitness centres and gyms in Boston, with a wide array of workout options, but for insurance purposes, many don't accept drop-ins. Here's a sampling that does.

Boston Body

6th Floor, 8 Newbury Street, at Arlington Street, Back Bay (1-617 262 3333/www.bostonbody.com). Arlington T. **Open** 8am-8.30pm Mon-Thur; 8am-3pm Fri; 8am-12.30pm Sat. **Rates** $89 1mth membership; $20 drop-in fee. **Credit** AmEx, MC, V. **Map** p277 H5.

Specialising in yoga and pilates for all levels, Boston Body offers private training and group classes. If you prefer to chill out instead of work out, book in for a healing treatment such as Thai massage.

Other location: 46 Austin Street, Newton, 1-617 969 2673.

Boston Sport Boxing Club

125 Walnut Street, at Cypress Street, Watertown (1-617 972 1711/www.bostonboxing.com). Harvard T then 71 bus. **Open** 4-11pm Mon-Thur; 4-9pm Fri; noon-5pm Sat. **Rates** $10 drop-in fee (call first). **No credit cards.**

The only full-time Olympic training centre in New England. Don't be put off by its professional credentials – the club attracts all types, levels and age groups. After working your way through circuit training, getting into the ring and sparring is optional.

Metropolitan Fitness

209 Columbus Avenue, at Berkeley Street, Back Bay (1-617 536 3006/www.bostonfitness.com). Back Bay T. **Open** 5.30am-11pm Mon-Wed; 5.30am-10pm Thur, Fri; 8am-8pm Sat; 9am-8pm Sun. **Rates** *Membership* $75 mth; $45 2wks; $30 1wk; $15 day pass. **Credit** AmEx, Disc, MC, V. **Map** p277 H6.

Metropolitan Fitness offers a wide array of workout options, including yoga, aerobics and kickboxing classes and a full gym.

Healthworks Fitness Center for Women

441 Stuart Street, at Dartmouth Street, Back Bay (1-617 859 7700/www.healthworksfitness.com). Back Bay or Copley T. **Open** 5.30am-10pm Mon-Fri; 7.30am-8pm Sat, Sun. **Rates** $20 drop-in fee. **Credit** MC, V. **Map** p277 H6.

If you're a woman who'd rather not shake, rattle and roll in the presence of the opposite sex, this gym's the place for you. As well as the usual workout facilities, classes (aerobics, step, pilates) and personal training, Healthworks also offers a spa, crèche, consultations on nutrition, massage, and pre- and post-natal fitness.

Other locations: 920 Commonwealth Avenue, Brookline, 617-731-3030; 36 White Street, Porter Square, Cambridge 1-617 497-4454; 1300 Boylston Street, Chestnut Hill, 1-617 383-6100.

Golf

Looking to swing a few? No problem. The following are public courses.

Fresh Pond Golf Course

691 Huron Avenue, at Fresh Pond Parkway, Cambridge (1-617 349 6282/www.freshpond golf.com). Alewife T. **Open** *Apr-Nov* dawn-dusk daily. **Rates** $19-$36; clubs $20. **Credit** MC, V.

Leo J Martin Memorial Golf Course

190 Park Road, Weston (1-781 894 4903/ www.state.ma.us/mcd/ljmartin.htm). Riverside T. **Open** *Apr-Nov* dawn-dusk daily. **Rates** $17-$25; clubs $15. **Credit** Disc, MC, V.

Newton Commonwealth Golf Course

212 Kenrick Street, Newton (1-617 630 1971/ www.sterlinggolf.com/newton). Boston College T. **Open** *Apr-Nov* dawn-dusk daily. **Rates** $18-$30; clubs $12. **Credit** AmEx, MC, V.

Putterham Meadows Golf Course

1281 West Roxbury Parkway, Brookline (1-617 730 2078). Chestnut Hill T. **Open** *Apr-Nov* dawn-dusk daily. **Rates** $31-$39; clubs $24. **Credit** AmEx, MC, V.

Franklin Park/William J Devine Golf Course

Franklin Park, 1 Circuit Drive, Dorchester (1-617 265 4084). Forest Hills T then 16 bus. **Open** 8am-5pm Mon-Fri; 7am-5pm Sat, Sun. **Rates** $16-$34; clubs $12. **Credit** AmEx, Disc, MC, V.

In-line skating

If you like to skate, you've come to the right place. Boston and nearby cities offer a plethora of paved trails and roadways for the inveterate eight-wheeler. Both novices and experienced skaters should check out the **Paul Dudley White Charles River Bike Path** or the **Minuteman Bikeway** *(see p226* **Cycling & mountain biking**). If you want to get in a good workout, hit the trail before 10am on sunny weekend mornings, otherwise you'll run into major traffic in the form of all the other runners, walkers, skaters and bikers with the same idea. Visit the InLine Club of Boston's website for details of more places to skate, plus races and events (www.sk8net.com).

If you want to hire or buy blades, try the **Beacon Hill Skate Shop** (135 South Charles Street, 1-617 482 7400), which, despite its name, is actually in the South End.

Polo

For those looking for a taste of sporting action combined with high-class tailgating, a trip to the **Myopia Polo Grounds** in Hamilton, Massachusetts, is a must. Polo matches are held every Sunday at 3pm (gates open at 1.30pm) throughout the summer and tickets cost $10. Call 1-978 468 7656 for details.

Pool & billiards

It's not uncommon to find a pool table plonked in the middle (or off to one corner) of a Boston bar. But focused players should cue up at **Big**

City (138 Brighton Avenue, 1-617 782 2020), the **Boston Billiard Club** (126 Brookline Avenue, 1-617 536 7665, www.bostonbilliardclub.com), and **Flat Top Johnny's** in Cambridge (1 Kendall Square, 1-617 494 9565, www.flattop johnnys.com). Those looking for a no-frills billiards experience (or who have automotive trouble) should try **Allston's Sully's Billiards**, located directly upstairs from Sully's Service Garage (445 Cambridge Street, 1-617 254 9851). The more fashion-conscious might want to head for **Felt** (533 Washington Street, 1-617 350 5555, www.feltboston.com), a club/restaurant where black-clad NYC-wannabes rack 'em up while enjoying a sesame seared salmon fillet.

Running

Local runners flock to the **Minuteman Bike Path** and the **Paul Dudley White Charles River Bike Path** on the weekend for long runs (*see p226* **Cycling & mountain biking**). A bonus of the Minuteman is that miles are marked on the path. Memorial Drive, the major road along the river in Cambridge, is closed to traffic between 11am and 6pm on Sundays from mid April to mid November, making it a great place to run, skate or cycle. Check out www.cambridgerunning.org for information on paths and the opportunity to meet up with others for Saturday runs.

Further afield, check out the trails in the three-square-mile (eight-square-kilmometre) **Middlesex Fells Reservation** (off Route 28 in Malden, Medford, Stoneham and Winchester, 1-781 322 2851, www.state.ma.us/mdc/fells.htm).

Skateboarding

With its cobblestone streets, cracked sidewalks and numerous handrails, stairs, curb cuts and ledges all concentrated within a small space, Boston is a great place to skateboard. In addition to the specially designated skateboard park in the suburbs listed below, the Metropolitan District Commission (MDC) playground in Brighton (between Soldiers Field Road and the Charles River) features rolling concrete banks and other great obstacles. The area in front of the Boston Medical Center (near the intersection of Massachusetts and Harrison Avenues) has enormous curved brick banks that attract skateboarders from all over the city, and the Christian Science Plaza on Huntington Avenue (*see p78*) is another good spot.

Messina Brothers Skateboard Park

John LeRoy Drive, at Braintree High School off Route 37, Braintree (1-781 794 8910). Braintree T then 236 bus.

For an old-school experience, hit Messina Brothers' 5,000 square feet (465 square metres) of asphalt with concrete ramps. You'll need to be dedicated though, as it's not the easiest (or quickest) place to get to.

Skiing

Aficionados of the sport have been known to make fun of New England skiing, with its rocky trails and slushy snow, but there is some good downhill action to be had in the northern states. In the last decade most New England resorts – including the big ones, **Killington**, **Sunday River** and **Sugarbush** – have brought the art of snow-making to a new level. In other words, as long as the temperature cooperates, there will be snow to ski on, regardless of snowfall. For a day's (or better a weekend's) excursion, zip up Route 93 North to Loon Mountain on the Kancamagus Highway or to Cannon Mountain in the Franconia Notch Parkway, both in nearby New Hampshire.

For those who can't afford to stray far from the city, try the **Blue Hills** (4001 Washington Street, Canton, 1-781 828 5070, www.thenew bluehills.com). It's not the most challenging terrain and snow conditions are entirely dependent on the weather, but it's just a 20-minute drive from Boston.

The **Ski Market** (860 Commonwealth Avenue, near Boston University Bridge, 1-617 731 6100) not only sells all sorts of ski and snowboard gear, but can be used as a resource for New England skiing and local events.

Swimming

When it comes down to it, your best swimming bet may well be your hotel pool. However, the Metropolitan District Commission operates all the public pools in the Boston area. These are open daily from late June to early September. Call 1-617 727 1300 to find the location of your nearest pool, or go to www.state.ma.us/mdc/ activ.htm and select 'pools'.

Tennis

Although most tennis playing in Boston takes place in members-only clubs, there are nearly 60 public tennis courts in the Boston area. Most of these are available on a first-come, first-served basis; some are lit, others aren't, and there's an unspoken understanding that players shouldn't monopolise courts for more than an hour. The Metropolitan District Commission runs a number of these. The most centrally located court is on **Boston Common**, on Beacon Street. For a list of other courts, visit the MDC's website (*see above* **Swimming**).

Trips Out of Town

Features

Colonial Villages

The picture-postcard settings that spawned a superpower.

Not everyone wears period garb in the **Minuteman National Historical Park**. *See p231.*

Thanksgiving turkeys, Minutemen, witches… Colonial New England conjures up certain stock images. And, as scores of tours, museums and monuments attest, the historical events that played out here – the Pilgrims' arrival at **Plymouth**, the Revolutionary War in **Lexington** and **Concord**, the witch trials in **Salem** – have had a profound and indelible impact on the area's identity. But there's more going on here than the occasional historical re-enactment. These villages are shaped as much by their backgrounds in industry and the arts as their involvement in American history. Concord and Lexington offer postcard images of pastoral scenery: roadside farms, apple orchards, town greens anchored by gleaming-white churches. The former mill towns have fostered a progressive genius in the many famous writers and social activists who have lived here. To the north, the seaside town of Salem appears to have repressed its vengeful puritanical spirit; today, the narrow cobbled streets, briny Atlantic breezes and excellent museums make it an appealing stop. And once you've exhausted the Pilgrim and Mayflower nostalgia in Plymouth, the South Shore beaches offer ample opportunity for relaxation.

Concord & Lexington

Concord and Lexington, neighbouring towns about half an hour west of Boston, are known as the battleground of American independence. The villages enjoy a friendly rivalry over who hosted the first rumblings of revolution; Lexington can claim the first shot, but Concord entertained the first fight. In fact, the first true battle in the American Revolution started in Lexington and ended in Concord, thus forever combining the two in the minds of many. It all began, in 1774, when the Provincial Congress delegated a division of elite militia soldiers known as the Minutemen. They were authorised to form 'for defence only'. But the Minutemen, in anticipation of future battles, had begun stockpiling weapons in the village of Concord. British generals caught word of the arsenal and sent 700 troops to make the 25-mile journey from Boston to Concord. Alerted by a trio of rebels (Paul Revere among them) sent on horseback, 77 Minutemen met the troops at Lexington Green. When the British soldiers arrived they ordered the Americans to drop their weapons. The colonists refused – and a battle began. During that first struggle, 18 Minutemen were killed or wounded, while not a single British soldier was injured. Emboldened by their victory, the British didn't stop to rest, but marched on to Concord where, unbeknown to them, more militia were marshalling. As the American troops awaited the Redcoats' arrival outside Concord, they spotted smoke rising from the town. Convinced that the British were burning their homes, they attacked a British patrol sent out to hold the Old North Bridge. It is said that the colonial troops were so enraged that Captain John Parker told the militia: 'Stand your ground. Don't fire unless fired upon, but if they mean to have a war, let it begin here!' And so it did. Two Americans and 11 British soldiers were killed there. With that, the war began in earnest (*see p9*).

With so many narrative placards and memorial statues, tourism is big business indeed. All the major sights of **Lexington** centre on **Lexington Green**, the triangular plot upon which the battle occurred. Today it is anchored by the **Minuteman Statue** and dotted with other markers and memorials. The statue is of Captain Parker, his famous quote engraved under his feet. Turning right as you come out of the green you'll see the yellow colonial house known as **Buckman Tavern**. Here the Minutemen assembled to await the arrival of British troops; they later used it as a field hospital. The tavern, one of the oldest buildings in the area, was already 85 years old at the time of the battle. Today it is staffed by knowledgeable young guides in period costume. The high bar counter is said to have been set at this level to prevent under-age drinking: if a boy's chin wasn't above the bar, he couldn't buy a beer. The tavern keepers tracked the sales of pints and quarts by chalking them up behind the bar, giving rise to the expression 'mind your Ps and Qs'.

Just behind the tavern is the small but perfectly informed **Lexington Visitors' Center**, which has a diorama outlining all the particulars of the battle. It also offers tours of the town's historically significant houses.

North of the green, on Hancock Street, sits the **Hancock-Clarke House**. On the night of the battle, largely by coincidence, rebels Samuel Adams and John Hancock were spending the night here, as guests of the owner, Rev Jonas Clarke. In the end, Revere awoke them in time, and they were hustled out of town to safety. He did not, however, warn the soldiers at Concord, as he was captured by the British. Today, the Hancock-Clarke house contains a permanent collection of the furnishings and paintings owned by the two families, as well as relics of that night in April 1775. About a mile east of the green is the **Munroe Tavern**. It was here that the British troops retreating from Concord stopped to rest and treat their injured, shooting the bartender who tried to flee after serving them. George Washington tried to redeem the bar's reputation by visiting it after the war, and several artefacts related to his stay are kept here today. Further along, at the intersection of Mass Avenue and Marrett Road, is the modern brick building that houses the **National Heritage Museum**. Colonial farm tools and Freemason propaganda mingle with rock concert posters and baseball memorabilia, making it a breezy respite from the rest of the area's emphatically colonial history.

Four miles (6.5 kilometres) from Lexington down Route 62 is the village of **Concord**. As well as playing a major role in the War of Independence, Concord is distinguished by its place in American letters. Ralph Waldo Emerson, Henry David Thoreau, Louisa May Alcott and Nathaniel Hawthorne all lived here at various points, and within a few short blocks, you'll find a group of houses that once contained an unparalleled flowering of American literary genius. But the first sites most visitors feel obliged to see are tied in to the country's earliest days. The most significant is the **Minuteman National Historical Park**, which marks the spot where the Battle of Concord took place after the British marched on victorious from Lexington. Once inside the park it's best to start at the **North Bridge Visitors' Center**, set on a hill overlooking the bridge and the Concord River. Inside there is a diorama alongside a collection of Revolutionary War memorabilia, including uniforms, weapons and tools from both sides of the battle. The helpful park rangers at the centre provide guided tours of the site. From there, it's just a short walk to the reconstruction of the **North Bridge**, where the 'shot heard around the world' was fired. It's worth stopping along the way to listen to recordings that tell the story of the battle and the area. The **Battle Road Trail** is a five-mile stretch that connects many of the park's points of interest.

Essayist and philosopher Ralph Waldo Emerson lived in two houses in town, but his primary residence was at what is now known as **Ralph Waldo Emerson House**. He lived here with his family from 1835 until his death in 1882; while he was on tour in Europe, his friend and fellow Transcendentalist Henry

Back to nature

One of the great things about Boston is the fact that it takes no time at all to escape from it. Within a half-hour (traffic permitting), you can drive to these attractive country trails, stretch your legs, breathe fresh air and get some idea of what the Transcendentalists were up to when they sought spiritual enlightenment in nature.

The **Great Meadows National Wildlife Refuge** (1-978 443 4661, http://easternmanwrcomplex.fws.gov) is a 3,600-acre (1,457-hectare) parcel of freshwater wetlands in Concord, offering some of the most serene landscapes in a region famous for them. Great Meadows teems with life: white-tail deer, cottontail rabbits, red fox and more than 220 species of birds. The sanctuary has several excellent trails to choose from, depending on your mood, time frame, and level of ambition. The Dike Path, a 2.7-mile (4.5km) loop in the Concord section of the park, is a fairly easy starting point. Long and flat, the trail runs along a glassy marsh pool lined with cattails, and the path is strewn with benches and helpful signs detailing the local wildlife, which is best viewed at dawn or dusk. **Getting there**: take Route 2 West for about ten miles (16km), following signs to Concord Center. Bear right onto Main Street, and turn left on to Route 62 East. After 1.5 miles (2.5km), turn left on to Monsen Road and follow signs for the refuge. About 30 minutes west of Boston.

The **Great Blue Hill** in Milton is the highest peak in eastern Massachusetts. At 635 feet (193 metres), it doesn't break any records, but at least you can conquer it in the course of an afternoon. The ascent takes roughly an hour, and cuts through rocky, wooded turf (this may sound intimidating, but it's easy enough for children). The observation deck at the summit yields spectacular panoramic views of the city. At the base of the hill, the Trailside Museum (1-617 698 1802) has several exhibits on local Native American history, as well as a small zoo of local creatures, including otters, owls and deer. **Getting there**: take Route I-93 South to Exit 2B for Route 138 North. Follow 138 North until signs for the Trailside Museum appear on the right. It's 15 minutes south of Boston.

According to local lore, the **Breakheart Reservation** (1-781 233 0834) in Saugus got its name during the Civil War, when soldiers training here were devastated by its isolation. Today the park's removal from civilisation is considered a major draw, and its network of woodland trails attracts thousands of visitors each year. The paved Saugus River path is short but sweet; though its steep hills can seem gruelling, all is forgiven at the top, where you can see all the way to New Hampshire on a clear day. Hikers looking for a real challenge should investigate the Ridge Trail, an invigorating series of ups and downs that culminate at Castle Rock, a granite outcrop. **Getting there**: From the I-93 in Boston, take exit 27 to Route 1 North. Take the exit for Lynn Fells Parkway, then follow signs to the park entrance at Forest Street. The journey is about 20 minutes.

Known as 'The Fells', **Middlesex Fells Reservation** (1-781 332 2851) in Stoneham/Winchester contains several types of terrain: forest, wetlands, meadows and jagged hills. Though the entire park is blessed with stunning scenery, its eastern section generally has fewer visitors than its western counterpart. The Rock Circuit Trail is a terrific, moderately challenging hike, marked by a series of small craggy hills that afford the occasional glimpse of downtown Boston; amateur rock climbers often use them for bouldering practice. On the western side, a short walk along Bear Hill Trail brings you to its 317-foot (97 metre) observation tower, which gives an awesome perspective on the reservation's blanket of oak and hemlock trees. **Getting there**: take I-93 North to exit 33 (Route 28 North). At the roundabout, take South Border Road to the Bellevue Pond entrance. Allow 20 minutes from Boston.

David Thoreau kept house. It contains original furnishings and many of Emerson's belongings. Another Emerson residence is the **Old Manse**, built by his grandfather, Reverend William Emerson, in 1770. Both RW Emerson and Nathaniel Hawthorne lived here at different times; RW with his wife from 1842 to 1847, and many of their personal effects are on display. Hawthorne's stories inspired by his time here brought him his earliest fame. Not far away is **Orchard House**, which once was home to the educator Bronson Alcott, another prominent Transcendentalist. However, its best-known resident was his daughter, Louisa May Alcott. Her *Little Women* was both written about and set at Orchard House. The house, filled with the family's effects, attracts thousands of fans of the book every year. A ticket includes a highly detailed tour. LM Alcott also lived at **The Wayside**, a neighbouring residence where, coincidentally, Hawthorne later came to spend his final years. The **Concord Museum**, built on the site of Emerson's orchard, contains a tidy collection of local relics, including the largest collection of Thoreau's belongings. The most famous possession is one of the lanterns that was hung in the Old North Church on the night of Paul Revere's famous ride, to signal the approach of British troops.

From the nearby town square, you can catch a glimpse of the steep embankment of **Sleepy Hollow Cemetery** on Bedford Street, the eternal home of Concord's most celebrated writers-in-residence. At the top of a hill, under the shade of enormous maple trees, lie the graves of Emerson, Thoreau, Alcott and Hawthorne. It's an especially apt tableau for Thoreau and Emerson, the naturalists who drew inspiration for their work from the serenity of Concord's landscape. Thoreau's best-known muse, though, lies just south of town. At **Walden Pond**, in a one-room cabin off Route 126, he lived in rustic meditation for a year or so from 1846. He wrote the ground-breaking essay *Walden* about the experience, but fame only came with *Civil Disobedience* three years later. The house in which Thoreau sought his simple life is long since gone – a pile of stones marks the spot – but the well-preserved **Walden Pond State Reservation** affords the kind of swimming and hiking the native seer advocated. A full-size replica of the original cabin, with painstakingly reproduced furnishings, is open to visitors. In summer, the pond's wooded banks can become quite crowded with Bostonians hoping to cool off.

Buckman Tavern

1 Bedford Street, Lexington (1-781 862 5598). **Open** *Apr-Nov* 10am-5pm Mon-Sat; noon-5pm Sun. **Admission** $5; $3 concessions. **Credit** MC, V.

Concord Museum

200 Lexington Road, Concord (1-978 369 9763). **Open** *Jan-Mar* 11am-4pm Mon-Sat; 1-4pm Sun. *Apr, May, Sept-Dec* 9am-5pm Mon-Sat; noon-5pm Sun. *June-Aug* 9am-5pm daily. **Admission** $8; $5-$7 concessions. **Credit** AmEx, MC, V.

Hancock-Clarke House

36 Hancock Street, Lexington (1-781 862 1703). **Open** *Mar-Oct* 10am-4.30pm daily. **Admission** $4; $2 concessions. **No credit cards**.

Minuteman National Historical Park

Lexington Green, off Route 2A, Lexington (1-781 674 1920/www.nps.gov/mima). **Open** *June-Sept* 9am-5.30pm daily. *Oct-May* 9am-4pm daily. **Admission** free.

Munroe Tavern

1332 Massachusetts Avenue, Lexington (1-781 862 1703). **Open** *Mar-Oct* 10am-4.30pm daily. **Admission** $4; $2 concessions. **No credit cards**.

Old Manse

269 Monument Street, Concord (1-978 369 3909). **Open** *Mid Apr-Oct* 10am-5pm (last tour 4.30pm) Mon-Sat; noon-5pm Sun. **Admission** $8; $5-$7 concessions. **Credit** AmEx, Disc, MC, V.

Orchard House

399 Lexington Road, Concord (1-978 369 4118). **Open** *Apr-Oct* 10am-4.30pm Mon-Sat; 1-4.30pm Sun. *Nov-Mar* 11am-3pm Mon-Fri; 10am-4.30pm Sat; 1-4.30pm Sun. **Admission** $8; $7-$5 concessions. **Credit** MC, V.

Ralph Waldo Emerson House

28 Cambridge Turnpike, Concord (1-978 369 2236). **Open** *Apr-Oct* 10am-4.30pm Thur-Sat; 1-4.30pm Sun. **Admission** $7; $5 concessions. **No credit cards**.

North Bridge. *See p231.*

Walden Pond State Reservation

915 Walden Street, Concord (1-978 369 3254/ www.state.ma.us/dem/parks/wldn.htm). **Open** 8am-5pm daily. **Admission** free.

The Wayside

455 Lexington Road, Concord (1-978 318 7825/ www.nps.gov/mima/wayside). **Open** *tours mid May-Oct* 2pm, 4pm Tue, Thur; 11am, 1.30pm, 3pm, 4.30pm Sat, Sun. **Admission** $4. **No credit cards**.

Where to stay

Concord has two historic inns: the 19th-century **Hawthorne** (462 Lexington Road, 1-978 369 5610, www.concordmass.com, $125-$265) and the 18th-century **Colonial Inn** (48 Monument Square, 1-978 369 9200, www.concordscolonial inn.com, $165-$250), which occupies a prime spot on the square and houses a well-received restaurant. For something a bit more intimate, the **North Bridge Inn** (21 Monument Square, 1-978 371 0014, ww.northbridgeinn.com, $165-$250) has six suites of various sizes. The **Battle Green Inn** (1720 Massachusetts Avenue, 1-781 862 3100, www.battlegreen inn.com, $79-$109) in Lexington, though unremarkable in appearance, offers pleasant, competitively priced rooms.

Getting there

By car

Lexington is nine miles (14.5km) north-west of Boston on Route 128 (I-95). Concord is 18 miles (30km) north-west of Boston and six miles (9.5km) west of Lexington. Take Route 2A from Lexington, or Route 2 from Boston.

By bus or rail

The MBTA Commuter Rail (*see pp248-249*) service covers both towns, Lexington by bus only, Concord by train only. Awkwardly, there is no public transport connection between the two. Both services leave from Boston's North Station.

Tourist information

Lexington Visitors' Center

Lexington Green, 1875 Massachusetts Avenue, Lexington (1-781 862 1450). **Open** 9am-5pm daily.

Minuteman National Historical Park Visitors' Center

Lexington Green, off Route 2A, Lexington (1-781 674 1920/www.nps.gov/mima). **Open** *June-Sept* 9am-5pm daily. *Oct-May* 9am-4pm daily.

North Bridge Visitors' Center

174 Liberty Street, off Monument Street, Concord (1-978 369 6993/www.nps.gov/mima). **Open** 9am-5pm daily.

Salem

There are few American towns with reputations as dark as that of Salem. While there is more to its history than the notorious Salem Witch Trials of 1692, the mass hysteria that consumed the town during seven months of that year still casts a pall on its name. According to lore, Tituba, an Arawak maid who practised voodoo, turned the interest of a group of repressed young Puritan girls towards magic and mystery, with devastating results; other stories attribute their behaviour to adolescent hysteria, or even ergot poisoning. The tragic conclusion of it all, the executions of more than 20 people – mostly elderly women – means that Salem's name will be forever linked with madness (*see p236* **Live at the witch trials**).

The contemporary residents, however, have managed to turn a black mark into both a local industry and a curious point of pride – or at least an identity. The city's police cars and its local newspaper sport caricatures of a witch's profile as their logos. In addition, the local high school calls its football team the Witches. Black magic associations aside, Salem is a lovely place. It has a slightly split personality: one side of it is darkly colonial, with red-brick buildings and cemeteries dating back to its earliest days, but it's also a beach town, with a brisk fishing trade and colourful summer houses by the coast. The colonial section makes a good starting point in terms of chronology because you move towards the more modern buildings as you get nearer the water.

Though Salem is small, it is sprawling enough to make getting from one end to the other a bit of a hike, but walking really is the best way to get around. Not surprisingly, Salem is overrun with witchcraft-related attractions, many of them closer to Hallowe'en spectacles than actual historical points of interest. The few sites worth investigating are mostly scattered around Salem Common, a scenic park in the middle of the oldest section of town. The **Witch House**, also known as the Jonathan Corwin House after the former inhabitant and witch trial judge, was where the 200 or more unfortunates suspected of witchcraft were questioned. The house is truly spooky, though probably more for its dearth of windows than for its ominous pedigree. The **Salem Wax Museum** displays re-creations of the characters involved in the trials. Nearby, and the best of the lot, the **Salem Witch Museum** features a very thorough (and even somewhat scary) mixed-media re-enactment of the Puritan hysteria. There's also a refreshingly enlightened exhibit on modern-day 'witches', including pagans and Wiccans.

Old downtown Salem is a National Historic District and site of architectural interest. Along Chestnut Street Samuel McIntyre, a native of Salem and a pioneer of the American Federalist style, designed a number of houses. In the heart of the area is the **Peabody Essex Museum**, an exceptional resource for international art and culture. Founded by the East India Maritime Company in the late 18th century, when Salem dominated the shipping trade to China, the Peabody collection documents the history of whaling and merchant shipping, and features an extensive collection of exhibits from sailors' travels. Renovations have recently brought several new galleries and exhibits, including Yin Yu Tang, a spectacular Qing dynasty merchant's house which was shipped over and reassembled in partnership with the Chinese government.

Salem's seafaring past is on display aboard the **Friendship**, a full-scale replica of a three-masted 1797 East India merchant ship. It is docked at the end of Derby Street, amid the nine-acre (3.6-hectare) **Salem Maritime National Historic Site**, which offers tours of reconstructions of wharves, warehouses and stores, as well as the old Customs House where Nathaniel Hawthorne worked before he wrote *The Scarlet Letter*. Salem's most famous son, Hawthorne took the inspiration for his other great novel from the **House of the Seven Gables**. It's an extraordinary building, large and gloomy, with a peaked roof and turrets, the former home of Hawthorne's cousin. Built in 1668, it is filled with period furniture, much of which is described in the book of the same name. Tours include Hawthorne's birthplace, which has since been moved to the grounds.

House of the Seven Gables

54 Turner Street, at Derby Street, Salem (1-978 744 0991). **Open** 10am-5pm Mon-Sat; noon-5pm Sun. **Admission** $11; $7.25 concessions. **Credit** AmEx, Disc, MC, V.

Peabody Essex Museum

East India Square, at Liberty Street, Salem (1-978 745 9500/1-866 745 1876/www.pem.org). **Open** 10am-5pm daily. **Admission** $13; $9-$11 concessions. **Credit** AmEx, Disc, MC, V.

Salem Maritime National Historic Site

174 Derby Street (1-978 740 1660/www.nps.gov/sama). **Open** 9am-5pm daily. **Admission** *tours* $5; $3 concessions. **No credit cards**.

Salem Wax Museum

288 Derby Street (1-978 740 2929/www.salemwaxmuseum.com). **Open** *July, Aug* 10am-10pm daily. *Sept-June* 10am-6pm daily. **Admission** $6; $4 concessions. **Credit** Disc, MC, V.

Salem Witch Museum

19½ Washington Square North, at Route 1A (1-978 744 1692/www.salemwitchmuseum.com). **Open** 10am-5pm daily. **Admission** $6.50; $4.50 concessions. **Credit** Disc, MC, V.

Witch House

310 Essex Street, at North Street (1-978 744 8815). **Open** *May-Nov* 10am-5pm daily. **Admission** $7; $4-$6 concessions. **Credit** MC, V.

Where to stay & eat

Salem offers fairly extensive dining options; the best bet is **Grape Vine** (26 Congress Street, 1-978 745 9335), a funky, well-priced New-American bistro facing Pickering Wharf. For something more upscale, try **Lyceum Bar & Grill** (43 Church Street, 1-978 745 7665); housed in the building where Alexander Graham Bell conducted his early telephone experiments, it offers contemporary American cuisine in refined surroundings.

Local lodging features a range of colourful possibilities. Aside from the usual chains, there are several historic choices. One is the **Salem Inn** (7 Summer Street, 1-800 446 2995, www.saleminnma.com, $129-$295), a complex of three 19th-century houses, all of which are on the National Register of Historic Places. Another is the **Hawthorne Hotel** (18 Washington Square West, 1-978 744 4080, www.hawthornehotel.com, $104-$285), which is nicely furnished, close to the sights and reasonably priced. Although not as old as its name would suggest, it offers a full hotel service in a grand manner. Cheaper still, a little further off the common, the **Amelia Payson** B&B (16 Winter Street, 1-978 744 8304, www. ameliapaysonhouse.com, $95-$155) is an 1845 Greek Revival structure with a piano in the parlour. The **Coach House Inn** (284 Lafayette Street, 1-800 688 8689, www.coachhousesalem.com, $105-$205), a 19th-century captain's mansion, is an elegant choice.

Getting there

By car

Salem is 16 miles (26km) north of Boston. Take Route I-95 North to Route 128 North, then Route 114 East into Salem. The journey takes about 30 minutes.

By rail

The journey by rail takes half an hour by MBTA Commuter Rail (*see pp248-249*) out of North Station.

Tourist information

Salem National Visitors' Center

2 New Liberty Street, Salem (1-978 740 1650). **Open** 9am-5pm daily.

Live at the witch trials

'An Army of Devils is horribly broke in upon the place which is our centre.' So wrote the Puritan preacher Cotton Mather in July 1692 as the madness that became known as the Salem Witch Trials swept through the village.

The long legacy of the shocking proceedings in Salem between February and September 1692 has proved a point of fascination in American folklore. By the time the witch hunt ended, 19 convicted witches had been executed, at least four accused witches had died in prison, and one man had been pressed to death. More than 100 others were arrested and imprisoned on witchcraft charges. Even animals were not immune to the mass hysteria – two dogs were executed as suspected accomplices.

It all started with the peculiar symptoms of Betty Parris, the six-year-old daughter of village minister Samuel Parris. With little provocation, she dashed about, diving under furniture, contorted in pain and complaining of fever. When three of Betty's playmates developed similar symptoms, Tituba, the Parris's slave, attempted a remedy: a 'witch cake' composed of rye and the urine of an afflicted victim. This, and her knowledge of voodoo, placed her under suspicion of witchcraft. Under pressure, Tituba confessed to consorting with the devil.

The 'victims', now numbering seven, were encouraged by their new-found power, and their accusations flowed. The paranoia and fear spread, and suddenly it seemed nobody was immune from allegations of witchcraft.

Even as they went about the business of killing their neighbours, the townspeople were stunned by the devil's intrusion into their quiet community. 'It cannot be imagined that in a place of so much knowledge, so many in so small a compass of land should abominably leap into the Devil's lap all at once,' wrote the Reverend John Hale in September 1692.

Over time, as accusations fell upon those with the purest of characters, the villagers began to have doubts. By the autumn of 1692, even the zealous father-and-son preaching team of Cotton and Increase Mather began to question the validity of the proceedings, and the sorry mess was brought to an end.

Throughout the centuries since, memories of the event refuse to die. Countless books have been written about it. In the 1950s, the playwright Arthur Miller wrote *The Crucible* to highlight the similarities he saw between Salem in 1692 and the anti-communist witch hunts of his time (subsequently adapted for the big screen in 1996). In the end, it seems the fascination in Salem lies not only in the mysticism of it all, but in the speed with which this brave new world of freedom and democracy turned on itself.

Plymouth

As you head south along the scenic coast between Quincy and Cape Cod, aka the South Shore, you come into the heart of colonial New England. Near Plymouth, the roadside retailers adopt faux 'Olde English' signage to emphasise the local heritage, and there are lots of 'towne shoppes'. In addition to the glut of historical attractions clustered near the old Pilgrim settlement, the South Shore contains hundreds of old colonial trails and parks that remain mostly uncorrupted by the tourist trade.

Famously, this is the spot where the Pilgrims landed in 1620 after their harrowing trip from England. The landmark in these parts is **Plymouth Rock** where, according to lore, they first stepped. But there's no evidence the Pilgrims ever saw the rock, much less stepped on it. Still, the legend alone makes it worth a look. The rock has been moved several times, even once broken in two, and it only came to rest at its present location, in a landscaped park on Water Street near the harbour, in 1867. The thing itself is rather unimpressive, especially compared to the neo-classical monument that both girds and dwarfs it. A replica of the ship in which the Pilgrims made their epic journey is docked close by. The **Mayflower II** is a full-scale version of the original, with a staff of performers in 17th-century garb who recount the tale of the Pilgrims' struggles. The boat seems tiny, and it's hard to imagine that the settlers spent months aboard it, much of that time amid violent storms.

Plymouth itself is charming, with narrow streets, and 17th- and 18th-century houses, many open to the public. The main attraction is the **Plimoth Plantation**, a huge, surreal re-creation of the 1627 settlement, developed by historians and archaeologists. The village is populated by actors who speak, work, play, eat and breathe 17th-century life. The Plantation pays painstaking – some might say obsessive –

attention to detail, and visitors can watch the 'settlers' stocking firewood, stuffing sausages and plucking geese. The effect is somewhere between a time warp and a mental ward, but, above all, it's extremely entertaining. Also worth seeing are the **Pilgrim Hall Museum**, with Mayflower-era artefacts and exhibits on the native Wampanoag tribe, and the epitaphs on **Burial Hill** (Carver Street), one of the oldest cemeteries in America and resting place of many of the first settlers.

Just south of the town centre is **Plymouth Long Beach**, a pretty three-mile (five-kilometre stretch of coastline, while **Morton Park**, near Summer Street, has swimming holes and woodland hiking trails. Other towns around Plymouth Bay include **Hull**, **Cohasset** and **Hingham**. Hull was evacuated during the Revolution after a military fort was constructed on one of its hills. Today its beaches do a brisk tourist trade. The **Hull Lifesaving Museum** tells the tale of local superhuman shipwreck rescues. Close by, Hingham and Cohasset are picture-perfect colonial villages with none of the tourist trade of Plymouth or Hull. The century-old **Minot's Ledge Lighthouse** in Cohasset is a classic piece of New England scenery. At 4 Elm Street, the small, seasonally open **Maritime Museum** commemorates local early American heritage; its neighbour, the **Captain John Wilson House** at No.2 is closed for restoration until 2005, but the exterior is worth a look (call 1-781 383 1434 for information on both). Peaceful and bucolic Hingham, the next hamlet over, is a good place to kill a few hours. Cove Park is great for a stroll, and the **Old Ordinary** (21 Lincoln Street, 1-781 749 0013) is a 14-room house museum with period furniture and a tap room.

Hull Lifesaving Museum

1117 Nantasket Avenue, Hull (1-781 925 5433). **Open** 10am-4pm Wed-Sun. **Admission** $2; $1.50 concessions; free under-18s. **Credit** MC, V.

Mayflower II

State Pier, Water Street, Plymouth (1-508 746 1622). **Open** *Apr-Nov* 9am-5pm daily. **Admission** $8; $6 concessions. **Credit** AmEx, MC, V.

Pilgrim Hall Museum

75 Court Street, Plymouth (1-508 746 1620/ www.pilgrimhall.org). **Open** *Feb-Dec* 9.30am-4.30pm daily. **Admission** $6; $3-$4 concessions. **Credit** AmEx, MC, V.

Plimoth Plantation

137 Warren Avenue, off Route 3A South at Exit 4, outside Plymouth (1-508 746 1622). **Open** *Apr-Nov* 9am-5pm daily. **Admission** $20; $12 concessions. Combined ticket with Mayflower II $22; $14-$20. **Credit** AmEx, MC, V.

Where to stay & eat

Dining around Plymouth is a briny business. Top-notch fish and shellfish at the self-service **Lobster Hut** (Town Wharf, 1-508 746 2270) are inexpensive and come with a view. The more upmarket **Isaac's** (114 Water Street, 1-508 830 0001) offers another great ocean vista and more elaborate seafood. In nearby Hull, residents swear by the lobster at **Jake's** (50 George Washington Boulevard, 1-781 925 1024), an award-winning local institution overlooking the bay. Hingham has many good restaurants, including **Tosca** (14 North Street, 1-781 740 0080) and **Stars On Hingham Harbor** (4 Otis Street, 1-781 749 3200).

Plymouth has a number of serviceable, if undistinguished, motels within convenient reach of downtown. A more pleasant choice, and one with its own private beach, is the **Pilgrim Sands Motel** (150 Warren Avenue, 1-800 729 72637, www.pilgrimsands.com, $80-$275), a few miles out of town. The **Auberge Gladstone B&B** (8 Vernon Street, 1-508 830 1890, 1-866 722 1890, www.aubergegladstone.com, $70-$170), a colonial mansion with modern furnishings, is another good option. If you're looking for water views, check out the **Cohasset Harbor Inn** (124 Elm Street, 1-781 383 6650, www.cohassetharborresort.com, $79-$209), a low-key hotel with two on-site restaurants.

Getting there

Plymouth is an hour south of Boston by train, or about halfway to Cape Cod by car. Organised tours are available – contact the **Plymouth Chamber of Commerce** (*below*) for details.

By car

Plymouth is 40 miles (64km) south-east of Boston on the I-93 (Southeast Expressway) to Route 3. Take Exit 6 (roughly 45 minutes' drive).

By bus or rail

MBTA Commuter Rail (*see pp248-249*) runs daily services from Boston's South Station. Buses also run out of South Station (*see p248*). Journey time is about an hour for both.

Tourist information

Plymouth Chamber of Commerce

15 Caswell Lane, Plymouth (1-508 830 1620/www.plymouthchamber.com). **Open** 9am-5pm Mon-Fri.

Plymouth Visitors' Center

130 Water Street, Plymouth (1-508 747 7533/1-800 872 1620). **Open** *Summer* 9am-8pm daily. *Spring/autumn* 9am-5pm daily. *Winter* 9am-5pm Mon-Sat.

Massachusetts Coast & Islands

Join the Mass exodus in summer.

Along the rocky coastline of Massachusetts you'll find seagulls, sand dunes and salty sea air. You'll also find lonely lighthouses, rattletrap clam shacks and gruff seafaring charm. There's lowlife too – if you know where to look. Many communities on the Massachusetts shoreline still rely on the Atlantic for their livelihood. This is what people are talking about when they refer to the 'real' New England.

Cape Ann is the lesser visited of the Bay State's two capes, and has managed to survive the past 200 years with minimal commercial interruption. Its pride, personality and picture-perfect panoramas are fully intact, unlike the holiday mecca and significantly more clogged **Cape Cod**. This wedge of New England is an area of extremes and asserts a rough loveliness: regal schooners are moored next to rickety old row boats; grand, multi-tiered homes are flanked by ramshackle cottages and shacks with the stability of card castles.

Cape Ann

Cape Ann includes Gloucester, Essex, Rockport and Manchester-by-the-Sea. These towns all started off with post-Pilgrim seafaring histories: shipbuilding, shipwrecks, brave sailors crossing the Atlantic, tragedy and heroism captured by poets and artists such as Winslow Homer and Henry Wadsworth Longfellow.

Gloucester, the largest of the towns, has been a centre of the fishing industry since 1623, and some 10,000 locals are said to have perished at sea over the years (Sebastian Junger's book *The Perfect Storm* and the subsequent film of the same name documented a 1991 tragedy). The town's tribute to these men, a bronze statue known as 'The Man at the Wheel', stands sentinel on the harbour promenade, just off Western Avenue. Right down the street is the more recent and equally poignant 'Fishermen's Wives' Statue', dedicated to those who've lost loved ones at sea. Rocky Neck, in East Gloucester, is the country's oldest working artists colony. Here, **Hammond Castle** is a full-scale stone replica of a medieval castle, built between 1926 and 1929 by John Jays Hammond Jr. You'll also find ample opportunity for whale-watching excursions and day-long fishing trips.

Essex relies on clamming as one of its principal industries, and the sweet, tender Essex clam is about as famous as a clam can get. In 1914, a clam-digging local named Lawrence 'Chubby' Woodman, opened a clam shack called **Woodman's** here (*see p241*). Whether Chubby actually 'invented' the fried clam is not important. What is important is the ones at Woodman's, where the motto is 'Eat in the rough', are the best on the coast. The main strip in Essex, known as the Causeway, is lined with antiques shops, most famously the White Elephant. Some look like cluttered junk shops, others resemble mini museums, and are priced accordingly.

Shipbuilding began in Essex in the mid 1600s, and by the 1850s the town was recognised around the world as the North

Top five Beaches

Crane Beach, Ipswich
A stunning stretch with 1,200 acres (485 hectares) of beach front, dunes and maritime forest. *See p240.*

Nauset Beach, Cape Cod
The heaviest surf and the liveliest crowd on the Cape. *See p243.*

Singing Beach, Manchester-by-the-Sea
Squeaky-clean sand and lapis sea. *See p240.*

South Beach, Martha's Vineyard
Volleyball heaven for a young, fun-loving set. *See p245.*

Wingaersheek Beach, Gloucester
Forget *The Perfect Storm* – this is the perfect beach. *See p240.*

American centre for schooner building. People are still building ships by hand there today, and you can learn about the history of the industry at the **Essex Shipbuilding Museum**.

Visitors poke around **Rockport**'s narrow streets lined with little gift shops and galleries. Bear Skin Neck has tons of tiny storefronts and cafés, although don't expect alcoholic revelry – Rockport has been dry since 1856, when 75-year-old resident Hannah Jumper was so outraged by the rampant alcoholism in town she led 200 women armed with hatchets and hammers to smash every bottle and keg in every bar.

The entrance to Rockport's main harbour, an old red building with rows of colourful buoys hanging off the outer wall and rugged jetties in the background, has been painted so often it's known by locals as 'Motif Number 1'.

Manchester-by-the-Sea is the most sleepy and residential of the four towns, although its **Singing Beach**, named after the rare 'singing' sand which chirps when you step on it, is one of the best in the whole state, and makes it a must-visit destination.

Other great Cape Ann beaches include **Long Beach** in Rockport, and **Wingaersheek** and **Good Harbor**, both in Gloucester. South of Gloucester, at **Rafe's Chasm Reservation**, the granite ledges open to a chasm 200 feet (60 metres) long and 60 feet (18 metres) deep, and the tides often produce some striking sights and sounds. East of town, **Pebble Beach** has an unusual shoreline of timeworn stones stretching into the horizon.

Although not in Cape Ann proper, Ipswich (www.ipswichma.com), north of Essex, boasts **Castle Hill**, the **Crane Wildlife Refuge** and **Crane Beach** (Argilla Road, 1-978 356 4354), which was all once part of the expansive estate of Chicago plumbing magnate Richard T Crane Jr. Crane Beach is a four-mile (6.5-kilometre) stretch of sand, home to the threatened piping plover. Income for wildlife preservation in this conservation area is raised by hiring out the regal Great House on Castle Hill, set in 165 acres (67 hecatres) of land with the Grand Alleé path running from its porches down to the bluffs overlooking Crane Beach.

Essex Shipbuilding Museum

66 Main Street, Essex (1-978 768 7541/www.essexshipbuildingmuseum.org). **Open** *mid May-Sept* noon-4pm Wed-Sun. *Oct-mid May* noon-4pm Sat, Sun. **Admission** $5, $3 concessions. **Credit** MC, V.

Hammond Castle

80 Hesperus Avenue, Gloucester (1-978 283 2080/www.hammondcastle.org). **Open** *mid May-mid June* 10am-3pm Sat, Sun. *Mid June-Sept* 10am-4pm Mon-Thur; 10am-3pm Fri-Sun (call in advance; hours are subject to private functions) **Admission** $8.50 adults; $5.50-$6.50 concessions. **Credit** MC, V.

Where to stay & eat

The most interesting choices include Rockport's **Addison Choate Inn** (49 Broadway, 1-800 245 7543, www.addisonchoateinn.com, $110-$165), a Greek Revival house from the 1850s, and the

Seaside stalwart **Woodman's** is famous for fried clams. *See p241.*

Paint it again: **Rockport**'s oft-rendered harbour. *See p240.*

Inn on Cove Hill (37 Mount Pleasant Street, 1-978 546 2701, www.innoncovehill.com, $95-$165), which was reputedly built with funds from a discovered cache of pirates' loot. The **Cape Ann Chamber of Commerce** (*see below*) runs a hotel reservation service on 1-800 321 0133.

For dining, of course there's **Woodman's** (121 Main Street, Essex, 1-800 649 1773, www.woodmans.com). In Gloucester **The Rudder** (73 Rocky Neck Avenue, 1-978 283 7967, closed in winter), in the heart of the Rocky Neck Art Colony, has a well-priced, eclectic menu, quirky decor and a festive atmosphere. The **Franklin Café** (118 Main Street, 1-978 283 7888), sibling to the venue in Boston's South End (*see p120*), offers funky comfort food.

Getting there

By car

Gloucester is 30 miles (48km) north-east of Boston on I-93 to Route 128 North; Rockport is 40 miles (64km) from Boston, and seven miles (11km) north of Gloucester on Routes 127 or 127A. Ipswich is 25 miles north-east of Boston. Take Route I-95 North to Route 1 North.

By bus or rail

MBTA Commuter Rail (*see p248*) runs trains to Gloucester and Ipswich from North Station. The bus service on the Cape Ann peninsula is run by the Cape Ann Transportation Authority (1-978 283 7916, www.canntrann.com).

Tourist information

Cape Ann Chamber of Commerce

33 Commercial Street, Gloucester (1-978 283 1601/ www.capeannvacations.com). **Open** 8am-5pm Mon-Fri.

Cape Cod

Order a Cape Codder at the bar, and you'll get a vodka and cranberry juice with a wedge of lime – a Cosmopolitan without the Cointreau. And that's the Cape right there: sharp, strong, and a splash away from being something fancy. It's a mix of swarthy, fisher-folk year-rounders and the summer crowd in their khaki shorts and Polo button-downs; of sweeping Cape estates and quaint old clapboard cottages. In summer, ask a Bostonian what they're up to for the weekend and invariably the answer will be: 'I'm heading to the Cape.'

Cape Cod was named after the fish found there by English explorer Bartholomew Gosnold. These days, cranberry-growing and tourism provide the region's economic support rather than the old industries of fishing, whaling, shipping and salt-making. It is the nation's largest producer of the red berries (thus the name of the cocktail), and the burgundy bogs add to the often austere landscape. As for tourism, you can expect the summer weekend traffic over Sagamore Bridge – the gateway to the Cape – to be backed up for miles.

The Cape is made up of 16 towns organised into three chunks: Upper (Wareham, Bourne, Sagamore, Sandwich, Falmouth and Mashpee); Mid (Barnstable, Dennis, Yarmouth, Brewster and Harwich); and Lower, or Outer (Chatham, Orleans, Eastham, Wellfleet, Truro and Provincetown). Within these larger towns are settlements such as Hyannis in Barnstable. Throughout parts of the Cape also runs the **Cape Cod National Seashore**, with 43,685 acres (17,686 hectares) of beaches, sand dunes, heathlands, marshes, freshwater ponds and a number of historic sites.

Rockin' with the Rockefellers

Although it's across the Massachusetts border in Rhode Island, **Newport** is a favourite summer seaside excursion for Bostonians. About an hour by car from Boston, the town has two main lures: its magnificent architecture and its Jazz Festival.

Newport was once the summer playground of America's wealthiest industrialists. The Rockefellers and the Vanderbilts came here and built what they called 'cottages'. The size of English manor houses, the sweeping mansions along Bellevue Avenue – each in a distinctly different style – are opulent testimony to the wealth of their owners. Some of these estates, most notably the **Breakers** – a 70-room Italian Renaissance-style pile built in 1895 for Cornelius Vanderbilt – are open to the public. Roam room after room of imported marble, gold leaf, chandeliers, precious antiques and art. Other tourable mansions in the vicinity include the **Elms** (*pictured above*), **Rosecliff** and **Marble House** (*pictured left*). Call 1-401 847 1000 or go to www.newportmansions.org for more details.

The history of the **Newport Jazz Festival** is equally lofty, boasting such names as Ella Fitzgerald, Dizzy Gillespie and Billie Holiday – and that was just in its inaugural year. Miles Davis played in Newport. So did Nina Simone and Charles Mingus, to name a few more. But it's not all scatting and saxophones – in 1959 the granddaddy of jazz festivals (celebrating its 50th anniversary in 2004) spawned the **Newport Folk Festival**. Bob Dylan, Joni Mitchell, Joan Baez and, more recently, Billy Bragg, Aimee Mann and Lyle Lovett, have all taken the Newport stage. Both events are held in August. Visit www.festivalproductions.net, or call 1-401 847 3700 for further information.

GETTING THERE

Newport is about an hour's drive from Boston. Take the I-93 South to Route 24 South, then on to Route 114 South. Bonanza buses (*see p248*) run daily services from Boston's South Station.

Sandwich was the first of the Pilgrims' Cape towns. In the 19th century the town became a centre of American glass-making; the plentiful scrub brush fuelled the artisans' ovens. Today its **Glass Museum** contains a wealth of examples of the work of those craftsmen. At the restored 17th-century **Dexter Grist Mill** on the corner of Main and Water Streets, you can still buy ground cornmeal. The nearby **Heritage Plantation** is a hotchpotch of objects ranging from antique cars to Currier & Ives prints. It includes several museums and a Shaker barn built on 76 acres (30 hectares) of grounds, and offers children rides on a 19th-century carousel.

Provincetown was the first place where Miles Standish and his *Mayflower* boatload of Pilgrims landed, on 11 November 1620 (they quickly decided against the site and moved on to that famous rock in Plymouth; *see p6*). Today Provincetown supports a booming tourist trade and a notorious nightlife on three-and-a-half miles (five-and-a-half kilometres) of beach. In summer it becomes the queer community's Disneyland destination and an anything-goes attitude pervades the scene. Tea dancing at the **Boat Slip** (161 Commercial Street, 1-508 487 1669), a midnight boogie at **Atlantic House** (4-6 Masonic Place, 1-508 487 3821) and a late pizza at **Spiritus Pizza** (190 Commercial Street, 1-508 487 2808) are part of the seasonal routine.

A year-round local artist community has long been established. The **Provincetown Art Association & Museum** has been offering exhibitions, lectures and classes since 1914, while **DNA**, a well-respected local gallery, shows daring contemporary work.

Woods Hole, on the Cape's south-west tip, is one of the world's great centres of maritime research. The **Woods Hole Oceanographic Institute**, which assembled the team that located the remains of the *Titanic* in 1985, has exhibitions on undersea exploration. The more visitor-friendly **Marine Biological Laboratory** gives guided tours at weekends. **Hyannis**, halfway out on the Upper Cape, is the transport hub of the area, with rail and airport services and ferries to **Nantucket** and **Martha's Vineyard** (*see p244*). It came to the forefront of popular awareness as the Kennedy's summer home and remains inseparably linked to visions of a suntanned JFK at the helm of a skiff. The family's well-known compound is walled off south of town in Hyannisport but there's an extensive photographic display at the **JFK Hyannis Museum**.

Chatham is a chic little town that has been continuously settled since the mid 17th century. In its earliest days, Chatham's perch on the shipping lanes made it a favourite location for 'moon-cussers', bands of pirate wreckers who roamed the beaches with false lights that led boats aground to be pillaged. The most prominent landmark today is one that guides sailors safely back to shore, the **Chatham Light** lighthouse. The town still plays host to a substantial population of fishermen and it accommodates the tourist trade in genteel style with its crafts and antiques shops downtown.

For a glimpse of primal New England, head south of town past the Chatham Light on to **Morris Island** for the ferry to the **Monomoy Island National Wildlife Refuge**. This barrier island, born out of a hurricane some 40 years ago, serves as a stopover point for bird migration in the Atlantic Flyway.

Along the Cape Cod National Seashore you'll find some of Massachusetts' loveliest and brightest beaches. **Nauset Beach**, at the southern tip outside East Orleans, has the best surf and draws the youngest, liveliest crowd. This last, narrow stretch of the Cape has managed to escape most of the horrors of commercialisation. **Wellfleet Harbor**, on the bay side, encloses the 1,000 acres (400 hectares) comprising the **Wellfleet Bay Wildlife Sanctuary**. Here the Massachusetts Audubon Society (www.massaudubon.org) sponsors tours and lectures and allows camping (for a fee, and for Audubon members only). Wellfleet and nearby Truro are known as artists' and writers' retreats. Edna Saint Vincent Millay and Edmund Wilson lived in Wellfleet in the 1920s; Edward Hopper liked the bleak light of the high dunes outside Truro. Most recently, Sebastian Junger penned his novel, *The Perfect Storm*, in his Truro holiday home.

DNA

288 Bradford Street, Provincetown (1-508 487 7700/ www.dnagallery.com). **Open** *Summer* 11am-7pm daily (call for off-season hours). **Admission** free.

Glass Museum

129 Main Street, Sandwich (1-508 888 0251/ www.sandwichglassmuseum.org). **Open** *Feb* 9.30am-5pm Wed-Sun. *Mar-Dec* 9.30am-5pm daily (last tour 4.15pm). Closed Jan. **Admission** $4.50; $1 concessions. **Credit** Disc, MC, V.

Heritage Plantation

67 Grove Street, Sandwich (1-508 888 3300/ www.heritagemuseumsandgardens.org). **Open** *May-Oct* 9am-6pm Mon, Tue, Thur-Sat; 9am-8pm Wed. *Nov-Apr* 10am-4pm Wed-Sat; noon-4pm Sun. **Admission** $12; $6-$10 concessions. **Credit** AmEx, MC, V.

JFK Hyannis Museum

397 Main Street, Hyannis (1-508 790 3077). **Open** *Summer* 9am-5pm Mon-Sat; noon-5pm Sun. *Spring, autumn* 10am-4pm Tue-Sat; noon-4pm Sun. *Winter* 10am-4pm Thur-Sat, noon-4pm Sun. **Admission** $5; $2.50 concessions. **Credit** AmEx, MC, V.

Marine Biological Laboratory

100 Water Street, Woods Hole (1-508 289 7623). **Open** 8am-5pm Mon-Fri. **Admission** free.

Provincetown Art Association & Museum

460 Commercial Street, Provincetown (1-508 487 1750/www.paam.org). **Open** *June* noon-5pm Thur, Sun; 8am-10pm Fri, Sat. *July, Aug* 8am-10pm daily. *Sept-May* noon-5pm Sat, Sun. **Admission** $2; **Credit** AmEx, Disc, MC, V.

Wellfleet Bay Wildlife Sanctuary

291 State Highway, Route 6A, Wellfleet Harbour (1-508 349 2615). **Open** *June-Oct* 8.30am-5pm daily. *Nov-Apr* 8.30am-5pm Tue-Sun. **Admission** $5; $3 concessions. **Credit** MC, V.

Woods Hole Oceanographic Institute

15 School Street, Woods Hole (1-508 289 2663). **Open** *Apr-Dec* 10am-4.30pm Tue-Sat; noon-4pm Sun. **Admission** $2 (additional donation requested). **No credit cards**.

Where to stay

Lodging is extremely varied the whole length of Cape Cod. Towns on the Cape Cod Bay side of the peninsula are more interesting and relaxing. Rates tend to drop the further down the Cape you are from Provincetown, though there are bargains there too, if you book well in advance. Off-season rates drop precipitously – the Cape has a wonderful austerity once the tourists have gone. In Sandwich, the **Village Inn** (4 Jarves Street, 1-800 922 9989, $110-$135) boasts a charming wraparound porch. In Barnstable, the **Beechwood** (2839 Main Street/Route 6A, 1-800 362 6618, www.beechwoodinn.com, $100-$190) nestles among the trees after which it is named. The historical district of Chatham has a number of carefully restored, period-furnished 19th-century inns, such as the **Chatham Bars Inn** (Shore Road, 1-800 527 4884, www.chathambarsinn.com, $150-$1,600), but they can be expensive in season.

To be where the action is, head to Provincetown's most luxurious lodging, the **Brass Key** (67 Bradford Street, 1-800 842 9858, www.brasskey.com, $110-$445). The **Commons** (386 Commercial Street, 1-508 487 7800, www.commonsghb.com) offers slightly lower prices and more history. Out of the centre, the charming **White Horse** (500 Commercial Street, 1-508 487 1790, $50-$75, studio apartments $125-$140) is a penny-saver's delight. For a free directory of gay- and lesbian-owned hotels, restaurants, bars and services, contact the **Provincetown Business Guild** (3 Freeman Street, No.2, 1-508 487 2313, www.ptown.org).

Where to eat & drink

Dining in Provincetown runs the gamut, but phone ahead wherever you go as off-season hours are unpredictable and sometimes non-existent. Upmarket interpretations of New American cuisine are the order of the day at **Front Street** (230 Commercial Street, 1-508 487 9715); decent contemporary Italian food can be had at reasonable prices at the venerable **Ciro and Sal's** (4 Kiley Court, 1-508 487 6444); and stylish light fare is served at **Café Heaven** (199 Commercial Street, 1-508 487 9639). It's worth driving to Wellfleet for dinner at **Aesop's Tables** (316 Main Street, 1-508 349 6450, closed in winter), which has an inventive touch with local ingredients. Provincetown also has a significant Portuguese community, émigrés from the Azores who came to work the fishing boats. Sample their cuisine at **The Moors** (5 Bradford Street, 1-508 487 0840), known for its spicy swordfish and pork.

Getting there

By car

The Sagamore Bridge, linking Cape Cod to the mainland, is 30 miles (48km) south-east of Boston on Route 3, the most direct route.

By bus

The Plymouth and Brockton bus (1-508 746 0378, www.p-b.com) runs every hour from Boston's South Station to Hyannis and then on to Provincetown. The Cape Cod Regional Transit Authority (1-800 352 7155, www.capecodtransit.org) and Bonanza (*see p248*) cover the mid-Cape region by bus. Provincetown runs local shuttle bus services in town in the summer months.

By boat

Bay State Cruises (1-617 748 1428, www.boston-ptown.com) runs a daily ferry from Boston to Provincetown in summer and at weekends in spring and autumn. The journey from Commonwealth Pier takes three hours.

Tourist information

Cape Cod Chamber of Commerce

Junction of Routes 6 & 122, Hyannis (1-508 362 3225/www.capecodchamber.org). **Open** 9am-5pm daily.

Martha's Vineyard & Nantucket

If locals aren't heading to the Cape, chances are they're off to the islands; every summer the beaches, bars, restaurants and air of exclusivity of Martha's Vineyard and Nantucket draw

Nauset Beach on Cape Cod. *See p243.*

thousands of tourists. Beautiful New England seascapes bring in money by the bucketload.

The first recreational use of Martha's Vineyard was for Methodist camp meetings in the summer of 1835. Today, summer residents include Spike Lee and Bill Clinton. **Edgartown** is the largest and oldest of the main towns. A walk along the harbourside, past the stately captains' mansions on Water Street, reveals the prosperity they brought back from the sea. The island's historical society keeps the **Vineyard Historical Museum** replete with scrimshaw, ships' models and other local artefacts. Nearby **South Beach**, also known as Katama, is the island's largest and most popular strand.

Oak Bluffs buzzes a bit more than the other Vineyard towns. It's got a collection of gingerbread cottages and the wonderful 1876 Flying Horses Carousel (corner of Oak Bluffs and Circuit Avenue, 1-508 693 9481), reputedly the country's oldest. A premier example of American folk art, it runs every day in summer until 10pm for a dollar a ride. Stick to Oak Bluffs for the island's liveliest late-night action, too. Avoid the pastel and khaki crowd and kick it with the locals at the **Rare Duck** (6 Circuit Avenue, 1-508 696 9352); enjoy a beer on the beach by the harbour at **Menemsha Blues** (6 Circuit Avenue Extension, 1-508 693 9599), or spot celebrities at the **Atlantic Connection** (19 Circuit Avenue, 1-508 693 7129).

Vineyard Haven (also known as Tisbury), on the north coast, was long the island's chief port and it's where the old colonial atmosphere is best preserved. One of the prettiest spots on the island is the town of **Aquinnah** on the western tip. The public beach there is famous for its dramatic mile-long cliffs of multi-coloured clay and the views from the trails above them.

While Martha's Vineyard is only a 45-minute ferry ride away, it takes over two hours on the open seas to get to Nantucket, making the 'Faraway Island' an apt nickname. In *Moby-Dick*, Herman Melville calls Nantucket 'a mere hillock, an elbow of sand; all beach without a background'. You can bet there's background now, in the form of eye-popping properties – and Nantucket is doing everything it can to control the development of its precious land.

For 150 years, the island was the centre of the world's whaling industry, and its streets and historic houses are soaked in that history. (The **Whaling Museum**, currently undergoing renovation, is scheduled to reopen in the spring of 2005.) In the 19th century, with the rise of the petroleum industry, a devastating fire in 1846, and the onset of the Civil War, the island's economy began to tumble. Between 1840 and 1870, the population decreased from 10,000 to 4,000. Nantucket was revived by tourism.

History still pervades the island, and through spring and summer, the Nantucket Historical Society offers guided walking tours of the historic downtown hub. Highlights include the last of the town's 18th-century mills, as well as the **Old Gaol**, a lock-up in which the prisoners were allowed to go home for the night.

Cobblestoned Main Street now reveals fleets of Range Rovers blocking traffic, women dripping in gold, and men in linen trousers and loafers, dangling keys to Lexus SUVs and million-dollar 'cottages'. The streets are lined with boutiques, antiques shops and upscale clothing stores. Conspicuous consumption aside, in its beaches, foggy moors and ubiquitous grey clapboard houses, Nantucket has a grace that is missing in mainland Massachusetts.

Bring a bicycle – or rent one at Young's Bicycle Shop (6 Broad street, Steamboat Wharf, 1-508 228 1151). Bike paths thread around the island, and having two-wheeled transport means you won't have to pay the prohibitively expensive car-ferry reservation, imposed to discourage drivers. A ride out to **Madaket**, will be rewarded with a long and lovely stretch of beach on the west side of the island. **Cisco Brewery and Triple 8 Vodka Distillery** (5 & 7 Bartlett Farm Road, 1-800 324 5550) is the island's very own oasis of beer, wine, and booze. Tucked away out of town, the brewery is open to the public and it's worth stopping in for the free samples.

Nantucket Historical Association

7 Fair Street, Nantucket (1-508 228 1894/ www.nha.org).

Vineyard Historical Museum

59 School Street, Martha's Vineyard (1-508 627 4441). **Open** *Apr-Sept* 10am-5pm Tue-Sat. *Oct-Mar* 10am-5pm Wed-Sat. **Admission** $7; $4 concessions. **Credit** Disc, MC, V.

Where to stay & eat

As a result of the celebrities on Martha's Vineyard, and the need to import most produce, dining out on both islands is not cheap. If you want to splash out on the Vineyard, **L'Etoile** (27 South Summer Street, 1-508 627 5187) has a renowned contemporary French menu. The always-packed **Black Dog Tavern** (Beach Street Extension, Vineyard Haven, 1-508 693 9223) is where everyone flocks to load up on a huge breakfast or watch the sunset – and invariably buy the T-shirt.

On Nantucket, pack a picnic with sandwiches from **Something Natural** (50 Cliff Road, 1-508 228 0504), or breakfast at Main Street mainstay **Arno's** (No.41, 1-508 228 7001). A decent dinner can be had at the **Brotherhood of Thieves** (23 Broad Street), followed by live music and more drinks at the **Chicken Box** (16 Dave Street, 1-508 228 9717).

Good, cheap accommodation can be found throughout the season in youth hostels on either island. **Hostelling International – Nantucket** is at 31 Western Avenue (1-508 228 0433, www.capecodhostels.org, $20-$25); while **Hostelling International – Martha's Vineyard** is in Edgartown (West Tisbury Road, Box 3158, 1-508 693 2665, www.capecod hostels.org, $20-$25). Beyond that, the cost per night is going to be pretty high, if you can even secure a room. In Edgartown, comfort and convenience at relatively modest prices can be found at the **Victorian Inn** (24 South Water Street, 1-508 627 4784, www.thevic.com, $105-$385), the former home of a whaling captain.

Prices run even higher among the swells of Nantucket, but the local landmark, **Jared Coffin House** (29 Broad Street, 1-508 228 2400, www.jaredcoffinhouse.com, $85-$375), is not too exorbitant and is packed with history. Nantucket has a wealth of B&Bs listed through services such as **Nantucket Accommodations** (1-508 228 9559).

Getting there

By car or air

Check with the ferry services about transporting cars to the islands, as there are restrictions. However, car rental firms abound and both islands have extensive shuttle bus services for most of the year, run by the Martha's Vineyard Transit Authority (1-508 693 9400, www.vineyardtransit.com) and the Nantucket Regional Transit Authority (1-508 228 7025). Cape Air (1-508 771 6944, flycapeair.com) has flights from Boston to Hyannis, Provincetown, Martha's Vineyard or Nantucket.

By boat

Martha's Vineyard and Nantucket are served by several ferry companies. The Massachusetts Steamship Authority (1-508 477 8600, www.steam shipauthority.com) has a year-round service from two Cape Cod locations: the trip from Woods Hole to Martha's Vineyard takes 45 minutes. The trip from Hyannis to Nantucket is two hours and 15 minutes, but a Steamship Authority high-speed ferry from Hyannis only takes about an hour. In summer, Island Queen (1-508 548 4800, www.islandqueen.com) and Pied Piper (1-508 548 9400, www.falmouthferry.com) ferries run from Falmouth to Martha's Vineyard; Hy-Line (1-508 778 2600, www.hy-linecruises.com) has a summer service to Nantucket.

Tourist information

Martha's Vineyard Chamber of Commerce

Vineyard Haven, Martha's Vineyard (1-508 693 0085/www.mvy.com). **Open** 9am-5pm Mon-Fri.

Nantucket Island Chamber of Commerce

48 Main Street, Nantucket (1-508 228 1700/ www.nantucketchamber.org). **Open** 9am-5pm Mon-Fri.

Directory

Features

Directory

Getting Around

Arriving & leaving

By air

Logan International Airport
Information 1-617 561 1800/ www.massport.com. Airport Ground Transportation 1-800 235 6426).
On a spit of reclaimed land to the east of Boston, the airport is just 3 miles (5km) from the downtown area. The airport's five terminals are lettered A to E and connected by a shuttle bus that also runs to Airport T station. Logan has recently expanded its international terminal.

Airlines

Aer Lingus 1-800 223 6537.
Air Canada/Air Canada Jazz 1-888 247 2262.
Air France 1-800 237 2747.
Alitalia 1-800 223 5730.
American Airlines 1-800 433 7300.
British Airways 1-800 247 9297.
Delta Air Lines 1-800 221 1212.
JetBlue Airways 1-800 538 2583.
KLM 1-800 374 7747.
Lufthansa 1-800 645 3880.
Qantas 1-800 227 4500.
Song 1-800 221 1212.
Swiss 1-877 359 7947.
United Airlines 1-800 241 6522.
US Airways 1-800 428 4322.
Virgin Atlantic 1-800 862 8621.

By bus

The **Logan Dart** bus line (1-800 235 6426) provides a non-stop transfer between the airport and South Station near downtown Boston. The fare is $5 one way. Buses leave from all five of the airport's terminals every 15 minutes between 6am and 8pm Sunday to Friday. Buses depart from Gate 25 at South Station every 15 minutes between 6am and 8pm.

Logan Express (1-800 235 6426) runs a bus service from the airport to Braintree, Framingham and Woburn. One-way fares cost $11.

Most out-of-town services arrive and depart from the **South Station Transportation Center** (700 Atlantic Avenue, at Essex Street), which is served by the following bus companies:

Greyhound
1-617 526 1801/1-800 231 2222.
For national services.
Peter Pan/Bonanza
1-401 751-8800/1-800 237 8747.
For the New England area, including services to Cape Cod. Also services to New York.
Concord Trailways
1-617 426 8080.
For New Hampshire and Maine.
Plymouth & Brockton
1-617 773 9401.
For buses to Plymouth and Cape Cod.
Vermont Transit
1-800 451 3292.
For buses to Vermont.

By rail

The national rail service **Amtrak** (1-800 872 7245/www.amtrak.com) runs from **South Station** and **Back Bay Station** (145 Dartmouth Street, at Stuart Street).

By T

The Massachusetts Bay Transport Authority or **MBTA** operates the local subway system known as the 'T'. Access to the Airport T station is by the Blue Line, which runs from State or Gov't Center stations – the journey takes about 15 minutes. Airport shuttle buses numbers 22 and 33 take passengers from the airline terminals to the T station. With the state of traffic in Boston, this is the quickest and cheapest way to access the airport.

Photocopied T maps are available from information booths in terminals A, C and E. *See also p249.*

By taxi

Taxis are directly outside the airport's baggage claim area. A cab ride to downtown Boston costs $20-$25, and $35-$40 to Cambridge, with an extra $1 toll for travelling through the Sumner Tunnel from Logan to Boston.

Station wagons, taxis with disabled access and credit card taxis are all available upon request. For a list of reputable firms *see p249*.

If you want to travel in style, advance booking can be made with **Carey Limousine** (1-617 623 8700) and the **Commonwealth Limousine Service** (1-617 787 5575).

By sea

Travelling by boat is the most pleasant way of getting to and from the airport.

The **Logan Water Shuttle** (1-800 235 6426) connects the free terminal shuttle bus with Boston's Long Wharf. (During the winter boats run every 30 minutes 8am-6pm Mon-Fri; 10am-6pm Sat-Sun. The summer schedule is more frequent, with boats every 20 minutes 7am-8pm Mon-Fri; and every 30 minutes 10am to 6pm Sat, Sun. Tickets are $10 one way). The journey takes approximately seven minutes.)

Harbor Express (1-617 222 6999) runs a similar service between the airport, the southern suburb of Quincy and Long Wharf, in downtown Boston near the Marriott Hotel.

City Water Taxis (1-617 422 0392) operates between 1 April and 31 October ($5-$10) and takes passengers from the airport to the World Trade Center, Congress Street (near South Station), Long Wharf (for Government Center and the North End), North Station and Charlestown, among other stops.

Public transport

Fares & tickets

Public transport in the Boston area is run by the MBTA and consists of the local subway system, known as the T, Commuter Rail and buses. Visitor's Passports are available for one-day ($7.50), three-day ($18) or weekly ($35) use, providing unlimited travel on the T and MBTA buses. For those planning longer stays, monthly passes are available for $44. Passes can be bought at the Airport, Gov't Center, Harvard, Alewife and Riverside T stations and North Station, South Station and Back Bay Station, as well as at the Boston Common and Prudential Center tourist information booths (*see p259*).

MBTA
(Information 1-617 222 3200/ 1-800 392 6100; pass program 1-617 222 5218; complaints 1-617 222 5215/www.mbta.com).

Subway

Boston's T was America's first subway, and is easy to use, efficient, and cheap, though recent fare hikes have caused a grumble or two. Tokens now cost $1.25 (65¢ for under-12s; 35¢ for senior citizens), and a trip on one of the Green or Red Line surface extensions can cost up to $3 (you pay the driver).

Trains run from 5.15am to 12.30am Mon-Sat and from 6am to 12.30am on Sundays. On Friday and Saturday nights you can catch the Night Owl bus service, which runs parallel to the subway lines, until 2.30am. (*See below* for more information.) Free subway maps are available from the larger stations such as Harvard, Gov't Center, Back Bay, South Station and Park Street.

'Outbound' and 'Inbound' services sometimes have different subway entrances. Inbound is always towards the downtown stations Park Street, State, Downtown Crossing and Gov't Center; Outbound is away from them.

Not many Bostonians (and even fewer visitors) know that each branch colour was chosen to reflect a characteristic of the area that each line covers. The Green Line, for example, was named in honour of the Emerald Necklace, the chain of parks that links Boston and the western suburbs. The Red Line, serving Harvard, pays homage to the Harvard Crimsons, the university's football team colour. The Blue Line is supposed to mirror the colour of the waterfront, and the Orange Line runs along Washington Street, originally known as Orange Street after William of Orange, king of England between 1689 and 1702.

Be aware that the Silver Line, which is marked on subway maps, is in fact a bus service (*see below*).

Bus

The MBTA runs around 150 bus routes in Boston and the suburbs. The flat fare is 90¢ (25¢ for senior citizens), and payment has to be in exact change. Bus transfers valid for two hours from the time of issue are available for no additional charge – always request one at the beginning of your journey.

Buses run from 5.30am to 1am daily. In an effort to become more party-friendly, the MBTA has instituted a Night Owl bus that runs Friday and Saturday nights from 12.30am to 2.30am. The rail bus routes run parallel to the subway lines. Some other bus routes like the 1 and 66 also continue later into the night.

The MBTA is currently also implementing a 'bus rapid transport' stategy, promising more frequent high-tech, environmentally friendly buses, with global positioning systems to prevent 'bunching up' on high-traffic routes. At the centrepiece of the strategy is the Silver Line, the first leg of which – between Downtown Crossing and Dudley Station – opened in 2002. Confusingly the Silver Line is marked on the subway map, and although the service is frequent (about every ten minutes), it's still not as fast as the subway, especially during rush hour.

The rail buses cost $2, the regular bus lines are $1.50, and trips to the suburbs cost $4. Routes and timetables are available from major T stops or the **MBTA central office** (10 Park Plaza, 120 Boylston Street).

Rail

Boston has three main train stations: **South Station** (700 Atlantic Avenue, at Summer Street), **Back Bay Station** (145 Dartmouth Street, at Stuart Street) and **North Station** (Causeway Street, at Friend Street). MBTA Commuter Rail runs from North Station and South Station, serving the Greater Boston area and Massachusetts as far away as Providence, Rhode Island.

Taxis & limousines

Taxis can be hailed on the street at any time of day or night, although it becomes difficult after 1am, when public transport has closed down for the night. Taxi ranks can be found near major hotels, outside main train stations and in Harvard Square, Cambridge.

Regular meter fares begin at $1.75 for the first quarter of a mile and then 30¢ for each eighth of a mile thereafter. If you have a complaint about a taxi service phone the police department's Hackney Hotline on 1-617 536 8294.

The following local taxi companies offer a 24-hour service and most accept major credit cards, but it is always best to phone to check first:

Boston Cab
1-617 536 2000.

Independent Taxi Operators Association
1-617 268 1313/426 8700.

Red Cab
1-617 566 5000.

Town Taxi
1-617 536 5000.

The **Boston Cab Association** (1-617 262 2227/536 5010) also provides limousines, while **Boston Coach** (1-800 672 7676) has vans, coaches, limousines and cars.

Driving

With the Big Dig (*see p28* **Bridging past and present**) at 92 per cent completion in 2004, driving in Boston isn't the purgatory it used to be. Still, despite obvious improvements brought about by the Central Artery Project, traffic in this town can still be frustratingly slow. If you must drive, here is some of the information you may need.

The three main highways that lead into town are the **I-95**, the **I-93**, which runs all the way to Vermont, and the **I-90** (the Massachusetts Turnpike, or 'Mass Pike'), which runs into New York State.

The speed limit on most major highways is 55 miles per hour. On sections of the Mass Pike this goes up to 65 miles per hour. Elsewhere in Boston, speed limits range from 20 to 50 miles per hour.

The **American Automobile Association** or AAA (1-800 222 4357/www.aaa.com) can provide members with maps on request. Some clubs – including the AA and RAC in the UK – have reciprocal arrangements with the AAA, which also entitles you to discounts at certain sights, museums and hotels. The AAA offers a free towing service to members (except on the privately run Mass Pike, which has its own patrol cars to aid breakdowns).

State law requires the wearing of seat belts. It's also a fineable offence to litter: throwing a wrapper out of a car window could end up costing you $1,000 or even your right to drive in the US.

Vehicle hire

If you want to hire a car, check whether an international driver's licence will be required, as some rental companies insist on both a foreign and international licence (available from the AAA, *see p250*). Many companies also require that a licencee be over 25 years of age, and all insist on payment with a major credit card. Also, the days when you could borrow a parent's or spouse's credit card are over. Most companies require that the card be in the driver's name.

Ask about basic US driving rules before heading out – some rules are different here. If you're driving with children under the age of five they must be in the back seat in an approved child-safety restraint. Car rental rarely includes insurance, so be sure to check exactly what is covered.

Major rental companies include:
Alamo 1-800 327 9633.
Avis 1-800 831 2847.

The Orient express

Commonly referred to as the 'Chinatown Bus', the Fung Wah travels between Boston and New York's Chinatowns for $10 each way. The ticket office (a table inside a bakery) is a stone's throw from South Station's bus station, yet it seems worlds away. There is no actual terminal, and Fung Wah employees' grasp of English can be limited, so confusion may arise as to where to board the bus. Usually it picks up right across the Surface Artery (the main road). If in doubt, head toward the gaggle of shabby-chic scenesters waiting on the side of the road with rucksacks in tow.

The service was originally provided as cheap transport for restaurant workers shuttling between the two cities' Chinatowns. While there are still a few Chinese travellers on each voyage, the clientele is increasingly comprised of students and thrifty city dwellers. If you'd never imagined yourself lusting after the organisation of a queue, try to get on the bus to New York on a Friday night around 6pm. It takes guile and determination, and perhaps some elbow throwing. While online reservation is available for a $1 fee, the ticket office has been known to oversell buses, leaving ticket holders to wait an extra hour for the next bus to depart. Late morning or early afternoon journeys might be a less jarring option.

If the bus is sold out, there is now formidable competition within a one-block radius, in the form of **Travel Pack** (1-888 881 0887, www.travelpackusa.com) and **Lucky Star** (1-888 881 0887, 1-617 426 8801, www.luckystarbus.com), which is why prices have stayed so low.

The journey to New York takes four and a half hours – not much longer than by air after you factor in the commute to the airport, security and baggage claim. For your peace of mind, Fung Wah promises that it's legitimised with 'permission' from the Federal Highway Authority, and also claims to be fully insured.

Fung Wah

Crown Royal Bakery, 68 Beach Street, at Hudson Street, Chinatown (1-617 338 1163/338 0007/www.fungwahbus.com). Buses depart hourly from 7am to 10pm, & at 11.30pm.

Budget 1-800 527 0700.
Dollar 1-800 800 4000.
Hertz 1-800 654 3131.
National 1-800 227 7368.

Parking

Parking can be very difficult in Boston. The number of spaces is trimmed by about five per cent each year, as the city has yet to comply with the Clean Air Act standards. You'll notice right away that, despite the city's ample public transportation, Bostonians still have that American love of cars. Thus the traffic congestion is dreadful and parking spaces are rare. In addition, many spaces are available only to locals with special parking deals.

The few spaces that do exist are metered and only available to non-residents for up to two hours between 8am and 6pm. A fine can cost $20 and retrieving a towed car can be well over $50. If you do get a ticket, phone the **Boston Office of the Parking Clerk** (1-617 635 4410).

If you must use a car while in Boston, the wisest thing to do is leave it in a parking lot and walk. Boston's two main car parks are under Boston Common (on Charles Street, directly opposite the Public Garden, 1-617 954 2096) and under the Prudential Center (800 Boylston Street, 1-617 267 1002). Other garages can be found at Government Center (50 New Sudbury Street, 1-617 227 0385), the New England Aquarium (70 East India Row, 1-617 723 1731) and at Zero Post Office Square (Congress Street, 1-617 423 1430).

Breakdown services

The AAA (1-800 222 4357) offers a 24-hour breakdown service (*see p249*). However, in case of a breakdown, your best bet is to contact local police or state highway patrol for help. They will, in turn, contact tow-trucks or local garages to move your car to safety.

24-hour fuel stations

Bowdoin Square Exxon

239 Cambridge Street, at Blossom Street (1-617 523 3394). **Credit** AmEx, Disc, MC, V.

Fenway Texaco Service

1241 Boylston Street, at Ipswich Street (1-617 247 7905). **Credit** AmEx, Disc, MC, V. **Map** p276 D7.

Cycling

Cycling is quite popular, especially in areas just outside the city like Cambridge and Jamaica Plain, which have less dense traffic. Cambridge's so-called bike lane, adjacent to street parking, has caused biker injury when parked car doors open in front of an oncoming cyclist. Revenge: at 5.30pm on the last Friday of the month Boston's Critical Mass (*www.bostoncriticalmass.org*) takes place. A huge group of cyclists departs from Copley Square, taking over the streets and forcibly holding up motorised traffic.

Walking

It's not called 'America's Walking City' for nothing. Walking through Boston's different neighbourhoods is a pleasurable and leisurely alternative to public transport.

Resources A-Z

Age restrictions

To drink and purchase alcohol in Boston, you must be 21 with proper ID (a passport should suffice, an out-of-state driving licence might not). Tobacco is sold only to those aged 18 and over, and ID is also required from anyone who looks younger than 30. Drivers must be 16 and over. The age for consensual heterosexual sex is 16 for women, 18 for men. The laws regulating gay sex are a bit blurry. As this guide went to press the Massachusetts Supreme Judicial Court had not repealed the state's ancient sodomy laws, but it has limited the law to cases that are non-consensual or committed in public places.

Business

Conventions & conferences

Boston Convention & Exhibition Center
415 Summer Street, at D Street (1-617 954 2000/www.mccahome.com). South Station T. **Open** depends on function.

Hynes Convention Center
900 Boylston Street, at Gloucester Street, Back Bay (1-617 954 2000/www.mccahome.com). Hynes/ICA T. **Open** 9am-5pm Mon-Fri. **Map** p276 F6.

World Trade Center
164 Northern Avenue, at Seaport Lane (1-617 385 5000/www.wtcb.com). South Station T. **Open** depends on function. **Map** p275 N5.

Couriers & shippers

DHL Worldwide Express
1-800 225 5345/www.dhl.com.
Phone for opening hours and pick-up locations.

Federal Express
1-800 463 3339/www.fedex.com.
Phone for opening hours and pick-up locations.

Metro Cab
1-617 242 8000.
A taxi company that offers package delivery 24 hours a day.

Symplex Courier Systems
1-617 523 9500/www.groundex.com.
Provides package delivery service 24 hours a day.

US Postal Service
1-800 222 1811/www.usps.gov.

Office hire/services

Kinkos
10 Post Office Square, at Milk Street (1-617 482 4400/www.kinkos.com). Downtown Crossing T. **Open** 24hrs daily. **Map** p275 L4.
Services include on-site computer rental, internet access, typesetting, printing, photocopying, faxing and mailing. Kinkos also sells stationery.
Other locations: 2 Center Plaza (1-617 973 9000); 1 Mifflin Place, Cambridge (1-617 497 0125); 187 Dartmouth Street (1-617 262 6188).

Sir Speedy
20 Province Street, at School Street (1-617 227 2237/www.sir-speedy.net). State T. **Open** 8.30am-5.30pm Mon-Fri. **Map** p274 K4.
Services at Sir Speedy include copying, printing, desktop publishing, binding and graphic and web design.
Other locations: 827 Boylston Street (1-617 267 9711); 76 Batterymarch Street (1-617 451 6491); 77 North Washington Street (1-617 523 7656).

Secretarial services

HQ Business Center
101 Federal Street, at Franklin Street (1-617 342 7000). Downtown. **Open** 8.30am-5pm Mon-Fri (open earlier/later upon request) **Credit** AmEx, Disc, MC, V. **Map** p275 L5.

Translators & interpreters

Boston Translation Co
Suite 510, 31 St James Avenue, at Arlington Street (1-617 859 9959). Arlington T. **Open** 8.30am-6pm Mon-Fri. **Credit** AmEx, MC, V. **Map** p277 H6.
Offers translation and interpreting services for all major languages.

Transperfect Translations
Suite 305, 15 Broad Street, at State Street (1-617 854 6566). Gov't Center T. **Open** 8.30am-6pm Mon-Fri. **Credit** AmEx, MC, V. **Map** p275 L4
As well as translation and interpreting services for all major languages, it also provides a multi-lingual secretarial service.

Consumer

Better Business Bureau
(1-508 652 4800/www.bosbbb.org).
If you are interested in receiving information on a particular company

Travel advice

For up-to-date information on travel to a specific country – including the latest news on safety and security, health issues, local laws and customs – contact your home country government's department of foreign affairs. Most have websites packed with useful advice for would-be travellers.

Australia
www.dfat.gov.au/travel

Canada
www.voyage.gc.ca

New Zealand
www.mft.govt.nz/travel

Republic of Ireland
www.irlgov.ie/iveagh

UK
www.fco.gov.uk/travel

USA
http://travel.state.gov

(and know its address) or wish to file a complaint about a US business, you can phone the above number.

Office of Consumer Affairs and Business Regulation

(1-617 727 7780/www.state.ma.us/consumer).
If you have a complaint to make regarding your consumer rights or a query regarding your responsibilities, OCABR should be able to help. Arbitration services for home improvement and car purchase are provided. Will make references to mediation or legal services.

Customs

Standard immigration regulations apply to all visitors. During your flight you will be handed an immigration form and a customs declaration form to be presented when you land at the airport. Fill them in carefully, and ask for another if you make a mistake. Be prepared to queue when you arrive at immigration for anything up to an hour, and expect to explain the nature of your visit (business and/or pleasure). If you don't have a return ticket and are planning a long visit, you will be questioned closely. Usually you will be granted an entry permit to cover the length of your stay.

US Customs allows visitors to bring in $100 worth of gifts duty free ($400 for returning Americans), 200 cigarettes (one carton) or 50 cigars and one litre of spirits (liquor).

Any amount of currency can be brought into the US, but a form, available from the airport, must be filled in for anything over $10,000. Prescription drugs must be clearly marked (and visitors should be prepared to produce a written prescription upon request).

No meat, meat products, seeds, plants or fruit can be taken through customs. For more detailed information on agricultural produce and customs phone the **US Department of Agriculture** (1-301 734 8295).

UK Customs & Excise allows returning travellers to bring in £145 worth of gifts and goods and an unlimited amount of money, as long as you can prove it's yours.

For further information contact the following agency:

Office of Immigration and Naturalisation

1st Floor, John F Kennedy Building, City Hall Plaza, Downtown (1-617 565 3879). Gov't Center T. **Open** 7am-3pm Mon-Fri. **Map** p274 K3.

Disabled travellers

Boston is generally well equipped for disabled travellers. Hotels must provide accessible rooms, museums and street curbs have ramps for wheelchairs, and buses on some routes are wheelchair accessible. However, it's always best to phone first to double-check.

Transportation Access Passes (TAP) entitle the disabled passenger to reduced fares on public transport. Passes are available for $3 from the **MBTA Senior and Access Pass Program Office** (Back Bay Station, 145 Dartmouth Street, 1-617 222 5976), and applications must be completed by a licensed health-care professional. The office also supplies a map that shows disabled access points to the T.

For information on access to more than 200 local arts and entertainment facilities contact **VSA Arts** (Massachusetts China Trade Center, 2 Boylston Street, at Washington Street, 1-617 350 7713/www.vsamass.org).

Airport Handicap Van

1-617 561 1769.
Runs a service for the disabled between the airport and various hotels to the Airport T stop. Phone the above number for details.

Lift Bus Program

1-800 543 8287.
For queries about bus access.

Massachusetts Office on Disability

1-617 727 7440/1-800 322 2020.
This governmental agency is a good source for enquiries into issues like rights enforcement and building access.

Electricity

The United States uses a 110-120V, 60-cycle AC voltage, rather than the 220-240V, 50-cycle AC voltage used in Europe. Laptops and most travel appliances are dual voltage and will work in the US and in Europe, but it is always a good idea to check with the manufacturer before you plug them in. Older computers in particular, have been known to blow. You will also need an adaptor for US sockets; they can be bought at the airport or at pharmacies.

Embassies & consulates

Australia

1601 Massachusetts Avenue NW, Washington, DC (1-202 797 3000/www.austemb.org).

Canada

Suite 400, 3 Copley Place, at Huntington Avenue, Back Bay (1-617 262 3760/www.canadianembassy.org). Copley T.
Map p277 G6.

New Zealand

57 North Main Street, Concord, New Hampshire (1-603 225 8228/ www.nzembassy.com/usa).

Republic of Ireland

3rd Floor, 535 Boylston Street, at Clarendon Street (1-617 267 9330). Copley T. **Map** p277 H6.

South African Consulate

9th Floor, 333 E 38th Street, New York (1-212 213 4880/ usaembassy.southafrica.net).

United Kingdom

Suite 1500, 1 Memorial Drive, by the Longfellow Bridge, Cambridge (1-617 245 4500/www.britainusa.com/boston). Kendall T.

Emergencies

This is a list of contacts for emergency services. For more information *see p253* **Health**.

Ambulance, fire brigade or police

For all emergency services in the US, dial 911. The call is toll-free from any payphone. 911 also works from most mobile phones.

Verizon (telephone) automated hotline

1-800 244 3737.

NStar information hotline

(Gas) 1-800 592 2000; (electric) 1-800 592 2000.

Massachusetts Poison Control Center

1-800 682 9211.

Boston Water and Sewer Commission

1-617 330 9400.

Gay & lesbian

Boston's South End is a highly concentrated gay neighbourhood. All around the Back Bay and Cambridge, an affectionate gay couple will rarely get a second look. There is also a large lesbian and transgender community in Jamaica Plain. *See also p200-206.*

Help & information

For HIV/AIDS information, *see below* **Health**.

Bay Windows

www.baywindows.com.
For details, *see* **Media: Newspapers**

Gay Men's Domestic Violence Project

Crisis Line 1-800 832 1901/ www.gmdvp.org.
The project offers shelter for battered men at a confidential address.

Out in Boston

www.outinboston.com.
The site provides information on what's on in the Boston gay scene along with a directory of useful addresses and phone numbers.

Health

Within the United States you will have to pay for any emergency medical treatment you might need – welcome to privatised health care. In most cases, emergency rooms will also want you to provide them with a credit card before they treat you. Be sure to contact the emergency number on your travel insurance before seeking treatment if you can, and you will be directed to a hospital that will deal directly with your own insurance company.

Accident & emergency

Brigham & Women's Hospital

75 Francis Street, between Huntington & Brookline Avenues, Brookline (1-617 732 5500/1-800 294 9999). Brigham Circle T. **Open** 24hrs daily.

Children's Hospital

300 Longwood Avenue, at Brookline Avenue, Brookline (1-617 355 6000/ 355 6611). Longwood T. **Open** 24hrs daily.

Franciscan Children's Hospital & Rehabilitation Center

30 Warren Street, at Commonwealth Avenue, Brighton (1-617 254 3800). Warren Street T. **Open** 24hrs daily.

Massachusetts General Hospital

55 Fruit Street, at Cambridge Street, (1-617 726 2000). Charles/MGH T. **Open** 24hrs daily. **Map** p274 J3.

Mount Auburn Hospital

330 Mount Auburn Street, at Memorial Drive, Cambridge (1-617 492 3500). Harvard T. **Open** 24hrs daily.

New England Medical Center

750 Washington Street, at Kneeland Street, Chinatown (1-617 636 5000). NE Medical Center T. **Open** 24hrs daily. **Map** p277 J6.

Alternative medicine

Langer Chiropractic Group

179 Elm Street, Somerville (1-617 625 5350). Porter or Davis T. **Open** *By appointment* Mon-Thur. **Credit** AmEx, Disc, MC, V.
Dr Langer is a specialist in chiropractic therapy, physiotherapy and massage.

Market Street Health

214 Market Street, at North Beacon Street, Brighton (1-617 787 3511). Cleveland Circle T then 86 bus. **Open** *Phone enquiries* 9am-2pm Mon-Fri. **No credit cards**.
Market Street Health offers a wide variety of complementary medicine and holistic therapies. Services offered here include acupuncture, chiropractic therapy, homeopathy, Chinese medicine, flotation, massage and yoga.

New England School of Acupuncture

34 Chestnut Street, Watertown (1-617 926 4271/www.nesa.edu). Central T then 70 bus. **Open** 9am-7.30pm Mon-Fri; 9am-3pm Sat. **Credit** varies.
The oldest college of acupuncture and oriental medicine in the country, this well-known school offers a wide array of alternative treatments.

Contraception & abortion

Planned Parenthood

1055 Commonwealth Avenue, at Babcock Street (1-617 616 1660/ www.pplm.org). Babcock St T. **Open** 8am-7pm Mon; 7.30am-7pm Tue-Fri; 7.30am-2pm Sat.

Dentists

Dental Referral Service

(1-800 511 8663). **Open** *Phone enquiries* 8am-8pm Mon-Fri.

Metropolitan District Dental Society

(1-508 651 3521). **Open** *Phone enquiries* 9am-4pm Mon-Fri.

Tufts Dental School

1 Kneeland Street, at Washington Street, South End (1-617 636 6828). NE Medical Center T. **Open** *Emergency walk-in clinic* 9am-10.30pm Mon-Fri. **Map** p277 J6.

Pharmacies & prescriptions (24-hour)

CVS

155-7 Charles Street, at Cambridge Street, Beacon Hill (1-617 523 1028/ www.cvs.com). Charles/MGH T. **Open** *Pharmacy* 7am-midnight daily. *Store* 24 hours daily. **Map** p274 H3.
Check the phone book or phone the number above to find the location of other branches in the Boston area. Not all locations are open 24 hours.

Psychiatric emergency services

Massachusetts General Hospital

(1-617 726 2994). **Open** 24hrs daily.
Acute psychiatric treatment is offered by the emergency room of Massachusetts General Hospital.

STDs, HIV & AIDS

AIDS Hotline

(1-800 235 2331). **Open** 9am-7pm Mon-Fri; 10am-2pm Sat.
AIDS Hotline offers advice on emotional issues, testing and insurance, as well as referrals to support groups for legal and financial advice.

Fenway Community Health Services

7 Haviland Street, Back Bay (1-617 267 0900/www.fenwayhealth.org). Hynes/ICA T. **Open** 7.30am-8pm Mon-Thur; 7.30am-7pm Fri; 8.30am-1pm Sat. **Map** p276 F7.

Helplines

Alcohol/drug abuse

Alcoholics Anonymous

(1-617 426 9444/www.aaboston.org). **Open** 9am-9pm Mon-Sat; noon-9pm Sun.

Volunteers (recovered alcoholics who have been through the programme) offer counselling and referral to detox houses and AA meetings.

Child-at-Risk Hotline

(1-800 792 5200). **Open** 24hrs daily.
An emergency service provided by the Department of Social Services, this hotline will refer concerned adults or abused children to other agencies for help.

Drug & Alcohol Hotlines

(1-800 327 5050). **Open** 24hrs daily.
This service provides a helpful information and education service on issues including substance abuse, referrals to detoxification centres within Massachusetts and advice on who to phone for out-of-state information.

Rape Crisis

(1-617 492 7273). **Open** 24hrs daily.
Rape Crisis is a hotline that takes messages from people who have suffered sexual abuse. A trained counsellor will phone back, usually within five minutes.

Samaritans Suicide Helpline

(1-617 247 0220/www.samaritans.org). **Open** 24hrs daily.
The Samaritans hotline is manned by trained and experienced counsellors 24 hours a day.

Samariteens Suicide Helpline

(1-617 247 8050). **Open** 24hrs daily.
A hotline that offers the same service as the Samaritans, but for teenage callers. Between 2pm and 11pm daily, the line is staffed by teen volunteers.

ID

The legal drinking age is 21 and Boston is serious about checking photo ID. Not all forms of out-of-state identification are accepted so it is best to carry your passport with you if you are likely to order a drink in a bar or buy alcohol. Alcohol is sold in liquor stores and a few supermarkets and convenience stores, and it is now legal to purchase alcohol on Sundays.

Insurance

It's advisable to take out comprehensive insurance cover before travelling to the United States: it's almost impossible to arrange once you are there. Make sure that you have adequate health cover since medical expenses can be high. *See p253* **Health** for a list of hospitals and clinics.

Internet

The best way to check your email when you're in Boson is to either use one of the public libraries with online facilities or to pay for the use of a computer at a copy/office centre – certain branches of Kinkos (*see p251*), Copy Cop and Gnomon Copy offer high-speed internet access. The main Boston Public Library at Copley Square offers free 'express' internet access (only 30 minutes at a time for non-members). You need to stop by the computer desk and make a reservation in advance. Another option is to swing by the free internet terminals in the Prudential Center mall, which are located near the entrance to the Sheraton hotel. Be warned, though: there are no seats and there is often a queue.

For hotels that offer modem or dataport facilities (listed under Room Services), see *p40-56.*

Internet access

The cybercafé trend never really caught on in Boston, and there is only one in a central location: **Tech Superpowers Cyber Café** (252 Newbury Street, at Fairfield Street, Copley T, 1-617 267 9716). It charges a minimum of $3 for 15 minutes, and $5 for an hour.

Left luggage

At this time, because of FAA restrictions, there are no luggage storage facilities at Logan Airport.

Legal help

If you run into legal trouble, contact your insurers or your national consulate. *See p252* **Embassies & consulates**.

Libraries

Boston Public Library

700 Boylston Street, at Copley Square, Back Bay (1-617 536 5400/www.bpl.org). Copley T. **Open** *General library & research* 9am-9pm Mon-Thur; 9am-5pm Fri, Sat; 1-5pm Sun. *Print department, rare books & manuscripts* 9am-5pm Mon-Fri. *Young adults' room* 9am-9pm Mon-Thur; 9am-5pm Fri, Sat; 1-5pm Sun. **Map** p277 G6.

Other locations: 25 Parmenter Street, North End (1-617 227 8135); 685 Tremont Street, South End (1-617 536 8241); 151 Cambridge Street, West End (1-617 523 3957).

Lost property

Airport

Logan Airport's lost and found department can be reached at 1-617 561 1714.

Public transport

The MBTA lost and found department is divided into different sections for each form of transport. If you lose something on a bus, phone 1-617 222 5000 (8.30am-5pm Mon-Fri. You can pick up valuable items 9am-6pm daily). Phone 1-617 222 3600 for property lost on Commuter Rail from North Station (6.30am-midnight Mon-Fri; 7am-11pm Sat, Sun). South Station's number is 1-617 222 8120 (7.30am-4.30pm Mon-Fri).

Each T line has a different number: **Blue Line** (1-617 222 5533); **Green Line** (1-617 222 5221); **Orange Line** (1-617 222 5403); and **Red Line** (1-617 222 5317). All are open 24 hours daily.

Taxis

If you lose something in a taxi, phone the police department's **Hackney Hotline** (1-617 536 8294). It's open 24 hours daily.

Media

Newspapers & magazines

Bay Windows

www.baywindows.com
Weekly newspaper for lesbians and gay men, focusing on Boston news, politics and the arts scene. The cover price is 50¢, though it's available free from many bars and shops in Back Bay and the South End.

Boston Globe

www.boston.com
The city's oldest and most popular daily newspaper, the *Boston Globe* takes a cautiously liberal line on most subjects, covering local politics quite well, but sometimes lacking on national and international stories. The paper's massive Sunday edition has also recently revamped its *Globe Magazine*. Thursday's paper includes *Calendar Magazine*, a guide to what's on in the city.

Boston Herald
www.bostonherald.com
The *Globe*'s slowly declining competitor is a raucous and conservative-leaning tabloid in the style of the *New York Post*. It has a strong following among working-class Bostonians and it has been very successful in unearthing local political scandals. Not surprisingly, the sports coverage is very extensive.

Boston magazine
www.bostonmagazine.com
A general-interest glossy monthly magazine with a mix of lifestyle features and occasional strong pieces on city issues; catering mostly to an upmarket audience. The annual 'Best of Boston' issue and the restaurant reviews are highly regarded.

Boston Phoenix
www.bostonphoenix.com
An irreverent free weekly, which takes an alternative line on the city's politics and culture. The arts section is excellent, featuring critical and smart coverage of music, film, theatre, dance and visual art. The entertainment and events listings are the most comprehensive you'll find. Available from sidewalk dispensers, clubs and cafés around the city.

Improper Bostonian
www.improper.com
A weekly lifestyle magazine distributed free from sidewalk dispensers on main streets. Newbury Street is the centre of its universe and the desperately enthusiastic and uncritical style and arts features are, well, desperate.

Stuff@Night
www.stuffatnight.com
A bi-monthly arts and lifestyle magazine published by the owners of the *Boston Phoenix*. The coverage is self-consciously hip, with lots of attention given to fashion and food. A good place to discover the current 'in' bars and nightclubs.

The Tabs
www.townonline.com
A chain of newspapers that caters towards a particular city or neighbourhood – the *Cambridge Tab*, the *Brookline Tab*, etc. Mostly focused on community issues and local arts coverage.

The Weekly Dig
www.weeklydig.com
Boston's little upstart freebie covers local goings-on from an indie standpoint. Columnists portray their strong political stances and take great pleasure in lashing out at anyone and anything in the Boston scene – from local politicos to other newspapers and their editors (particularly the *Dig*'s older rival the *Phoenix*).

Radio

WERS (88.9 FM)
A very good semi-professional college radio station run by students at Emerson College. Daily slots dedicated to folk, jazz, world music, reggae and hip hop. Lots of interviews, live performances and local music coverage. Listen for ticket giveaways to small shows around Cambridge and Allston.

WGBH (89.7 FM)
A public radio station that airs the main NPR (National Public Radio – the US equivalent of the BBC) news shows ('Morning Edition' and 'All Things Considered'), in addition to a mix of classical music, folk, blues and jazz.

WBUR (90.9 FM)
A public radio station dedicated almost completely to news and talk. The very worthwhile nationally syndicated programmes 'Car Talk' and 'The Connection' are just two of the shows that are produced here.

WBOS (92.9 FM)
'Adult Alternative', which means Barenaked Ladies, Sting, Dave Matthews Band and the like.

WJMN (94.5 FM)
Mainstream hip hop and R&B.

WHRB (95.3 FM)
Harvard University's station plays a pleasing combination of classical and jazz during the day, though punk, indie, rock and hip hop take over in the wee hours.

WBCN (104.1 FM)
A long-standing rock station, now focusing on 'alternative' and hard rock, plus a smattering of local music.

WRKO (680 AM)
Talk radio and news programmes.

WEEI (850 AM)
A station for the die-hard Red Sox and Celtics fan. That would be just about everyone in Boston, then.

TV

National networks dominate the airwaves in Boston, however, the local PBS (Public Broadcasting Service) station, **WGBH**, is one of the best in the country, producing acclaimed shows such as *Nova* and *Frontline*. Below are the local channels and the national networks with which they are affiliated:
WGBH, Channel 2 and 44, PBS
WBZ, Channel 4, CBS
WCVB, Channel 5, ABC
WHDH, Channel 7, NBC
WFXT, Channel 25, Fox

Money

The US dollar ($) equals 100 cents (¢). Coins range from copper pennies or cents (1¢) to silver nickels (5¢), dimes (10¢) and quarters (25¢).

Paper money 'bills' come in denominations of $1, $5, $10, $20, $50, and $100, which are confusingly all the same size and colour.

Since counterfeiting of $50 and $100 bills is a booming business, many small shops will not accept them. If you have to use a $50 or $100 bill, ask first, especially if your payment is only a few dollars. On the whole it is better to restrict your paper money to denominations of $1, $5, $10 and $20. Tax is applied to hotels (12.45%), meals (5%) and retail purchases (5%), excluding food from supermarkets and clothing.

Banks & bureaux de change

Most banks are open from 9am to 5pm Monday to Friday, and some are open from 9am to noon on Saturday. You will need some kind of photo identification, such as a passport, to transact any business like cashing travellers' cheques or obtaining cash from a credit card. If you arrive in Boston after 5pm, change money at the airport or, if you have US dollars travellers' cheques, buy something in order to get some change. If you want to cash travellers' cheques at a shop, ask first if a minimum purchase is required. You can obtain cash on a credit card account from certain banks. Check with your credit card company before you leave, and be prepared to pay interest rates that vary daily. *See also p256* **ATMs**.

American Express Travel Services
1 State Street, Downtown (1-617 723 8400/www.americanexpress.com). State T. **Open** 8.30am-5.30pm Mon-Fri. **Map** p275 L4

Fleet Bank
100 Federal Street, Downtown (1-617 434 5501/www.fleet.com). Downtown Crossing or South Station T. **Open** 8.30am-5pm Mon-Fri. **Map** p275 L5.
Check the phone directory for the location of other branches.

Citizens Bank

28 State Street, at Congress Street, Downtown (1-617 725 5500/ www.citizensbank.com). Gov't Center T. **Open** 8.30am-5pm Mon-Fri. **Map** p275 L4.
Check the phone directory for the location of other branches.

OneUnited Bank

133 Federal Street, at Summer Street, Downtown (1-617 457 4400/www.oneunited.com). South Station T. **Open** 9am-5pm Mon-Fri. **Map** p275 L5.

Thomas Cook Currency Services

1-800 287 7362/ www.thomascook.com.
Phone for exchange rates and the location of the nearest branch.

Travelex

1-800 287 7362/www.travelex.com. **Open** 7am-10pm daily.
This bureau de change is located in Terminal C and Terminal E of the airport.

Western Union

1-800 325 6000/ www.westernunion.com.
Western Union is still the most reliable way to get money wired from one country to another.

ATMs

Automated Teller Machines (ATMs or cashpoints) are easy to find. Most machines will accept American Express, MasterCard and Visa and selected international debit and cash cards – tap in your usual PIN number. There is a fee, of course. You can get directions to the nearest ATM location by calling Visa Plus System (1-800 843 7587) or Mastercard (1-800 424 7787). If you have forgotten your PIN number or have de-magnetised your card, most banks will dispense cash to card holders with valid ID. You can also get cash back at supermarkets if you pay with a card bearing the Cirrus or Plus logo (with your usual PIN).

Credit cards

Less disastrous if you're robbed, and accepted almost everywhere, credit (and not debit) cards are required by almost all hotels, car rental agencies and airlines. Your stay will be made much more pleasant if you 'don't leave home without them'. The major credit cards most often accepted in the US are American Express, Discover, MasterCard and Visa. If you lose your credit card (or your travellers' cheques) call the appropriate number below.

Lost or stolen credit cards

American Express
1-800 221 7282.
Discover
1-800 347 2683.
MasterCard
1-800 307 7309.
Visa
1-800 336 8472.

Lost or stolen travellers' cheques

American Express
1-800 221 7282.
Thomas Cook
1-800 223 7373.
Visa
1-800 227 6811.

Opening hours

Opening hours vary depending on the business and time of year. Shops tend to open around 10am and close around 7pm. Many stay open later during the tourist season. Banks are open 9am to 4pm or 5pm Monday to Friday, and some are open 10am to 1pm on Saturdays. Post offices are usually open from 8am to 5pm Monday to Friday and 8am to noon on Saturdays.

Police stations

For emergencies dial 911. Otherwise, call the Boston Police at 1-617 343 4240. Headquarters is at 40 New Sudbury Street, Downtown. Another branch is at 650 Harrison Avenue, South End, 1-617 343 4250. For more information check www.ci.boston.ma.us/police.

Postal services

Post office opening hours in Boston are usually 9am to 5pm Monday to Friday, with limited hours on Saturday. Contact the **US Postal Service** (1-800 222 1811/ www.usps.com) for information on your nearest branch and mailing facilities (be ready with a post- or zipcode).

Stamps can be bought at any post office as well as at many hotels, grocery stores and convenience stores. It costs 37¢ to send a one-ounce (28g) letter within the US. Each additional ounce costs 23¢. Postcards mailed within the US cost 23¢; for international postcards it's 70¢. Airmailed letters to anywhere overseas costs 80¢ for the first ounce and 80¢ for each additional ounce. Express mail costs extra and guarantees 24-hour delivery within the US, and two- to three-day delivery to international destinations with no guarantee. Call 1-800 275-8777 for more information on various deadlines. **Western Union** (1-800 325 6000) will take a telegram over the phone and charge it to your phone bill.

See also p251 **Business: Couriers & shippers**.

Fort Point Station

25 Dorchester Avenue, behind South Station, Downtown (1-617 654 5302). South Station T. **Open** 24hrs daily.
If you have no definite address while you are travelling and you're not sure where you will be staying, have it marked General Delivery and posted to Fort Point Station. Proof of identity is needed when picking up mail.

Mailboxes Etc

167 Milk Street, Downtown (1-617 734 3744/www.mbe.com). Gov't Center T. **Open** 8.30am-5.30pm Mon-Fri; 9am-2pm Sat. **Map** p275 L4.
This is a very useful national chain offering shipping and packaging services, plus mailbox rentals, office supplies and many other things that come in handy when you're on the road.

Religion

Here are just a few of the many places of worship in and around Boston. Check the *Yellow Pages* for more.

Baptist

First Baptist Church of Boston

110 Commonwealth Avenue, at Clarendon Street, Back Bay (1-617 267 3148/www.first baptistchurchofboston.org). Copley T. **Service** 11am Sun. **Map** p277 H5.

Sacred Heart Church

49 Sixth Street, at Otis Street, Cambridge (1-617 547 0399). Harvard T then 69 bus. **Services** 9am Mon, Wed-Fri; 6pm Tue; 7.30am, 5pm Sat; 9am, 11am Sun.

Buddhist

Cambridge Zen Center

199 Auburn Street, Cambridge (1-617 576 3229/www.cambridge zen.com). Central T. **Map** p278 C3.
Nightly practice at 7pm.

Episcopal

Church of Christ, Scientist

250 Massachusetts Avenue, at Huntington Avenue, Back Bay (1-617 450 2000/www.tfccs.com). Symphony T. **Services** noon, 7.30pm Wed; 10am, 7pm Sun. **Map** p276 F8.

Church of the Advent

30 Brimmer Street, West End (1-617 523 2377/www.theadvent.org). Charles/MGH T. **Services** 7.30am Mon-Fri; 9am Sat; 8am, 9am, 11.15am Sun. **Map** p274 H4.

Old North Church (Christ Church)

193 Salem Street, at Hull Street, North End (1-617 523 6676/ www.oldnorth.com). Haymarket T. **Services** 9am, 11am Sun. **Map** p275 L2.

Jewish

Jewish Religious Information Services

177 Tremont Street, at Boylston Street, Downtown (1-617 426 2139). Boylston T. **Open** 9am-4pm Mon-Thur. **Map** p274 K5.
The Jewish Religious Information Services is a useful organisation that provides referrals to other groups, organisations, temples and synagogues throughout the area, as well as advice on kosher foods and restaurants.

Temple Israel

Longwood Avenue, at Plymouth Street, Brookline (1-617 566 3960/ www.tisrael.org). Longwood T. **Services** 5.45pm Fri; 10.30am Sat.

Methodist

Old West Church

131 Cambridge Street, at Staniford Street, Downtown (1-617 227 5088/www.oldwestchurch.org). Gov't Center T. **Services** 11am Sun. **Map** p274 K3.

Muslim

Islamic Society of Boston

204 Prospect Street, at Massachusetts Avenue, Cambridge (1-617 876 3546/www.isboston.org). Central T. **Services** 5.15am, 1pm, 4.30pm, 7.20pm, 9.30pm daily. **Map** p278 C3.
The Islamic Society acts both as a religious organisation and an information service.

Presbyterian

Church of the Covenant

67 Newbury Street, at Berkeley Street, Back Bay (1-617 266 7480/ www.churchofthecovenant.org). Arlington or Copley T. **Services** 10am Sun. **Map** p277 H5.

Quaker

Beacon Hill Friends House

6 Chestnut Street, at Charles Street, Beacon Hill (1-617 227 9118/ www.bhfh.org). Charles/MGH T. **Open** *Office* 9am-5pm Mon-Fri. *Meetings* 10.30am Sun. **Map** p274 J4.
The Friends House also has rooms for rent (in the Quaker style) for $70-$85 per night.

Safety & security

Boston is one of the safest cities in the United States. However, as in any big city, it's wise to be aware of the basic safety precautions. Don't fumble with your map or wallet in public; always plan where you're going and walk with brisk confidence; avoid walking alone at night; avoid parking in questionable areas (if in doubt, use valet parking when you can) and keep your car doors locked when parked and while driving.

Central Boston is generally well lit, but pedestrians should probably avoid Boston Common, the Public Garden and the walkways along the Charles River after dark. It's also useful to know that the couple of blocks along Washington Street, between Avery and Stuart Streets, are what's left of the Combat Zone – the old red-light district.

Smoking

Not long ago, smoking was allowed in bars and certain areas of some restaurants. The laws regulating where puffing was and wasn't permitted were quite confusing for everyone involved. Now things are easy: smoking has been banned in all public places, including bars, clubs and restaurants. Much to the dismay of smokers and many bar owners, the unpopular law forces smokers outside on to the pavement to get their fix. Some places have set up beer gardens with space heaters to help smokers get through Boston's brutal winter months. Bars have complained of a decline in business since the law's inception. Regardless, the rest of Massachusetts is expected to follow the lead of the Boston ban.

Study

As Boston has the world's largest number of colleges and universities per square mile, the choices for study are plentiful. The city is a great place to be a student with loads of youth-orientated activities, and there is a wide variety of courses and summer schools on offer each year.

Listed below is the most basic contact information for some of Boston's largest colleges and universities:

Boston College

40 Commonwealth Avenue, Chestnut Hill, MA 02467 (1-617 552 8000/ www.bc.edu).
Founded in 1863, BC is one of the oldest Jesuit universities in the US. Boasting top athletic programmes and high-quality academics, BC hosts more than 13,000 undergrads and graduate students on its 115-acre (46-hectare) campus, which is located in the suburbs six miles (9.7km) from downtown Boston. Annual tuition and other costs add up to over $37,000.

Boston University

930 Commonwealth Avenue, Boston, MA 02215 (1-617 353 2000/ www.bu.edu).
BU is the largest university in Boston and the third-largest independent university in the United States. With more than 30,000 students, including a large international contingent, BU offers a range of degrees and programmes. It sprawls along Commonwealth Avenue, west of downtown Boston. Famous alumni include Dr Martin Luther King Jr, Geena Davis, Nina Totenberg and *Seinfeld* actor Jason Alexander. Studying here isn't cheap, however. Annual tuition costs, including fees, room and board, exceed $38,000.

Emerson College

120 Boylston Street, Boston, MA 02116 (1-617 824 8500/ www.emerson.edu).
The nation's only four-year college devoted to the exclusive study of the performing arts and communication, Emerson links education with hands-on experience in studios, editing booths and workshops. It is a fairly small college, with a famously artistic student body. Its radio station, WERS (88.9 FM), consistently earns awards for its programming. Tuition alone costs $22,000 a year here.

Harvard University

Massachusetts Hall, Harvard Yard, off Massachusetts Avenue, Cambridge, MA 02138 (1-617 495 1000/www.harvard.edu).
The oldest and most prestigious university in America, enrolling about 6,600 undergrads (in Harvard College) and more than 11,000 graduate students. The Harvard Law, Medical and Business schools are also among the best in the world and the university's massive endowment ($11 billion) and reputation have guaranteed its steady growth and excellence. This is one of the most difficult colleges in the world to get into. Undergraduate tuition costs about $27,500 annually; the total expense per year is almost $40,000.

Massachusetts Institute of Technology

77 Massachusetts Avenue, Cambridge, MA 02139 (1-617 253 1000/www.mit.edu).
MIT is considered one of the top science and technology universities in the world. More than 4,300 students pay tuition in excess of $29,000 each year to attend. Men at the school bemoan the 61:39 male-female ratio. Students are required to take a six-subject core course that includes calculus, physics, chemistry and biology; eight terms of humanities; plus laboratory and writing classes. Still, its primary emphasis is science and technology. Undergrads may also cross-register in courses at Wellesley and Harvard.

Northeastern University

360 Huntington Avenue, Boston, MA 02115 (1-617 373 2000/ www.neu.edu).
The second-largest college in Boston, with nearly 12,000 undergrads, Northeastern is located in Back Bay, between the Museum of Fine Arts and Symphony Hall. Tuition costs $26,750 per year and students are encouraged to participate in 'co-operative education', which combines study with paid professional employment.

Suffolk University

8 Ashburton Place, Boston, MA 02108 (1-617 573 8000/ www.suffolk.edu).
Located on Beacon Hill, Suffolk sits plum in the heart of Boston. More than 6,000 full- and part-time graduate and undergraduate students are enrolled. Suffolk's Law School is especially renowned.

Tufts University

Bendetson Hall, Medford, MA 02155 (1-617 628 5000/www.tufts.edu).
With more than 8,000 students on three campuses, Tufts is based in Medford, just north-west of Boston proper. Its campus sits on prime real estate, perched on a hill overlooking the city. A private university, it was founded in 1852. Here, too, tuition plus room, board and other costs exceeds $38,000 a year.

University of Massachusetts at Boston

100 Morrissey Boulevard, Dorchester, MA 02125 (1-617 287 5000/www.umb.edu).
Established in 1964, UMass Boston represents one of several branches of the state-wide University of Massachusetts. Everybody, absolutely everybody, calls this system UMass. Situated on the Columbia Point peninsula, UMass is blessed with one of the prettiest campus locations in the city. The university's Boston location has a student population of around 12,000, but it has many more students at its other locations throughout the state. More than 37% of the university's students are 30 or older; minority students make up 35% of the population.

Telephones

Dialling & codes

The area codes for metropolitan Boston (including Cambridge, Somerville and Brookline) are 617 and 857. The first ring of suburbs is in the 781 and 339 area codes, which are considered a local call from metropolitan Boston. The northern suburbs and north coast are served by 978 and 351; the western and southern suburbs (including Cape Cod and the islands) are served by 508 and 774. Western Mass is also served by area code 413. These are all long-distance calls from Boston.

Calls made from all nine area codes of Massachusetts should be dialled using all 10 digits – area code + seven-digit phone number. So, even when calling within the city, it is necessary to include 617 before the bulk of the number. If you are trying to reach a Boston number from elsewhere within the US, you will have to dial 1 + area code and the seven-digit numbers. Area codes are included in the listings of this guide.

When calling Boston from abroad, dial the international access code of the country from which you are calling (00 from the UK), followed by the US country code (1), the area code and the number as before. Note that toll-free calls generally start with 1-800 or 1-888, while expensive per-minute calls usually start with 1-900 or 1-976. However, many hotels add a surcharge on all numbers.

Making a call

A local call costs 50¢; operator, directory and emergency calls are free. Public payphones only accept nickels, dimes and quarters – not ideal for long-distance calls. To make a call from a public phone, pick up the receiver and check for a dial tone before parting with your money; many pay phones in the US are broken and battered, and once you put your money in, it's gone. Some phones require you to dial the number first and wait for an operator or recorded message to tell you how much change to deposit. To make a collect (reverse charge) call, dial 0 for the operator followed by the area code and phone number. For help, dial 0 for an operator.

One of the most convenient ways to make a call is to use a phone card. These can be purchased at many retail outlets and range in price from $5 to $50, with a cost as low as 3¢ per minute. Read the card info carefully before buying; some have a 'connection charge'.

European-style prepaid phone cards that you insert directly into public phone booths instead of coins can be used in some special phone booths. Alternatively, you can charge calls to your MasterCard with AT&T (1-800 225 5288).

Telephone directories are available at many public phones and most hotels. If you can't find one, dial directory assistance (1-617 555 1212) for local numbers.

Useful numbers

Operator assistance 0.
Emergency (police, ambulance, fire) 911.
Directory assistance 1 + area code + 555 1212.

International calls

To phone abroad from Boston dial 011 followed by the country code, the area code and phone number. Country codes include:
UK 44, Ireland 353, Australia 61, New Zealand 64. To call other nations, check the White Pages of the telephone book which provides a full list of city and country codes.

Mobile phones

Whereas in Europe mobile phones work on the GSM network at either 900 or 1800 megahertz, the US does not have a standard mobile phone network that covers the whole country. This means that many European handsets will not work, and travellers from Europe may need to rent a handset and service once they arrive. Try **Cingular** (222 Newbury Street, at Exeter Street, 1-617 266 6975), which offers a prepaid service. US visitors to Boston should check in advance with their service provider whether they will be able to use their mobile phone.

Local service providers

Nextel
1-800 639 8359.
AT&T
1-800 462 4463.
Sprint PCS
1-800 480 4727.

Time & date

Massachusetts operates on Eastern Standard Time, which is five hours behind Greenwich Mean Time and one hour ahead of Central Time (Manitoba to Texas), two hours ahead of Mountain Time (Alberta to Arizona and New Mexico) and three hours ahead of Pacific Time (California).

Daylight Saving Time is observed from the first Sunday in April to the last Sunday in October, when clocks are put forward one hour.

Also, note that, in the US, dates are written in month, day and year order; so 12/5/04 is 5 December 2004, and not 12 May.

Tipping

Unlike in Europe, tipping is a way of life in the US. The growth of the service industry here is based largely on cheap labour. Waiters and bartenders in particular often make little more than $2 per hour outside of tips. Thus, Americans tip much more than people in other countries. Interestingly, this has spawned the myth that US residents throw their money around trying to impress people by tipping heavily. In reality, they're just aware how little their waiter earns. So, if you want good service and happy and healthy waitstaff, here are some basic guidelines for tipping in Boston:

Bellhops & baggage handlers
$1-$2 per bag.
Hotel maids
$1 a night.
Hotel concierges
$3-$5.
Bartenders
15% of the bill.
Cabbies, hairdressers & food delivery 15%-20% of the bill.
Valets, counter staff
$1-$3 depending on the size of the order and any special arrangements
Wait staff
15%-20% if no service is included in the bill.

Toilets

A few public toilets can be found in Boston – in Copley Place, Prudential Center and Faneuil Hall Marketplace.

Tourist information

Boston Common Information Booth

147 Tremont Street, Back Bay (1-617 426 3115/advance information 1-800 888 5515). Park Street T. **Open** 8.30am-5pm Mon-Fri. **Map** p274 J5.

Boston National Historical Park Service

15 State Street, at Congress Street, Downtown (1-617 242 5642/ www.nps.gov/bost). State T. **Open** 9am-5pm daily. **Map** p275 L4.
A useful source of information on Boston and New England; there's also a bookshop.

Cambridge Office of Tourism

Office 352, 18 Brattle Street, at Mount Auburn Street, Cambridge (1-617 441 2884/1-800 862 5678/ www.cambridge-usa.org). Harvard T. **Open** 9am-5pm Mon-Fri. **Map** p278 A2.
For general enquiries on Cambridge. The office also publishes the *Cambridge Visitor Guide*, which has information on local accommodation, sights and attractions as well as maps, a seasonal calendar of events and a walking tour map. The office also runs the Visitor Information Booth in Harvard Square, which has a touch-screen service to help you find your way around Cambridge.

Cambridge Visitor Information Booth

Harvard Square, Cambridge (no phone). Harvard T. **Open** 9am-5pm Mon-Sat. **Map** p278 B2.

Greater Boston Convention & Visitors Bureau

Suite 105, 2 Copley Place, Boston, MA 02116 (1-617 536 4100/1-888 733 2678/www.bostonusa.com). **Open** *Phone enquiries* 8.30am-5pm Mon-Fri.
The Greater Boston Convention & Visitors Bureau (GBCVB) provides information on attractions, restaurants, performing arts and nightlife, shopping and travel services. The main office operates as a telephone information service, but the bureau also runs visitor information centres at various locations in the city.

Massachusetts Office of Travel & Tourism

(1-617 727 3201/recorded information 1-800 447 6277/UK office 020 7978 7429/www.mass-vacation.com). **Open** *Boston office* 8.45am-5pm Mon-Fri. *UK office* 9am-5.30pm Mon-Fri.
The Office of Travel & Tourism has a telephone information service and also publishes a free magazine called *Getaway Guide*, which includes information about attractions and lodgings, a map and a seasonal calendar of events covering the state of Massachusetts.

Prudential Center Tourist Booth

Between Boylston Street & Huntington Avenue, Back Bay (advance information 1-800 888 5515/www.prudentialcenter.com). Hynes/ICA or Prudential T. **Open** 9am-5pm daily. **Map** p277 G6.

Travelers Aid Society

17 East Street, at Atlantic Avenue, Downtown (1-617 542 7286/ www.travelersaid.org). South Station T. **Open** 8.30am-5pm Mon-Fri. **Map** p275 L5.
A non-profit social service agency that has been helping travellers since 1920. These days, though, most of the organisation's work is with homeless families. However, volunteers also provide information on Boston and will help stranded travellers, but only those with serious financial problems.
Other locations: Logan Airport, Terminal E (1-617 567 5385).

Visas & immigration

See also p260 **New passport regulations**.
Under the Visa Waiver Scheme, citizens of the UK, Japan and all West European countries (except for Portugal, Greece and the Vatican City) do not need a visa for stays in the United States of less than 90 days (business or pleasure) – as long as they have a passport that is valid for the full 90-day period and a return or onward ticket. An open standby ticket is acceptable.

Canadians and Mexicans do not need visas, but they may be asked for proof of their citizenship. All other travellers, including those

New passport regulations

All travellers entering the United States under the Visa Waiver Program must present a machine-readable passport (MRP), which has been the standard-issue (burgundy) passport in the UK since 1988. However, at some point in the future, all visitors to the US will be required to present a passport with a biometric identifier (a microchip encoded with information such as fingerprints). The deadline for this requirement was, at the time of writing, under review. At a congressional hearing on 21 April 2004, the State Department lobbied for a two-year postponement of the original deadline, which stated that any passport issued after 26 October 2004 would require a biometric identifier. Call your nearest US Embassy and check http://unitedstatesvisas.gov or www.travel.state.gov/vwp.html for a final decision.

Meanwhile, all Visa Waiver Program travellers should expect to have their fingerprints scanned and a digital photo taken when they arrive. This extra measure is supposed to add just 15 seconds to the arrival process, but queue times have increased. Also, children can no longer travel on their parents' passports.

Those travellers applying for a visa after 26 October 2004 will need to submit biometric data for an identifier, which will be added to their visa. Plenty of time should be allowed for visa applications (a process that can easily take anything from two to three months).

from Australia and New Zealand, must have a visa. Full information and visa application forms can be obtained from your nearest US embassy or consulate. If you require a visa urgently, apply via the travel agent when you book your ticket.

Weights & measures

The US uses the imperial system. Here are a few basic metric equivalents.

1 foot = 0.3048 metre
1 mile = 1.6093 kilometre
1 square yard = 0.836 square metre
1 pound = 0.4536 kilogramme
1 pint (16fl oz) = 0.4732 litre

When to go

Weatherwise, the best time of year in Boston is the autumn. Temperatures are generally in the low 70s°F (20s°C) and the skies are clear for days. Of course, this also means that the city is packed to bursting-point. Prices soar (even more than usual in this expensive town) and booking a hotel room becomes difficult. It's the time when students of over 60 colleges are returning to town; many professional conventions take place, and autumn foliage sightseers are arriving by the busload. In other words, it is, without question, the best of times and the worst of times to find yourself in Boston.

Summer is much quieter, and in general more laid-back. Bostonians are more relaxed and it's a lot easier to get around town. But the downside is that temperatures can soar to the 80s°F and 90s°F (high 20s°C and 30s°C) with almost 100 per cent humidity. This can make sightseeing arduous and sleeping quite difficult. It's worth making sure your hotel has air-conditioning.

Spring is also a quieter time of year, when blossom appears and the city is quite beautiful. But the weather can also be very unpredictable at this time of year, and temperatures can range, day-by-day, from the high 40s°F to the low 70s°F (10°C-20°C). It also tends to be a particularly rainy season, so bring an umbrella.

Winter tends to be grey, cold and dreary, which is why the hotel rates drop. The city is lovely after a light dusting of snow, but there can be debilitating blizzards in January and February, during which the city comes to a standstill.

Whichever season you choose to visit Boston, make sure you pack layers of clothing. The old saying 'If you don't like the Boston weather, wait ten minutes' holds true. Hat, gloves and scarf are essential in winter; shorts are preferable in the summer. An umbrella or waterproof gear is a good idea at any time of year.

Public holidays

New Year's Day
1 January.
Martin Luther King Day
Third Monday in January.
Presidents' Day
Third Monday in February.
St Patrick's Day
17 March.
Memorial Day
Last Monday in May.
Independence Day
4 July.
Labor Day
First Monday in September.
Columbus Day
Second Monday in October.
Veterans Day
11 November.
Thanksgiving Day
Last Thursday in November.
Christmas Day
25 December.

Weather forecast

Phone 1-617 936 1234 or 1-617 637 1212 for free daily weather info, or check the Massachusetts weather on the web at www.rainorshine.com.

Working in the US

Foreigners seeking work in the US must enlist a US company to sponsor them for an H-1 visa, which permits the holder to work in the US for five years. It will also have to convince the Immigration department that no American could do the job. Contact your American embassy for details.

Women

Boston is a safe city for women, but it's still a good idea to use common sense and avoid deserted streets at night. One nuisance is the loutish frat boys roaming the streets after the bars close. They're mostly harmless, but do enjoy shooting their mouths off after a dozen pints with their brothers.

Further Reference

Books

Non-fiction

Jack Beatty: *The Rascal King: The Life and Times of James Michael Curley, 1874-1958*
Thoroughly researched biography of the charismatic Boston mayor.
David Hackett Fischer: *Paul Revere's Ride*
Brilliant account of the legendary ride to Lexington, related as a historical narrative.
Sebastian Junger: *The Perfect Storm*
Tale of a crew of Gloucester fishermen caught up in the 'Hallowe'en Gale' in the North Atlantic in 1991; it was brought to the big screen in 2000.
Noel Riley Fitch: *Appetite for Life: The Biography of Julia Child*
All about America's favourite TV chef and Boston icon.
Barney Frank: *Improper Bostonians: Lesbian and Gay History from the Puritans to Playland*
Comprehensive history of homosexuality in Boston.
Doris Kearns Goodwin: *The Fitzgeralds and the Kennedys: An American Saga*
The story behind America's answer to royalty.
J Anthony Lukas: *Common Ground: A Turbulent Decade in the Lives of Three American Families*
The 1970s busing crisis, through the eyes of an Irish-American, a black and a white middle-class family.
Dan McNichol and Andy Ryan: *The Big Dig*
Tells the story of the biggest highway project in US history.
Robert S Morse: *25 Mountain Bike Tours in Massachusetts: From the Connecticut River to the Atlantic Coast*
Guidelines and trips for the ambitious recreational biker.
Douglass Shand-Tucci: *The Art of Scandal: The Life and Times of Isabella Stewart Gardner*
Biography of Boston's famous patron of the arts and the inspiration behind Isabel Archer in *Portrait of a Lady.*
Dan Shaughnessy: *The Curse of the Bambino*
Entertaining look at the Red Sox 'curse' by local sports journo.

Fiction

Nathan Aldyne: *Canary; Cobalt; Slate; Vermillion*
Four tongue-in-cheek mystery novels set in the gay communities of Boston and Provincetown, circa 1980.
Nathaniel Hawthorne: *The Scarlet Letter; The House of the Seven Gables*
Two American – and New England – classics by the Salem native.
Henry James: *The Bostonians*
The tale of Varena Tarrant, James's Boston feminist.
Henry Wadsworth Longfellow: *The Works of Henry Wadsworth Longfollow*
Includes the famous poem *Paul Revere's Ride.*
Robert Lowell: *Life Studies* and *For the Union Dead*
The poet's account of growing up privileged in Boston and hating it.
Norman Mailer: *Tough Guys Don't Dance*
Boston's ultimate cynic tells another hard-edged tale.
Robert McCloskey: *Make Way for Ducklings*
The classic children's tale about ducks in the Boston Public Garden.
Michael Patrick McDonald: *All Souls*
The bittersweet story of a family growing up together in South Boston's Irish ghetto.
Herman Melville: *Moby-Dick*
The great American novel. Melville's 19th-century romance with the sea.
Henry David Thoreau: *Walden*
The Transcendentalist's most famous work, written while living in isolation in a cabin for two years, two months and two days.
John Updike: *Roger's Version*
The writer's updated take on *The Scarlet Letter.*

Film

A Civil Action (1998)
John Travolta stars in the real-life tale of a town near Boston that was poisoned by a chemical company, sued and lost.
The Crucible (1996)
Film version of the Pulitzer Prize-winning play about the Salem Witch Trials, with Wynona Ryder.
Good Will Hunting (1997)
Academy Award-winning film by and about South Boston residents. Filmed on location all over town, particularly in Southie and in Cambridge around MIT.
Legally Blonde (2001)
Bubbly West Coast blonde (Reese Witherspoon) sets out to win her blue-blooded Boston fraternity crush by attending Harvard Law School. The film was not actually filmed in Cambridge.
Love Story (1970)
Ali MacGraw and Ryan O'Neal star in the classic weepie set in Harvard.
Mona Lisa Smile (2003)
Chick flick based on Wellesley College's campus in the '50s, starring Julia Roberts.
Mystic River (2003)
Clint Eastwood directs this serious drama starring Sean Penn – check out his take on the Boston accent.
Next Stop, Wonderland (1998)
Wonderful, low-budget romantic comedy with nods toward Boston's old and new immigrant communities. Filmed all over the city.
No Cure for Cancer (1994)
Concert film with local comedian Denis Leary, who both typifies and spoofs Boston's angry young Irish.
Prozac Nation (2001)
Christina Ricci acts out Elizabeth Wurtzel's famous novel about being stressed and depressed at Harvard.

Average temperatures

	High (°F/°C)	Low (°F/°C)
January	36/2	23/-5
February	38/3	24/-4
March	45/7	32/0
April	57/14	41/5
May	67/20	50/10
June	77/25	59/15
July	82/28	65/18
August	80/27	64/18
September	72/22	57/14
October	63/17	47/8
November	52/11	39/4
December	40/4	27/-3

Learning the lingo

When a Boston native tells you to 'pahk the cah ovah by Hahvahd Yahd', you may wonder where all the r's have got to. They're not gone, they've just relocated – ask someone if they grew up in Southie, and they may well answer 'Yeahr I did.'

The Boston accent, so often mangled by Hollywood, sports a pedigree that goes back four centuries. Boston's first settlers, mostly Puritans from East Anglia, brought with them the slighted 'r' of 'yahd' and the broad 'a' of 'bahthroom.' Later waves of immigrants, particularly the Irish in the 19th century, infused the local dialect with their own linguistic quirks. Today, the accent is fading downtown, but thrives in Boston's older neighbourhoods and the suburbs just outside the city.

'Bawstin' English is renowned as one of the most difficult American accents for outsiders to understand. Add in some unique regional slang, a whacking number of place names with inscrutable pronunciation, and a tendency among locals to do the neat trick of mumbling while talking at top speed, and you may feel you've stumbled across a foreign language. Have no fear – a little practice and you'll be well on your way to comprehension. Just knowing how to pronounce 'Woburn' will set you apart from the garden-variety tourist.

Here's a brief guide to some odd pronunciations, place names, and colloquialisms you'll hear about town:

Quincy: Pronounced 'Quinnzie'
Woburn: Pronounced 'Woobuhn'
JP: Jamaica Plain
Southie: South Boston
Comm Ave: Commonwealth Avenue
Mass Ave: Massachusetts Avenue
Mem Drive: Memorial Drive
The Pit: The centre of Harvard Square
The Pike: The Massachusetts Turnpike
The Pru: The Prudential Tower
Shattered: Very, very drunk
Khakhis: What you use to unlock the 'cah' (car)
Tonic: Old Boston word for soft drink
Jimmies: Chocolate sprinkles on top of ice-cream
Frappe: A milkshake – pronounced 'frap'
Spa: Convenience store that sells food
Packie: A liquor store (short for package store)
Bang a U-y: Make a U-turn
Hang a louey: Take a left
Big Dig: The most expensive highway project in US history
The Pats: The New England Patriots
The Sox: Boston's beloved and beleaguered baseball team, the Red Sox

TV shows

Ally McBeal
Quirky legal drama, written and directed by the respected writer David E Kelly. Set in, occasionally filmed in, Boston.

Boston Public
Another David E Kelly drama set in Beantown. Stressed out high-school teachers deal with unwieldy students. Sensational sensationalism.

The Practice
Quirky legal drama, written and directed, again, by David E Kelly. Set in, and occasionally filmed in, Boston.

Two Guys and a Girl
Rather dull sitcom set in Boston.

Music

Aerosmith: *Toys in the Attic* (1975)
Essential album by the '70s rock band before they quit doing drugs.

Boston: *Boston* (1976)
The city's namesake band's namesake release was one of the best-selling albums of all time.

The Cars: *Greatest Hits* (1978)
Hugely popular new wave band from the late 1970s.

Dropkick Murphys: *Do or Die* (1998)
Irish-American working class punk anthems to shout along with.

Tom Lehrer: *The Remains of Tom Lehrer* (2000)
Box set of snarky satire from Harvard University.

The Lemonheads: *Car, Button, Cloth* (1996)
Funny, sad, wonderful songs by this quirky, adorable Boston band.

Mission of Burma: *Signals, Calls and Marches* (1981)
Boston's indie godfathers are back together and playing to sold-out audiences all over the country.

Morphine: *Cure for Pain* (1993)
The quirky Boston rock band with no guitar that was fronted by the late Mark Sandman.

Pixies: *Doolittle* (1989)
Boston's own: on classics like 'Monkey Gone to Heaven' these guys (and one girl) had it all – the rock, the quirks and the hooks.

Johnathan Richman and the Modern Lovers: *Modern Lovers* (1988)
Influential Boston-based true musician's band.

Websites

www.bostonphoenix.com
The website of local weekly paper the *Boston Phoenix*. Great for tracking down what's happening where in the city.

www.justanotherscene.com
This huge site is ground zero for the local underground rock scene.

www.bostonusa.com
Website of the Greater Boston Convention & Visitors Bureau. Excellent for all kinds of information about the city.

www.boston.com
The website of the *Boston Globe*, the city's daily broadsheet.

www.cityofboston.gov
Official website with a section for visitors. Access to everything from free outdoor concerts to maps.

Index

Note Page numbers in **bold** indicate section(s) giving key information on a topic; *italics* indicate photographs.

Accommodation

Restaurants & Cafés

Pubs & Bars

Advertisers' Index

Please refer to the relevant sections for addresses/telephone numbers

Place of interest and/or entertainment
Railway stations
Subway
Parks
Hospitals/universities
Neighbourhood .... BACK BAY

Maps

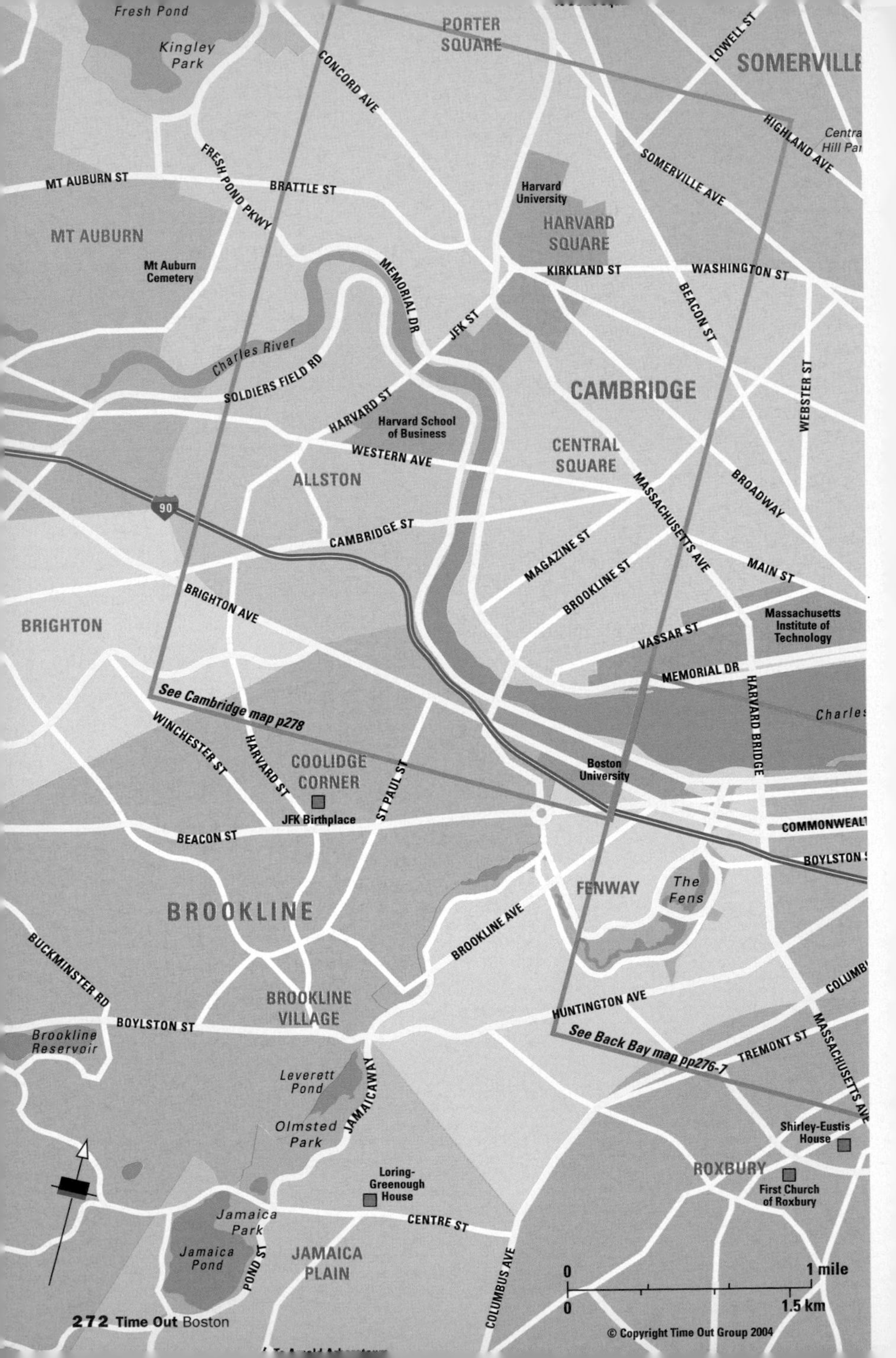
Fresh Pond
Kingley Park
PORTER SQUARE
SOMERVILLE
LOWELL ST
CONCORD AVE
HIGHLAND AVE
Central Hill Park
SOMERVILLE AVE
FRESH POND PKWY
MT AUBURN ST
BRATTLE ST
Harvard University
HARVARD SQUARE
MT AUBURN
Mt Auburn Cemetery
MEMORIAL DR
KIRKLAND ST
WASHINGTON ST
BEACON ST
JFK ST
Charles River
SOLDIERS FIELD RD
CAMBRIDGE
WEBSTER ST
HARVARD ST
Harvard School of Business
WESTERN AVE
CENTRAL SQUARE
ALLSTON
MASSACHUSETTS AVE
BROADWAY
90
CAMBRIDGE ST
MAGAZINE ST
BROOKLINE ST
MAIN ST
BRIGHTON AVE
BRIGHTON
Massachusetts Institute of Technology
VASSAR ST
MEMORIAL DR
HARVARD BRIDGE
Charles
See Cambridge map p278
WINCHESTER ST
HARVARD ST
COOLIDGE CORNER
ST PAUL ST
Boston University
JFK Birthplace
BEACON ST
COMMONWEALTH
BOYLSTON ST
FENWAY
The Fens
BROOKLINE
BROOKLINE AVE
BUCKMINSTER RD
BROOKLINE VILLAGE
HUNTINGTON AVE
COLUMBUS
BOYLSTON ST
Brookline Reservoir
See Back Bay map pp276-7
TREMONT ST
MASSACHUSETTS AVE
Leverett Pond
JAMAICAWAY
Olmsted Park
Shirley-Eustis House
Loring-Greenough House
ROXBURY
First Church of Roxbury
Jamaica Park
CENTRE ST
Jamaica Pond
POND ST
JAMAICA PLAIN
COLUMBUS AVE
0
1 mile
0
1.5 km

Greater Boston

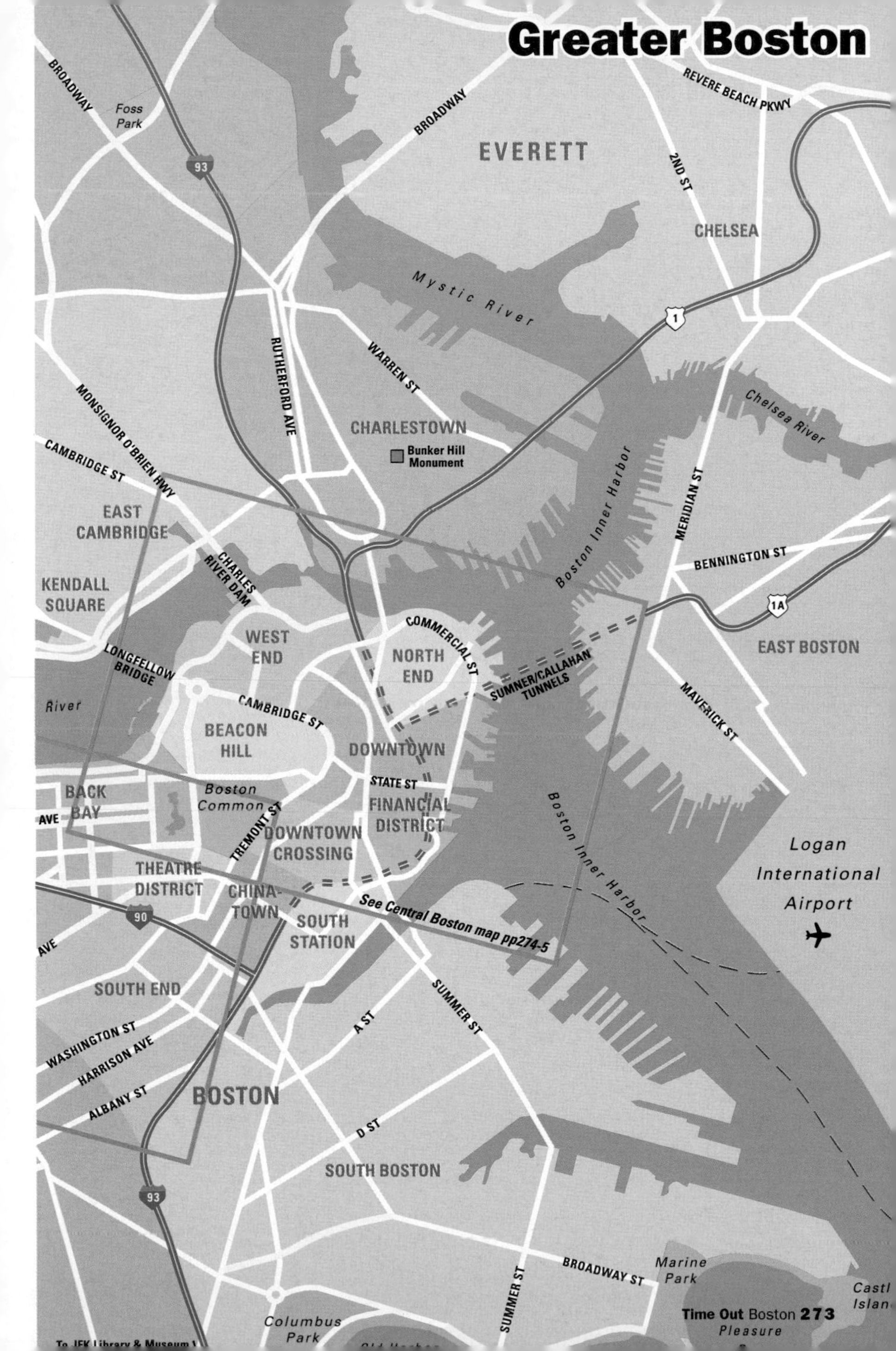

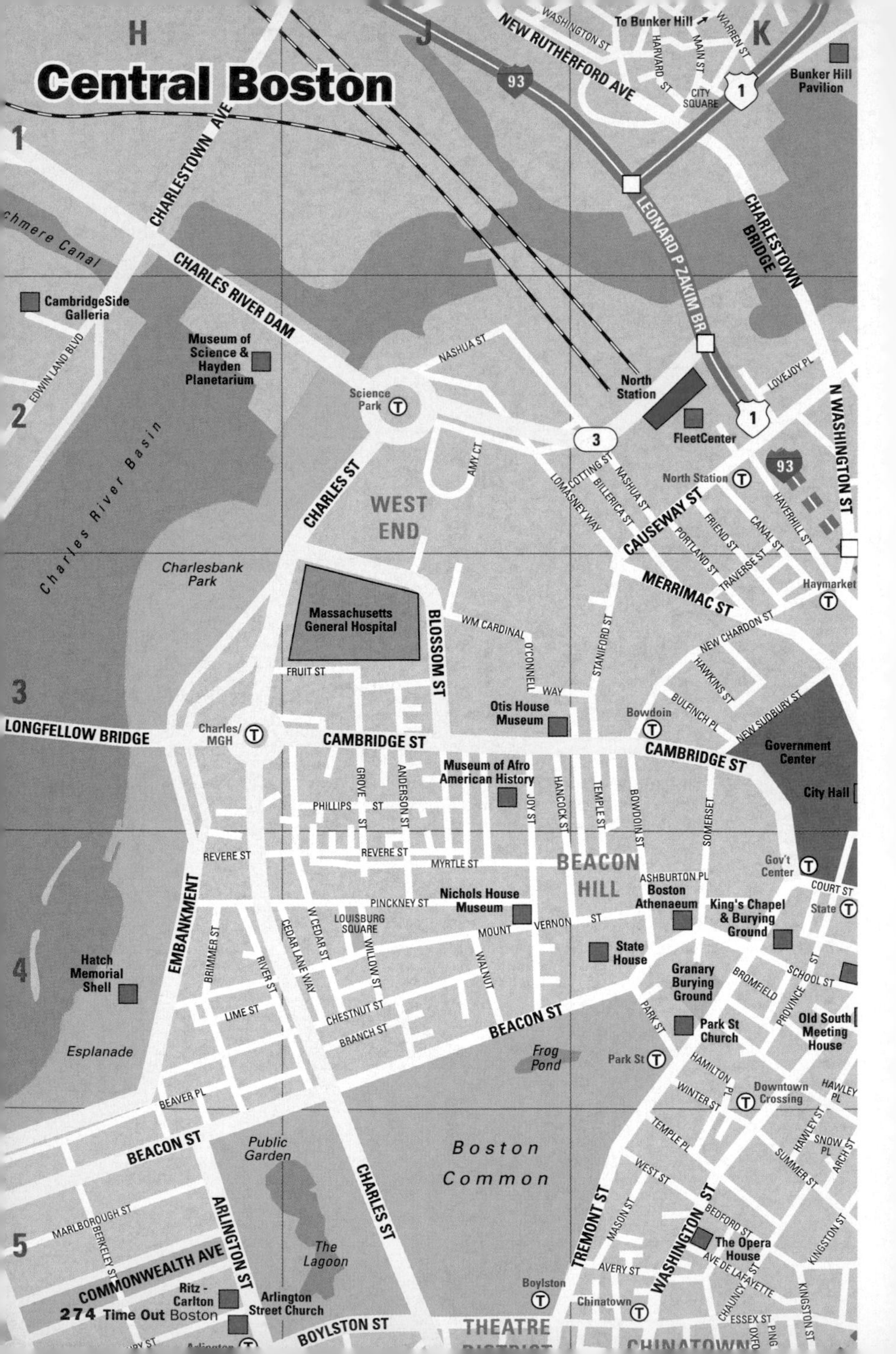
Central Boston
H
J
K
1
2
3
4
5
CHARLESTOWN AVE
CHARLES RIVER DAM
CambridgeSide Galleria
EDWIN LAND BLVD
Museum of Science & Hayden Planetarium
Science Park
Charles River Basin
Charlesbank Park
NEW RUTHERFORD AVE
WASHINGTON ST
To Bunker Hill
WARREN ST
HARVARD ST
MAIN ST
CITY SQUARE
Bunker Hill Pavilion
LEONARD P ZAKIM BR
CHARLESTOWN BRIDGE
North Station
FleetCenter
NASHUA ST
LOVEJOY PL
N WASHINGTON ST
AMY CT
WEST END
CHARLES ST
COTTING ST
LOMASNEY WAY
BILLERICA ST
CAUSEWAY ST
PORTLAND ST
FRIEND ST
CANAL ST
HAVERHILL ST
TRAVERSE ST
MERRIMAC ST
Haymarket
Massachusetts General Hospital
BLOSSOM ST
WM CARDINAL
O'CONNELL WAY
STANIFORD ST
NEW CHARDON ST
HAWKINS ST
BULFINCH PL
NEW SUDBURY ST
FRUIT ST
Otis House Museum
Bowdoin
LONGFELLOW BRIDGE
Charles/MGH
CAMBRIDGE ST
Government Center
City Hall
Museum of Afro American History
GROVE ST
ANDERSON ST
PHILLIPS ST
JOY ST
HANCOCK ST
TEMPLE ST
BOWDOIN ST
SOMERSET
REVERE ST
MYRTLE ST
BEACON HILL
Gov't Center
ASHBURTON PL
EMBANKMENT
Nichols House Museum
PINCKNEY ST
Boston Athenaeum
King's Chapel & Burying Ground
COURT ST
State
LOUISBURG SQUARE
W CEDAR ST
CEDAR LANE WAY
BRIMMER ST
RIVER ST
WILLOW ST
MOUNT VERNON ST
WALNUT
State House
Hatch Memorial Shell
Granary Burying Ground
BROMFIELD
SCHOOL ST
PROVINCE
LIME ST
CHESTNUT ST
BRANCH ST
BEACON ST
PARK ST
Park St Church
Old South Meeting House
Esplanade
Frog Pond
Park St
HAMILTON PL
WINTER ST
Downtown Crossing
HAWLEY PL
BEAVER PL
HAWLEY ST
SNOW PL
ARCH ST
TEMPLE PL
SUMMER ST
Public Garden
Boston Common
WEST ST
MARLBOROUGH ST
BERKELEY ST
ARLINGTON ST
The Lagoon
TREMONT ST
MASON ST
WASHINGTON ST
BEDFORD ST
The Opera House
KINGSTON ST
COMMONWEALTH AVE
AVERY ST
AVE DE LAFAYETTE
Ritz - Carlton
Arlington Street Church
Boylston
Chinatown
CHAUNCY ST
ESSEX ST
BOYLSTON ST
THEATRE

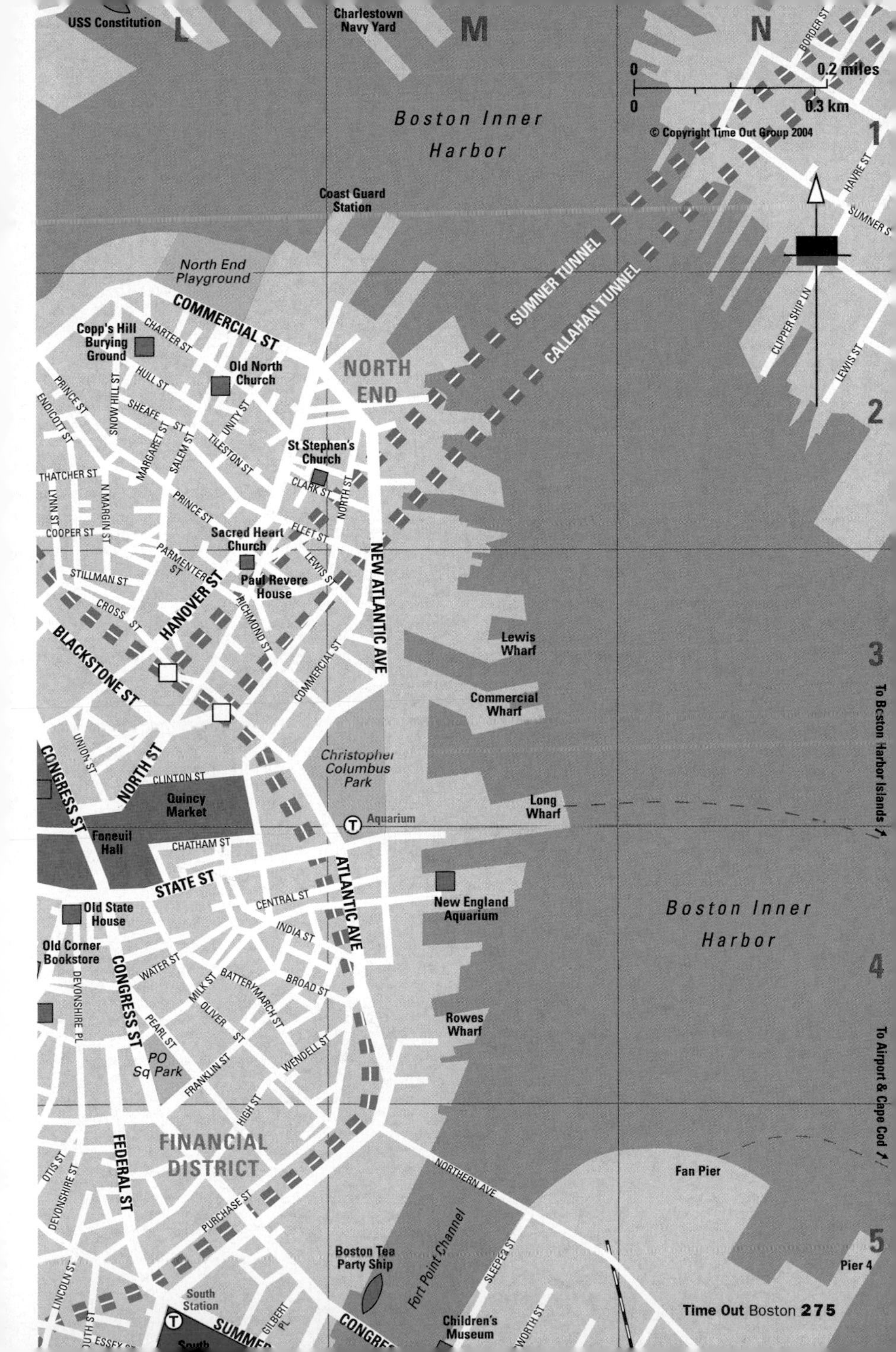

USS Constitution
Charlestown Navy Yard
L
M
N
0
0.2 miles
0
0.3 km
© Copyright Time Out Group 2004
Boston Inner Harbor
Coast Guard Station
North End Playground
SUMNER TUNNEL
CALLAHAN TUNNEL
COMMERCIAL ST
Copp's Hill Burying Ground
Old North Church
NORTH END
St Stephen's Church
Sacred Heart Church
Paul Revere House
NEW ATLANTIC AVE
HANOVER ST
BLACKSTONE ST
NORTH ST
CONGRESS ST
Quincy Market
Faneuil Hall
STATE ST
Old State House
Old Corner Bookstore
ATLANTIC AVE
New England Aquarium
Aquarium
Lewis Wharf
Commercial Wharf
Long Wharf
Christopher Columbus Park
Rowes Wharf
Boston Inner Harbor
PO Sq Park
FINANCIAL DISTRICT
FEDERAL ST
Fan Pier
Pier 4
Boston Tea Party Ship
Fort Point Channel
Children's Museum
South Station
NORTHERN AVE
To Boston Harbor Islands
To Airport & Cape Cod
1
2
3
4
5

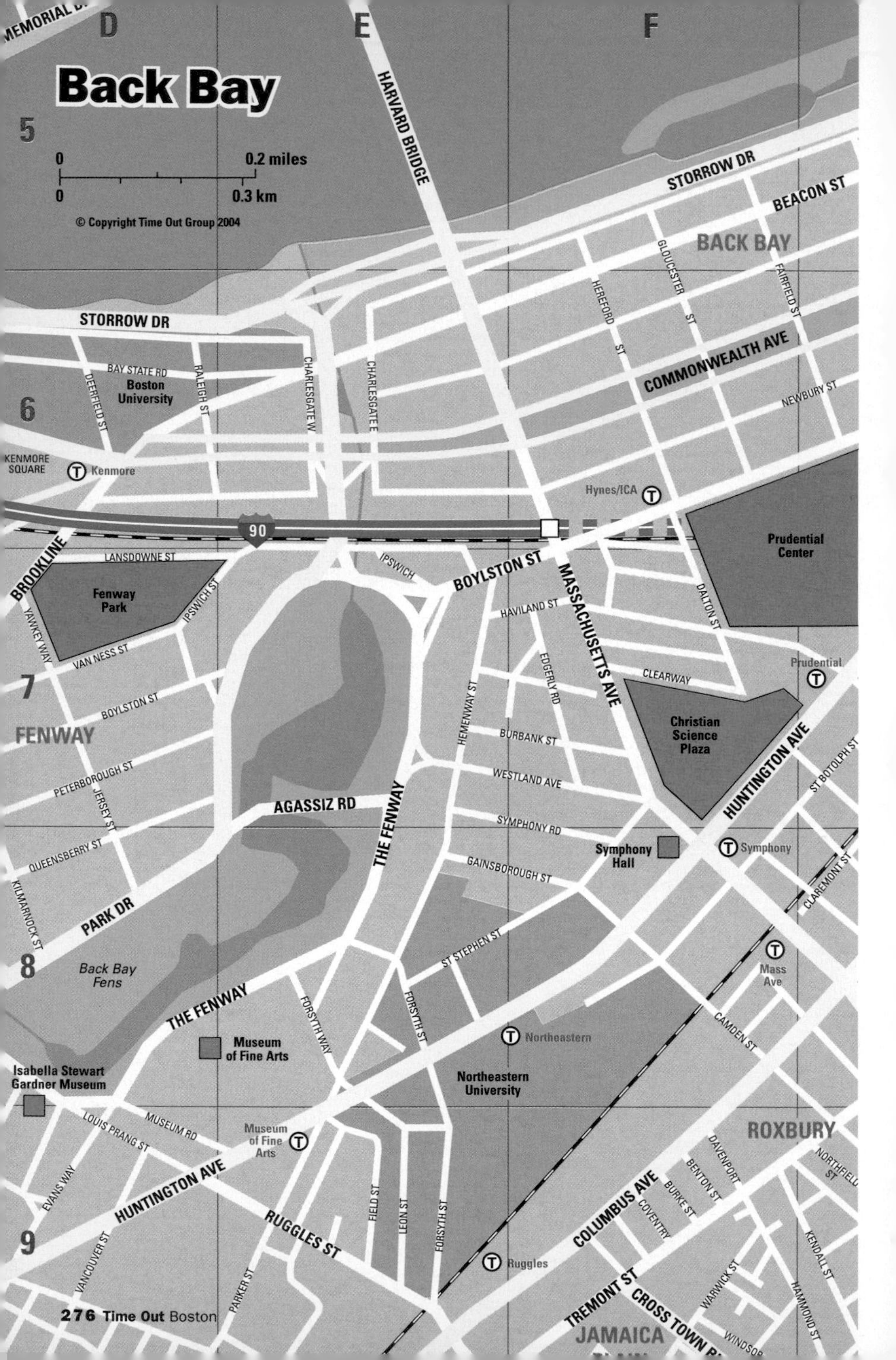
Back Bay
D
E
F
5
6
7
8
9
0
0.2 miles
0
0.3 km
© Copyright Time Out Group 2004
MEMORIAL D
HARVARD BRIDGE
STORROW DR
BEACON ST
BACK BAY
GLOUCESTER ST
HEREFORD ST
FAIRFIELD ST
COMMONWEALTH AVE
NEWBURY ST
BAY STATE RD
Boston University
DEERFIELD ST
RALEIGH ST
CHARLESGATE W
CHARLESGATE E
KENMORE SQUARE
Kenmore
Hynes/ICA
90
Prudential Center
BROOKLINE
LANSDOWNE ST
IPSWICH
BOYLSTON ST
MASSACHUSETTS AVE
Fenway Park
IPSWICH ST
YAWKEY WAY
VAN NESS ST
HAVILAND ST
DALTON ST
EDGERLY RD
CLEARWAY
Prudential
HEMENWAY ST
Christian Science Plaza
FENWAY
BOYLSTON ST
BURBANK ST
HUNTINGTON AVE
ST BOTOLPH ST
PETERBOROUGH ST
WESTLAND AVE
JERSEY ST
AGASSIZ RD
SYMPHONY RD
QUEENSBERRY ST
THE FENWAY
Symphony Hall
Symphony
GAINSBOROUGH ST
CLAREMONT ST
KILMARNOCK ST
PARK DR
ST STEPHEN ST
Back Bay Fens
Mass Ave
THE FENWAY
FORSYTH WAY
FORSYTH ST
CAMDEN ST
Museum of Fine Arts
Northeastern
Isabella Stewart Gardner Museum
Northeastern University
MUSEUM RD
LOUIS PRANG ST
Museum of Fine Arts
ROXBURY
DAVENPORT
NORTHFIELD ST
BENTON ST
EVANS WAY
HUNTINGTON AVE
COLUMBUS AVE
BURKE ST
COVENTRY
FIELD ST
LEON ST
FORSYTH ST
RUGGLES ST
KENDALL ST
VANCOUVER ST
Ruggles
WARWICK ST
TREMONT ST
CROSS TOWN
HAMMOND ST
PARKER ST
JAMAICA
WINDSOR

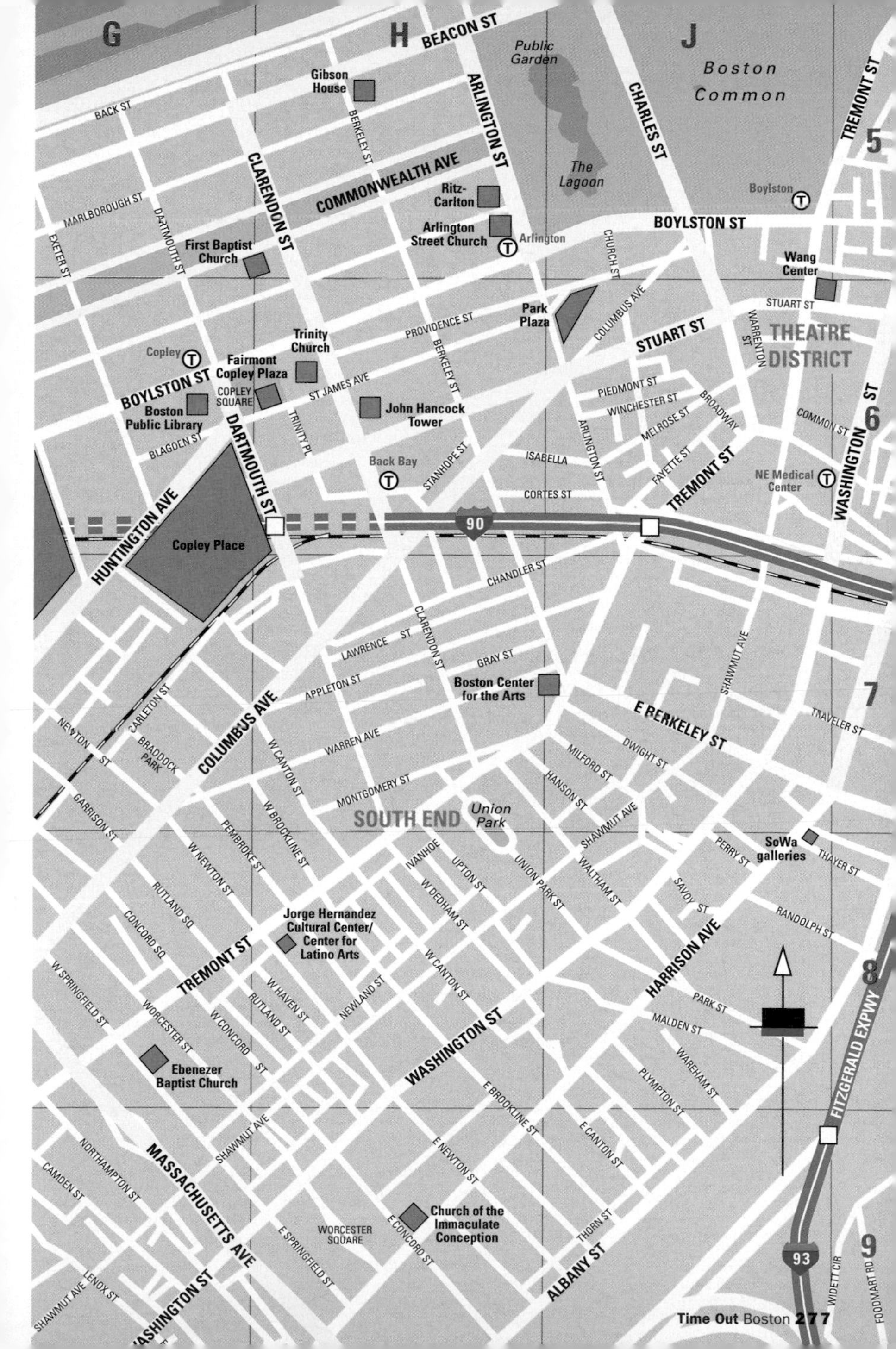
G
H
J
5
6
7
8
9
BEACON ST
Public Garden
Boston Common
The Lagoon
Gibson House
BACK ST
BERKELEY ST
ARLINGTON ST
CHARLES ST
TREMONT ST
COMMONWEALTH AVE
CLARENDON ST
Ritz-Carlton
Boylston
MARLBOROUGH ST
DARTMOUTH ST
EXETER ST
First Baptist Church
Arlington Street Church
Arlington
BOYLSTON ST
CHURCH ST
Wang Center
STUART ST
Park Plaza
COLUMBUS AVE
PROVIDENCE ST
WARRENTON ST
THEATRE DISTRICT
Trinity Church
Copley
Fairmont Copley Plaza
COPLEY SQUARE
ST JAMES AVE
BOYLSTON ST
Boston Public Library
TRINITY PL
John Hancock Tower
PIEDMONT ST
WINCHESTER ST
MELROSE ST
BROADWAY
COMMON ST
BLAGDEN ST
Back Bay
STANHOPE ST
ISABELLA
ARLINGTON ST
FAYETTE ST
NE Medical Center
WASHINGTON ST
CORTES ST
HUNTINGTON AVE
Copley Place
90
CHANDLER ST
CLARENDON ST
LAWRENCE ST
GRAY ST
SHAWMUT AVE
APPLETON ST
Boston Center for the Arts
CARLETON ST
E BERKELEY ST
TRAVELER ST
NEWTON ST
BRADDOCK PARK
WARREN AVE
COLUMBUS AVE
W CANTON ST
DWIGHT ST
MILFORD ST
HANSON ST
MONTGOMERY ST
GARRISON ST
W BROOKLINE ST
SOUTH END
Union Park
SHAWMUT AVE
PEMBROKE ST
IVANHOE
UPTON ST
UNION PARK ST
WALTHAM ST
PERRY ST
SoWa galleries
THAYER ST
W NEWTON ST
W DEDHAM ST
SAVOY ST
RUTLAND SQ
CONCORD SQ
Jorge Hernandez Cultural Center/ Center for Latino Arts
W CANTON ST
HARRISON AVE
RANDOLPH ST
TREMONT ST
W HAVEN ST
NEWLAND ST
PARK ST
W SPRINGFIELD ST
WORCESTER ST
W CONCORD ST
RUTLAND ST
MALDEN ST
WASHINGTON ST
FITZGERALD EXPWY
Ebenezer Baptist Church
WAREHAM ST
E BROOKLINE ST
PLYMPTON ST
NORTHAMPTON ST
SHAWMUT AVE
MASSACHUSETTS AVE
E CANTON ST
E NEWTON ST
CAMDEN ST
Church of the Immaculate Conception
WORCESTER SQUARE
E CONCORD ST
THORN ST
E SPRINGFIELD ST
93
LENOX ST
WIDETT CIR
FOODMART RD
SHAWMUT AVE
WASHINGTON ST
ALBANY ST

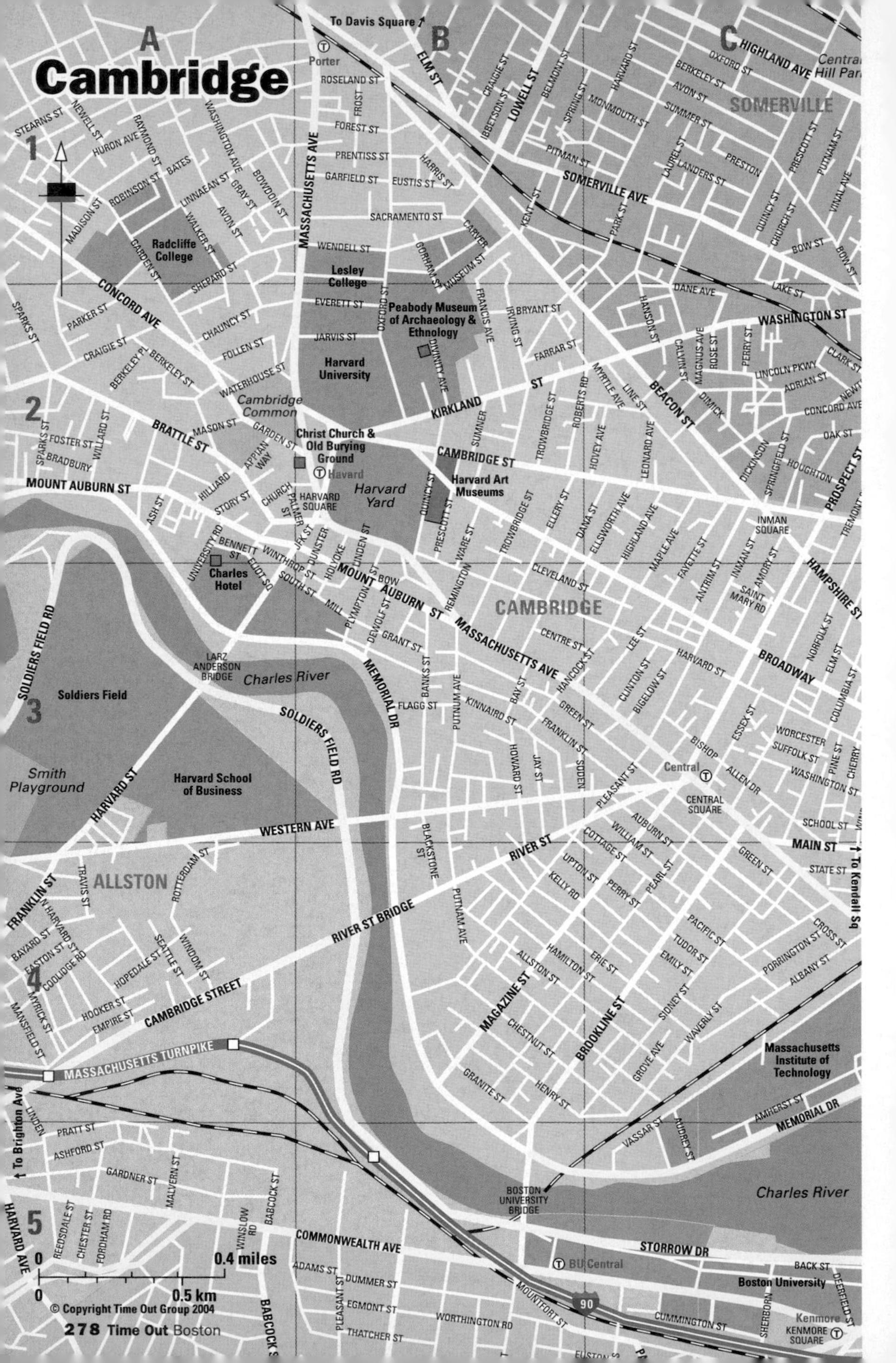
Cambridge
A
B
C
1
2
3
4
5
To Davis Square
Porter
Radcliffe College
Lesley College
Peabody Museum of Archaeology & Ethnology
Harvard University
Cambridge Common
Christ Church & Old Burying Ground
Harvard
Harvard Yard
Harvard Art Museums
HARVARD SQUARE
Charles Hotel
INMAN SQUARE
SOMERVILLE
Central Hill Park
CAMBRIDGE
LARZ ANDERSON BRIDGE
Charles River
Soldiers Field
Smith Playground
Harvard School of Business
ALLSTON
Central
CENTRAL SQUARE
To Kendall Sq
Massachusetts Institute of Technology
BOSTON UNIVERSITY BRIDGE
BU Central
Boston University
Kenmore
KENMORE SQUARE
To Brighton Ave
MASSACHUSETTS TURNPIKE
90
MASSACHUSETTS AVE
CONCORD AVE
BRATTLE ST
MOUNT AUBURN ST
KIRKLAND ST
CAMBRIDGE ST
SOMERVILLE AVE
WASHINGTON ST
BEACON ST
HIGHLAND AVE
PROSPECT ST
HAMPSHIRE ST
BROADWAY
MAIN ST
WESTERN AVE
RIVER ST
RIVER ST BRIDGE
CAMBRIDGE STREET
MEMORIAL DR
SOLDIERS FIELD RD
HARVARD ST
FRANKLIN ST
MAGAZINE ST
BROOKLINE ST
COMMONWEALTH AVE
STORROW DR
HARVARD AVE
0
0.4 miles
0
0.5 km

Trips Out of Town

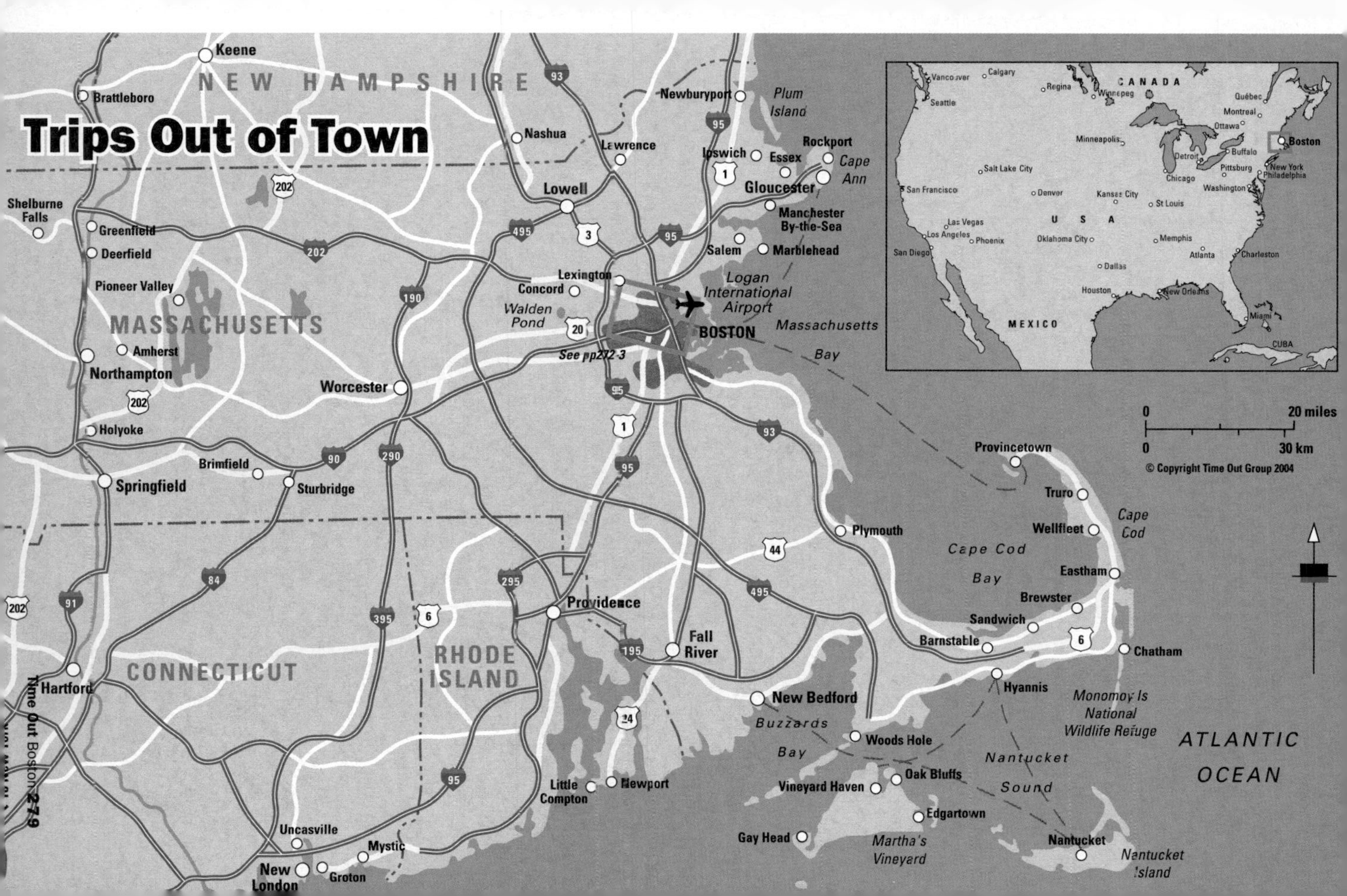

Street Index

MBTA Subway Map

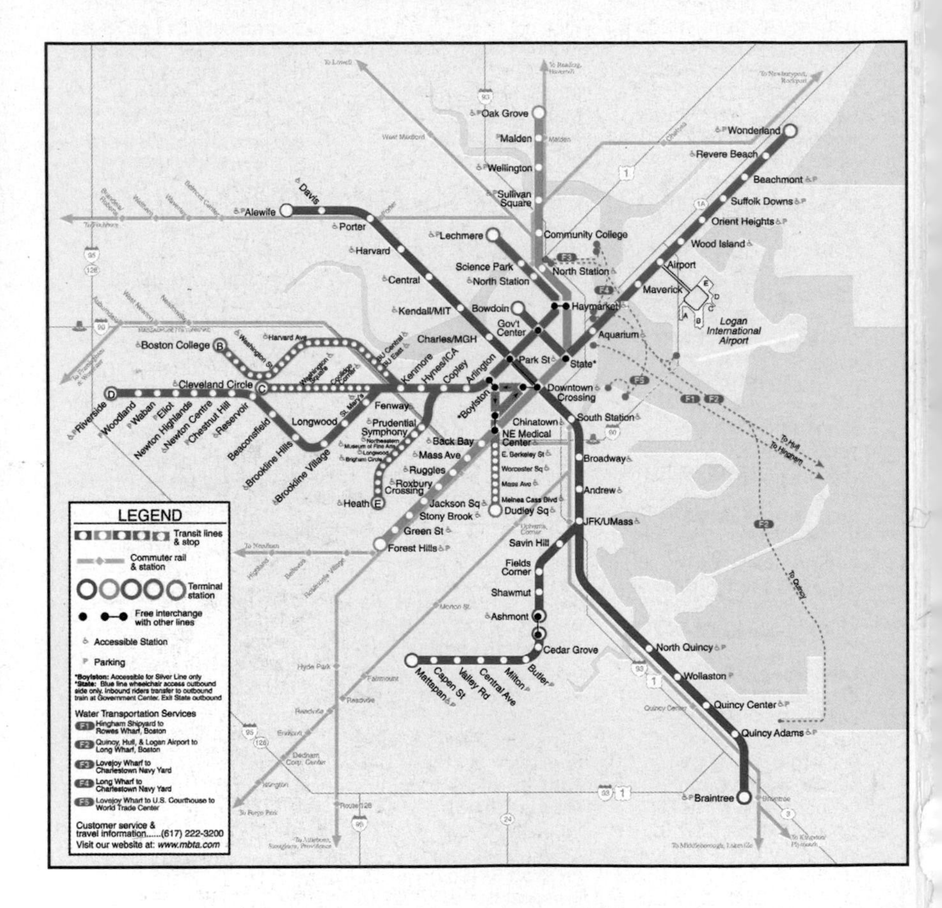